S0-ARX-555

E DU

E D

THE CENTURY POLITICAL SCIENCE SERIES

LATIN AMERICA AND
THE UNITED STATES

Latin America
AND
The United States

GRAHAM H. STUART

Author of *American Diplomatic*
and Consular Practice

FIFTH EDITION

New York: APPLETON-CENTURY-CROFTS, Inc.

Copyright, 1955, by

APPLETON-CENTURY-CROFTS, INC.

*All rights reserved. This book, or parts
thereof, must not be reproduced in any
form without permission of the publisher.*

5114-11

Library of Congress Card Number: 55-5020

Copyright, 1938, 1943, by D. Appleton-Century Company, Inc.

Copyright, 1922, 1928, by The Century Co.

PRINTED IN THE UNITED STATES OF AMERICA

327.73
S92d

Fr 15 Ag 57
recl. Mi 22864

16 Jy 57   SVS (Lot Am S)

To

A. W. S.

PREFACE TO THE FIRST EDITION

THE purpose in writing this book has been to give a brief and accurate survey of the diplomatic and commercial relations between the United States and those Latin-American countries with which our interests have been most closely related. The increasingly friendly relations brought about by the World War, the development and expansion of commercial relations, the improved facilities for communication and travel, have made evident the vital importance of our future relations with the nations of this hemisphere. This need has been shown by the demand of our colleges and universities for more courses dealing with Latin-American history, geography, institutions, diplomatic policies, and commercial possibilities.

This volume, designed primarily as a text for classes in American diplomacy, and for those studying our relations with Latin America, will, it is hoped, also appeal to that part of the general public which is interested in the bases and development of American foreign policy. To make it the more useful for reference, the citation of the documentary sources of much of the material has been considered essential. In addition, supplementary reading lists have been appended to each chapter to give the student opportunity to obtain the background necessary for a complete understanding of the facts presented. The maps have been specially prepared for the volume to give the reader a clearer conception of the general features of Latin-American geography, and for that reason have been made as simple as possible.

Every effort has been made to present the facts fairly and accurately, with particular emphasis upon those phases of American diplomacy which have hitherto received least attention. For example, the diplomatic relations between the United States and Mexico preceding the Mexican War have been sketched very briefly, inasmuch as this material is already available in excellent form. On the other hand, our recent relations with the Caribbean countries and Central America, and our diplomatic relations with Argentina, Brazil, and Chile have been given more detailed attention owing to the greater difficulty of obtaining satisfactory material on these subjects.

The author wishes to express his deep obligation to Professor Frederic A. Ogg, the editor of the series, for his careful reading and revision of the manuscript and for his many helpful suggestions and improvements. Grateful acknowledgment is also given to the librarians of the Wisconsin Historical Society for their constant and invaluable assistance, and in par-

ticular to Mrs. R. D. Evans for aid in collecting the documentary materials
and to Miss Mary Foster and Miss Marjorie Park for their coöperation in
the search for material.

G. H. S.

PREFACE TO THE FIFTH EDITION

The Good Neighbor policy of the Roosevelt administration, followed by
the outbreak of war in the Western Hemisphere, has brought about a new
era in the relations of the United States with Latin America. The present
edition seeks to indicate the many resulting changes. Considerable new
material has been added covering totalitarian and Communist subversive
activities and the implementation of the Good Neighbor policy. The
author's grateful acknowledgment is due to Professors Martin B. Travis Jr.
and James T. Watkins IV of Stanford University for their most helpful
criticism and advice.

G. H. S.

CONTENTS

MAPS

LATIN AMERICA AND THE UNITED STATES

1

The New
Pan Americanism

Just as individuals, influenced by their several environments, follow out definite courses of action, so nations, reacting to certain geographical, economic, and strategic stimuli, evolve policies that fix the broad outlines of their world relations. For Great Britain, the control of the seas has been the dominating factor; her whole foreign policy, her great navy, her far-flung empire, are part and parcel of it. For France the eastern frontier has been a perpetual sword of Damocles; the Russian Alliance, the Triple Entente, and the harsh clauses of Versailles were merely rings of defense in a policy of protection against Germany. The Russian giant, hemmed in by the frozen seas of the north, the Siberian wastes on the east, and powerful neighbors on the west, steadily pursued a policy of expansion towards the open water, with Constantinople and control of the Mediterranean arteries as the goal of his ambition.

The keynote of the foreign policy of the United States was sounded by Washington in the memorable proclamation of neutrality of 1793; and its *motif* was outlined in the farewell address of 1796. The new nation must not have part in the political broils of Europe. The great ocean had isolated us—"Why forego the advantages of so peculiar a situation?" The Monroe Doctrine, enunciated a generation later, merely added a corollary to this policy by making it objective as well as subjective. And for fully a century the United States, confronted with what seemed an unlimited field for inland expansion, pushed its frontier westward and maintained its isolation.

The war with Spain, however, brought a new situation. The Monroe Doctrine could easily be stretched to the Spanish West Indies, but could it be made to reach across the Pacific? While still debating the question,

1

the United States became a world power. The Hague conferences, the peace of Portsmouth, relief of the legations endangered by the Boxer Rebellion, the Conference of Algeciras, found the United States participating; and its rôle was not without honor.

Naturally enough, the results of the Spanish war aroused in Europe a feeling of jealousy towards the new world power that had appeared in the west; international society is commonly conservative and prone to frown upon the upstart state. But this feeling was not confined to Europe. Latin America, which might have been expected to acclaim the new-found freedom of the unhappy Cubans, looked instead with regret towards the conquered Spaniard and with fear towards the Yankee victor. *Quis custodiet custodem?* Texas and Mexico were not forgotten, and Cleveland's assertion of the sovereignty of the United States over the Western Hemisphere still echoed in the Andes. *Cuba libre* had a pleasing sound. But how about Puerto Rico?

The events of the next few years were not of such character as to allay Latin-American suspicions. The Platt Amendment was looked upon no more favorably in South America than in Cuba. The policy of President Theodore Roosevelt in Santo Domingo, and the "big-stick" policy in general, was viewed with alarm. Again, when Colombia refused to accept the terms of the United States for a canal concession, and as a result lost possession over her province of Panama, all Latin America looked askance at its powerful neighbor on the north. Washington's policy of isolation seemed to have been thrown overboard; Monroe's doctrine was no longer recognizable.

Fortunately, for a period at any rate, the peak of American imperialism had been reached. In 1905 Elihu Root became Secretary of State, and in the following year he visited South America. The sincerity and cordiality of his utterances, and the friendly attitude of the United States towards closer American coöperation, opened a new era in Pan American relations. The Wilson administration, from the outset, favored closer relations with Latin America, and one of the earliest statements of the President thus outlined his policy: "One of the chief objects of the new administration will be to cultivate the friendship and deserve the confidence of our sister republics of Central and South America and to promote in every proper and honorable way the interests which are common to the peoples of the two continents." This attitude was maintained throughout the trying Mexican situation and through the stress of World War I, and one of the last official acts of President Wilson was to send Secretary Colby on an official mission to South America to counteract influences working against the United States. The success of this visit was so great that it evoked a very cordial farewell message from President Irigoyen of Argentina, whose attitude towards the United States throughout the war had been decidedly unsympathetic.

The Harding administration, with the Department of State under the able guidance of Secretary Hughes, not only recorded itself as supporting the excellent policies promulgated by Secretary Root, but made a unique record in its efforts to settle a number of outstanding and thorny disputes in the Caribbean area. The prompt ratification of the treaty with Colombia, affording some reparation to the latter for her loss of sovereignty over Panama, made an auspicious beginning. The withdrawal of the marines from the Dominican Republic and the promise of a better situation in Haiti gave encouragement to the anti-imperialists. The decision to raise the legation at Havana to an embassy, and the naming of General Crowder for the post, was more than a friendly gesture, while the surrender of the Isle of Pines to Cuba was a real if belated contribution to the inviolability of treaty obligations. The appointment of an able administrator in the person of Judge Towner to the governorship of Puerto Rico, in place of the time-serving politician who had first received the post, augured well for an immediate improvement in the conditions in Puerto Rico. Even the impasse with Mexico was finally broken and the Obregón government recognized.

But perhaps the outstanding achievement of the Harding administration in its Caribbean policy was the Central American Conference at Washington, which not only resurrected the Central American Court of Justice but also brought about a limitation of armament on land as well as on water among the five Central American Republics. It was in his speech of welcome to the delegates of this conference that Secretary Hughes laid down certain bases of conduct governing the United States in its relations with its Caribbean neighbors which might well serve subsequent administrations: "The government of the United States has no ambition to gratify at your expense, no policy which runs counter to your national aspirations, and no purpose save to promote the interests of peace and to assist you, in such manner as you may welcome, to solve your problems to your own proper advantage. The interest of the United States is found in the peace of this hemisphere and in the conservation of your interests." The value of the statement was enhanced by the sincerity of its author.

The Coolidge administration was less fortunate in the results of its dealings with Latin-American neighbors. Neither by training, experience, nor temperament was Secretary Kellogg suited to handle the delicate problems which faced the United States in Mexico and the Caribbean. The relations with Mexico required a finesse and tact which were wholly wanting in Washington. A policy of smug self-righteousness and thinly veiled threats bolstered up by the bogy of Bolshevism set in motion a strong current of bitter hostility not only below the Rio Grande but also south of Panama. The vacillating intervention in Nicaragua swelled the torrent of ill-will. The utter failure of the Tacna-Arica arbitration was an added blow to our prestige. Criticism of American policies in Latin America became so pronounced that on February 22, 1927, Senator Borah introduced a resolution to empower the Senate Foreign Relations Committee "to investigate and study conditions and policies bearing upon the relationship between Central American countries, Mexico and the United States and to visit such countries." Secretary Kellogg protested vigorously and the investigation idea was dropped; but with this change the proposal was approved by the Foreign Relations Committee.

The constant criticism of American policies in the Caribbean area brought forth a remarkable speech from President Coolidge on the occasion of the meeting of the United Press Association in New York City in April, 1927. After advocating the naïve theory that the press should always support an administration in its dealings with foreign powers, he laid down a rather startling extension of the Wilsonian principle that recognition be accorded only to constitutionally established governments. The Coolidge policy not only accepted this responsibility but asserted that such recognition, by its evidence of approval, entailed the support of the United States. Having enunciated a frank policy of intervention, President Coolidge thereupon fixed the sphere of its operation in specific terms: "Toward the governments of countries which we have recognized this side of Panama we feel a moral responsibility that does not attach to other nations." If this was a blunt notice of American hegemony over its weaker neighbors to the South, it at least had the merit of confining "manifest destiny" to a definite area.

Nevertheless the next principle laid down by President Coolidge allowed for no bounds or barriers. "Our government has certain rights over and certain duties toward our own citizens and their property wherever they may be located. The person and property of a citizen are a part of the general domain of the nation, even when abroad. . . . Wherever he goes these duties of our government must follow him." Such policies, if followed to their natural conclusion, would constitute a *real politik* for the Western Hemisphere which might be very difficult to reconcile with any policy of Pan American solidarity.

Fortunately, the well conceived good will trip of President-elect Hoover to various countries of the Caribbean and South America directly after his election in 1928 was an auspicious augury for a period of more friendly relations between the United States and Latin America. The excellent results of the 1929 Washington Conference on Arbitration and Conciliation which produced two conventions, providing for the settlement by arbitration of all justiciable disputes and the submission of all others to commissions of inquiry, furnished substantial proof of the coöperative attitude of the United States. The withdrawal of all marines from Nicaragua gave even more concrete evidence to our Latin-American neighbors that "Yankee imperialism" was no longer to be feared.

President Franklin D. Roosevelt was eager to continue this policy of conciliation and friendship so that the United States might enter the forthcoming Seventh Pan American Conference with a record unmarred by any word or act which might indicate a departure from a policy of sincere coöperation. The keynote of his attitude was sounded in his inaugural address when he declared that he would "dedicate this nation to the policy of the good neighbor—the neighbor who respects his obligations and respects the sanctity of his agreements in and with a world of neighbors." Secretary of State Hull was an able coadjutor to his chief in carrying out the Good Neighbor Policy. He was able to bring about a coördinating and strengthening of inter-American peace machinery at the Montevideo Conference and he was even more successful in his efforts to break down tariff barriers in the Americas by his program of reciprocal trade agreements. The abrogation of the Platt Amendment was another important step on the road to Pan American solidarity. The crowning achievements of the Roosevelt administration were the Buenos Aires Conference, which definitely established the principle of non-intervention among the republics of the Western Hemisphere and the acceptance of the forward-looking Declaration of American Principles at the Lima Conference with adequate machinery to make it effective.

The Good Neighbor Policy of President Roosevelt was not wholly immune to Congressional criticism owing to the very considerable financial outlays made in Latin America. Senator Hugh Butler of Nebraska, who made a trip through Latin America in the summer of 1943, alleged that the Good Neighbor Policy had become the policy of the rich uncle and that some six billion dollars had been expended, much of it profligately. Senator McKellar denied the allegations categorically and proved that the total expenditure for 1941-1943 amounted to less than one and one-half billion dollars, of which more than one billion had been used to purchase strategic materials and ships. In fact, the total expenditure for non-war purposes was about $178 million.

President Harry S. Truman followed in the footsteps of his predecessor and supported the Good Neighbor Policy by words and deeds. He went personally to the Inter-American Conference for the Maintenance of Continental Peace and Security held in Brazil in September, 1947, and declared to the assembled delegates: "The United States seeks world peace—the peace of free men. I know that you stand with us. United we can constitute the greatest single force in the world for the good of humanity."

Although the Truman administration was vitally concerned with the European Recovery Program, every effort was made to aid the Latin-American republics financially through the Export-Import Bank and through the Institute of Inter-American Affairs.

During World War II and after its conclusion vigorous efforts were made to strengthen inter-American military coöperation. Military missions were sent to all Latin-American countries which requested them and by 1946 the United States had seventeen military missions in thirteen Latin-American countries. President Truman on May 6, 1946, submitted a bill to the Congress authorizing a program of military coöperation with the other American states which would permit the Army and Navy to transfer military and naval equipment by sale or otherwise to countries coöperating. Although Congress failed in both 1946 and 1947 to pass the Inter-American Military Coöperation Act, the Departments of War and Navy furnished surplus military equipment including fighters, bombers, and armored cars which had cost over $37 million. This was in addition to the $400 million worth of combat supplies furnished through Lendlease during the war. It should be noted that from 1951 on most of our foreign aid was for direct military purposes in a program aimed at the security of the United States. Although Latin America was the least threatened of the various areas of the world, military assistance appropriations to this region through June 30, 1953, totaled about $90 million.

To indicate the extent of practical aid extended to Latin-American countries by the United States it could be shown that from 1940 to 1950 the United States through the Institute of Inter-American Affairs and predecessor agencies supported programs of health and sanitation, agriculture, and education in the American republics to the amount of almost $60 million. About 900 experts from the United States coöperated in agricultural problems, about 300 professors were exchanged, and other trained officials helped in technical and social welfare problems. For the fiscal year 1952 the United States contributed about $18 million for technical assistance and for 1953 almost $22 million was authorized. It should be noted also that some 650 American technicians as of September, 1953, were working continuously in Latin America with about 12,000 Latin Americans in various joint projects. Nevertheless, in post-war economic assistance from the United States, the Latin-American states fared very poorly in comparison with other areas of the world. At the beginning of 1953 the Middle East and Africa had received about $1½ billion, the Far East $5⅛ billion, and Europe almost $23½ billion, as against about $¾ billion to Latin America.

The Republican administration of Dwight Eisenhower not only continued to support the technical assistance program but increased slightly the 1954 appropriation for aid to the Latin-American republics to $22,342,000.

As a further evidence of his intention to follow a more coöperative policy with the republics to the south, President Eisenhower shortly after his inauguration despatched his brother Milton to make a survey of the Latin-American countries and the possibilities of working out programs of mutual advantage. Accompanied by representatives of the Departments of State, Treasury, and Commerce, Dr. Eisenhower visited ten states and reported that on the whole, political relations with the United States were quite good and the concept of hemisphere solidarity was cherished by all. Among his recommendations were the elimination of misunderstandings, fair trade and tax policies, expanded public loans and technical coöperation, and in crises the President be authorized to make grants of food from surplus stocks to the Latin-American countries. The $9 million emergency grant of food to Bolivia on October 14, 1953, may well have been the result of an informal recommendation made by Milton Eisenhower.

The entrance of the United States into both World Wars, despite every effort to remain neutral, is conclusive proof that in the present condition of world politics no great nation can withdraw itself from an active participation in international affairs, and yet maintain its position and prestige. This is especially true in the case of a nation that aspires to leadership in the Western Hemisphere. *Noblesse oblige* must be an important factor in the policy of great nations, just as it has been in the lives of great men; and before undertaking obligations it behooves a nation to understand clearly the responsibility it is assuming. If the policy of non-interference in European affairs permitted the United States to pay little attention to European diplomacy—and surely our participation in two World Wars proved the lack of foresight in such a policy—on the other hand, the Monroe Doctrine, which has heretofore been regarded as the backbone of our foreign policy, demands as an absolute condition of its maintenance, not only very careful attention to the affairs of the Latin-American republics, but also a thorough and comprehensive understanding of their problems and their policies.

The most casual study of the relations between the United States and the Latin-American republics will indicate that the great republic in the north has made until recently little effort either to understand the difficulties that have sorely tried her younger and less powerful neighbors or to study their racial characteristics and customs with the friendly appreciation necessary to good relations between states. Nor is it sufficient in a democracy where public opinion plays an important part in foreign affairs to confine knowledge of foreign policies and peoples to the select few who make up the government. Such understanding should be widespread among the peoples themselves, so that public opinion, based upon an intelligent comprehension of the facts, can act as a lever towards more friendly coöperation, rather than as a spur to jealous and rival aspirations. To bring about this better relationship, which can be accomplished only by a better mutual understanding, every possible point of contact and every avenue of approach should be utilized.

The first and most important means of understanding and knowing foreign peoples is to be acquainted with their language. Hitherto this aid to an understanding between ourselves and South America has been almost completely overlooked. Only recently have our schools and colleges given Spanish the recognition long accorded German and French, and even today Portuguese, the language of the largest of all the South American states, appears in the curricula of few of our educational institutions. A real effort is now being made to lower the language barrier.

It is not sufficient to know the language of a foreign country. There must be also some understanding of that country's history, institutions, government, and policies. It must be confessed that until recently the educational institutions of the United States have done very little to stimulate interest in these aspects of Latin America. A glance at the courses of study announced by the various institutions and colleges of the United States in recent bulletins still indicates the scant attention paid to Latin-American history and affairs. When our great colleges and universities manifest so little interest in bringing Latin-American affairs to the attention of their students, it is not surprising that in the secondary schools even less interest is shown. As a consequence, the ignorance of the ordinary well educated American citizen concerning all things south of the border is veritably limitless.

Undoubtedly there has been a remarkable increase in the attention devoted by the average American citizen to European and Asiatic affairs during the past few years; but the affairs of the great nations of Latin America, with which his real interests are far more closely related, have not yet been brought to his attention for the consideration which they merit. Before we can expect to interest the American public in the problems and policies of its neighbors on the south, an educational campaign must be waged which will give the people some conception of the actual situation in the great Latin-American republics. Surely a proper realization of the importance of maintaining cordial relations between the United States and South America did not exist in the mind of the American business man who wrote to the United States legation in Buenos Aires to inquire whether the shops there used glass in their windows. If this Denver merchant had realized that Buenos Aires was approximately seven times as large as his own city, and was the capital of a country that did business to the amount of more than a billion and a quarter dollars at the time, he would not have wondered whether the South Americans had yet reached the stage of civilization in which they were no longer content to use oilpaper for their windows.

A well known South American commercial authority has declared that the great work of Pan Americanism can be accomplished only if based upon close commercial relations, which are the proper foundations for continental harmony in America. The first World War gave the United States a marvelous opportunity to seize the position long held by Great Britain as the leading trader with the South American republics, and we were not slow to take advantage of the situation. Between 1913 and 1920 the commerce of the United States with Latin America showed a gain of about 400 per cent.

This supremacy brought about by Europe's misfortune and the liberal Underwood tariff of 1913 was seriously jeopardized, however, by the depression years and the super-protective Hawley-Smoot tariff act of 1930. Although after the first World War the United States had set the pace in the race towards economic nationalism, we finally learned that tariff walls keep domestic products within as well as foreign products without. Our foreign customers not only adopted equally high tariffs, but invented new devices such as quotas, exchange control systems, clearing and compensation agreements, government import monopolies to strangle import trade. The trade of the United States with the Latin-American countries which had increased by leaps and bounds during the first World War and had been maintained at a high level until 1930 suffered a disastrous decline. Exports from the United States to Latin America dropped from $911,749,000 in 1929 to $215,944,000 in 1933, and the imports of the United States from Latin America fell from $1,014,127,000 in 1929 to $316,040,000 in 1933. Nor could we allege the depression as the sole cause, inasmuch as the relative share of this trade going to Great Britain, Italy, Brazil, and Japan had materially increased.

The administration of Franklin Roosevelt, pledged to a policy of economic rehabilitation, was able to persuade the Congress to pass the Trade Agreements Act of June 12, 1934. The excellent results of the new liberal commercial policy were soon evident. The first of the bilateral reciprocity trade agreements was signed with Cuba on August 24, 1934, whereby mutual tariff concessions were made on a wide range of subjects. Trade statistics vividly and accurately tell the story of the beneficial results. The total trade between the two countries in the four months September to December, inclusive, of 1933, amounted to $29 million. During the same period of 1934, the first four months of the operation of the new treaty, trade jumped to $65 million, an increase of 125 per cent. The success of the Cuban agreement stimulated the speedy completion of others. During the year 1935 four more reciprocity trade agreements with Latin-American republics were signed, namely, with Brazil, Haiti, Colombia, and Honduras. During 1936 similar agreements were signed with Nicaragua, Guatemala, and Costa Rica. In 1937 an agreement was signed with El Salvador, the following year one with Ecuador, and in 1939 one with Venezuela. In 1939 negotiations were begun with Argentina, but the agreement, the first comprehensive commercial treaty between the two countries since 1855, was not signed until 1941. The war situation of 1942 encouraged even closer commercial relations in the Americas, and Peru, Uruguay, and Mexico entered into trade agreements with the United States in that year. When Paraguay signed a similar agreement in 1946, it brought the total number to sixteen.

The success of the trade agreement program was so clearly manifest that the act was renewed nine times by the Congress to continue in force until 1955. The statistical record of the total foreign trade of Latin America between the two World Wars indicated that a determined drive had been instituted on the part of Germany, Great Britain, and Japan for a greater share in these markets, but that the strong position of the United States had not been seriously undermined. The effectiveness of the reciprocal trade agreement program and the general friendliness engendered by the Good Neighbor Policy have been invaluable assets to the United States in maintaining its excellent trade position against ever keener competition. As a result, by 1953 the trade with Latin America amounted to about $3 billion in each direction.

Any renewal of an arbitrary interpretation of the Monroe Doctrine will continue to be a stumbling-block to our commercial expansion. We must realize that South America no longer either needs or desires our protection, except as we may coöperate with her to protect the mutual interests of the two Americas. Furthermore, this coöperation must be upon terms of equality, an equality that will be achieved only when an interchange of ideas, knowledge, and sympathy shall supplement commerce in products and exchange. President Wilson expressed this fact in most happy phraseology in his address before the Southern Commercial Congress at Mobile: "It is a very perilous thing to determine the foreign policy of a nation in the terms of material interest. It is not only unfair to those with whom you are dealing, but it is degrading as regards your own actions. Comprehension must be the soil in which shall grow all the fruits of friendship."

The growing interest of the United States in Latin America has been reflected not only in the attitude of the President and State Department in official pronouncements, but also in the increased number of courses on Latin-American life and culture which have become available to students in the higher institutions of learning. For example, whereas in 1931 only 206 colleges and universities in the United States were giving courses in any way dealing with Latin-American institutions or affairs, in 1947 the number had increased to 769. The number of courses given in the Latin-American field had increased over 600 per cent: 436 in 1931, 2804 in 1947.[1]

Despite this progress in scholastic facilities, the schools must give a larger place to Latin America in their curricula, not merely in the teaching of its languages and geography, but also in the teaching of its history, literature, and political science. Increased attention to the study of foreign policy and diplomacy is especially needed in the institutions of higher learning in the United States. The Monroe Doctrine has too long been regarded as a sort of holy of holies in all questions of American foreign policy, perhaps most of all by the people who have the most hazy conceptions of what the doctrine really means. Exchange professorships and scholarships afford a most excellent means of developing a just and accurate percep-

---

[1] Estillita Hart, "Courses in Latin America in Institutions of Higher Learning in the United States, 1946-47," *Dept. of Cultural Affairs, Pan American Union* (Washington, D. C., 1948).

tion of mutual values and points of view, and should be given every encouragement. Even before the Buenos Aires Conference gave impetus to the idea, the University of Chile had taken the lead in this matter, arranging exchanges of professors with the University of Washington and the University of California. In 1921 the National University of Mexico organized a summer school for foreigners, giving particular attention to courses in Mexican and Spanish-American archæology, geography, history, literature, and institutions. In the 1924 session some 250 teachers and students from the United States attended.

This movement was given additional momentum by the provisions of the cultural conventions signed [2] at the Inter-American Conference for the Maintenance of Peace: 1—Convention for the promotion of inter-American cultural relations; 2—Convention on interchange of publications; 3—Convention concerning artistic exhibitions; 4—Convention concerning the peaceful orientation of public instruction; and 5—Convention covering facilities for educational and publicity films. Intellectual coöperation, once sporadic and limited, will be organized to obtain maximum results under more ideal conditions. Annual fellowships will support the exchange students; government funds will meet the expenses of visiting professors; thus will circulate among the Americas persons of prestige in the related realms of education, science, and technical progress.

As evidence of substantial progress in this direction the United States awarded sixty-six travel grants during the 1941 and 1942 fiscal years to outstanding Latin Americans for visits to the United States and twelve to North Americans to travel in Latin America. From January 1, 1940, to January 1, 1942, twenty-seven Latin-American students were received by the United States and nineteen graduate students sent by the United States under the first of these conventions. About 1750 students from the other American republics were enrolled in our colleges in the academic year 1941-1942. [3]

In the fiscal year 1945-1946 the Department of State made grants-in-aid to send forty-seven American professors to American republics and brought seven American professors to the United States. The United States also assisted in the maintenance of twenty-seven independent and two branch cultural centers in the American republics.

The increase in the number of Latin-American students attending secondary schools and universities has been so rapid that Dr. Milton

[2] All of these conventions were approved by the United States Senate on June 29, 1937, except the one on interchange of publications.

[3] *The Program of the Department of State in Cultural Relations* (Washington, D. C., 1942).

Eisenhower was able to report in 1953 that 5000 students from a single Latin-American republic were studying in our universities and secondary schools and that 75 per cent of all Latin Americans who studied abroad came to the United States. Also in 1953 the United States government granted 135 scholarships to Latin American students and brought 565 Latin Americans to the United States.

The press can play quite as important a part as the schools and colleges. The opportunities are vast and the possibilities limitless. In this connection full credit must be given to the great South American papers, such as *La Prensa* and *La Nación* of Buenos Aires,[4] *El Mercurio* of Chile, *Jornal do Brazil,* and numerous others, which for some time have maintained special correspondents and representatives in the United States, and since January, 1919, have become members of the Associated Press.

Except for despatches carried on special occasions such as during the Washington and Buenos Aires Conferences, far too little attention has been given in the columns of the daily press of the United States to important events in the countries of Latin America; while, on the other hand, the great dailies of South America have shown their resentment by adopting in many cases an antagonistic and unfriendly tone in discussing items of news from the United States. Now that great journals in the United States like the *New York Times, New York Herald Tribune, Christian Science Monitor, Philadelphia Public Ledger,* and others, have opened special sections for the presentation of news and feature articles on the republics of Latin America, a great improvement may be looked for. It may also be hoped that some American newspaper will soon establish a South American edition, just as *La Prensa* has already established a United States edition with so much success in New York. For, as Señor Collao, publisher of the New York edition of *La Prensa,* has declared: "The daily paper is the most able resource that both the government and people can find to express their purposes and needs, and as a promoter of more friendly relations by the abolition of misunderstanding, ignorance, and prejudice." A recommendation to the press and news agencies that greater interest and space be devoted to news relating to the nations of America was approved at the Seventh Pan American Conference at Montevideo.

Some mention should also be made of the periodicals devoted to Pan American affairs. There are several very excellent ones. In addition to the *Bulletin of the Pan American Union,* now the *Américas,* which is described

---

[4] These two great newspapers are temporarily in eclipse, the first having been taken over by the Péron government and the second subject to rigid controls.

later, special note should be made of *Panorama,* a quarterly devoted to inter-American cultural matters published by the Department of Cultural Affairs of the Pan American Union, whose articles may appear in Spanish, Portuguese, or English. Two other periodical publications of the Pan American Union are the *Annals of the Organization of American States,* which contains the official documents of the Organization of American States, and *Ciencias Sociales* published six times a year to present new developments in the social sciences. A publication which fills a real need is the *Hispanic American Report* which presents a monthly summary on current developments in Spain, Portugal, and Latin America. It has appeared regularly since November, 1948, and is published by Stanford University under the direction of Professor Ronald Hilton. The *Hispanic American Historical Review* is a scholarly publication appearing quarterly, devoted primarily to articles in the field of political, economic, social, and diplomatic history of the Hispanic American countries.

A few fine magazines of general interest published in Latin America might be noted: *Carteles,* a popular weekly devoted to politics and current events, published in Havana, Cuba; an excellent weekly news magazine, *Tiempo,* published in Mexico City and distributed in the United States and Puerto Rico under the title *Hispano Americano;* a somewhat similar weekly, though more restricted in its scope, *Semana,* published in Bogotá, Colombia. *Veritas,* a beautifully illustrated monthly published in Buenos Aires; *Revista do Brasil,* Brazil's most important literary monthly; and *Vea,* a widely circulated current affairs weekly published in Santiago de Chile. *Sur,* while published as a leading Argentine literary magazine, has become continental in appeal, with a solid reputation outside Latin America. Mention should also be made of the Latin-American editions of *Time* and the *Readers Digest,* both of which have been phenomenally successful. International Rotary now publishes an edition in Spanish, *Revista Rotaria.*

In conclusion, one further way of bringing about mutual sympathetic understanding between the two Americas may be suggested, namely, increased travel for pleasure and sightseeing by the people of the Americas in the countries of their neighbors. Let the phrase, "See America First" be changed to "See the Americas First." No better means of increasing transportation facilities can be imagined than a passenger-carrying trade that demands it. Both continents contain natural scenic wonders in profusion, and no traveler in a foreign land returns without a better understanding and appreciation of the customs, life, and aspirations of the peoples with whom he has come into personal contact. The proposal made at the Montevideo Conference that a tourist passport be issued and viséed gratis for all persons traveling in the Americas might be very helpful as a means of achieving these purposes.

By thus utilizing every avenue to a better understanding, the republics of North and South America can acquire that mutual respect which is the indispensable foundation of friendship, and will thereby approach a unity of purpose and an effectiveness of coöperation that will translate into a living reality the ideal of the new Pan Americanism. The great differences in race, religion, temperament, and manner will be bridged by sympathetic friendliness; unjust suspicions of ulterior motives can be explained away. The first World War, which brought the two continents into a closer financial and commercial relation, also united them for a time in the struggle for democratic ideals. The United States has proved upon various occasions that she regards the rights of humanity of infinitely more consequence than the rights of property; the republics of Latin America have shown their appreciation of this spirit and have not stood aloof. The time has at last arrived when the republics of the Western Hemisphere can coöperate effectively on the basis of the principles laid down over a century ago by John Quincy Adams—"disinterestedness, cordial good will, and fair and equal reciprocity." But they have come to realize that such coöperation can achieve lasting results only when functioning in the spirit of the precepts enunciated by Elihu Root—"with sympathy and understanding, with kindly consideration and honorable obligation."

SUPPLEMENTARY READINGS

DUNCAN AIKMAN, *The All American Front* (New York, 1940).

GERMÁN ARCINIEGAS, *The State of Latin America* (New York, 1952).

CARLETON BEALS, *Pan America* (Boston, 1940).

SAMUEL FLAGG BEMIS, *The Latin American Policy of the United States* (New York, 1943).

ADOLPH A. BERLE, JR., *New Directions in the New World* (New York, 1940).

F. CARABALLO Y SOTOLONGO, *El imperialismo norte-americano* (Habana, 1914).

HAROLD E. DAVIS, *The Americas in History* (New York, 1953).

STEPHEN DUGGAN, *Latin America* (Boston, New York, 1936).

WALDO FRANK, *America Hispana* (New York, 1931).

E. GIL, *La Evolution del Pan-Americanismo* (Buenos Aires, 1933).

LAWRENCE GRISWOLD, *The Other America* (New York, 1941).

JOHN GUNTHER, *Inside Latin America* (New York, 1941).

CLARENCE H. HARING, *South America Looks at the United States* (New York, 1928).

HUBERT HERRING, *The Good Neighbors* (New Haven, Conn., 1941).

—— *America and the Americas* (Claremont, 1944).

S. G. INMAN, *Latin America* (New York, 1942).

PRESTON E. JAMES, *Latin America* (New York, 1950).

MIGUEL JORRÍN, *Governments of Latin America* (New York, 1953).

AUSTIN F. MACDONALD, *Latin American Politics and Government* (New York, 1954).

DANA G. MUNRO, *The Latin American Republics* (New York, 1950).

H. K. NORTON, *The Coming of South America* (New York, 1931).

EZEQUIEL PADILLA, *Free Men of America* (Chicago and New York, 1943).

LUIS QUINTANILLA, *A Latin American Speaks* (New York, 1942).

J. FRED RIPPY, *Historical Evolution of Hispanic America* (New York, 1945).

FRANCISCO A. RIZZUTO, *Anatomia de los Problemas Americanos* (Buenos Aires, 1941).

J. ROA, *Positive and Negative Factors in Inter-American Relations* (Havana, 1940).

W. S. ROBERTSON, *Hispanic American Relations with the United States* (New York, 1923).

WILLIAM L. SCHURZ, *Latin America* (New York, 1949).

ROLAND H. SHARP, *South America Uncensored* (New York, 1945).

GEORGE H. SOULE, *et al.*, *Latin America and the Future World* (New York, 1945).

M. UGARTE, *The Destiny of a Continent* (New York, 1925).

A. K. WEINBERG, *Manifest Destiny* (Baltimore, 1935).

CHARLES WERTENBAKER, *New Doctrine for the Americas* (New York, 1941).

ARTHUR P. WHITAKER, *The United States and South America: The Northern Republics* (Cambridge, 1948).

T. R. YBARRA, *America Faces South* (New York, 1940).

J. M. YEPES, *Le Panamericanisme* (Paris, 1936).

❦ 2 ❦

Coöperation by Conference

MANY methods and agencies have been employed to bring about mutual sympathy and understanding between the independent republics of the Western Hemisphere. One of the most effective has been a series of Pan American conferences and congresses. The idea underlying these conferences was put forth by Bolívar in 1824, when, as the head of the Republic of Peru, he suggested that representatives of the independent states of America meet at Panama, with the object of establishing "certain fixed principles for securing the preservation of peace between the nations of America, and the concurrence of all those nations in defense of their own rights." [1] This conference took place two years later, but only four governments participated—Peru, Colombia, Central America, and Mexico. Owing to the cordial support of the idea by Henry Clay, then Secretary of State, President John Quincy Adams appointed two plenipotentiaries for the United States. Strong opposition developed in Congress, however, and the necessary appropriations were not made in time to enable our delegates to take part.[2] Although a number of excellent agreements and proposals were signed, the times were not yet ripe for employing arbitration and mediation in the settlement of international disputes, and the conference had no tangible results.

Nevertheless when, one hundred years later, the Republic of Panama invited representatives of the states of the Western Hemisphere to join with her in the Panama Congress of 1926 to further the ideals fostered by the great *Libertador*, one of the most interesting items on the agenda

[1] *International American Conference, Senate Executive Document No. 232*, 51st Cong., 1st Sess., Part IV, Vol. IV, p. 155.

[2] For an interesting discussion of the reasons for the failure of American participation see J. B. Lockey, *Pan-Americanism: Its Beginnings* (New York, 1920), pp. 313-316; for the attitude of the United States, *ibid.*, Chap. X.

17

was the consideration of Bolívar's project of a league of nations for the states of the new world.

Bolívar clearly saw how advantageous it would be if the nations could get together in conference at regular intervals, not only to become better acquainted, but also to settle the various disputes that were bound to arise between them. He therefore suggested an amphictyonic assembly of plenipotentiaries empowered to use good offices, mediation or arbitration. It was to negotiate treaties for the preservation of peace and interpret treaties when difficulties arose. In fact it had many elements of likeness to the Council and Assembly which were to function later at Geneva.

But not only did Bolívar see the need of providing machinery to settle disputes. He believed that it was even more important to eliminate causes of friction. Therefore he constantly urged the guarantees of territorial integrity upon the basis of the *status quo*. He also realized the dangers of secret alliances with foreign powers and urged that they be forbidden except when accepted by all members of the confederation. Friendly intercourse and the elimination of economic and political barriers were regarded as prerequisites of effective coöperation. Even social problems were not overlooked, and provision was made for the complete extirpation of the African slave trade. Finally, the sanction of force was made available as a last resort, and careful consideration was given to effecting the best possible coöperation in times of emergency.

Looking back today, we are compelled to admire the sheer audacity of Bolívar in attempting to give the states of the Western Hemisphere an international law for their mutual relations almost simultaneously with the establishment of their internal governmental organizations.[3]

The next serious attempt to bring about a joint conference of the independent nations of North and South America was initiated by the United States. On November 29, 1881, James G. Blaine, Secretary of State, invited the governments of all the independent states of the two continents to send representatives to Washington to participate in a congress "for the purpose of considering and discussing the methods of preventing war between the nations of America."[4] However, as the War of the Pacific (between Chile and Peru) was still in active progress, the conference did not take place until 1889. President Cleveland had been authorized by Congress in 1888 to issue a call to all the independent Latin-American countries to send representatives to meet at Washington; but President

[3] G. H. Stuart, "Simon Bolívar's Project for a League of Nations," *Southwest Polit. and Soc. Sci. Quar.*, Vol. VII (Dec. 1926), p. 238.

[4] *Int. Amer. Conf., loc. cit.*, p. 256.

Harrison had the honor of inaugurating the First International American Conference. All the independent republics except the Dominican Republic were represented, and Mr. Blaine, who once more held the office of Secretary of State, was chosen to preside. The program outlined for consideration was an extensive one, and included measures tending to promote peace and prosperity, the establishment of uniform customs regulations, a uniform system of weights and measures, laws for the protection of patents, copyrights, and trademarks, and the formulation of a definite plan of arbitration for the settlement of all disputes among the American nations. One of the noteworthy agreements of this congress was to incorporate into American international law the principle of arbitration as a means of settling disputes among the American nations. But the governments were not yet ready to go so far as their representatives.

Of more practical importance was the establishment of the Bureau of American Republics, devoted to the encouragement of Pan American commerce, friendship, and peace. This international organization became the nucleus of a system known now as the Organization of American States. A Council composed of a representative from each of the twenty-one American republics is the executive body of this regional organization for the maintenance of peace and may serve in a consultative capacity in the case of disputes between the American states. Representatives from the larger states on the Council enjoy the rank of ambassadors but are not a part of the diplomatic missions, while many smaller states prefer to be represented by their regularly accredited diplomatic officer in Washington. The Organization of American States formulates policy in conferences held every five years or in meetings of their foreign ministers held whenever one state so requests. The Pan American Union now serves as the Secretariat of the Organization of American States and is administered by a Secretary General and an Assistant Secretary General chosen by the Council.

It collects, compiles, and distributes information of all sorts regarding the commerce, laws, progress, and general development of all the American republics. It also acts as a permanent commission of the international conferences of the American states, to keep their records and archives, to assist in obtaining ratification of treaties and conventions as well as compliance with the resolutions adopted, and to prepare the program and regulations of each conference.[5] Its *Monthly Bulletin,* published in English, Spanish, and Portuguese, and superbly illustrated, was for many

[5] For summary of functions see Art. 83 of *The Charter of the Organization of American States,* in the Appendix.

years a veritable storehouse of information concerning the conditions, possibilities, and latest development of the Pan American republics. When the *Bulletin* ceased publication with the October, 1948, issue a new magazine called the *Américas* took its place. This monthly also published in an English, Spanish, and Portuguese edition presents the panorama of the Americas in literature, art, music, economy, and industry in a somewhat more vivid and popular way. At approximately the same time a new quarterly entitled *Annals of the Organization of American States* was published by the Pan American Union in Spanish, English, Portuguese, and French which contained the documents of the Organization for the period. The Union also publishes special reports and pamphlets containing information on various subjects of practical value. It has a well equipped library containing about a hundred thousand volumes, and is especially rich in official documents of the various republics. It is housed in two magnificent buildings costing more than a million dollars, the greater part of which was contributed by Andrew Carnegie, and its budget for 1955 amounted to about $3 million. Under the able management of its first Director General, John Barrett, who resigned in 1920 after fourteen years of service, the Union did a great work towards Pan American understanding and peace. His successor, Dr. Leo S. Rowe, who served more than a quarter of a century was a man peculiarly well equipped to continue its work and enlarge the scope of its influence. Upon his tragic death in December, 1946, the governing board chose Dr. Alberto Lleras, an eminent Colombian statesman and the first Latin American to serve in this capacity. Dr. Lleras announced his resignation at the Caracas Conference in March, 1954, and his successor is the distinguished Chilean publicist and statesman Carlos Davila.

With the success of the First International American Conference so clearly manifested, it was to be expected that other conferences would be called to enlarge upon and follow up its work. The second conference was summoned in October, 1901, at the suggestion of the United States and Mexican governments. Its sessions were held in Mexico City. Perhaps its most important result was that all the American nations became parties to the Hague Convention of 1899 for the pacific settlement of international disputes.[6] The third conference met at Rio de Janeiro in 1906, and Elihu Root, who as Secretary of State of the United States was making an official tour of South America, represented the United States. His speech at this conference remains one of the greatest expositions of the vital need of a mutual and sympathetic understanding among the Amer-

[6] *Second Int. Amer. Conf., Sen. Doc. No. 330, 57th Cong., 1st Sess.*

ican nations. The entire speech is worthy of quotation, but the following sentences indicate his message:

No nation can live unto itself alone and continue to live. Each nation's growth is a part of the development of the race. . . . There is not one of all our countries that can not benefit the others; there is not one that will not gain by the prosperity, the peace, the happiness of all. . . . We wish for no victories but those of peace; for no territory except our own; for no sovereignty except the sovereignty over ourselves.[7]

The Fourth International American Conference assembled at Buenos Aires on July 12, 1910. All the American republics were represented except Bolivia, and although Philander C. Knox, Secretary of State of the United States was elected an honorary president his dollar diplomacy had not endeared him to Latin America. The conference took up and debated an extensive list of subjects, and adopted a number of important conventions and resolutions. Among the most noteworthy were resolutions relating to patents, trademarks, and copyrights; extending the existence and powers of the Pan American Railroad Committee; providing for the encouragement of steamship communication between the republics of the American continent; providing for the exchange of professors and students between the universities of the American continent; recommending the uniformity of consular documents and custom-house regulations; and, finally, providing for the establishment of a section of commerce, custom-house, and statistics in the Bureau of American Republics, which was to be known henceforth as the Pan American Union.[8]

Between the Fourth and Fifth International American Conferences many vital changes had occurred affecting the relations both between the Latin-American nations and the United States, and between the Latin-American nations and Europe. All of the Latin-American republics except Mexico, Ecuador, and the Dominican Republic[9] had become members of the League of Nations, and Latin America was well represented both on the Council and in the World Court. Where formerly the conferences had limited their discussions almost entirely to problems of a social and economic character, the agenda of the fifth conference included certain rather delicate political questions. In addition to problems of agriculture, commerce, transportation, and health, one noted such

[7] *Third Int. Amer. Conf., Sen. Doc. No. 365*, 59th Cong., 2nd Sess.; Elihu Root, *Latin America and the United States* (Cambridge, Mass., 1917), p. 6.

[8] *Fourth Int. Amer. Conf., Sen. Doc. No. 744*, 61st Cong., 3rd Sess.

[9] The Dominican Republic was admitted to the League in 1924, Mexico in 1931, and Ecuador in 1934.

subjects as the codification of international law, the reduction of military and naval armament, measures tending to bring about a closer association of the American republics, and questions arising out of the encroachment by a non-American power on the rights of an American nation.[10]

When the conference opened in Santiago, Chile, on March 25, 1923, Mexico, Peru, and Bolivia were found to be unrepresented, Mexico because of her failure to obtain the recognition of the United States, and Peru and Bolivia because of the failure to settle the Tacna-Arica dispute. The American delegation headed by Henry P. Fletcher, and including Senator Kellogg, who subsequently became Secretary of State, and Dr. L. S. Rowe, Director General of the Pan American Union, found itself entrusted with the rather difficult task of averting drastic action on the part of the smaller Latin-American states in regard to the reorganization of the Pan American Union and a clarification of the Monroe Doctrine.

As regards the reorganization of the governing board of the Pan American Union, a separate organization was proposed to consist of representatives other than the regularly accredited diplomatic agents of the American republics at Washington, a body which might ultimately become the council of an American League of Nations. The United States opposed this idea but conceded that states not possessing diplomatic representation at Washington should be represented on the governing body of the Union by special representatives.[11] It was also agreed that henceforth instead of the Secretary of State of the United States acting *ex officio* as chairman of the governing board, the latter would elect its president and vice-president.

The conference sidestepped action on a specific interpretation or a joint sanction of the Monroe Doctrine, to neither of which the United States would subscribe, by adopting an innocuous resolution entrusting to the governing board of the Pan American Union "the task of studying the bases...relative to the manner of making effective the solidarity of the collective interests of the American continent." [12]

Although the committee on the limitation of armament recommended the limitations of the Washington Conference of 1922 as to tonnage of capital ships and airplane carriers and caliber of guns thereon, of greater importance was the work of the committee in securing the adoption of a convention generally known as the Gondra Treaty for the investigation

[10] *Report of Delegates of U. S. A. to Fifth Int. Conf. of Amer. States* (Washington, D. C., 1924), Appendix I.

[11] This change was incorporated in Article V of the Resolution on the Organization of the Pan American Union adopted by the Conference.

[12] *Report of Delegates of U. S. A. to Fifth Int. Conf. of Amer. States,* Appendix XII.

of disputes between American states by a commission of inquiry modeled upon those set up by the Hague Conventions and the Bryan treaties. Señor Augustin Edwards, president of the conference, has been quoted as regarding this treaty as "the most important ever signed on the American continent for the promotion of peace." [13]

Opinion seems to differ radically as to the real success of the conference. Certainly as regards coöperation along nonpolitical lines, as much if not more progress was made than in any of the previous conferences. Conventions for the protection of trademarks, the publicity of customs documents, and on uniformity of nomenclature for the classification of merchandise were adopted. The Hague Convention for the suppression of the drug traffic was approved, simplification of passports and visas and their ultimate elimination recommended, and closer coöperation for stamping out disease resolved upon. But whenever political issues were discussed there was noticeable throughout the conference a marked antagonism toward the United States, particularly on the part of the smaller states in the Caribbean area. For the first time in such a gathering the long smoldering fears of American imperialism were given free expression. Nevertheless, although the United States did not escape open criticism, the very fact that frankness prevailed relieved the tension to a considerable extent and made for results of a more lasting character.

The Sixth International American Conference met from January 16 to February 20, 1928, in Havana, Cuba. It came at a time when the United States was being harshly criticized throughout Latin America for its intervention in Nicaragua. President Coolidge, as a special honor to Cuba on the thirtieth anniversary of her independence, as well as to placate Latin America, made a hasty trip to Havana, in order to proclaim in person the friendliness of the United States towards all Latin America. Delegates from all the Latin-American countries were present. To make the gesture of friendship the more emphatic the most eminent delegation ever sent by the United States to an international conference was chosen to represent us. Headed by former Secretary of State Hughes, it included Henry P. Fletcher, former Ambassador to Chile, Mexico, and Belgium, and at the time to Italy, ex-Senator Oscar W. Underwood, Dwight W. Morrow, Ambassador to Mexico, Dr. James Brown Scott of the Carnegie Endowment, President Ray Lyman Wilbur of Stanford University, and Dr. L. S. Rowe, Director General of the Pan American Union.

[13] G. H. Blakeslee, *The Recent Foreign Policy of the U. S.* (New York, 1925), p. 143.

Although on the surface the agenda of the Sixth Conference [14] seemed to have avoided all contentious political subjects, the proposal to establish the Pan American Union upon a conventional basis instead of the hitherto less formal basis of successive resolutions offered the Latin-American delegates an oportunity to try to curb the over-preponderant influence which it was claimed the United States exerted both on the governing board and in the administration of the Union. Projects for the codification of international law for the American continent placed the United States on the defensive in regard to such questions as intervention, recognition, and the equality of states.

While a felicitous speech of generalities by President Coolidge indicated a keen desire on the part of the United States to inspire confidence and good will, an address made by Mr. Hughes before the United States Chamber of Commerce in Havana made an even more favorable impression, owing to its frank reference to Nicaragua and Haiti.

Asserting that the first pillar of Pan Americanism was independence, Mr. Hughes declared it to be the firm policy of the United States to respect the territorial integrity of the American republics. But the second pillar was stability and the United States desired to encourage stability in the interest of independence. Her entrance into Santo Domingo and withdrawal upon the establishment of a stable government proved it. "We would leave Haiti at any time that we had reasonable expectations of stability. . . . We are at this moment in Nicaragua; but what we are doing there and the commitments we have made are at the request of both parties and in the interest of peace and order and a fair election. We have no desire to stay. We entered to meet an imperative but temporary exigency; and we shall retire as soon as possible."

The conference decided that all sessions, both plenary and full committee, should be open to the public—an innovation. The United States accepted the Mexican-Peruvian proposal for governmental reorganization of the Pan American Union to permit each nation to decide whether a special delegate or its diplomatic representative should be employed. An additional proposal for the regular rotation of the Chairman, Vice Chairman and Director General was defeated, however, the conference agreeing that the Director General should attend the conference as an *ex officio* member instead of as a member of one delegation, and his expenses should be paid pro rata by all the member states.

A cause of serious disagreement came when the committee on codifica-

[14] *Sixth Int. Conf. of Amer. States. Special Handbook for the Use of Delegates* (Pan American Union, Washington, D. C., 1927).

tion of international law discussed the third article of the project concerning the existence, equality, and recognition of states. This article declared that "no state may intervene in the internal affairs of another." [15] With the American marines actively engaged in the pursuit of Sandino in Nicaragua the subject was of more than academic interest. The United States disputed the correctness of the rule, making a distinction between political intervention for permanent possession, and temporary interposition for humanitarian or other limited purposes. Furthermore its inclusion in a code would be futile since it was contrary to the accepted practice of international law. The sixth conference agreed to adopt obligatory arbitration for the settlement of justiciable disputes, and provided for an arbitration and conciliation conference to be held at Washington within the next year to draw up a collective Pan American arbitration convention which should outlaw aggressive warfare in the Western Hemisphere.

In the questions of a less political nature the conference was able to make a signal progress. The excellently drawn code of private international law prepared by Dr. Bustamente was approved, an aviation convention for the regulation of aircraft communication between the American republics was accepted, with a reservation to the effect that special arrangements between any two states for reciprocal convenience might be permitted provided it impaired in no respect the rights of other parties to the convention. The amendment permitted the United States to make special arrangements for the protection of the Panama Canal.

The treaty on the rights and duties of neutrals in the event of war which placed belligerent submarines under the same rules as other vessels of war in visit and search, and subjected armed merchant vessels to the rules of neutrality in respect to the time for remaining in port, coaling, and provisioning, was approved. Treaties placing aliens abroad on the same footing as nationals and establishing the right of asylum were signed although the United States entered a formal reservation to the latter. The copyright convention was revised and recommendations made for an inter-American automobile highway extending from Canada to Patagonia, for a Pan American railway, better river navigation and improved cable, telegraph, and radio communications. A Pan American pedagogical congress was agreed upon, as well as the creation of a Pan American institute of geography and history.

The Havana Conference from many points of view was unique. Political questions which hitherto had been completely eliminated from the

[15] *International Commission of Jurists—Public International Law Projects* (Pan American Union, 1927), p. 8.

agenda were brought up and discussed frankly without fear or favor. The United States made every effort to explain its position of *primus inter pares* and owing to the excellent choice of its representatives was remarkably successful. Every Latin-American state was represented, and at the conclusion of the conference their representatives could leave with the assurance that they had at last come into their own as equal participants in the fraternity of American nations.

Supplementing the Havana Conference by which it was authorized, the Conference of American States on Conciliation and Arbitration met at Washington on December 10, 1928. With the exception of Argentina, all the independent American states were represented. Secretary of State Kellogg and ex-Secretary of State Hughes acted as delegates for the United States. Two treaties were signed at this conference, one on arbitration and the other on conciliation.

The general treaty of inter-American arbitration has been called one of the most advanced multilateral arbitration pacts ever concluded. It followed the Kellogg-Briand Pact in its general form, condemned war as an instrument of national policy, and provided for settlement of all justiciable questions by arbitration. Only two subjects were excluded—domestic questions and questions concerning third states. Any existing international tribunal might be used or a special one set up.

The general convention of international conciliation was based upon the Gondra Treaty of 1923. It retained the commissions of inquiry of that treaty, but gave them also the character of commissions of conciliation. It covered all controversies between states not settled by diplomacy, it defined the procedure to be used and made it arbitrary, it set up permanent bodies at Washington and at Montevideo to bring about conciliation, and it approved the right of any state to offer mediation.

These two treaties, which seemed to provide for the settlement of any dispute which might arise between the states of the Western Hemisphere, were signed by all the states present. Before the seventh international conference met in Montevideo in 1933 a large majority of the twenty-one republics had ratified one or the other of these conventions, and ten states, including the United States, had ratified both.

Despite the tragic failure of the Geneva Disarmament Conference and the London Economic Conference of 1933, the republics of the Western Hemisphere were unwilling to postpone the meeting of the Seventh Pan American Conference scheduled to convene at Montevideo December 3, 1933. Not only were all American republics represented, half of them by their ministers of foreign affairs, but also, for the first time, it was proposed to admit official observers from Spain, Portugal, and the League of Nations. Action on this radical change in the organization of the conference was postponed to the eighth meeting, however. An eminent delegation from the United States, headed by Secretary of State Hull, included J. Reuben Clark, former Ambassador to Mexico, Alexander W. Weddell, Ambassador to Argentina, and J. Butler Wright, Minister to Uruguay, all outstanding authorities on Latin-American affairs.

In his address of welcome President Terra of Uruguay declared that "the American ideal of peace must not be buried in the swamps of the Chaco." Yet thousands of Bolivian and Paraguayan soldiers had already been slaughtered and buried in the swamps of the Chaco and thousands of others faced the same fate. The problem was complicated by the fact that since a Commission of American Neutrals and an ABC Peru Commission had both failed to bring about a settlement, a League of Nations Commission was now engaged in trying to work out a solution. For this reason, the United States and Brazil,[16] both non-League powers, were unwilling to bring the Chaco dispute, which was not on the agenda, into the conference. But, when it could not be avoided, the conference prevailed upon Bolivia and Paraguay to declare a truce for the period of the conference. It also passed a resolution submitted by Secretary Hull urging both peoples to accept judicial processes for the settlement of their dispute, as recommended by the League of Nations Commission. As a concrete suggestion the conference adopted an Argentine proposal that, contingent upon the approval of the League Commission, a conference be held at Buenos Aires including the ABCP powers, as well as the two disputants, to settle the Chaco question by considering the economic and geographic problems of Bolivia and Paraguay.

The principal achievement of the conference was the coördinating and strengthening of inter-American peace machinery. Before the Montevideo conference opened, all of the Latin-American states except Argentina and Bolivia had ratified the Gondra Conciliation Treaty concluded at the Santiago conference in 1923. Less than half of the states had ratified the arbitration and conciliation treaties of 1929. All but five had accepted the Kellogg-Briand Pact and all but four had joined the League of Nations. In an effort to establish a standard method of procedure for the settlement of disputes in the Western Hemisphere, Foreign Minister of Argentina, Saavedra Lamas, had drafted a Latin-American anti-war pact, modeled upon the Pact of Paris. In addition to outlawing wars of aggres-

[16] Brazil had withdrawn from the League in 1928.

sion and compelling a settlement of disputes by legal means, it outlawed aggression in settling territorial questions and followed the
Hoover-Stimson doctrine of nonrecognition of territorial changes brought
about by force. As a sanction the signatory powers agreed to exercise the
political, judicial, and economic means authorized by international law,
as well as the influence of public opinion, "but in no case shall they resort
to intervention, either diplomatic or armed." Although the United States
had previously refused to adhere, at the conference Secretary Hull agreed
to sign the Argentina anti-war pact and also supported the proposal of
Argentina and Chile to consolidate the peace machinery by having non-
signatory powers sign the five peace pacts available to Latin-American
states. As conclusive evidence of its good neighborly intentions before
the conference ended, the United States delegation accepted with explanatory reservations a convention on the rights and duties of states
wherein it was agreed "no state has the right to intervene in the internal
or external affairs of another." [17]

In regard to tariffs and currency stabilization, Secretary Hull took the
lead in recommending a plan for reducing tariffs through the negotiation
of bilateral or multilateral reciprocity treaties. As proof of its earnest
intent the United States signed a reciprocity treaty with Colombia on
December 15, the first of its kind since 1902. The conference voted to
hold a Pan American financial conference at Santiago, Chile, in 1934,
when stabilization of currency and all other thorny financial problems
might be placed on the agenda.

With these political subjects out of the way, the conference had little
difficulty in obtaining agreement upon questions of a technical, social,
or cultural nature. A general extradition treaty was signed, binding for
the first time all American countries and standardizing procedures. In a
comprehensive resolution, the conference established the procedure for
carrying on the future work of codifying international law and provided
for a juridical section of a purely administrative character in the Pan
American Union. A general convention on nationality clarified the allegiance of the individual as to nation of origin, status of inhabitants in
the case of transferred territory, and the effects of matrimony or its dissolution upon the nationality of husband, wife, or children. To sum up
the achievements of the Montevideo Conference: it effected an armistice
in the Chaco, strengthened and correlated the peace machinery of the

[17] Article 8 of Convention on Rights and Duties of States, ratified by the U. S.
June 29, 1934.

Americas, took a practical step towards better trade relations, and enhanced the standing of the United States as a good neighbor.

In his opening speech to the United States Congress on January 3, 1936, President Roosevelt declared that "at no time in the four and a half centuries of modern civilization in the Americas had there existed, in any year, any decade or any generation, in all that time, a greater spirit of mutual understanding, of common helpfulness and of devotion to the ideals of self-government than exist today in the twenty-one Republics. . . . This policy of the 'good neighbor' among the Americas is no longer a hope— it is a fact, active, present, pertinent and effective." To give further concrete illustration of his intention to continue this policy, President Roosevelt on January 30 sent personal letters to the presidents of the other American republics proposing that an extraordinary inter-American conference be summoned to meet in Buenos Aires to determine how the maintenance of peace among the Americas might best be safeguarded. As a tentative suggestion to this end he proposed that the conference give attention to: the prompt ratification of existing peace agreements, their amendment in accordance with experience, and the creation of new instruments of accord.

It should be noted that one of the weaknesses of existing machinery for the maintenance of peace had been the failure of certain states to ratify the agreements already signed; for example, neither of the belligerents in the destructive war in the Chaco had ratified the Inter-American Conciliation and Arbitration Treaties of 1929. A vital need to organize peace was recognized to be the consideration of measures to secure the prompt ratification of existing treaties and conventions for the maintenance of peace. It should further be noted that the republics of the Western Hemisphere were for the most part parties not only to five different treaties of a purely continental character, but to four instruments of a universal character, all designed for the maintenance of peace as well as to some half dozen declarations against war and the forcible acquisition of territory. The conference proposed to consider the possibility of coordinating these instruments and incorporating them in a single instrument.

Under the heading of economic problems, an elaborate agenda was prepared. It was proposed to consider every phase of trade restriction which might hinder closer economic relations and if possible inaugurate substantial reforms. Every type of trade agreement was to be taken up, the question of the most favored nation clause, exchange control, and a tariff truce.

An important subsidiary subject was the improvement of means of communication in the Western Hemisphere. It was noted that substantial progress had been made towards the carrying out of the proposed Pan American Highway system; for example, on July 1, 1936, the highway from Mexico City to Laredo, Texas, was formally dedicated after having been in use for several months. This magnificent road runs for over 750 miles from the United States border through dry plains, a subtropical jungle, and towering mountain peaks to Mexico City. The paved roadway is twenty-one and a half feet wide—it required the construction of over three thousand bridges and culverts, and although it runs from practically sea level to over eight thousand feet, the whole trip can be made in high gear. A route had also been laid out from Mexico City to the Guatemalan border, and much of it had already been completed. A survey had also been made to continue this route to Panama City.

Steamship accommodations had also been improved considerably. In addition to the long-established Grace Line on the west coast, the Moore-McCormack Line on the east, and the Great White Fleet of the United Fruit Co. in the Carribbean, Lykes Brothers Steamship Co. inaugurated a service between Mobile and the west coast of South America. The Alcoa Steamship Company offered improved service in the Caribbean and to the east coast ports, and the Standard Fruit and Steamship Co. and the Shephard Steamship Co. carried freight to the west and east coasts of South America.

With the advent of commercial aviation the communication problem changed to such an extent that the United States became more accessible to Latin America than was Europe. Pan American Airways established a commuting service to all Latin-American capitals. Panagra, Braniff, American, Chicago and Southern, Colonial, Eastern, National, and Western Air Lines established flights between the Americas. Colombian Air Lines connected Bogotá and Barranquilla with Miami, and Venezuela Airlines joined New York with Caracas via Havana.

The delegation from the United States to the Buenos Aires Conference, a large and representative one, was headed by Secretary of State Hull and included Assistant Secretary of State Sumner Welles and Alexander Weddell, Ambassador to Argentina. President Franklin D. Roosevelt showed his intense interest by being present and giving the opening address of the Conference. He urged the necessity of striving to prevent war in the Western Hemisphere by every honorable means and to avoid the creation of conditions giving rise to conflict. Although he did not mention the Monroe Doctrine he indicated that the United States was willing to participate in a multilateral agreement providing for mutual consultation in case of external aggression. He concluded his address by emphasizing the importance of satisfactory commercial relations as a fundamental bulwark of permanent peace.

Three concrete peace proposals were introduced and unanimously agreed upon. The first was a convention for the maintenance of peace. It provided that should the peace of the American republics be threatened by any source either at home or abroad, the signatory powers should consult with each other immediately with a view to coöperative action to preserve the peace of the American continent. According to Secretary of State Cordell Hull "this proposal represents the strongest assurance of peace which this continent has ever had." It should be noted, however, that a very important part of the United States proposal, namely, a permanent body consisting of the foreign ministers of each state to carry out the provisions, does not appear in the convention as accepted.

The second convention coördinated existing treaties for the maintenance of peace. It repeated the obligations and pledges under the Kellogg-Briand Pact, the Inter-American Conciliation and Arbitration Treaties of 1929, and the Saavedra Lamas Anti-War Treaty. To carry out these principles the more effectively, provision was made for individual or joint offers of good offices or mediation and a reminder to the parties to a controversy of their obligations under existing treaties.

Upon threat of war the parties concerned agreed to a delay of six months for consultation before beginning hostilities. Upon the outbreak of war the signatory powers agreed to adopt a common attitude of neutrality, and in order to prevent the spread of hostilities they might impose restrictions upon the sale or shipment of munitions and upon any sort of financial assistance to the belligerents.

The third proposal was a protocol of nonintervention. According to its terms, the internal affairs of any of the parties was inadmissible of intervention by any one of them and violations should give rise to mutual consultation. The protocol reaffirmed the nonintervention doctrine adopted in Montevideo in 1933.

The Buenos Aires Conference had as its aim the maintenance of peace in the Western Hemisphere through mutual consultation and coöperative action. Consultation was the keynote of the Conference, and the conventions were pitched accordingly. The United States, by definitely giving up the right of intervention, had finally agreed to the position of equality in the commonwealth of nations of the Western Hemisphere. The conference marked the completion of another important link on the good neighbor highway.

As the world's political conditions became ever more critical the desire for still closer coöperation for peace in the Americas was strengthened. The eighth Pan American Conference which met in Lima, Peru, December 9, 1938, afforded this opportunity. The agenda included plans both for an American League of Nations and a Pan American Court of Justice. "Hemisphere defense" was the keynote of the Conference.

The United States delegation of twelve was headed by Secretary of State Hull and included Assistant Secretary of State Berle, Ambassador to Peru Steinhardt, Minister to the Dominican Republic Norweb, and Chief Justice Cuevas of the Puerto Rican Supreme Court.

In spite of the opposition of Argentina it was quickly evident that the American republics were determined to take further steps toward strengthening the machinery for continental defense. Although the idea of an American League of Nations was discarded, the twenty-one states finally agreed to support a project of American coöperation which was designated by the conference as the Declaration of Lima. This Declaration reaffirmed the principle of continental solidarity and the decision to defend it against all foreign intervention. In case the peace, security or territorial integrity of any American republic should be threatened it was agreed to make effective this solidarity by consultations as established by conventions in force. To facilitate such consultative action the Declaration provided that "the Ministers of Foreign Affairs of the American republics, when deemed desirable and at the initiative of any one of them, will meet in their several capitals by rotation. . . ."

By this Declaration a definite procedure of consultation was established which could be quickly utilized in an emergency. It was signal success for Secretary Hull in his efforts to obtain unanimous action against a threat of autocratic aggression.

Perhaps the next most important result of the Conference of Lima was a Declaration of American Principles which the governments of the American republics proclaimed as essential to the preservation of world order under law. The substance of these principles had been presented by Secertary Hull in a statement released on July 16, 1937. Summarized, the Declaration established the following canons of international conduct: intervention and the use of force as instruments of national or international policy are proscribed; international differences must be settled by peaceful means and international law must govern relations between states; the faithful observance of treaties is an indispensable rule of international conduct and revision must be obtained by agreement of the signatory powers; intellectual and economic coöperation are essential to national and international well being and world peace can only be achieved by international coöperation based upon these principles.

The Lima Conference established a precedent by not signing a single treaty or convention. All of its projects were formulated as resolutions, declarations, or recommendations, of which 112 were accepted. As in previous conferences the majority of resolutions pertained to nonpolitical subjects. Resolutions were approved committing the Americas to establish liberal trade practices and equality of treatment, to improve transportation and communication, to increase the exchange of professors and students, to protect Indian art, literature, language, and culture, and to coöperate in various ways conducive to better relations and understandings.

Although no alliance for defense was established and no new machinery for the elimination of war was set up, the twenty-one republics of the Western Hemisphere agreed unanimously to consult and if necessary to act for their mutual defense. In the words of Secretary Hull "the American Republics have made it clear to the world that they stand united to maintain and defend the peace of this hemisphere, their territorial integrity, their principles of international relations, their own institutions and policies."

The nations who subscribed to the Declaration of Lima little expected that in less than a year they would be called upon to give effect to its basic principles. Yet when on September 1, 1939, Herr Hitler loosed the Nazi hordes upon Poland, the repercussion in the New World was such that the American republics unanimously agreed to consult as to a joint policy of hemisphere defense.

On September 23, 1939, the representatives of the twenty-one republics assembled at Panama City in the first Inter-American Consultative Conference of Foreign Ministers. Undersecretary of State Sumner Welles who headed the delegation of the United States well expressed the sentiments of the Conference when he characterized it as "a meeting of American neighbors to consider in a moment of grave emergency the peaceful measures which they may feel it wise to adopt . . . so as best to insure their national interests and the collective interests of the nations of the New World."

The most important problem was the security of the Western Hemisphere and the Conference faced it resolutely. A general declaration of neutrality of the American republics was adopted which not only included the generally accepted canons of conduct as to neutral rights and duties, but added several of special application to the Western Hemisphere. The American republics might bring together and place in a single port under guard belligerent merchant vessels which had sought refuge in their waters. Bona fide transfers of flags of American merchant vessels in American waters were permitted. Defensive armament on merchant vessels was conceded, but belligerent submarines could be excluded from the territorial waters of a state.

The most original and drastic action of the Conference was a joint resolution entitled the Declaration of Panama whereby the American republics declared that, so long as they were neutral, they were, as of inherent right, entitled to have those waters adjacent to the American continents free from the commission of any hostile act by a non-American belligerent. A remarkable feature of the resolution was the promulgation of a protective zone approximately 300 miles wide encircling the continents south of Canadian territorial waters. The resolution contemplated no extension of the three-mile marginal sea but rather an extension of the adjacent waters as a zone free from belligerent activities as an essential means of self-protection.

As might have been expected violations were not long in materializing. The scuttling of the *Graf von Spee* by the Nazi captain in Uruguayan territorial waters, December 13, 1939, and various sinkings by the British within the protective zone brought about a joint protest through the President of Panama on December 23, 1939. Great Britain, France, and Germany were advised that consultations were being carried out looking towards penalizing future violations by forbidding access to supplies or repairing of damages in American ports to belligerents guilty of the commission of warlike acts within the security zone.[18]

With a view to studying further the problems of neutrality, the Conference authorized the governing board of the Pan American Union to set up an Inter-American Neutrality Committee of seven experts for the duration of the war. This committee met at Rio de Janeiro and, on April 27, 1940, set forth a lengthy recommendation which in substance favored the maintenance of the security zone as an open sea for the commercial traffic of every state but prohibited any sort of belligerent act within the zone.[19]

[18] *Department of State Bulletin,* Vol. I, No. 26 (Dec. 23, 1939), p. 723.
[19] Pan American Union, *Decrees and Regulations on Neutrality, Supp. No. 2* (Law and Treaty Series No. 14), pp. 38-48.

Another important result of the Panama Conference was the setting up in Washington on November 15, 1939 of the Inter-American Financial and Economic Advisory Committee consisting of one expert representing each of the American republics. The Committee's function was to establish a program of coöperation between the American republics to protect their economic and financial structures, maintain their fiscal equilibrium, safeguard the stability of their currencies, and develop their industries and commerce.

The second meeting of ministers of foreign affairs of the American republics convened in Havana, Cuba, from July 21 to 30, 1940. The meeting was called to meet the threat of Nazi aggression in the Western Hemisphere through the possible seizure of Dutch, Danish, and French colonies following the subjugation of the mother countries. Agreement was quickly obtained to cover any such possible contingency. Condemning violence in every form and refusing to recognize force as a basis of rights, the American republics refused to accept any transfer or attempt to transfer any interest or right in the Western Hemisphere. In the case of such an attempt thus threatening the peace of the continent, provision was made for the taking over and the provisional administration of such a region by an Inter-American Commission of Territorial Administration.

A supplementary declaration known as the Act of Havana authorized the creation of an emergency committee to cover situations arising prior to the promulgation of the convention. The declaration further permitted any state in an emergency to act singly or jointly with others in any manner required by its own defense or in defense of the continent. This action was the first unanimous recognition by Latin America of the value of the principle of the Monroe Doctrine for the defense of the Americas. A number of resolutions were aimed at subversive activities, and attempted their control by restricting the political activities of foreign diplomatic and consular representatives, regulating more closely the issuance of passports, and coördinating police and judicial measures for mutual defense. The American republics were getting prepared to stand together against the totalitarian menace.

The Third Conference of Ministers of Foreign Affairs of the American republics held at Rio de Janeiro from January 15 to 28, 1942, was convened as a result of the arrival of the war in the Western Hemisphere. The Japanese attack on Pearl Harbor was a flagrant act of aggression which gave the two Americas an opportunity to prove that promised coöperation meant more than high sounding declarations.

The Caribbean republics did not wait for the conference to indicate their whole-hearted support of the United States. The day after the attack on Pearl Harbor, Costa Rica, the Dominican Republic, Guatemala, Haiti, Honduras, Panama, and El Salvador declared war upon Japan and followed this within a few days with similar declarations of war against Germany and Italy. Cuba declared war on Japan on December 9, and on Germany and Italy on December 11. Nicaragua declared war on all three of the Axis powers on December 11. Thus, within four days after the United States became a belligerent, nine of the Latin-American republics had joined her in the conflict.

On December 8, Mexico condemned Japanese aggression, severing diplomatic relations the same day, and with Germany and Italy three days later. Colombia broke relations with Japan December 8, and Venezuela with the three Axis powers December 31. The other Latin-American republics promised to honor their obligations, refrained from regarding the United States as a belligerent, and put into effect various measures to restrain Axis activities—an auspicious background for the forthcoming conference.

Undersecretary of State Sumner Welles, who headed the American delegation, expressed the appreciation of the United States government at the declarations of solidarity and support, but he also made it clear that the only certain method of stamping out the Axis methods of poisoning inter-American intercourse was by the severance of diplomatic relations. Mr. Welles' address was well received, but it was the eloquence and idealism of Mexican Foreign Minister Padilla and the obstinacy and diplomatic acumen of Brazilian Foreign Minister Aranha which prevented the conference from foundering upon the rocks of Axis subversive activities.

A resolution sponsored by Colombia, Mexico, and Venezuela declaring that the American republics "cannot continue diplomatic relations with Japan, Germany and Italy" appeared to have unanimous support. However the Argentinian representative at first vacillated then balked, and he was supported by the representative from Chile. As a compromise, the wording of the resolution as finally voted merely "recommended rupture of diplomatic relations" as each country should determine. The sentiments of the Conference were shown when Peru, Uruguay, Bolivia, Paraguay, Ecuador, and Brazil broke off relations with the Axis powers before the Conference closed.

The final act of the Rio Conference comprised forty-one declarations and resolutions. In addition to recommending severance of diplomatic relations they urged the production and exchange of strategic materials essential to hemisphere defense and the formulation of a coördinated plan for economic mobilization. Complete coördination of transportation facilities was recommended and the improvement of all inter-American communications by land, water, and air, including the construction of the unfinished sections of the Pan American Highway. An economic boycott of the Axis powers was approved, with reservations by Argentina and Chile, and several resolutions were aimed at the combatting of subversive activities and the control of dangerous aliens. It was recommended that an Inter-American Joint Defense Board composed of military and naval technicians appointed by each government should be set up in Washington to study and recommend measures for the defense of this continent. The Board met for the first time March 20, 1942 and functioned effectively for hemisphere defense.

The Rio Conference, although based upon idealistic principles, was realistic in its methods and its proposals. The United States needed freedom of action, bases, and strategic materials; the Latin-American republics needed protection, financial assistance, and supplies. The Conference provided for a mutually advantageous exchange.

During the course of World War II the overfriendly attitude of Argentina to the Axis powers provoked retaliatory measures on the part of the United States, resulting finally in a formal request upon the part of Argentina that an Inter-American Conference of Foreign Ministers be held to consider her relations with the other American republics. The United States countered by suggesting a conference of the American states coöperating in the war to consider war and post-war problems. The proposal of the United States was accepted with the understanding that the Argentine situation be placed upon the agenda.

The Inter-American Conference on Problems of War and Peace met in Mexico City during February-March, 1945. All the republics except Argentina, which had not declared war upon the Axis, were represented. The United States delegation was headed by Secretary of State Stettinius and included Senators Connally and Austin. Foreign Minister Padilla of Mexico was elected President of the Conference.

After various resolutions had been passed for closer collaboration in the war effort, such as establishing the Inter-American Defense Board upon a permanent basis and strengthening the coöperation against subversive Axis propaganda, the Conference took up the problem of post-war international organization. The Latin-American states desired a strong regional agreement against aggression, whereas the United States was concerned lest regional agreements should interfere with the new world organization which was to be established.[20] The resulting compromise known as the Act of Chapultepec placed aggression against an American state either by a non-American state or an American state on a parity. In either case the signatory states would consult as to what action should be taken. Aggression was defined as armed trespass and various measures such as severing diplomatic relations, imposing an economic boycott, and using armed force were to be utilized. A treaty of such a character was to be concluded after the war to constitute a regional arrangement for the security of the Western Hemisphere but consistent with the purposes and principles of the general international organization.

A very important resolution was passed to reorganize and strengthen the inter-American system by having the International Conferences of American States meet every four years and Foreign Ministers meet annually. The governing board of the Pan American Union was to be composed of *ad hoc* representatives with the rank of Ambassador and they were given broader powers. The Chairman of the Board was to be elected annually and not be eligible for immediate re-election. The Director General was to be chosen for a ten-year term and not be eligible for re-election. A draft charter including these and other changes was to be prepared and presented at the next Conference of the American States.[21]

At the end of the Conference a resolution was passed deploring Argentinian policy and expressing the wish that Argentina would change its policy so that it might adhere to the Final Act of the Conference and be incorporated into the United Nations. An understanding was reached at the Conference that if Argentina would declare war on the Axis and curtail further Axis activities in Argentina, the United States would support the admission of Argentina in the forthcoming conference at San Francisco to draw up a charter for the United Nations.

Although it was expected that a Conference of Foreign Ministers of the American Republics would meet in 1946 to formalize the provisions of the Act of Chapultepec by concluding a treaty of mutual assistance, it was not until August 15, 1947, that such a conference met in Rio de Janeiro.[22] All of the Latin-American republics except Nicaragua were represented and the Conference completed its work in less than three

[20] The American delegation itself was divided on this issue to such an extent that the Mexican representative suggested an adjournment until the American delegation make up its collective mind.

[21] *Final Act of the Inter-American Conference on Problems of War and Peace* (Washington, D. C., 1945).

[22] The United States had delayed the Conference because of Argentina's failure to comply with the obligations assumed after the Conference at Mexico City.

weeks. The Treaty of Reciprocal Assistance signed at Rio de Janeiro on September 2, 1947, condemned war and provided for peaceful procedure for the settlement of all disputes in the Inter-American System. An attack against one American state was an attack against all and each undertook to assist the state attacked, individually and collectively, until the Security Council of the United Nations should take measures to maintain security. The states were to consult when the peace of the Americas was threatened and sanctions might be employed beginning with the suspension of diplomatic relations and ending with the use of force. Aggression was defined as unprovoked attacks or armed invasion.

This regional agreement looking towards the maintenance of security in the Western Hemisphere which became operative in 1948 when Costa Rica, the fourteenth republic, deposited its ratification, was the successful culmination of the continuous efforts of almost a half century to achieve coöperation for mutual defense. The fact that action could be taken by a two-thirds vote made the procedure the more effective. It was up to the next conference to perfect the organization of American states.

As previously noted, a draft charter for the organization of the American republics had been prepared and was the principal item on the agenda of the Ninth International Conference of American States which met in the spring of 1948 in Bogotá. In spite of a bloody revolution which cost over a thousand lives and destroyed many of the fine public buildings in Bogotá, the Conference carried out the program contemplated.

The United States had noted a gradually mounting antagonism in the Latin-American countries as a result of its inability to carry out the European Recovery Program and at the same time meet the economic and financial needs of its neighbors to the south. To reverse this trend the American delegation headed by Secretary of State Marshall not only included such diplomatic experts in Latin American affairs as Assistant Secretary of State Norman Armour, Director of the Office of American Republics Paul C. Daniels, and Ambassador Willard L. Beaulac, but also Secretary of the Treasury John W. Snyder, Secretary of Commerce W. Averell Harriman, and Head of the World Bank John J. McCloy.

The Charter of Organization of the American States as finally adopted at Bogotá not only put the Organization upon a permanent treaty basis, but made a number of important changes long considered necessary. The Inter-American Conference was made the supreme organ for the formulation of policy; it would meet at least once every five years; each state would be represented and have one vote. The Meeting of Consultation of Ministers of Foreign Affairs was retained to consider problems of an urgent nature and it could be convened upon the request of any state. The former governing board of the Pan American Union was now established as the Council of the Organization of the American States with each state having a representative possessing the status of ambassador. It was given authority to consider all matters submitted by the International Conference or the Organ of Consultation and it might serve provisionally as the Organ of Consultation. It could draft and submit proposals to the governments or to the Conferences of the American States. As aids, three agencies were established: the Inter-American Economic and Social Council, the Inter-American Council of Jurists, and the Inter-American Cultural Council. The Pan American Union under the Charter became the permanent organ and secretariat of the Organization.

Perhaps the next most important achievement of the Ninth Conference was the American Treaty on Pacific Settlement, also known as the "Pact of Bogotá." By the terms of this treaty the American Republics accepted the obligation to "settle" all disputes by peaceable means. The procedures provided are good offices, mediation, investigation and conciliation, judicial settlement, and arbitration. This treaty was the successful culmination of the sustained effort to bring about obligatory peaceful settlement of disputes in the Western Hemisphere.

On the economic side Secretary Marshall stated that President Truman had requested an increase of $500 million in the Export-Import Bank allocation for Latin-American loans. It was also promised that the Economic Coöperation Administration would finance a part of Latin-American exports to Europe in United States dollars. That the allocation did not reach the amount expected was due to the policy of Argentina fixing a price for her cereals, meats, and hides far above the world market price. An elaborate Economic Agreement was signed which provided for financial and technical coöperation, for the approval and safeguarding of private investment, and the improvement of transportation facilities in the Western Hemisphere.

Inasmuch as individual rights were being eliminated in all countries behind the Iron Curtain, the Ninth International Conference adopted an American Declaration of the Rights and Duties of Man far more inclusive than the Bill of Rights in the United States Constitution. Also, in order to go on record as regards the threat of Soviet Communism, the Conference approved a declaration and resolution stating that "by its anti-democratic character and its interventionist tendency the political activity of international communism or any totalitarian doctrine is incompatible with the concept of American freedom. . . ." [23]

The Ninth International Conference at Bogotá, by setting up an improved organization of the American states upon a treaty basis, pointed the way for the establishment of regional organizations for the maintenance of peace in other parts of the world as envisaged by the Charter of the United Nations.[24] The Charter of the Organization of American States went into effect December 13, 1951, when Colombia was the fourteenth state to complete ratification.

The Senate of the United States approved the ratification of the Charter of the Organization of American States on August 28, 1950. A world crisis had occurred three months earlier when the Communist forces in North Korea had violated the 38th Parallel and marched south. The Security Council of the United Nations immediately voted that a breach of the peace had occurred and called upon all members of the United Nations to render assistance. One day later, June 28, the Organization of American States unanimously adopted a resolution declaring its firm adherence to the actions of the Security Council and reaffirming the pledge of continental solidarity. Within a month seventeen of the republics had promised at least token assistance.

When it was seen that the Communist aggression threatened the security of the entire world the United States felt that a meeting of the American Ministers of Foreign Affairs was required to consider the situation. The date set was March, 1951, the place, Washington, and the agenda covered political, military, and economic coöperation for the defense of the Americas abroad and their security at home. The United States felt that greater aid to the United Nations forces in Korea was needed and that the Latin-American Republics should tighten their internal controls against Communism. All twenty-one republics of the Western Hemisphere were represented; President Truman welcomed the delegates and Secretary of State Dean Acheson was elected President of the Conference. Both President Truman and Secretary Acheson stressed the immediate dangers of Communist imperialism to the democratic countries of the Western Hemisphere and the need to combat them effectively.

On the whole the Conference was successful in its aims. The principles of the United Nations were sustained and specific efforts to strengthen the Inter-American Defense Board and to provide strategic materials and

[23] Final Act, XXXII.

[24] For texts of treaties, conventions, resolutions, and commentary thereon see *Ninth Int. Conf. of Amer. States, Dept. of State Pub. 3263* (Washington, D. C., 1948). For *Charter of the Organization of American States* see Appendix.

to aid with troops where possible were agreed upon. Resolution VIII of the Final Act recommended adequate legislation be adopted in every American republic to prevent and punish subversive acts of international Communism and no state made any reservations to this resolution.

The Tenth International Conference of American States scheduled to meet in Caracas, Venezuela, March 1, 1954 was the first to be held under the Charter signed at Bogotá in 1948. The United States was particularly desirous of including in the agenda consideration of "the intervention of international Communism in the American republics." The Latin American states were for the most part less interested in Communism than in economic questions but Guatemala alone opposed its inclusion. The Eisenhower administration had promised that the Republicans would not neglect Latin America, but except for Dr. Milton Eisenhower's visit no concrete evidence for change in policy was visible. The Latin American states were in a mood to demand action.

All the twenty one republics were present except Costa Rica who by refusing to attend showed her disapproval of the military dictatorship in Venezuela. The United States delegation headed by Secretary of State John Foster Dulles included former Assistant Secretary of State for Latin American Affairs John M. Cabot, his successor Henry F. Holland, Assistant Secretary of State for Economic Affairs Samuel C. Waugh, Legal Advisor Herman Phleger, United States Ambassador to Venezuela, Fletcher Warren and the United States Representative on the Council of the Organization of American States, John C. Dreier.

Secretary Dulles, supported vigorously by the delegates of Cuba, Peru and the Dominican Republic, was determined to obtain priority for discussion of the Communist menace. Foreign Minister Toriello of Guatemala, supported by Argentina, was equally insistent against it. The United States won out and its draft resolution condemned International Communist activity directed against the political system of the Western Hemisphere as a threat to its peace and security, and recommended positive measures be taken for its extermination. The vote was 17 to 1 in favor, with only Guatemala voting in the negative and Argentina and Mexico abstaining.

Secretary Dulles pledged the intention of the United States to obtain better economic relations and it was agreed to hold an economic conference in Rio de Janeiro in 1955. The Conference voted a resolution requesting that industrialized states refrain from any restrictions on the imports of raw materials which was clearly aimed at the United States.

It also by a vote of 19 to 1—only the United States refraining—passed a resolution calling for the elimination of colonialism and "foreign occupation" of territory in the Western Hemisphere. A resolution favoring the guarantee of human rights and freedoms to all persons received the support of all the states except Guatemala which abstained.

In all, the Conference passed some 117 resolutions, declarations, recommendations, agreements and approved motions. The United States had succeeded in impressing its neighbors with the danger of Communism and obtained their support in combatting it. We recognized the need for closer economic coöperation and would have the opportunity to prove it at Rio. On the other hand the enthusiastic support of the United States by a Trujillo-dominated Dominican Republic and the failure of the United States to support the position taken by democratic Uruguay led one delegate to declare that the United States preferred "docile dictators to difficult democracies."

In addition to the general periodic international conferences of American states numerous special conferences have been held, particularly since World War I, covering, among others, the fields of health, commerce, finance, transportation, agriculture, child welfare, and education. Space prevents more than the most summary consideration of these congresses.

Public health and sanitary problems have particularly engaged the interests of the republics of the Western Hemisphere. The Second International American Conference of 1901 recommended the establishment of a Pan American Sanitary Bureau which was accomplished the following year. Since that time thirteen international sanitary conferences of the American republics have taken place, the last held in Ciudad Trujillo in October, 1950. As a result of these conferences a Pan American Sanitary Code has been promulgated and put into effect in all of the twenty-one republics. As a result of more efficient sanitary conditions, quarantine regulations have been materially liberalized throughout the Western Hemisphere. Subjects such as public health organization, vital statistics, infant hygiene, and the control of such diseases as yellow fever, leprosy, malaria, tuberculosis, and typhus fever regularly appear on the agenda. In 1947 the Directing Council of the Pan American Sanitary Organization was created to serve as the executive body of the Pan American Sanitary Organization between the quadrennial sessions of the Pan American Sanitary Conference. This Directing Council held its fifth meeting in Washington, D. C., from September 24 to October 3, 1951. This Directing Council also serves as the Regional Committee of the World Health Organization, according to an agreement between PASO and WHO approved June 30, 1949, at the second World Health Assembly.

To celebrate the fiftieth anniversary of the Pan American Sanitary Organization a special Congress met at Havana in 1952 to review the technical bases of public health practice.

Under the auspices of the Pan American Sanitary Bureau four Inter-American Congresses in Radiology have been held, the first in 1943 and the latest in Mexico City in 1952.

Closely affiliated with the work of the Sanitary Conferences has been that of the four Pan American Conferences of National Directors of Health held every five years in Washington since 1926. At these confer-ences it has been possible to consider the technical problems of tracking down and eliminating the sources of infection. At the third conference the recently discovered jungle type of yellow fever, the bubonic plague, typhus, malta fever, and malaria were all discussed at length. Some twenty-two resolutions covering every phase of public health were adopted. The ten Pan American Conferences on Child Welfare, the first meeting in Buenos Aires in 1916, and the tenth to be held in Panama City in 1954 should be mentioned in passing. These conferences have con-sidered exhaustively problems of the health, social welfare, and education of the child. As Katherine Lenroot, former Chief of the Children's Bureau, has aptly remarked, these conferences have met "to take counsel for America's children." On a somewhat broader front the regional Inter-American Red Cross Conferences the first of which met in Buenos Aires in 1923, and the most recent in Mexico City in 1951, have been devoted largely to the problems of disaster relief, health and social assistance, and public nursing.

Five Pan American commercial conferences have been held to obtain an informal but comprehensive exchange of news and information be-tween official and unofficial commercial representatives, trade experts, businessmen, and others interested in the improvement of business con-ditions and the development of trade. The first four of these conferences were held in Washington under the auspices of the Pan American Union: the first in February, 1911, the second in June, 1919, the third in May, 1927, the fourth in October, 1931, the fifth at Buenos Aires under the auspices of the Argentine government in May-June, 1935. These confer-ences have regularly supported the lowering of customs barriers and the simplification of customs, port and consular procedure, improved trans-portation facilities, and the settlement of commercial disputes by arbitration. All twenty-one republics were present at the fifth conference and some sixty-four conclusions were approved, four in the form of conventions. These conventions related to measures for the suppression of smuggling; to the creation of Pan American commercial boards in each republic to coöperate with the Pan American Union in gathering and distributing commercial information; to the establishment of a Pan American tourist passport; and to the creation of transit facilities for airplanes operating on regularly established commercial lines.

It was to be expected that the subjects of transportation and communication which had received some attention in both the commercial and financial conferences, as well as in the periodic Pan American conferences, would also be the basis of more specialized treatment. Although all of the states in the Western Hemisphere are members of the Universal Postal Union, it was decided in 1921 to establish a regional postal organization in the Americas. The first Congress was held in Buenos Aires in 1921 and the second was held in Mexico City in 1926. At the third Congress of the Postal Union of the Americas held in Madrid in 1931 Spain joined and has remained a member ever since. The most recent meeting was the Sixth Congress, held in Madrid in 1950. Conventions regarding parcel post, money orders, air mail in the Americas, and upon other kindred subjects have been signed at these meetings.

Five Pan American Highway Congresses have been held, the first in Buenos Aires in 1925 and the fifth in Lima in 1951. The problems of railway transportation were first considered in 1910. The seventh Pan American Railway Conference was held in Mexico City in 1950. Not only are the states of the Western Hemisphere represented in the International Civil Aviation Organization, but they have held regional conferences as well, as, for example, the South American Regional Air Navigation Meeting held in Lima in 1947 and the South Atlantic Regional Air Navigation Meeting in Rio de Janeiro the same year. A joint meeting of these two organizations was held in Buenos Aires in 1951. Four Inter-American Travel Conferences have been held and the fifth is scheduled to meet in Panama City in 1954. The first Inter-American Radio Conference was held in Havana in 1937 and the fifth in Montevideo in 1952.

The agricultural problems of the American republics have also been considered jointly in conference; the first Inter-American Conference of Agriculture was held in Washington, D. C., in 1930 and the fourth in Montevideo in 1950. On March 19, 1943, President Calderón Guardia of Costa Rica and Vice-president Wallace of the United States jointly inaugurated the Inter-American Institute of Agricultural Sciences in Turrialba, Costa Rica. This Institute had aided the American republics with advisory services in animal husbandry, the control of plant and animal diseases, livestock raising, soil conservation, and in other technical matters. Its research work in the production of coffee, cocoa, vegetable fats and oils, and fiber have benefited industry throughout the Americas.

Perhaps the most extensive agenda subjects considered for any Pan American conferences are those of the Scientific Conferences whose aim has been "to increase the knowledge of things American and to disseminate and make the culture of each American country the heritage of all American republics." Nine of these conferences have been held, the first in Santiago, Chile, in 1907-1908, the latest in Havana in 1950. At the second conference at Washington in 1915-1916 more than two hundred delegates were in attendance from the Latin-American countries and more than a thousand from the United States, making it one of the greatest international scientific meetings in the world's history.

At the eighth Pan American Scientific Congress held in Washington, D. C., in 1940, an Inter-American Statistical Institute was established whose Executive Committee in January, 1946, named a Committee on the 1950 Census to provide for a uniform census of the American states. This committee had its third meeting in Bogotá in 1950 in connection with the second meeting of the Institute.

Other Pan American conferences which might be considered under the head of intellectual coöperation have been the five meetings of the Pan American Institute of Geography and History, the first in Rio de Janeiro in 1933, and the most recent in Santiago, Chile, in 1950; and the two Inter-American Congresses on Education, the first in Havana in 1930 and the second in Santiago, Chile, in 1934.

An Inter-American Seminar on Elementary Education held in Montevideo in 1950 was declared to be the initial step toward insuring the right to education for the present school-age generation in the Americas.

Other conferences of a miscellaneous nature might be noted to indicate the variety of such meetings. The architects of the Western Hemisphere have been meeting regularly since 1920 to consider such problems as housing, new construction methods, and town planning. Their eighth conference was held in Mexico City in 1952. There have been six Inter-American Press Congresses, three Pan American Congresses of Mining Engineers and Geology, two Pan American Pharmaceutical Congresses, ten Inter-American Indian Congresses, and three Pan American Congresses of Physical Education. An Inter-American Conference on the

Rehabilitation of the Crippled and Disabled was held in Mexico City in July, 1948.

When it is realized that the American states also participate regularly in the bimonthly meetings of the Council of the American States in Washington and in the meetings of the three technical organs of the Council—the Inter-American Economic and Social Council, the Inter-American Council of Jurists, and the Inter-American Cultural Council—one can appreciate the importance and vast ramifications of the conference system in the Americas.

SUPPLEMENTARY READINGS

MARY MARGARET BALL, *The Problem of Inter-American Organization* (Stanford, Calif., 1944).

HARRY BERNSTEIN, *Modern and Contemporary Latin America* (Philadelphia, 1952).

LAURENCE DUGGAN, *The Search for Hemisphere Security* (New York, 1949).

JAMES W. GANTENBEIN, *The Evolution of Our Latin American Policy* (New York, 1950).

E. O. GUERRANT, *Roosevelt's Good Neighbor Policy* (Albuquerque, 1950).

LIVINGSTON HARTLEY, *Our Maginot Line* (New York, 1939).

HUBERT HERRING, *America and the Americas* (Claremont, 1944).

JOHN T. P. HUMPHREY, *The Inter-American System* (Toronto, 1942).

RUTH D. MASTERS, *et al.*, *Handbook of International Organizations* (Washington, D. C., 1945).

Participation of the United States in International Conferences (Washington, D. C., 1941–).

J. B. SCOTT, *International Conferences of American States, 1889-1928* (New York, 1931).

Strength of the International Communist Movement, Special Subcommittee on Security Affairs (Washington, D. C., Oct. 15, 1953).

❦ 3 ❦

The Monroe Doctrine

IN ANY discussion of the relations between the United States and Latin
America the Monroe Doctrine must necessarily occupy a prominent
place. To the average citizen of the United States the Monroe Doctrine
seems to possess almost as important a niche in the structure of American
institutions as the Declaration of Independence and the Constitution.[1]
Yet this same normal American, if pressed to give an exact explanation of
what is meant by the Monroe Doctrine, would have great difficulty in
making himself clear. He would probably define it ultimately in some
such general terms as, "America for the Americans," or "Europe must keep
her hands off," or some other expression whose meaning would approximate the idea that the United States should mind her own business and
take care of the affairs of the Western Hemisphere, and the nations of the
Eastern Hemisphere should do the same. And the interpretation would
not be wholly inaccurate; for, in the words of Professor Hart, the Monroe
Doctrine is a national policy based upon "the daily common-sense
recognition of the geographical and political fact that the United States
of America is by fact and by right more interested in American affairs,
both on the northern and southern continents, than any European power
can possibly be."[2]

If the Monroe Doctrine were merely a question of an understanding
between the United States and Europe, it might well be considered as one
whose solution had at last been reached. Sixty-three nations of the world
voluntarily signed the Covenant of the League of Nations, thereby giving
their assent to Article XXI, which states: "Nothing in this covenant shall
be deemed to affect the validity of international engagements, such as

[1] Mary Baker Eddy, writing at the time of the first hundred years' anniversary of
the Monroe Doctrine declared, "I believe in the Monroe Doctrine, in our Constitution
and in the laws of God." (*N. Y. Times*, Dec. 2, 1923.)

[2] A. B. Hart, *The Monroe Doctrine* (Boston, 1916), p. 2.

48

treaties of arbitration, or regional understandings like the Monroe Doctrine, for securing the maintenance of peace." Although the term "regional understanding" more accurately describes Woodrow Wilson's proposed development of the doctrine than its accepted meaning, Europe was willing to subscribe to the doctrine under its original name. In fact, the very same doctrine, which Lord Salisbury declared to be a novel principle which "no statesman, however eminent, and no nation, however powerful, are competent to insert into the code of international law," [3] was declared by representatives of Great Britain at the Paris Conference to have become an international understanding "consistent with the spirit of the covenant; and, indeed, the principles of the League as expressed in Article X represent the extension to the whole world of the principles of this doctrine." [4] The same doctrine, which Bismarck declared to be an "international impertinence," and von Bülow "a theory launched venturesomely upon the blue waves of conjectural politics," was recognized to such an extent by Germany at the outbreak of World War I that the German ambassador at Washington assured the United States government that Germany had no intention, in case of victory, to seek expansion in South America. Furthermore, Dr. Dernburg, recognized as representing the German government unofficially, declared that "Germany has not the slightest intention of violating any part or section of the Monroe Doctrine." [5] Finally, France, which under the Second Empire committed the grossest violation of the principles of the doctrine by engineering the Maximilian expedition, has now recognized the fact that the Monroe Doctrine is bound up inseparably with the safety of the United States; and, in the words of M. Paul Deschanel, "It issued from the vitals of reality, just as the Constitution of the United States itself." [6]

But, whether or not we consider the Monroe Doctrine a settled policy as regards the future relations between the United States and Europe, the question remains open as regards our relations with the independent republics of Latin America. However fixed the North American may be in his belief that in the past the Monroe Doctrine has been the sheet-anchor of safety for the storm-tossed republics to the south, he must recognize the fact that there has been a strong belief throughout Latin America

[3] In his answer to Mr. Olney, Lord Salisbury gives an impartial and judicial interpretation of the Monroe Doctrine. See *Foreign Relations of the United States*, 1895, Part I, p. 563.

[4] Quoted by A. B. Hall, *The Monroe Doctrine and the Great War* (Chicago, 1920), p. 153.

[5] *New York Times*, Oct. 25, 1914.

[6] *Les Questions Actuelles de Politique Etrangère dans l'Amérique du Nord* (Paris, 1911), p. 231.

that the original Monroe Doctrine has very little value for any country but
the United States. Undoubtedly, many men of high position and great
authority in the states of Latin America have paid tribute to the doctrine
for the very substantial assistance it gave to the Latin-American republics
at a time when friendly intercession was most advantageous. At the
Fourth Pan American Conference, Dr. Victoriano de la Plaza, Minister of
Foreign Affairs in Argentina, was whole-hearted in his praise. "This
condition of precarious autonomy and liberty of action," he said, "and the
constant danger of being subjugated or suffering the mutilation of their
territory, would have continued among those weak states but for the
wise and famous declarations of President Monroe." [7] That a fine appreciation of the true spirit and meaning of the doctrine may be found in
South America the following quotation from the eminent Argentinian
authority on international law, Dr. Luis M. Drago, will indicate:

The Monroe Doctrine is in fact a formula of independence. It imposes no
dominion and no superiority. Much less does it establish protectorates or relation
of superior to inferior. It creates no obligations and no responsibilities between
the nations of America, but simply calls upon all of them, with their own means
and without aid, to exclude from within their respective frontiers the jurisdiction
of European powers. Proclaimed by the United States in the interest of their
own peace and security, the other republics of the continent have, in their turn,
proceeded to adopt it with an eye alone to their own individual welfare and
tranquillity. . . . Thus understood, the Monroe Doctrine, which in the end is
nothing more than the expression of the will of the people to maintain their
liberty, assures the independence of the states of that continent in respect to
one another as well as in relation to the powers of Europe. [8]

Señor Alejandro Alvarez, the Chilean delegate to the fourth Assembly
of the League of Nations, went so far as to declare that the Monroe
Doctrine was more valuable to South America than Article X of the
League Covenant because American naval and military forces stood ready
to enforce the Monroe Doctrine.

On the other hand, there is also a very strong sentiment prevailing
among many worthy representatives of Latin-American countries, that,
as far as the republics of Latin America are concerned, the Monroe Doctrine has long since outlived its usefulness. The conditions that called
into existence the original statement of President Monroe have passed
away, never to return. The subsequent policy of the United States, which
masked itself under the doctrine of Monroe, was aimed at Latin Amer-

[7] *Fourth Int. Conf. of Amer. States, Sen. Doc. No. 744,* 61st Cong., 3rd Sess., Vol. I,
p. 12.
[8] Hart, *op. cit.,* p. 253.

ica as well as at Europe and Asia. When Secretary Olney declared that "today the United States is practically sovereign on this continent, and its fiat is law upon the subjects to which it confines its interposition," and used this interpretation of the Monroe Doctrine to interfere in a dispute in South America, the inference seemed clear that the United States considered itself sovereign on *both continents*. The great republics of South America keenly resented any such attitude. When the United States took over the Panama Canal, on the ground that the act was justified by the interests of civilization, the South American countries could not fail to note that the interests of civilization and those of the United States were surprisingly alike. Dr. Lucio M. Moreno Quintana, an eminent Argentine lawyer and a grandson of a former president of the country, has expressed what is unquestionably the sentiment of the great majority of Latin Americans: "The Monroe Doctrine is not a doctrine of America for the Americans, but of America for the North Americans. It has served as an admirable instrument for the United States to separate Europe from America and to establish its hegemony over the latter. The United States has been at all times preoccupied in obtaining concessions of every kind at the cost of the sovereignty of the rest of the American states. The doctrine is dangerous because it is North American imperialism hidden under a principle of international law." [9]

Just so long as a large number of our Latin-American neighbors felt that the Monroe Doctrine was a selfish policy, based upon the desire of the United States to exclude European powers from interfering with the political interests of the Western Hemisphere merely in order to have a better opportunity to act in a similar fashion itself, our relations with Latin America could not be established upon a satisfactory basis of mutual confidence. But, before casting aside the Monroe Doctrine as an inseparable barrier to a more friendly *rapprochement* between the United States and the Latin-American republics, let us consider the doctrine from two standpoints. First, has the Monroe Doctrine of the past been a policy that, while safeguarding the interests of the United States, has been a menace as well as a benefit to the great powers of Latin America? Second, can the Monroe Doctrine of the future be so interpreted that it will become a real Pan American doctrine, a policy whose maintenance will be the bulwark of defense for the other twenty American republics as well as for the United States?

In order to answer the first question, it is necessary to review briefly both the circumstances that called forth the doctrine, and the manner

[9] *New York Times,* Oct. 13, 1920.

in which it has been extended by the various presidents who have had occasion to interpret it.

The Spanish dependencies in the New World had very little reason to cherish a keen spirit of loyalty to the mother country. Spain had ever looked upon them as a fruitful field of exploitation, and had considered no regulations too severe to accomplish this result. Therefore, when Napoleon placed his brother Joseph upon the throne at Madrid in 1808, the slight thread of allegiance that still bound the Spanish colonies to the Old World snapped, and a series of revolutions in South America followed. By the end of the year 1810 virtually all of the Spanish colonies in South America had declared their independence, although they still acknowledged a half-hearted allegiance to the deposed Ferdinand VII. As long as the Peninsular War raged in Europe, the colonies were left mostly to their own devices. Upon the restoration of Ferdinand, an attempt was made to bring them once more under his selfish and autocratic rule. But, having enjoyed the benefits of freedom, the colonies were unwilling to go again under the yoke; and the real struggle for independence began.

From the outset the United States viewed the contest with close attention, and in 1815, by issuing what virtually amounted to a proclamation of neutrality, she accorded the struggling colonies the status of belligerent states.[10] Monroe, then Secretary of State, while unwilling to recognize them outright, declared in a despatch in December, 1815, that the colonies would probably gain their independence, and that it was to the interest of the United States that they should do so. Henry Clay was outspoken in his demands for recognition, and upon several occasions introduced bills authorizing the necessary appropriation for ministers to those governments in South America that had really established their independence. In 1820 such a resolution passed the House. President Monroe was not yet ready to act; [11] but when, in 1822, the victories of San Martín in the south and Bolívar in the north had virtually wiped out all chance of Spanish control, he felt that he need delay no longer, and in a special message to Congress on March 8, 1822, he declared that the time for recognition had come.[12] This recognition did not come any too soon, for in the autumn of this same year, at the Congress of Verona, the three powers of the Holy Alliance, with France in their leading-strings, declared that the system of representative government was incompatible with mon-

---

[10] *American State Papers, Foreign Relations*, Vol. IV, p. 1.
[11] *Annals of Congress*, 16th Cong., 1st Sess., pp. 2223 *ff*.
[12] *Amer. State Papers, For. Rel.*, Vol. IV, p. 818.

archical principles, and mutually engaged not only to put an end to representative government in Europe, but to prevent its being introduced in those countries where it was not yet known.

Although Great Britain had never joined the so-called Holy Alliance, she was an equal partner in the Quadruple Alliance, whose duty also it was to safeguard Europe from further dangers of revolution. She took part in the conference at Aix-la-Chapelle in 1818, but, unable to back the reactionary policies of Metternich, did not participate in those that followed at Troppau or Laybach. A state with the democratic tendencies already shown by Great Britain could not join whole-heartedly in the suppression of constitutional government, and Castlereagh preferred to follow his allies hesitantly and at a distance.[13] When, at the Congress of Verona, Prince Metternich won over Czar Alexander I to his policy of using the concert of powers to crush out democracy wherever it should be found, the Duke of Wellington, representing Great Britain, was instructed to withdraw. George Canning, who now held the portfolio of foreign affairs in the place of Castlereagh, realized only too well that if the Quintuple Alliance aided Ferdinand to recover his possessions in the New World, Great Britain would see the large and profitable trade which she was now carrying on with the South American states restricted once more to Spanish merchants and Spanish ships. In a despatch to the Duke of Wellington, the English representative at Verona, he pointed out that now that American questions were more important than European ones to the British, the opportunity was afforded to turn the situation to their advantage.[14]

Canning hereupon protested against the reactionary policy of the allies, and, with that as an excuse for withdrawing from the European concert, he turned towards the United States. He was justified in expecting the United States to support Great Britain in any program based upon the recognition of the independence of the South American colonies, since the United States in 1819 had proposed the recognition of Buenos Aires, intimating that if Great Britain should adopt similar measures it would be highly satisfactory to the United States. Nor could he afford the time for diplomatic soundings, for the success of the French troops in restoring Ferdinand showed that if the allies' further plans of bringing back the Spanish colonies were to be checked there must be haste.

[13] Viscount Castlereagh, *Correspondence, Despatches, etc.*, 12 vols. (London, 1853), Vol. XII, pp. 311-318.
[14] Duke of Wellington, *Despatches, Correspondence, etc.*, 2nd ser., 8 vols. (London, 1867), Vol. I, p. 511.

On August 16, 1823, Canning approached Richard Rush, the American minister, suggesting a joint diplomatic action against European intervention in America, and four days later he put his ideas into a formal proposal. The substance of the proposition was somewhat as follows: Assuming the recovery of the colonies by Spain to be hopeless, the question of recognition was one of time and circumstances; under these conditions, would it not be an act of wisdom for the two powers to announce publicly that they neither aimed at taking any portion of the colonies themselves, nor were willing to see any portion of them transferred to any other power with indifference? [15] However, when Rush suggested that Great Britain recognize the colonies forthwith, Canning admitted that such a move was not feasible at the time. The American minister thereupon reported the situation to his home government and awaited instructions, confident that some diplomatic action was bound to occur.

Before considering the great step which the United States was now about to take in the development of her foreign policy, one other factor that entered into the situation must be noted. In 1821 the Czar of Russia had issued a ukase claiming the Pacific coast down to the fifty-first degree, and at the same time declaring that Bering Sea and the North Pacific were closed seas and subject to his exclusive jurisdiction. Adams protested vigorously both against the establishment of new colonial possessions on this continent and at the exorbitant pretensions to exclusive jurisdiction over territory whose title was in dispute.[16] Both Monroe and Adams felt that the time had come when it must be decided whether the United States should join with Great Britain in a strong stand for the independence of the Latin-American states against further encroachments of the powers of Europe, or whether it would be better for the United States to take the stand alone, as the foremost republic in the Western Hemisphere. At first the sentiment of virtually all the statesmen whom Monroe consulted—Jefferson, Madison, Calhoun, and Rush—seemed to favor a joint declaration, and the President himself inclined in that direction. John Quincy Adams alone vehemently opposed a joint declaration, pointing out that Canning's object seemed to be to obtain a public pledge from the government of the United States against its own acquisition of any part of the Spanish-American possessions as much as against the forcible interference of the Holy Alliance. He also made it clear that the United States would be safer in disclaiming all intention of interfering with European concerns, and in issuing a declaration made solely by the

---

[15] For text see J. B. Moore, *Digest of International Law*, Vol. VI, p. 389.
[16] *Amer. State Papers, For. Rel.*, Vol. IV, p. 861.

United States for an American cause.[17] His views finally prevailed, and it was at length agreed that inasmuch as the South American states were free and independent, they, and not Great Britain and the United States, had the right to dispose of their condition.

President Monroe issued his famous message on December 2, 1823, and although considerable space was given to the expression of the policy of the United States in regard to the attitude and intentions of Europe, the gist of the doctrine may be summed up in two sentences. The first concerned colonization, and was in answer to the Russian ukase of 1821. It declared that "the American continents, by the free and independent condition which they have assumed and maintain, are henceforth not to be considered as subjects for future colonization by any European powers." The second answered the threat of the Holy Alliance, and asserted that "the political system of the allied powers is essentially different . . . from that of America. . . . We owe it, therefore, to candor, and to the amicable relations existing between the United States and those powers, to declare that we shall consider any attempt on their part to extend their system to any portion of this hemisphere as dangerous to our peace and safety." [18]

As was to have been expected, a message that so simply and so completely phrased a true American policy based upon the firm foundation of self-protection, was received enthusiastically in both North and South America. Speaking in behalf of the Panama Mission, April 14, 1826, in the House of Representatives, Daniel Webster declared that "one general glow of exultation, one universal feeling of the gratified love of liberty, . . . pervaded all bosoms." [19] In the words of Señor de Manos Albas, "It [the pronouncement] rang through the world like a peal of thunder; it paralyzed the Holy Alliance, and defined, once and for all time, as far as Europe is concerned, the international status of the newly constituted American republics." [20] Even though its enunciation was due primarily to the realization upon the part of the United States that the preservation of the independence and democratic systems in the South American countries was closely bound up with the protection of her own independence, nevertheless the nations of South America realized

[17] J. Q. Adams, *Memoirs* (Philadelphia, 1874-1877), Vol. VI, pp. 177 *ff*.

[18] For full text see J. D. Richardson, *Messages and Papers of the Presidents*, Vol. II, p. 209.

[19] J. W. McIntyre [ed.], *The Writings and Speeches of Daniel Webster* (Boston, 1903), Vol. V, p. 203.

[20] Joseph Wheless, "Monroe Doctrine and Latin America," in *Annals of Amer. Acad.*, Vol. LIV (July, 1914), p. 66.

clearly that such a policy, maintained by their more firmly established neighbor on the north, was precisely the bulwark needed until they could strengthen themselves sufficiently to stand entirely alone. It is not surprising that Colombia proposed that this doctrine be ratified at the projected Congress of Panama as one of the bases of Pan-Americanism; for such a policy well represented "the gospel of the new continent." [21]

If the American doctrine as laid down by President Monroe could have been forever confined to the two fundamental concepts just outlined, perhaps today this policy would be the unanimously accepted basis of a true Pan American policy. But the doctrine as laid down by Monroe was merely an attempt to meet the situation that confronted him by a policy whose aim was safety for the United States. It contradicted two principles of international law generally accepted at the time: the right of intervention, and the right of taking possession of unoccupied territory. The statesmen of Europe were not slow in expressing their disdain and contempt for these new and presumptuous principles. Châteaubriand declared that such a doctrine "ought to be resisted by all the powers possessing either territorial or commercial interest in that hemisphere"; while Canning, who boasted publicly that he had called into existence the New World to redress the balance of the Old, in his private correspondence expressed himself in an entirely different vein.[22] Even Congress was unwilling to commit itself unreservedly to the new principles, especially as Henry Clay, who introduced a joint resolution doing so, interpreted the doctrine to mean that the United States was ready to insure the independence of the South American republics.[23] Therefore, although the doctrine was to remain the basis of our foreign policy henceforth, it was not recognized as a principle of international law.

Nor, on the other hand, was its interpretation to be rigidly circumscribed by the original limits laid down by Monroe. Rather, it was to be shaped in accordance with the conditions that successive presidents were called upon to confront. As a result, the original doctrine has been expanded as circumstances demanded, and this expansion has been the result of two forces, American interest and American power. A brief consideration of the important occasions when the doctrine has been invoked will give evidence of its changing character.

[21] For an excellent account of contemporary opinion of the doctrine in Hispanic America see J. B. Lockey, *Pan-Americanism: Its Beginnings* (New York, 1920), Chap. VI; see also W. S. Robertson, "South America and the Monroe Doctrine," *Polit. Sci. Quar.*, Vol. XXX (Mar., 1915), p. 82.

[22] W. S. Robertson, "The Monroe Doctrine Abroad, 1823-1824," in *Amer. Polit. Sci. Rev.*, Vol. VI (Nov., 1912), p. 546.

[23] For text of resolution see Moore, *op. cit.*, Vol. VI, p. 404.

In 1827 the Argentine Republic, which was then at war with the Empire of Brazil, sent an inquiry to Henry Clay, asking that he outline the scope of the declarations made by President Monroe. Clay replied that the war between the two states could in no way be considered analogous to the conditions that provoked President Monroe's message, since it was a war "strictly American in its origin and its objects." [24] A few years later in 1833, when Great Britain resumed occupation of the Falkland Islands, Buenos Aires protested that the action of Great Britain was a clear violation of the Monroe Doctrine. Inasmuch as the United States had already been forced to take action against the treatment accorded American fishermen by the Argentinians during their brief possession of the islands, and as the British could lay title to a claim antedating the seizure by Buenos Aires, the United States acknowledged the British sovereignty.[25]

The first enlargement of the doctrine so as to preclude the transfer of American territory from one foreign country to another seems to have been made in connection with Cuba. In 1825 Mr. Clay, in a letter to the American minister to France, declared that the United States could not consent to the occupation of Cuba or Puerto Rico "by any other European power than Spain under any contingency whatever," [26] and the same sentiments were repeated by Mr. Van Buren in 1829 and 1830 in notes to the American minister to Spain.[27] Mr. Forsythe, in 1840, declared that the United States would prevent at all hazards any voluntary transfer on the part of Spain of her title to Cuba, whether it was temporary or permanent, just as she would assist Spain with both military and naval resources in preserving it or recovering it.[28] This enlargement of the doctrine was just as advantageous to the free republics of Latin America as to the United States, for any transfer of colonies would most likely be from a weak power, such as Spain, to one of the stronger and more dreaded European states, and therefore an event to be feared equally by the United States and Latin America.

The earliest enlargement of the doctrine that seemed to be aimed at the Latin-American nations as well as at Europe came with the first message of President Polk. Up to 1845, the United States, when insisting upon a maintenance of the status quo in the Western Hemisphere, had, it is

[24] Ibid., p. 434.
[25] Ibid., p. 435. See also infra, Chap. 16.
[26] Ibid., p. 447.
[27] Ibid., pp. 448-449.
[28] Ibid., p. 450. For a more detailed discussion of the Cuban question see infra, pp. 192-202.

true, alluded only to Europe. But there was no reason to believe that the inhibition was not equally applicable to the United States herself. Directly after the annexation of Texas, however, Polk declared that "the people of this continent alone have the right to decide their own destiny"; and that "should any portion of them, constituting an independent state, propose to unite themselves with our confederacy, this will be a question for them and us to determine without any foreign interposition"; [29] and the declaration was followed by the annexation of New Mexico and California. Well might the Latin-American states now begin to wonder whether the Monroe Doctrine was an unmixed blessing. In his message of April 29, 1848, President Polk went even further in his free interpretation of the Monroe Doctrine by urging the annexation of Yucatan, which at that time was so upset by an Indian insurrection that the authorities offered to transfer the "dominion and sovereignty of the peninsula" in return for immediate aid. Inasmuch as similar proposals had been made to Great Britain and Spain, President Polk seized the occasion to assert that the United States could not consent to a transfer of this colony to any European power.[30] Under the circumstances, Polk's assertion could mean nothing else than that the United States interpreted the Monroe Doctrine to prevent a Latin-American state from accepting the dominion of a European nation, even if the Latin-American state desired such a transfer of sovereignty. However, Yucatan soon withdrew its offer, so that Polk was not forced to put his interpretation to the test.

Following Polk's administration, the doctrine to a certain extent disappeared from view. Mr. Clayton, Secretary of State through President Taylor's short presidency, struggled against admitting British rights in Central America, but he was finally forced by circumstances to give Great Britain joint rights in any inter-oceanic canal that might be constructed on the isthmus. It may be conceded that the Clayton Bulwer treaty did not constitute an infringement of the Monroe Doctrine.[31] But a situation was soon to arise in Mexico which was to provoke a serious violation of the doctrine on the very borders of the United States.

After the disastrous war with the United States, the rival factions struggling for power in Mexico brought the unfortunate country into bankruptcy and anarchy, and the attention of the United States was finally called to the fact that Spain, Great Britain, and France were about to

---

[29] Richardson, *op. cit.*, Vol. IV, p. 398.

[30] *Ibid.*, p. 582.

[31] For a discussion of the Monroe Doctrine in its relation to the Panama Canal see *infra* Chap. 5; also *Sen. Doc. No. 194*, 47th Cong., 1st Sess.

employ strong measures to protect the interests of their citizens on Mexican soil. In a despatch to our minister to Mexico, dated September 20, 1860, Secretary Cass thus indicated the general position of the United States: "While we do not deny the right of any other power to carry on hostile operations against Mexico, for the redress of its grievances, we firmly object to its holding possession of any part of that country, or endeavoring by force to control its political destiny. This opposition to foreign interference is known to France, England, and Spain, as well as the determination of the United States to resist any such attempt by all means in its power." [32] President Buchanan, who had already recognized the Juarez government in Mexico in 1859, intimated in his annual message of 1860 that his position was the same, to the point "of resisting, even by force should this become necessary, any attempt by these governments to deprive our neighboring republic of portions of her territory— a duty from which we could not shirk without abandoning the traditional and established policy of the American people." [33]

When the European powers decided upon armed intervention in Mexico, the United States was, unfortunately for the maintenance of this traditional policy, at the very brink of the war for the Union. A convention was signed October 31, 1861, by Great Britain, France, and Spain, outlining their plan of action. The United States was invited to accede to it, but it was made very clear that operations would be begun regardless of our adherence. Secretary Seward realized the difficulty of the situation, and, while refusing to depart from our traditional policy by entering into a European alliance, he was unable to protest very vigorously against the joint intervention. [34] The British and Spanish, however, whether because they were desirous of respecting our wishes after their claims had been met, or whether because they were dissatisfied with the attitude of the French, withdrew their forces early in 1862. The French, while disclaiming any ulterior motives, pushed forward their forces, seized the city of Mexico, took control of the government, and had the assembly change the government to a monarchy and offer the crown to Archduke Maximilian of Austria. Even when Maximilian had been persuaded to accept, Mr. Seward was unable to do more than declare that the permanent establishment of a foreign and monarchical government in Mexico would be found neither easy nor desirable. [35] The House of Representatives was

[32] Moore, *op. cit.*, Vol. VI, p. 481.
[33] Richardson, *op. cit.*, Vol. V, p. 646.
[34] For text of the note and Secretary Seward's reply see *House Ex. Doc. No. 100,* 37th Cong., 2nd Sess., pp. 185-187.
[35] Moore, *op. cit.*, Vol. VI, p. 495.

not so diplomatic, and voiced a vigorous protest by a resolution unanimously carried April 4, 1864. But Mr. Seward informed the French minister that the President had not departed in any way from his previous policy.[36] However, with the close of the Civil War the tone of the Secretary's protests changed, and his note of December 16, 1865, boldly asserted that the sincere friendship between the two nations would be brought into imminent jeopardy unless France desisted from "the prosecution of armed intervention in Mexico to overthrow the domestic republican government existing there." [37] Louis Napoleon was now more interested in the European situation arising out of the growing dispute between Austria and Prussia than in his Mexican enterprise, and in the spring of 1866 he decided to withdraw his troops. With the withdrawal of the French the power of Maximilian began to crumble, and, in less than a year after the departure of the first detachment of French troops, the unfortunate prince paid for his ill-fated Mexican expedition with his life.

The principles of the Monroe Doctrine were vindicated once more in the most serious attempt that had yet been made to impose European domination upon the independent republics of the Western Hemisphere, although nowhere in the diplomatic correspondence is the doctrine mentioned by name. From the standpoint of Latin America, no objection could possibly be raised to the Seward doctrine in regard to Mexico. The United States, torn by the Civil War, could not protest effectively against European intervention, but the United States, reunited, could and did make her protest effective.

Secretary Seward's well considered policy had to some extent lulled the latent fear in the Latin-American states that the United States was preserving their independence for its own advantage, but the ill considered expressions of President Johnson again aroused their resentment. In his fourth annual message, dated December 9, 1868, Johnson delivered himself of these astonishing sentiments: "Comprehensive national policy would seem to sanction the acquisition and incorporation into our Federal Union of the several adjacent continental and insular communities as speedily as it can be done, peacefully, lawfully, and without violation of national justice, faith, or honor. . . . The conviction is rapidly gaining ground in the American mind that, with the increased facilities for intercommunication between all portions of the earth, the principles of free government as embraced in our Constitution would prove of sufficient

[36] *Ibid.*, Vol. VI, pp. 496-497.
[37] *Ibid.*, p. 501.

strength and breadth to comprehend within their sphere and influence the civilized nations of the world." [38] This was either a most extraordinary extension of the Monroe Doctrine, or else the promulgation of a new and all-embracing Pan American doctrine, with the United States as the chief beneficiary. Fortunately for future Pan American relations, President Johnson was at the close of his term, and, in view of the fact that he had been estranged from Congress throughout the greater part of it, his statements did not receive the attention which they would otherwise have commanded.

President Grant and his Secretary of State, Hamilton Fish, returned to the common interpretation of the doctrine, as aiming to protect the feeble powers of America against European intervention, but in such a way as to secure and maintain their confidence. Secretary Fish was careful to make it clear to the neighboring states that the United States did not covet their territories and was ready to aid them to the fullest extent in any steps which they might take to protect themselves against anarchy. But, while emphasizing the unselfish attitude of the United States in offering its protection against Europe, he was careful to safeguard the interests of his country in regard to the proposed isthmian canal. It was his expressed opinion that the canal was an American enterprise, to be undertaken under American auspices. [39] Secretary Evarts took the same stand, declaring that the paramount interest of the United States in the project of interoceanic communication seemed indisputable. [40] When the French company under the direction of de Lesseps indicated its intention to start construction of a canal, President Hayes pointed out that "the policy of this country is a canal under American control; ... it will be the great ocean thoroughfare between our Atlantic and Pacific shores, and virtually a part of the coast-line of the United States." [41]

Secretary Blaine, in Garfield's administration, opposed the idea of a joint guaranty and control of an interoceanic canal by the European powers as a direct infringement of the Monroe Doctrine, but when communicating his views to Great Britain he put himself in a very weak position by omitting to mention the Clayton-Bulwer treaty of 1850. [42] When the British Foreign Minister called his attention to this *lapsus memoriæ*,

[38] Richardson, *op. cit.*, Vol. VI, p. 688.
[39] *For. Rel. of the U. S.*, 1870, pp. 254 *ff.*; see also *Sen. Ex. Doc. No. 112*, 46th Cong., 2nd Sess., p. 48
[40] *Sen. Ex. Doc. No. 112*, 46th Cong., 2nd Sess., p. 18.
[41] Richardson, *op. cit.*, Vol. VII, p. 585.
[42] *For. Rel. of the U. S.*, 1881, p. 537.

Mr. Blaine attempted to prove that the situation had so changed that the treaty was no longer of value.[43] Needless to say, Great Britain disagreed with this doctrine, and had little difficulty in supporting her position. Unsuccessful here, Blaine turned his attention to strengthening the bonds of friendship between the republics of the two Americas by a Pan American conference, though before he could bring his plans to fruition he was no longer Secretary of State.

Up to this point the Monroe Doctrine had been interpreted, with very few exceptions, as protective of American institutions and territory against Europe. Now a new and disturbing extension of the doctrine was at hand. It was preceded by a period of strained relations between the United States and Chile. The protection accorded President Balmaceda and refugees of his party by the United States minister, and the unfortunate *Baltimore* incident, provoked feelings of bitterness on both sides. President Harrison expressed in no uncertain terms the intention of the United States to protect her citizens in those states whose governments were too weak to do it. But it remained for President Cleveland, through his Secretary of State, Mr. Olney, to declare that: "To-day the United States is practically sovereign upon this continent, and its fiat is law upon the subjects to which it confines its interposition. Why? . . . It is because, in addition to all other grounds, its infinite resources combined with its isolated position render it master of the situation and practically invulnerable as against any or all other powers." [44]

The occasion that provoked this expression, it is true, was brought about by Venezuela, who wished to use the power of the United States to protect her against British encroachments. Nevertheless the Latin-American republics might well look with perturbation upon this new extension of the Monroe Doctrine. As Señor Alvarez has pointed out, such an interpretation does not properly come under the Monroe Doctrine, but under a policy whose basis is the safety of the United States through its hegemony on this continent.[45] Even such a policy might well have as an essential corollary the protection of the Latin-American republics. But such a bold statement of overweening power was pregnant with sinister possibilities, and the influences hostile to the closer relations between the United States and its Latin-American neighbors were not slow to avail themselves of the opening. This doctrine as announced by President Cleveland has been termed the doctrine of paramount interest, and the

[43] *Ibid.*, p. 554.
[44] Moore, *op. cit.*, Vol. VI, p. 553.
[45] Alejandro Alvarez, "Latin America and International Law," in *Amer. Jour. of Int. Law*, Vol. III (April, 1909), p. 269.

President put himself on record as willing to go to war, if necessary, to enforce it. In spite of Lord Salisbury's protestations that international law could never sanction any such novel principle, President Cleveland maintained his point, and Great Britain finally accepted American intervention. In the Venezuela controversy President Cleveland stood upon a doctrine whose observance was necessary "to our peace and safety as a nation and to the integrity of our free institutions." But it is essential to note that his stand was also useful to Venezuela in supporting her claims.[46]

After the Spanish-American War had extended our jurisdiction to certain of the Spanish colonies, it became a matter of even greater interest to Latin Americans to know just how far our peace and safety would lead us in intervening in their destinies. President Roosevelt's action in regard to Colombia and the Panama Canal, and the passage of the Platt Amendment by Congress, were events that cast shadows of a most dubious sort before the eyes of all Latin-American countries. Neither were the utterances of President Roosevelt of such a character as to dissipate apprehension. In the annual message of 1904 he enunciated what is generally known as the "big-stick" policy, as follows: "Any country whose people conduct themselves well can count upon our hearty friendship. If a nation shows that it knows how to act with reasonable efficiency and decency in social and political matters, if it keeps order and pays its obligations, it need fear no interference from the United States. Chronic wrong-doing, or an impotence which results in a general loosening of the ties of civilized society, may in America, as elsewhere, ultimately require intervention by some civilized nation, and in the western hemisphere the adherence of the United States to the Monroe Doctrine may force the United States, however reluctantly, in flagrant cases of such wrong-doing or impotence, to the exercise of an international police power." [47]

This statement of policy was merely the prologue to the taking over and administration of the finances of the Dominican Republic. Although the Senate refused to ratify the protocol, the President, under the guise of an executive agreement, carried out his plan, and the Senate later gave its sanction. When President Taft followed the same course in his dealings with Nicaragua and Honduras, and President Wilson in his action in Haiti, well might the states of Latin America believe that the Monroe

[46] For a discussion of the Venezuela affair see J. H. Latané, *The United States and Latin America* (New York, 1920), pp. 238-249; also Raúl de Cardenas, *La Politica de los Estados Unidos en el Continente Americano* (La Habana, 1921), pp. 123-132.

[47] A. H. Lewis, *Messages and Speeches of Theodore Roosevelt* (Washington, D. C., 1906), Vol. II, p. 857.

Doctrine, in its new interpretation, meant intervention by the United States to prevent intervention by Europe.

One other notable extension of the Monroe Doctrine which is based primarily upon the principles of self-defense occurred in 1912, when an American company attempted to sell out certain concessions in Lower California around Magdalena Bay to a Japanese concern. The result was the following Lodge resolution, which received the indorsement of the Senate: "*Resolved,* That when any harbor or other place in the American continents is so situated that the occupation thereof for naval or military purposes might threaten the communications or the safety of the United States, the government of the United States could not see without grave concern the possession of such harbor or other place by any corporation or association which has such a relation to another government, not American, as to give that government practical power of control for naval or military purposes." [48]

Although this particular phase of an American doctrine was aimed at Japan, it seems reasonable to assume that the same policy would be invoked by the United States as against any other interests or concessionaires who might be supposed to have the support of their government.

If these extensions of the Monroe Doctrine were uniformly of a nature tending to protect the United States, regardless of the rights of the other republics of the New World, the hostility with which the doctrine is generally regarded in South America would be easy to understand. But other phases of the doctrine have been brought out which show that the United States, in its insistence upon self-protection, has not wholly lost sight of the rights of its Latin-American neighbors. In numerous addresses delivered during his memorable visit to South America in 1906 Elihu Root gave an interpretation of the doctrine that all South America was only too glad to accept. In Uruguay he asserted that the declaration of Monroe was "an assertion to all the world of the competency of Latin-Americans to govern themselves." [49] We have already quoted a portion of his eloquent address at the Pan American Conference in Rio de Janeiro in which he outlined an all-American policy for the United States. Some years later Mr. Root, in an address welcoming Dr. Lauro Müller, Foreign Minister of Brazil, declared that "there is neither to the Monroe Doctrine nor any other doctrine or purpose of the American government any corol-

---

[48] For text see *Amer. Jour. of Int. Law,* Vol. VI (Oct., 1912), p. 437. See also T. A. Bailey, "The Lodge Corollary of the Monroe Doctrine," *Polit. Sci. Quar.,* Vol. 48, p. 238.

[49] Elihu Root, *Latin America and the United States* (Cambridge, Mass., 1917), p. 58.

lary of dominion or aggression, or aught but equal friendship." [50] In fact,
in an address before the American Society of International Law on April
22, 1914, Mr. Root went so far as to assert that, outside of the one apparent extension of the doctrine by President Polk, there has been no other
change or enlargement of the Monroe Doctrine since it was first promulgated.[51]

President Wilson was particularly successful both in enunciating and
in maintaining this friendly policy towards Latin America. On March 11,
1913, very shortly after his inauguration, he declared: "The United States
has nothing to seek in Central and South America except the lasting interests of the peoples of the two continents." [52] And a little later he was
more definite: "The United States will never again seek one additional
foot of territory by conquest." [53] Yet even President Wilson was forced
to follow the Roosevelt doctrine in the case of Haiti; nor was American
administration there so satisfactory as to escape very serious criticism.
But in the Caribbean, particularly, the United States cannot brook European intervention, and to act as policeman in the region has been regarded
as essential to our peace and safety.

One of the most important interpretations of the Monroe Doctrine
was made by Secretary of State Hughes in a notable speech made in 1923
upon the occasion of the celebration of the centenary of the Monroe
Doctrine.[54] The address, delivered before the American Bar Association
at Minneapolis on August 30, 1923, was entitled "Observations on the
Monroe Doctrine." In the course of his remarks Secretary Hughes made
certain categorical assertions which had considerable influence upon subsequent interpretations of the doctrine. In the first place, he declared:

... the Monroe Doctrine is not a policy of aggression; it is a policy of self-
defense.... *Second,* as the policy embodied in the Monroe Doctrine is dis-
tinctively the policy of the United States, the Government of the United
States reserves to itself its definition, interpretation and application.... *Third,*
the policy of the Monroe Doctrine does not infringe upon the independence
and sovereignty of other American states.... *Fourth,* so far as the region of the
Caribbean Sea is concerned it may be said that if we had no Monroe Doctrine
we should have to create one.... Our interest does not lie in controlling foreign
peoples; that would be a policy of mischief and disaster. Our interest is in

[50] *Ibid.,* p. 243.
[51] Elihu Root, *Addresses on International Subjects* (Cambridge, Mass., 1916),
p. 112.
[52] E. E. Robinson and V. J. West, *The Foreign Policy of Woodrow Wilson* (New
York, 1917), p. 180.
[53] *Ibid.,* p. 201.
[54] C. E. Hughes, *Address before the Fifty-sixth Annual Meeting of the American Bar
Association* (Washington, D. C., 1928).

having prosperous, peaceful and law-abiding neighbors with whom we can coöperate to mutual advantage. *Fifth,* it is apparent that the Monroe Doctrine does not stand in the way of Pan American coöperation; rather it affords the necessary foundation for that coöperation in the independence and security of American states.

These utterances clarified the current interpretation of the doctrine and seemed to eliminate reasonable fears on the part of the South American countries. On the other hand, it might be called a "big brother" doctrine in the Caribbean area, and fraternal admonitions are not always cordially welcomed. Nevertheless, every nation has both a right and a duty to protect its essential interests, and the Monroe Doctrine was ever fundamentally a policy of self-protection for the United States. Nor did the United States object to similar declarations of policy on the part of its Latin-American neighbors; for, as Secretary Hughes declared on January 20, 1925, "While this doctrine was set forth and must be maintained as the policy of the United States, there is no reason whatsoever why every one of the our sister republics should not have and formulate a similar principle as a part of its foreign policy...." [55]

But when we come to the Coolidge-Kellogg policy in the Caribbean, as exemplified particularly in the sending of marines to Nicaragua, the fears of the Latin-American nations seemed to be justified. In the words of *La Nación* of Buenos Aires: "We do not recall that the right of intervention by force has ever been pronounced to such a disquieting extent as it is done today by the government of the United States. The Monroe Doctrine in the hands of Kellogg seems to retain its defensive quality for the United States but to lose its quality as a dignified guaranty of safety to small neighbors. Nicaragua does not fear to be made a colony by some European country but must suffer the military domination of the United States. This fact creates a precedent whereby the independence of American countries will be subordinated to the amount of dollars which the United States invests therein, thus replacing the Monroe Doctrine which for a century has been the resplendent shield of the moral greatness of the United States." [56]

Upon the advent of the Hoover administration, Secretary of State Stimson delegated Undersecretary of State J. Reuben Clark to prepare a memorandum on the Monroe Doctrine which should give a comprehensive historical presentation of its origin and development. Mr. Clark's memorandum which was published in 1930 as an official document by the

[55] *Amer. Jour. of Int. Law,* Vol. 19 (Apr., 1925), p. 368.
[56] *New York Times,* Jan. 6, 1927.

Department of State interprets the doctrine in a fairly restrictive fashion. The Big Stick corollary of President Theodore Roosevelt is declared to be unjustified by the terms of the doctrine. The doctrine according to this interpretation neither prevents Europe from waging war against the Latin Americas, nor does it relieve Latin-American states of their responsibilities as independent sovereignties. Although "the United States determines when and if the principles of the doctrine are violated and . . . we alone determine what measures shall be taken to vindicate the principles of the doctrine . . . so far as Latin America is concerned, the doctrine is now, and always has been, not an instrument of violence and oppression, but an unbought, freely bestowed, and wholly effective guaranty of their freedom, independence, and territorial integrity against the imperialistic designs of Europe." [57]

The Hoover administration gave concrete evidence that it intended to carry out a nonimperialistic policy when the United States and the Latin-American states at the 1928 Washington Conference on Conciliation and Arbitration signed two treaties condemning war as an instrument of national policy and agreeing to settle all juridical disputes by arbitration, and all others by conciliation.

Franklin D. Roosevelt in his first inaugural address of March 4, 1933, dedicated the United States "to the policy of the good neighbor." Speaking before the governing board of the Pan American Union on Pan American Day, April 12, 1933, he interpreted this policy as it affected our relations with Latin America: "The essential qualities of a true Pan Americanism must be the same as those which constitute a good neighbor, namely, mutual understanding and, through such understanding, a sympathetic understanding of the other's point of view. . . . In this spirit the people of every republic on our continent are coming to a deep understanding of the fact that the Monroe Doctrine . . . was and is directed at the maintenance of independence by the peoples of the continent. It was aimed and is aimed against the acquisition in any manner of the control of additional territory in this hemisphere by any non-American power." [58]

Now to answer our question as to whether the Monroe Doctrine has been a menace as well as a benefit to the Latin-American republics. Let us briefly summarize the interpretations from the viewpoint of Latin America. Undoubtedly the idea of no transfer by one European nation to another of its territory in the New World is satisfactory to the Latin

[57] J. Reuben Clark, *Memorandum on the Monroe Doctrine* (Washington, D. C., 1930).

[58] U. S. Department of State, *Press Releases*, Vol. VIII, No. 451 (Apr. 15, 1933).

Americans; but when this interpretation is extended to prevent voluntary transfer of allegiance, it becomes an arbitrary interference with sovereign rights. When, on the other hand, transfer of territory to the United States is regarded as permissible, from the Latin-American viewpoint the doctrine becomes dangerous. President Johnson's ill considered words as to American expansion merely aroused antagonism, but President Hayes' carefully considered statement of the United States coast-line extending to Panama inspired fear. Finally, the Cleveland-Olney doctrine of American supremacy on this continent, followed by the Roosevelt doctrine of responsibility for the behavior of badly governed republics, provoked openly manifested hostility. Although Secretary Root, President Wilson, Secretary Hughes, and President Franklin D. Roosevelt have done much to allay this antagonism, the judgment of the average Latin American undoubtedly was that the Monroe Doctrine of the past at any rate has been a menace, as well as a benefit, to the Latin-American countries.[59]

This brings us to our second question: Can the Monroe Doctrine of the future be so interpreted that it will be regarded as a true Pan American doctrine? If the doctrine of the present could be restored to the original formula, there would be little question of its acceptance by South America. But such a doctrine would be entirely unnecessary; the conditions no longer demand such a policy. The Americas no longer possess uncolonized territory, nor do the more powerful Latin-American states look to the United States to prevent European intervention. Hence a return to the original doctrine of Monroe would render the doctrine obsolete, and therefore futile as a Pan American doctrine. On the other hand, to continue the Monroe Doctrine as a policy which conforms itself to the new problems that arise, and whose interpretation may be based upon selfish advantage as well as upon self-preservation by the United States, will never be acceptable to the Latin-American nations as a true Pan American policy.

Several solutions of this *impasse* have been proposed. A practical suggestion has been to enlarge gradually the powers of the Pan American Union so that it shall come to have jurisdiction over all questions that might arise to disturb the peace of the Western Hemisphere. In a special memorandum on the Monroe Doctrine and the League of Nations which Mr. Barrett prepared for the American representatives at the Paris Peace Conference, he pointed out that in the Pan American Union we already had "a practical, peace-preserving, and successfully working, although

[59] For critical detailed indictment of the Monroe Doctrine from the Latin-American point of view see Gaston Nerval, *Autopsy of the Monroe Doctrine* (New York, 1934).

limited and voluntary, American league of nations." It was further suggested that the American governments give the supreme council of the Pan American Union, or some similar body to be created, authority not only to initiate and effect mediation, adjudication, and arbitration, but to enforce its conclusions without the interference of the Old World powers. This solution, which is based upon the practical results already achieved by an established organization, seems well within the bounds of possibility, and that such a solution would be accepted by the republics of Latin America might well be taken for granted. In the words of Señor Calderon, minister from Bolivia: "If the Monroe Doctrine is the proud determination of the United States to keep the whole American continent free from any contamination of foreign autocrats, the Pan American Union is the agreement of all the republics to live together, linked by the great ideals of democracy, not looking down upon the weaker or the less advanced ones, but determined to help them and to forge ahead in a united and free effort to reach the goal of popular welfare, free and peaceful development, and the elimination of pauperism and anarchy." [60]

Another solution, one that has received much attention, is based upon the address made by President Wilson to Congress on January 22, 1917, in which he proposed that "the nations should with one accord adopt the doctrine of President Monroe as the doctrine of the world; that no nation should seek to extend its policy over any other nation or people, but that every people should be left free to determine its own policy, its own way of development, unhindered, unthreatened, unafraid, the little along with the great and powerful." [61] This idea was later incorporated into the covenant of the League of Nations as Article X, stating that "the members of the League undertake to respect and preserve as against external aggression the territorial integrity and existing political independence of all members of the League."

This proposal was bitterly opposed on the ground that such a doctrine would withdraw us from our isolation and involve us in all the disputes of Europe. It was also asserted that by extending the Monroe Doctrine to the world its value as an American doctrine would be completely lost. Space prevents even the barest consideration of this controversy, other than to point out that a policy of isolation for the United States is neither possible nor desirable, and that the extension of the Monroe Doctrine to the world would mean not only that the world would recognize the doctrine, but that it would join with the United States in guaranteeing its

[60] *Jour. of Int. Relations,* Vol. X (Oct., 1919), p. 133.
[61] Robinson and West, *op. cit.,* p. 369.

observance. However, Article X, by fixing a definite guaranty mutually enforceable by and binding upon the member states, pledged more in relation to the world than the Monroe Doctrine ever did in relation to the Western Hemisphere. To obviate this objection, and to secure the adherence of the United States to the League, Article XXI was added, which declared that such regional understandings as the Monroe Doctrine are not incompatible with the Covenant of the League. Whether these two principles, a Monroe Doctrine that guarantees nothing except the safety of the United States, and Article X, which guarantees the territory and independence of the member nations of a world league, are mutually sympathetic or antagonistic, is now academic.[62] But—as was pointed out by Señor Paredes, Minister of Foreign Affairs in Salvador, in a communication to our State Department early in 1920—even if the League of Nations had become a permanent institution, with the United States a member, it would have been necessary to interpret the Monroe Doctrine. For, as Señor Paredes says, "since the doctrine will be forthwith transformed into a principle of universal public law, *juris et de jure, . . .* the necessity of an interpretation of the genesis and scope of the Monroe Doctrine not only in the development of the lofty purpose of Pan Americanism but in order that that doctrine may maintain its original purity and prestige, is rendered all the more urgent." [63]

Some eight years later when Costa Rica was asked to reconsider its intention of withdrawing from the League of Nations, Foreign Secretary Castro again requested a definition of the scope of the doctrine as interpreted by the League under Article XXI, "since the inclusion of various American nations in the League and the fact that this doctrine is mentioned in the Statute by which it was created fully justify its definition by the League." [64] Inasmuch as Señor Castro in the very next sentence pointed out that the "doctrine in question constitutes a unilateral declaration" it was manifestly impossible for the League of Nations with the United States outside to give an acceptable definition. Consequently, when Mexico entered the League of Nations in 1931 and Argentina took her place in 1933, both made reservations declining to recognize the Monroe Doctrine under Article XXI of the Covenant.

It is therefore evident that if the Monroe Doctrine is to be maintained

[62] A subsequent interpretation of Article X, adopted by the League Assembly at Geneva, weakened it to such an extent that it became hardly more than a Monroe Doctrine for the signatory nations.

[63] *New York Times,* Feb. 8, 1921. See also S. G. Inman, *Problems in Pan-Americanism* (New York, 1921), pp. 179-194.

[64] League of Nations, *Official Journal* (Oct., 1928), pp. 1606-07.

by the United States as a policy essential to its peace and safety, and at the same time accepted by the Latin-American countries as a policy in no way inimical to their rights and interests, some form of a multilateral pact must be envisaged. Colonel House had such a solution in mind when he initiated negotiations during the Wilson administration for a Pan American pact embodying mutual guarantees of territorial integrity and political independence among all the American republics. Argentina and Brazil appeared very friendly to the idea, but Chile was less inclined to support the proposal and no definite results came of it.

At the Montevideo Conference of 1933 Dr. Puig Casauranc of Mexico suggested that the Roosevelt administration carry out the New Deal in foreign policy and express itself in inter-American affairs not by words alone but by a revision of the Monroe Doctrine. When Secretary Hull replied by definitely accepting for the United States the principle of non-intervention in the Western Hemisphere the corner stone was laid for such a multilateral pact.

When the twenty-one American republics convened in Buenos Aires in 1936 for the Inter-American Conference for the Maintenance of Peace the foundation for the erection of a joint policy of Pan American action for mutual protection in the Western Hemisphere was already prepared. The bogey of intervention had been laid and Secretary Hull's willing acceptance and support of the Saavedra Lamas Peace Pact had changed the latent suspicions of Argentina to cordial interest in coöperation with the United States. Not only was the Montevideo convention of 1933 accepted as a fundamental principle that "no state has the right to intervene in the internal or external affairs of others" reaffirmed, but another convention was formulated and approved by the terms of which the various American governments pledged themselves to consult with each other first, in the event that the peace of the American republics was menaced; second, in the event of war between American states; and third, in the event of an international war outside America which might menace the peace of the American republics. This consultative pact so clearly takes care of any situation envisioned by the Monroe Doctrine in its original or recent interpretations by joint action on the part of all the American republics that it was aptly named by the delegates the "Monroe Doctrine Convention."

The outbreak of war in Europe resulting from the Nazi attack upon Poland at first merely provoked the New World to strengthen its bulwarks of neutrality. But at the same time lest aggression invade its portals, the foreign ministers of the twenty-one republics in conference at Panama in 1939 resolved that in case continental security should be endangered by a threatened change of territorial sovereignty in the Western Hemisphere a meeting for consultation should be held immediately.[65]

The quick downfall of Holland and the incredibly sudden collapse of France left their colonial possessions in the New World wholly without protection. All America was aroused. Both houses of Congress rushed through resolutions in June 1940 declaring that the United States would not only refuse to acquiesce in any attempt to transfer any region in the Western Hemisphere from one non-American power to another but proposed to consult immediately with the other American republics in case of such a threat.[66] Secretary of State Hull thereupon instructed our representatives in Europe to notify all governments concerned to this effect. Thus the United States indicated that the Monroe Doctrine was still a vital principle in the Western Hemisphere and the American republics would unite to enforce it.

Forthwith a second conference of foreign ministers met at Havana in July 1940, and Secretary of State Hull in his opening address proposed "the establishment of a collective trusteeship to be exercised in the name of all the American republics" [67] where the existing status of any American region was threatened by cession or transfer. The Conference except for Argentina was unanimously in favor of such a proposal. As finally accepted, the Act of Havana and a Convention on the Provisional Administration of European Colonies and Possessions in the Americas categorically prohibited the transfer of territories in the Western Hemisphere from one non-American state to another, and in case such action was threatened provision was made for the taking over and provisional administration of any such region by an Inter-American Commission of Territorial Administration. In case of an emergency any state could act *singly* or jointly with others in any manner required by its own defense or in defense of the continent.[68]

By this unanimous action of the representatives of the twenty-one republics, the Monroe Doctrine was accepted as a fundamental living principle of continental defense, and its maintenance was recognized to be of joint concern to all of the American republics. Furthermore, to prevent the possibility of a *fait accompli* before joint action was possible, the

---

[65] For text of the resolution see *Dept. of State Bull.*, Vol. I, No. 15 (Oct. 7, 1939), p. 334.

[66] S. S. Jones and D. P. Meyers, *Documents on American Foreign Relations, 1939-1940*, Vol. II (Boston, 1940), p. 89.

[67] *Dept. of State Bull.*, Vol. III, No. 57 (July 27, 1940), p. 46.

[68] *Ibid.*, Vol. III, No. 61 (Aug. 24, 1940), pp. 138, 145-148.

United States or any other power could act immediately and by itself to prevent its violation. The Monroe Doctrine had at last become a doctrine of continental security voluntarily and unanimously accepted.

The threat to the democratic systems of the New World inherent in the recent development of autocratic systems in the Old has brought about a situation somewhat comparable to that existing when the original Doctrine of Monroe was enunciated. Today, however, the United States no longer need take the sole responsibility for the maintenance of security in the New World. The will and ability to coöperate are manifest; the machinery for joint consultation has already been set up. President Franklin D. Roosevelt repeated on several occasions during his trip to South America a felicitous phrase: "Each one of us had learned the glories of independence. Let each one of us learn the glories of interdependence." Such a principle in which the peace and safety of one assumes the support and protection of all should effect a coöperation and solidarity among the nations of the Western Hemisphere whereby joint responsibility of the American republics replaces the now outmoded original Doctrine of Monroe.

SUPPLEMENTARY READINGS

A. Alvarez, *The Monroe Doctrine* (New York, 1924).

H. D. de Barral de Montferrat, *De Monroë à Roosevelt 1823-1905* (Paris, 1906).

M. D. de Beaumarchais, *La Doctrine de Monroe* (Paris, 1898).

Hiram Bingham, *The Monroe Doctrine, an Obsolete Shibboleth* (New Haven, 1913).

F. Capella y Pons, *Monroeism* (Paris, 1913).

Raúl de Cárdenas, *La Política de los Estados Unidos en el Continente Americano* (La Habana, 1921), pp. 89-186.

J. Reuben Clark, *Memorandum on the Monroe Doctrine* (Washington, D. C., 1930).

R. G. Cleland, *One Hundred Years of the Monroe Doctrine* (Los Angeles, 1923).

A. L. Delle Piane, *Doctrina de Monroe* (Montevideo, 1930).

T. B. Edington, *The Monroe Doctrine* (Boston, 1905).

Wilson Leon Godshall, *American Foreign Policy* (Ann Arbor, 1937), Chap. V.

A. B. Hall, *The Monroe Doctrine and the Great War* (Chicago, 1920).

A. B. Hart, *The Monroe Doctrine* (New York, 1916).

John B. Henderson, *American Diplomatic Questions* (New York, 1901), Chap. IV.

Herbert Kraus, *Die Monroe Doktrin* (Berlin, 1913).

T. H. Mahoney, *The Monroe Doctrine* (Boston, 1921).

GASTON NERVAL, *Autopsy of the Monroe Doctrine* (New York, 1934).

CARLOS PEREYA, *El Mito de Monroe* (Madrid, 1931).

CARLOS PEREYA, *La Doctrina de Monroe* (Mexico, 1908).

DEXTER PERKINS, *The Monroe Doctrine 1823-1826* (Cambridge, Mass., 1927).

———, *The Monroe Doctrine 1826-1867* (Baltimore, 1933).

———, *The Monroe Doctrine 1867-1907* (Baltimore, 1938).

———, *Hands Off: A History of the Monroe Doctrine* (Boston, 1941).

HECTOR PETIN, *Les États-Unis et la Doctrine de Monroë* (Paris, 1900).

ERNESTO QUESADA, *La Doctrina Monroe, Su Evolución Histórica* (Buenos Aires, 1920).

W. F. REDDAWAY, *The Monroe Doctrine* (Cambridge, Mass., 1898).

C. H. SHERRILL, *Modernizing the Monroe Doctrine* (New York, 1916).

D. Y. THOMAS, *One Hundred Years of the Monroe Doctrine* (New York, 1927).

CAMILO BARCÍA TRELLES, *La Doctrina de Monroe y la Cooperación Internacional* (Madrid, 1931).

BENJAMIN H. WILLIAMS, *American Diplomacy* (New York, 1932), Chap. IV.

❦ 4 ❦

Undermining the
Monroe Doctrine

I. THE TOTALITARIAN THREAT

DEMOCRACIES unfortunately are prone to possess two dangerous tendencies: wishful thinking and overconfidence. Britain wanted to do business as usual and was confident that the royal fleet made her sea girt isle impregnable—came the tragedy of Dunkirk. France was content with the *status quo* and possessed confident assurance that the Maginot Line would maintain it, but the line was turned. The Western Hemisphere has its vast ocean frontiers and its much publicized Monroe Docrine, but oceans are highways as well as barriers and the Monroe Doctrine was not contrived to prevent economic penetration and still less subversive propaganda. Totalitarian influences became deeply entrenched in the Western Hemisphere before either the North or South American republics realized the danger.

Not that warning was not given. Both Fascist and Nazi frankly boasted of their intentions. Virginio Gayda, the newspaper mouthpiece of Mussolini, on June 7, 1940, declared that "when the United States participates too indiscreetly in European affairs . . . the United States automatically grants European powers the right of retaliation, to be taken today or in any other period of American history and on American territory." [1] The Fuehrer was even more explicit when he boasted "We shall create a new Germany in South America. . . . Mexico is a country that cries for a capable master. . . . We shall create a new Germany in Brazil. . . ." [2]

One of the weapons employed most effectively by the Nazis to accom-

[1] *Giornale d'Italia,* June 7, 1940.
[2] Herman Rauschning, *The Voice of Destruction* (New York, 1940), pp. 61-67.

plish their ends was the stimulation of jealousy and hostility among Latin Americans by making invidious contrasts between the Yankees and their neighbors to the south. A subtle example is shown by a sentence from an editorial in the *Voelkischer Beobachter* of February 15, 1939: ". . . The biggest obstacle in the way of the Pan American policy of the Yankees is the deep chasm between the prosperity civilization of North America and the Iberian culture of Latin America. . . ." German newspapers and German publicists constantly strove to weaken the increasingly closer ties engendered by the good neighbor policy by a continuous campaign of detraction and innuendo. Although clearly a brazen attack upon the morale of the people of Latin America, the Nazis were confident that the Yankees were too stupid to appreciate the danger and the Latins would not be averse to implied support against the powerful neighbor to the north. Unfortunately, their reasoning was correct. The United States continued to be primarily interested in business as usual and the Latin-American republics were not unaccustomed to dictators and totalitarian methods. They appreciated the increasing attention showed to them but they did not take *der Führer* too seriously.

Apparently the United States, in spite of a constantly increasing loss of trade with the larger South American states to the benefit of Germany, failed to realize the threatening political implications. For example, in 1936 when the United States was buying twice as much from Chile as was Germany, the Reich exported to Chile about $2 million worth of goods more than the United States. In 1937 the Chilean State Railways bought over $3 million worth of railway equipment from Germany and in 1938 the Chilean National Air Lines were equipped with Junkers J. V86 although the bids of American firms were lower and Chilean pilots preferred American planes. During the same year Germany took away from us even our leading position in Brazilian imports, and only the outbreak of war in 1939 prevented a similar loss in Argentina.

The Nazis, however, were not content with economic gains. They were determined to bring Latin America under political control as well. The situation seemed tailored to their purpose. Although not well entrenched in Mexico or the Caribbean area, it was estimated that there were about two million German nationals in South America of whom the majority possessed German citizenship, even though not born in the Reich. Furthermore, they were well concentrated. In the southern departments of Chile, from Valdivia and Osorno to Puerto Montt, some 30,000 German farmers kept in such close touch with the Reich that their output of skins, wool, lentils, oats, and wine was contracted for far in advance of its production. In the northern territories of Argentina, such as Misiones, Formosa, and Chaco, and in the provinces of Corrientes and Entre Rios there were about a quarter of a million Germans, who practically dominated both the industry and agriculture of the region. But it was in the southern states of Brazil where there had been established a veritable *Deutschland über meer.* Reliable figures gave a conservative estimate of approximately a million Germans in the states of Sao Paulo, Santa Catharina, and Rio Grande du Sul. In some of the towns of Santa Catharina almost two-thirds of the people speak German in their daily lives instead of Portuguese.

The Nazis also counted upon the nationals of their Axis allies for strong support. With approximately six million of Italian blood and about a quarter million Japanese and an undetermined number of Falangistas who wished to restore Spanish influence and culture in the western hemisphere, this attitude seemed justified. The Nazis soon discovered, however, that they were badly mistaken in this hope. The Italians in South America assimilate quickly with both Spanish and Portuguese races. In Argentina where about half of the Italian stock is found they consider themselves Argentinians and are proud of it. The great Salocchi bank, in Peru, the Banco Italiano, may be Fascist-minded, but its Peruvian depositors of Italian race on the whole are not. Uruguay, which has a large Italian stock, is one of the most liberal minded republics in South America. The Latin citizens of the South American republics whether born in Spain, Italy, or Portugal are patriotic nationals of their adopted countries and react accordingly. The Italians resented Mussolini's attempts to export Fascism and even more his subservience to his Nazi master. Jokes on Mussolini and the Fascists were very popular among the Argentines whether of Italian or Spanish antecedents. One which was often quoted referred to the automobile racer who got extra speed from his car by putting Perelli (Italian) tires on his frontwheels and Dunlops (English) on the rear. Another referred to the man in a restaurant who ordered spaghetti, then Worcestershire sauce. When the sauce arrived he found the spaghetti had disappeared.

It was therefore the Nazis primarily whose activities were a real menace to the unified defense of the Western Hemisphere. It was they who, in the picturesque language of Sumner Welles, were the "human termites gnawing at the foundations of our Inter-American system." If we try to estimate just how great was the danger, we must divide South America into two parts—one, that section lying for the most part north of the bulge of Brazil and including Venezuela, Colombia, Ecuador, and Peru, and, the second and far larger part, including Argentina, Bolivia, Brazil, Chile, and Uruguay. In the northern sector, except for a potential threat to the Panama Canal, the problem was never very serious. In the southern sector we must confess that although Hitler could hardly take it over by telephone as has been alleged if he won the battle of Europe, he was in an excellent position to bring about the quick demise of the Monroe Doctrine in most of the area south of the equator, save Peru.

Let us take a brief glance at the situation in this northern section.[3] Starting with Colombia, we find there were only about 4000 Germans, but they were very well organized and some of them owned large and strategically located estates, with reference to the great oil pipe-lines. One of these, a 2500 acre tract south of Cartagena, owned by Dr. Hans Neumüller, an ardent Nazi, was only a stone's throw from an oil pipeline that delivered 54,000 barrels daily. Another Nazi, Adolph Held, owned an extensive estate across from Tenerife, where the Andean pipe-line crossed the river. Held, who incidentally was on the United States blacklist, had two air fields upon his estate.

Up to 1939 the German air line Scadta—the oldest commercial line in South America, was a direct threat to the Panama Canal. It was finally taken over by Arianca, a line owned partly by Pan American Airways and partly by the government of Colombia. The small German Arco line which controlled some forty landing fields in Southeastern Colombia only about 500 miles from the Panama Canal resisted all efforts to take it over until the autumn of 1941. In his broadcast of September 11, 1941, President Franklin D. Roosevelt mentioned a dangerously strategic German air field between Barranquilla and Cartagena on the Neumüller estate which the Colombian government, when the matter was brought to its attention, promised to investigate immediately.

Although the leader of the Colombian conservatives, Dr. Laureano Gómez, formerly minister to Germany, was reported very anti-Yankee— the taking of the Canal Zone via Panamanian independence still rankles— the United States' position was too strong to cause us much worry. The country with an investment of a quarter of billion dollars which controlled the oil industry and took most of Colombian coffee, bananas, and platinum had a full house before the draw. The well arranged visit of President-elect Alfonso Lopez to the United States in the summer of 1942

[3] The facts presented in this chapter are based for the most part upon information obtained in the various United States embassies and legations in South America where the writer was given every opportunity to survey the situation in the spring of 1941.

strengthened materially the bonds of friendship between the two countries.

There was no Nazi problem for the United States in Venezuela. Living principally upon oil which American and British companies controlled the government was pro-United States and pro-British. We had a naval mission there and our new base at Trinidad completely controlled the approach by sea. Port of Spain in Trinidad is on the direct line of the Pan American Clippers from Miami to Rio and on the east-west run Pan American joins Port of Spain with La Guaira, Maracaibo, and the Panama Canal. A mere glance at the map shows the strategic value of this service. With less than 5000 Germans to work upon, Herr Goebbels wasted little time in Venezuela. In fact Venezuela was the first republic of South America to sever diplomatic relations with the Axis powers.

Ecuador, which straddles the equator, had about 6000 Germans and the names Hindenburg and Adolph Hitler were still found on its busses. Where the United States had a minister, a diplomatic secretary, and a naval attaché with three or four clerks in its legation,[4] Germany had, until the severance of diplomatic relations, a staff of twenty-five. Where we had a half dozen in our consulate in Guayaquil, Germany had three times as many. The Sedta Air line—a German company—was formerly a real threat to the Panama Canal but Panagra first duplicated its runs and finally brought about its suspension. The United States had sent two missions, one naval and one military, to take the place of the Italian military mission withdrawn in 1940. Subsequently Ecuador leased us a base on the Galapagos Islands—a concession which was of as great a strategic value in the Pacific as Trinidad was in the Atlantic. The Nazis tried to fish in the troubled waters of the boundary dispute between Ecuador and Peru, but their catch was inconsequential.

Peru had long been regarded as very friendly to the United States. Standard Oil of New Jersey had a monopoly of its oil, the Cerro de Pasco Mining Corporation controlled Peru's copper and much of its gold and silver. The Vanadium Corporation was American and W. R. Grace and Company, an American concern, ran the Grace Line to the west coast, had sugar and cotton plantations, and was half owner of Panagra. The Japanese and the Italians far outnumbered the Germans, and Nazi efforts were completely checkmated. The great German sugar

[4] The United States has raised this post to an embassy.

family, the Gildermeisters, were not Nazis; in fact, there was some Jewish blood in the direction of Casa Grande, their vast sugar company. The fact that the Peruvian military airport at Talara was built entirely out of German materials was due to the same reason that the American Cerro de Pasco Company had their aerial tramway built by a German company—the Nazi bids were lower.

In 1941, resenting German violation of governmental regulations, Peru canceled the Lufthansa Airway Service, confiscated its planes, and gave the rights to Panagra. It also nationalized the Italian Caproni airplane plant, sent the Italian air mission home and invited in an American mission. Although one of the principal newspapers, *El Commercio* of Lima, was decidedly pro-Nazi and some of the leaders in the army had decidedly Nazi predilections, the Gestapo organization found to its dismay that President Manuel Prado was friendly to the United States, and his foreign minister, Solf y Muro, almost equally so; even the famous Aprista, Haya de la Torre, formerly very critical of Uncle Sam, was a strong believer in the Good Neighbor Policy. When the United States declared war upon Germany, Peru promised the United States every assistance; at the Rio Conference she made good on her promise and before the conference adjourned, she broke all diplomatic relations with the Axis powers.

Coming to the larger and more important part of South America south of the Equator the situation was not so satisfactory. In Bolivia, Chile, Argentina, Uruguay and Brazil the Nazis were more numerous and better organized. It is in this area that Germany made the greatest economic advances and her political infiltration was most powerful. Commercial inducements, military missions, schools, news services, radio programs, every instrumentality for drawing this tier of states into the orbit of the swastika was effectively used. And coördinating all these subversive activities were the German embassies, legations, and consulates whose officers, abusing their privileges and immunities, served as agents for Dr. Goebbels' Ministry for National Enlightenment and Propaganda, and Heinrich Himmler's even more dangerous Gestapo organization known as U. A. 1 (*Überwachtungsstelle Ausland*). It was in this region that the destruction of democratic morale by the promulgation of subversive propaganda was most aggressively conducted.

Bolivia, the least important of these countries in influence, but of vital importance to the United States because of its tin, was still suffering a bad hangover from the Chaco War. Whatever the real causes, Bolivia believed that her army trained by the German General Hans Kundt could easily conquer backward Paraguay. When it failed, a whipping boy was required and Standard Oil was at hand. Its $17 million property was confiscated. The President at the time was German Busch, who immediately afterwards set up a totalitarian state with himself at its head. When he committed suicide or was assassinated in 1939, the Nazi press claimed it was murder and the United States was in some way cause of it. But whatever the cause, the results were disastrous for the Nazi organization. When the European situation became very serious, Bolivia immediately turned towards the United States, in spite of the fact that three-fourths of the big firms in Bolivia were German and German propaganda both by radio and by press flooded the country. When in May, 1941, the United States made a deal to purchase Bolivia's total production of tungsten for three years for about 25 million dollars, and at the same time was able to force out the important German Lloyd Aereo Boliviano with its 4000 miles of airways and substitute Panagra, Nazi elements attempted a *coup*. But before the putsch came off, President Peñaranda acted. A letter from the Bolivian military attaché in Berlin to the German minister in La Paz fixing the date for the *coup d'état* was intercepted and published. Although the German minister declared it was a forgery, he was dismissed, a number of pro-Nazi Bolivians arrested, four pro-Nazi newspapers closed, and the Nazi menace in Bolivia was eliminated at least for the time. To strengthen the new situation the first air mission from the United States to Bolivia was sent in November, 1941, to take the place of the hitherto well entrenched Italian advisors. When the United States entered the war, Bolivia immediately accorded us non-belligerent status, and early in 1942, severed diplomatic relations with Germany and Japan. On April 7, 1943, Bolivia formally declared war upon the Axis powers and on April 20 she declared her adherence to the principles of the Atlantic Charter.

To North American travelers, Chile seems the nearest approach to home of any of the Latin-American republics. To North American financiers, the riches of the Chilean Andes have encouraged investments to the value of over a half billion dollars: Guggenheim in nitrates, Anaconda-Kennecott and Braden in copper, Bethlehem in iron. To the Germans, Chile beckoned agriculturally. The earliest German colonists in South America settled in Chile in the sixteenth century. In 1840 many families came and by the 50's there were some 2000 Germans in Chile—for the most part engaged in agriculture in the southern provinces from Valdivia to Puerto Montt. Later Germany sent engineers and officials to the nitrate fields and military missions to the Chilean army. Authoritative sources gave these estimates as to the German population of Chile: About 18,000 born in Germany; 40,000 of German descent; 20,000 of mixed marriages, and 9,000 refugees, mostly Jews, making a total of 87,000.

The Germans in Chile whether in commerce, agriculture, or industry not only retained their identity but maintained close connections with the Reich. Therefore, with the advent of Hitler a fallow field was afforded to his agents of propaganda. The German embassy at Santiago was enlarged to eleven principal officers not counting clerks (forty employees in all), some of whom under the title of press and cultural attachés devoted all of their time to preaching the gospel of Naziism. It was claimed that the German embassy spent over $100,000 a month on this work, a considerable part of which was obtained by forced levies on German firms and nationals. It has been asserted that the Nazi propaganda in Chile, carried on by the press, the radio, and the hand-outs from the German embassy was so overpowering that it brought about a confusion of ideas in the minds of the Chilean people as to just what were the national ideals, with a corresponding weakening of faith in democracy.[5]

The Chilean army was modeled to a considerable extent upon the German system. In fact, for almost fifty years German army officers on missions had advised as to its training. The Mauser rifle was still used and the Krupp factories furnished its artillery. The military police known as carabineros were also German trained—their former instructor Otto von Zipellius was regarded as chief of the Nazi party in Chile. In June, 1941, the German government presented a schooner for training purposes to the Chilean navy and in presenting it Ambassador von Schoen declared that a new link had been forged between the German and Chilean navies.

There were a considerable number of primary and secondary schools in Chile whose curricula were entirely in German. But the excellence of the Chilean public school system—it is one of the best in South America—made Chile's problem of the foreign language school less serious than it was in Argentina and Brazil. However, in the very excellent Santa Maria Technical College at Valparaiso, with a $5 million endowment which is sufficient not only to give free tuition but also free board and room to the fortunate students who enter by competition, all of the professors were German as was most of the technical equipment.

[5] See Hugo Fernandez Artucio, The Nazi Underground in South America (New York, 1942), p. 162.

Since Chile controlled the only other water route between the Atlantic and Pacific except via the Panama Canal it was vital for the United States to keep the Straits of Magellan open. In spite of the overwhelming German character of the population in the southern territories, Nazi principles were never overly popular. The success of Hitler kindled in some the pride of race, but the majority were well content to have *der Führer* win his victories in Europe. Furthermore, the Popular Front government was completely awake to the totalitarian menace. The United States was popular with the Chileans, and with the return to Chile of the eight Chilean newspapermen who, through the invitation of Ambassador Bowers, lived the life of American reporters, and the still larger number who came as guests of the United States under the auspices of the Coördinator's Office the neighbor to the North was even better understood than before.

It must be confessed that Chile's attitude in refusing to sever relations with Germany and Japan at the Rio Conference seemed to indicate that Nazi propaganda had been more successful than the United States had expected. Nevertheless, when Chile's new President, Juan Antonio Rios, accepted President Roosevelt's invitation to visit the United States in October, 1942, it was thought in many quarters that Chile would break with the Axis powers before that time. When it was evident that Chile intended to remain neutral for the time being, Sumner Welles forced the issue by declaring publicly that Axis espionage in certain South American states had resulted in the sinking of ships and the loss of lives in the western hemisphere. Although Chile vigorously protested and postponed the Rios visit, a change in Chilean foreign ministers followed and the new cabinet took a strong stand against all German nationals accused of subversive activities. With public opinion thoroughly aroused the Chileans finally took the decisive step and broke relations with the Axis powers on January 20, 1943.

For many reasons Argentina was regarded as the focal point of Nazi propaganda in all Latin America. The Argentine Republic had a larger percentage of its nationals who were born in Europe than any other Latin-American republic and of these, some 60,000 were born in Germany. Another 125,000 were born in Argentina but of German parents. This gives the Argentinian a natural predilection for Europe rather than for the "crude aggressive Caliban" of the north.

The center of the German propaganda organization during World War II was the German Embassy in Buenos Aires. Ambassador von

Thermann had the largest staff of any foreign mission in Argentina. In addition to the counselors and regular diplomatic secretaries, there were press and cultural attachés whole sole function was propaganda. The German Embassy with its staff of over forty, was almost twice as large as the United States Embassy and Consulate General combined. It was estimated that its annual expenditures were more than ten times the amount available to the embassy of the United States. The German government maintained fourteen consulates outside of Buenos Aires, the United States one. The Embassy saw to it that copies of Hitler's speeches translated into Spanish were mailed to all post office boxes within two days after their delivery. The Embassy also issue a mimeographed daily bulletin entitled "Off Cable News from Berlin," the general tone of which was decidedly anti-United States and anti-British.

The Nazi organization in Buenos Aires was founded in 1933 by an employee of the Banco Germanico under the name of the German Benevolent and Cultural Society. This organization possessed an elaborate card index of the names of German nationals giving the business and family connections of the individual including those living in the Reich. All social affiliations were listed and the individual's income and its sources. It was expected that a minimum of 10 per cent would be contributed for the needs of the organization and collection was made regularly by accredited agents. If payment was not made, pressure was used; if that was not sufficient the Gestapo had harsher means and finally if necessary, close relatives in Germany paid the penalty for the recalcitrant objector. Such extreme measures were rarely necessary.

The Argentine army was very sympathetic to Nazi influences which was natural, since for twenty-five years it had been advised by German military missions. When the mission was not reappointed in 1940, its chief, General Niedenfuhr, was made military attaché, dividing his time between Rio and Buenos Aires. The retired officers, were very influential and very pro-Nazi.

The Nazi influence in the school system of Argentina was particularly strong. The German schools were the most important in numbers and influence of all the foreign schools in the Republic. Out of 284 foreign schools at the outbreak of World War II 203 were German, with an approximate attendance of 13,500 pupils. Among the best known were the Goethe Schule, the Germania Schule, and the Colegio Aleman. The majority were under the strict control of an Inspector from the Ministry of Kultur in Berlin.

The Nazis paid particular attention to the press in Buenos Aires. The most outstanding Argentine newspapers, *La Prensa, La Nación, El Mundo,* and *La Razón* were objective in their reporting, and although critical of our tariff policies they were otherwise quite friendly to the United States. Even the more sensational papers such as *Crítica* and *Noticias Gráficas* were pro-British and anti-Nazi; therefore the Nazis had to establish their own organs. They first took over the old *Deutsche La Plata Zeitung,* gave it a Spanish language supplement and colored the news and editorials with pro-Nazi hues. Next they got control of *Crisol* which commenced a series of vitriolic attacks upon President Roosevelt, whose name they alleged to be Rosenfeldt. The Good Neighbor Policy was merely camouflaged Yankee imperialism. In 1940 the Nazis set up a new so-called nationalistic newspaper called *El Pampero* with an elaborately equipped establishment. Its monthly stipend from the German embassy was 60,000 pesos and it had a forced subscription among the Nazi organizations and a wide distribution in Argentine army circles. It attacked the United States and Great Britain upon every possible occasion.

It was hoped that the military revolt of June 4, 1943, which forced the resignation of President Ramón S. Castillo, might bring about a break with the Axis powers. However, the new government of General Ramirez, although promising loyal coöperation with the other American republics, declared for a continuation of the previous policy of neutrality. In spite of popular demonstrations in favor of the democracies, the provisional government suppressed the Communist newspaper *La Hora* and permitted the pro-Nazi *El Pampero* to continue publication.

Uruguay has long rivaled Brazil and Peru in her friendship for the United States; nevertheless the small but effective Nazi organization here went so far as to prepare a plan by which German technicians after an insurrection were to take over the work of Uruguayan officials and transform the state into a German agricultural colony. Much credit is owing to Professor Fernández Artucio for unearthing the plot and disclosing it in a book entitled "Los Nazis en el Uruguay." He followed it up with numerous radio addresses appealing for Congressional action. Congress finally investigated and found so much evidence that twelve leading Nazis were arrested. They were later released, but in September, 1940, eight of them were rearrested and charged with treason against the state. The German subversive organizations were dissolved, their newspapers and radio suspended for a period and all activities driven under ground. It is reported that the Counselor of the German embassy in Rio publicly declared in March, 1941, that "Montevideo is our weakest spot in Latin America."

Paradoxically enough, Brazil which has long had the closest commercial and political ties with the United States of all Latin America had at the same time the most dangerous Nazi organization in South America. Brazil had the largest number of Germans, about 50,000 born in the Reich, and a million to a million-and-one-half of German blood. They were for the most part concentrated in the southern states of São Paulo, Paraná, Santa Catharina, and Rio Grande do Sul.

The German Embassy in Rio in 1941 was known to have available some two-and-a-half million dollars for propaganda purposes. Former Ambassador Karl Ritter became so obnoxious to the Brazilian government through his opposition to the suppression of local Nazi organizations and to his support of one of the members of his embassy accused of complicity in the Integralista coup of 1938 that he was finally declared *persona non grata*. The cultural attaché of the Embassy was also the chief of the Trans Ocean News Agency which purveyed radio and cable news from abroad to all Latin-American newspapers that would take it. There were some twenty-eight papers in Brazil alone which subscribed to its services. The German embassy was the largest of all the foreign representations. It had one of the most magnificent residences in Rio and its chancellery took even more extensive quarters during World War II. It is difficult to state the exact number who were employed inasmuch as a large number of its clerks and employees were not listed in the diplomatic list, but it was estimated that its total staff was over a hundred. At the request of the German Embassy, the Brazilian Minister of War, General Dutra, and the Brazilian Chief of Staff, General Goes Montero, were decorated in 1940 for their valuable services to Germany in Brazil.

Closely in touch with the German Embassy were many important commercial concerns such as Compania Chimica Merck, Bayer Ltd., and various banks and motor companies. The Condor Syndicate was the most important airway in South America, except for Pan American. It formerly coöperated with the Italian L.A.T.I. which flew till recently from Dakar to Natal, and its network of lines spanned many areas of strategic rather than commercial value. The inability to obtain fuel and make essential repairs finally grounded it even before Brazil declared war upon the Axis powers.

The German Protestant Church in southern Brazil was impressed into the propaganda machine. It was reputed to have some 200 pastors and bishops who served as Nazi agents. At one time it was estimated that there were 3000 German schools in southern Brazil and the number of German cultural, benevolent, and athletic societies was legion.

In spite of this Axis predominance, the Vargas régime was able gradually to impose a series of restrictive measures. Portuguese was made compulsory in the schools, the foreign language press was forbidden, all airplane pilots had to be Brazilian nationals, and alien political activity was strictly prohibited.

The Japanese attack upon the United States strengthened the hands of President Vargas and Foreign Minister Aranha in their efforts to strengthen continental solidarity. Señor Aranha played a leading role at Rio in bringing about a break with the Axis powers. When German submarines began to sink Brazilian ships, President Vargas decreed corresponding confiscation of Nazi assets in Brazil. All fifth column suspects were rounded up and interned. When finally five Brazilian ships were sunk in three days in August, President Vargas hesitated no longer. Brazilian aircraft were ordered to sink Axis submarines on sight and on August 22, 1942, a formal declaration of war was issued. The results of years of Nazi propaganda were wiped out when the concrete evidence of Nazi methods was brought home to the Brazilian people.

The United States has done its share to combat Naziism and its ideologies in all parts of South America. Missions, military, naval, and air, have been made available to all. Loans for defense, stabilization, or constructive purposes of any sort may be readily obtained. Economic and technical experts may be had for the asking. And, as a more positive procedure, the elaborate black list of all firms affiliated with or utilizing German companies or their products proved to be very effective.

Although the totalitarian threat of the Nazis and the Facists has been overcome, a new totalitarian danger has recently arisen in Argentina known as Peronismo. Dictatorships have been the rule rather than the exception in Latin America but the dictatorship of Perón is not confined to Argentina. It is an aggressive totalitarian menace to all South America. Although aimed particularly at the United States it is a threat of equal concern to the South American republics. Masking under promises of protection and aid to the worker and support for trade unions, the movement is both imperialistic and totalitarian. Perón has already organized an inter-American labor federation (ATLAS) which is seeking to undermine the Inter-American Regional Organization which is supported by the United States. Perón is also trying to build a political economic bloc of South

American states under the aegis of Argentina and has already persuaded Chile to enter into a close economic relationship. Imperialistic Peronismo is as yet in the embryonic stage, but the growth of totalitarianism can be exceedingly fast.

II. THE MENACE OF COMMUNISM

Another and perhaps an even more insidious and deadly threat to the democratic system of the Americas is the aggressive imperialistic brand of Soviet Communism. Whereas Naziism and Fascism needed a German or Italian soil to nurture the ferment, Soviet Communism needs only a dissatisfied minority to propagate its destructive theories. In the Latin-American republics where exploitation of the masses is a commonplace whether by the foreign capitalist or by the national politician, the glittering promises of Communism are more persuasive and alluring than the realities of a none too successful democracy.

The fact that large holdings of land by the few has long been a basic feature of the economy of Latin America has given rise to glaring abuses which are easily capitalized upon by the subversive agent. Similarly, the exploitation of mineral resources which require large outlays of capital tends to bring in the foreign entrepreneur whose only interest is profit, with small regard for the interests or rights of the native. Thus, countries like Mexico, Chile, and Bolivia, where land, oil wells, and mines were exploited by wealthy national or foreign interests, or the Central American states whose bananas were almost completely controlled by the United Fruit Company, were fertile fields for Communist infiltration.

So long as Communism in Latin America was essentially Marxian it was largely confined to an honest struggle to better the conditions of the lower classes. One of the great Marxian Communists, José Carlos Mariátegui of Peru, was a patriotic intellectual who was solely interested in agrarian reform for the benefit of the people of Peru. He saw the Indians in a state of beggary and, knowing the excellent conditions existing among the Incas with their communal farms, he favored a modified form of communal life. It was only after his death in 1930 that the South American Communist movement came under the direction of the Soviet Comintern, and the great Socialist leaders such as Luis Carlos Prestes in Brazil and Vincente Lombardo Toledano in Mexico, although not inscribed party members, were the leaders of the Soviet Communist Fifth Column in Latin America.

Inasmuch as certain radical movements such as the Aprista in Peru and the Popular Front in Chile were making considerable progress, the

Communist International agreed to use them where it seemed feasible instead of provoking revolution. The procedure is well described by the one-time Peruvian Communist, Eudocio Ravinas, as the "Yenan Way." In fact, discussing it in Moscow at Stalin's suggestion with Mao Tse-Tung and Li Li Siang, Ravinas was directed to go to Chile, and utilizing the middle and professional classes as well as the working class and the peasants, to convert the Popular Front to an all-out Communist movement.[6] The procedure to be employed was unscrupulous opportunism.

Proceeding from Moscow to Santiago de Chile, the Communist group headed by Ravinas, who worked under the pseudonym Jorge Montero, was able to infiltrate the Radical party, establish a Communist newspaper called *Popular Front*, and supported by outstanding radicals like Gonzales Videla, win a number of seats in the Senate and Assembly in the 1937 elections. In 1938 on a platform of *pan, techo, y abrigo* (bread, roof, and overcoat) they joined with the radicals in the Popular Front and elected Aguirre Cerda president. As might have been expected, they then refused to coöperate with the Socialists in the Congress or to take any positions of responsibility, and encouraged strikes and lockouts. When in 1940 the Socialist Minister of Development went to the United States to obtain badly needed credits, the Communists denounced him as the tool of Yankee imperialism. This brought a split between the Communists and the other parties of the left which, although it wrecked the Popular Front, did not prevent the Communists from gaining additional seats in the 1941 Congressional elections.

The Communists were forced to cease their campaign against the United States when Hitler attacked Russia, and Stalin became an ally of the democracies. The new president of Chile, Juan Antonio Rios, elected in 1942, was a Radical but bitterly anti-Communist, and although the Communists voted for him as against former Dictator Ibanez, he included none of them in his cabinet. The Communists after encouraging a series of strikes brought matters to a head in 1946 when they staged a great demonstration which threatened the police, who fired into their ranks killing and wounding many of the strikers. This action antagonized many of the more conservative elements and in the next election the Communists joined the Radicals and Socialists to help elect Gabriel Gonzales Videla, a left-wing Radical. He rewarded them by giving them three cabinet posts—the first American government to so honor the Communist party.

President Gonzales Videla quickly recognized his mistake. The Com-

[6] See Eudocio Ravinas, *The Yenan Way* (New York, 1951), Chaps. V, VI.

munists attacked him immediately for not vetoing all Conservative measures and when he accepted the resignation of the three Communist
cabinet members they encouraged strikes in the copper mines. Gonzales
Videla now took drastic action. He dismissed the Communist governors
and provincial heads, obtained emergency powers from the Congress
permitting him to seize all essential industries and run them by the
army. He broke the strikes, severed diplomatic relations with the Soviet
Union and its satellite states, and persuaded the Congress to pass a law
making the Communist Party illegal.

The unions still had a Communist core, however, and in March, 1952,
President Gonzales Videla was forced to proclaim a state of emergency
in the northern provinces of Antofogasta and Tarapaca when the unions
controlled by Communists refused to settle a strike which was paralyzing
the vital nitrate fields. In July some 13,000 office workers in these same
mines staged a walk-out to protest ratification of a United States-Chilean
mutual security pact.

When General Carlos Ibanez was elected in September, 1952, the Communists were encouraged because he had campaigned against the law
making the Communist party illegal; nevertheless, in his first message to
the Congress on May 21, 1953, he attacked international Communism as
conspiring against peace and endorsed the Organization of American
States and the Inter-American Reciprocal Assistance Treaty. He imple-
mented his statement by refusing to allow the sale of copper to Communist countries. Although the Chilean Communists who must swear to
dedicate their lives "to emancipate the peoples oppressed by North American imperialism" operate openly except in elections, the stand taken by
the Ibanez administration precludes any serious danger to the inter-American system.

If the Communist Party obtained its first Cabinet members in Chile, it
was in Brazil where it made its most rapid advances and obtained its
largest popular vote of any country in the Western Hemisphere. The story
of Communism in Brazil is closely intertwined with its soldier leader, Luis
Carlos Prestes, a colorful character whose famous ten-year successful
struggle with a small following in the hinterlands against more than a
dozen different generals sent by President Arturo Bernardes to capture
him, has become a famous Latin-American Odyssey.

Beginning their operations clandestinely about 1922, the Communists
were outlawed by the government in 1927 and practically disappeared.
When in 1930 Getulio Vargas became President, Prestes returned to Brazil

and for a time supported the government. However, when Vargas suspended the constitution and dissolved Congress, Prestes broke with the government and fled the country. The next few years he spent in Russia and became a full-fledged Communist. Returning to Brazil in 1935, he staged an unsuccessful revolt against the government and Vargas retaliated by proclaiming "a state of grave internal commotion" and throwing thousands of suspected Communists into jail. Prestes was given a sentence of seventeen years at hard labor and later thirty more years were added to his sentence as accessory to a murder committed while he was in prison.

Prestes remained in jail and the Communist party in abeyance until 1945 when Vargas pardoned Prestes and the latter reciprocated by urging that Vargas remain in power although he was not a candidate for election. Vargas next legalized the Communist party which campaigned strenuously for local, state, and congressional offices. Fearing that Vargas would stage a *coup d'état* to retain power, the army acted, forced him to retire and turned the power over to the president of the Supreme Court. The presidential elections were now held peacefully and to the surprise of all, Vargas was elected to the Senate and his candidate, General Dutra, became President. But even more incredible, the Communist Party received more than 600,000 popular votes, obtained fourteen seats in the Chamber of Deputies, and elected Luis Carlos Prestes to the Senate.

Stimulated by their success, the Communists put on a strong campaign in the 1947 elections and did even better than before. They obtained about 800,000 votes, elected two Senators, fourteen Deputies, sixty odd members of the state legislatures, and the largest number of any one party in the city council of Rio de Janeiro. Senator Prestes speedily made known his opposition to the United States policy towards China and Jugoslavia and he demanded the immediate return of the air bases to Brazil. However, when asked in a Senate debate which country he would support in a war between Russia and Brazil, he replied "Russia," his inexcusable blunder ruined his cause.

President Dutra about a month after the elections directed a petition be presented to the Supreme Electoral Tribunal requesting the dissolution of the Communist Party on the grounds that it opposed democracy and was under the control of a foreign power. The Electoral Tribunal obliged and the President removed all Communists from appointive positions and closed all Communist clubs. It took several months to expel the Communists from Congress, but by the beginning of 1948 the Communist Party in Brazil was driven underground.

This did not mean that the Communist menace was obliterated. When Assistant Secretary of State Edward Miller and head of the Foreign Policy Planning Staff George Kennan visited Rio de Janeiro in March, 1950, the Communist press was bitterly critical and the American Embassy was smeared with inscriptions "Go away spies Kennan and Miller." In 1951 the *Revista Militar*, the organ of the influential *Club Militar*, was suppressed because of its harsh attacks upon the United States and its constant publication of Red propaganda. That the army was infiltrated by Communist agents was shown when on April 30, 1952, Minister of War General Ciro Cardosa warned all officers that the presence of Communists in the Brazilian army had been positively established and subsequently the prosecutor in charge of cases against officers accused of Communist activity was relieved of his post on suspicion of Communist sympathies.

President Vargas who had again been inaugurated President in January, 1951, quickly took a strong stand against Communism. He ordered all state and territorial governors to prevent a meeting anywhere in Brazil of the Communist "Continental Peace Congress" which Communist leader Prestes had projected for March, 1952. When early in 1953 it was discovered that a nationwide Communist drive was attempting to defeat the United States-Brazilian military aid treaty signed March 15, 1952, the police throughout the country were instructed to ban all "peace" meetings organized by the outlawed Communist party. Although urged by some members of his Cabinet to enter into diplomatic relations with the Soviet government, no such action has yet been taken.

Despite the constant menace to the United States through infiltration into Brazilian government organizations and the army, the present attitude of the Brazilian government is to attack Communism whenever and wherever it shows itself interfering in public affairs. Otherwise it is permitted to spread its propaganda by means of its score of daily newspapers and thirty odd weeklies, ignored and unmolested by the government. On July 9, 1954, a military court acquitted 44 army officers accused of Communism.

Communism in Argentina since the Perón era has been complicated by the fact that Peronism has as one of its appealing vote-catching assets, aid to the masses—the shirtless ones. This has been cleverly joined with support for the labor unions, at least for those labor unions that will coöperate with Perón. Although Communism in Argentina goes back as far as 1922, it wasn't until 1929 that it showed any real strength. In 1930 it was outlawed and had little political influence until 1943 when

Perón became interested in organizing and using labor for his purposes. At this time the labor organizations had split over whether to coöperate with Communism. It was only natural that Perón, an innate Fascist, should take the anti-Communist side. Although Russia had opposed the entrance of Argentina into the United Nations, Perón saw the possibility of using the Soviets as a counter balance to the United States. The Communist Party was legalized in December, 1945, and a Soviet trade mission sent in 1946 was enthusiastically received. In 1947 the *Partido Communisto Argentina* pledged in its convention support of Perón in all policies consistent with the Communist program. U. S. Ambassador George Messersmith was particularly singled out for Communist abuse and in November, 1948, his successor, James Bruce, declared that President Truman was much concerned about Communism in South America, particularly in Argentina.[7]

It was not long after this that the Communist leaders in Argentina split and the Stalinist wing headed by Victorio Codovilla and Rodolfo Ghiholdi became anti-Perón and the "Dissident" group headed by Rodolfo Puiggros supported him. Moscow, however, ceased its propaganda campaign against Perón, and Communist infiltration into the General Confederation of Labor was stepped up. The split seemed to have been sufficiently patched up by the end of 1952 for the Communist Party to pledge full coöperation for Perón's second Five Year Plan. Nevertheless, in March of 1953 after Codovilla had revisited Moscow the Communist Party again turned against Perón and attacked his apparent intention to coöperate with the Eisenhower administration. It also violently opposed Perón's Union of Latin American Labor Organizations (ATLAS). Although ATLAS subsequently took a strong stand against the Communist-dominated World Federation of Trade Unions and the pro-Communist Confederation of Labor of Latin America led by Vincente Lombardo Toledano of Mexico, the Argentine government did not object to signing a mutually advantageous trade treaty with Moscow on August 5, 1953. Perón's "Third Position" makes it possible for him to march with either Washington or Moscow as the situation seems to warrant.

International Communism has not succeeded in obtaining a substantial hold in any of the other South American republics. In Bolivia there is no Communist Party as such, although the Revolutionary Party of the Left (PIR) is based upon a Marxist ideology and its leader, José Antonio Arce, denounces "American imperialism" upon all occasions.

[7] *New York Times,* Nov. 4, 1948.

Haya

In Peru Victor Raul de la Torres' Aprista party of democratic socialism has never accepted the Marxian philosophy and although its leader has flirted with various agents from Moscow, no agreement was ever reached. Since APRA offered a haven for those who might normally have gone Communist, no Communist Party existed in Peru until 1929. Even then its activities were confined to organizing workers rather than engaging in political matters. However, in 1945 under the name of *Vanguardia Socialista* the Communists cast almost 70,000 votes. Today its enmity towards APRA is so bitter that it is unable to attack the United States with the destructiveness that an undivided hostility might permit.

In Colombia the Communists are divided into three groups, none very important. When the Leftist Liberal, Dr. José Eliecer Gaitán, was assassinated in April, 1948, at the time of the Bogotá Conference, the Communists were alleged to have instigated and carried out the destructive riots which followed. However, impartial observers concede that while the Communists unquestionably helped in the orgy of violence, they were not the group which initiated the trouble. As a result of the uprising Colombia severed diplomatic relations with Russia and the country today is so completely under the control of the Conservatives that in the 1953 Congressional elections only Conservative candidates' names appeared on the ballot. The unseating of President Laureano Gomez in June, 1953, has brought about a more liberal trend which should weaken Communism still further.

The Communists in Venezuela were not recognized as a legal party until 1945, and their principal achievement has been to obtain a considerable following among the oil workers. They are not particularly close to Moscow and under the dictatorship of President Perez Jimenez their activities are largely clandestine.

In Ecuador Communism is practically of no importance politically due to the strength of the Socialists. Their principal strength is among the stevedores and agricultural workers.

Uruguay gives the Communists complete freedom to function, but since 1946 they have been losing influence and at present have no Senators and only three representatives in the Assembly. They have opposed the United States foreign policy but are not controlled by Moscow. The Communist Party has been outlawed in Paraguay.

Although there is a Communist Party in Mexico and it obtained about 40,000 votes in the presidential election of 1946, it has never played an important role. On the other hand, Mexico's leftist labor leader, Vincente Lombardo Toledano, who has been sympathetic to Soviet policies, has considerable influence throughout Latin America. Born into a wealthy family, well educated, a brilliant writer and orator, he became intellectually intrigued with Marxian Communism and the Soviet experiment. He decided to reorganize Mexican labor and since President Cardenas in his campaign had urged Mexican workers to unite, Toledano found the President *muy simpatico.* In February, 1936, a new national federation of labor unions was organized under the direction of Toledano and named *Confederacion de Trabajadores Mexicanos* (CTM). It became very powerful during the Cardenas régime and it was in Mexico that a new inter-American labor organization was set up in 1938 called the *Confederacion de Trabajadores de la America Latina* (CTAL) and Lombardo Toledano was elected president of the organization.

The policy of CTAL throughout World War II followed the Soviet lead. So long as this coincided with that of the anti-Nazi allies, the Latin-American groups coöperated, but with the Cold War and the outlawing of the Communist Party in several South American states, the position of Toledano as a fellow traveler became difficult. He was ousted from the head of CTM and in 1949 he was refused a visa by the United States when he wished to attend a CIO congress. President Miguel Aleman, elected in 1946, took a strong stand against Communism, and in 1951 the Communist Party was denied official recognition by the Mexican government.

This did not affect Lombardo Toledano, who now headed the so-called Popular Party and who still professed Marxian Communism. During the spring of 1952 Toledano was regarded as a serious coalition candidate for the presidency, but the Communists were unable to procure the 35,000 signatures required for legal registration. When Toledano, as candidate of the Popular Party and supported by the Communists, only obtained about 2 per cent of the entire vote, the Communists turned towards General Henrique Guzman of the Federation of Peoples Party as their future standard bearer. Toledano retaliated by stating in his newspaper, *El Popular,* that he would henceforth support President Ruiz Cortines and his policy of "honesty and morality in government."

During 1953 the Communists confined their efforts largely to converting the rural school teachers to Marxism, to getting rid of the religious schools, and to increasing the use of Communist textbooks, but with little success due to strong governmental opposition. In the labor union field the Communists were losing strength and dominated only two out of the ten or more labor organizations. Politically the Mexican Communists had become of little value to the Soviet infiltration program.

At the present time perhaps the chief Communist menace to the United States lies in the Caribbean area with Cuba and Guatemala the two focal points. In both the Dominican Republic and Haiti, Communists mask under the name of Popular Socialists and in 1946 both countries authorized their appearance on the ballot. Subsequently they have been driven underground and have little influence today. The only Central American republic other than Guatemala where the Communists have had any substantial influence is Costa Rica where in 1944 under the name of *Partido Vanguardia Popular* they elected four deputies to the Congress. However, the recently elected President Jose Figueres has taken a strong stand against Communism and has promised that his country will remain "faithful to the ideals of Western democracy."

The Communists in Cuba first gained importance during the scandalous administration of President Machado, and helped to bring about his overthrow. In the strike-ridden period which followed, the Communists increased in strength and influence until Colonel Baptista became President in 1940. During the second World War the Communists known as the Popular Socialist Party coöperated with the government temporarily, but about 1947 they broke with President Grau San Martin and went into opposition. At this time they were very well organized, polled close to 200,000 votes, were influential in the General Confederation of Cuban Workers whose membership reached half a million, and they possessed a well edited, popular daily newspaper in *Hoy*. In the 1948 elections, however, the Communist candidate, Dr. Juan Marinello, received less than 150,000 votes, the smallest of all the parties participating. When in 1952 ex-President Baptista seized control of the government by a *coup d'état*, the Communist power was already on the decline.

On July 26, 1953, an abortive uprising against the Baptista régime took place which the authorities claimed was at least partially instigated by the Communists. The government immediately suspended their newspaper *Hoy* and declared its editor and other Communist leaders would be seized and tried. However, the Communist leaders were able to escape, although all their publications and literature were seized and destroyed. On November 10, 1953, the government outlawed the *Partido Socialista Popular* with all of its affiliations such as the Socialist Youth Organization and the Federation of Democratic Women, a part of the Soviet world "peace" movement. Both the daily newspaper *Hoy* and the weekly *Ultima Hora* were banned. The Minister of Information declared that Cuba has now become a bastion against Communism in the Americas.

Whereas the Communist position in Cuba has become less important, that in Guatemala until the Castillo Armas revolt in June, 1954, correspondingly increased in influence and power if not in numbers. Furthermore, the Guatemalan Labor Party which is the official name of the Communist Party took its orders directly from Moscow and served as the local agent of Soviet propaganda and subversive action in the Caribbean. The strength of Communism in Guatemala sprang from the fact that the group was very well organized and had been supported openly by the past two administrations in control of the government. Under the presidency of Dr. Juan Jose Arevalo Communists were given many important governmental positions. At the end of his term in 1951 he supported a coalition of leftists including Communists which succeeded in electing Colonel Jacobo Arbenz Guzman. The candidate of the moderate elements, Colonel Francisco J. Arana, the principal opponent of Colonel Arbenz, was ambushed and murdered during the campaign.

The Arbenz administration, although supported by a coalition of parties in which the Communists were a decided minority, was anti-United States and against business organizations controlled by North Americans. The disproportionate influence wielded by the Communists in the government—they had only four of the fifty-one seats controlled by the government—was due to their close organization, concrete program, and unscrupulous tactics. Each of the four Communist Congressmen held an important committee chairmanship, Communists held important positions in the Ministry of Foreign Affairs and in the Labor Department and practically controlled the agencies for social security and land reform. They dominated both the press and the radio and they held key positions in the labor union movement. Guatemala had consequently become the base of operations for the Soviet Union's plan to divide and conquer in the Western World.

Inasmuch as bananas have become one of the most profitable export crops of Guatemala and the United Fruit Company is the principal producer and exporter of this fruit, the government centered its attack upon this company. The Agrarian Law passed in 1952 permits the confiscation of any plantation in excess of 644 acres which is not cultivated by the owner or for his account. Inasmuch as United Fruit has large holdings not under cultivation, but held in reserve to compensate for cultivated lands attacked by the Panama disease, 234,000 acres have already been expropriated under this law. At the same time other foreign companies, the Empresa Electrica and the International Railways of Central America, are being seriously threatened. When it is realized that these three companies employ over 15,000 men with a total annual payroll of about $10 million or about 34 per cent of all the wages earned in Guatemala, the implications of confiscation are evident.

The Guatemalan Communists have been a constant threat to the governments of the other Central American states. They have infiltrated the Caribbean Legion which from its Guatemalan base has been an effective instrument of subversive action. When the Organization of Central American States, established in 1951 as a regional union, wished to investigate the Communist threat in Central America, Guatemala first blocked the proposal and when outvoted, withdrew from the Organization.

The United States has not been unaware of the Communist menace in Guatemala. On February 25, 1952, Representatives John W. McCormack and Joseph W. Martin, Jr., majority and minority leaders, respectively, agreed that the Soviet government had established a beachhead in Guatemala and that the troubles of the United Fruit Company and other American enterprises were a direct result of the Communist dominated labor unions taking their orders from Moscow. The United States government protested the seizure of 234,000 acres owned by United Fruit Company in an *Aide-Memoire* dated August 18, 1953, declaring that the offer of $600,000 in 3 per cent twenty-five year "agrarian bonds" bore not the slightest resemblance to a just evaluation." [8] Assistant Secretary of State for Inter-American Affairs, John Moors Cabot, speaking in Washington October 14, 1953, accused Guatemala of "openly playing the Communist game." The official Guatemalan newspaper even went so far as to join with the Communists in their lying and wholly discredited accusations of bacteriological warfare by the United States aviators in Korea. However, Mr. Cabot took the stand that the determination as to whether the activities of the international Communist conspiracy to destroy free governments were prejudicing the independence of Guatemala and that of the neighboring republics was "essentially a matter of inter-American rather than unilateral concern." In other words, where formerly such a threat was a clear violation of the Monroe Doctrine to be met by immediate and effective action unilaterally by the United States, today the Republics of the Western Hemisphere have pledged themselves on numerous occasions, particularly by Resolution 32 of the Bogotá Conference of 1948, and by Resolution 93 of the Caracas Conference of March, 1954,

[8] *Dept. of State Press Release* No. 464, Aug. 28, 1953.

to protect the Western Hemisphere from subversive activities of this sort. The steadily increasing strength of the Communist movement in Guatemala was finally broken by the anti-Communist revolution led by Carlos Castillo Armas in June, 1954.

SUPPLEMENTARY READINGS

DUNCAN AIKMAN, *The All American Front* (New York, 1941).

HUGO FERNANDEZ ARTUCIO, *The Nazi Underground in South America* (New York, 1942).

SAX BRADFORD, *The Battle for Buenos Aires* (New York, 1943).

ALBERT E. CARTER, *The Battle of South America* (New York, 1941).

WALTER M. DANIELS, ed., *Latin America and the Cold War* (New York, 1952).

THEODORE GEIGER, *Communism versus Progress in Guatemala* (Washington, 1953).

JOHN GUNTHER, *Inside Latin America* (New York, 1941).

HUBERT HERRING, *Good Neighbors* (New Haven, 1941).

RAFAEL LARCO ITARRERA, *La Ultima Carta de la Democracia* (Lima, 1952).

MIGUEL JORRÍN, *Governments of Latin America* (New York, 1953).

RAY JOSEPHS, *Latin America—Continent in Crisis* (New York, 1948).

AUSTIN MACDONALD, *Latin American Politics and Government* (New York, 1949).

N. P. MACDONALD, *Hitler Over Latin America* (London, 1940).

JACINTO ODDONE, *The Landowning Bourgeoise* (Buenos Aires, 1936).

HERMAN RAUSCHNING, *The Voice of Destruction* (New York, 1940).

EUDOSIO RAVINES, *The Yenan Way* (New York, 1951).

K. D. SINGER, *Germany's Secret Service in South America* (New York, 1942).

ROBERT STRAUZ-HUPÉ, *Axis America* (New York, 1941).

5

Anglo-American
Isthmian Diplomacy

FROM the time when Columbus started on his famous quest of a new route to an old world, a shorter waterway from Europe to farther Asia has been the dream of navigators. Columbus believed that he had found a new route to India, but he realized that there remained the task of finding a passage by which he could cross between the great land masses and circle the globe. With the discovery of the Pacific by Balboa, the search for the secret of the strait was prosecuted with increased diligence, but in vain. Magellan finally discovered the secret, but his solution *via* the Straits of Magellan or Cape Horn was too long to be satisfactory, and the quest continued. When Cortez, by numerous expeditions, became virtually certain that no natural waterway connected the two great oceans, he proposed to construct one. Charles V took much interest in the project; and, according to the historian Gomara, four routes were considered practicable, *i.e.*, those of Darien, Panama, Nicaragua, and Tehuantepec.[1] Thus not only was an interoceanic canal regarded from the earliest times as feasible, but the four routes considered most practicable up to our own time were among the first to be considered.

Early in the nineteenth century new interest in the idea was provoked by the interesting surveys and reports of the great scientist Alexander von Humboldt. After five years of exploration in Central and South America, he urged the construction of an artificial waterway, and he went so far as to discuss the possibilities of nine different routes, although he, too, regarded the four routes already mentioned as particularly worthy

[1] See Report of J. T. Sullivan on *Problem of Interoceanic Communication, House Ex. Doc. No. 107*, 47th Cong., 2nd Sess., Chaps. I and II.

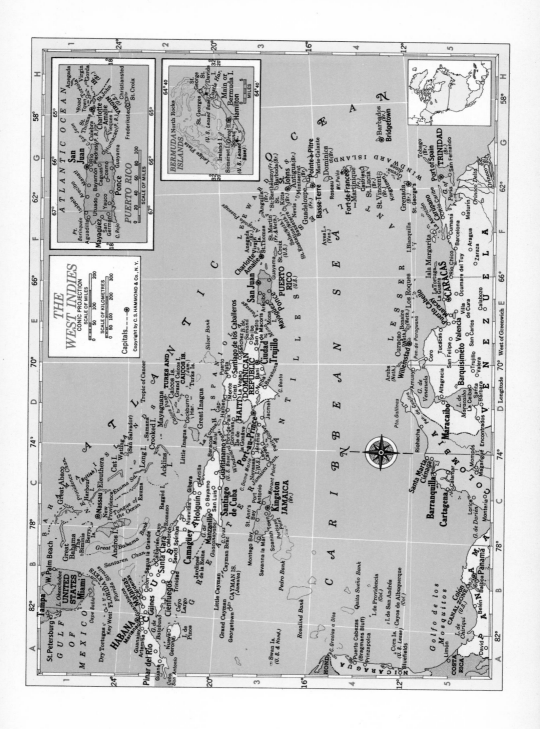

THE WEST INDIES

CONIC PROJECTION

SCALE OF MILES

0   50   100   200   300

SCALE OF KILOMETERS

0   50   100   200   300

Copyright by C. S. HAMMOND & Co., N. Y.

Capitals......⊛

PUERTO RICO

SCALE OF MILES

0   20   40   60   80   100

BERMUDA ISLANDS

MILES

0   2   4   6

of investigation.[2] Spain was finally aroused once more to the advantage that would accrue to her through the possession of such a waterway, and in 1814 the project was authorized by the Cortes. With the outbreak of the revolutions throughout Latin America the project lapsed, and it remained for the newly liberated republics to resume its consideration. As early as 1823 the matter came before the congress of Central America, and in the following year Señor Cañas, the diplomatic representative of this federation at Washington, drew the attention of the United States to the importance of a canal linking the two oceans and urged that the United States coöperate with his country in the construction of such a waterway. Henry Clay, Secretary of State, was interested in the project and promised to instruct the American representative to investigate and make a report.[3]

At approximately the same time the United States was invited to send representatives to the Panama Congress, called at the instance of Bolívar, at which the canal question was one of several subjects to be considered. Owing to strong opposition in Congress, the American representatives were not sent until it was too late to participate in the congress, but in their instructions the canal project was considered a proper subject for consideration. The sole limitation was that such a canal should not be under the control of any one nation, "but its benefits be extended to all parts of the globe upon the payment of a just compensation or reasonable tolls." [4] Although nothing substantial came of the Panama Congress, the importance and need of a trans-isthmian canal persisted, and in the next few years various projects were launched. An American company obtained the concession for a canal in Nicaragua; but, although the cost was estimated at only five million dollars, that sum could not be raised. The King of Holland, who had been represented by General Werweer at the Congress of Panama, also obtained a contract to construct a canal by the Nicaragua route; a company was formed, and the United States was sufficiently interested to consider the desirability of obtaining a majority of the shares. The revolution in the Netherlands, resulting in the separation of Belgium from Holland, forced an indefinite postponement of the project.[5]

[2] For complete citations see *House Report No. 145*, 30th Cong., 2nd Sess., pp. 169-204.

[3] *House Rep. No. 322*, 25th Cong., 3rd Sess., pp. 15, 16.

[4] J. B. Moore, *Digest of Int. Law*, Vol. III, p. 2, or *Report of International American Conference*, Vol. IV, Hist. Index, pp. 143 *ff*.

[5] *House Rep. No. 322*, pp. 17-33.

The Panama route was also being seriously considered at this time, and Bolívar went so far as to have the route surveyed. But the engineers reported that there was a difference of three feet between the levels of the two oceans, a factor that enormously increased the difficulty of the project. Nicaragua realized the particular interest that the United States had in an interoceanic canal, and on June 16, 1825, the congress of the Central American Confederation passed a decree offering liberal concessions to stimulate the construction of a canal. Bids were received and the contract was awarded to an American financial group; whereupon a company, capitalized at five million dollars, was formed under the name of the "Central American and United States Atlantic and Pacific Canal Company." Sufficient funds, however, were never subscribed.[6] About a decade later, in reply to another decree of the Central American congress offering the United States prior rights, a Senate resolution authorized the President to open negotiations with the governments of both Central America and New Granada in regard to protecting the rights of such companies as should undertake to open communication between the Atlantic and Pacific oceans, and to secure forever "the free and equal right of navigation of such canal to all nations, on the payment of such reasonable tolls as may be established."[7] President Jackson appointed Mr. Charles Biddle to undertake the necessary negotiations. But Biddle did not carry out his instructions in the proper fashion, and in his next message to Congress the President declared it inexpedient to enter into negotiations with foreign governments upon the subject.[8] President Van Buren sent Mr. John L. Stephens upon a similar mission in 1839, but after surveying the route and estimating the cost at twenty-five millions, he declared that in his opinion the country was too unsettled to risk the undertaking.[9]

Among the most interesting of the early projects for a canal was the one launched by Prince Louis Napoleon while he was a prisoner in the fortress of Ham. In 1845 he secured a concession from the Nicaraguan government for the construction of a canal, and when he finally escaped, he published a brochure on the subject, pointing out the possibilities of the Nicaragua route and emphasizing the great political interest of England in the execution of this project to create a new center of enterprise in Central America, which would prevent any further encroachments

[6] *Ibid.,* p. 125.
[7] Moore, *op. cit.,* Vol. III, p. 3.
[8] *Senate Journal,* 24th Cong., 2nd Sess., p. 100; for Biddle's report see *House Rep. No. 322,* 25th Cong., 3rd Sess., pp. 38-44.
[9] *House Rep. No. 145,* 30th Cong., 2nd Sess., p. 236.

from the north. With the fall of the July monarchy, Louis Napoleon found more interesting and vital matters to engage his attention.[10]

It was about this time that the United States took the first important step to secure control of the trans-isthmian route in Panama. On December 12, 1846, the American *chargé* signed a treaty with the Republic of New Granada, which, among other things, guaranteed to the United States "that the right of way or transit across the Isthmus of Panama upon any modes of communication that now exist, or that may be hereafter constructed, shall be open and free to the government and citizens of the United States"; and in return the United States guaranteed to New Granada "the perfect neutrality of the before-mentioned isthmus, with the view that the free transit from the one to the other sea may not be interrupted or embarrassed in any future time while this treaty exists." As a natural corollary, the United States also guaranteed the sovereignty of New Granada over this territory.[11] In other words, although "perfect neutrality" clearly meant that all nations should have equal right to free passage across the isthmus, and was so interpreted by Polk in his message to Congress, February 10, 1847,[12] it was understood both by the President and the Senate that by guaranteeing this neutrality the United States accepted a responsibility that was justified only because of the fundamental importance which the trans-isthmian route already possessed for the United States. This treaty was approved unanimously by the United States Senate.

Owing to the discovery of gold in the recently acquired California, the importance of the treaty was speedily demonstrated. The difficulties of overland travel were such that the sea route, with the short passage across Panama, became the most practicable avenue for the great horde of gold-seekers and settlers. Relying upon the terms of the new treaty, an American company constructed a railway across the isthmus from what is now Colon to Panama—a road that, since its completion in 1855, has been one of the most profitable short lines ever laid down. Another American company established a second interoceanic route through Nicaragua, by means of the lakes and short stretches of land travel, but it never attained the sucess of the Panama Railroad route.[13] It was in connection with the rights to construct a canal by the Nicaragua route that the United States came into conflict with Great Britain, a conflict that was

[10] See B. Jerrold, *The Life of Napoleon III* (London, 1874), Vol. II, pp. 320-330.
[11] W. M. Malloy, *Treaties, Conventions, etc., of the U. S.* (Washington, D. C., 1910), Vol. I, p. 302.
[12] J. D. Richardson, *Messages and Papers of the Presidents*, Vol. IV, p. 512.
[13] For a more complete account of this undertaking see Chap. 14.

settled only by the much criticized and wholly unsatisfactory Clayton-Bulwer treaty.

The attempts of Great Britain to obtain territory in Central America dated back to the seventeenth century, and, although her claims rested upon very uncertain grounds, by the middle of the nineteenth century she had practically established her sovereignty over the Mosquito Coast, the Bay Islands, and Belize. When, however, in 1848 Great Britain forced the withdrawal of the Nicaraguans from San Juan del Norte (Greytown)—a certain terminus of any interoceanic canal through Nicaragua—the United States deemed it necessary to act. Secretary Buchanan sent Mr. Hise as a special agent to Nicaragua in 1849, but with very indefinite instructions as to what action he should take, other than a vague implication that the Monroe Doctrine should be maintained. Hise succeeded in signing a convention giving the United States rights virtually equivalent to those acquired in the treaty of 1846 with New Granada. But, as this directly contravened the British claims, our government was not ready to back up his negotiations.[14]

The administration of President Taylor, which had come into office the same year, despatched a new emissary, Mr. Squier, to negotiate with Nicaragua, with the admonition that he should not involve the United States in any unnecessary controversy. He not only signed a treaty with Nicaragua obtaining the concession for the canal, but also another with Honduras, whereby the United States virtually obtained control of Tigre Island in the Gulf of Fonseca. When the British government answered this action by sending a squadron which took possession of the island, the United States found itself in an awkward predicament.[15] It was necessary to come to an agreement with Great Britain, and Mr. Lawrence, the American minister at London, entered into negotiations. When, however, he demanded that as a preliminary to the settlement of the question Great Britain should withdraw her protectorate from the Mosquito territory, Lord Palmerston was unwilling to continue. In his anxiety to settle the dispute, Mr. Clayton, the American Secretary of State, decided to go over the head of his representative and come to a settlement, if possible, with Sir Henry Bulwer, the British minister at Washington. The British representative saw the advantage of coming to an agreement at a time when the United States was willing to compromise, and the famous Clayton-Bulwer treaty was negotiated.[16]

[14] For text see *Sen. Ex. Doc. No. 112*, 46th Cong., 2nd Sess., p. 92.
[15] For text and correspondence see *British and Foreign State Papers*, Vol. XL, pp. 997-1002; also Chap. XIII.
[16] For correspondence see *Sen. Ex. Doc. No. 194*, 47th Cong., 1st Sess. ,pp. 55-82.

The principal provisions of this treaty may be summarized as follows: Great Britain and the United States promised never to obtain or maintain any exclusive control over the proposed Nicaragua canal; they would neither erect fortifications commanding the canal, nor occupy, colonize, or exercise dominion over any part of Central America; the two powers agreed to guard the safety and neutrality of the canal and to invite other nations to join with them in doing the same; they promised to support any company that would construct the canal in accordance with the spirit of the convention; and finally, in order to establish a general principle, they agreed to extend their protection to any other practicable communication, whether by canal or railway, across the isthmus, and particularly to the proposed interoceanic communication by way of Tehuantepec or Panama.[17] The precedent against joint action established by John Quincy Adams was seemingly forgotten.

Hardly had the treaty been signed before difficulties arose concerning its interpretation. Great Britain regarded the treaty as definitely establishing her rights in the regions to which she had already laid claim, future settlements only being prohibited, while the United States confidently expected that the British would immediately withdraw from the Mosquito Coast and the Bay Islands. When Great Britain continued to maintain her position on the east coast of Nicaragua, and when in 1852 she formally annexed the Bay Islands by proclamation, her interpretation of the treaty seemed to be receiving *de facto* recognition. However, the United States continued to protest, and by a supplementary agreement, known as the Dallas-Clarendon treaty of 1856, an attempt was made to settle the question by the withdrawal of the British protectorate from the Mosquito Indians in return for obtaining a protectorate over the Bay Islands under the nominal sovereignty of Honduras.[18] When this convention failed of ratification, another attempt was made the following year, but with similar results; so that President Buchanan, in his message of December 8, 1857, declared that the wisest course would be to abrogate the treaty by mutual consent.[19] Great Britain was willing, provided that the United States would accept the *status quo ante* as the basis of the abrogation. But, as this was the last thing that the United States desired, the President did not press the matter. When, in 1860, the British signed a treaty with Nicaragua restoring a nominal sovereignty over the Mosquito

[17] For text with accompanying notes see Hunter Miller, *Treaties and Other International Acts of the United States of America* (Washington, D. C., 1937). Vol. V, pp. 671-703.

[18] *Sen. Ex. Doc. No. 194*, p. 138.

[19] *Ibid.*, p. 126.

Coast, the United States was forced to accept this solution.[20] A treaty of amity and commerce between the United States and Nicaragua, signed at Washington, November 6, 1857, known as the Cass-Yrisarri treaty, gave the United States equal rights with Nicaragua over any interoceanic route, in return for a guaranty of neutrality. This treaty, however, was never ratified by the Nicaraguan congress.[21]

During the Civil War period the United States was forced to lay aside both the Monroe Doctrine and all projects for the construction of an interoceanic waterway. Hardly, however, had the war come to an end before interest in a trans-isthmian canal revived, and at the same time feeling grew stronger that the waterway must be under American control. In 1867 the United States and Nicaragua ratified the Dickinson-Ayon treaty, which gave the United States the right to construct a canal in return for guaranteeing Nicaragua's neutrality.[22] About the same time Mr. Seward entered into the negotiations with Colombia to obtain exclusive rights for an isthmian canal, and a treaty to this effect was signed in 1869, but was not ratified either by the Senate of the United States or by the Colombian congress. An even more advantageous treaty, signed by the representatives of the two countries in 1870, met a similar fate.[23] In the same year President Grant appointed an Interoceanic Canal Commission, which conducted a number of important surveys, including the Darien, Nicaragua, Tehuantepec, and Panama routes, and after very careful consideration of the data obtained reported unanimously, in 1876, in favor of the Nicaragua route, from Greytown to Lake Nicaragua by the San Juan River and thence to Brito on the Pacific coast.[24]

In the meantime an adventurer, Gogorza, appeared in Paris with a canal concession obtained from Colombia, and succeeded in interesting certain of the imperialists in the scheme.[25] A company was promoted to push the project, and Ferdinand de Lesseps, justly famous as the builder of the Suez Canal, became interested in it. Surveys were made, and an International Engineering Congress was held at Paris in 1879, under the presidency of de Lesseps, to consider the execution of the project. Various routes were considered, but de Lesseps favored the Panama route and his advice was ultimately taken. The Universal Oceanic Canal Company purchased a concession for $10 million, its president, de Lesseps, went

[20] *Ibid.*, p. 151.
[21] *Ibid.*, p. 117.
[22] *Sen. Ex. Doc. No. 112*, p. 130.
[23] *Ibid.*, pp. 34-84; also see *House Rep. No. 224*, 46th Cong., 3rd Sess., p. 24.
[24] *Sen. Ex. Doc. No. 15*, 46th Cong., 1st Sess., p. 1.
[25] *For. Rel. of the U. S.*, 1876, pp. 87-93.

to Panama; and early in 1880 he announced that plans had been completed for a tide-level canal whose cost was estimated at $168 million by the International Technical Commission.[26]

The prospect of early construction of an interoceanic canal under European control aroused the United States, and President Hayes took occasion to present his views of such an undertaking in a special message to Congress, March 8, 1880.

The policy of this country is a canal under American control. The United States cannot consent to the surrender of this control to any European powers. If existing treaties between the United States and other nations, or if the rights of sovereignty or property of other nations, stand in the way of this policy, . . . suitable steps should be taken by just and liberal negotiations to promote and establish the American policy on this subject, consistently with the rights of the nations to be affected by it. . . . An interoceanic canal across the American isthmus will essentially change the geographical relations between the Atlantic and Pacific coasts of the United States and between the United States and the rest of the world. It will be the great ocean thoroughfare between our Atlantic and Pacific shores and virtually a part of the coast-line of the United States. Our mere commercial interest in it is larger than that of all other countries, while its relation to our power and our prosperity as a nation, to our means of defense, our unity, peace, and safety, are matters of paramount concern to the people of the United States.[27]

Congress also became concerned about the matter, and passed a resolution declaring it to be in the interest of the people of the United States that its government should insist that its consent be a necessary condition precedent to the construction of any ship-canal across the isthmus.[28] Urged on by similar sentiments, Mr. Evarts attempted to make a treaty with Colombia whereby any concession for an interoceanic canal hitherto made, or to be made in the future, by Colombia should be subject to the rights of the United States, as guarantor of the neutrality of the isthmus and of the sovereignty of Colombia, over isthmian territory.[29] The Colombian government, however, was unwilling to concede any such rights to the United States; so that our government was forced to rest content with such powers as the treaty of 1846 guaranteed. At the same time, renewed interest was manifested in other trans-isthmian routes, particularly that by way of Tehuantepec, where Captain James B. Eads proposed to construct a great ship-railway, by which the largest ships could be transported from one ocean to the other by rail. The House Committee

[26] For text of Salgar-Wyse concession see *Sen. Ex. Doc. No. 112*, p. 84.
[27] Richardson, *op. cit.*, Vol. VII, p. 585.
[28] *Sen. Miscellaneous Doc. No. 42*, 46th Cong., 3rd Sess.
[29] *Sen. Doc. No. 237*, 56th Cong., 1st Sess., pp. 473-499.

reported favorably but no guaranties from the government could be obtained.[30]

The idea grew that the Clayton-Bulwer treaty was hampering the legitimate aspirations of the United States for a canal under its own control, and President Garfield, who came into office in 1881, directed his Secretary of State to take measures looking to the abrogation of the treaty. Instead of taking up the matter directly with the British government, Mr. Blaine sent a circular despatch to the United States ministers in Europe, outlining the American attitude towards the proposal to establish a trans-isthmian canal under European guaranty. He pointed out that such a guaranty was entirely unnecessary, because by the treaty of 1846 the United States had already guaranteed the neutrality of the isthmus, and this guaranty required reinforcement, accession, or assent by no other power. Furthermore, he said that the proposed European guaranty would be offensive to the United States, since the proposed canal would be the chief means of transportation between the Atlantic and Pacific states and would be, to all intents and purposes, a part of our coast line. This being the case, the passage of armed vessels of a hostile power during any war to which the United States or Colombia might be a party would be no more admissible than over the railway lines joining the Atlantic and Pacific shores of the United States or of Colombia.[31]

The remarkable feature of this communication was not so much its expression of principles, which showed, after all, no radical departure from former statements on the subject, but the fact that, although a copy of it was sent to the British Foreign Office as well as to the other European chancelleries, no mention was made, even in the British copy, of the Clayton-Bulwer treaty. This was the more surprising in that the statement on the passage of armed ships was in direct violation of the second article of that treaty. At first, Great Britain ignored the despatch. But at length, about four months after it was received, Lord Granville pointed out that the position of the United States and Great Britain with reference to the canal was determined by the convention commonly known as the Clayton-Bulwer treaty, and that her Majesty's government relied with confidence upon the observance of all the engagements of that instrument.[32]

Shortly before this reply was received, Mr. Blaine, apparently realizing that a formal treaty could not be disposed of in this cavalier fashion, sent

[30] See *House Rep. No. 322*, 46th Cong., 3rd Sess.
[31] *For. Rel. of the U. S.*, 1881, pp. 537-540.
[32] *Ibid.*, p. 549.

a special despatch to the British government through Mr. Lowell, dated November 19, 1881, in which he attempted to show that the conditions of the Clayton-Bulwer treaty were no longer existent. In the first place, the treaty had been drawn up more than thirty years before, when the position of the United States on the Pacific Coast was entirely different. Again, whereas the intention of the treaty was to put Great Britain and the United States on an equal basis in respect to the canal, the present arrangements insured control by Great Britain, on account of her superior naval strength, unless the United States should be allowed to fortify the canal. In the third place, now that other nations had become interested in a canal project, the United States, by the terms of this treaty, was prohibited from asserting the rights acquired by the treaty with Colombia signed earlier than the Clayton-Bulwer treaty. Finally, the treaty had been made on the implied understanding that both nations would immediately subscribe funds for undertaking the work; now that nothing had been done, and the United States no longer needed outside aid, there was no reason for either side to regard itself as bound by the treaty's terms.[33]

Lord Granville had little difficulty in exposing the weakness of Mr. Blaine's arguments, both in this despatch and in one of November 29 which followed it. The British possessions in North America had also shown considerable development, and it could hardly be supposed that the statesmen who were parties to the treaty had not envisaged certain changes of condition.[34] Neither was Mr. Frelinghuysen, who followed Mr. Blaine as Secretary of State, more successful than his predecessor, although he was on more familiar ground when he based his objections on the Monroe Doctrine and the traditional policy of the United States in opposing European intervention in American political affairs.[35] The weak point, of course, was the fact that the Monroe Doctrine had not been regarded as a bar to making the treaty; therefore it could hardly be advanced as a reason for abrogating it. Needless to say, the diplomatic correspondence of the United States during this period did very little to improve the country's position; in fact, so easily and completely were its arguments refuted that its position diplomatically was even weaker than before. Nor did Great Britain confine her activities to the exchange of notes with the United States. At the first intimation of American action against the Clayton-Bulwer treaty, the British government protested that

[33] *Ibid.*, pp. 554-559.
[34] *British and Foreign State Papers*, Vol. LXXIII, p. 873.
[35] *Ibid.*, p. 892; or see *Sen. Ex. Doc. No. 194*, for correspondence.

Nicaragua had never paid the indemnity promised to the Mosquito Indians by the treaty of 1860, and forced the case to arbitration before the Emperor of Austria. The award was wholly favorable to the British, not only in that it was declared that Mosquitia was not subject to regulations of Nicaragua, but in that it gave Great Britain the right, in case the terms of the treaty were not strictly observed, to intervene to protect her own interests.[36]

Mr. Frelinghuysen also attempted direct action by negotiating a treaty with Nicaragua in December, 1884, which provided for the construction of a canal by the United States under the joint protection of the United States and Nicaragua, the United States agreeing to guarantee the territorial integrity of Nicaragua.[37] But when Grover Cleveland became President in 1885, he recalled this treaty from the Senate, and declared in his first annual message that whatever highway should be constructed joining the two oceans "must be for the world's benefit, a trust for mankind." [38] There was no change in this attitude until 1899, when John Hay undertook to obtain the abrogation of the troublesome Clayton-Bulwer treaty, and succeeded quite as brilliantly as his predecessors had ignominiously failed.

In the meantime de Lesseps had made a spectacular beginning upon his stupendous undertaking. The actual work of construction was started February 1, 1881, and a veritable army of engineers and laborers was employed. Unfortunately for the success of the enterprise, de Lesseps remained in France, apparently failing to realize the prodigal and extravagant methods that were being employed. Useless and expensive equipment was purchased; the officers and directors were housed magnificently; an expensive campaign of propaganda was maintained to stimulate enthusiasm for the undertaking; and no matter how rapidly money flowed in, it was used up even more rapidly. The Engineering Congress at Paris had originally estimated the cost of the canal at $114 million and had figured that it could be built in seven or eight years. At the end of eight years almost $400 million had been spent and the work was not one third completed. The company went into bankruptcy, and the investigation that followed showed that the undertaking had been managed in a most corrupt and wasteful manner. The scandal was so great that all hope of ever constructing the canal by private means seemed eliminated.[39]

[36] *British and Foreign State Papers,* Vol. LXXII, p. 1212.
[37] Richardson, *op. cit.,* Vol. VIII, pp. 256-260.
[38] *Ibid.,* p. 324.
[39] For an excellent summary of the reasons for the French failure see W. F. Johnson,

In the United States, where the Nicaragua route still seemed preferable, various attempts to organize companies to construct a canal by this route met with varied success. In 1890 the Maritime Canal Company, which held a concession from Nicaragua, was chartered by Congress and began work at Greytown. After three years work, its capital was used up and the company went into the hands of a receiver. In 1895 Congress authorized a commission to report on the cost of completing the abandoned canal and the original estimate of $67 million was raised to $133 million. Under these conditions the government was not willing to back a resumption of work.[40] Various proposals were made in Congress to purchase the Maritime Company's franchise and property, but nothing came of them. Upon the outbreak of the war with Spain, all projects were dropped. Nevertheless, the fact that the battleship *Oregon* had to travel 13,400 miles, instead of 4600 by the canal route, to arrive at the West Indies, where she was needed, from San Francisco, where she was stationed, showed conclusively the vital need of a trans-isthmian waterway.

At the close of the war, agitation was renewed; and this time Congress made the generous appropriation, March 3, 1899, of $1,000,000 for a commission to make an exhaustive investigation of the relative merits of the Nicaragua and Panama routes. Moreover, since it was realized that no satisfactory solution could be arrived at until the Clayton-Bulwer treaty was out of the way, the Senate authorized the President to secure its abrogation, if possible. Somewhat isolated in Europe on account of the unpopularity of the Boer War, Great Britain had shown herself quite friendly towards the United States during the Spanish-American War, and the conditions were now exceedingly favorable for opening up negotiations on the subject. In fact, as early as December 7, 1898, Mr. Hay had made overtures through our representative, Mr. White, who was instructed to approach the British authorities in a "frank and friendly spirit of mutual accommodation, and ask whether it may not be possible to secure such modification of the provisions of the Clayton-Bulwer treaty as to admit such action by the government of the United States as may render possible the accomplishment of a work which will be for the benefit of the entire civilized world." [41]

Four Centuries of the Panama Canal (New York, 1907), Chap. VII; see also *For. Rel. of the U. S.*, 1884, p. 119, for report on difficulties encountered.

[40] For complete report see *House Rep. No. 2126*, 54th Cong., 1st Sess., pp. 122-129.

[41] *Diplomatic History of the Panama Canal*, Sen. Doc. No. 474, 63rd Cong., 2nd Sess., p. 1.

Both Lord Salisbury and Mr. Balfour were willing to consider the suggestion favorably, and Lord Pauncefote, the British ambassador to the United States, was forthwith instructed to enter into negotiations on the subject. A treaty was signed by Mr. Hay and Lord Pauncefote on February 5, 1900, which provided that an isthmian canal might be constructed and operated by the United States, but that it must be neutralized in accordance with the principles of the Clayton-Bulwer treaty.[42] This convention was not satisfactory to the American Senate, which had expected a complete abrogation of the treaty. Accordingly, it proposed a number of alterations. One of these authorized the United States to take such measures as should be necessary to secure the defense of the canal and the maintenance of public order by its own forces; Article III, providing for the adherence of other powers, was stricken out; and provision was made for the express abrogation of the Clayton-Bulwer treaty.

These amendments were not satisfactory to Lord Lansdowne, the new British Minister of Foreign Affairs, who, in a lengthy communication, set forth his objections to them.[43] After conferring with Lord Pauncefote and with leading senators, Mr. Hay accordingly proceeded to secure a fresh convention. In the course of several months of friendly negotiations all differences were ironed out, and on November 18, 1901, the second Hay-Pauncefote treaty was signed. This instrument the Senate ratified the following month by a vote of 72 to 6.

Article I of the new treaty expressly abrogated the Clayton-Bulwer treaty. Article II provided that the canal might be constructed directly or indirectly under the auspices of the United States government, which should have the exclusive right to regulate and manage it. Article III provided for the neutralization of the canal under substantially the same rules as those governing the Suez Canal. The most important of these rules was the first, which declared that the canal should be free and open, on terms of entire equality, to the vessels of commerce and of war of all nations observing these rules, with no discrimination in respect to traffic charges or otherwise, and that the conditions and charges should be just and equitable. Although no provision regarding fortification was laid down, the United States was given the right to establish such military police as would protect the canal from lawlessness; and since the canal was to be completely immune in time of war, the logical inference was that the United States, which was charged with its defense, would not be prevented from erecting such fortifications as would insure its

[42] *Ibid.*, p. 289.
[43] *Ibid.*, p. 11.

protection. The fourth article stipulated that no change of territoria'
sovereignty or of international relations of the country or countries
traversed by the canal should affect the general principle of neutralization or the obligations assumed under the treaty.[44]

As far as Great Britain was concerned, the United States was now
free to proceed with the construction of a canal over whatever route
should appear most practicable. A source of constant friction between
the two great Anglo-Saxon countries had been removed, amicably and to
the ultimate advantage of each. Great Britain had made the greater concession; it remained to be seen whether the United States would be duly
appreciative of this fact when questions should arise involving the new
treaty's interpretation.

SUPPLEMENTARY READINGS

C. L. G. ANDERSON, *Old Panama and Castilla del Oro* (Washington, D. C.,
    1911).

H. ARIAS, *The Panama Canal* (London, 1911).

I. E. BENNETT, *History of the Panama Canal* (Washington, D. C., 1915).

JOHN BIGELOW, *Breaches of Anglo-American Treaties* (New York, 1917), pp.
    37-164.

FARNHAM BISHOP, *Panama Past and Present* (New York, 1913).

ARTHUR BULLARD, *Panama, the Canal, the Country, and the People* (New York,
    1914).

P. BUNAU-VARILLA, *Panama, Creation, Destruction, and Resurrection* (New
    York, 1914).

Diplomatic History of the Panama Canal, Sen. Doc. No. 474, 63rd Cong., 2nd
    Sess.

MILES P. DuVAL, JR., *Cadiz to Cathay* (Stanford University, 1940).

J. B. HENDERSON, *American Diplomatic Questions* (New York, 1901), Chap. II.

W. F. JOHNSON, *Four Centuries of the Panama Canal* (New York, 1907).

L. M. KEASBY, *The Nicaragua Canal and the Monroe Doctrine* (New York,
    1896).

J. H. LATANÉ, *The United States and Latin America* (New York, 1920), pp.
    144-183.

C. H. A. FORBES-LINDSAY, *Panama and the Canal Today* (Boston, 1910).

W. D. McCAIN, *The United States and The Republic of Panama* (Durham,
    N. C., 1937), Chap. I.

J. C. RODRIGUES, *The Panama Canal* (New York, 1885).

NORMAN THOMSON, *Colombia and the United States* (London, 1914).

ANTONIO J. URIBE, *Colombia y los Estados Unidos* (Bogota, 1931).

M. W. WILLIAMS, *Anglo-American Isthmian Diplomacy* (Washington, D. C.,
    1916).

[44] *Ibid.*, p. 292.

❦ 6 ❦

Colombia, The United States, and the Panama Canal

Just two days before the Hay-Pauncefote treaty was signed, the Walker Commission, after a thorough investigation of both the Nicaragua and Panama routes, reported in favor of the Nicaragua route. It estimated that the interests of the French company were not worth more than $40,000,-000; and inasmuch as the French had estimated their holdings at $109,-141,500, there was no need to consider the Panama route farther.[1] When, however, the Hepburn bill, providing for the construction of the canal by the Nicaragua route, passed the lower house almost unanimously, the French company became panic-stricken and offered to sell out to the United States at the figure fixed by the commission. As a result of this offer, the commission filed a supplementary report recommending the adoption of the Panama route.[2] Each route had its strong advocates in Congress, but the offer of the French company to sell at the very low figure set by the American commission gave the advantage to those favoring the Panama route. An amendment to the Hepburn bill was introduced by Senator Spooner, authorizing the President to purchase the rights and property of the Panama company for not more than $40 million, and to secure the necessary rights from Colombia for the construction of the canal, with the proviso that, if a satisfactory arrangement could not be made with both the French company and Colombia within a reasonable time, he should proceed with the construction by the Nicaragua route.[3] The adoption of this amendment virtually spelled defeat for the proponents of the Nicaragua route, although without a

[1] *Sen. Doc. No. 54,* 57th Cong., 1st Sess.
[2] *Sen. Doc. No. 123,* 57th Cong., 1st Sess.
[3] *U. S. Stat. at Large,* Vol. XXXII, Part I, p. 481.

vigorous campaign by M. Philippe Bunau-Varilla, the former chief engineer of the Panama Company, which did much to make the American congressmen realize the superior advantages of the Panama project, the fight for the Panama route might not have been won.[4]

The Spooner amendment became law with the President's signature June 28, 1902, and shortly afterwards Attorney-General Knox, after an investigation in Paris, declared that the French company could give a clear title. There remained the task of acquiring the right of way from Colombia. Negotiations were immediately begun with Señor Concha, the Colombian minister to the United States. But, now that the United States was willing to proceed by the Colombian route, Colombia seemed disposed to drive a very stiff bargain. So unsatisfactory were the Colombian replies that Mr. Hay finally called the attention of the Colombian minister to the fact that if a satisfactory treaty could not be arranged with Colombia, the President was authorized to proceed with the construction of a canal by another route.[5] When, on December 1, the Colombian minister left Washington unexpectedly, without giving the reasons for his departure, the negotiations were put in the hands of Señor Herran, the Colombian *chargé d'affaires*, who proceeded with them in a far more conciliatory manner. As a result, a compromise was soon arranged, and the Hay-Herran treaty was signed on January 22, 1903, and approved by the Senate on March 17 of the same year. This treaty authorized the French company to transfer its properties and concessions to the United States; it also gave the United States exclusive right to construct and operate the canal for one hundred years, with an option to continue the arrangement for similar periods, and the full control over a strip of land three miles wide on each side of the canal, not including the cities of Colon and Panama. Colombia was to maintain her sovereignty over the territory, and was to have the right to transport over the canal at all times her vessels, troops, and munitions of war without payment of any charges. As a price for these concessions, the United States promised to pay Colombia $10,000,000 in cash and an annuity of $250,000.[6]

To complete the transaction, there remained only the ratification by the

[4] For the detailed story of the various influences working for and against the choice of the Panama route see P. Bunau-Varilla, *Panama, the Creation, Destruction, and Resurrection* (New York, 1914), especially Chap. XXII; also see *The Story of Panama*, hearings on the Rainey resolution before the House Committee on Foreign Affairs (Washington, D. C., 1913).

[5] *Diplomatic History of the Panama Canal*, Sen. Doc. No. 474, 63rd Cong., 2nd Sess., p. 256.

[6] *Ibid.*, p. 277.

Colombian senate. But this was never obtained. The Colombian government was determined to profit to the uttermost, and, now that it appeared that the Panama route was definitely decided upon, the terms that the United States offered were no longer deemed satisfactory. A perusal of the correspondence between the American representative at Bogotá, Mr. Beaupré, and Mr. Hay, shows that from the moment the opportunity was given to Colombia to obtain what had hitherto been considered favorable terms, public sentiment turned against the treaty. When a circular was issued by the government to the press, inviting discussion, it was quickly discovered that public opinion towards the treaty had changed "from approbation to suspicion and from suspicion to decided opposition." [7] The attitude of President Marroquin towards the treaty had at first seemed most favorable, but in his message to congress, which convened on June 20, he was completely noncommittal. He pointed out that the government was in a dilemma—it must either ratify the treaty and suffer a loss to its sovereignty, or refuse and sacrifice a great financial opportunity. It is doubtful, however, whether the second horn of the dilemma was not interpreted in a double sense by both the president and congress. It would undoubtedly be a real sacrifice financially if the United States should turn once more to Nicaragua. But would it not be also a sacrifice if the present offer should be accepted when there was a possibility of obtaining better terms? In fact, it soon developed that the treaty would never pass unless better terms were secured. General Reyes finally suggested to Mr. Beaupré that two amendments were necessary to obtain the ratification of the treaty: first, that the French company pay $10 million for the right to transfer its concessions; and second, that the United States raise its cash payment from $10 million to $15 million.[8] When the Colombian government learned that the United States would not even consider these changes, the treaty came up for a vote in the senate on August 12, and was unanimously rejected.

From the viewpoint of international law, the Colombian government was wholly within its rights in rejecting the treaty, and from a business viewpoint, if better terms could be obtained from the United States, this was the time to get them. The situation, however, presented other angles than these. The United States was the only nation that was prepared to carry out the stupendous task from which not merely the United States and Colombia, but the whole world, would profit. It had made what seemed to be a fair offer, and the Colombian representative

[7] *For. Rel. of the U. S.*, 1903, p. 134.
[8] *Ibid.*, p. 163.

had accepted it. Then the Colombian senate rejected the offer, after intimating that certain increased indemnities would make the ratification possible. Somewhat later, a senatorial committee drafted a new report in which the indemnity was again increased and the terms were made still more difficult.[9] If the United States should accept this draft, there was nothing to prevent the Colombian senate from rejecting the new proposition and again raising the terms.

In the meantime the people of the province of Panama, who were vitally interested in the acceptance of the treaty, saw their interests jeopardized by a government acting, as it seemed, in entire disregard of everything except its own interests. On the other hand, the French company, whose concession would lapse in October, 1904, saw its last opportunity to recoup a part of its great loss.[10] The Colombian government should have realized that the hostility of the United States was not so much to be feared as the desperate ventures of those people whose immediate interests were far more closely involved. It was a combination of these interests that ultimately resulted in the undoing of the Colombian plans.

There is an abundance of evidence to show that the Colombian government was not ignorant of the dangerous game that it was playing. Early in June, 1903, M. Bunau-Varilla, the former chief engineer of the Panama company, in a cablegram to President Marroquin pointed out that, if the Hay-Herran treaty were not ratified, either the Nicaragua route would be chosen or the Isthmus of Panama would revolt and receive the protection of the United States.[11] It was also reported that Senator Obaldia, the newly appointed governor of Panama, had stated to the Colombian president, in accepting the position, that in case the department found it necessary to revolt to secure the canal he would stand by Panama.[12] However, the Colombian government was determined to stand upon its rights and exact the terms that it considered proper to demand under the circumstances.

The story of how M. Bunau-Varilla engineered the revolution in Panama reads more like an Arabian Nights' tale than the narrative of an actual series of events occurring in the matter-of-fact twentieth century. The inhabitants of the isthmus had sent a Dr. Amador to the United

[9] *Ibid.* (No. 139, Inclosure). For a detailed account of the Colombian action see Miles du Val, Jr., *Cadiz to Cathay* (Stanford University, 1940), Chap. IX.

[10] By the payment of $1 million the company had secured a six-year extension from the government; but there was the possibility of the decree being declared null and void.

[11] Bunau-Varilla, *op. cit.*, p. 267.

[12] *For. Rel. of the U. S.*, 1903, p. 193.

States to see what chance there was of obtaining the aid of this country in bringing about a revolution, if no satisfactory arrangement could be reached with Colombia. After having approached various officials in Washington, the representative from Panama was convinced that no aid could be expected from the United States, and was about to return, when M. Bunau-Varilla appeared. When the latter learned that Panama was ripe for revolution if financial backing and military protection from the United States could be secured, he promised to do what he could to obtain them. The first step was to ascertain, if possible, what the intentions of the United States were, and what attitude would be taken if a revolution should break out. M. Bunau-Varilla was fortunate enough to secure an interview with President Roosevelt, and, although the Panama question came up only in the most casual way, it was apparent that the President still favored the Panama route. The other factor that M. Bunau-Varilla counted upon was the clause in the treaty of 1846 whereby the United States guaranteed to New Granada that the free transit of the isthmus from the one sea to the other should never be interrupted or obstructed. An interview with Mr. Hay confirmed his belief that, in case of trouble on the isthmus, the United States naval forces would be on hand to maintain open communications across the isthmus, as they had already done on several earlier occasions.

Basing his plan upon these rather frail supports, M. Bunau-Varilla promised Dr. Amador $100,000 in cash from his own funds and the protection of the United States navy within forty-eight hours after a revolution should be declared. The only conditions were that the Panamanians should stage their own revolution, and that they should appoint M. Bunau-Varilla as their official representative in Washington, with plenary powers. Dr. Amador accepted the terms and promised that the revolution would take place within one week of his return home. When he arrived at Panama, the emissary found that his confederates needed more definite assurance of American protection. He therefore sent a cipher cablegram to M. Bunau-Varilla asking for the immediate despatch of an American cruiser. His confederate was equal to the occasion. Various press despatches had already reported that the *Nashville* had left Kingston on October 31, with sealed orders. Taking it for granted that its destination was Colon, M. Bunau-Varilla computed the time of its arrival, and cabled the Panamanians that an American cruiser would arrive in two and a half days. The conspirators were satisfied, and when the *Nashville* sailed into the bay, they immediately proclaimed the independent Republic of Panama, and, confiding in the assistance of the great American republic, proceeded to arrest Colombian officers and troops who had already landed.[13]

The part that the United States played in the Panama Revolution has been much criticized, but evidence showing that this country started the revolution or gave it encouragement in advance, other than by the interpretation which the Panamanians put upon the appearance of the *Nashville* in the harbor, must be open to suspicion unless the whole account of M. Bunau-Varilla is to be regarded as deliberately misleading.[14] However, after the revolution was started, the Colombians may be considered as having just grounds for complaint at the American action. The treaty of 1846, it is true, gave the United States the right to protect the neutrality of the isthmus and to keep the transit open. But it could hardly be interpreted to mean that, to carry out these provisions, the United States was given the right to prohibit Colombia from maintaining its sovereignty upon the isthmus against revolutionary uprisings. In fact, since the United States was expected to assist New Granada in maintaining her sovereignty against foreign nations, might it not even be expected that the same guaranty would hold in the case of revolutionary uprisings? Certainly the following orders, given to the commanders of the *Nashville* and the *Dixie* by the Navy Department, can hardly be justified under the broadest interpretation of the treaty: "Maintain free and uninterrupted transit. If interruption threatened by armed force, occupy the line of railroad. Prevent landing of any armed force with hostile intent, either government or insurgent, either at Colon, Porto Bello, or other point." [15]

This message was sent on November 2, 1903. On the following day our government went even farther, when orders were given to prevent Colombian troops at Colon from proceeding to Panama.[16]

The *Nashville* arrived at Colon on the evening of November 2, but Commander Hubbard did not prevent the disembarkment of Colombian troops which arrived that night on the *Cartagena*. These troops remained in Colon under Colonel Torres, while the superior officers left for Pan-

[13] M. Bunau-Varilla gives a most vivid account of the whole affair in his book, *op. cit.*, pp. 284-366.

[14] J. C. Freehof in his book, *America and the Canal Title* (New York, 1916), discounts the truth of M. Bunau-Varilla's statements and upon circumstantial evidence asserts collusion between President Roosevelt and M. Bunau-Varilla. Mr. Hall, in his statement before the House Committee on Foreign Affairs in the hearings on the Rainey resolution, also implicates President Roosevelt, but he is inclined to attribute the revolution to the machinations of Mr. William Nelson Cromwell, the American legal adviser of the Panama Canal Company.

[15] *Dip. Hist.*, p. 362.

[16] *Ibid.*, p. 363.

ama. That same day the revolution started in Panama, and these officers were seized by the revolutionary forces; and when Colonel Torres attempted to transport his troops to Panama by the railway, he was prohibited from doing so by the orders of Commander Hubbard of the *Nashville*. When Colonel Torres threatened to kill every American citizen in Colon unless the Colombian generals in Panama were released, Commander Hubbard landed his marines and prevented bloodshed. In the meantime, the revolutionists gained complete control in Panama, a declaration of independence was drawn up, a provisional government was formed, and notice of the separation from Colombia was sent to Vice-Consul Ehrman of the United States. A part of the Colombian forces threw in their lot with the Panamanians; the rest were allowed to depart, and the revolution was over. M. Bunau-Varilla was appointed official confidential agent of the Republic of Panama at Washington, and on November 6, 1903, Secretary Hay cabled the American consul that he was to enter into relations with the new state of Panama as the responsible government of the territory. The independence of the new republic was assured when the United States refused to permit the landing of Colombian troops on the isthmus, on the ground that the act would precipitate civil war and disturb the free transit that the United States was pledged to protect.

With the new Republic of Panama recognized and its independence guaranteed by the United States, and with M. Bunau-Varilla representing it at Washington, the construction of the canal by the Panama route was assured. On November 18, 1903, the Hay-Bunau-Varilla treaty was signed at Washington; it was ratified by Panama in December, and by the Senate of the United States in February of the following year. By the terms of this treaty the United States promised to maintain the independence of the Republic of Panama. In return for the sum of $10,000,000 in gold, and an annual subsidy of $250,000, beginning nine years after the ratification of the treaty, the Republic of Panama granted to the United States the use, occupation, and control of a zone of land ten miles wide, extending across the isthmus from Colon to Panama. Provision was made also for the use and occupation of any other lands and waters outside of the zone necessary to the canal's construction, operation, or protection. The canal was to be neutral in perpetuity, and the Republic of Panama was to have the right to transport over the canal its vessels, troops, and munitions of war at all times without paying charges of any kind. The treaty, in effect, made the United States virtually sovereign over as much of the isthmus as was necessary for the exercise of full control over the canal.[17] The pathway was now clear of all diplomatic obstacles, and it remained for the United States only to begin the work of construction.

Inasmuch as all Latin America nourished very bitter resentment towards the United States for its part in the Panama Revolution, and since the United States had upon several occasions offered to make reparation, and has finally settled the controversy by a convention signed by both parties in 1921,[18] it is pertinent at this point to examine the affair in a judicial manner from the viewpoint of the various participants, and to determine, if possible, precisely how much blame the United States should assume. As to fomenting the revolution, the evidence seems to prove conclusively that the United States was guiltless. We have already shown that M. Bunau-Varilla has voluntarily assumed all of the credit or discredit for engineering the affair. Upon numerous occasions President Roosevelt publicly and privately denied categorically that he was implicated in the slightest degree in the plottings that went on in the United States. In a letter to Dr. Albert Shaw, editor of the *Review of Reviews,* dated October 10, 1903, he declared: "I cast aside the proposition made at this time to foment the secession of Panama. Whatever other governments can do, the United States can not go into the securing, by such underhand means, the cession. Privately, I freely say to you that I should be delighted if Panama were an independent state, or if it made itself so at this moment, but for me to say so publicly would amount to an instigation of a revolt, and therefore I can not say it." [19] In a special message to Congress, on January 4, 1904, the President declared the injurious insinuations of complicity by this government in the revolutionary movement in Panama to be "as destitute of foundation as of propriety." "No one connected with this government," he said, "had any part in preparing, inciting, or encouraging the late revolution on the Isthmus of Panama"; and he added that, "save from the reports of our military and naval officers, . . . no one connected with this government had any previous knowledge of the revolution." [20] Finally, John Hay, whose reputation for straightforward integrity is unimpeachable, in an official reply to General Reyes, the Colombian representative, declared that "any charge that this government, or any responsible member of it, held intercourse, whether

[17] *Ibid.,* p. 295.
[18] See p. 127.
[19] J. B. Bishop, *Theodore Roosevelt and His Time* (New York, 1920), Vol. I, p. 279.
[20] *Ibid.,* p. 292.

official or unofficial, with agents of revolution in Colombia, is utterly without justification." [21]

Of the more substantial grievances of Colombia, as summed up by General Reyes in a statement of grievances presented to the United States, the following seem to be the most important:

(1) American cruisers were sent into Colombian waters with orders to prevent Colombian troops from landing to suppress any revolutionary uprising that might occur; (2) A military officer of the United States prevented the railway from carrying Colombian troops from Colon to Panama at the very time when their arrival would have impeded any revolutionary attempt; (3) in time of peace between the two countries the United States prevented by force the landing of troops where they were necessary to reëstablish order; (4) Two days after the revolutionary movement began, Panama was recognized by the United States as a sovereign and independent republic; (5) Fourteen days later the American government signed a treaty with the Republic of Panama, which not only recognized and guaranteed its independence but agreed to open a canal.[22]

In replying to these charges, Mr. Hay pointed out that, while Colombia manifestly sought to deal fairly with the United States as long as the Nicaragua route was being considered favorably, after an agreement was made with the duly accredited Colombian representative and with the French company, a very different attitude was taken. As a result of this shift of policy, trouble was threatened by the inhabitants of Panama, whose vital interests were being menaced. Advice to this effect came to the United States through its officials and the press, and in order to maintain order on the transit route the government took steps, as it had on previous occasions, to be ready for any emergency. The treaty of 1846 was signed with the implied obligation that an interoceanic passage was to be constructed, and the guaranty of the sovereignty of New Granada by the United States was given for this purpose. But the great design of the treaty of 1846 remained unfulfilled, and it finally became apparent that it could be fulfilled only by the construction of a canal by the government of the United States; yet by the repudiation of the Hay-Herran convention the Colombian government showed its intention to violate the spirit of the treaty. The declaration of independence of the Republic of Panama created a new situation. Another civil war threatened not merely the rights of the United States but the interests of the whole civilized world. The Republic of Panama stood for those interests; the government of Colombia opposed them. Compelled to cast her influence into the

[21] *Dip. Hist.*, p. 492.
[22] *Ibid.*, p. 481.

scale, the United States, in no wise responsible for the situation, recognized the independence of Panama.[23]

From these statements it would seem that, although the United States did not foment the revolution, her protection of the revolutionists made the movement successful; that, while the United States had the right to keep the transit across the isthmus open, she could scarcely claim the right to prevent the landing of soldiers to put down a rebellion against the sovereign state that granted this right; that, even if the United States had the right to recognize the independence of Panama any time after such independence was won, she hardly had the right to guarantee this independence against Colombia by forbidding the disembarkation of its troops. On the other hand, it was not merely for the benefit of the United States that the canal was to be built, but for the benefit of the whole world. Nor would any country profit more from its construction than Colombia herself. Finally, the people in the province of Panama were exceedingly desirous of seeing the canal constructed, as is shown by the prompt ratification of the Hay-Bunau-Varilla treaty by the municipal councils of Panama, and it seems that the government at Bogotá should have shown some consideration for their wishes. Therefore, even though extenuating circumstances could be found to justify the action of the United States, the fact remained that Colombia was wronged, and it was only fitting that a settlement be made of such a character not merely that Colombia would cease to feel bitter but that she would come to realize that her great neighbor on the north desired her friendship upon a basis of equality and justice.

Various attempts to this end were made before a successful compromise was effected. On October 21, 1905, the Colombian government suggested that a just, equitable, and complete diplomatic adjustment of the differences between the two nations be arrived at, and failing that, the question be submitted to arbitration.[24] Elihu Root, then Secretary of State, pointed out in his reply that an arbitration tribunal could not pass upon the question without passing upon the justice of Panama's stand in declaring her independence, whereas the United States had already taken an affirmative stand upon that question.[25] Further negotiations were carried on, and owing to the friendly attitude of General Reyes, the Colombian president, and to the favorable impression made by Secretary Root's visit to South America in the summer of 1906, an agreement was finally

[23] *Ibid.*, p. 491.
[24] *Ibid.*, p. 576.
[25] *Ibid.*, p. 583.

embodied in a tripartite protocol, signed in Washington, August 17, 1907, by the representatives of Colombia, Panama, and the United States. The tripartite treaties resulting were known as the Root-Cortes-Arosemena treaties, one between Colombia and the United States, a second between Panama and the United States, and the third between Panama and Colombia. Colombia was to have the liberty at all times to transport war-ships and troops through the canal without paying duty; its agricultural and manufactured products were to be admitted to the canal zone on the same basis as those of the United States; its mails were to receive similar treatment; Panama was to transfer the first ten annual rental payments of $250,000 advanced by the United States to Colombia as her share of the Colombian foreign debt; finally, Panama was to be recognized by Colombia, and boundaries were to be definitely drawn.[26] The United States ratified these treaties early in 1909. But, despite the earnest support of President Reyes, public opinion ran so strong against them in Colombia that their mere presentation to Congress caused the downfall of the administration backing them, and the exile of the Colombian minister who negotiated them.

Another serious effort to adjust the situation was made during the Taft administration, when the American minister to Bogotá was authorized to make further proposals to Colombia. The tripartite treaties were to be ratified, and in addition the United States offered to pay $10 million for a concession to build a canal by the Atrato route and for the lease of two small islands in the Caribbean as coaling stations. Once more the Colombian congress rejected the proposals and demanded arbitration of the whole question or compensation for all the moral, physical, and financial losses that Colombia had sustained as a result of the separation of Panama. Mr. du Bois, the American minister to Colombia, made several further attempts, but they were unavailing, and it remained for the Wilson administration to try its hand. Mr. Bryan, as Secretary of State, was very desirous of arriving at a settlement, and suggested that Colombia make a proposition. Colombia consented and its proposal carried three main clauses: first, the United States should express regret for what had happened; second, Colombian merchant-ships, war-ships, troops, products, and mails should pass through without paying duties, and the products of Colombia for consumption in the canal zone should have the same treatment as the goods of the United States; third, the United States should pay $50 million as indemnity.[27]

[26] *Ibid.*, pp. 314-325.
[27] *For. Rel. of the U. S.*, 1913, p. 324.

In its counter-proposal the United States offered to express sincere regret that anything should have occurred to mar the relations of cordial friendship between the two countries; to permit Colombian war-ships and troops to pass through the canal free of duty, and the products of its soil and industry, its citizens and its mails, to pass through and be admitted on the same basis as those of the Unied States; and to pay an indemnity of $20 million.[28] Our government finally raised the indemnity to $25 million. But when the treaty came before the Senate and its terms were published, Mr. Roosevelt denounced it bitterly as the "Colombia blackmail treaty," calling it "an attack upon the honor of the United States, which, if justified, would convict the United States of infamy." [29] The opposition to the treaty became so great, and the new problems raised by the World War had become so urgent, that further consideration of the agreement did not take place till 1919. At this time the Committee on Foreign Relations reported the treaty out, amending it by giving support to President Roosevelt's position and eliminating the expression of regret on the part of the United States; but, even with this change, the Senate refused to approve it.

Hardly had President Harding been inaugurated before he indicated in no uncertain manner that he desired an early settlement with Colombia. In a message to the Senate, dated March 9, 1921, he called attention to the impending treaty and suggested that "the early and favorable consideration of this treaty would be very helpful at the present time in promoting our friendly relationships." [30] Yielding to the request of the new President, the Senate began discussion of the treaty in open session on April 24. When Senator Lodge, chairman of the Committee on Foreign Relations, not only spoke in favor of ratification but indicated that Colonel Roosevelt before his death had also signified his approval of coming to a settlement, it was evident that the treaty would have little difficulty in securing the necessary two-thirds majority. Another factor which undoubtedly had considerable influence was the hostile attitude of the Colombian government towards important American oil concessionaires. It was very evident that a *quid pro quo* was essential if the Standard Oil interests were to be allowed to carry on their extensive explorations.[31] The question came to a decision on April 20, 1921, and was approved

[28] *Ibid.*, p. 328.

[29] Theodore Roosevelt, *Fear God and Take Your Own Part* (New York, 1916), pp. 305-342.

[30] *Cong. Rec.*, Vol. LXI, No. 2, p. 81.

[31] J. Fred Rippy, "The United States and Colombian Oil," *Foreign Policy Reports*, Vol. V, No. 2 (Apr. 3, 1929).

by a vote of 69 to 19; [32] and ratifications were exchanged at Bogotá on March 1, 1922. At last this affair, which according to a former United States minister to Colombia, was felt by the people of Latin America to be "the only real injustice committed by the United States against Latin-American people," had been settled in a manner acceptable to both.

On the other hand, the Hay-Bunau-Varilla treaty of 1903 between the United States and Panama gave rise to certain difficulties of interpretation immediately upon the beginning of active construction of the canal. Secretary Hay in a letter to Senator Spooner before the treaty had passed the Senate had already emphasized the disproportionately advantageous character of the treaty to the United States, and pointed out that there were "many points in this treaty to which a Panamanian patriot could object." [33] The chief source of dispute was raised in regard to the assumption of full rights of sovereignty on the part of the United States in the Canal Zone. For example, the Panamanian government objected to the establishment of post offices and customs houses since the powers of the United States government were limited to measures necessary for the construction and maintenance of the Canal. The United States, however, claimed full sovereign powers within the limits of the Zone.[34] To adjust these difficulties, Mr. Taft, then Secretary of War, proceeded to Panama and formulated a temporary agreement to serve as a *modus operandi* during the period of construction of the Canal. This agreement was embodied in a series of executive orders issued by the War Department in 1904, 1905, and 1911, and the Panama Canal Act of August 12, 1912, validated these orders until Congress should otherwise provide.[35]

In spite of the Taft agreement, numerous disputes arose, particularly through the establishment by the United States of commissaries which did a very extensive business in the Zone, and through other acts of sovereignty such as issuing exequaturs to foreign consuls to perform their functions within the Zone. To improve the situation the State Department on September 1, 1922, declared that the Taft agreement was no longer satisfactory and recommended its termination in order that a

[32] For text see *Treaty Series, No. 661* (Washington, D. C., 1922), or *Cong. Rec.*, Vol. 41, No. 2, p. 378. The treaty as finally approved eliminated the so-called apology clause, paid Colombia $25,000,000 and gave her equal rights with the United States in the use of the Canal.

[33] A. L. P. Dennis, *Adventures in American Diplomacy* (New York, 1928), p. 341.

[34] That even in the United States there was a very decided difference of opinion as regards the status of the United States in the Zone is shown later by a Supreme Court decision handed down January 6, 1930, in the case of the Luckenback Steamship Company vs. the United States, *U. S. Supreme Court Reports*, 74:356.

[35] *U. S. Stat. at Large*, Vol. XXXVII, Part I, p. 560.

new treaty with Panama might be negotiated.[36] In accordance with a joint resolution approved February 12, 1923, the President terminated the Taft agreement by an executive order issued May 28, 1924, to take effect beginning June 1, 1924. Relations henceforth between the Canal Zone and the Republic of Panama were governed by the treaty of 1903.

Negotiations were immediately begun by the State Department looking towards a new treaty covering various questions such as the acquisition of further lands for canal purposes and the protection of the Canal, new customs regulations, the rights of radio communication and aërial navigation in Panama and its more efficient control, further regulations concerning the sanitation of Panama City and Colon, and more definite arrangements as to the status of Panama currency in the Canal Zone. A treaty covering these and other subjects was signed at Washington, July 28, 1926, by representatives of the Republic of Panama and by Secretary Kellogg and Francis White representing the United States.[37]

Upon publication of the treaty, considerable comment was aroused by certain provisions of the agreement. Particular note was taken of the first paragraph of Article XI, which stated that "The Republic of Panama agrees to coöperate in all possible ways with the United States in the protection and defense of the Panama Canal. Consequently the Republic of Panama will consider herself in a state of war in case of any war in which the United States should be a belligerent; and in order to render more effective the defense of the Canal will if necessary in the opinion of the United States government, turn over to the United States in all the territory of the Republic of Panama, during the period of actual or threatened hostilities, the control and operation of wireless and radio communications, aircraft, aviation centers, and aërial navigation."

The question was immediately raised as to whether such a military alliance on the part of Panama did not conflict with her obligations under the Covenant of the League of Nations. It was reported from Geneva that League officials were of the opinion that Article XI of the treaty conflicted with Articles II, XI, XVI and XX of the Covenant. It would appear that the objections were well taken, for an automatic entrance into war upon the part of Panama at the behest of the United States would violate categorically her promise under the Covenant to utilize various peaceful agencies before the final resort to war. Opposition to the treaty quickly developed in Panama, and on January 26, 1927, the National Assembly passed a resolution requesting President Chiari to reopen

---

[36] *Sen. Doc. No. 248*, 67th Cong., 2nd Sess.
[37] Text in *Cong. Rec.*, Vol. 68, Pt. 2, pp. 1846-1852.

negotiations for an agreement more satisfactory to the interests of Panama.[38]

No further action was taken, however, until Franklin D. Roosevelt became president. At that time the devaluation of the dollar and the attempt to pay the annual $250,000 rental for the Canal in sixty per cent paper dollars brought matters to a crisis. The situation afforded an excellent opportunity to put the Good Neighbor Policy into operation and maintain the financial integrity of the American government. The United States proposed a complete revision of the Treaty of 1903 and a settlement of all outstanding disputes. Negotiations which began in Washington in 1934 were finally terminated on March 2, 1936, when four agreements were signed by the two powers.[39] The first was a general treaty revising the convention of November 18, 1903, two others related to radio communication in Panama and the Canal Zone, and the fourth was concerned with the construction of a trans-isthmian highway between the cities of Panama and Colon.

The general treaty made certain fundamental changes in the relations between the two governments. The United States accepted stricter limitations on the conduct of business and the right of residence in the Canal Zone. The annual rental of the Canal was henceforth to be 430,000 balboas, thus avoiding difficulties due to devaluation. In case of threat of aggression endangering Panama or the Canal the two governments were to consult for mutual defense. Inasmuch as Article I of the new treaty superseded Article I of the treaty of 1903 wherein was found the guarantee of Panamanian independence, this provision for joint consultation and action took on additional importance.

Perhaps the next most important provision of the new treaty from the Panamanian standpoint was Article II whereby the United States renounced further grants of lands and water in addition to those already under the jurisdiction of the United States outside of the Zone. According to Article II of the original treaty, such expropriation of territory was authorized in so far as it was necessary for the construction, operation, and protection of the Canal, but the Panamanians felt that the Canal authorities had abused the privilege. Little opposition was raised to giving the United States the 167 square miles of territory outside of the Zone covered by Lake Gatún and its shores, nor an additional several thousand

---

[38] *New York Times,* Jan. 27, 1927.

[39] For text of the General Treaty of Friendship and Coöperation see *U. S. Treaty Series,* No. 945; for the Trans-isthmian Highway Treaty see *ibid.,* No. 946; for text of the Radio Convention which has been ratified by Panama but not by the United States see *Sen. Doc. Exec. C,* 74th Cong., 2nd Sess., p. 7.

acres along the Chagres River, but when in 1918 the United States insisted upon taking over about five-sixths of the beautiful island of Taboga—Panama's finest health resort—for the defense of the Canal, the whole of Panama rose in protest.[40] Although the United States reduced materially its expropriation in Taboga, other demands for concessions followed. The new agreement, while renouncing the right of expropriation on the part of the United States, recognized the joint obligation for the operation and defense of the Canal, and if need arose necessary measures should be taken.

Owing to the political implications of Article X of the new treaty providing for joint consultation in case of aggression, the treaty was considered in executive session by the United States Senate and on April 29 it was decided to await Panamanian action before final disposition should be taken. After an acrimonious debate, the Panama National Assembly approved the Treaty and the three conventions on December 24, 1936.

No further action was taken by the United States until February, 1939, when by an exchange of notes between Secretary of State Hull and the Foreign Minister of Panama it was agreed that the United States might determine when an emergency existed which required consultation and that under some circumstances consultation might have to follow military action.[41] With this reassuring clarification of Article X, the Treaty was resubmitted to the Senate on July 24, 1939, and ratification approved the following day. Ratifications were immediately exchanged with Panama and the treaty proclaimed July 27, 1939.

The ever darkening world situation enhanced both the importance of our relations with Panama and the strategic value of the Panama Canal. In the spring of 1939 the United States raised its legation at Panama City to an Embassy and, with the outbreak of war in Europe in the fall, immediate steps were taken to enlarge the canal by a new set of locks and to build a strategic highway across the isthmus. In order to afford better defense the United States requested the use of a number of areas outside the Canal Zone for the installation of air bases, searchlights, and aircraft detectors under the provisions of Article X of the 1936 treaty.

The government of President Arnolfo Arias debated the proposal at some length and only assented after a considerable delay. By a manifesto dated March 5, 1941, the Republic of Panama acceded to the request of

[40] For a detailed account of this problem see W. D. McCain, *The United States and the Republic of Panama* (Durham, N. C., 1937), Chap. VII.

[41] *U. S. Treaty Series, No. 945*, pp. 63-64.

the United States government providing that occupation cease at the end of the war and that adequate compensation be granted.[42] President Arias again showed a leaning towards the Axis when he issued a decree refusing to permit American-owned vessels sailing under Panamanian register to be armed for self-defense. Resentful of this policy of obstruction, certain leaders of the government taking advantage of the fact that President Arias was visiting in Havana without the necessary constitutional permission, took over on October 9, 1941, and elected Ricardo Adolfo de la Guardia to exercise the presidency. When certain allegations were made in the press that the United States supported the *coup*, Secretary Hull issued a categorical denial and gave a detailed statement of the facts as reported to the State Department.[43]

The new administration immediately rescinded the decree prohibiting the arming of merchant ships and coöperated actively in a program of defense. Panama declared war upon Japan the day after Pearl Harbor and on May 18, 1942, signed an agreement with the United States permitting the use by the armed forces of the United States of numerous defense areas in the Republic outside of the Canal Zone. The largest of these was the Rio Hato air base situated almost eighty miles southwest of the Canal for which the United States was to pay an annual rental of 10,000 balboas. For the other public lands utilized, the annual rental payment was one balboa, while private lands were to be paid for at an annual rental of 50 balboas per hectare. The United States had the right to use the waters adjacent to these lands and to construct necessary highways for their effective utilization. All lands taken over amounting to 134 pieces by the end of the war were to be evacuated one year after the definite treaty of peace.[44]

At the same time certain adjustments were made to improve the relations between the two countries. The United States relinquished the Panama Railroad's real estate holdings in the cities of Colon and Panama except such as were essential to the operation and protection of the Canal, and conveyed to Panama the waterworks and sewerage systems lying within the Republic's jurisdiction. The United States also proposed to liquidate the credit of two and one half million dollars made available to Panama by the Export-Import Bank for the construction of Panama's share of the Chorrera-Rio Hato Highway, a road constructed primarily for the defense requirements of the Canal and the United States.

[42] *New York Times*, Mar. 6, 1941.
[43] *Dept. of State Bull.*, Vol. V, No. 121 (Oct. 18, 1941), p. 293.
[44] *Ibid.*, Vol. VI, No. 152 (May 23, 1942), p. 448.

When the agreement was submitted to the Senate of the United States for its approval certain objections were raised due to the fact that the proposal was made in the form of a joint resolution. By this procedure it was pointed out that a change in a treaty would be made by a majority vote of the Congress instead of by a two-thirds vote of the Senate. However, when the resolution came to a vote on December 4, 1942, the Senate approved it by a vote of 40-29 which more than met the two-thirds requirement.

Although all the lands taken over were to be relinquished one year after the treaty of peace, the refusal of Soviet Russia to agree to a peace treaty with Germany influenced the United States to request the retention of some fourteen bases, including that of Rio Hato, after the treaties were signed with Italy and the Balkan states. A treaty with Panama permitting the retention of the Rio Hato base and certain others for ten years was signed by representatives of the two powers on December 10, 1947. Although President Jiménez favored the treaty, strong opposition developed in the country and the National Assembly refused to approve its ratification. The United States thereupon ordered all bases evacuated immediately to the surprise and dismay of many Panamanians who would suffer considerable economic loss by the withdrawal.

Dissatisfaction still existed in Panama concerning the terms of the 1903 Treaty and in the fall of 1953 negotiations were begun in Washington looking towards its revision. It was reported that Panama wished a higher annual rental, better opportunities, and fairer treatment for Panamanian workers in the Canal Zone, further restrictions on the American commissaries, and permission to serve ships passing through the Canal. President José Antonio Remon made an official visit to Washington in September, 1953, and made public a statement that Panama was willing to afford any facilities necessary for the building and maintenance of the United States military bases for common defense. President Eisenhower agreed that the United States would return to Panama all lands not required for the maintenance of the Canal and would favor equality of treatment and opportunity for Panamanian workers in the Canal Zone. By the middle of 1954 the provisions of the draft treaty had not yet been agreed upon.

One other difficulty of a diplomatic nature must be mentioned here, although not strictly within the scope of our Latin-American relations. The Hay-Pauncefote treaty provided that the Canal should be open to vessels of all nations on terms of entire equality; but the Panama Canal Act of August 24, 1912, provided that no tolls should be levied on the coastwise vessels of the United States.[45] The British government protested against this exemption and suggested that the question be submitted to arbitration. The United States claimed that "all nations" meant all nations except the United States, since the remission of tolls was merely a subsidy to our shipping and therefore not a discrimination against foreign shipping.[46] Neither was the United States willing to submit the question to arbitration. However, upon the advent of the Democratic administration, President Wilson took the position that a great nation like the United States was hardly justified in quibbling about the interpretation of a clause in order to advance its financial interests, and hence he asked Congress that the tolls-exemption clause be repealed. After a spirited debate, Congress granted his request, carefully stipulating, however, that such action should not be construed as a relinquishment of the right of the United States to discriminate in favor of its vessels by exempting them from the payment of tolls for passage through the canal.[47]

This act held throughout the Wilson administration. But inasmuch as its repeal was demanded in the Republican platform of 1920 and in President Harding's speech of acceptance, the question was again raised in Congress in 1921. There seems to be little doubt that when the treaty was drawn the phrase "all vessels" was meant to be taken literally, and, considering our general attitude towards nations that hold treaties to be mere "scraps of paper," it would seem both politic and just to maintain the treaty in its spirit rather than to seek profit through the loop-hole of legal technicalities. However, party pledges had to be redeemed, and the Senate, after a heated discussion, finally passed the tolls-exemption clause.[48] Although not openly recanting his stand as a candidate, the President was apparently not very desirous of having the bill come to him for his signature, particularly at a time when the United States was planning to receive Great Britain and her allies as guests in a conference looking towards disarmament—a meeting whose sole chance of success lay in the implicit confidence of the participants in the inviolability of their pledged agreements. The bill was therefore sent to the House, where, as a former President once remarked, it was "relegated to innocuous desuetude," and without any noticeable grief on the part of its friends.

It would not be proper to conclude this chapter without a word concerning the Canal itself. As an engineering feat it stands unparalleled— in the words of a former British ambassador, Lord Bryce, "it is the greatest

[45] Dip. Hist., p. 328.
[46] For. Rel. of the U. S., 1913, p. 540.
[47] U. S. Stat. at Large, Vol. XXXVIII, p. 385.
[48] Cong. Rec., Vol. 41, No. 125, pp. 6893 ff.

liberty man has ever taken with nature." Culebra Cut, a nine-mile channel, nowhere less than 300 feet in width and averaging 120 feet in depth was hewn through a mountain. This great ditch, which necessitated the excavation of more than 100 million cubic yards of material, or about twenty-five times as much as was used in the largest of the Egyptian pyramids, was perhaps the greatest feat. Yet the Gatun Dam, a mile and a half long, half a mile wide at its base, and containing more than 20 million cubic yards of material, or more than five times as much as is found in the Cheops pyramid, ranks well with it. The problem of obtaining sufficient labor, the question of health, and the task of stamping out yellow fever and malaria were difficulties almost commensurate with the engineering problems. Work on the Canal was started in 1904 and completed within a decade, at a cost of $375 million. With the fortifications added, the total cost of construction has been about $500 million, and the cost of maintenance is approximately four millions annually.

Largely because of the vulnerability of the Canal to bombing in time of war the Congress in 1939 authorized the construction of a third series of locks approximately a mile distant from the present Canal. The new locks were to be large enough to permit the passage of battleships and commercial vessels larger than any yet afloat. However, after considerable sums had been spent, the requirements of World War II forced the postponement of further construction.

By the law effective July 1, 1951, the operation and maintenance of the Canal was transferred to a new agency—The Panama Company. The provisions of this law required the company to be self-supporting and to reimburse the United States Treasury for the net cost of administering the Canal Zone government and as nearly as possible for the net direct investment of the United States. By reducing the interest charges to 1.95 per cent for 1952 and 2.05 per cent for 1953 and crediting the agency's accounts for tolls for the hitherto toll-free transit of government vessels, the Canal is expected henceforth to be a self-sustaining agency.

From the beginning, the need for the Canal has been demonstrated, and during the first thirteen months of its operation, in spite of the European war, 6½ million tons of merchandise were carried through it. In the fiscal year ending June 30, 1952, 6524 commercial vessels, carrying over 33 million tons of cargo, went through the waterway, and in addition 744 government vessels were towed through. The total revenues for this period were $30,409,499.[49] Although the Canal cannot be regarded as a

[49] *First Annual Reports, Panama Canal Company, Canal Zone Government* (Washington, D. C., 1953).

paying investment in a strictly commercial sense, a route which cuts off 7873 miles in traveling by water from New York to San Francisco, and 8868 miles between New Orleans and San Francisco, which brings the United States 3000 miles nearer the Chilean nitrate fields, and the western grain markets of the United States 5000 miles nearer to Europe, has a value to humanity that can never be measured in dollars and cents alone.

SUPPLEMENTARY READINGS

WILLIS J. ABBOT, *Panama and the Canal* (New York, 1914).

H. ARIAS, *The Panama Canal* (London, 1911).

I. E. BENNETT, *History of the Panama Canal* (Washington, D. C., 1915).

J. B. BISHOP, *The Panama Gateway* (New York, 1913).

P. BUNAU-VARILLA, *Panama, Creation, Destruction, and Resurrection* (New York, 1914).

JACQUES CROKAERT, *La Mediterranée americaine* (Paris, 1927).

Diplomatic History of the Panama Canal, Sen. Doc. No. 474, 63rd Cong., 2nd Sess.

MILES P. DUVAL, JR., *And the Mountains Will Move* (Stanford, 1947).

———, *Cadiz to Cathay* (Stanford, 1940).

P. J. EDER, *Colombia* (London, 1913).

J. F. FRASER, *Panama and What It Means* (New York, 1913).

J. C. FREEHOF, *America and the Canal Title* (New York, 1916).

F. J. HASKIN, *The Panama Canal* (New York, 1914).

HOWARD C. HILL, *Roosevelt and the Caribbean* (Chicago, 1927).

C. H. HUBERICH, *The Trans-Isthmian Canal* (Austin, Texas, 1904).

EMORY R. JOHNSON, *The Panama Canal and Commerce* (New York, 1916).

C. LLOYD JONES, *The Caribbean Since 1900* (New York, 1936), Chaps. XII, XIII.

WILLIAM D. MCCAIN, *The United States and the Republic of Panama* (Durham, N. C., 1937).

HUGH GORDON MILLER, *The Isthmian Highway* (New York, 1929).

D. C. MINER, *The Fight for the Panama Route* (New York, 1940).

N. J. PADELFORD, *The Panama Canal in Peace and War* (New York, 1942).

E. T. PARKS, *Colombia and the United States—1765-1934* (Durham, N. C., 1935).

J. FRED RIPPY, *The Capitalists and Colombia* (New York, 1931).

ANDRÉ SIEGFREID, *Suez and Panama* (New York, 1940).

D. H. SMITH, *The Panama Canal* (Baltimore, 1927).

The Story of Panama, hearings on the Rainey resolution (Washington, D. C., 1913).

NORMAN THOMSON, *Colombia and the United States* (London, 1914).

ANTONIO JOSÉ URIBE, *Colombia y los Estados Unidos de América* (Bogotá, 1926).

✿ 7 ✿

Mexico and the United States

IF ONE were to form an impression of Mexico solely from the reports of some of the numerous organizations and committees in the United States engaged from time to time in investigating Mexican affairs, one might well believe that Mexico, like all Gaul, is divided into three parts—first and most important, the foreign oil interests; second and largest, the country given over to bandits and outrages; third, and of little consequence, the Mexican government. But Mexico is a land that does not disclose itself to the casual observer. Where the representative of big business would see nothing but rich deposits of mineral oil, the archæologist would discover prehistoric temples, monoliths, painted caves, and picture-writing, all giving evidence of a marvelous prehistoric civilization. Where the politician would find nothing but revolution and anarchy, the historian would note the traces of the Toltecs, the great civilized race that came and went before Columbus, and the Aztecs, who, under the glorious rule of the Montezumas, made Mexico City the Venice of America. Mexico is indeed, as an observant writer has described it, a land of contrasts: "It is a land of mystery and a land of commonplace dirt and existence. Areas of fabulously rich soil contrast with arid desert regions. . . . On the one hand, romance, adventure, chivalry, sacrifice, lofty ideals; on the other, oppression, cruelty, sordid ambition, pestilence. Great wealth confronts the direst poverty. The lights are always strong, the shadows always dark." [1] There are no tales in the world's history more thrilling than the conquest of Mexico by Cortez and his little band of adventurers; nor can one find more striking examples of the ruthless exploitation of helpless natives than are recorded of the Spanish taskmasters during the centuries following the conquest. From Montezuma to Diaz the fabric of Mexican history has been shot through with the "cursed love of gold."

[1] E. D. Trowbridge, *Mexico To-day and To-morrow* (New York, 1919), p. 1.

The diplomatic relations of the United States with Mexico may be said to have begun January 27, 1823, when by the appointment of Mr. Joel R. Poinsett as minister, the republic's independence was recognized. From that time to the present, there has been no period when our State Department has not been vitally interested, directly or indirectly, in our nearest Latin-American neighbor. Our first treaty with Mexico was negotiated in 1826, but was not satisfactory to the Senate and was withdrawn. Two years later a treaty of limits was concluded, and in 1831 a treaty of amity and commerce was signed, which is still in force.[2] Despite the friendly attitude of the United States and the exceptional ability of its first minister, both the country and its representative were from the first suspected and antagonized; and in 1829 Mr. Poinsett's recall was demanded. The new minister, Anthony Butler, was a most unfortunate choice. An American historian has well observed that his sole qualifications for the post were "an acquaintance with Texas and a strong desire to see the United States obtain it." [3]

When, early in 1836, Texas declared its independence, Mexican hostility towards the United States became very bitter, on the grounds that this country was the chief backer of the rebellion. There was even thought of breaking off diplomatic relations. However, there is little evidence to show that our government failed in its duties of neutrality, although the occupation of the Nacogdoches region as a protection against raiding Indians might be proved an exception. But whether justified or not, this incident fanned the flames of Mexican hatred, and our recognition of Texas early in 1837 added fuel. In 1842 President Santa Anna, "worthy son of the father of lies," as his Mexican opponents termed him, began his war for the reconquest of Texas, and at the same time the Mexican Minister of Foreign Relations accused the United States of permitting its citizens to give aid to the Texans.[4] Daniel Webster, then Secretary of State, denied the allegations promptly and categorically.[5] On the other hand, the government of the United States had serious grounds for provocation, in that upon several occasions American citizens had been mistreated, and even shot, by agents of the Mexican government. Furthermore, a large number of private claims for whose payment the American government had long been demanding action were ignored as long as possible; and

---

[2] J. B. Moore, *Digest of Int. Law*, Vol. V, p. 778. For text see Malloy, *Treaties, Conventions, Etc.* (Washington, D. C., 1910), Vol. I, p. 1085.

[3] J. H. Smith, *The War with Mexico* (New York, 1919), Vol. I, p. 62.

[4] *British and Foreign State Papers*, Vol. XXXI, p. 801.

[5] *House Ex. Doc. No. 266*, 27th Cong., 2nd Sess., pp. 7-15.

when a settlement was finally reached, evasion of full payment was attempted.[6]

The annexation of Texas in 1845 by joint resolution of Congress made a conflict between the two countries inevitable. The Mexican minister at Washington was recalled and a deaf ear was turned to all efforts of the United States to resume friendly relations. A brief ray of hope appeared when a confidential agent sent by President Polk succeeded in obtaining the promise of a resumption of diplomatic relations; but when Mr. Slidell, the newly appointed American minister, arrived, the Mexican government would not receive him. Although ordered by Polk to remain in Mexico, he was unable to accomplish anything, since almost immediately after his arrival the war faction got control of the government.[7]

It seems necessary to say a word here about the almost universally accepted tradition that Polk was eager for war with Mexico and forced it upon her. In reality, his diary, his private correspondence, and even his actions, show that he was most unwilling to force the issue. When we take into consideration the delicate situation that the Oregon question had brought about between this country and Great Britain, it would seem incredible that Polk should have deliberately engaged the country in war with Mexico. As to the sending of a large force of troops to Texas, it must be remembered that Mexico had broken off diplomatic relations and had been threatening to begin war at any moment. If it be conceded that the United States had the right to annex the sovereign state of Texas, it must surely be conceded that it had the right to protect its newly acquired territory from an attack momentarily expected. The only justifiable objection to Polk's conduct is the order sending Taylor and his forces forward to the east bank of the Rio Grande opposite Matamoros into territory claimed by Mexico. Yet this order was not given until January 13, 1846, when the diplomatic outlook seemed hopeless. With this advance, war was almost certain to come, and the first engagement—an attack upon an American reconnoitering expedition—took place virtually a month after the arrival at the Rio Grande. Polk might have postponed the war; but when we find, on the one hand, the American minister, who did all in his power to bring about a peaceful settlement, declaring, "We shall never be able to treat with her [Mexico] on fair terms until she has been taught to respect us," [8] and, on the other, a Mexican editor writing,

[6] J. B. Moore, *International Arbitrations*, Vol. II, p. 1209.
[7] For the correspondence of Mr. Slidell see *Sen. Ex. Doc. No. 337*, 29th Cong., 1st Sess., pp. 18-67.
[8] *Sen. Ex. Doc. No. 337*, p. 57.

"The American forces did not advance to the Rio Grande until after the war became inevitable, and then only as an army of observation," [9] we can hardly lay all the blame for the Mexican War at the door of President Polk. If the United States must be held guilty of instigating the war, as many historians have asserted, it would be more just to fix the blame upon the same internal causes that were to bring about the Civil War— the demand for territory which should be open to slavery, and the struggle for supremacy between the North and the South.[10]

Fortunately, the war was too one-sided to be very long drawn out. The first real engagement was fought at Palo Alto May 8, 1846, and with Scott's entrance into Mexico City, September 14, 1847, after the brilliant capture of the heights of Chapultepec, the fighting was virtually over. The United States never had as many as fifty thousand men in the field at one time, and the total casualties in the field, including sickness, probably did not run as high as fifteen thousand. Peace was concluded by the treaty of Guadalupe Hidalgo, signed February 2, 1848. The United States commissioner, Nicholas P. Trist, having already been recalled, was really without power to conclude the treaty. But he realized that his country was sufficiently anxious to conclude peace to waive technicalities.[11] The treaty's terms, although increasing the territory of the United States by more than half a million square miles, including New Mexico and Upper California, were not wholly unfair to Mexico. As the treaty itself stated, a great part of the territory was occupied by savage Indian tribes, and most of it was under only nominal control of the Mexican government. Furthermore, the United States engaged itself to pay $15 million for this territory, besides assuming and paying all claims against Mexico to an amount not exceeding $3¼ million.[12] Even conceding that this amount in no way represented the actual value of the territory, it must be remembered that this sum was greater than that paid for Louisiana, a much larger and more valuable region. Besides, the United States was in the position of a conqueror who had to pay all the expenses of its conquest. The boundaries and certain other provisions proved not entirely satisfactory to the United States, but a new convention was signed December 30, 1853—the so-called Gadsden purchase—whereby Mexico, for the sum of $10 million, ceded the Mesilla Valley and released the United

[9] Quoted by J. H. Smith, op. cit., Vol. I, p. 155.
[10] For a detailed and authoritative treatment of this period see G. L. Rives, The United States and Mexico, 1821-1848, 2 vols. (New York, 1913).
[11] See Moore, Digest of Int. Law, Vol. V, pp. 780 ff.
[12] Text in Malloy, op. cit., Vol. I, p. 1107.

States from liability imposed by stipulations of the former treaty.[13]

The decade following the war with the United States was a time of revolution and anarchy.[14] Nevertheless, real progress was made by the overthrow of the clerical party, which resulted in the passage of laws bringing the army and the clergy within jurisdiction of the ordinary courts of justice and forcing the sale of church lands and property. The exceedingly democratic constitution of 1857 was also a product of this period, though to put its principles into practice required an electorate more experienced in democratic government than Mexico possessed or could hope to possess for many years.[15] On the other hand, the public finances were in a deplorable state. Such a situation in a weak state that has borrowed heavily from foreign powers is always dangerous, and Mexico was no exception to the rule. Large sums had been obtained from Great Britain, France, and Spain, and the recurring changes of government had prevented regular payments. When in 1858 the full-blooded Indian, Benito Juarez, *ex-officio* vice-president, became president *de jure* through a revolutionary uprising against the constitutional president, the United States, unable to maintain diplomatic relations with the faction in control, withdrew its minister. In the following year President Buchanan, relying upon the ultimate success of the Juarez government, which had been maintaining itself successfully at Vera Cruz, sent a minister, thereby recognizing Juarez as the "only existing government." The forecast proved correct, and in December, 1860, the Juarez government gained complete control and entered the city of Mexico in triumph. As might be expected, the treasury was empty; hence the new government was forced to issue an order suspending payments for two years on its national and foreign obligations.[16]

This decree brought a strong protest from the British and French ministers, who demanded its immediate repeal. When the Mexican government failed to comply, diplomatic relations were severed. As the Spanish representative had previously been given his passport, owing to his open support of the church party, Spain was already prepared to act. A conven-

---

[13] *Ibid.*, p. 1121. The treaty was again revised when the United States on April 17, 1937, agreed to the abrogation of the long obsolete Article VIII which gave the right to the United States to transport troops across the Isthmus of Tehuanepec.

[14] Five successive revolutionary governments had been recognized by the United States in the course of a few months. See special message of President Pierce of May 15, 1856, J. D. Richardson, *Messages and Papers of the Presidents,* Vol. V, p. 368.

[15] For the text of this interesting document see *House Ex. Doc. No. 100,* 37th Cong., 2nd Sess., p. 140.

[16] *British and Foreign State Papers,* Vol. LII, p. 294.

tion for joint action was therefore signed in London, providing for seizure of the ports and customs as guarantees of payment, and the United States was invited to participate.[17] With the Civil War already begun, our government was not able to protest effectively; [18] nor did Seward feel that we should depart from our traditional policy of abstaining from alliances with foreign nations. The three powers therefore proceeded to send fleets and seize Vera Cruz. It was soon perceived, however, that the French had disembarked with an entirely different purpose from that of their allies. Napoleon III, *rêveur et conspirateur,* felt the need of accomplishing some brilliant exploit to shed luster upon his weakening régime, and Mexico offered the opportunity. The leader of the French expedition was therefore instructed to advance upon the Mexican capital and establish a stable government, if the situation so warranted. The British and Spanish governments refused to follow the French lead, and the plan for joint action came to an end. Soon afterwards the British and Spanish withdrew, while the French finally pressed on and occupied the capital. In order that the imperialistic design of Napoleon III might not be too apparent, a junta and assembly of Mexican citizens were selected, who, after deliberation, adopted a limited monarchy as the new form of government, with a sovereign bearing the title of Emperor of Mexico. The imperial crown was offered to Prince Maximilian, archduke of Austria. If he should not accept, Napoleon III was to indicate another Catholic prince.[19] Unfortunately for Maximilian, he was prevailed upon to accept, and with much pomp and ceremony he entered the Mexican capital on June 12, 1864. In order to maintain the expensive requirements of an imperial court, to satisfy the more pressing claims, and to keep in the field an army strong enough to sustain the government against Juarez and his followers, new loans were floated in Paris, plunging the country still more hopelessly in debt.

Another difficulty that confronted Maximilian was the American attitude. While bending all effort to maintain the Union, the United States could do little more than look askance at the French intervention. Yet its hostile attitude was very apparent, and at no time would it consider the recognition of the imperial government. On April 7, 1864, it was resolved by the House of Representatives that "the Congress of the United States are unwilling by silence to have the nations of the world under the impression that they are indifferent spectators of the deplorable events

[17] *Ibid.,* Vol. LI, p. 63, or *House Ex. Doc. No. 100,* p. 134.

[18] Seward did, however, protest; see *ibid.,* p. 217, for his notice to France.

[19] A very interesting collection of documents regarding the intervention has been assembled in *Sen. Ex. Doc. No. 11,* 38th Cong., 2nd Sess.

now transpiring in the Republic of Mexico, and that they think fit to declare that it does not accord with the policy of the United States to acknowledge any monarchical government erected on the ruins of any republican government in America under the auspices of any European power." [20] Although Seward did not think it expedient at the time to accept this as a statement of the government's policy, he conceded that it was the unanimous sentiment of the American people.

After the end of the Civil War the United States firmly but courteously demanded that the French forces be withdrawn, and Napoleon III, already worried by the European situation, thought it best to comply.[21] Maximilian was not able to resist long after the French forces were reëmbarked, and on May 16, 1867, he was compelled to surrender to the republican forces under General Diaz. In spite of protests from Europe and the United States, he was courtmartialed and shot. Napoleon's dream of a great western empire dominated by France, and assuring him the support of Austria, proved equally vain with the Plombières conference and the pact with Cavour, simililarly intended to assure him the enthusiastic support of a united Italy.[22]

Following the short-lived imperial régime, Juarez once more reëstablished himself, and although he was forced to maintain a constant struggle against sectional uprisings, he retained control of the government until his untimely death in 1871. He is still regarded as the father of constitutional government in Mexico, for it was due principally to his efforts that the liberal constitution of 1857 was established and maintained.

The political history of Mexico has been scarred by many revolutions, uprisings, and rapid changes of government, but the period from 1876 to 1911 will always remain a notable exception. On November 26, 1876, Porfirio Diaz, a pure-blooded Indian, gained control of the government. He had himself elected president in 1877, and thereafter, with the exception of a single term, he ruled Mexico during the next thirty-four years. There has been much dispute as to the real advantages to Mexico of the Diaz régime. From the viewpoint of law and order, nothing better could have been desired. By means of an efficient rural police, well paid and well mounted, bandits were pursued relentlessly. A bandit soon discovered that but two opportunities were left for him: to continue his

[20] Moore, *Digest of Int. Law,* Vol. VI, p. 496.
[21] *Ibid.,* pp. 498-503. See also *House Ex. Doc. No. 73,* 39th Cong., 1st Sess., Part II, and *Sen. Ex. Doc. No. 6,* 39th Cong., 1st Sess.
[22] For a concise, well documented account of the French intervention in Mexico, see J. H. Latané, *The United States and Latin America* (New York, 1920), Chap. V.

trade, with the certainty of an early demise at the hands of a firing squad, or to enlist in the *rurales*. "It takes a thief to catch a thief," was never better illustrated.

In its relations with foreign powers, the government of Diaz was very successful. To establish financial credit, the president recognized the need of foreign capital, and he determined to encourage it. But although his government was quickly recognized by foreign governments—the United States alone delayed till 1878—yet, owing to the danger of civil strife, capital was very loath to enter. Railways were especially needed. But, in order to get them built, extremely liberal inducements and concessions had to be offered; and these had to be strengthened by onerous guarantees. In some cases, even a share of the customhouse revenues was demanded. But, with the realization that Diaz was in earnest, governments encouraged their citizens to invest in Mexico. The following passage in a communication to our minister from Mr. Blaine, the Secretary of State, dated June 1, 1881, shows the excellent impression already made at that time:

It is a source of profound satisfaction to the government of the United States that the political situation of Mexico is so apparently and assuredly in the path of stability, and the administration of its constitutional government so regular, that it can offer to foreign capital that just and certain protection without which the prospect even of extravagant profit will fail to tempt the extension of safe and enduring commercial and industrial enterprise. It is still more gratifying that, with a full comprehension of the great political and social advantages of such a mode of developing the material resources of the country, the government of Mexico cordially lends its influence to the spirit of welcome and encouragement with which the Mexican people seem disposed to greet the importation of wealth and enterprise in their midst.[23]

In a report made to the House of Representatives in the session of 1883-1884 on the trade between Mexico and the United States, it was shown that most liberal concessions had been made to corporations of the United States for the construction of railroads in Mexico. The subventions alone amounted to some $90 million, and Mr. Thomas Nickerson of Boston, president of the Mexican Central Railroad, stated that about $30 million of American capital had been invested in railroads in Mexico in the past two years. It was also pointed out that already about 1800 miles of railroad had been constructed in Mexico by citizens of the United States. The results of these improvements were shown in the growing volume of commerce. The total value of the commerce of the United

[23] *For. Rel. of the U. S.*, 1881, p. 761.

States with Mexico in 1877 was about $11 million. In 1882 it had more than doubled, while the revenues of Mexico had increased from $17,800,-000 to $34,000,000. Well might the report say, in concluding, that "the line of policy adopted by the Mexican government since the restoration of the republic, of aid in promoting the construction of railroads to connect that country with the United States, and the persistency with which that policy has ever since been pursued, commends Mexico to the favorable consideration of the more advanced nations of the globe." [24] The policy was unquestionably ideal for the foreign investor.

To carry out such a policy in a country that had so long been unused to political restraint required a strong executive. It was not enough to check robbery on the highways: it must also be abolished in the government. Diaz himself was honest, and he intended that his subordinates should be the same. Hardly had he come into power before the first payment on claims amounting to more than four million dollars owing the United States came due, and he proposed to meet it. He cut officials' salaries, including his own, and weeded out large numbers of superfluous public servants. Real reforms could, however, hardly be introduced and firmly established within a four-year term. Yet a law forbade reëlection until a term had intervened. Diaz showed his respect for law by refusing to run again at the end of this first term, although unquestionably Congress would have repealed the law preventing it. One of his own followers, Gonzalez, was elected, and Diaz was given control of the department of public works. But, becoming convinced that his presence cast a shadow over the administration, he resigned and withdrew from national politics. The Gonzalez administration, which had started under the most favorable auspices, came to an end under a cloud of odium and distrust. More subventions were granted than the government could meet and still pay its officials. The foreign capitalists received their installments and the government officers went without pay, unless they resorted to corrupt methods. The foreign debt rolled up to huge proportions. A nickel currency was introduced which had most unfortunate results, and when the Gonzalez administration came to an end the country turned to Diaz unanimously.

For the next twenty-seven years Diaz was reëlected with unfailing regularity, and with no opposition until 1910. He felt that he was best fitted to govern Mexico, and in order to do it effectively he needed full power. The result was a despotism, benevolent perhaps, but unquestionably a one-man government. He laid down a program embracing peace

[24] *House Ex. Doc. No. 85, 48th Cong., 1st Sess.*

at home and credit abroad, and he put it through, regardless of obstacles. Banditry was virtually abolished; railway mileage was increased from 400 to 15,000; the national income was increased from $20 million to over $100 million annually; government bonds were raised to par from 10 cents on the dollar, and at the same time interest rates were reduced from 10 or 12 per cent to 4 per cent; imports were increased eightfold and exports sixfold; silver mines raised their output from $21 million to $125 million; even education was not entirely overlooked, and at the close of the Diaz régime there were three times as many schools as at the beginning. Finally, to the president's credit it must be observed, that at the end of his administration, with unlimited opportunities for self-aggrandizement, his total fortune amounted to about a quarter of a million dollars.[25]

If we could leave the Diaz régime with a mere statement of the many material benefits which it conferred upon Mexico, Porfirio Diaz would rank as one of the world's great statesmen. But, unfortunately, there is a reverse side to the picture. A scientific form of government which functioned very effectively, which kept peace at home and friendship abroad, had been established, but almost wholly in the interest of the *cientificos* who controlled it. The financiers, the large land-owners, and the government officials found the system most satisfactory. But how did it meet the needs of the great mass of Indians who constituted about three-fourths of the population? It must be conceded that it did nothing for the peon except to exploit him. The land was held in great estates, some containing as high as half a million acres. There the peon and his family had to live in a condition bordering upon slavery; there he must give his service to the farmer at a starvation wage, and often take out all his pay in trade at the *hacienda,* or plantation store. It was estimated that almost 80 per cent of all the farm and plantation laborers in Mexico were slaves, or peons. The Diaz government must be held responsible for encouraging, rather than frowning upon, the peonage system. A still greater blot upon it was the inhuman treatment of the Yaqui Indians. With full cognizance of the government, these unfortunates, among the highest type of Indians found in the western hemisphere, were unjustly dispossessed of their lands and then sold into virtual slavery in Yucatan to work in the henequen plantations. Therefore, even if we conceded that Diaz was "the master builder of a great commonwealth," as one of his

[25] For complete statistics on Mexican finances during the Diaz government see the *Mexican Year Books, 1908-14* (London, 1908-1914). For a well written, unbiased account of the Diaz régime see David Hannay, *Diaz* (New York, 1917).

biographers has termed him,[26] in the last analysis his building could not endure because the foundation was laid upon special privilege. He was a great administrator, and he raised Mexico to a higher level, economically and politically, than it had ever attained before. But he accomplished this result as an arbitrary tyrant rather than as a democratic ruler, and at the expense of the most numerous class of the Mexican people.

The very fact that the whole Mexican political system depended upon the vigor of the man in control was the cause of its utter collapse when that prop was withdrawn. The system was extremely centralized, very much like France under Napoleon I. The executive power counted for everything in the state, and that rested in the president's hands. The governors in the various states were nominated by the president and responsible to him, although the formalities of popular elections in accordance with constitutional formulæ were regularly carried out. Although on paper the legislative bodies, both federal and state, appeared quite as representative as the corresponding bodies in the United States, they were, in reality, wholly dominated by the executive. As long as Diaz was vigorous enough to direct the state in person, the system worked. But gradually he was forced, through weakness arising from advanced age, to allow his ministers more and more power. The result was an apparent sacrifice of Mexican natural resources of every sort through the *científicos* to various foreign interests, particularly English and American.

In 1910 President Diaz, at the age of eighty years, once more stood for reëlection, although he had declared publicly in 1908 that he was serving his last term. The opposition, long repressed, might have endured Diaz—he could not live forever—but it refused to accept his choice for the vice-presidency, Señor Corral, one of the leaders of the hated *científicos*. A leader appeared in the person of Francisco Madero, a weak but impassioned theorist, who gained added prestige from the fact that he was fighting for democratic principles in spite of being a member of the wealthy land-owning class. At first his campaign for a democratic election was ridiculed; but at length, taking alarm, the government had him seized and imprisoned at San Luis Potosí. It was from this place that he issued his famous plan, declaring the recent elections illegal because the public had been excluded by violent means from participating, and assuming provisionally the presidency of Mexico. The plan further fixed November 20, 1910, as the day for the armed protest to begin. However, the most important feature of the plan was the clause of Section 3,

[26] José F. Godoy, *Porfirio Diaz, The Master Builder of a Great Commonwealth* (New York, 1910).

promising a revision of the decrees dispossessing small proprietors of their land, which was to result in restitution to the former owners.[27]

After issuing the plan, Madero fled across the border to San Antonio; but, returning in November, he soon had a large following. Other outbreaks were led by Orozco in the north and Zapata in the south, and in February, 1911, Gonzalez, governor of Chihuahua, joined his state troops to the revolutionists. The government seemed wholly unable to stem the fast rising revolutionary tide, and although Diaz, in his message to Congress on April 1, 1911, promised a correction of local abuses, electoral reform, division of the large estates, and a reform in the judicial system, it was too late.[28] To prevent further bloodshed, he resigned, May 25, and early on the following day he left for Europe. A provisional government was set up, and Madero entered Mexico City in triumph on June 8. In the election held in October of the same year he was elected president by an overwhelming majority.

Even if the new executive had possessed the organizing ability and the will to achieve of Diaz, it would have been very difficult to put into effect the socialistic clauses of the San Luis manifesto. To expect such action from the visionary theorist who now held the reins of government was futile. It was not sufficient that Madero honestly desired to give Mexico a truly democratic government, since he lacked every attribute that would have rendered the accomplishment of his program possible. Before the inauguration, Zapata was stirring up trouble against the new administration, and Orozco quickly followed suit. The situation soon became so critical that the United States was forced to send a warning to the Madero government that American property must be protected, and to make the warning doubly sure a similar warning was sent to General Orozco.[29] The situation of Americans in Mexico throughout the period when Madero held office was so critical that the United States was forced to keep extra troops on the border constantly, in anticipation of emergencies, and an American transport was sent to bring back Americans desiring to leave.

Madero's inability to keep in check the revolutionary movements was not so detrimental to his success as his failure to remain popular. He soon fell under the control of a set of politicians with members of his own family at their head. He was accused of lending more than half a million dollars to his brother Gustavo from the funds of the public treasury;

[27] For the text of the plan and an excellent summary of the events leading up to it see *For. Rel. of the U. S.*, 1911, pp. 348-354.

[28] *Ibid.*, p. 445.

[29] *For. Rel. of the U. S.*, 1912, p. 787.

of failing to comply with the promises made to the working classes; of filling all the important public offices with members of his own family; finally, of permitting the same exploitation of the nation's natural resources by foreign capitalists that had gone on under Diaz, save that now the chief operator was the Standard Oil Company rather than the Pearson Syndicate.[30] In a long despatch dated August 28, 1912, Mr. Henry Lane Wilson, the American ambassador, thus summed up the situation, after noting the wide area given over to devastation and slaughter:

In the midst of this appalling situation in the north and in the south, the federal government sits apathetic, ineffective, and either cynically indifferent or stupidly optimistic. This peculiar phase of the situation I believe to be largely due to the character of the president, who is one day a Diaz come again and the next day an apostle of peace, the apologist for important bandits and criminals and the enemy of monopolies, landholders, and privileged characters and classes. To such an extent has this wavering and unsettled policy been carried that it has lost the president the confidence and support of all classes, and today he stands practically alone, sustained only by the sympathy of his numerous family, the administration office-holders, and the useful and established apprehension that the evils which exist are less than those which might be anticipated with his downfall.[31]

A brief period of respite was obtained by the Madero government through the recapture, with little difficulty, of Vera Cruz, which Felix Diaz, nephew of the former president, had seized. But the day of settlement was merely postponed. On February 8, 1913, the younger Diaz started a revolt in Mexico City, and throughout the next ten days—the *decena trágica*—the capital was the scene of continuous fighting. Civilians were in constant danger, and the situation finally appeared so hopeless that Ambassador Wilson called a conference of the foreign ministers, and it was unanimously decided that President Madero be asked to resign to avert further bloodshed. But the president was firm in his resolve to maintain his position, and replied that if necessary he would die in defense of his rights as legally elected president.[32] On February 18, General Huerta, in command of the government forces, suddenly turned against the president and ordered his arrest. A truce was patched up, and on February 20 a provisional government was established, with General Huerta in control. The American ambassador urged immediate recognition of this government. But before the negotiations were completed the

[30] For a critical account of this period see E. I. Bell, *The Political Shame of Mexico* (New York, 1914).
[31] *For. Rel. of the U. S.*, 1912, p. 830.
[32] *Ibid.*, 1913, p. 711.

situation was altered by the murder of both President Madero and Vice-president Suarez while being conducted from the National Palace to the penitentiary. The official version of the affair as given out by the Huerta government was that two groups of armed men attempted to release the prisoners, and in the fight that ensued both the president and vice-president lost their lives.[33] Other accounts, however, indicated that the two prisoners were placed against a wall and shot. Whatever the truth may be, a strong reaction immediately set in against the provisional government, particularly in the states of Sonora and Coahuila. Foreign recognition was also delayed, notably that of the United States and Great Britain, although Ambassador Wilson urged the Taft administration to grant recognition to prevent worse confusion.[34] But President Taft, at the end of his term, was unwilling to bring possible embarrassment upon his successor by inaugurating a policy that the latter would not be able to carry out. Hence the matter was turned over intact to the Wilson administration.

SUPPLEMENTARY READINGS

H. H. BANCROFT, *History of Mexico* (New York, 1914).

U. R. BURKE, *A Life of Benito Juárez* (London, 1894).

J. H. CORNYN, *Díaz y México*, 2 vols. (Mexico, 1910).

C. R. ENOCK, *Mexico* (New York, 1909).

C. M. FLANDRAU, *Viva Mexico* (New York, 1937).

JOSÉ F. GODOY, *Porfirio Díaz* (New York, 1910).

ERNEST GRUENING, *Mexico and Its Heritage* (New York, 1928).

DAVID HANNAY, *Díaz* (New York, 1917).

MAURICE HUDSON, *Mexico, Yesterday, Today, Tomorrow* (Philadelphia, 1945).

J. H. LATANÉ, *The United States and Latin America* (New York, 1920), Chap. V.

R. J. MACHUGH, *Modern Mexico* (London, 1913).

W. R. MANNING, *Early Diplomatic Relations between the United States and Mexico* (Baltimore, 1916).

A. H. NOLL, *From Empire to Republic* (Chicago, 1903).

H. I. PRIESTLY, *The Mexican Nation* (New York, 1923).

J. F. RAMIREZ, *México durante su guerra con los Estados Unidos* (Mexico, 1905).

MIGUEL REBOLLEDO, *México y los Estados Unidos* (Mexico, 1917).

J. F. RIPPY, *The United States and Mexico* (New York, 1926).

[33] *Ibid.*, p. 732.

[34] *Ibid.*, p. 741. For a first hand account of the events of this period see Henry Lane Wilson, *Diplomatic Episodes in Mexico, Belgium, and Chile* (New York, 1927), Chaps. XXIX-XLIV.

G. L. RIVES, *The United States and Mexico, 1821-1848,* 2 vols. (New York, 1913).

MATÍAS ROMERO, *Mexico and the United States* (New York, 1898).

LESLEY B. SIMPSON, *Many Mexicos* (New York, 1941).

J. H. SMITH, *The War with Mexico* (New York, 1919).

E. D. TROWBRIDGE, *Mexico To-day and To-morrow* (New York, 1919).

❧ 8 ❧

Our Recent Relations
With Mexico

THE advent of the Wilson administration found the situation virtually unchanged. In Sonora, opposition to the Huerta régime continued strong; while in Coahuila, Governor Venustiano Carranza declared his intention of inflicting summary vengeance upon the usurping government. His "Constitutionalist" movement was soon supported by other well known leaders, among whom were two destined to play very important parts, Francisco Villa and Alvaro Obregón. However, as General Huerta continued to strengthen his authority, the European governments, Spain and Great Britain taking the lead, extended recognition. In a long despatch to Washington, dated May 15, 1913, the American ambassador, Mr. Henry Lane Wilson, strongly urged that the United States also extend recognition to the established Mexican government. On June 9 he wrote that, "at the risk of being considered intrusive and insistent, I must again urge upon the President that on the highest grounds of policy—which in this case I understand to be the conserving and the extension of our material interests in Mexico, the restoration of peace, and the cultivation of sentiments of friendship and respect with a neighboring and friendly nation— we should, without further delay, follow the example of all governments accredited here but two, and accord official recognition to the present provisional government." [1]

President Wilson preferred to follow a policy of "watchful waiting," but, in order to show his friendly intentions towards the Mexican people, he sent John Lind, ex-governor of Minnesota, as his personal representative to offer the good offices of the United States in an attempt to establish peace upon a satisfactory basis. His instructions to Mr. Lind made it

[1] *For. Rel. of the U. S.*, 1913, p. 807.

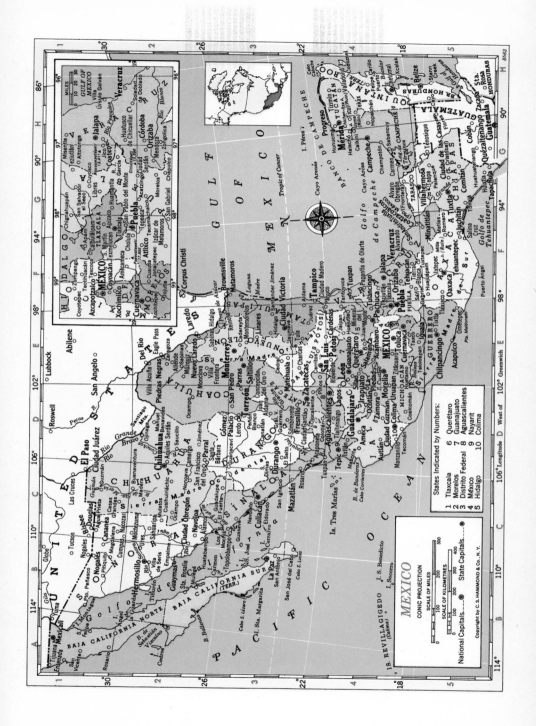

MEXICO

CONIC PROJECTION

SCALE OF MILES

SCALE OF KILOMETERS

National Capitals
State Capitals

Copyright by C. S. HAMMOND & Co., N. Y.

States Indicated by Numbers:

1 Tlaxcala
2 Morelos
3 Distrito Federal
4 México
5 Hidalgo
6 Querétaro
7 Guanajuato
8 Aguascalientes
9 Nayarit
10 Colima

clear that such a settlement was conditioned upon (1) an immediate cessation of fighting; (2) an early and free election; (3) General Huerta's consent not to be a candidate for president; (4) an agreement by all parties to abide by the results of the election.[2] Although the envoy was received courteously enough by the Mexican government, it categorically refused to treat with him on the basis outlined, and the only result of his mission was to inspire in Huerta and his party a more bitter hatred towards the United States.

This feeling showed results in a number of incidents. On April 9, 1914, a paymaster of the U. S. S. *Dolphin,* landing at Tampico with a crew to obtain supplies, was arrested by an officer and squad of General Huerta's army. Two American sailors who had remained in the boat were forced to land, although the American flags at the bow and stern should have protected them. General Huerta ordered their release and expressed his regret, but refused to meet Admiral Mayo's demand that he salute the flag of the United States. A few days later an orderly from U. S. S. *Minnesota* was arrested at Vera Cruz while ashore in uniform, and was forced to spend some time in jail. President Wilson upheld Admiral Mayo, and when it was finally seen that Huerta would not comply, the American fleets were ordered to establish a pacific blockade of the Mexican coasts.

In his review of the situation before Congress, President Wilson pointed out that "a series of incidents have recently occurred which cannot but create the impression that the representatives of General Huerta were willing to go out of their way to show disregard for the dignity and rights of this government, and felt perfectly safe in doing what they pleased, making free to show in many ways their irritation and contempt." [3] On April 21, in order to prevent the German steamer *Ypirango* from landing a consignment of arms, the American forces shelled Vera Cruz and then landed and seized the custom-house; after rather sharp fighting, they occupied the city completely.[4] When this was followed by an embargo on the shipment of arms into Mexico, and a complete severance of diplomatic relations, it was believed, both in the United States and in Mexico, that armed intervention was at hand. At this critical juncture Argentina, Brazil, and Chile tendered their good offices to effect a settlement of the difficulties, and their proffer was accepted. General Huerta, now almost at the end of his financial resources, and worried by

[2] *Ibid.,* p. 822.
[3] *Cong. Rec.,* Vol. 51, p. 6908.
[4] For the details of the Vera Cruz affair, see J. P. Tumulty, *Woodrow Wilson as I Know Him* (New York, 1921), p. 150.

the continued successes of the Constitutionalists under Villa and Carranza, could hardly afford to refuse. Carranza also was invited to suspend hostilities and send representatives to Niagara Falls, though it was hardly to be expected that, with success so near at hand, he would do so. Torreon had fallen to Villa early in April, and the Constitutionalists had captured Tampico on May 13, a week before the conference opened. The deliberations lasted six weeks, but with no practical results other than allaying South American fears in regard to the Mexican policy of the United States.[5] A fortnight after the adjournment of the conference, General Huerta, realizing the hopelessness of his cause without American recognition, turned over the government to Señor Carbajal and left the country.

President Wilson has been much critized for his failure to recognize Huerta, and it has been asserted that much of the subsequent bloodshed and anarchy which ultimately forced American intervention could have been averted by a prompt recognition of the latter's *de facto* government. Such speculation *a posteriori* seems rather futile, considering the fact that at no time during his control of the Mexican government was Huerta able to put down the various factions that refused to recognize his authority. More proper complaint may be lodged against the grounds on which the President refused recognition, namely, that Huerta had employed unconstitutional methods to gain the presidency. Was not such an attitude in reality intervention in the domestic concerns of a foreign country? Were the methods employed by Carranza to gain control of the government any more constitutional?

Whatever may be said for or against the policy of watchful waiting, it soon became decidedly unpopular in the United States. Hardly had Carranza entered Mexico City before Villa raised a new revolt in the north, while Zapata continued his depredations in the south. The government was finally compelled to take refuge at Vera Cruz, and Mexico City became the plaything of all factions—the Constitutionalists occupying and reoccupying the city four different times. On June 2, 1915, President Wilson addressed a strong plea to the leaders of the various factions to act together for the relief of their prostrate country, declaring that, while the United States did not desire or claim the right to settle the affairs of Mexico for her, yet she could not stand indifferently by and do nothing to serve her neighbor.[6] When this produced no results, our government held a conference with the six ranking Latin-American representatives,

[5] The protocols of the conference may be found in the publications of the World Peace Foundation, Vol. VI, No. 1 (Feb., 1916).

[6] E. E. Robinson and V. J. West, *The Foreign Policy of Woodrow Wilson* (New York, 1917), p. 268.

and a joint note, signed by the United States and the ministers from Brazil, Chile, Argentina, Bolivia, Uruguay, and Guatemala, was despatched, August 11, 1915, to Carranza and Villa. The two leaders were asked to meet at some neutral place to exchange ideas on the creation of a provisional government which should take the first steps necessary to the constitutional reconstruction of the country.[7] General Villa accepted forthwith, but General Carranza declared that he could not consent to the discussion of the domestic affairs of the republic by mediation or on the initiative of any foreign government. Nevertheless, when Carranza gave pledges that his government would guarantee that the lives and property of foreigners in Mexico would be respected, and that damages caused by the revolution would be settled, President Wilson, on October 19, 1915, authorized his *de facto* government to be recognized by the United States.

Enraged by this triumph of his rival, Villa swore vengeance upon the United States, and on January 10, 1916, eighteen Americans holding passports of safe conduct issued by the *de facto* government were taken from a train at Santa Ysabel and shot in cold blood. On March 9 Villa raided the little town of Columbus, New Mexico, killing seventeen Americans and carrying away horses. The American government thereupon ordered General Pershing to pursue the bandits across the border, with orders to capture them or destroy their band. Instead of coöperating, the Carranza government seemed desirous of thwarting the purpose of the expedition, and, as American troops continued their vain quest farther and farther inland, it showed itself openly hostile. Finally General Jacinto Trevino issued a pronunciamiento informing General Pershing that if he moved his troops farther south, east, or west he would be attacked.

President Wilson had been patient, but his forbearance had a limit, and he immediately ordered 150,000 militia under arms and despatched them to the border. In a long despatch to the Mexican government, dated June 20, 1916, Secretary Lansing reviewed the whole situation and made it clear that the American troops were in Mexico to accomplish a duty that had been forced upon it through the impotence of the Mexican authorities. Therefore the demand of the Mexican government for "the immediate withdrawal of the American troops" could not be entertained.[8] The day after the despatch of this note the situation was rendered still more grave by an attack upon the American troops at Carrizal, in which some soldiers on each side were killed and seventeen American soldiers were taken captive. The United States government notified American

---

[7] *Amer. Jour. of Int. Law,* Vol. X (Apr., 1916), p. 364.

[8] This correspondence may be found in *ibid.,* Supp., pp. 179-225.

citizens to leave Mexico, and, with American troops massed on the border, war seemed inevitable. A demand for the immediate release of the prisoners and a definite statement of the Mexican government's purposes finally aroused Carranza to the danger of his position. The captives were released, and Carranza proposed that an offer of mediation on the part of Spain and several Latin-American countries be accepted. The United States thereupon suggested a joint conference, with three commissioners from each side, to arrange a settlement. This solution was accepted by the Mexican government, which named as its delegates Luis Cabrera, Minister of Finance, Alberto Pani, president of the Mexican International Railways, and Ignacio Bonillas. The United States was represented by Franklin K. Lane, Judge George Gray, and John R. Mott.

The conference convened September 6 at New London, Connecticut, and continued, with several recesses, until November 24. The Americans were especially insistent on the protection of foreigners and their interests in Mexico, while the Mexicans urged the immediate withdrawal of American troops from Mexican soil. A protocol was finally signed providing for the withdrawal of General Pershing's army within forty days, provided no new raids should occur in the meantime, the United States reserving the right to send an army into Mexico to capture bandits who had invaded American territory. Claims for damages and plans for economic development were left to future negotiations.[9] Although the Carranza government did not ratify the protocol, in accordance with the recommendation of the American commissioners the American troops were ordered withdrawn, and on January 2, 1917, diplomatic relations were resumed with the appointment of Henry P. Fletcher as American ambassador to Mexico. Villa remained at large, and Carranza gained added prestige for his successful baiting of the United States; but President Wilson had the satisfaction of preventing intervention from becoming war at a time when there was a greater need for American troops and resources in Europe than in Mexico.

Another very important problem that the government had to solve was the devising of some means whereby the dictatorship could be resolved, with the least possible friction, into a constitutional régime. To this end, a constitutional convention was called to adopt a new constitution in place of the one of 1857, and the delegates assembled at Queretaro in February, 1917. As it was hoped in 1857 to make Mexico a democratic state by giving her a democratic constitution modeled upon the constitution of the United States, so now, sixty years later, it was hoped to

[9] Text of protocol, *ibid.*, Vol. XI (Apr., 1917), p. 403.

solve the various social and economic problems by incorporating their remedies in a constitutional formula.[10] In the framework of government the new constitution followed the constitution of 1857, and as amended provides for a president elected for a single six-year term, with duties very similar to the duties of the President of the United States, and a bicameral congress, the senate consisting of two members from each state and two from the federal district, chosen directly for a six-year term, and the house elected directly for a three-year term. The federal system was maintained, such powers as were not granted to the national government being reserved to the states. The constitution began with a very elaborate bill of rights and ended with a series of temporary articles regulating the procedure in the first election to be held under it.

The new provisions of most interest to the United States were those concerning the ownership of land and natural resources. Article XXVII declared the ownership of lands and waters to be vested originally in the nation, which has the right to transmit title thereof to private persons. Necessary measures were to be taken to divide large landed estates and to develop small holdings. The ownership of all minerals, phosphates, petroleum, and hydrocarbons is vested directly in the state, is inalienable, and may not be lost by prescription. As to the legal capacity to acquire ownership of lands, it was provided that "only Mexicans by birth or naturalization, and Mexican companies, have the right to acquire ownership in lands, waters, and their appurtenances, or to obtain concessions to develop mines, waters, or mineral fuels in the Republic of Mexico. The nation may grant the same right to foreigners, provided they agree before the department of foreign affairs to be considered Mexicans in respect to such property, and accordingly not to invoke the protection of their governments in respect to the same, under penalty in case of breach, of forfeiture to the nation of property so acquired. Within a zone of 100 kilometers from the frontiers and 50 kilometers from the seacoast, no foreigner shall under any conditions acquire direct ownership of lands and waters."

It can be easily seen that the provisions of this article, especially when it is realized that most of the oil-producing property lies within the 50-kilometer zone, are almost completely prohibitive of further foreign exploitation of Mexican oil resources. However, the more immediate question was in regard to the effect it would have on property already acquired. Article XIV of the constitution seemed to answer this in declar-

[10] The text of the constitution of 1917 may be found in *Investigation of Mexican Affairs*, Sen. Doc. No. 285, 66th Cong., 2nd Sess., Vol. II, p. 3123.

ing: "No law shall be given retroactive effect to the injury of any person whatsoever." But another provision in Article XXVII (Sec. IV) declared that commercial stock companies may not acquire, hold, or administer rural properties, but only lands in an area absolutely necessary for their establishments, which the executive of the union or of the state in each case shall determine. This seemed like a dangerous exercise of the executive power, and even before the constitution was signed and promulgated, Secretary Lansing, in a despatch to Charles Parker, representing American interests at Queretaro, protested against this paragraph, pointing out that "the objection to a provision so capable of capricious application appears evident. The precise conditions under which the power vested in the executive may be exercised are not defined. No safeguards are afforded against unwise or arbitrary executive acts." [11] After considerable correspondence on the subject, it was apparent that, while the new constitution did not interfere with any wells already drilled, it did prevent foreign companies from sinking new wells unless they waived their nationality and organized as Mexican corporations.

The opposition to Article XXVII upon the part of the American oil interests, particularly as to the interpretation placed upon it by Carranza in a series of executive decrees promulgated at different times during the year 1918, formed the bone of diplomatic contention during the remaining part of the Carranza régime. A decree of February 19, 1918, imposing certain taxes on the surface of oil lands, as well as on the rents and royalties derived from their exploitation, seemed to indicate an intention to separate the ownership of the surface from that of the mineral deposits of the sub-surface, thereby confiscating private property under the guise of taxation without just compensation. Both the American government [12] and the oil companies protested, but with little apparent effect upon the intentions of the Mexican government. The Mexican authorities contended that the decrees were merely fiscal legislation, which operated similarly upon its own citizens and upon foreigners, and that therefore Mexico, in the exercise of its sovereign rights, could not admit the interference of foreign governments in the mattter. If the foreigners felt themselves prejudiced by the decree, the Mexican courts were open to afford them legal remedies.[13] Mr. Frank L. Polk summed up the American case in an emphatic but friendly fashion in a long note to Mr. Fletcher, the American ambassador, on December 13, 1918. He pointed

[11] *Ibid.*, p. 3121.
[12] See note of Ambassador Fletcher dated Apr. 2, 1918, *ibid.*, p. 3157.
[13] For a full statement of the Mexican case see the note of E. Garza Perez, Aug. 17, 1918, to Henry P. Fletcher, *ibid.*, p. 3161.

out that the Mexican attitude regarding the decrees—namely, that merely because they applied equally to Mexican citizens and foreigners the question was one of internal sovereignty, and afforded no rightful basis for interposition by the governments of interested foreigners whose property rights were jeopardized—was not in accordance with international law. "While the Mexican government may see fit to confiscate vested property rights of its own citizens, such action is in equity no justification for the confiscation of such rights of American citizens, and does not stop the government of the United States from protesting on behalf of its citizens against confiscation of their property." Mr. Polk then went on to show that Mexican citizens had, by their participation in molding governmental policies, a weapon in addition to judicial remedies which foreigners did not possess; therefore, he argued, friendly representations were not out of place.[14] President Carranza finally turned the matter over to the Mexican congress; but no "organic act" on the subject was passed until some years later.

It is impossible to find an absolutely impartial account of the oil question under the Carranza régime, but a few statements on both sides will afford a basis for a fair approximation. Mr. Frederic R. Kellogg, general counsel of the Pan-American Petroleum and Transport Company, sums up the complaints of the oil interests somewhat as follows: Many regulations of a harassing nature to prevent development were adopted; the government allowed the filing of claims against the oil properties by persons claiming to be entitled to acquire them under the Carranza decrees; concessions to drill upon lands comprised within titles held by petroleum companies were granted to Carranza's favorites; no company was allowed to drill on its own land unless it had a drilling permit, and no permit would be granted unless the company agreed to abide by the terms of any petroleum law that might be enacted in the future; Carranza sent his armed forces into the oil regions, resulting in a series of murders and assaults upon the employees of the companies; finally, a campaign of vilification against the companies was conducted in Mexico and the United States, accusing them of being tax-dodgers, fomenting rebellion against the Carranza administration, and even seeking to bring about armed intervention by the United States to subserve their own greed and financial ambitions.[15]

On the other side, Mr. Joseph F. Guffey, president of the Atlantic Gulf Oil Corporation, declared that the chief offenders in respect to propa-

---

[14] *Ibid.*, p. 3163.
[15] *Ibid.*, p. 3270.

ganda were the so-called associations ostensibly formed for the protection of American rights in Mexico. As to confiscation, he asserted that

... the Mexican government is not attempting to confiscate oil properties developed and operated by American companies. If such were its purpose, it could easily double or treble the export tax of eleven cents per barrel which was collected on all oil exported from Mexico in 1919. ... All these companies have to do to conform to Mexican requirements is to recognize the constitution, renounce all oil concessions and leases obtained prior to its promulgation, and take out new permits. This process does not invalidate the occupancy of these properties by oil companies, but simply recognizes the government's right to levy taxes or collect a royalty on oil production. ... President Carranza I regard as an intelligent, constructive, and honest statesman; he has done more for Mexico and the Mexican people than any other president in its history.[16]

But without question one of the best sources of information upon Mexican conditions during the Carranza régime is the voluminous testimony offered before the Fall subcommittee on the investigation of Mexican affairs, which lasted from August 8, 1919, until May 28, 1920.[17] Hearings were held in Washington, New York, and in various cities and towns along the border, and, in all, more than two hundred and fifty witnesses were examined. Mr. Edward L. Doheny's account of his long struggle against climatic conditions, governmental interference, and discouragement on the part of stockholders is a story of success against odds which rivals the epic tales of the forty-niners. Incidentally, Mr. Doheny brought out the fact that the oil companies, instead of hiring Palaez to protect them against the Carranza régime, were paying him under duress with the connivance of the Carranza authorities, who themselves were wholly unable to give adequate protection. The payments had also been advised by the American State Department.[18]

Whether or not one is in favor of intervention, an unbiased perusal of this report indicates clearly that Mexico under the Carranza régime was not a safe place for an American citizen, whether he was mine-owner, oil-producer, or the proprietor of a ranch. The report further made it clear not only that there was a vast amount of American capital in Mexico,[19] but that it went there under the protection of, and in many cases at the urgent solicitation of, the Mexican government. It would also seem that

[16] *New York Times,* Feb. 26, 1920.

[17] By a Senate resolution the committee was directed to investigate the matter of damages and outrages suffered by citizens of the United States in Mexico, the proper indemnities, and what measures should be taken to prevent a recurrence of such outrages.

[18] *Investigation of Mexican Affairs,* Vol. I, p. 285.

[19] The report gives $1,057,770,000 as the exact figure, p. 3322.

until the Carranza government came into power the Mexicans were, for the most part, very well disposed towards Americans and often preferred to work for them rather than for their own countrymen. Finally, despite a good deal of popular suspicion of Senator Fall's Mexican policy, it must be conceded that every effort was made to get at the entire truth of the situation, and that the attempts to prove that a plot existed in the United States to force armed intervention in Mexico failed because no substantial facts were brought forth to substantiate the assertions.

While the Fall sub-committee was at work, a new revolution was started which carried Carranza out of power and down to his death. Like Diaz, Carranza was unable to resign himself to letting the supreme power slip from his fingers. Inasmuch as the constitution prevented a second term, his only chance of retaining control lay in procuring the election of someone who would be subservient to him. The two strongest candidates, General Alvaro Obregón and General Pablo Gonzalez, were not men of this sort. Hence Señor Bonillas, the Mexican ambassador to the United States, was picked; the point was pressed that the country ought to have a civilian president; and Bonillas was pledged the support of a civilian party. Whatever may have been his qualifications, Señor Bonillas was handicapped by his long absence from the country and by his lack of a strong personal following.

President Carranza had signified his intention to allow the elections to be held without any governmental interference. Nevertheless, it was not long before Candido Aguilar, the president's son-in-law, came out for Bonillas, and soon it was manifest that government dictation was again to be reckoned with. The power of the government to bring about the election of its own candidate in Mexico is notorious. The only hope for Obregón and Gonzalez was a revolution, and on April 23, 1920, General Obregón and a number of influential leaders raised a revolt in the state of Sonora. The so-called Agua Prieta plan had been adopted, which declared that the sovereignty of Mexico rested in the people; Carranza, it was contended, had violated it; therefore he must give over his power to a provisional president, namely, Governor de la Huerta of Sonora, who should be supreme commander of the state until the elections were to be held. The plan further decreed that the constitution of 1917 should continue to be the fundamental law of the republic.

The revolution spread very rapidly, particularly after leaders like Generals Alvarado, Gomez, and Palaez went over to Obregón, and Gonzalez withdrew his candidacy in Obregón's favor. Early in May, Carranza was forced to flee from the capital, and the revolutionists entered it the same day. Unfortunately for Carranza, he fell in with a small band supposed to be a part of the forces of Palaez, but under the command of Carrera. These men offered to act as guides. But during the night an attack was made upon the sleeping-quarters of General Carranza, and he was shot, presumably by the pretended escort. In the meantime, Congress had chosen Adolfo de la Huerta provisional president, and he postponed the elections from July to September, in order that the provisional government might have time to pacify the country. The delay was necessary, for Gonzalez, apparently repenting his self-effacement, had started a new revolution. But even Mexico was war weary; the revolt was speedily put down, and Gonzalez captured and tried for treason. He was acquitted with the understanding that he would leave the country. Pancho Villa, who also had promised to be good, soon grew tired of inaction and raised a revolt. Realizing the difficulty of capturing him, the government finally got an agreement under which he was to lay down his arms, provided each of his eight hundred followers should receive a tract of land and Pancho himself be given a large estate, with the privilege of keeping fifty retainers at government expense.

On September 5, 1920, Alvaro Obregón was elected president; and his party, the Liberal Constitutionalists, gained control of both houses of congress. Before taking office, he made a tour of the Mexican states, in the course of which he crossed the boundary and spent some ten days on the American side. He was enthusiastically received, and at El Paso he declared that he felt sure that Mexico was already recognized by the American people, if not by their government. In a speech at Dallas, October 17, he assured his hearers that Mexico would recognize all legal foreign debts and all legal rights of Mexicans and foreigners alike. On December 1, 1920, he was inaugurated. But, although the new government was recognized the same month by Japan, Brazil, Holland, and Germany, the Wilson administration, whose term was soon to expire, thought it best to allow the question of recognition on our own part to be handled by the incoming administration. President Obregón called a special session of congress to meet February 7, 1921, and in his address to the body he stressed the need of legislation to institute a modern banking system, the establishment of an agrarian policy that would encourage the restoration of the land to the people, and the solution of the problem arising from the application of Article XXVII to the nation's petroleum resources.[20]

With men like Señor Calles as Secretary of Interior and Premier, and

[20] Text may be found in the *Mexican Review,* Vol. IV, No. 8 (March, 1921), p. 4.

Señor de la Huerta as Secretary of Treasury to assist him, President Obregón was enabled in a very short time to establish peace and order in Mexico. His attitude towards American investors was firm in maintaining the rights of the Mexican nation, but fair in respecting rights honestly acquired. However, the Harding administration refused to consider the question of recognition until certain preliminary questions were settled.

Secretary Hughes outlined his policy in a general way on June 7, 1921. He insisted that the fundamental question was the safeguarding of American property rights against confiscation. "This question is vital," he declared, "because of the provisions inserted in the Mexican Constitution promulgated in 1917. If these provisions are to be put into effect retroactively, the properties of American citizens will be confiscated on a great scale. This would constitute an international wrong of the gravest character, and this government could not submit to its accomplishment. If it be said that this wrong is not intended, and that the Constitution of 1917 will not be construed to permit, or enforced so as to effect, confiscation, then it is important that this should be made clear by guaranties in proper form."

According to Secretary Hughes, the best way to obtain such guaranties was for the two governments to sign a treaty of amity and commerce in which Mexico would agree to safeguard the rights of property which attached before the Constitution of 1917 was promulgated.[21] Such a treaty of some eighteen articles was presented by United States *Chargé d'Affaires* Summerlin to the Mexican government on May 27, 1921,[22] but President Obregón had already rejected recognition upon such a basis, declaring that "the acceptance and signing of a convention to obtain recognition would be equal to placing in doubt the rights that Mexico has to all the privileges international law establishes.[23]

A series of notes between the two governments now followed which culminated with Secretary Hughes' note of instruction dated July 28, 1922, in which he stated that if the Mexican authorities were not willing to sign a treaty binding Mexico to respect the valid titles acquired under Mexican laws prior to the Constitution of 1917, then the question remained in what manner such assurances should be given.[24]

On March 31, 1923, Minister Pani made a lengthy response, claiming that the accomplished acts of the Mexican government since the cor-

[21] *New York Times,* June 8, 1921.
[22] For text see *United States Daily,* May 15, 1926.
[23] *New York Times,* May 21, 1921.
[24] *United States Daily,* May 19, 1926.

respondence began were such as to affect advantageously the solution of the diplomatic problem. He then cited among other "acts" the signing of the Lamont-Huerta agreement, on June 16, 1922, for the adjustment of the Mexican debt; the negotiations already begun between the Secretary of the Treasury and the representatives of the principal oil companies; and the five *amparo* (injunction) decisions of the Mexican Supreme Court, which had defined in an unmistakable manner the non-retroactive character of Article XXVII.[25] He also justified the agrarian policy as being humane and economic, and insisted that the damages to American agricultural properties were insignificant in comparison with the vital advantages to the Mexican people.[26]

Apparently moved by this plea, President Harding on May 2, 1923, appointed Charles Beecher Warren, former ambassador to Japan, and John Barton Payne, former Secretary of the Interior, as American commissioners to meet two Mexican commissioners for the purpose of exchanging impressions. The conference convened in Mexico City on May 15, 1923, and lasted till August 15 of the same year.[27] The two outstanding issues were the questions arising from the confiscation of American agricultural lands to provide *ejidos* or communal lands to villages who had never had them or had been deprived of them, and the dispute regarding the nationalization of the sub-soil deposits whereby rights possessed by American owners of the property were confiscated.[28]

In the case of the agricultural lands the United States insisted that the indemnity should be paid in cash and according to their just value, and that payment by bonds not convertible into money on the basis of their par value could not be considered as indemnification under the rules of international law.[29] Nevertheless, realizing that an urgent social emergency existed, the United States' commissioners agreed that if the Mexican government would make a statement that its claim to expropriate lands of American citizens for *ejidos* did not constitute a precedent for the expropriation of any other kind of property except for due compensation made in cash, the United States government would consider whether under the circumstances it would be willing to accept for its citizens

[25] For the Mexican embassy's official statement regarding the Supreme Court's ruling see *New York Times,* July 8, 1922; for the decisions *ibid.,* Aug. 9, 1922.

[26] *United States Daily,* May 19, 1926.

[27] *Proceedings of the United States—Mexican Commission Convened in Mexico City May 14, 1923* (Washington, D. C., 1925).

[28] For a careful and, on the whole, impartial presentation of the legalistic point of view see Antonio Gomez Robledo, *The Bucareli Agreements and International Law* (Mexico City, 1940).

[29] *Proceedings of the United States—Mexican Commission,* p. 29.

federal bonds of Mexico in payment for the lands taken, providing that the *ejidos* did not exceed a specified area of 1755 hectares (4335 acres). Furthermore such action was contingent upon the conclusion of a general claims convention between the two governments under which those dispossessed might present their claims for loss or damage. The Mexican commissioners accepted this formula.[30]

In the case of sub-soil deposits, the Mexican commissioners conceded that those owners of the surface prior to May 1, 1917, who had performed "some positive act" indicating their intention to exploit the sub-soil deposits were protected against nationalization, but insisted that all who had not, had forfeited their rights.[31] Here also, however, a compromise was obtained whereby to those owners who had not performed a "positive act" were given preferential rights to the sub-soil as against third parties. Here again the United States' right to make reservations in behalf of its citizens was recognized.[32]

With these understandings approved by the chief executives of both countries, the government of President Obregón was formally recognized by the United States on August 31, 1923. Shortly afterwards two claims conventions were signed, a general one at Washington on September 8, 1923, covering claims arising since July 4, 1868, the date of the former claims convention,[33] and a special convention signed at Mexico City on September 10, 1923, covering claims arising from losses occurring during the revolutionary activities lasting from November 20, 1910, to May 31, 1920.[34]

President Obregón had at last won his long fight for recognition, but too late to profit greatly by it, for his term of office was almost ended and the constitution forbade his immediate reëlection. Nevertheless he was now able to support openly and effectively the candidacy of General Plutarco Calles, his Secretary of the Interior and a leader of the socialist and labor groups. When a revolution broke out, engineered by Adolfo de la Huerta, former Minister of Finance and chief candidate of the opposition, the United States showed its friendliness to the newly recognized government by sending a large consignment of arms to the Obregón forces, and placing an embargo on all shipments of arms to the revolutionists. A little later the Navy Department ordered a division of six destroyers to Tampico where de la Huerta was attempting to maintain a

[30] *Ibid.*, pp. 37-44.
[31] *Ibid.*, pp. 20-23.
[32] *Ibid.*, pp. 47-49.
[33] *U. S. Treaty Series*, No. 678.
[34] *Ibid.*, No. 676.

blockade, and the State Department requested the governor of Texas to permit 2000 Mexican federal troops en route from Sonora to cross Texas territory to enter Mexico by El Paso. This seemed to be stretching the bonds of friendly neutrality and the question of our benevolent attitude was raised in Congress. Congressman Fairchild asked that the Harding doctrine against the sale of arms to any foreign power be made the official doctrine of the United States and he was supported by Senators King, Borah, and Johnson in the Senate.[35] Senator Robinson introduced an even more drastic bill in the Senate which would prevent any officer, agent, citizen, or corporation of the United States from selling arms and munitions to any foreign government or its agents.[36] But the Mexican government had the arms and the revolution was soon put down.

During the year 1924 the relations between the two countries were exceedingly cordial. The appointment of Mr. Charles Beecher Warren as ambassador to Mexico indicated the intention of the United States to support the understandings recently arrived at. When for personal reasons he was forced to resign a few months later, he declared that never since the Diaz régime had relations between the two countries been on a more friendly basis. General Calles, who had been elected by a large majority, paid a visit to the United States before his inauguration and was received, both officially and unofficially, in a most cordial fashion.

Unfortunately for the continuance of amicable relations, on March 4, 1925, Secretary Hughes resigned and former Senator Frank B. Kellogg took over the affairs of the State Department. One of his first official acts was to ask Ambassador Sheffield, who had taken Mr. Warren's post, to report to Washington. After conferring with him, Secretary Kellogg on June 12, 1925, gave to the press what one of his former colleagues termed "an unmannerly and unjustifiable" statement. Noting that conditions in Mexico were not entirely satisfactory, Mr. Kellogg declared that we were looking to the Mexican government to restore properties illegally taken and to indemnify American citizens. He understood from the press that another revolutionary movement might be impending. If so, Secretary Kellogg concluded, "it is now the policy of this government to use its influence and its support in behalf of stability and orderly constitutional procedure, but it should be made clear that this government will continue to support the government in Mexico only so long as it protects American lives and American rights and complies with its international engagements and obligations. The government of Mexico is now on trial before

[35] *New York Times,* Jan. 1, 1924.
[36] *Ibid.,* Jan. 9, 1924.

the world. . . . We have been patient and realize, of course, that it takes time to bring about a stable government, but we cannot countenance violation of her obligations and failure to protect American citizens." [37]

President Calles resented the implications of this statement and regretted that Mr. Kellogg showed the interest of the United States in the maintenance of order in Mexico by suggesting that revolutionary movements were said to be impending. As for the government of Mexico being on trial before the world, such was also the case with that of the United States, as well as those of other countries, "but if it is to be understood that Mexico is on trial in the guise of defendant my government absolutely rejects with energy such imputation which in essence would only mean an insult." [38]

However, this diplomatic flurry was merely an ominous portent of a much more serious situation to follow. Although there had been constant recriminations between the two powers in regard to the provisions of Article XXVII of the Constitution of 1917, concerning agrarian reform and the nationalization of the sub-soil deposits, no action had as yet been taken by the Mexican Congress to put these provisions into effect. But in December, 1925, the Mexican Congress passed two laws to remedy this situation—laws generally known as the land law and the petroleum law. [39]

The petroleum law repeated the provision of the Constitution asserting inalienable ownership of sub-soil deposits by the nation; it required foreigners to comply with the constitutional provisions regarding the waiving of nationality and the right to invoke diplomatic protection in so far as Mexican owned property was concerned; it also enforced the clause prohibiting ownership of lands or waters within fifty kilometers from the sea coast and one hundred kilometers from the frontiers. A new feature of the law required all holdings to be confirmed by concessions to be granted for a period of not more than fifty years from the time when exploitation was begun. Furthermore, the concessions to be confirmed must have arisen in lands where exploitation was begun or the contract made prior to May 1, 1917. Detailed regulations for the concessions were also included.

The land law also repeated the constitutional restrictions, and included foreigners participating in Mexican corporations. It was further provided that Mexican companies owning rural property for agricultural purposes

[37] *Ibid.*, June 13, 1925.
[38] *Ibid.*, June 15, 1925.
[39] For text of the land law see C. W. Hackett, "The Mexican Revolution and the United States, 1910-1926," *World Peace Foundation Pamphlet*, Vol. IX, No. 5, p. 414; for petroleum law, *ibid.*, p. 425.

would not be granted a permit if there remained in the hands of aliens 50 per cent or more of the total interests of the company. Foreign persons holding 50 per cent or more of total interests could hold the amount in excess of 50 per cent till their death, and their heirs were given five years to dispose of their holdings with an extension if considered necessary. Corporations were granted ten years to dispose of excess holdings.

Even before the passage of these laws, Secretary Kellogg, through the American ambassador, submitted certain inquiries regarding them, and on November 17, 1925, he sent an *aide-mémoire* of personal message to the Mexican Minister of Foreign Affairs in the hope "that the clouds which I perceive on the horizon of friendship between the United States and Mexico may be removed." [40] President Calles replied directly through his Minister of Foreign Affairs that there was "absolutely no cause for perceiving clouds, and that the legislation was merely aimed at dispelling the vagueness of the constitutional provisions and would in no way violate the obligations of Mexico under international law."

The ensuing correspondence which began with the *aide-mémoire* of November 17, 1925, ended exactly a year later with the final reply of the Mexican government dated November 17, 1926. Inasmuch as it amounts to some 50,000 words and much of it is repetitious, perhaps the simplest method of approach would be to note the issues involved and the attitude of both parties in regard to them.

The issues in dispute pertained to a difference in interpretation in regard to the four following subjects:

(1) the alleged retroactive features of the land law; (2) the alleged retroactivity of the petroleum law; (3) the insistence on the part of the Mexican government that foreigners owning property agree to submit themselves to Mexican jurisdiction in all disputes concerning their property, on penalty that their property be forfeited if they should invoke the protection of their government; (4) the nature of the agreements formulated at the Conference in Mexico City by the four commissioners in May, 1923.

As to the engagements of 1923, President Calles insisted that they were merely an "exchange of views" and "did not result in any formal agreement other than that of the claims conventions which were signed after the resumption of diplomatic relations." [41] Furthermore, although Mexico recognized the declarations made by its commissioners, the conferences of 1923 were not a condition for the recognition of the government of

---

[40] This correspondence has been published as *Sen. Doc. No. 96*, 69th Cong., 1st Sess.

[41] Reply of Mexican Minister of Foreign Affairs, Nov. 27, 1925, *ibid.*, p. 5.

Mexico and could never be given that character.[42] Finally, the Mexican government refused to recognize the binding force equivalent to a treaty or a constitutional precept in the outlines of policy presented at the conference, since the declarations of neither side took the form of a synallagmatic agreement.[43]

Secretary Kellogg's stand on the binding nature of the oral agreements of the conference is clearly and succinctly stated in his last note of October 30, 1926: "The declarations of the Mexican and American commissioners on that occasion, subsequently ratified by an exchange of notes between the two governments, constituted, in the view of my government, solemn and binding undertakings which formed the basis and moving consideration for the recognition of the Mexican government by this government." [44]

However, inasmuch as the appointment of the two American commissioners was not approved by the Senate, nor was the agreement itself submitted to the Senate for its approval, it could hardly be considered as of the same binding force as a formal treaty. Furthermore, in the minutes of the meeting of the commission on August 2, it is stated that the policy of the present President of Mexico is conditioned within the limitations of his constitutional power and "is not intended to constitute an obligation for an unlimited time on the part of the Mexican government to grant preferential rights to such owners of the surface or persons entitled to exercise their rights to the oil in the sub-soil." [45] Under these circumstances, the legislative branch or a subsequent executive would hardly appear to be legally bound.

In regard to the disagreement due to the Mexican government's insistence that foreign property owners bind themselves not to invoke the diplomatic protection of their government, but agree to submit themselves as Mexicans to Mexican laws in disputes over property under penalty of forfeiture of their property if such protection is sought, a compromise seems to have been reached in the correspondence. In his note of October 7, 1926, Foreign Minister Saenz declares: "The Mexican government therefore does not deny that the American government is at liberty to intervene for its nationals; but that does not stand in the way of carrying out an agreement under which the alien agrees not to be the party asking for the diplomatic protection of his government. In case of in-

[42] *Ibid.*, p. 34.
[43] U. S. Dept. of State, *American Property Rights in Mexico* (Washington, D. C., 1926), p. 11.
[44] *Ibid.*, p. 26.
[45] *Proceedings of the United States—Mexican Commission,* 1923.

fringement of any international duty such as a denial of justice would be, the right of the American government to take with the Mexican government appropriate action to seek atonement for injustice or injury which may have been done to its nationals would stand unimpaired. Under these conditions neither would the American government have failed to protect its nationals nor the Mexican government to comply with its laws." [46]

It might be noted, however, that this so-called Calvo clause seems to have been interpreted to some extent in favor of the position taken by the United States in the decision rendered by the General Claims Commission on March 31, 1926, in the case of the North American Dredging Company of Texas v. United Mexican States, even though the Commission dismissed this case and thus sustained the position of the Mexican agent. The Commission found the Calvo clause neither upheld unanimously nor universally rejected by authorities on international law, but it did reject as unsound the right of Mexico or any other nation "lawfully to bind all foreigners by contract to relinquish all rights of protection by their governments. . . . This provision did not and could not deprive the claimant of his American citizenship and all that that implies. It did not take from him his undoubted right to apply to his own government for protection if his resort to the Mexican tribunals or other authorities available to him resulted in a denial or delay of justice as that term is used in international law." [47]

The third point under dispute was the alleged retroactivity of the land law, which required foreign persons and corporations to divest themselves of majority control of corporations owning rural properties for agricultural purposes. According to the terms of this law, corporations were required to dispose of their stock in excess of 50 per cent within ten years, while individuals were allowed to retain such majority stock till their death and their heirs were given five years to dispose of it. Secretary Kellogg insisted that this provision of the law was "manifestly retroactive," since it required the alien owner of rural properties legally acquired under the laws of Mexico "to divest himself of the ownership, control and management of his property." [48] Minister Saenz maintained that the law in the case of individuals was not retroactive nor confiscatory, since it permitted possession till the death of the owner and therefore was

---

[46] *American Property Rights in Mexico*, p. 14.
[47] *Amer. Jour. of Int. Law*, Vol. 20 (Oct., 1926), p. 800.
[48] *Sen. Doc. No. 96*, p. 23.

merely a limitation upon the right of inheritance, which is in strict conformity with international law.[49] In the case of alien moral persons (corporations) Minister Saenz declared that "in all legislation it is admitted that the law is free to amplify, modify, or restrict the capacity of that class of persons," and since the article referred to future rights, that is those arising from the period of time subsequent to ten years, "its effects cannot be regarded as retroactive, since there was no acquired right but merely expectation of a right."[50]

The final point in dispute covered the parts of the petroleum law which were claimed to be retroactive. Under the mining codes of 1884, 1892, and 1909, owners of the surface were given right to exploit subsoil deposits of petroleum without special concession of the Mexican government. But Article XXVII of the Constitution of 1917 vested direct ownership of all minerals and petroleum in the nation. According to the minutes of the proceedings of the United States Mexican Commission of 1923, the Mexican executive agreed to enforce the principles of the decisions of the Supreme Court in the five *amparo* cases, which held that Article XXVII of the Constitution was not retroactive in respect to all persons who previous to May 1, 1917, had performed some positive act manifesting the intention of the owner of the surface to exercise his rights. The executive further agreed to grant preferential rights to those owners who had not performed any positive act.[51] However the petroleum law of 1925 changed these vested titles into concessions of fifty years' duration and made no provision for granting preferential rights to those owners who had not performed some positive act.

Secretary Kellogg insisted that the provisions of the petroleum law and the regulations issued thereunder which required the owners to apply for confirmation of their titles within one year, and to accept concessions for not more than fifty years from the time when exploitation began "would be nothing but a forced exchange of a greater for a lesser estate ... a statute so construed and enforced is retroactive and confiscatory, because it converts exclusive ownership under positive Mexican law into a mere authorization to exercise rights for a limited period of time. . . ."[52] Furthermore, not only did Secretary Kellogg object to the fact that no preferential treatment seemed to be accorded to owners who had failed to perform some positive act, but he rejected the entire Mexican doctrine

[49] *Ibid.*, p. 11.
[50] *Ibid.*, p. 30.
[51] *Proceedings of the United States—Mexican Commission*, p. 47.
[52] *American Property Rights in Mexico*, p. 4.

that no vested right was acquired until some positive act had been performed.[53]

The Mexican government claimed that a concession of fifty years' duration which might be renewed for another thirty years protected the working of any property discovered up to date, and that such a system founded upon concessions was even more secure than the system of private ownership. Therefore, although it might seem that the exchange of a title for a concession lessened the right, it was not so in practice. The Mexican case closed with an invitation to the United States to point out any specific case which violated international law, and if the Mexican government should fail to correct such violations it would be disposed to accept in justice the resulting claims of the American government.[54]

Indeed, when we come to the facts of the situation it would seem as though the foreign oil companies for the most part accepted the new legislation. The oil laws went into effect on January 1, 1927, and according to a statement issued by Minister of Labor Morones, 125 out of the 147 oil companies operating in Mexico agreed to accept them.[55] According to figures submitted by Mr. W. W. Liggett to the Senate Sub-Committee on Foreign Relations, out of 28,493,914 acres under development for oil, only 1,660,579 remained for which concessions had not been asked, and of this latter acreage 87 per cent was owned or controlled by Edward Doheny, Harry F. Sinclair, and Andrew Mellon.[56]

Apparently the peak of the difficulties had been passed, and four events occurred in the fall of 1927 which presaged an era of better relations. The first was the appointment of Mr. Dwight W. Morrow as ambassador to Mexico to succeed Mr. Sheffield, who had resigned in June. Although a representative of the financial interests, Mr. Morrow was noted for his broad-minded outlook and outstanding ability, and when in presenting his letter of credence he declared that "we shall not fail to adjust outstanding questions with that dignity and mutual respect which should mark the 'international relationship of the two sovereign and independent states'" it was indicated that a policy of compromise and coöperation on the part of the United States could now be anticipated.[57] The second was the repeal by President Calles on October 27 of the decree prohibiting the purchase of goods in the United States by Mexican departments. The third was the unanimous decision of the Mexican Supreme Court

[53] *Ibid.*, p. 5.
[54] *Ibid.*, pp. 21, 25.
[55] *New York Times,* Feb. 20, 1927.
[56] *Cong. Rec.,* Vol. 68 (Mar. 3, 1927), p. 5580.
[57] Harold Nicolson, *Dwight Morrow* (New York, 1935), p. 316.

rendered on November 17, 1927, granting an appeal restraining the Department of Industry, Commerce, and Labor from cancelling certain drilling permits of the Mexican Petroleum Company, an American concern which had not applied for a concession. The decision declared Articles XIV and XV of the petroleum law, which required companies to exchange their titles for fifty-year concessions within one year, unconstitutional in so far as they applied to the case at bar.[58] As a direct result of this decision President Calles recommended to the Mexican Congress the passage of a law amending these two articles so as to confirm all rights derived from lands where exploitation or contracts for exploitation had been entered into previous to May 1, 1917, by issuance of concessions without limit of time. The Mexican Congress passed such a law on December 27, 1927,[59] and on March 27, 1928, regulations were signed by President Calles validating in perpetuity all oil titles obtained before May 1, 1917.[60] The fourth was the non-stop flight of Colonel Lindbergh on December 14, 1927, from Washington to Mexico City. This event had an immediate and remarkable repercussion on public opinion both in Mexico and in the United States, and made for a very considerable improvement in the mutual friendliness and appreciation of the two peoples.

Although Ambassador Morrow had little difficulty in settling the oil controversy, he found the agrarian problem far more complex. He was able by personal efforts to obtain the reversal of some flagrant seizures of American-owned properties and he gave encouragement to American claimants to bring action in the Mexican courts, but the problem itself remained unsolved. Apparently he hoped that the Mexican government would soon abandon its policy of seizing lands and devote itself to improving land already taken.[61]

The religious problem engaged Ambassador Morrow's attention particularly.[62] In Febuary, 1926, a series of orders was issued for the arrest and deportation of foreign priests, for the nationalization of all church property not yet held by the state, and for the closing of all schools, convents and orphan asylums giving religious instruction in violation of Article XXVII of the Constitution. Although there was considerable outcry in church circles in the United States, and the House of Representa-

[58] *United States Daily,* Nov. 19, 1927.

[59] Text in *ibid.,* Jan. 6, 1928.

[60] For an authoritative discussion of the settlement see J. Reuben Clark, "Oil Settlement with Mexico," *Foreign Affairs,* Vol. VI (July, 1928), p. 600.

[61] Nicolson, *op. cit.,* p. 335.

[62] See Wilfrid H. Calcott, *Liberalism in Mexico 1857-1929* (Stanford University, 1931), Chap. XV, for a brief survey.

tives asked Secretary Kellogg for information, the State Department contented itself with a request that American churchmen should not be made to suffer unduly in the enforcement of the law. President Coolidge on September 8, 1926, declared that he regarded the church and state conflict in Mexico as purely an internal question in which the United States could have no interest save in the protection of American rights.[63]

However, Ambassador Morrow, although recognizing the inadvisability of intervening in the struggle between Church and State, was intrigued by the problem, and when Father Burke at the Havana Conference in January, 1928, suggested that Morrow arrange an interview for him with President Calles, the Ambassador agreed to take the matter under consideration. He finally arranged a secret meeting on April 4 at which he was present and during which a temporary compromise was drafted. The following month Morrow persuaded Calles to receive Monsignor Ruíz y Flores, the senior prelate of the Mexican bishops who had sought refuge in Texas. The previous agreement was confirmed and the situation looked quite hopeful when General Obregón, who had been slated to replace President Calles, was murdered July 17, 1928, by a young Catholic. Public opinion was so aroused that hostility flamed anew and the proposed compromise was dropped for the time being.

The next year Morrow again took up the question and persuaded President Portes Gil to receive as emissaries of the Pope, Monsignor Ruíz and Archbishop Diaz. A new agreement was reached on June 19, 1929, which was approved two days later by the Vatican. Although the Church question was by no means settled, a working agreement had been reached which permitted the Church once more to carry on religious services.[64]

Exactly one day before President Hoover's inauguration in 1929 a revolt broke out in Mexico and the new administration decided to utilize its power under the Arms Embargo Resolution of 1922,[65] and while supplying arms and munitions to the government it placed an embargo on all shipments to the rebels. When Secretary of State Kellogg refused to recognize the rebels as belligerents and his successor Secretary of State Stimson, refused to receive the revolutionary agent sent to Washington, the insurrection collapsed.

Throughout the Hoover administration the relations between the United States and Mexico were exceedingly friendly. J. Reuben Clark, who had been Ambassador Morrow's right-hand man, was appointed as

[63] *New York Times,* Sept. 9, 1926.

[64] Arnold Toynbee called this achievement Mr. Morrow's "greatest diplomatic triumph."

[65] 42 *U. S. Stat. at Large,* 361.

Ambassador when Mr. Morrow resigned to enter the Senate, and he ably carried on the Morrow policies. The newly elected Mexican President, Ortiz Rubio, following the precedent set by President Hoover, made a good-will visit to the United States before entering upon his official duties. His cordial reception strengthened the desire for closer coöperation on both sides of the Rio Grande.

It was during this era of good feeling that Genaro Estrada, Mexican Foreign Minister, in a statement to the press on September 30, 1930, gave utterance to a doctrine subsequently called the "Estrada Doctrine" or "Doctrina Mexicana." It was to the effect that recognition of a government should be granted automatically, regardless of the origin of the government. "The Mexican government," he declared, "does not grant recognition which implies judgment; it confines itself to the maintenance or withdrawal, as it may seem advisable, of its diplomatic agents. . . ." [66] This doctrine was erroneously stated to be a repudiation of the Monroe Doctrine, but Estrada, himself, publicly disclaimed any such intention.

It was somewhat of a paradox that although President Franklin D. Roosevelt inaugurated his administration with the Good Neighbor Policy the Mexican government was a little dubious regarding the new representative of the United States sent to Mexico City to interpret it. The appointment of Josephus Daniels to supplant J. Reuben Clark seemed a rather inauspicious beginning. Mexico had not forgotten that Mr. Daniels had been Secretary of the Navy when Vera Cruz had been shelled and occupied.[67] But since Franklin D. Roosevelt was Assistant Secretary of the Navy at the same time, to have declared Daniels *persona non grata* would have been highly inadvisable. Fortunately, Mr. Daniels manifested such an earnest desire to carry on the sympathetic and friendly policy of his predecessors that he quickly overcame the initial feelings of misgiving.

Another potential cause of trouble which had failed of satisfactory settlement over a long period of time was the question of claims. We have already mentioned the ratification of the two claims conventions of 1923.[68] The first or General Claims Convention covered claims dating back to 1868, and the other, a Special Convention, covered all claims arising during the revolutionary period 1910-1920. A third group known as the agrarian claims arose from the expropriation of American lands subsequent to August 29, 1927, under the Mexican agrarian program.

[66] *Bulletin of the Pan American Union*, Vol. 58, No. 3 (Mar., 1934), p. 161.

[67] The story is told that President Roosevelt and Mr. Daniels had completely forgotten the incident when the appointment was made.

[68] *Supra*, p. 171.

At the advent of the Roosevelt administration out of some 6,500 claims filed under the General and Special Conventions only a few hundred had been settled.[69] All agrarian claims had been excluded pending informal diplomatic discussion between the two governments.

A final settlement was first obtained in the case of the revolutionary claims. Since by 1931 the Special Claims Commission had made awards on none of the 3,176 filed, it was finally decided to make a settlement *en bloc*. By a treaty signed April 24, 1934, the revolutionary claims were to be settled by the payment of a sum proportionate to the final settlement of similar European claims.[70] The total sum was fixed at $5,448,-020.14, payable with interest by annual sums of $500,000 which were to be deposited to the credit of the United States government in January of each year. The ninth of these annual payments was made by Mexico on January 2, 1943, and payment for the revolutionary claims was made by 1945.

A new Special Claims Commission to allocate these awards was set up in 1935 and it completed its work by May, 1938. The Commission considered 2833 claims, of which 1475 were disallowed, and 1358 were allowed wholly or in part. The total amount of the awards allowed before reduction on a percentage basis was $9,135,041.79, thus giving each approved claimant 57 per cent of the original amount allowed.[71] It might be noted that the claims from the Santa Ysabel massacre which the previous commission had disallowed were awarded $92,910.[72]

In the question of recompense for the seizure of agricultural lands a spirited correspondence between the two governments ensued during the year 1938. Secretary Hull pointed out that between 1915 and 1927 one hundred sixty-one moderate-sized properties of American citizens had been taken, and subsequent to 1927 additional properties valued at more than $10 million had been expropriated. After considerable argument the Mexican government proposed that each side appoint a commissioner who should jointly determine the value of the confiscated properties by May 31, 1939, and as proof of its good intentions the Mexican government agreed to a first payment of $1 million in May, 1939.[73]

After three payments totaling $3 million had been made under this

[69] A. H. Feller, *The Mexican Claims Commissions, 1923-1934* (New York, 1935), pp. 60, 68.

[70] *U. S. Treaty Series*, No. 883.

[71] *Special Mexican Claims Commission—Report to the Secretary of State* (Washington, D. C., U. S. Government Printing Office, 1940).

[72] *Ibid.*, p. 104.

[73] S. S. Jones and D. P. Myers, *Documents on American Foreign Relations, 1938-39* (Boston, 1939), pp. 87-121.

agreement, a convention was signed in Washington on November 19, 1941, providing for a global settlement of both the argricultural claims and all claims filed by the two governments with the General Claims Commission. Under the terms of this convention Mexico agreed to pay a total sum of $40 million, $3 million at the date of ratification and the balance of $34 million by payments of $2½ million annually. It was further provided that other claims would be subject to agreements to be concluded as soon as possible.[74] As we shall see later this convention was merely one of a series of agreements covering the solution of a number of problems including the confiscation of the petroleum properties all of which were signed at this same time.

The armistice in the struggle between Church and State which Ambassador Morrow had obtained in 1929 had by no means settled this question. The Church was not reconciled to the drastic limitations imposed upon its representatives and their work and it sought assistance in the United States. Early in 1935 the Knights of Columbus were persuaded to work towards obtaining American intervention. Failing to interest Secretary Hull in such a policy, appeal was made to both houses of Congress where less discretion obtains. Representative Higgins wished to withdraw recognition, and recall Ambassador Daniels, while the resolution which Senator Borah introduced, although not so extreme, protested the antireligious campaign and practices of the Mexican government, and authorized the Committee on Foreign Relations to conduct an investigation into the situation.[75] When nothing came of this effort some 242 members of the House of Representatives petitioned President Roosevelt to take some action. When the Knights of Columbus continued the campaign to involve the United States, President Roosevelt wrote a personal letter to the Supreme Knight declaring that no American citizen in Mexico had complained during the year that his religious freedom had been interfered with and as regards Mexican citizens the United States intended to continue its policy of nonintervention.[76] Cardinal Mundelein a fortnight later eulogized President Roosevelt's foreign policy and decried self-appointed spokesmen for the Catholics in America, whereupon the agitation for intervention died down.

A more serious threat to friendly relations arose in 1937, when the Mexican government once again threatened to confiscate foreign concessions in order to nationalize the oil industry.

[74] For text of the convention see *Cong. Rec.*, Vol. 88, No. 21 (Jan. 29, 1942), p. 861.
[75] For text of the Borah Resolution see *New York Times*, Feb. 1, 1935.
[76] For text of letter see *ibid.*, Nov. 18, 1935.

The Mexican workers in the oil fields staged many strikes during the year 1937 demanding a substantial increase in pay. On December 18, 1937, the Mexican Federal Board of Conciliation and Arbitration ruled that foreign-owned oil companies must increase wages one-third and improve the pension and welfare system. Claiming that such changes meant an annual increase of operating costs of about $7,200,000, the companies sought a permanent injunction. However, the Mexican Supreme Court upheld the award and the Federal Labor Board declared the new wage scale became effective on March 7, 1938. When the companies refused to comply President Cárdenas by a degree dated March 18 announced that the oil properties would be nationalized and indemnification made within ten years. Claiming a "manifest denial of justice" the oil companies appealed to their respective governments.[77]

Secretary of State Cordell Hull issued a statement March 30 conceding the right of the Mexican government to expropriate properties within its jurisdiction but questioning the ability of the Mexican government to make adequate compensation for the large number of properties confiscated. He did hope, however, that a fair and equitable solution might be found.[78] President Cárdenas replied immediately to Ambassador Daniels that "Mexico will know how to honor its obligations of today and its obligations of yesterday." [79]

Nevertheless in spite of this rather vague assurance of compensation, the expropriation of the oil properties soon became a *cause célèbre* in the diplomatic relations of the two countries.[80] There was no question about the popularity of confiscation among the Mexican people. A celebration staged in Mexico City on March 26 brought out a quarter of a million people, and President Cárdenas received wide popular support in his effort to float an internal loan to pay for the seizure. But even with payment conceded there was a wide difference of opinion as to the value of the oil properties. The American oil companies placed their minimum value at $262 million, whereas, Mexico estimated that after paying back taxes and back compensation to workers the companies would have about $10 million coming to them.

If the expropriation was stimulating to Mexico politically it was ex-

[77] See *ibid.*, Dec. 31, 1937; Mar. 4, 8, 19, 1938.
[78] *Ibid.*, Mar. 31, 1938.
[79] *Ibid.*, Apr. 2, 1938.
[80] For the Mexican case see United States of Mexico, *The True Facts About the Expropriation of the Oil Companies' Properties in Mexico* (Mexico City, 1940). For the companies' side see Standard Oil Co., N. J., *The Reply to Mexico* (New York, 1940).

ceedingly detrimental economically. The peso dropped from 3.60 to 6 to the dollar, capital took flight, production of oil diminished, while prices received were lower. Distribution was a serious problem and no considerable market was available except in the Axis powers.[81] Skilled technicians were difficult to obtain and replacements of outworn equipment was a serious problem due to the hostile influence of the dispossessed companies.

But above all the situation was dangerous to the new development of cordial relations. The Roosevelt administration was unwilling to see the well established structure of the Good Neighbor Policy jeopardized, and it was willing and anxious to make every effort towards obtaining a fair settlement.

As a first step the United States government encouraged the companies to enter into direct negotiations with the Mexican government. Donald R. Richberg, representing the companies, had numerous conferences with President Cárdenas, and at first a compromise seemed possible.[82] When a deadlock ensued, Under Secretary Welles, on August 14, 1939, made a compromise proposal while at the same time reiterating the necessity for "adequate, effective, and prompt payment for the properties seized." [83] No action was taken on his suggestion, and on December 2, 1939, the Mexican Superior Court unanimously upheld the expropriation as constitutional both as regards movable and immovable property.[84]

The matter was reopened in 1940 by an informal memorandum delivered by Ambassador Nájera on March 16 which failed completely to meet the question at issue. In his reply of April 3, Secretary Hull again stressed the requirement of adequate and prompt compensation and pointed out that the Mexican government had been somewhat remiss hitherto in the payment of claims. He then proposed arbitration for all the questions involved by a tribunal clothed with authority not only to determine the amount to be paid but also the means to make the payment effective.[85]

In the reply of May 1, the Mexican government ruled out arbitration as incompatible in this case since the matter in dispute was domestic in nature and already nearing solution. It was also noted that a private and direct settlement had been made with the Sinclair interests which it was

[81] It has been claimed that Mexico sold about 10 million barrels to the three totalitarian powers. See A. W. MacMahon and W. R. Dittmar, "The Mexican Oil Industry Since Expropriation," *Polit. Sci. Quar.*, Vol. LVII, No. 2 (June, 1942), p. 164.

[82] Donald R. Richberg, *The Mexican Oil Seizure* (New York, n.d.).

[83] S. S. Jones and D. P. Myers, *Documents on American Foreign Relations 1939-1940* (Boston, 1940), p. 217.

[84] See Roscoe B. Gaither, *Expropriation in Mexico* (New York, 1940), Chap. VIII.

[85] Jones and Myers, *op. cit.*, pp. 234-238.

claimed represented approximately 40 per cent of the investment of American nationals in the oil industry.[86] This settlement was for $8½ million plus the delivery of 20 million barrels of oil over a four-year period at a determined price. Incidentally, the asking price of the Sinclair interests had been $32 million. Inasmuch as a presidential election was in the offing, and President Cárdenas was not up for reëlection, the principal oil companies preferred to wait and to hope for a more friendly attitude on the part of the new administration.

Various events now clearly foreshadowed a settlement. Early in November, 1940, President Cárdenas placed an embargo on oil and scrap iron going to Japan and declared that he expected an early, definite, and satisfactory settlement of all pending questions. The visit of Vice-president Wallace as President Roosevelt's special representative at the inauguration of General Avilo Camacho on December 1, 1940, was more than a friendly gesture. The fact that President Cárdenas had to ask the congress for $12,000,000 to bolster the operating deficit of the oil industry was undoubtedly a persuasive element. Finally the success of the Axis powers in overwhelming Europe and the Far East tended to cement the republics of the New World more closely together.

An understanding satisfactory to Mexico and the United States covering not only the oil question but also claims, trade, stabilization of currency, credits, and purchase of silver was announced on November 19, 1941. As regards the expropriation of petroleum properties it was agreed that each government would appoint an expert to determine the just compensation to be paid American owners whose rights and interests in the petroleum industry had been jeopardized by the acts of expropriation. Five months were allowed to fix the amount, and the Mexican government agreed to make an immediate deposit of $9 million cash on account.[87] The two experts Morris L. Cooke, representing the United States, and Manuel J. Zevada, representing Mexico, began their work in Mexico City in January, 1942, and on April 17, 1942, they reported that the valuation of the American-owned oil companies was $23,995,991. The companies were released from all claims present and future except for unpaid taxes and duties and private claims now pending.[88] Apparently the settlement was based upon a physical valuation of the properties without giving consideration to the value of the subsoil rights. According to valuations set by the companies, the payment amounted to only

[86] *Dept. of State Bull.*, Vol. 11, No. 45 (May 4, 1940), pp. 465-470.

[87] L. M. Goodrich, *Documents on American Foreign Relations 1941-1942* (Boston, 1942), Vol. IV, p. 421.

[88] *Ibid.*, p. 425.

seven cents on the dollar, and at first they refused to accept it. However since the United States government declared the evaluation to be final, the manner and conditions of payment were agreed upon by an exchange of notes on September 29, 1943. Mexico had made the $9 million cash deposit at the time of settlement and now agreed to pay the remaining $20,137,700.84 including interest, in five payments—the last on September 30, 1949. The oil companies, with no support from the government, accepted the settlement.

As to the other agreements announced on November 19, 1941, we have already discussed that of claims.[89] The third concerned the negotiation of a reciprocal trade agreement, and this was signed December 23, 1942, the fifteenth of its kind with an American republic. The other agreements were to assist Mexico in its financial position by the stabilization of the Mexican peso in terms of the dollar by the purchase of pesos, to aid silver mining by purchasing newly mined silver at thirty-five cents an ounce up to six million ounces monthly,[90] and to help finance the highway construction program in Mexico by requesting the Export-Import Bank to accept certain of these highway bonds as security for credits.[91]

Long before the United States entered the war, Mexico had given this country her whole-hearted support. At the Conferences of Panama and Havana her representatives took the lead in supporting continental solidarity and all-out measures for American defense, and even before Pearl Harbor Mexico had agreed to reciprocal use of strategic airports and bases.[92] Before going to the Rio Conference, Mexico severed diplomatic relations with the Axis and at the Conference Foreign Minister Padilla thrilled the delegates with his impassioned plea for support of the men who fell on Wake and in the Philippines "to defend human liberties and the common destiny of America."

Early in April, 1942, Foreign Minister Padilla visited the United States and on April 8 he and Under Secretary of State, Sumner Welles, issued a joint statement covering a program of close economic coöperation. Through funds obtained from the Mexican government and Export-Import Bank certain basic industries such as a steel and tin plate rolling mills were to be established to meet Mexican consumers' needs and to supply goods required by the war efforts of the United States. Arrangements were made for the survey of the Mexican railway transportation

[89] See above, p. 175.
[90] This was the most criticised agreement in the Senate because of the vast amount of unused silver already stored in the treasury vaults of the United States.
[91] Goodrich, *op. cit.*, p. 359.
[92] *U. S. Treaty Series,* No. 971.

system; experts were commissioned to explore the feasibility of constructing small cargo vessels in Mexico, and it was agreed that a high-octane gasoline plant should be constructed as soon as the necessary equipment might be spared.[93]

With the declaration of war upon the Axis powers by Mexico on May 22, 1942, the two governments entered into still closer military relationships. The 1941 agreement for the reciprocal use of air bases was enlarged, United States warships were permitted to use Mexican bases and territorial waters, and United States troops and planes could cross Mexican territory. Under lend-lease provisions Mexico was authorized to purchase war equipment to the value of approximately thirty million dollars. Through a Joint Mexican-United States Defense Commission, close liaison was established for protection of the long and exposed coast line. All Axis nationals were removed from coastal areas; financial transactions of Axis enterprises were subjected to full governmental control; and the United States black list was more rigidly enforced. The two neighbors were as one against the common foe.

As an earnest of the intention of the United States to coöperate loyally, President Franklin D. Roosevelt met President Avila Camacho in Monterrey, Mexico, in April, 1943, and the two agreed to an increased exchange of goods. During 1944 a plan of economic coöperation known as the "Mexico Plan" was developed whereby the two governments worked out jointly a unified industrial program in a single pattern rather than giving consideration to unrelated individual requests for industrial goods.

One of the most important developments towards better relations between the two countries occurred during the war period when on February 3, 1944, Mexico and the United States signed a water treaty relating to the utilization of the waters of the Colorado and Tijuana Rivers and the Rio Grande. The rapid expansion of agricultural areas along the common boundary increased the need for more water for irrigation. The treaty proposed by engineers and diplomats was based upon the principles of the Good Neighbor Policy and settled a problem which had long vexed the two governments. It provided for flood control and increased materially the amount of water available to each country for agricultural and industrial uses. Both the American and Mexican Senates approved the treaty with large majorities and ratifications were exchanged in Washington November 8, 1945, and the treaty became effective immediately.

[93] *Dept. of State Bull.*, Vol. VI, No. 41 (Apr. 11, 1942), p. 325.

One of the problems which still faces the two countries is a product of World War II. The need for workers to harvest crops and help in the maintenance of railroads in the Western states during the war was met by annual agreements for the temporary immigration of Mexican workers (*braceros*) into the United States. Elaborate guarantees as to wages and conditions of labor were embodied in the agreements and the results were mutually satisfactory. However, after the war a large number of Mexican laborers known as "wetbacks" (having swum the Rio Grande) entered the United States illegally and such persons were exploited by certain farm interests. It was alleged that many thousands of these laborers came in annually and produced a situation unfair to American labor.

A diplomatic incident occurred in 1948 when the Mexican Secretary of Foreign Affairs sent a note to Washington protesting the action of the American Immigration Service which allowed some 4000 "braceros" to cross the border illegally to be employed by American farmers. The United States claimed that Mexico had failed to send the number of "braceros" agreed upon, and Mexico replied that workers were forbidden to go to the United States because of discriminatory practices which were being permitted. The United States finally sent a formal apology and the incident was considered closed.

In 1950-1951 an effort was made by a mixed commission representing the United States and Mexico to prepare an acceptable accord in treaty form covering the temporary immigration of Mexican workers. A compromise was worked out, but it would run only through 1952. Meanwhile the United States Congress in 1952 passed legislation strengthening control over the "wetbacks" and fairer and more effective regulation of the *braceros* was instituted.

The problem seems to have been temporarily settled by an agreement signed March 10, 1954, which renewed the Migratory Labor Agreement of 1951, and which will run until December 31, 1955. This not only clarified the 1951 agreement but also changed it to prevent the flow of illegal workers into the United States. President Eisenhower declared that the basic purpose of the agreement was to enable the United States to give Mexican migratory labor the protection of its laws.[94] However many thousands of "wetbacks" still remain in the United States and in the first quarter of 1954 from 700 to 2000 illegal entrants were being shipped back to Mexico daily. Over a million "wetbacks" were deported in 1953.

Another problem which faced the two countries had a more satisfactory ending. When *aftosa*, hoof and mouth disease, attacked Mexican cattle

[94] *Dept. of State Bull.*, Vol. XXX, No. 770 (March 29, 1954), pp. 467-8.

and sheep in 1947, it threatened the cattle industry in the United States. At first it was proposed to shoot the diseased cattle and recompense the owners. The United States aided with experts and cash but the Mexicans resented the procedure. The next procedure attempted was quarantine and vaccination. It was a stupendous job, but after some 17 million animals were vaccinated, the United States having contributed over $150 million to the cost, by the fall of 1952 the disease was eradicated.

President Truman carried on the friendly policy initiated by his predecessor. On March 3, 1947, he made the first official visit to Mexico City ever made by an American president and the following month President Alemán returned the visit and in a special joint session of the Congress he promised an effective continuation of the Good Neighbor Policy on both sides of the border. One concrete example of the desire to cement the "Era of Good Feeling" was shown by the two governments' decision in 1950 to restore battle flags captured by each other in the War of 1847.

Although it is somewhat premature to evaluate the policies of President Adolfo Ruiz Cortines, elected in July, 1952, and President Dwight Eisenhower, elected in November, 1952, the two presidents have already met personally and promised to coöperate loyally. The occasion of their meeting was the dedication on October 19, 1953, of the Falcon Dam on the Rio Grande seventy-five miles down from Laredo. This vast structure five miles long and built at a cost of some $47 million, of which the United States contributed 58.6 per cent and Mexico 41.4 per cent, could be mutually advantageous to the two countries in regard to irrigation, flood control, and the development of power. President Eisenhower declared that the project had given the world "a lesson in the way neighbor nations can and should live—in peace, in mutual respect, in common prosperity." President Ruiz Cortines called the project "the tangible result of that friendly spirit which it is our duty to maintain and to make universal."

In concluding this chapter, a few facts must be given indicating the great importance of Mexico both in its natural resources and in its trade possibilities. In size, Mexico ranks fourth among the twenty-one American republics, having an area of approximately 767,000 square miles, which means a territory almost as large as the United States east of the Mississippi. In natural resources, Mexico is one of the richest countries in the world in proportion to its area. Its mineral resources easily take first place, and silver, gold, copper, lead, and mineral oils are found in almost unlimited quantities. Taxes were paid on more than 30,000 mining properties in 1910, and the mineral output for the year 1909-1910 was between $80 million and $90 million. Mexico has long been renowned for her famous silver mines; in 1803 Humboldt calculated that Mexico had produced, even at that time, silver valued at more than $1,750,000,000. During the period from 1788 to 1810 the Valencia mine in Guanajuato produced annually almost $1½ million worth of silver, while from 1800 to 1804 the Catorce mine in San Luis Potosí produced more than $10 million worth of bullion. Recent figures show a greatly increasing output. The highest silver production seems to have been in 1930, when it reached a value of over $105 million. The gold output for the same year was valued at about $13,860,000.

It is, however, the oil deposits that have been Mexico's most prolific source of wealth during the past decades. In 1910, about 3,300,000 barrels of petroleum were exported; in 1915 this rose to almost 33,000,000 barrels, and in 1920 to about 155,000,000 barrels. In 1915 Mexico produced less than 8 per cent of the world's petroleum; in 1920, more than 25 per cent. Although the effect of subsequent stringent legislation on the oil companies is shown by the fact that whereas in 1935 the world production reached the all time high of over a billion and a half barrels, the Mexican oil fields only furnished 40 million barrels, or about 2½ per cent of the world's output; nevertheless, the value of its reserves and potential production are still of great significance in the world's need of raw materials. Although expropriation reduced production to some 35 million barrels during 1942 and 1943, by 1947 production had passed 50 million barrels, and by 1952 it had reached 80 million.

Mexico and the United States are good customers of each other, and before 1914 about 50 per cent of Mexico's imports and about 75 per cent of its exports were from and to the United States. Immediately following the war there was an increase in the percentage of imports from the United States and the exports to the United States increased still more rapidly.

With the coming of the depression and the period of high tariffs the trade dropped very rapidly and the lowest point was reached during 1932 and 1933. The figures for the total trade between the United States and Mexico for the years 1920, 1935, 1940, and 1950, as given by the Foreign Commerce Yearbooks are as follows:

MEXICAN TRADE WITH THE UNITED STATES

	1920	1935	1940	1950
Imports from U. S.	$207,854,197	$65,574,000	$96,940,000	$409,613,000
Exports to U. S.	180,191,075	42,467,000	75,780,000	433,186,000

Although the 1940 figures amount in value to less than half of those in 1920, the trend is decidedly upward, and 1950 and 1952 showed a considerable increase over 1920.[95] The *percentage* of Mexico's trade with the United States which in 1940 furnished about 80 per cent of her imports and took almost 90 per cent of her exports was also on the increase.

Even though the foreign trade of the entire world has suffered grievously during the past few years, the internal conditions existing in Mexico during the past two decades have been an added liability, both to the country's purchasing power and to the utilization of its national wealth and resources. It is manifest that an immense commercial increase would be possible if a government were established which, while carefully protecting the sovereign rights of Mexico and safeguarding the interests of its citizens, could, by encouraging the legitimate investment of foreign capital, utilize a greater part of the vast riches of the country for the benefit of its citizens. But although Mexico realizes well enough that foreign capital alone has the magic power to open up the fabled riches of her mineral wealth, this genie, once summoned, is very difficult to control; and it is at this point that the United States can aid both Mexico and herself by continuing to maintain a generous, broadminded policy towards her economically weaker neighbor to the south. Such a policy must be based upon an attitude of friendly coöperation rather than upon selfish exploitation; but it is to be hoped that Mexican statesmen may be sufficiently far-seeing to realize that it can be ultimately successful only when based upon justice and fair dealing on both sides of the Rio Grande.

SUPPLEMENTARY READINGS

CARLETON BEALS, *Mexican Maze* (New York, 1931).
E. I. BELL, *The Political Shame of Mexico* (New York, 1914).
G. H. BLAKESLEE, ed., *Mexico and the Caribbean* (New York, 1920).
F. BULNES, *The Whole Truth About Mexico* (New York, 1916).
MANUEL CALERO, *Un decenio de política mexicana* (Mexico, 1920).
TOMME CLARK CALL, *The Mexican Venture* (New York, 1953).
J. M. CALLAHAN, *American Foreign Policy in Mexican Relations* (New York, 1932).
WILFRID H. CALLCOTT, *Liberalism in Mexico* (Stanford University, 1931).
STUART CHASE, *Mexico, a Study of Two Americas* (New York, 1931).
HOWARD FRANCIS CLINE, *The United States and Mexico* (Cambridge, 1953).
GEORGE CREEL, *The People Next Door* (New York, 1926).
JOSEPHUS DANIELS, *Shirt Sleeve Diplomat* (Chapel Hill, 1947).

[95] Official figures from the Statistical Abstract of the United States for 1952 place Mexico's imports from the U. S. at $666,429,000 and her exports to the U. S. at $410,579,000.

E. J. Dillon, *Mexico on the Verge* (New York, 1921).

Frederick Sherwood Dunn, *The Diplomatic Protection of Americans in Mexico* (New York, 1933).

A. H. Feller, *The Mexican Claims Commissions, 1923-1934* (New York, 1935).

T. E. Gibbon, *Mexico under Carranza* (Garden City, N. Y., 1919).

Wendell C. Gordon, *The Expropriation of Foreign Owned Property in Mexico* (Washington, D. C., 1941).

E. Gruening, *Mexico and Its Heritage* (New York, 1928).

S. G. Inman, *Intervention in Mexico* (New York, 1919).

C. Lloyd Jones, *Mexico and Its Reconstruction* (New York, 1921).

Betty Kirk, *Covering the Mexican Front* (Norman, Okla., 1942).

R. H. K. Marett, *An Eye Witness of Mexico* (London, 1939).

Harold Nicolson, *Dwight Morrow* (New York, 1935).

T. Esquivel Obregon, *México y Los Estatos Unidos ante el Derecho Internacional* (Mexico, 1926).

Virginia Prewett, *Reportage on Mexico* (New York, 1941).

H. I. Priestly, *The Mexican Nation* (New York, 1923).

J. F. Rippy, *The United States and Mexico* (New York, 1926).

J. Fernandez Rojas, *De Porfirio Diaz a Victoriano Huerta* (Mexico, 1913).

Frank Tannenbaum, *The Struggle for Peace and Bread* (New York, 1950).

Charles A. Thomson, "Mexico's Challenge to Foreign Capital," *Foreign Policy Reports,* Vol. XIII, No. 11 (Aug. 15, 1937).

William C. Townsend, *Lázaro Cárdenas: Mexican Democrat* (Ann Arbor, 1952).

E. D. Trowbridge, *Mexico To-day and To-morrow* (New York, 1919).

Nathaniel and Sylvia Weyl, *The Reconquest of Mexico* (New York, 1939).

R. de Zayas, *The Case of Mexico* (New York, 1914).

❦ 9 ❦

Colonial Cuba
and Its International Relations

THE American colonies had hardly gained their independence before the new republic stretching along the North Atlantic seaboard felt the growing pains of expansion. With a vast expanse of desirable territory spreading westward, ever beckoning to the adventurous hunter and farmer, it is not strange that the newly established nation should continue to look westward for remoter frontiers. The opening up of the great Northwest Territory and its early division into states gave added stimulus. When, furthermore, Napoleon succeeded in gaining control of the extensive Louisiana territory for France, the eyes of the American statesmen were turned south as well as west. In 1802 President Jefferson declared that the day that France takes possession of New Orleans "we must marry ourselves to the British fleet and nation"; [1] and when General Le Clerc's disastrous campaign in Haiti forced Napoleon's hand, the President was quick to seize the opportunity. Strict constructionist though he was in domestic policies, he realized that he must be an opportunist abroad. If Paris was worth a mass, surely Louisiana justified straining the Constitution.

The Floridas were regarded as of even greater importance to the United States than the Louisiana territory, and it was with the purpose of obtaining the Floridas that Livingston set out on his memorable mission in 1801. After Louisiana was obtained, including West Florida, according to the interpretation of the purchasers, it was merely a question of time before east Florida would fall into the orbit of the rapidly expanding republic. In fact, in 1811 Congress authorized President Madison to use

[1] P. L. Ford, ed., *The Writings of Thomas Jefferson*, 10 vols. (New York, 1892-1899), Vol. VIII, p. 145.

the army and navy to seize and occupy all or any part of east Florida.[2] But the need was hardly sufficient to proceed to this extremity, and in 1819 Spain was finally persuaded to cede the Floridas and all title to lands that the United States claimed as an integral part of the Louisiana Purchase.

A mere glance at the map of the Caribbean shows the strategic importance of Cuba to the country that possesses New Orleans and Florida. It also shows the interest which a nation possessing the Bahamas and Jamaica would have in seeing to it that Cuba should not fall into the hands of a dangerous rival. Therefore, from the beginning of the nineteenth century the United States and Great Britain continued to cast watchful eyes upon each other, lest the Pearl of the Antilles should slip from the ever-weakening grasp of Spain into the outstretched arms of a more dangerous rival.

The importance of the island of Cuba to the United States in the formative period of American foreign policy is perhaps best expressed by Secretary J. Q. Adams in a note dated April 28, 1823, to the American minister in Spain:

These islands [Cuba and Puerto Rico] from their local position are natural appendages to the North American continent, and one of them (Cuba) almost in sight of our shores, from a multitude of considerations has become an object of transcendent importance to the commercial and political interests of our Union. Its commanding position, with reference to the Gulf of Mexico and the West Indian Seas; the character of its population; its situation midway between our southern coast and the island of St. Domingo; its safe and capacious harbor of Havana, fronting a long line of our shores destitute of the same advantage; the nature of its productions and its wants furnishing the supplies and needing the returns of a commerce immensely profitable and mutually beneficial, give it an importance in the sum of our national interests with which that of no other country can be compared. Such indeed are between the interests of that island and of this country, the geographical, commercial, moral, and political relations, . . . that in looking forward to the probable course of events for the short period of half a century it is scarcely possible to resist the conviction that the annexation of Cuba to our Federal Republic will be indispensable to the continuance and integrity of the Union itself.[3]

In the same despatch Mr. Adams pointed out that if the control of Spain was terminated Cuba must look either to the United States or Great Britain. The government of the United States had been confidentially informed that Great Britain was so eager to obtain Cuba that she

---

[2] *Amer. State Papers, For. Rel.,* Vol. III, p. 571.
[3] J. B. Moore, *Digest of Int. Law,* Vol. VI, p. 380.

had offered Gibraltar in exchange. Whether or not this was true, "the transfer of Cuba to Great Britain would be an event unpropitious to the interests of the Union." [4] That Great Britain was not ignorant of the American attitude is shown by a sentence from the diary of Lord Ellenborough, a member of Wellington's cabinet, dated February 8, 1830: "The Americans declared they could not see with indifference any state other than Spain in possession of Cuba." [5] In fact, as early as 1819, when there was some talk in London of the British taking over Cuba, Mr. Rush, the American minister, asked Lord Castlereagh about these reports, but the latter denied any knowledge of such developments. [6] In 1823, when Canning was specially interested in obtaining the coöperation of the United States, he denied emphatically that England desired Cuba. [7] He by no means implied, however, that his government would look with equanimity upon such a desire on the part of the United States.

France also still had certain interests in the Caribbean region; for, though Guadeloupe and Martinique were very small relics of her once glorious trans-Atlantic empire, the nation that had so recently disposed of Louisiana, and that, during her long occupation of Haiti, had been Cuba's nearest island neighbor, could not be expected to lose all interest in this region of buried hopes. The *London Times* in 1825 accurately characterized Cuba as "the Turkey of trans-Atlantic politics, tottering to its fall, and kept from falling only by the struggles of those who are contending for the right of catching her in her descent."

Although the United States' real interest in Cuba dates from her possession of Florida, the earlier history of the island was associated with that of the mainland closely enough to warrant a brief sketch of Cuban history. Discovered by Columbus on his first voyage in 1492, the island was taken possession of in the name of the King of Spain, and named Maria. But its Indian name, Cuba, persisted, and the Spaniards finally adopted it. The Indians themselves were speedily exterminated by merciless treatment of the Spanish *conquistadores*.

During the sixteenth and seventeenth centuries the island was of little importance to Spain except as a naval base. In fact, it was a liability rather than an asset, owing to its use as a rendezvous by pirates and freebooters, and also the great difficulty that Spain found in protecting it against the English, French, and Dutch buccaneers. The French burned Havana in 1538, and again partially destroyed the city in 1554. The

[4] *Ibid.*, p. 383.
[5] *Ibid.*, p. 56.
[6] J. M. Callahan, *Cuba and International Relations* (Baltimore, 1899), p. 196.
[7] *Ibid.*, p. 199.

English navigator Drake threatened the island in 1585; but, although his thirty ships passed close to the harbor, and all Havana was prepared to resist the attack, no attempt at landing was made. In the following year the French fired upon Santiago, landed their forces, and looted the town. Philip II finally realized that Cuba deserved more consideration than merely to be utilized as a strategic base for the exploitation of Mexico, and he constructed the great forts of Punta and Morro to protect his "bulwark of the Indies, key to the New World" against the "corsair-caked Caribbean." [8]

But even the famous Morro Castle was not strong enough to save Cuba from the intrepid British in the Seven Years' War. In 1762 the Earl of Albemarle with 10,000 troops from England and 4,000 from the North American colonies, laid siege to the stronghold, and after more than a month of mining and sapping took it by assault. Although the capture came in the "sun-setting time of the age of plunder," it was estimated that treasure and property to the value of about $16 million were obtained. It was of even greater importance to Great Britain since she now held the key to both Mexico and Louisiana. Yet, in spite of Cuba's manifest value, by the treaty of Paris, signed February 10, 1763, England returned the island to Spain and received in exchange Florida, which, as Pitt declared at the time, was certainly no equivalent. As one imaginative writer put it, "But for that, Washington and his associates might have failed—the French Revolution might have been postponed—and the House of Hanover at this moment have been ruling over the present United States." [9]

If Spain made a good bargain with her enemy England, she made an even better one with her ally France, whose king out of his generous heart unconditionally ceded to Spain the Louisiana territory. Cuba was now of the greatest strategic and economic importance to Spain, and Havana, which during the short British occupation was opened to the trade routes of the world, was once more closed. Nevertheless, in the short period of English control Cuba had tasted of the forbidden fruit of free trade, and the experience was never forgotten.

During the American war of independence Spain was drawn in by France against England, but her interest in the American colonies was purely selfish, as is shown by the instructions given by the governor-

---

[8] For an interesting and authoritative narrative of this period of Cuban history see I. A. Wright, *The Early History of Cuba, 1492-1586* (New York, 1916).

[9] Anon., "The Conquest of Cuba," *Atlantic Monthly*, Vol. XII (Oct., 1863), pp. 462-475.

general of Cuba to an agent, urging upon Congress the capture of St. Augustine, Florida, in order that it might be restored to Spain.[10] Later, when Jay appeared at Madrid seeking a treaty granting free navigation of the Mississippi, he was not even granted official recognition. However, before peace was signed, in 1783, Spain showed herself more liberal towards her West Indian possessions than Great Britain, for both Havana and Santiago were opened to foreign commerce. In fact, the commercial code of 1778, which opened nine ports of entry in Spain and twenty-four in her colonies, was a model of liberality for the time.

The French Revolution made the trade between the West Indies and the American colonies exceedingly brisk, but Cuba was not to pass unscathed through the period that followed. A French squadron blockaded the island in 1794 and caused much hardship to the inhabitants. During the Napoleonic era Cuba was threatened alternately by Great Britain and France, and when by the treaty of San Ildefonso, signed October 1, 1800, Napoleon recovered Louisiana and then sent an expedition to Santo Domingo, well might Jefferson feel that France could no longer remain our "natural friend." Spain had equal cause for alarm. Napoleon could hardly confine his operations to Santo Domingo, with Cuba at his mercy, nor be content with Louisiana, when the wealth of Mexico lay at his feet. Both the United States and Spain had reason to feel thankful over his forced change in plans, for the failure of the expedition against Santo Domingo, and the prospect of an immediate rupture with England, gave Louisiana to the United States and gave Spain a new lease on her colonies. But, as Mr. Slidell declared in 1859, "From the day we acquired Louisiana the attention of our able statesmen was fixed on Cuba. What the possession of the mouth of the Mississippi had been to the people of the west, that of Cuba became to the nation." [11]

We have noted the increasing interest that the United States felt in Cuba after being assured of the possession of the Floridas, as shown by the instructions given by John Quincy Adams to our minister in Spain. Jefferson also, in a note to President Monroe dated October 24, 1823, indicated his feeling on the subject: "I candidly confess that I have ever looked on Cuba as the most interesting addition which could ever be made to our system of states. The control which, with Florida Point, this island would give us over the Gulf of Mexico, and the countries and isthmus bordering on it, would fill up the measure of our political well

---

[10] Francis Wharton, *Diplomatic Correspondence of the American Revolution* (Washington, D. C., 1889), Vol. III, pp. 412-415.

[11] *Sen. Rep. No. 351*, 35th Cong., 2nd Sess., p. 1.

being." [12] Therefore at this period, when the Spanish colonies in Mexico and South America had virtually established their independence, and when the United States had received trustworthy information that Cuba also was planning a revolt with the purpose of seeking admission to the Union, American statesmen saw the need of great diplomatic caution. When Calhoun urged the acceptance of the Cuban proposal, Adams wisely opposed on the ground that it might mean war with England. It would be wiser, he thought, to say "that our relations with Spain would not allow us to encourage such a proposal." [13] In fact, at a cabinet meeting March 17, 1823, when President Monroe proposed to offer to Great Britain a mutual promise not to take Cuba, both Adams and Calhoun opposed.[14]

The European situation soon worked itself out in such a way that both Great Britain and France were forced to declare themselves in regard to Spanish possessions in America. Although by the fall of 1823 French armies were in full control of Spain, Canning had already notified them "that, as England disclaimed all intention of appropriating to herself the smallest portion of the late Spanish possessions in America, she also felt satisfied that no attempt would be made by France to bring any of them under her dominion either by conquest or by cession from Spain." [15] Great Britain was apparently as anxious concerning the ultimate fate of the Spanish colonies as was the United States. In August of the same year Canning made his famous proposal to the American minister concerning a joint declaration looking towards recognition, to include a definite statement that neither nation aimed at the acquisition of any portion of the Spanish possessions itself, and that neither could see any portion of those possessions transferred to any other power with indifference. Although Adams was unwilling to join with Great Britain in exactly the manner specified, the message of President Monroe, dated December 2, 1823, showed clearly enough our stand in regard to European intervention. Cuba and Puerto Rico were saved to Spain, but, by the same token, her other possessions were irretrievably lost.

When, in 1825, Mexico and Colombia proposed a joint action against Cuba, the United States did all in her power to save the island for Spain. Clay gave Poinsett, our minister to Mexico, instructions indicating clearly that, while the United States was not looking to the acquisition of Cuba,

[12] Ford, op. cit., Vol. X, p. 278.
[13] Callahan, op. cit., p. 125.
[14] Memoirs of John Quincy Adams (Philadelphia, 1874-1877), Vol. VI, p. 138.
[15] F. E. Chadwick, The Relations of the United States and Spain, Diplomacy (New York, 1909), p. 178.

yet if the island was to become a dependency of any one of the American states, its geographical position proclaimed that it should be attached to the United States.[16] Mr. Everett, the new minister to Spain, was also instructed to point out to the government at Madrid the danger of continuing a hopeless war against the revolted colonies if it desired to keep possession of Cuba and Puerto Rico.[17] Clay even went so far as to instruct Mr. Middleton, our minister to Russia, to urge the Czar to use his influence with Ferdinand VII to the end that Spain might sacrifice her pride and make peace, thereby saving these valuable islands.

A large French fleet touched at Havana in August, 1825, and caused much anxiety among the powers, which were particularly interested in maintaining the *status quo* in the West Indies. Canning wrote to the British minister at Paris that "as to Cuba you cannot too soon, or too amicably, of course, represent to Villèle the impossibility of our allowing France (or France us, I presume) to meddle in the internal affairs of that colony. We sincerely wish it to remain with the mother country.... The Americans (Yankees, I mean) think of this matter just as I do."[18] Clay wrote in a similar vein to Mr. Brown, the American minister at Paris, that the United States "could not consent to the occupation of those islands by any other European power than Spain under any contingency whatever."[19] Canning once more tried to inveigle the United States into coöperating with Europe by proposing a tripartite agreement between Great Britain, France and the United States, disclaiming any intention of occupying Cuba. But Clay felt that the proposal might encourage Spain to continue her hopeless struggle.[20] Inasmuch as France also refused to participate, the matter was dropped.

It was during this same year (1825) that the question arose of the participation of the United States in the Congress of Panama. Although President Adams and Secretary Clay heartily supported the project, the Senate was not so enthusiastic, and the arguments of its members against "this new and untried experiment of a congress of nations" shows a marked resemblance to more recent diatribes on a similar subject. Among other objections raised was the possibility that a discussion of the probable destiny of the islands of Cuba and Puerto Rico might be forced

[16] W. R. Manning, *Early Diplomatic Relations between the United States and Mexico* (Baltimore, 1916), p. 105.

[17] *Ibid.*, p. 108.

[18] E. J. Stapleton, *Official Correspondence of George Canning* (London, 1887), Vol. I, p. 275.

[19] *Amer. State Papers, For. Rel.*, Vol. V, p. 855.

[20] A. G. Stapleton, *Political Life of Canning* (London, 1831), Vol. III, p. 154.

upon the United States. As long as the war between Spain and the colonies continued, the United States must preserve its independence of action; the mere participation in such a congress would interfere with the influence that the United States now possessed as an interested but impartial third party.[21] In fact, one of the objects of the Congress as indicated by the government of Colombia was: "To consider the conditions of the island of Puerto Rico and Cuba; the expediency of a combined force to free them from the Spanish yoke; and the proportion of troops which each state should contribute for that purpose; and to determine whether the islands shall be united to either of the confederated states or be left at liberty to choose their own government." [22]

The slavery question also entered prominently into the discussion, for if Cuba and Puerto Rico were freed, slavery would be abolished there, as it had been in the other liberated colonies, and such a prospect was unendurable to representatives from the southern states. In fact, during the next twenty-five years the American policy of maintaining the *status quo* in the West Indies, and of guaranteeing the sovereignty of Spain over the islands of Cuba and Puerto Rico, was based upon the fear of independence for the islands—including, as it would, the freeing of the slaves—almost as much as upon the fear of aggression on the part of Great Britain or France.

The annexation of Texas in 1845 increased the interest of the United States in Cuba, and in December of that year, a resolution was introduced in the Senate, authorizing the President to negotiate with Spain for the cession of Cuba to the United States. Early in the following year a similar resolution came up in the House. The war with Mexico and the resulting increase of territory to the United States kindled Polk's ardor for expansion, and Cuba offered an excellent outlet. In a long despatch (June 17, 1848) to Mr. Saunders, our minister to Spain, Secretary Buchanan enumerated the manifest advantages that would accrue to the United States from the possession of Cuba: possession of a naval station at Havana would enable us to command the Gulf of Mexico; under American control the island would become exceedingly prosperous and serve as a most profitable market; it would increase the strength and security of the Union, and it would give the United States "a free trade on a more extended scale than any which the world had ever witnessed." Nor would the advantages accrue solely to the United States. Cuba, appreciating

[21] See *Report of the Sen. Com. on For. Affairs.* This report, with other diplomatic documents, may be found in the *Historical Appendix, International American Conference, Sen. Ex. Doc. No. 232, 51st Cong., 1st Sess., Vol. IV, pp. 53 ff.*

[22] *British and Foreign State Papers,* Vol. XII, p. 894.

the advantage of annexation, was ready to rush into our arms. Spain must realize the distracted condition of the island and the danger of a successful revolution; else the island might be wrested from her by Great Britain. Under these circumstances, "the President has arrived at the conclusion that Spain might be willing to transfer the island to the United States for a fair and full consideration." The maximum price stipulated was $100 million.[23] Mr. Saunders was, however, given to understand that Spain, "sooner than see the island transferred to any power, would prefer to see it sunk in the ocean."

Failing to acquire the Pearl of the Antilles by peaceful means, certain ardent spirits in the United States were willing to compass it by a mode less justifiable. The discovery of gold in California showed the value of the isthmus in giving an almost all-water route to the west. But the ultimate possession of such a route made the possession of Cuba all the more necessary to protect it. The slave states were more than ever desirous of securing additional territory open to slavery. Therefore it is not surprising that when a Cuban patriot, Narciso López, attempted to recruit an expedition on American soil to free Cuba, he found much assistance in high quarters. A Venezuelan by birth, López had served in the Spanish army, had played a considerable part in Spanish politics, and had finally been made governor of Trinidad. Losing office through a turn of the political wheel, he engaged in business in Cuba, but with little success. In 1848 he attempted to stage a revolt near Cienfuegos, but the plot was disclosed and López was forced to flee the country. He went to New York and started the preparation of an expedition which should have the prestige of a great name at the head. Both Jefferson Davis and Robert E. Lee were approached, and when they refused López decided to lead the expedition himself. He had little difficulty in collecting the nucleus of a force, but a proclamation by President Taylor, issued August 11, 1849, warning all American citizens against participation in such enterprises, had a deterrent effect. The two vessels in which the expedition planned to leave New York were seized by the authorities, though the filibusters themselves were not held.

López' next expedition was in the beginning somewhat more successful. Some 750 men were collected, and in the spring of 1850 they succeeded in sailing from New Orleans in three vessels, making a landing at Cardenas. Failing to receive the assistance expected from the natives, and faced with an openly mutinous crew, López was forced to return to Key West. Upon information lodged by a Spanish war-ship which had followed

[23] Moore, *op. cit.*, Vol. I, pp. 584-587.

the expedition, the boat was seized and López was arrested. Sufficient evidence to convict the leader of violating the neutrality laws was not forthcoming.

A third (and last) expedition, which left New Orleans the following year, was even less fortunate, and its results were far more serious. A proclamation by President Fillmore on April 25, 1851, stating that persons who violated our neutrality laws not only would be subject to the penalties of our own laws, but would forfeit all claims to protection, had no effect.[24] The expedition, consisting of about 400 eager adventurers, sailed from New Orleans without clearance, August 3, 1851. A landing was made at Bahía Honda, whence López, with most of the troops, advanced to Las Pozas, where it was hoped an uprising would take place. Meanwhile, Colonel Crittenden, a former American army officer who had served creditably in the Mexican War, was left with a small force in command of the baggage. Attacked by an overwhelming force, Crittenden attempted to escape by sea, but, with fifty of his followers, he was captured by the Spanish and carried to Havana. Here the unfortunate filibusters were given a quick military trial and shot as pirates. López and his force withstood several serious attacks, but, obtaining no assistance from the natives, they were finally routed and dispersed. Some were shot on the spot, others were taken prisoners; López himself was publicly garroted. It was apparent enough that Cuba was not yet prepared to fight for independence. Nevertheless, the execution of Crittenden and his men aroused such a wave of hostility towards Spain and Spanish rule in Cuba that riots broke out in New Orleans and Key West, and throughout the United States the feeling was born that Cuba must be freed, even though it should take all the forces of the United States to accomplish it.[25]

Expeditions of this sort were looked upon with warm disapproval by Great Britain and France, as well as Spain, and there were rumors, in the autumn of 1851, that a treaty had been entered into between France, Spain, and Great Britain to guarantee Cuba to Spain.[26] On April 23, 1852, at the request of Spain, Great Britain and France again invited the United States to enter into a triple agreement disclaiming all intentions of obtaining possession of Cuba.[27] Webster replied that not only did the United States have no designs upon Cuba itself, but it was willing to assist Spain in preserving it. At the same time, the United States could not

[24] *Ibid.*, Vol. III, p. 788.
[25] For an authoritative and detailed account of the López expedition see Robert G. Caldwell, *The López Expedition to Cuba* (Princeton, N. J., 1915).
[26] Moore, *op. cit.*, Vol. VI, p. 458.
[27] *Sen. Ex. Doc., No. 13*, 32nd Cong., 2nd Sess., p. 7.

acquiesce in its cession to a European power.[28] In July the matter was again brought forward by the British and French governments, but Webster's death intervened, and the duty of answering fell to Edward Everett, the new Secretary of State. He replied in an able fashion. He pointed out that Cuba was mainly an American question. It commanded the approach to the Gulf of Mexico; it barred the entrance of the Mississippi; and it stood at the doorway of our intercourse with California by the isthmus route. The United States could not bind herself indefinitely as to her future relations with the island—"it would be as easy to throw a dam from Cape Florida to Cuba in hope of stopping the flow of the Gulf Stream as to attempt by a compact like this to fix the fortunes of Cuba now and hereafter." [29] The invitation was respectfully declined.

Such an answer did not mean that the United States looked favorably upon filibustering expeditions. In fact, the note stated that the President had thrown the whole force of his constitutional power against all illegal attacks upon the island. But were there not justifiable means? The Pierce administration, which came into power in 1853, was expected to find and use them. It was "our manifest destiny to move on with the world of progress," and if Cuba impeded our march, acquisition presented no terrors. The appointment as our minister to Spain of Pierre Soulé—a man who had openly lauded López and had urged the government not to delay too long in plucking the Cuban fruit from the Spanish tree—showed that not even diplomatic amenities were to be preserved in our methods.

Hardly had Soulé arrived at his post before he was forced to demand redress for the unfriendly treatment accorded the *Black Warrior*, an American steamship calling at Havana. For some time relations between the United States and Spain had been strained by the autocratic and hostile methods employed by the captain-general of Cuba towards American merchantmen. In 1852 the *Crescent City* was refused a landing, on the ground that its purser had written an article derogatory to the government of the island. In the following year, on a flimsy excuse, the *Ohio* was refused the landing privilege. In the case of the *Black Warrior* the entire cargo of cotton was confiscated because the ship's manifest had the cotton entered as "ballast." This had been done regularly, in accordance with the instructions of the collector, on previous occasions, since the cargo was merely in transit. On this particular occasion the authorities declared the method illegal, and when the captain refused

[28] *Ibid.*, p. 8.
[29] Moore, *op. cit.*, Vol. VI, p. 469. The correspondence has been published in pamphlet form by Little, Brown & Co. (1853) under the title, *Correspondence on the Proposed Tripartite Convention*.

to discharge his cargo, the Spanish authorities took over the boat and did it for him. The United States was aroused, and Soulé was authorized to demand a prompt disavowal of the act and an indemnity of $300,000 for damages done to the owners. Soulé presented the demand, and when several days passed without an answer, he put his demands in a more forcible manner, giving the Spanish government forty-eight hours in which to comply. This note provoked a curt rejoinder on the part of the Spanish Minister of Foreign Affairs. Before the situation became more serious, however, a settlement was patched up between the owners of the vessel and the Cuban authorities.[30]

In the United States the whole affair was closely bound up with the question of slavery. The southern states were anxious to obtain Cuba, and were willing to go so far, if necessary, as to make the affair a pretext for war with Spain. Although Pierce was not disposed to proceed to extremities, he was desirous of obtaining Cuba, and he had already sent Soulé confidential instructions giving him full powers to negotiate for its purchase. Spain apparently would make no reparation for the insult to the American flag. But Marcy, the Secretary of State, considered it "less important to settle an account with Spain as to the past than to make satisfactory arrangements for the future." [31] As the best means of making such arrangements, he suggested that Soulé confer with the American representatives in Paris and London. This proposal resulted in a conference at Ostend, Belgium, participated in by the three ministers, who embodied the results of their deliberations in the famous "Ostend manifesto."

This document is one of the curiosities of American diplomacy. In its fervid style, its astonishing proposals, and its naïve excuses it stands unrivaled. Not merely does it point out the value of the island to the United States, and reasons why it should be obtained, but it indicates the advantages that would accrue to Spain through its sale, even going so far as to suggest to her ways of spending the money received. "But if Spain, dead to the voice of her own interests, and actuated by stubborn pride and a false sense of honor, should refuse to sell Cuba to the United States, . . . then by every law, human and divine, we shall be justified in wresting it from Spain, if we possess the power." [32] Naturally, Pierce was forced to ignore an invitation to become a party to any such international hold-up game as this, and Soulé, who undoubtedly was

[30] For the correspondence concerning the *Black Warrior* affair see *House Ex. Doc. No. 93*, 33rd Cong., 2nd Sess., Vol. 10, pp. 30-120.

[31] *Ibid.*, p. 123.

[32] *Ibid.*, pp. 127-132.

chiefly responsible for the document, threw up his position in disgust. An American diplomatic official at Paris aptly remarked that Soulé sought Cuba for "manifest destiny," Mason for the Southern Confederacy, and Buchanan for the presidency. Despite the fact that Buchanan obtained the presidency and continued to urge the purchase of Cuba, the slavery question was now too closely tied up with the Cuban problem to permit of the island's purchase, even though Spain were willing. "Manifest destiny" was shackled by the growing opposition to slavery.

In the following decade, as Cuba became of steadily diminishing importance in American affairs, its relations with the mother country grew more serious. When Napoleon seized control of the government in Spain, the Cuban provincial council showed its fidelity by taking an oath to preserve the island for its legitimate sovereign. Instead of rewarding the "ever-faithful isle" for its devotion, the restored Bourbons in 1825 gave the governor-general "all the powers which by the royal ordinances are granted to the governors of besieged cities"—in other words, full autocratic powers over the persons, property, and administration of the island. Not many men could be intrusted with such despotic authority without abusing it, and the governors-general of Cuba were no exception. So that, despite the fact that Cuba remained, after the Latin-American revolutions, almost the sole relic of Spain's once vast trans-Atlantic empire, the desire for independence was by no means dormant even in Cuba. Between 1823 and 1830 a number of revolutionary schemes were hatched, though all proved abortive. In 1844 a threatened insurrection of slaves was stamped out in a savage fashion. We have already noted the failure of the López expedition. Not until 1868 did the first serious revolt on the island break out.

The causes of the so-called Ten Years' War—the insurrection dragged along in a desultory fashion for about that length of time—are not hard to discover. In the first place, Spain regarded the island merely as a source of revenue. In the year 1868 the revenue from the island approximated $26 million, and virtually none of it was used for Cuba's benefit. The public offices in the island carried very good salaries, but all were in the hands of Spaniards. The corruption among officials was notorious, the "perquisites" in some cases reaching as high as 70 per cent of the total receipts. In the second place, Spain virtually monopolized not only Cuba's exports but also its imports, and the duties were laid just as heavily upon necessities as upon luxuries. Flour was taxed so heavily that wheat bread almost ceased to be an article of food for the common people. Finally, representation in the Cortes, which at one time had been granted, only to be withdrawn later, was felt to be essential to any permanent improvement in the government of the island.

When Isabella II was driven from the throne of Spain by the revolution of 1868, the Cubans seized the opportunity to declare their independence and to organize to maintain it. Carlos Manuel de Céspedes, a wealthy planter and an ardent patriot, raised a body of some 15,000 men, and at the outset the patriots were generally successful. A constitution was promulgated April 10, 1869, and the legislature, which met in accordance with its provisions, elected Céspedes president. But without assistance the patriots could not hope to withstand the well equipped troops that Spain continued to send against them; and finally, upon promises of a general amnesty, representation in the Spanish Cortes, and a few other reforms, peace was brought about by the treaty of El Zanjon, February 10, 1878.[33]

From the beginning, the United States took a keen interest in the war. On March 27 the captain-general of the island, Domingo Dolce, issued a proclamation declaring that any vessels carrying men, arms, or ammunition found in the waters near the island, whatever their destination, should be seized, and persons on board immediately executed.[34] The United States protested immediately and emphatically. On April 4 the Count of Valmaseda, in command at Bayamo, issued a proclamation to the effect that every man above fifteen found away from his home without a reason would be shot and that unoccupied habitations and those not floating a white flag would be burned.[35] Mr. Fish, Secretary of State under President Grant, wrote the Spanish plenipotentiary: "In the interest of Christian civilization and common humanity, I hope that this document is a forgery. If it be indeed genuine, the President instructs me in the most forcible manner to protest against such mode of warfare." [36]

President Grant, who from the beginning of his term of office showed a decided friendliness to the Cubans, authorized General Sickles, the American minister to Spain, to tender the good offices of the United States to bring to a close the civil war ravaging the island. The bases suggested were: the independence of Cuba, an indemnity to Spain, the abolition of slavery in the island, an armistice pending the negotiations for the settlement.[37] Although some of the leaders of the Spanish govern-

[33] Text may be found in *Sen. Doc. No. 79*, 45th Cong., 2nd Sess., p. 16.
[34] *Sen. Doc. No. 7*, 41st Cong., 2nd Sess., p. 12.
[35] *Ibid.*, p. 20. Bayamo itself was burned to the ground and its inhabitants dispersed or slaughtered.
[36] *Ibid.*, p. 21.
[37] *House Ex. Doc. No. 160*, 41st Cong., 2nd Sess., pp. 13-16.

ment were willing to accept, public opinion opposed and the proffer was withdrawn.

The affair, however, which most aroused the United States against Spain, bringing the two nations to the brink of war, was the seizure of the steamer *Virginius* and the execution of her captain and crew. The *Virginius* was a merchant-vessel sailing under the American flag and registered in New York as an American-owned vessel. However, her cargoes consisted principally of contraband of war destined for Cuba; and for several years she had been successful in landing them, despite the vigilance of the Spanish cruisers. On October 23, 1873, she cleared from Kingston, Jamaica, for Puerto Limón, Costa Rica, though her actual intention was to land men and arms in Cuba. On October 31 she was captured on the high seas by a Spanish cruiser and taken into Santiago de Cuba. The Spanish commandant, General Burriel, summoned a court-martial, and within a week's time fifty-three of the passengers and crew were summarily condemned and shot, despite strong protests upon the part of the American and British consuls. Such a performance was not merely "a dreadful, a savage act," but it was directly contrary to international law, because the vessel was a neutral lawfully provided with papers; even if she were engaged in blockade-running or in carrying contraband, the maximum penalty should have been confiscation of the ship and cargo.

General Sickles, the American minister at Madrid, was instructed to demand the restoration of the *Virginius* with the survivors, a salute to the flag of the United States, and punishment of the guilty officials. At first Spain seemed inclined to support the United States in its stand, but later Castilian pride came to the front, and a curt and most unsatisfactory reply was returned. Spain could not consent to be thus addressed by the representatives of a foreign nation, and if reparations were to be made it would be only after a thorough investigation had been carried out by her representatives.[38] Recriminations became mutual, and it was only after General Sickles had asked for his passports that Spain agreed to consider the American demands. Owing either to the uncomprising attitude of General Sickles, or to the Spanish government's fear of a popular uprising, the negotiations were transferred to Washington. A protocol was finally reached, whereby Spain agreed to restore the *Virginius,* together with the surviving passengers and crew, and to salute the flag of the United States, unless she could prove before December 25, 1873, that

[38] The complete diplomatic correspondence regarding this incident may be found in the *For. Rel. of the U. S.*, 1874, pp. 922-1117; *ibid.*, 1875, Part II, pp. 1144-1256.

the *Virginius* was not entitled to carry the American flag. The Madrid government actually succeeded in furnishing proof that the vessel was both owned and controlled by Cubans; therefore the salute was waived. The vessel and survivors were turned over to the United States. But on its way north, under convoy, the ship foundered off Cape Hatteras. Spain also admitted the illegality of the capture and the summary execution of the crew, and finally paid an indemnity of $80,000 to the families of those executed. But the Spanish commandant guilty of the execution not only escaped punishment, but was later promoted to a higher grade.[39]

Meanwhile the Cuban insurrection dragged along, and the United States continued to look for means of putting an end to the devastating struggle. The whole situation, as far as the United States was concerned, was summed up in a long, carefully worded despatch from Secretary Fish to Caleb Cushing, the new American representative at Madrid, on November 5, 1875. In this state paper Mr. Fish enumerated the cases of arbitrary seizure, confiscation of American property, and arrest and execution of American citizens without trial, and protested vigorously against the continuance of a struggle on the very borders of the United States, disturbing to its tranquillity and commerce and conducted in a most barbarous fashion. "It will be apparent that such a state of things cannot continue. . . . In the opinion of the President, the time has arrived when the interests of this country, the preservation of its commerce, and the instincts of humanity alike demand that some speedy and satisfactory ending be made of the strife that is devastating Cuba. . . . The President hopes that Spain may spontaneously adopt measures looking to a reconciliation and to the speedy restoration of peace and the organization of a stable and satisfactory system of government in the island of Cuba. In the absence of any prospect of a termination of war or of any change in the manner in which it has been conducted on either side, he feels that the time is at hand when it may be the duty of other governments to intervene, solely with a view of bringing to an end a disastrous conflict, and of restoring peace in the island of Cuba." [40]

A copy of this note was sent to the American representatives in Europe, and when its contents became known it provoked considerable discussion, which was increased by President Grant's message of December 7, 1875. Great Britain, whose coöperation was particularly desired, decided, in the words of Lord Derby, that "if nothing were contemplated beyond

---

[39] For the trial of General Burriel see *ibid.*, 1876, pp. 486-535.
[40] *Report of Senate Committee on Foreign Relations Relative to Affairs in Cuba*, No. 885, 55th Cong., 2nd Sess., pp. 44-52.

an amicable interposition having peace for its object, the time was ill chosen and the move premature." [41] The other powers were no more willing to intervene than Great Britain, particularly at a time when the young Alfonso was struggling manfully against the revolution of Don Carlos. Owing to the superlative ability of Mr. Cushing and the high esteem in which he was held, Mr. Fish's communication was received by Spain in the friendly spirit in which it was sent, and in his reply Señor Calderon, the Spanish Foreign Minister, emphasized the recent satisfactory progress in putting down the revolution, and promised the abolition of slavery and the introduction of administrative reforms leading to representation of the inhabitants in the Spanish Cortes. In conclusion, he asked for a frank statement concerning the precise things which the United States would wish Spain to do. [42]

After emphatically disclaiming any intention on the part of the government of the United States to annex Cuba, Mr. Fish summed up the President's desires under four heads: first, mutual and reciprocal observance of the treaty obligations, with a friendly interpretation of the doubtful provisions; second, the establishment of peace, order, and a liberal government in Cuba; third, gradual but effectual emancipation of the slaves; fourth, improvement of commercial facilities and the removal of the obstructions now existing in the way of trade and commerce. [43] Spain's acceptance of these proposals eliminated, for the time being, any further discussion of intervention. However, the Madrid government urged that before there could be any hope of improvement the revolution must be put down, and a new general and additional troops were forthwith despatched to the island. In October, 1877, a number of the Cuban leaders surrendered, and early in February, 1878, the Ten Years' War came to an end. The terms of peace gave promise of a real improvement in the situation of the Cubans. Yet the habits of centuries can not be broken up by the good intentions of a day. The Spanish system of exploitation had become part and parcel of the island's administration, and Spanish officials were still employed to look out for Spanish interests. But two results of the revolution were manifest to the world: the seed of independence had taken firm root in the island of Cuba, and the United States could not remain an impartial witness to any attempts to prevent its growth.

As a result of the Ten Years' War, there was some improvement in the

[41] *Ibid.*, p. 162.
[42] *Ibid.*, pp. 96-99.
[43] *Ibid.*, pp. 102-106.

attitude of Spain towards Cuba, but little change in the actual conditions. The island was granted representation in the Spanish Cortes, but, owing to the limited suffrage, the majority of the delegates represented the Peninsulares, or Spanish element. Even when, in 1892, the tax qualification for the suffrage was reduced from twenty-five dollars to five dollars, the Spanish authorities who controlled the elections saw to it that the results were virtually the same. Seventeen years of comparative peace followed; yet it was the apathy of exhaustion rather than the tranquillity of satisfied hopes. In fact, the promises held out by the Spanish government were never realized. The sole noteworthy reform was the gradual abolition of slavery. In summing up the situation, Estrada Palma declared that the parliamentary representation was illusory, all officials of the island were Spaniards, taxes were levied upon everything conceivable, and about 95 per cent of the amount collected was devoted to the maintenance of the army and navy in Cuba, to the interest on the public debt, and to the salaries of the Spanish officeholders. The Cubans had no security of person or property; nor was there freedom of speech, press, or religion.[44]

These were the underlying causes of the outbreak of the revolution in 1895. The passage of the Abarzuza law in February, 1895, by the Spanish Cortes, creating a farcical council of administration, seemed to bring matters to a head.[45] The economic crisis engendered by the termination of reciprocity relations with the United States in 1894, thus closing Cuba's principal market for sugar, undoubtedly aided materially in strengthening the discontent. After the tragic death of the patriot, José Martí, in the beginning of the insurrection, the revolutionists were under the general command of Máximo Gómez, and they were financially supported by the juntas organized in the United States. The revolution spread rapidly, and from the outset the insurgents ruthlessly destroyed all property and plantations that might be useful to the enemy. Spain spared no effort to check the revolution, and when Governor-General Campos failed to put down the insurgents, General Weyler was placed in command. The struggle on the Cubans' part soon degenerated into guerrilla warfare. They gave notice that they would destroy all the resources of the island rather than surrender. General Weyler retaliated by forcing all the inhabitants of certain provinces to concentrate in the towns held by the Spanish troops or be considered rebels.[46] Great numbers of noncombatants were thus brought together, and, as no provision for feeding and

[44] Sen. Rep. No. 885, 55th Cong., 2nd Sess., pp. 1 ff.

[45] Hannis Taylor, "A Review of the Cuban Question," North Amer. Rev., Vol. CLXV (Nov., 1897), pp. 610-635.

[46] Text of decree in Sen. Rep. No. 885, p. 549.

housing them had been made, the brutal nature of the decree was soon apparent. The innocent women and children were forced to starve in the towns, while the able-bodied men remained at large and joined revolutionary bands.

On June 12, 1895, President Cleveland issued a proclamation recognizing that a state of insurgency existed in Cuba, and insisting upon the maintenance of American neutrality.[47] However, as the horrors of the struggle increased and the American press took up the campaign in Cuba's behalf, Congress also was drawn into the affair, and early in 1896 a resolution passed both houses urging that the President recognize Cuban belligerency. This, Cleveland refused to do. But public opinion steadily grew more hostile towards Spain; and the destruction of American property on the island, together with the great falling off of American trade, added fuel to the flames. Although the President refused to recognize Cuban belligerency, he authorized Secretary Olney to give the Spanish ambassador some words of admonition. In this way, Spain was given to understand that the United States could not contemplate with complacency another ten years of Cuban insurrection; and the good offices of the United States were tendered, with all assurance that the offer was prompted only by the friendliest feeling towards Spain. "The United States," it was specifically asserted, "has no designs upon Cuba and no design against the sovereignty of Spain."[48] The Spanish reply was a courteous refusal of the offer, and the United States was forced to let the matter drop temporarily, although, in his message to Congress in December of the same year, Cleveland declared that future American action would be determined when Spain's inability to deal successfully with the insurrection had become manifest, and that, although American conduct would be guarded by right and not by might, a situation might be presented in which our obligations to the sovereignty of Spain would be superseded by higher obligations.[49]

Hardly had the McKinley administration assumed office before it was compelled to take action; for the situation was growing steadily worse. In May, 1897, the President asked Congress to appropriate $50,000 for the relief of destitute Americans in Cuba, and in December he issued a public appeal for funds to aid in combating the Cuban famine. A slight gleam of hope for better conditions appeared when the new Sagasta ministry recalled General Weyler and promised Cuba a new constitution, with a

[47] *For. Rel. of the U. S.*, 1895, p. 1195.
[48] *Ibid.*, 1897, p. 540.
[49] *Ibid.*, 1896, p. xxix.

local parliament and a fair share of autonomy. In his annual message of December, 1897, McKinley noted the new policy of Spain, and declared that it was honestly due to Spain that she should be given a reasonable chance to realize her expectations. Unfortunately for Spain, her policy of reform was given no opportunity to materialize. General Blanco could not undo the terrible results of the reconcentration policy of General Weyler, although he made very earnest efforts to do so. Not only were the insurgents wholly averse to acceptance of semi-autonomy in the place of independence, but the Spanish party in Cuba was equally indignant at the liberality of the new program. Rioting against the newspapers backing autonomy became so serious that on January 13, 1898, the American consul-general, Mr. Lee, telegraphed that he was uncertain whether Blanco could control the situation, and that if it should be demonstrated that Americans were in danger, ships should be promptly sent.[50] The next day all was quiet; but the idea of sending a war-ship struck root, and on January 24 the President ordered the *Maine* sent to Havana on a "friendly visit." The American consul-general realized that the times were not propitious for a friendly visit and advised that the step be postponed six or seven days. But the battle-ship was already on its way, and on January 25 it anchored in Havana harbor.

The struggle between the Cuban insurgents and the Spaniards was soon to be merged in a direct conflict between Spain and the United States. On February 9, 1898, a New York newspaper published a private letter written by Señor Dupuy de Lome, the Spanish minister, to a friend in Cuba, in which he characterized President McKinley as a "weak ... would-be politician who tries to leave a door open behind himself while keeping on good terms with the jingoes of his party." [51] Although it was a questionable piece of journalism to publish a letter of this character that had been purloined from the mails, the Spanish minister showed an inexcusable lack of diplomatic discretion in expressing his opinions so frankly. The United States immediately demanded his recall—although not until after the discredited diplomat, realizing that his position had become untenable at Washington, had sent in his resignation. But public opinion, already aroused against Spain through her dilatory attitude in ameliorating the condition of Cuba, became increasingly hostile. And, as if other circumstances were not sufficiently irritating in the relations between the two countries, on the night of February 15 the *Maine* was blown up at its anchorage in Havana harbor, with the loss of two hundred

[50] *Ibid.*, 1898, p. 1025.
[51] For the full content of the letter see Moore, *op. cit.*, Vol. VI, pp. 176-177.

and sixty men, including two officers. A wave of indignation swept over the United States, and the demand for war was virtually unanimous. The few who counseled delay until a court of inquiry could fix the blame were scarcely heard in the popular clamor. Fortunately, democratic governments are so constituted that they function slowly; and the utter unpreparedness of the United States for war was an added incentive to move with deliberation.

An American court of inquiry was immediately constituted to determine the cause of the disaster. After twenty-three days of careful investigation it reported that the *Maine* was destroyed by a submarine mine, but that no evidence could be obtained sufficient to fix the responsibility upon any person or persons. A Spanish board of inquiry, making a separate investigation, reported that the explosion was due to internal causes.[52] The real cause will probably never be known.[53]

Even before the publication of the report on March 28, there was every indication that, no matter what the findings might be, the United States and Spain had reached an *impasse* in regard to Cuba. Spain found Consul-General Lee in sympathy with the insurgents and suggested his recall. The United States rejected the suggestion. Buoyed up by the virtual certainty of American intervention the Cubans would accept nothing less than independence. Proposals for the purchase of the island by the United States were tentatively raised in both Spain and the United States; but neither party was anxious for such a solution. From the American point of view, the one condition upon which a peaceful adjustment was possible was an immediate armistice to be granted by Spain to the Cubans. Instructions from Washington to General Woodford, the American minister at Madrid, declared, under date of March 26, that the President desired peace, but that there was no hope for peace through the Spanish arms. The United States did not want the island, but wanted peace to prevail in it. The suggestion was made that if Spain would revoke the reconcentration order and maintain the people until they could support themselves, and also offer the Cubans full self-government, with reasonable indemnity, the President would gladly assist in the consummation of the plan.[54] On the following day the same proposals were renewed, in somewhat more specific form, asking (1) an armistice for six months, during

[52] For the American report see *Sen. Doc. No. 207*, 55th Cong., 2nd Sess. The Spanish report is in *Sen. Rep. No. 885*, 55th Cong., 2nd Sess., pp. 566 ff.

[53] A later investigation upon the raising of the *Maine* in 1911 strengthened the view that an outside explosion caused the sinking: *Report of the U. S. Naval Board in 1911, House Doc. No. 310*, 63rd Cong., 2nd Sess.

[54] *For. Rel. of the U. S.*, 1898, p. 704.

which negotiations for peace between Spain and the insurgents might be undertaken through the friendly offices of the United States; (2) immediate revocation of the *reconcentrado* order; (3) agreement that, if peace were not arranged by October 1, the President of the United States should be accepted as final arbitrator between Spain and the insurgents.[55] The report on the *Maine* made to Congress, March 28, was bound to bring speedy action. Therefore, if the President was to succeed in obtaining a peaceful settlement, Spain must give him an immediate assurance that his offer was accepted.

Madrid's reply, on March 31, was not satisfactory, in that, instead of granting an immediate armistice, its offer conditioned a truce upon the insurgents asking for it, a proposal that they were most unlikely to make. On April 5, through the intervention of the Pope, the Queen, indeed, conceded an unconditional suspension of hostilities for six months, thus meeting the President's demand. But the latter had already prepared his message and had decided to place the responsibility for future action upon Congress. Undoubtedly he realized that to surrender control of the situation meant war. But who can say that, even if he had accepted the eleventh-hour promise of Spain, war would ultimately have been averted? Perhaps a Roosevelt or a Wilson could have dominated Congress; but there still remained the question of Spain's ability to placate the Cubans.

In his message delivered to Congress on April 11, 1898, President McKinley reviewed the situation in a judicial manner, describing conditions in the island and recounting the offers of mediation made by the United States. Since this method of settlement had failed, only forcible intervention was left, and he justified this course of action upon four grounds: first, in the cause of humanity, i.e., it would put an end to the bloodshed and misery at our door; second, it would protect American citizens and their property in Cuba; third, it would put an end to the wanton destruction and devastation of the island; fourth, and most important, "the present condition of affairs in Cuba is a constant menace to our peace." The destruction of the *Maine* was mentioned merely as impressive proof of the intolerable state of things in the island.[56]

Congress was only too willing to grant the President the powers that he asked for. After stormy debates in both houses, a joint resolution was passed, recognizing the independence of Cuba, demanding the immediate withdrawal of the Spanish forces from the island, granting the President

[55] *Ibid.*, p. 712.
[56] J. D. Richardson, *Messages and Papers of the Presidents*, Vol. X, p. 147; or *For. Rel. of the U. S.*, 1898, p. 750.

power to use the entire land and naval forces to carry the resolution into effect, and, finally, disclaiming any intention on the part of the United States to exercise sovereignty over the island except to establish peace, and, that accomplished, to leave the government and control of the island to its people.[57]

As soon as the President signed the resolution, the Spanish minister at Washington asked for his passports, and his action was approved by the Spanish Foreign Minister. On April 25, 1898, Congress passed the declaration of war, dating the outbreak as of April 21. Admiral Sampson had already received orders to blockade Cuba with the South Atlantic Squadron, and Commodore Dewey had left Hong Kong to engage the Spanish squadron at Manila. Foreseeing the outcome, the Navy Department had more than a month earlier ordered the battle-ship *Oregon*, lying at Puget Sound, to join the Atlantic Squadron. Her 15,000-mile journey around Cape Horn dramatically demonstrated to the United States the need strategically of an isthmian canal.

Both sides realized that the issue lay upon the sea; and it was fortunate for the United States that such was the case. But there is no necessity to tell the story of the conflict here. Dewey's overwhelming victory at Manila Bay, followed by the complete destruction of Cervera's fleet at Santiago, virtually sealed the defeat of Spain. The mechanistic era of warfare had come, and America had made the greater progress. "Spanish dominion in America, in which there had been much both of glory and of shame, with splendid episodes of heroic endeavor, noble self-abnegation, and great attainment, was to end in the final sacrifice, nobly met, on the sea which through generations witnessed so many conflicts of the two races." [58]

On July 22, 1898, through M. Jules Cambon, the French ambassador at Washington, Spain asked of the President upon what basis the conflict could be ended and a satisfactory political status in Cuba established. President McKinley outlined his terms, which were later incorporated in the protocol of August 12. In brief, the agreement provided (1) the relinquishment by Spain of all sovereignty over Cuba; (2) the cession of Puerto Rico and other Spanish West Indies, together with an island in the Ladrones, to the United States; (3) the occupation by the United States of Manila pending the signing of a treaty of peace which should determine the disposition of the Philippines; (4) the immediate evacuation by Spain of Cuba, Puerto Rico, and the other islands of the West Indies

[57] *U. S. Stat. at Large*, Vol. XXX, p. 738.
[58] Chadwick, *op. cit.*, p. 587.

under her sovereignty; (5) the appointment by Spain and the United States of not more than five commissioners each, to meet in Paris not later than October 1, 1898, to negotiate a treaty of peace; (6) the suspension of hostilities upon the signing of the protocol.[59]

In the peace negotiations which followed, Spain made every effort to turn over the Cuban debt, either to the Cubans or to the United States, along with the sovereignty of the island. But the American commissioners stood fast against the proposal, on the ground that the debt was created by Spain for its own purposes and through its own agents and not for the benefit of Cuba. The treaty signed December 10, 1898, was almost identical with the terms of the protocol, except for the clauses regarding the Philippines.[60] The United States at last had the opportunity to pacify Cuba and then withdraw as it had promised—a quixotic proceeding most highly incredible to a skeptic world.

SUPPLEMENTARY READINGS

EDWIN F. ATKINS, *Sixty Years in Cuba* (Cambridge, Mass., 1926).

R. CABRERA, *Cuba and the Cubans* (Philadelphia, 1896).

WILFRID H. CALCOTT, *The Caribbean Policy of the United States 1890-1920* (Baltimore, 1942).

J. M. CALLAHAN, *Cuba and International Relations* (Baltimore, 1899).

I. E. CANINI, *Four Centuries of Spanish Rule in Cuba* (Chicago, 1898).

F. E. CHADWICK, *The Relations of the U. S. and Spain, Diplomacy* (New York, 1909).

A. S. DRAPER, *The Rescue of Cuba* (Boston, 1910).

ISIDRO FABELA, *Los Estados Unidos Contra La Libertad* (Barcelona, n. d.) pp. 19-120.

H. E. FLACK, *Spanish American Diplomatic Relations Preceding the War of 1898* (Baltimore, 1906).

R. T. HILL, *Cuba and Porto Rico* (New York, 1899).

RAMÓN INFIESTA, *Historia Constitucional de Cuba* (Havana, 1942).

W. F. JOHNSON, *The History of Cuba*, 5 vols. (New York, 1920).

J. H. LATANÉ, *The United States and Latin America* (New York, 1920), Chap. III.

FITZHUGH LEE, *Cuba's Struggle against Spain* (New York, 1899).

C. H. FORBES-LINDSAY, *Cuba and Her People of To-day* (Boston, 1911).

CHAS. MORRIS, *Our Island Empire* (Philadelphia, 1899), Sect. I.

A. G. ROBINSON, *Cuba and the Intervention* (New York, 1905).

HORATIO RUBENS, *Liberty: The Story of Cuba* (New York, 1932).

HUDSON STRODE, *The Pageant of Cuba* (New York, 1934).

ENRIQUE JOSÉ VARONA, *De la colonia a la republica* (Havana, 1919).

[59] *For. Rel. of the U. S., 1898*, p. 828.
[60] *Ibid.*, p. 831.

A. H. Verrill, *Cuba, Past and Present* (New York, 1914).

Herminio Portell Vilá, *Historia de Cuba en relaciones con los Estados Unidos y España*, 4 vols. (Habana, 1936-1941).

I. A. Wright, *Cuba* (New York, 1910).

Z. Zaragoza, *Las insurreciones en Cuba*, 2 vols. (Madrid, 1872).

✿ 10 ✿

The Independence
of Cuba

THE official transfer of the island took place January 1, 1899, and thereupon the trusteeship of the United States began. The task assumed was truly stupendous. Disease and starvation were prevalent; civil government had disappeared; even the public buildings were unfit for occupancy. Major-General John R. Brooke, the first military governor, began a general program of rehabilitation, including the distribution of more than 5,000,000 rations, the supplying of medicine, the reorganization of civil government, particularly in the cities—all with the avowed purpose, as announced in a proclamation of January 1, 1899, "to give protection to the people, security to persons and property, to restore confidence, to build up waste plantations, to resume commercial traffic, and to afford full protection in the exercise of all civil and religious rights." [1] Major-General Leonard Wood took over the work in 1899, and in his three years as governor-general made a record of administrative efficiency which still sheds luster upon his name. [2] Undoubtedly his methods were at times autocratic, and necessarily he made some enemies; but when, on May 20, 1902, the government was transferred to the duly elected president and congress of Cuba, with a system of civil government established and successfully functioning, with a public-school system completely reorganized, with sanitary conditions thoroughly regulated and controlled, and with the plague of yellow fever virtually stamped out, well might President Palma

[1] *House Doc. No. 2*, 56th Cong., 1st Sess., p. 7.
[2] Even as harsh a critic as Carleton Beals concedes that "our first intervention in Cuba stands as a model of fine trusteeship," *The Crime of Cuba* (New York, 1934), p. 172. Elihu Root declared that Wood had done "one of the most conspicuous pieces of work ever done by an American." Philip C. Jessup, *Elihu Root* (New York, 1938), Vol. 1, p. 287.

declare to the retiring governor-general, in accepting the transfer: "I take this solemn occasion, which marks the fulfilment of the honored promise of the government and people of the United States in regard to the island of Cuba, and in which our country is made a ruling nation, to express to you, the worthy representative of that grand people, the immense gratitude which the people feel towards the American nation, towards its illustrious President, Theodore Roosevelt, and towards you for the efforts you have put forth for the successful accomplishment of such an ideal." [3]

From the outset of the intervention, the United States had not forgotten that by the terms of the joint resolution of April 20, 1898, the government and control of the island were to be left to its people as soon as pacification was accomplished. As an evidence of good faith, on July 25, 1900, the military governor ordered that a general election be held on September 15 to put into effect the following program: (1) to elect delegates to a convention to frame and adopt a constitution; (2) as a part thereof, to provide for and agree with the government of the United States upon the relations to exist between Cuba and the United States; and (3) to provide for the election by the people of officers under this constitution and the transfer of the government to these officers. [4] As an indication of what the United States considered essential under the second heading, on February 9, 1901, while the convention was in session, instructions were sent to Major-General Wood by the Secretary of War, Mr. Root, outlining the following provisions: (1) no government organized under the constitution should make any treaty impairing the independence of Cuba or grant any right to any foreign power without the consent of the United States; (2) no such government should contract any debt in excess of the capacity of the ordinary revenues to pay the interest; (3) the government should consent that the United States reserve the right of intervention in order to preserve independence and a stable government; (4) the acts of the military government should be validated and maintained; and (5) the United States should be given the right to acquire and maintain a naval station. [5]

While appreciating the decisive help rendered by the United States, and grateful for it, the delegates to the convention would not concede the right of the United States to impose conditions clearly violating that

[3] *House Doc. No. 2,* 57th Cong., 2nd Sess., p. 124.
[4] For text of the order see *For. Rel. of the U. S.,* 1902, p. 358.
[5] *House Doc. No. 2,* 57th Cong., 1st Sess., pp. 43-47.

independence which it had guaranteed to maintain. They realized that the United States had some claims to special consideration, and they made counter-proposals to this effect.[6] But undoubtedly they also feared too close a relationship with a powerful neighbor whose appetite had just been whetted by conquest. *L'appétit vient en mangeant,* and Cuba was a particularly toothsome morsel. Therefore the convention drew up a constitution which completely ignored the question of relations between the two countries. However, Senator Platt, chairman of the Senate Committee on Relations with Cuba, while conceding that Cuba was privileged to establish her own government without let or hindrance, held that the United States, by virtue of its intervention, had certain rights in the island which ought to be safeguarded. The result was the Platt Amendment to the Army Appropriation Bill, which passed both houses and received the President's signature.[7] The terms of this amendment have become such an important factor in the relations between the two countries that the most salient clauses deserve quotation in full:

(1) That the Government of Cuba shall never enter into any treaty or other compact with any foreign Power or Powers which will impair or tend to impair the independence of Cuba, nor in any manner authorize or permit any foreign Power or Powers to obtain by colonization or for military or naval purposes, or otherwise, lodgment in or control over any portion of said Island.

(2) That said Government shall not assume or contract any public debt to pay the interest upon which, and to make reasonable sinking-fund provision for discharge of which, the ordinary revenues of the Island, after defraying the current expenses of the Government, shall be inadequate.

(3) That the Government of Cuba consents that the United States may exercise the right to intervene for the preservation of Cuban independence, the maintenance of a government adequate for the protection of life, property, and individual liberty, and for discharging the obligations with respect to Cuba imposed by the Treaty of Paris on the United States, now to be assumed and undertaken by the Government of Cuba.

(4) That all acts of the United States in Cuba during its military occupation thereof are ratified and validated, and all lawful right acquired thereunder shall be maintained and protected.

(5) That the Government of Cuba will execute, and as far as necessary extend, the plans already devised or other plans to be mutually agreed upon, for the sanitation of the cities of the Island to the end that a recurrence of epidemic and infectious diseases may be prevented, thereby assuring protection to the people and commerce of Cuba, as well as to the commerce of the Southern ports of the United States and the people residing therein.

[6] *For. Rel. of the U. S.,* 1902, p. 360.
[7] Secretary of War Root prepared the original draft; see Jessup, *op. cit.,* Vol. I, p. 310.

(6) That the Isle of Pines shall be omitted from the proposed constitutional boundaries of Cuba, the title thereto left to future adjustments by treaty.

(7) That to enable the United States to maintain the independence of Cuba, and to protect the people thereof, as well as for its own defense, the Government of Cuba will sell or lease to the United States lands necessary for coaling or naval stations at certain specified points, to be agreed upon with the President of the United States.

(8) That by way of further assurance the Government of Cuba will embody the foregoing provisions in a permanent treaty with the United States.[8]

Needless to say, this benevolent protectorate thrust in so unceremonious a fashion upon the Cubans was welcomed neither by the convention nor by the people. A delegation of five members of the convention was sent to Washington to protest. But, although they were received in a most friendly fashion by President McKinley and Secretary Root, they were given to understand that the Platt Amendment could not be modified. After considerable discussion, the convention finally accepted the Platt Amendment on June 12, 1901, and it became an appendix to the constitution.[9] The assurance of Secretary Root that intervention was not synonymous with intermeddling or interference with the Cuban government, but a formal action based upon just grounds for the preservation of Cuban independence or the maintenance of an adequate government, gave the Cubans somewhat more confidence in the attitude of this country.[10]

As provided for by the constitution, the elections were held in December of the same year. Tomás Estrada Palma was elected president, and on May 20, 1902, Governor-General Wood turned over the government of the island to him. With a cash balance of more than $600,000 in her treasury, with her independence guaranteed, and assured of the good wishes of the government and the people of the United States, Cuba was ushered into the family of nations.[11]

The United States had given the insular republic an excellent start, but there remained the problem of the country's economic rehabilitation.

[8] U. S. Stat. at Large, Vol. XXXI, p. 897, or House Doc. No. 2, 57th Cong., 1st Sess., p. 47. The treaty embodying these provisions was ratified July 1, 1904; see For. Rel. of the U. S., 1904, p. 243. Naval stations were at first leased at Bahía Honda and Guantánamo, but since 1912 only the latter has been retained. Political pressure exerted by American landowners on the Isle of Pines delayed until 1925 the ratification of the Hay-Quesada Treaty of 1904 relinquishing all American claim to the Isle.

[9] For a full treatment of the Cuban attitude during this period see A. G. Robinson, Cuba and the Intervention (New York, 1905), pp. 207-277.

[10] House Doc. No. 2, 57th Cong., 2nd Sess., p. 48; text of the Cuban constitution, ibid., p. 102.

[11] For an account of the turning over of the government see House Doc. No. 2, 57th Cong., 2nd Sess., pp. 69 et seq.

This was dependent principally upon the immediate recovery of two industries, sugar and tobacco, and in the case of sugar it was vitally necessary that the United States make a reduction in her tariff. General Wood, Secretary Root, and President Roosevelt recognized the need, and the President, in his message to Congress, December 3, 1901, declared that "in the case of Cuba, however, there are weighty reasons of morality and national interest why the policy [of reciprocity] should be held to have a peculiar application, and I must earnestly ask your attention to the wisdom, indeed to the vital need, of providing for a substantial reduction in the tariff duties on Cuban imports into the United States." [12] Congress, however, seemed more inclined to listen to the selfish arguments of the beet-sugar growers' lobby, and not until two years later did President Roosevelt force his reciprocity measure through. This commercial convention, proclaimed December 17, 1903, gave Cuba the advantage of a 20 per cent reduction on sugar, and on other products of the soil imported into the United States, over the tariff act of 1897 or any tariff law that might subsequently be enacted.[13] The advantage to Cuba was speedily shown. The trade of the United States with Cuba during the fiscal year 1905 (the first full year under the reciprocity treaty) showed an increase of approximately $10,000,000 worth of Cuban imports into the United States, namely, $86,304,259 in 1905 as against $76,983,418 in 1904.[14] The percentage of increase in our exports to Cuba was even greater, showing that fair commercial treatment of our island neighbor was a very profitable investment.

These early figures, however, gave no indication of the tremendous increase that was to come when Cuba should be completely rehabilitated. In 1910 the value of our imports from Cuba was $122,528,037, and our exports were valued at $52,858,758.[15] In 1920 our imports from Cuba amounted to the remarkable figure of $721,693,880, while our exports had increased to $515,208,731—a total trade value of approximately $1,250,000,000, or almost one-tenth of our total world trade.[16] These figures were abnormal, however, owing to the excessive cost of sugar and the huge crop marketed, but the figures of 1925 show Cuba to have had the largest trade with the United States of all the Latin-American countries. In 1925 Cuba imported from the United States goods to the value of $185,617,496, while her exports to the United States amounted to

[12] *Ibid.*, 1901, p. xxxi.
[13] *Ibid.*, 1903, p. 375.
[14] *Foreign Commerce and Navigation of the United States*, 1905, p. 33.
[15] *Ibid.*, 1910, p. 30.
[16] *Ibid.*, 1920, p. x.

$262,613,978 making a total value of $448,231,474, which was almost 5 per cent of our total world trade.[17]

The political relations between the two governments remained uneventful until 1906. The election of 1905 produced a bitter struggle between the Liberals and the Moderates, and President Palma, reëlected by the Moderates, was accused by the Liberals of resorting to violence, intimidation, and bribery to retain his position. Early in 1906 an armed uprising against the government started in the provinces of Pinar del Río and Havana. On August 27 President Palma issued a proclamation granting amnesty to all insurgents who would lay down their arms,[18] but when this failed of its purpose he secretly requested the American consul-general at Havana to ask President Roosevelt to despatch two vessels at once, since the government forces were unable to quell the rebellion.[19] The American government was loath to intervene and pointed out the dangers of this course. But when President Palma threatened to resign, President Roosevelt sent the Secretary of War, Mr. Taft, and the Assistant Secretary of State, Mr. Bacon, to Havana to attempt to reconcile the difficulties.

Upon the arrival of the commissioners in Havana, September 19, 1906, they interviewed the leaders of the various factions, and finally urged as a solution that President Palma remain in office with a coalition cabinet, while the members of congress stand for reëlection. When the Moderates refused and the President insisted upon resigning, the commissioners established a provisional government under the authority of the President of the United States, and issued a proclamation to the Cuban people setting forth the causes for this action and defining afresh the position of the United States towards Cuba.[20]

On October 10, Governor Taft announced that active organized hostilities had ceased, and issued a proclamation of full and complete amnesty to all who had participated in the uprising. Three days later he turned the government over to Charles Magoon, who was, as events proved, to act as provisional governor for the next three years.

Although Governor Magoon has been subjected to almost scurrilous abuse by many Cuban writers, it is by no means justified by the facts. His policies may not always have been the wisest ones, but it must be remembered that for the most part he merely executed the orders emanating

[17] Pan American Union, *Latin American Foreign Trade in 1925* (Washington, D. C., 1927).
[18] *For. Rel. of the U. S.*, 1906, Part I, p. 459.
[19] *Ibid.*, p. 473.
[20] *Ibid.*, p. 489.

from the War Department. His methods of administration may not have been as rigorous as could be desired, but there are but few administrators with the force and personality of a Governor Wood. Perhaps a more suitable appointment might have been made; nevertheless, Mr. Magoon was an outstanding authority on Cuban law, and had had successful administrative experience in the Canal Zone. And in spite of the many accusations of his loose handling of funds, no proof has ever been presented which reflects upon the inherent honesty of the man.[21]

One of the most useful acts of the provisional government was the taking of a complete census as the basis for the new electoral lists, and the returns showed the total population of Cuba in 1908 to be 2,048,980, an increase of 25 per cent as compared with the returns of the census of 1899. A new electoral law was promulgated on April 1, 1908, the provincial and municipal elections were held on August 1 in an orderly fashion, and the results were quietly accepted. The general elections were equally peaceful, and the Liberal candidate, General José Miguel Gómez, defeated the Conservative candidate, General Mario Menocal, by a majority of more than 70,000 votes. The provisional government thereupon convoked congress, and President Gómez was inaugurated, on January 28, 1909, at which time Governor Magoon relinquished the administration to the duly elected representatives of the Cuban people. A number of much-needed public improvements, particularly in the matter of sanitation, had been carried out; necessary legislative decrees had been promulgated, among the most noteworthy being the new electoral law (decree 899 of 1908); and after paying all contracts and other obligations as far as practicable, $2,860,000 in cash was turned over to the new government.[22]

Once more the people of Cuba were put in full command of their ship of state, with the best wishes of the United States for a long and prosperous voyage. General Gómez proved himself a strong-minded leader, and he appeased the more restless spirits by appointing them to political office, thus materially strengthening his position. However, before his term of office expired, serious charges of corruption were brought against his government. It was claimed that the public offices were being sold to the highest bidder, that concession-hunters were finding lucrative opportuni-

[21] For a detailed study of the Magoon Administration, see D. A. Lockmiller, Magoon in Cuba (Chapel Hill, N. C., 1938).

[22] For an excellent summary of the period of the American occupation see Republic of Cuba, Reports of Provisional Administration, Vol. II (Havana, 1908-1909). For more critical surveys see Leland H. Jenks, Our Cuban Colony (New York, 1928), Chap. VI, and Russell H. Fitzgibbon, Cuba and the United States (Menasha, Wis., 1935), Chap. V.

ties at the people's expense, and that the government was even going
so far as to buy off the newspapers to avoid unpleasant publicity. The
government was also threatened by the veterans of the war of independence, who proscribed all office-holders of Spanish sympathies and
forced the suspension of the civil service rules. Fearing that with the
elections approaching the disorder might get beyond control, the American Secretary of State, Mr. Knox, sent a warning to the Cuban government, early in 1912, that intervention might be forced upon the United
States if the disorders were allowed to develop.[23] For a time, the warning
had a tranquillizing effect. But when, in the summer, a negro revolt
broke out in the eastern end of the island, the United States felt it necessary to land marines and to concentrate a number of naval vessels at
Key West. The government now rose to the occasion and put down
the revolt, and the American troops were forthwith withdrawn.

President Gómez had agreed not to stand for reëlection, and the two
leading candidates were Vice-President Zayas, the principal Liberal
candidate, and General Menocal, the choice of the Conservatives. The
election proved to be unexpectedly peaceful, and, owing to the split
in the Liberal ranks, General Menocal was elected. The new president
was a native Cuban and a veteran of the war with Spain. A civil engineer
by profession (he had studied at Cornell University), he was, at the time
of his election, the managing director of the Cuban American Sugar
Company. He had already shown remarkable administrative ability and
was reputed to be one of the wealthiest planters on the island. Financially disinterested, he made a valiant effort to eliminate graft in the
administration, and under his leadership the island made substantial
economic progress. Imports, valued at approximately $120,000,000 in 1912,
rose to over $200,000,000 in 1916; while exports increased from $146,000,-
000 to $336,000,000. During his administration the production of sugar
increased from 1,750,000 tons to more than 3,000,000 tons.

Notwithstanding the excellent results of his administration, Menocal
was strongly opposed when he sought reëlection in 1916. The Liberal
factions united on Dr. Zayas, and the results were so close that both sides
claimed the victory. In certain cases second elections were ordered; but
the Liberals, with ex-President Gómez as their leader, revolted before
they were held. On February 10, 1917, Secretary Lansing appealed to the
Cubans not to plunge the country into civil war,[24] and on February 13

[23] *For. Rel. of the U. S.*, 1912, p. 240.
[24] *New York Times*, Feb. 13, 1917. See also Raimundo Cabrera, *Mis malos tiempos*
(Habana, 1920), pp. 116-117.

he warned them that the United States would not recognize any government set up by violence.[25] The rebels, however, refused to lay down their arms, and early in March American marines were landed. At the same time the American government promised its aid to the Cuban government to reëstablish order and put down the rebellion. The revolution subsided as quickly as it had flared up, and in May, 1917, President Menocal again took the oath of office.[26]

Despite the fact that Cuba now entered the World War as the ally of the United States, the second Menocal administration began even more successfully than the first. In fact, by depriving the world of German beet-sugar the war stimulated to an extraordinary degree the production of Cuban cane-sugar. The crop for 1918 amounted to somewhat more than 4,000,000 tons, or about a million tons increase over the production for the preceding year, while the 1919 crop was even greater. As an indication of the tremendous wave of prosperity that had suddenly engulfed the island, President Menocal, in an interview with an American press correspondent in December, 1919, pointed out that the volume of deposits in banks and savings institutions had increased 1000 per cent in the preceding six years, land values had increased 500 per cent, and the volume of foreign commerce for 1919 would pass the billion-dollar mark.[27] Unfortunately, these values were considerably inflated, and towards the close of 1920, when the whole world began to experience the troubles of financial readjustment, the situation became very critical. A moratorium declared in October, 1920, was extended to June 15, 1921. A foreign loan seemed essential, and at the request of the Cuban government the State Department of the United States sent a financial adviser to consider the possibilities of a loan by American bankers. When this solution failed, a bill was put through the insular congress providing for a sliding scale of liquidation of obligations, and this measure went into effect on February 1, 1921.

For several reasons, the elections of 1920 were particularly important. They were to be held under the 1919 census and the electoral laws as newly revised by General Crowder; President Menocal was ineligible for a third term and had promised that the elections would be conducted with absolute impartiality; and General Gómez, the former Liberal leader, was

[25] *New York Times*, Feb. 15, 1917. Cabrera, *op. cit.*, p. 124.

[26] For a sprightly account of the American intervention see the article by George Marvin, "Keeping Cuba Libre," *World's Work*, Vol. XXXIV (Sept., 1917), pp. 553-567.

[27] L. J. de Bekker, "Cuba and Her President," *The Nation*, Vol. CX (Feb. 21, 1920), p. 230.

now opposed by Dr. Zayas, whom he had supported against Menocal. When the results came in, Dr. Zayas was found to be elected by a considerable majority. But the Gómez faction, alleging fraud and intimidation, refused to accept the results. General Crowder was again sent for, and finally he persuaded the opponents to abide by secondary elections in the districts where fraud was charged. These were held on March 15, 1921, and, as the Gómez adherents remained away, Zayas was again declared elected. The Liberals made a final protest through the abstention of their representatives when Congress convened on April 3. At the same time, General Gómez appealed personally to President Harding to set up a provisional government. But when the United States formally recognized Dr. Zayas as the duly elected president, General Gómez gave up the contest.

Owing to the government's economic difficulties, General Crowder remained in Havana to investigate the financial situation and if possible to suggest reforms. The Cuban government was anxious to float a $50,000,-000 loan in the United States, but as this was impossible under the Platt Amendment unless the revenue were sufficient to meet amortization and interest, a new tax measure had to be passed and the approval of Washington obtained. At the request of the Cuban government, Albert Rattibone, former Assistant Secretary of the Treasury, was sent by the State Department to act as financial adviser to consider possibilities of a loan by American banking interests.

An investigation showed that the second Menocal administration had been extremely wasteful of public funds; many illegal contracts had been awarded, some at exorbitant rates, piling up obligations far in excess of the government's ability to pay.[28] It was essential that a program of domestic economies be instituted immediately, with a strong and honest administration to put it into effect. General Crowder persuaded President Zayas to appoint a new cabinet, which was henceforth known as the Honest Cabinet. This cabinet, formed on June 16, 1922, included Dr. Céspedes, former Cuban minister to Washington, Colonel Despaigne, administrator of customs under Palma, and Captain Pokorny, a graduate of West Point and aid to General Crowder.

A program of reform covering a revision of contracts, a drastic curtailment of expenditures, and the elimination of graft as far as possible was immediately instituted.[29] On September 15, 1922, a law was passed for the establishment of a commission for the examination and audit of the

---

[28] C. E. Chapman, A History of the Cuban Republic (New York, 1927), p. 426.
[29] Ibid., pp. 427-439.

Cuban debt. The commission was organized in November and all claims had to be filed by the following March. Some 25,471 claims were filed, totaling $45,150,673.57.[30] The budget was set at about $55 million and a loan of $50 million agreed upon at 5½ per cent.[31] This was bought by J. P. Morgan & Co. at 96.77, which was a very small discount considering the general financial condition.

The financial situation now cleared rapidly. The fiscal year 1922-1923 closed with a surplus of income over expenditures of approximately $12 million, the bulk of which was appropriated to the retirement of the Cuban public debt. Among other debts paid was the war loan made to Cuba by the United States, thus giving Cuba the credit of being the first government to make a full settlement with the United States of the obligations contracted during the war,[32] an achievement largely due to General Crowder.

Unfortunately the Zayas administration soon wearied of being so completely divorced from the fleshpots, and early in April, 1923, the President dismissed four of his reform cabinet, including the Secretary of the Treasury and the Secretary of Public Works. General Crowder, whose post, in January, 1923, had been changed from special agent to ambassador, was no longer able to exert the same pressure for economy. As one investigator frankly stated it: "President Zayas threw off the 'vicious intermeddling of Washington,' placed fourteen members of his family in strategic positions in the administration, and his forces thus distributed laid siege to the public treasury."[33]

The scandal became so great that in August, 1923, an organization known as the Veterans and Patriots Association was founded, to combat the evils connected with the administration of the lottery and the passage of the notorious Tarafa bill for the consolidation of the railways, a piece of legislation which closed practically all the private ports and compelled sugar companies to utilize only the public service railways. When Ambassador Crowder protested against the reorganization of the lottery in such a way as to increase rather than to diminish the graft, the Cuban Congress passed a joint resolution condemning interference on the part of the United States.[34] Secretary Hughes thereupon called Ambassador Crowder back to Washington for a conference on the Cuban

[30] U. S. Commerce Reports, Aug. 6, 1923, p. 383.

[31] Text of Cuban law authorizing loan in Commercial and Financial Chronicle, Nov. 11, 1922; for its application see U. S. Commerce Reports, Feb. 12, 1923, p. 453.

[32] U. S. Trade Information Bulletin, No. 191 (Feb. 11, 1924).

[33] H. K. Norton, "Self Determination in the West Indies," World's Work, Vol. 51 (Nov., 1925), p. 81.

[34] See editorial in the Outlook, Vol. 134 (Aug. 29, 1923), p. 654.

situation, but it soon became apparent that a hands off policy was decided upon.[35]

The Veterans and Patriots Association now decided to act, and its leader, General Garcia Velez, Cuban minister to London, proceeded secretly to New York, and on March 22, 1924, made a scathing denunciation of the Zayas administration.[36] He was forthwith dismissed from the diplomatic service and the newspaper organ of the Association was suppressed for publishing the accusations. The revolution which followed was a complete fiasco, due partly to poor leadership but also to the fact that President Coolidge immediately (May 2, 1924) issued a proclamation forbidding the sale of arms and ammunition to the revolutionists, while approving two days later the sale of war materials to the government.[37] Apparently the United States, while looking askance at corruption in the Cuban administration, was wholly opposed to a clean-up by revolution— a policy which could hardly be met with enthusiasm by either imperialists or moralists in the United States, although it seemed a satisfactory interpretation of the Platt Amendment to the majority of Cubans.

President Zayas apparently at length came to realize that he could hope for no further favors at the hands of the electorate, and although renominated by the Popular Party he withdrew in favor of General Gerardo Machado, the nominee of the Liberals. The latter was thus able to defeat the Conservative candidate, ex-President Menocal, by a substantial majority, and he was peacefully inaugurated on May 20, 1925.

President Machado began his administration possessing both the confidence and support of Washington and pledged to improve the economic situation of the island. He had solemnly declared that he would not stand for reëlection and had repeated the promise on July 26, 1927, about a month after his term had been prolonged for two years by his henchmen in the Cuban Congress.[38] Nevertheless, he did run again in 1928 and saw to it that he was reëlected with practically no opposition and this time for a six years' term.

As early as 1927 sinister evidence was accumulating to the effect that Machado was crushing all opposition to his policies to the extent of imprisoning and assassinating his adversaries.[39] However, inasmuch as the Sixth Pan American Conference was to meet at Havana in January, 1928,

[35] Chapman, op. cit., pp. 446-449.
[36] New York Times, Mar. 23, 1924.
[37] Ibid., May 3, 4, 1924.
[38] Raymond L. Buell, "Cuba and the Platt Amendment," Foreign Policy Reports, Vol. V, No. 3 (Apr. 17, 1929), p. 39.
[39] See Carleton Beals, op. cit., for a graphic portrayal bitterly hostile to Machado.

the Cuban Ambassador in Washington made every effort to refute all such allegations and little attention was paid to them in the United States. However, on April 17, 1928, Senator Shipstead introduced a resolution charging the Machado administration with maintaining a dictatorship under which numerous assassinations, imprisonments and deportations had taken place, the National University had been closed, and private property of Cubans and Americans had been seized. A report was asked as to whether the obligations of the Platt Amendment did not require some action under the circumstances.[40] The Cuban Ambassador protested the resolution and United States Ambassador at Havana, Noble B. Judah, took issue with the statements contained and emphasized the cordial relations between the two countries.[41] President Machado also resented the possibility of intervention, and on December 31, 1928, he declared that the Platt Amendment no longer existed.

With the advent of the Hoover administration a special effort was made to understand and coöperate with the Latin-American states. Trained ambassadors and ministers were sent to every one of the Latin-American states except Cuba and subsequent events raised doubts as to the advisability of the single exception. The new Ambassador, Harry F. Guggenheim, was financially connected with numerous companies interested in Latin America and as a conservative businessman he stood consistently behind President Machado and the maintenance of a strong, stable government. Unfortunately, the depression cut the price of sugar to such an extent that bankruptcy threatened the Cuban government and such a situation was not conducive to political stability.[42]

The internal political situation became so serious in the fall of 1930 that the question of intervention was raised in the Senate by Senator Walsh, and the State Department issued a statement on October 3 declaring that a close watch was being kept upon affairs in Cuba, but it was made clear that no intervention was contemplated and only a state of anarchy could provoke it.[43] In August, 1931, a rebellion under ex-President Menocal was quickly suppressed, and again the United States refused to intervene. In fact, the White House characterized as a "midsummer dream" the report that the United States contemplated intervention in Cuba. As an evidence of its complete impartiality, the United States placed no embargo on shipments of arms to the rebels.

[40] *Cong. Rec.*, 70th Cong., 1st Sess., Vol. 69, p. 6591.
[41] *New York Times*, Apr. 19, May 29, 1928.
[42] The average price of sugar dropped from 2.64 cents per pound in 1926-27 to .72 cent in 1931-32.
[43] *New York Times*, Oct. 3, Dec. 13, 1930.

The situation now became steadily worse. With the collapse of the revolt of 1931 a secret society known as the ABC, consisting largely of young professional men and students, was organized to seek to overthrow the government. President Machado retaliated by creating a secret police, the so-called Porra, which soon became notorious for its inhuman and murderous practices. The *ley de fuga* was revived and the police made abundant use, and even misuse, of it.[44] In fact, as conservative an authority as Sumner Welles declared that by the beginning of 1933 "Cuba was a country economically prostrate, ruled by a tyrannical dictatorship to which 95 per cent of the people were fanatically opposed, a country . . . in which bombings, terrorism, and murder were daily occurrences." [45]

The United States could not escape some responsibility inasmuch as the Hawley-Smoot tariff of 1930 had aided materially in Cuba's economic collapse, while the Platt Amendment gave the government which had the support of the American administration an almost invulnerable moral as well as legal standing. Although Ambassador Guggenheim had employed financial experts at his own expense to help solve the serious financial and economic problems of the island, his open support of President Machado made him subject to ever increasing suspicion and to the most violent criticism. Nor did the fact that the Chase National Bank of New York had loaned the Machado government some $160 million make his position more tenable.

The situation had become so serious that President Franklin D. Roosevelt shortly after his inauguration despatched, as ambassador, his Assistant Secretary of State Sumner Welles, an able career diplomat with considerable experience in Latin-American countries, with authority to negotiate a new commercial convention to relieve the economic strain, and to tender his good offices to help put an end to the intolerable political situation.[46] Ambassador Welles' efforts were frustrated partly by Machado's intransigence and partly by the bitter hostility which still smoldered against the ruthless President. A general strike on August 4 was followed a week later by a revolt of the army. Not only did the President and his Cabinet resign but they found it expedient to flee from the country.[47] The rioting and looting which followed were such that the United States as a precautionary measure ordered several warships to

[44] See article by Russell Porter, *New York Times*, Feb. 4, 1933.

[45] Sumner Welles, *Relations Between the United States and Cuba*, Dept. of State, Latin American Series, No. 7 (Washington, D. C., 1934), p. 6.

[46] *Ibid.*, p. 7.

[47] For a detailed account of the attempted mediation and the specific reasons for its failure see Charles A. Thomson, "The Cuban Revolution: Fall of Machado," *Foreign Policy Reports*, Vol. XI, No. 21 (Dec. 18, 1935).

Cuban waters. President Roosevelt was careful to state that neither intervention nor the slightest interference with the internal affairs of Cuba was intended.[48] In fact, the United States accorded immediate recognition to the de Céspedes government and endeavored to coöperate in every way. But the new government did not satisfy the more liberal elements and in less than three weeks a coup d'état brought into office another provisional government headed by a committee of five which in turn chose Dr. Grau San Martín as provisional president.

Inasmuch as the new government was opposed by a considerable number of the groups which had ousted Machado, the United States refused it recognition. As an evidence of his sympathetic attitude towards Latin-American susceptibilities, President Roosevelt on September 6, 1933, invited the diplomatic representatives of Argentina, Brazil, Chile, and Mexico to discuss the situation and assured them that the United States would avoid intervention except as a last resort. On September 11 Secretary Hull declared that the United States was not antagonistic to any political organization and would "welcome any government representing the will of the people of the republic and capable of maintaining law and order throughout the island." [49] In spite of failure to receive American recognition and several serious uprisings against its authority, the Grau San Martín government endured until the middle of January, 1934. It had shown itself consistently hostile to the United States and on November 15 President Grau had written a personal letter to President Roosevelt requesting the recall of Ambassador Welles.[50] As Mr. Welles had only undertaken the mission as an emergency measure, he returned to his position as Assistant Secretary of State, and Jefferson Caffery, another career diplomat, replaced him in Havana. However, since Washington had not recognized the Grau régime, Mr. Caffery could only serve as the personal representative of President Roosevelt.

The real power in Cuba after the downfall of de Céspedes was a Sergeant Fulgencio Batista (who had now quickly risen to the rank of colonel). Seeing the utter impotence of the Grau régime, Colonel Batista transferred his support to Colonel Carlos Mendieta, a popular Nationalist leader with considerable ability. Mendieta became provisional president January 18, 1934, and four days later President Roosevelt, after inviting

[48] U. S. Dept. of State, *Press Releases*, Aug. 15, 1933.

[49] For respective positions of Hull and Welles see *Foreign Relations of the United States. Diplomatic Papers, 1933. The American Republics*, Vol. V, pp. 270-588 (Washington, 1952).

[50] Charles A. Thomson, "The Cuban Revolution: Reform and Reaction," *Foreign Policy Reports*, Vol. XI, No. 22 (Jan. 1, 1936), p. 268.

the diplomatic representatives of the Latin-American republics to confer with him, instructed Mr. Caffery to establish relations with President Mendieta.[51] To give more concrete evidences of its support, Assistant Secretary of State Welles on behalf of the United States publicly promised four constructive measures to help Cuba: (1) a fair sugar quota; (2) a new commercial treaty; (3) stimulation of trade by utilization of the new Export and Import Bank; and (4) a modification of the permanent treaty with Cuba.[52]

It was the fourth provision that was the most important in the eyes of the Cubans, for it was the Platt Amendment which was regarded as the cause of the existence and continuance of a situation such as had existed under President Machado. The provision which permitted the United States to intervene to maintain a government adequate for the protection of life, property, and individual liberty was a bulwark of protection to the administration in power. It served as a two-edged sword. The government could use the threat of intervention as an effective means of stifling armed opposition by the Cubans and if that failed there was always the chance that intervention would prefer the maintenance of the *status quo*. Furthermore, the fact that the United States had the right to intervene seemingly made it lean backward in a policy of nonintervention to prove to Latin America as a whole its anti-imperialistic policy.

The United States did not delay in the fulfilment of its promises. On May 29, 1934, President Roosevelt signed a treaty between the United States and Cuba which abrogated the Platt Amendment. In submitting the treaty to the Senate the President declared: "By the consummation of this treaty this Government will make it clear that it not only opposes the policy of armed intervention but that it renounces those rights of intervention and interference in Cuba which had been bestowed upon it by treaty." [53]

By the terms of the new agreement the Treaty of 1903 was abrogated, the acts of the United States during its military occupation were validated, the arrangement for the United States naval station at Guantánamo was maintained, and provision was made for reciprocal suspension of communications between certain ports in case of outbreak of a contagious disease. The Senate approved the treaty two days after it was signed, an example of almost unprecedented speed. The Cuban government was equally prompt and ratifications were exchanged on June 9.

[51] U. S. Dept. of State, *Press Releases*, Jan. 27, 1934.
[52] Welles, *op. cit.*, pp. 14-16.
[53] For text of the treaty see U. S. Dept. of State, *Treaty Information Series*, No. 56 (Washington, D. C., May 31, 1934).

Hardly was the ink dry on the new political arrangement before announcement was made of a new commercial agreement. The Hawley-Smoot tariff of 1930 had been particularly injurious to the Cuban sugar trade, which was the island's basic industry.[54] The Chadbourne Plan for world control of the sugar industry which Cuba wholeheartedly supported had proved a dismal failure. The United States alone could furnish relief and the first step was the Costigan-Jones Act signed May 9, 1934, which permitted a larger quota of Cuban sugar. On the same day the import duty on sugar was reduced 25 per cent. But the greatest boon to Cuban prosperity was the preferential trade agreement signed August 24, 1934. Under this agreement the tariff on sugar was reduced from 1.5 cents to .9 cent per pound. Duty on Cuban rum was reduced from $4.00 to $2.50 a gallon. Reductions in duties were made in tobacco and fresh fruits. In return, the United States secured substantial reductions in the duties on its exports of foodstuffs, textiles, machinery and automobiles, lumber and many other articles. In its first month of operation the new agreement increased the exchange of commodities between the two countries over 60 per cent. The great value to Cuba is shown by the fact that her average exports to the United States during 1932-1934, the two years preceding the trade agreement, amounted to $51 million whereas in the two years after the agreement the average was $133 million.[55]

Unfortunately, the efforts of the United States to aid Cuba both politically and economically did not have an immediate stabilizing effect upon the internal situation. The year 1935 opened with student strikes, followed by a strike of government employees, and finally by a general strike. President Mendieta was forced to suspend constitutional law and proclaim a state of siege. The situation became so serious that the State Department declared that the new treaty of relations of May 29, 1934, abolished the former special relationship, and wished it made emphatically clear that the United States would not intervene directly or indirectly in the political concerns of the Cuban people. Three candidates aspired to the presidency to succeed Mendieta and Dr. Harold W. Dodds of Princeton University was invited to come to Havana and serve as adviser. He accepted and early in December flew to Havana where he worked out a

[54] For a carefully prepared study of the sugar industry in Cuba see *Problems of the New Cuba* (New York, Foreign Policy Association, 1935), Chaps. X-XIII.

[55] U. S. Dept. of State, *Analysis of Cuban-American Trade During the First Two Years Under the Reciprocal Agreement* (Washington, D. C., Jan. 19, 1937). Two supplementary trade agreements were signed with Cuba, the first December 18, 1939, and the second December 3, 1941, to balance the conditions resulting from the second World War. See *Dept. of State Bulletin,* Vol. I, No. 26 (Dec. 23, 1939), p. 729; *ibid.,* Vol. V, No. 131 (Dec. 27, 1941), p. 603.

comprehensive voting plan. Elections held January 10, 1936, gave a majority to Miguel Mariano Gómez, who was inaugurated on May 20. However, Colonel Batista was still the real power in Cuba, and before the year was out he had Gómez impeached and Vice-president Laredo Bru inducted into the presidency. It was a source of criticism to some that Ambassador Caffery seemed to be on most cordial terms with Colonel Batista. But the United States had definitely ceased meddling in Cuba's internal political problems and it looked with sympathetic approval upon the efforts of its former ward to put her house in order.

The United States was not disappointed, for both internal conditions in Cuba and the relations between the two countries continued to improve steadily. In 1938 Colonel Batista accepted an invitation of the War Department to visit the United States for the armistice day ceremonies, and he received a very cordial reception. Shortly after his return he retired from the army and became a candidate for the presidency. During his campaign he pledged the immediate and unreserved aid of Cuba in case the United States should be drawn into the war.

Batista was elected President of Cuba, July 14, 1940, and was inaugurated in October of the same year. As war threatened to engulf the western hemisphere, the two governments jointly engaged in a policy of the closest coöperation. As evidence of our appreciation of Cuba's importance, the United States sent as ambassador Assistant Secretary of State, George Messersmith, one of the ablest of our career diplomats. During 1941 the Export-Import Bank authorized a loan of $25 million to diversify Cuban production and another of $11 million to grind an additional 20 per cent of sugar above the quota assigned for export to the United States. A considerable sum for the purchase of war materials for defense needs was authorized under the Lend Lease Act.

Arrangements were made annually between the Commodity Credit Corporation of the United States and the Cuban Stabilization Institute for the disposition of the Cuban sugar crop for the duration of World War II at a mutually satisfactory price. The Cuban financial situation was so satisfactory at the end of the war that in 1949 the government of Cuba began the payment of some $6 million due to American firms for services and supplies dating back to 1924. Incidentally, the European War had stimulated very considerably the production of Cuba's strategic minerals such as manganese, copper, nickel, chromium, tungsten, and antimony.

With the Japanese attack upon the United States, Cuba was among the first of the Latin-American republics to declare war upon the Axis powers. She also took prompt and effective action against enemy aliens, placing them in a concentration camp on the Isle of Pines. On June 18, 1942, an agreement was signed whereby the Cuban government offered facilities to the United States War Department for training aviation personnel and for operations against enemy underseacraft.[56] An all-embracing agreement coördinating military and naval measures for the duration of the war was signed September 7, 1942, which provided for the most complete coöperation of the two countries upon a basis of reciprocity.[57] For the first time in its history, Cuba imposed compulsory military service. Various air bases were leased to the United States and a large one near Havana valued at $20 million was retained until May 20, 1946, and then turned back to Cuba.

President Batista's term of office expired in 1944 and although he could have elected his candidate, he permitted an honest election and Grau San Martín received a large majority. The United States which had refused to recognize him as president in 1933 now accorded recognition immediately. His régime was sufficiently popular to permit the election as president in 1948 of one of his cabinet ministers, Carlos Prío Saccarás, a bitter opponent of Communism.

During the Prío administration in 1949 a disgraceful incident threatened to mar the very friendly relations existing between the two countries. The beautiful statue of the Cuban patriot, José Marti, in Havana's Central Park was desecrated by three drunken sailors on shore leave from a United States naval vessel. Quick action by the Cuban police prevented mob violence. The next day United States Ambassador Butler apologized publicly, promised that the sailors would be punished, and he deposited a wreath at the foot of the statue.

Before Prío's administration ended in 1952 Ex-president Batista, whose candidacy for another term was not succeeding too well, engineered another *coup d'état* and seized control of the government. He suspended the constitution of 1940 and set up a provisional government which promulgated a new constitutional code suspending all political parties, but he promised that a presidential election would be held in 1953. However, in February, 1953, he declared that due to "conspiratorial activities" the elections would be postponed until June 1, 1954. A serious but abortive revolt in July, 1953, brought about a new postponement of the general elections until November 1, 1954. The new régime was promptly recognized by the United States and by most of the Latin-American republics. Just before Prío's administration ended, a military aid pact

[56] *Dept. of State Bulletin*, Vol. VI (June 20, 1942), p. 553.
[57] *Ibid.*, Vol. VII (Sept. 12, 1942), p. 752.

was signed with the United States and in 1953 the United States sent both military aid and technical assistance to Cuba.

A beautiful new embassy building which cost a million and a half dollars to build was completed in 1953 by the United States on the Malecón drive near the monument to those who lost their lives on the ill-fated battleship *Maine*. But of much greater importance has been the policy of the United States to send top-flight career diplomats to the Havana post. With experienced Foreign Service officers such as Sumner Welles, Jefferson Caffery, Butler Wright, George Messersmith, Robert Norweb, and Willard Beaulac serving as ambassadors, few capitals of the world have been favored with abler representatives from the United States than the island of Cuba.

SUPPLEMENTARY READINGS

CARLETON BEALS, *The Crime of Cuba* (Philadelphia, 1934).

RAYMOND L. BUELL, "Cuba and the Platt Amendment," *Foreign Policy Reports*, Vol. V, No. 3 (Apr. 17, 1929).

RAIMUNDO CABRERA, *Mis malos tiempos* (Habana, 1920).

WILFRID H. CALCOTT, *The Caribbean Policy of the United States 1890-1920* (Baltimore, 1942).

RAÚL DE CARDENAS, *La Política de los Estados Unidos en el Continente Americano* (La Habana, 1921), pp. 187-212.

C. E. CHAPMAN, *A History of the Cuban Republic* (New York, 1927).

RUSSELL H. FITZGIBBON, *Cuba and the United States, 1900-1935* (Menasha, Wis., 1935).

Foreign Policy Association, *Problems of the New Cuba* (New York, 1935).

H. F. GUGGENHEIM, *The United States and Cuba* (New York, 1934).

HOWARD C. HILL, *Roosevelt and the Caribbean* (Chicago, 1927), Chaps. IV, VIII.

LELAND H. JENKS, *Our Cuban Colony* (New York, 1928).

W. F. JOHNSON, *The History of Cuba*, 5 vols. (New York, 1920).

C. LLOYD JONES, *The Caribbean Since 1900* (New York, 1936), Chaps. II, III.

C. H. A. FORBES-LINDSAY, *Cuba and Her People of To-day* (Boston, 1911).

D. A. LOCKMILLER, Magoon in Cuba (Chapel Hill, N. C., 1938).

DANA G. MUNRO, *The United States and the Caribbean Area* (Boston, 1934), Chap. I.

FERNANDO ORTIZ, *Cuban Counterpoint: Tobacco and Sugar* (New York, 1947).

RAFAEL MARTINEZ ORTIZ, *Cuba, los primeros anos de independencia*, 2 vols. (Paris, 1921).

DIEGO DE PEREDA, *El Nuevo Pensamiento Político de Cuba* (La Habana, 1943).

DEXTER PERKINS, *The United States and the Caribbean* (Cambridge, Mass., 1947).

J. FRED RIPPY, *The Caribbean Danger Zone* (New York, 1940).

HERMINIO PORTELL VILÁ, *Historia de Cuba en relaciones con Los Estados Unidos y España*, 4 vols. (Havana, 1936-1941).

❦ 11 ❦

Puerto Rico–A Study
in American
Territorial Government

IN THE foreign relations of the United States previous to the war with
Spain, Puerto Rico [1] had generally been regarded as a sort of natural
appendage to Cuba. In the public statements made by American statesmen regarding Cuba, mention was sometimes made of Puerto Rico, but,
even when nothing was said, it was generally understood that Puerto
Rico would follow in the wake of Cuba if that island should ever transfer
its allegiance from Spain. Perhaps that is one of the reasons why, in the
Foreign Relations of the United States, Cuba plays such a prominent part,
while Puerto Rico is virtually unmentioned. Undoubtedly another reason
is the uneventfulness of the island's history as compared with that of
Cuba. Not having the importance which Cuba derived from its size
and its proximity to the mainland, and possessing no mineral resources
to incite the cupidity of the early Spanish adventurers, Puerto Rico, from
the time of its discovery by Columbus until its surrender to the United
States, probably received as generous treatment from the Madrid government as obtained anywhere in the great Spanish colonial dominion.

So long as Spain held most of the Americas south of the Rio Grande,
she could hardly be expected to pay much attention to such an insignificant possession as Puerto Rico. However, during the wars for independence Spain came to a realization of the importance of attaching

---

[1] The change in spelling from Porto Rico to Puerto Rico was approved by Act of
Congress, *S.J. Res.* 36, and signed by the President on May 17, 1932. The United
States Geographic Board adopted the spelling Puerto Rico in 1891 but changed back
to Porto Rico in 1900 to conform to the spelling found in the treaty of annexation.

her colonies to herself through fair dealing; and a royal decree of 1815 was very generous. The result was a heavy influx of whites, many of them Spanish sympathizers, driven from the revolting countries of the empire. Although the governor-general of Puerto Rico had powers as despotic as those of the governor-general of Cuba, there was considerably less complaint of their abuse. In 1870 the island was made a province of Spain with representation in the Spanish Cortes. A little latter, in 1874, the provincial constitution was abrogated. But the provincial deputations were reëstablished in 1877; only now they were partially dependent upon the governors-general. The next step towards self-government did not come till 1897, when Spain granted a form of autonomous government similar to that offered to Cuba. But the troops of the United States took over the island before its organization under the new system was completed.[2]

From October 18, 1898, when the Spanish troops withdrew, until May 1, 1900, when the Foraker act establishing civil government went into effect, the island was under military rule. The guiding principle under the three military governors, Generals Brooke, Henry, and Davis, was to interfere as little as possible with the existing native institutions. The greatest difficulty was the complete lack of knowledge, on the part of the Americans, of the methods of administration under the local laws. As General Davis writes: "Judicial procedure was strange, and the temperament, mode of life, and manners of the inhabitants differed greatly from those with which Americans are conversant. . . . At the time of my arrival not a page of the voluminous laws of the island, all of Spanish origin, had been translated into English. Those laws, upon which the whole fabric of society was based, were as a sealed book and had been so to my predecessors."[3]

The problems of the military government included policing the island, remedying the lack of sanitation, reorganizing the judicial system, and introducing financial reforms. There was much disorder and murder; pillage and arson were common offenses of the natives against the Spaniards. The sanitary condition of the cities was impossible according to American standards, and an immediate and thorough cleaning up was essential. In the first six months of the American control, more than 750,000 Puerto Ricans were vaccinated, smallpox was stamped out, and steps were taken to isolate lepers. The reorganization of the courts and legal procedure

[2] For a description of the government preceding 1897 and the proposed reforms, see the *Report of Brig.-Gen. G. W. Davis, House Doc. No. 2*, 56th Cong., 1st Sess., p. 484.
[3] *Ibid.*, p. 483.

was the most difficult problem, for, as General Davis reported: "The system of laws that prevails here is the outgrowth of quite a thousand years of human experience, and can not be struck down or radically changed in a day nor yet in a year." [4] For instance, proceedings under the writ of habeas corpus were authorized; but through inability to understand the purpose of the writ it remained virtually a dead letter. The district insular courts were reduced from fifteen to six; and each of the sixty-nine towns retained its municipal court, though upon a modified and improved basis. The insular supreme court of appeals was retained; while for the trial of offenders violating United States law a provisional court under the authority of the president was created, consisting of one law judge and two army officers.[5] The stamp taxes placed upon all deeds, notes, and bills of exchange, and the *consumo* tax upon necessities of life, such as bread and rice, were immediately abolished by the military government, and an excise tax was substituted.

The military government was faced with new and difficult problems, and it solved them in a highly creditable manner. In fact, Dr. Rowe was of the opinion "that during the early stages of our occupation of Porto Rico military government was not only desirable, but the only means of solving the immediate problems of government." [6] But, as he also said, a military régime could not be continued, because such a system is repugnant to the political standards of the American people. The principal reason why civil government was not sooner established was the fear of Congress that, on this basis, legislation in regard to the insular possessions might be subject to the restrictions of the Constitution. To avoid misunderstanding on this point, the Foraker act provided that native inhabitants should be deemed citizens of Puerto Rico instead of citizens of the United States, and tariff duties of 15 per cent of the Dingley tariff were placed upon goods imported into the United States from Puerto Rico, which was possible only if the island was regarded as foreign territory.[7] There was considerable uncertainty as to whether such territory as Puerto Rico, once incorporated into the United States, could be considered "foreign." But the insular cases, particularly Downes *v.* Bidwell, determined that Puerto Rico had not become a part of the United States for purposes of the constitutional provision "that all duties, imposts, and excises shall be uniform throughout the United

---

[4] *Ibid.,* p. 502.

[5] *Ibid.,* p. 504. See also Leo S. Rowe, *The United States and Porto Rico* (London, 1904), Chap. XII, for an excellent survey of the reorganization of the judicial system.

[6] *Ibid.,* p. 127.

[7] *U. S. Stat. at Large,* Vol. XXXI, Chap. 191, Sects. 2 and 7.

States." The court's ruling is often summarized by the phrase, "the Constitution does not follow the flag." Justice White reasoned in the concurring opinion: "To concede to the government of the United States the right to acquire, and to strip it of all power to protect the birthright of its own citizens and to provide for the well-being of the acquired territory by such enactments as may in view of its conditions be essential, is in effect to say that the United States is helpless in the family of nations.... Although the House of Representatives might be unwilling to agree to the incorporation of alien races, it would be impotent to prevent its accomplishment, and the express provisions conferring upon Congress the power to regulate commerce, the right to raise revenue, and the authority to prescribe uniform naturalization laws would be in effect set at naught by the treaty-making power." [8]

As established by the Foraker act, the government of the island included, first, a governor appointed by the President for a four-year term, who had the powers generally conferred upon governors of organized territories, such as to grant pardons and reprieves, appoint certain officials, veto laws, and see that the laws are executed. He was to be assisted by an executive council consisting of a secretary, attorney-general, treasurer, auditor, commissioner of the interior, and commissioner of education, also appointed by the President for four years, and by five others who were required to be native inhabitants. This executive council was also to act as the upper branch of the legislative assembly, the lower branch being a house of delegates consisting of thirty-five members elected biennially by the qualified voters. The council was to prescribe the regulations and date for the first election. The courts already established by General Davis were continued, except that a United States district court was provided to take the place of the provisional court. [9]

Perhaps the most noteworthy feature of this system of government was the executive council, which had both administrative and legislative powers; although a somewhat similar organ was found in the American colonies prior to the independence. It was to be expected that this body, whose members were for the most part experienced in parliamentary practice, would take ascendancy over the lower house, whose members

[8] 182 U. S. 288. See also the analysis by Dr. Rowe, *op. cit.*, Chap. III, and that by P. Capo Rodriguez, *Amer. Jour. of Int. Law*, Vol. X, pp. 317 ff., and Vol. XIII, pp. 483 ff.

[9] *U. S. Stat. at Large*, Vol. XXXI, Chap. 191. For an analysis of the workings of the government see W. F. Willoughby, *Territories and Dependencies of the United States* (New York, 1905), Chap. IV.

were uniformly devoid of parliamentary training. In fact, nearly two-thirds of all the bills passed in the first session originated in the upper chamber. As summarized by Charles H. Allen, the first civil governor, the results of this first session consisted not so much in what the body did as in what it refrained from doing, for among the thirty-six acts passed "not one foolish expression of the legislative will is to be found, and not one of these acts will be speedily repealed." [10]

Governor Allen's conclusions on the success of the new plan of government are worthy of consideration. In the first place, he pointed out that American occupation found the island inhabited by a race of people of different language, religion, customs, and habits, with virtually no acquaintance with American methods, and with the commerce and trade in the hands of the Spaniards. Therefore, with the people wholly unfitted, without careful training and preparation, to assume the management of their own affairs, he felt that "Congress went quite as far as it could safely venture in the form of government already existing in the island, ... and with good men devoted to the work, the island will develop faster under such form, its people through experience and education will advance more rapidly in their knowledge of the civic virtues under a guidance of present methods than could be gained in any other way." [11]

That the Puerto Ricans were not entirely satisfied with the system of government is evidenced in the successive reports of the governors. In the third annual report (for 1902-1903) Governor William H. Hunt declared that the majority of all the people wanted territorial government, but that, in his opinion, a change in the government at that time would be a mistake. The creation of a House of Delegates had already conferred much power upon the people, considering their autocratic government in the past. The inhabitants were justified in looking forward to full incorporation within the political body of the United States, but such a transition could not be successfully consummated without relying heavily upon the young people still in the schools, who would not be able to take their share of responsibility for some years to come.[12] The complaint sometimes raised that the Puerto Ricans were not given a full share of the appointments seems hardly just, for a summary found in the fifth annual report indicates that of the total number of government employees 2548 were Puerto Ricans, as compared with 313 Americans; while in

[10] *First Annual Report of Charles H. Allen, Governor of Porto Rico* (Washington, D. C., 1901), p. 76.

[11] *Ibid.*, p. 98.

[12] *Third Annual Report of the Governor of Porto Rico* (1903), p. 13.

salaries the Puerto Ricans were getting $1,220,567 as against $355,200 received by Americans.[13]

One complaint of the Puerto Ricans, however, was fully justified, namely, that based on the uncertainty of their status as citizens. Governor Winthrop, in 1905, made it clear that this situation was creating a spirit of discontent and unrest prejudicial to the American administration. As he pointed out, under the Spanish régime Puerto Ricans were classed as citizens of Spain, and it was naturally difficult for them to understand why citizenship of the sovereign country should be denied to them under the more free and liberal government of the United States. He urged very strongly the granting of citizenship by Congress, on the ground that it would greatly improve the feeling of loyalty with which the Puerto Ricans regarded the United States, and would instill in them a healthy feeling of patriotism as being citizens of the country and not merely citizens of the dependency of the country.[14]

Another serious cause of discontent was the fact that the governors were, for the most part, political appointees of the President, and had neither experience nor interest in the problems of colonial government. Ignorant as they were of the Spanish language, rarely holding the office more than a year or two (Governor Yager's seven-year term is the notable exception), it could hardly be expected that the governors would be qualified to appreciate the Puerto Rican point of view. Mr. Frank H. Richmond, who served as Assistant Attorney-General of Puerto Rico, and later as associate judge of the district court of San Juan, characterized the Puerto Rican appointees as "noted for the seriousness with which they take themselves and the amateurish pettiness of their activities; the calmness with which they assume that they are doing these people good and that the little they know of business and administration is superior to methods in vogue on the island for three centuries." [15] The bitter opposition on the part of the Puerto Ricans to Governor E. Mont Reily, President Harding's appointee, and the serious charges brought against him, indicated that stalwart political henchmen do not furnish the best material for satisfactory governors of our colonial possessions.[16]

Almost from the beginning of the island's administration under the Foraker act, a marked antagonism was manifested on the part of the House of Delegates towards the executive council, and on several occa-

[13] *Fifth Annual Report* (1905), p. 41.
[14] *Ibid.*, p. 42.
[15] *The Eclectic Magazine,* Vol. CXLVII (Dec., 1906), p. 487.
[16] See the interesting characterization of Mr. Reily by Mr. Davila, the Puerto Rican representative at Washington in Congress, *Cong. Record,* Mar. 2, 1922.

sions serious deadlocks occurred. In 1909 the situation was brought to a head when the lower house refused to vote the appropriation bills for the ensuing year unless the upper house would accept certain legislative measures which were generally conceded to be very radical in their scope, and in one case in direct violation of the Foraker act. The executive council refused to recede, and the session terminated with the appropriation measures unpassed. The governor immediately called a special session, which merely resulted in another deadlock. He then cabled to Washington a full statement of the situation,[17] and President Taft, in a special message, laid the matter before Congress, then in extra session. Pointing out the advantages already secured by the Puerto Ricans under American control, the President recommended an amendment to the Foraker act providing that, when the assembly should adjourn without making the necessary appropriations, sums equal to the appropriations of the previous year should be available from the current revenues.[18] Congress immediately took up the subject, and the so-called Olmstead Amendment was passed, which provided that "if at the termination of any fiscal year the appropriations necessary for the support of government for the ensuing fiscal year shall not have been made, an amount equal to the sums appropriated in the last appropriation bills for such purpose shall be deemed to be appropriated." This amendment brought the organic act into agreement, in this matter, with the organic acts of Hawaii and the Philippines.[19]

In order to obtain further information President Taft directed the Secretary of War, Mr. Dickinson, to visit the island and investigate the situation. The emissary was accompanied by General Edwards, chief of the Insular Bureau, whose bureau now had jurisdiction over the island by virtue of the second paragraph of the amendment of 1909; also by Colonel Kean of the medical department. Secretary Dickinson's report made it clear that on two subjects Puerto Rican sentiment was unanimous, namely, citizenship and the organization and selection of the upper house. On the first the inhabitants demanded the granting of American citizenship to all Puerto Rican citizens collectively, and on the second they asked the substitution of an elective senate for the existing executive council, thus separating the executive from the legislative functions. Secretary Dickinson advised that American citizenship should in some way be conferred upon the Puerto Ricans, but not collectively, as there

[17] *Sen. Doc. No. 40*, 61st Cong., 1st Sess., p. 7.
[18] *Ibid.*, p. 1.
[19] *U. S. Stat. at Large*, Vol. XXXVI, Part I, p. 11.

were many of Spanish decent who did not wish to become citizens. In regard to the senate, he recommended that a senate be created, to consist of thirteen members, all citizens of Puerto Rico or of the United States and resident for not less that one year in Puerto Rico, eight to be appointed by the President and the remainder to be elected by the Puerto Ricans. The separation of the executive and legislative departments was also recommended. Other suggestions were that elections for all insular offices be held only once in four years instead of biennially; that a department of health be created, with jurisdiction over matters of health, sanitation, and charities; and that a department of agriculture, commerce, and labor also be added. In conclusion, the secretary gave it as his opinion that the people of Puerto Rico had, on the whole, an excellent government, and that the people of the United States could look with just pride upon the administration of affairs they had given there. The island was peaceable and generally prosperous; health conditions had improved; and the people were, in the main, contented. There were many criticisms as to the judgment, ability, sense, and industry of various officials who had been there since American occupation. But the universal testimony was that the administration had been honest and free from favoritism.[20]

As a result of this investigation, a bill was introduced in Congress by Mr. Olmsted, chairman of the Committee on Insular Affairs, embodying substantially the recommendations enumerated. In a well documented and comprehensive speech the author of the measure pointed out the conditions and needs of the island, and urged the passage of the bill as a means of ending the unsatisfactory status of the island—that of "a disembodied shade in an intermediate state of ambiguous existence," as Chief Justice Fuller expressed it.[21] The lower house finally passed the bill, amended in several matters. But it was by no means satisfactory to the Puerto Ricans. In a message to Congress dated February 23, 1910, the House of Delegates protested vigorously against its passage, on the ground that it curtailed, rather than increased, the liberties granted by the Foraker act. Incidentally they also indicatea in no uncertain language their dissatisfaction with the latter act, declaring that "the regimen by the Foraker act is absurd and despotic, installing the higher house by presidential appointment without the intervention of the people, mingling and confusing the legislative and executive powers, and leaving the Porto Ricans without a definite and recognized personality in the law of nations." Inasmuch as the minority report of the Committee on Insular Affairs very

20 *House Doc. No. 615,* 61st Cong., 2nd Sess. Text of a proposed bill included.
21 *Cong. Record,* Vol. 45 (May 25, 1910), pp. 6862-6876.

strongly upheld the Puerto Rican contention, the Olmsted bill never became a law.[22]

The next attempt to remedy the political situation in Puerto Rico came in March, 1914, when Mr. Jones, chairman of the Committee on Insular Affairs, reported out a bill to supersede the Foraker act. No action, however, was taken at this time. Early in 1916 another bill of similar character was introduced and unanimously recommended for passage by the Committee on Insular Affairs. This time the sentiment in Congress was very favorable, and a brilliant speech made by the commissioner from Puerto Rico, Mr. Rivera, in behalf of the bill was received with applause.[23] This measure, commonly known as the Jones Act, passed both houses after considerable debate and became the organic law of Puerto Rico on March 2, 1917.[24]

Although this act did not go quite so far as some of the Puerto Ricans wished, it did attempt to meet the demands of the majority, and it successfully remedied the chief defects of the Foraker act. In the first place, a bill of rights guaranteed the individual rights and liberties of the Puerto Ricans in exactly the same manner that these rights are guaranteed by the federal constitution and the constitutions of the various states. American citizenship was granted collectively, but provision was made that those who did not wish to become American citizens could avoid it by making a declaration to this effect. The executive department was made to consist of a governor appointed by the President, and the heads of the following departments: justice, finance, interior, education, health, and agriculture and labor. Of these executive heads, the Attorney-General and the Commissioner of Education were to be appointed by the President with the consent of the Senate of the United States, while the other four were to be appointed by the governor with the advice and consent of the Senate of Puerto Rico. These departmental heads were to constitute an executive council; but all legislative duties were withdrawn. Another important executive officer was the auditor (also appointed by the President), whose duty it was to examine, audit, and settle all financial accounts of the central and municipal governments of the island.

The legislative department was to consist of two houses, a senate of nineteen members elected for terms of four years, two each from the seven senatorial districts and five at large, and a house of thirty-nine mem-

[22] *House Report No. 750*, 61st Cong., 2nd Sess., Pt. 2.
[23] *Cong. Record*, Vol. 43 (May 5, 1916), p. 7470.
[24] *U. S. Stat. at Large*, Vol. XXXIX, p. 951.

bers, also elected quadrennially, one from each of the thirty-five representative districts and four at large. The executive council was given the power to arrange the district; and, with a view to preventing gerrymandering, the districts were required to be contiguous and compact and of approximately equal population. Future redistricting was given over to the legislature of Puerto Rico. The legislature was to meet biennially, and the governor was authorized to call special sessions if, in his opinion, the public interest required it. Bills were to be passed by a majority vote, except in case of a veto by the governor; if vetoed, repassed by a two-thirds vote, and still refused approval by the governor, a bill must be transmitted to the President of the United States, who by signing it would make it law. Furthermore, all laws enacted by the insular legislature must be reported to the Congress of the United States, which reserved full power of annulment.

The qualifications for voters were to be prescribed by the legislature, except that American citizenship and age of twenty-one or over must be requirements, and property qualifications must not be imposed. The electors of Puerto Rico were authorized to choose a resident commissioner to the United States for a four-year term, whose salary of $7500 was to be paid by the United States, and who was granted approximately the same privileges (except voting) possessed by members of the House of Representatives.

The courts already organized were to be maintained, but jurisdiction over their organization and procedure was given to the legislature, except in the case of the District Court of the United States for Puerto Rico. The judge of this tribunal was to be appointed by the President, and the range of its jurisdiction was defined in the organic act.

The government under the new act was promptly put into effect, and in his report for 1917 Governor Yager declared that the measure was received everywhere with satisfaction. Celebrations were held in various municipalities of the island manifesting the gratification of the people. Under the provision for the renunciation of citizenship, only about 290 in the whole island made application, while more than 800 persons born in Puerto Rico of alien parents made a voluntary declaration of allegiance, thus accepting American citizenship.[25] The first elections under the act were conducted in an orderly fashion in spite of many spirited contests. In the first legislative session some friction arose between the governor and the senate, principally over the senate's slowness to confirm the governor's appointments, and it culminated in an attempt of the legislature

[25] *Report of the Governor of Porto Rico, 1917*, p. 1.

to take a recess of two and one-half months instead of *sine die*. The governor refused to accept this interpretation of the organic law. But a compromise was agreed upon whereby the legislature reassembled pursuant to adjournment, adjourned immediately, and then reconvened at the call of the governor for a special session.[26]

Upon the entrance of the United States into the first World War, the Puerto Ricans found themselves shouldered with the obligations and duties of citizenship before they had fairly begun to enjoy its benefits. The selective service act was extended to Puerto Rico, and more than 120,000 men were registered under its provisions. Officers' training camps were established and some 425 men received commissions. Liberty Loan campaigns were carried on and the total amount subscribed amounted to more than $12¼ million. Campaigns for food conservation and production were undertaken, branches of the Red Cross and YMCA were organized. As an example of the people's generosity, in a campaign for new Red Cross headquarters in San Juan $10,000 was raised within twenty-four hours by the subscriptions of forty-five merchants.[27]

The ideals of the first World War so nobly maintained while the nations were actively participating, so sadly distorted in the period of settlement, are still a vital part of the world's imponderables. World peace and good will cannot obtain until the peoples of the various nations and states shall adopt such principles and practices in their international relations as have proved effective and satisfactory in their domestic intercourse. Nor can the exercise of these principles be confined merely to the relations between the so-called sovereign states. The relationships between sovereign states and their colonies, dependencies, protectorates, spheres of influence, and territorial possessions must be an important factor in the world politics of the future. The obligations of the great powers, the states whose importance and prestige are such that they are made mandatory or protecting powers, must be fulfilled in the broad spirit of world humanity. Areas of exploitation will always be breeding-places for international jealousies and disputes, and the United States has publicly proclaimed its adherence to a policy of unselfish guardianship of the rights of minorities and backward peoples. Does its policy, as exemplified in the control of Puerto Rico, square with these doctrines?

The unfortunate appointment by President Harding on May 11, 1921, of E. Mont Reily, a time-serving politician, to the post of governor, did

[26] *Ibid., 1918*, p. 4.

[27] Clarence Ferguson, "The People of Porto Rico and the War," *Overland Monthly,* Vol. LXXIII (Apr., 1919), p. 300.

not square with these doctrines, and hardly did the new governor arrive on the island before he was involved in serious difficulties with the Puerto Ricans. His dismissal of administrative officers and judges without hearing or without cause, and the filling of their posts by wholly inexperienced politicians, his insistence on increases in salaries for his particular henchmen, his utter disregard of Puerto Rican interests and needs,[28] soon brought about a demand on the part of the Puerto Rican Senate that he be dismissed, and a petition to this effect was laid before the Senate of the United States on March 7, 1922.[29] A series of resolutions was introduced in the Congress of the United States to investigate conditions in Puerto Rico, but Governor Reily finally relieved the situation by resigning on February 16, 1923. The appointment of Representative Horace M. Towner of Iowa, a fortnight later, did much to allay the increasing hostility of the Puerto Ricans, and the president of the Puerto Rican Senate immediately cabled his congratulations upon the excellence of the choice.

Governor Towner, who, as chairman of the House Committee on Insular Affairs, was thoroughly acquainted with the situation in the island, entered upon his duties April 6, 1923. He declared that he hoped to lead but not to coerce, to advise but not to impose, and he carried out this policy. Speaking before the House of Representatives on January 11, 1924, in favor of permitting the Puerto Ricans to elect their own governor, Resident Commissioner Davila thus characterized Governor Towner: "At present we have in Porto Rico an able, diplomatic and sagacious executive. Governor Towner is one of the best governors the island has ever had. . . . Should our people have the power to elect their own governor, Horace M. Towner might be the choice of the people. He has won the hearts of the people by his fairness and justice and his sympathetic understanding of their methods." [30] When in 1927 it was rumored that Governor Towner was to be removed because of ill health a delegation was immediately despatched to Washington, headed by the president of the Puerto Rican Senate and the speaker of the House, to present a concurrent resolution and a memorial urging the retention of Governor Towner "because of his great ability as an executive, his untiring energy and his devotion to the fulfilment of his duties, because of the absolute spirit of justice and impartiality which forms his character . . . his retention is absolutely indispensable for the continuation of the work

[28] See the speeches of the Puerto Rican Representative, Mr. Davila, in the *Cong. Record*, Vol. 62, Part 4, pp. 3301-3309; Part 5, pp. 5024-5031; Part 12, pp. 13170-71.
[29] *Ibid.*, Part 4, p. 3479.
[30] *Ibid.*, Vol. 65, Part I, p. 861.

undertaken by him for the solution of our social, economic, and political problems. . . ." [31]

Nevertheless, the Puerto Ricans realized that so long as governors were appointed by the President of the United States, and largely upon a political basis, a Mont Reily might be their future lot as often as a Towner. Therefore in January, 1924, a delegation representing all the political parties in the island and headed by Governor Towner came to Washington to plead for certain changes in the Jones Act which might bring about full self-government under American sovereignty. Perhaps the most important change desired was the right of the islanders to elect their own governor.

After hearings by committees of both houses, a bill acceptable to the various political parties of Puerto Rico, to Governor Towner, and to the War Department of the United States [32] was drawn up. The outstanding feature was the provision that, beginning with the year 1932 and thenceforth, the qualified electors of Puerto Rico should elect the governor, provided that he be subject to removal by the President of the United States for due cause and to impeachment by the Puerto Rican legislature. The bill also provided that the office of vice-governor be abolished, and that the head of the department of education and the attorney-general, as well as the other heads of departments, be appointed by the governor with the advice and consent of the Senate of Puerto Rico instead of by the President of the United States with the consent of the United States Senate. The bill also provided for a separate department of labor.

Although this bill was passed unanimously by the Senate on May 15, 1924, and received the approval of the Insular Affairs Committee of the House, it failed to come to a vote in the House. In 1926 the House did pass such a bill but on this occasion the session adjourned before the Senate could again act. Although President Coolidge had in 1925 favored the principle of an elective governor, in a letter to Governor Towner dated February 28, 1928, he showed no sympathy for Puerto Rican autonomy and declared that "Porto Rico had a greater degree of sovereignty over its internal affairs than does the government of any State or Territory of the United States." [33] A very elaborate and impartial study made at this time by a group of experts under the auspices of the Brookings Institution proposed as a more satisfactory arrangement an amendment of the Organic Act with a view first to perfecting the island's government

[31] *United States Daily*, Mar. 20, 1927.
[32] *Cong. Record*, Vol. 65, Part 9, p. 8599 *ff*.
[33] *Hearings Before Committee on Insular Affairs*, 70th Cong., 1st Sess., May 16, 1928 (Washington, D. C., 1928), p. 27.

machinery and then making the appointment of Governors from the island itself.[34]

The island was able to appreciate the friendly attitude of the government and people of the United States when in the autumn of 1928 it was visited by the most destructive hurricane on record in the West Indies. Due to advance warnings the loss of life was not over 300, but the property damage reached almost $100 million. A half million people were left homeless, without food or clothing. The $10 million coffee crop, ready for harvest, was almost completely destroyed. The American Red Cross expended over $3 million in relief and rehabilitation, while the United States government appropriated $2 million for repair and rebuilding of schoolhouses and roads and another $6 million for loans to be made to individual planters and fruit growers.[35] In spite of this assistance the conditions in the island for a considerable period afterwards were pitiful in the extreme. And hardly had the island partially recovered from the disaster of 1928 before it was again stricken by the terrific hurricane of 1932.

In President Hoover and his appointee as governor of the island, Theodore Roosevelt, the Puerto Ricans found sympathetic and useful friends; both labored to bring about an amelioration of conditions in the island. President Hoover visited the island in person and urged Congress to make further appropriations in its behalf. Governor Roosevelt lost no opportunity to appeal for assistance both publicly and privately, for his investigations showed that "poverty, sickness and hunger stalk the island."[36] It was during the Hoover administration that Congress, by joint resolution and in accordance with the desire of the people of Puerto Rico, changed the spelling of the name to Puerto Rico, the original and correct form.[37]

The Democratic platform of 1932 had promised ultimate statehood for Puerto Rico and the politicians in the island were not disposed to allow the promise to be forgotten. But the Roosevelt administration realized that the economic situation of the island was more critical than the political, and appointed a committee of eminent Puerto Ricans to formulate a plan for economic rehabilitation. The Puerto Rico Policy Commission, as it was called, was headed by Dr. Carlos E. Chardón, Chancellor

[34] *Porto Rico and Its Problems* (Washington, D. C., 1930), Chap. V.

[35] *29th Annual Report of the Governor of Porto Rico* (Washington, D. C., 1930), pp. 7-9.

[36] Theodore Roosevelt, "Puerto Rico," *Foreign Affairs*, Vol. XII (Jan., 1934), p. 271.

[37] *Sen. Rep.*, 71st Cong., 2nd Sess., Vol. II, Report No. 1116.

of the University of Puerto Rico, and the report is generally known by his name.[38] The program as outlined in the Chardón Report recommended: the purchase of sugar lands and mills by the United States so as to cut production of sugar and at the same time distribute the marginal lands in the form of ten-acre subsistence farms; the reduction of holdings of large landowners for redistribution to the landless agricultural class; the rehabilitation of the coffee, citrus, and tobacco industries; the establishment of farm credit; and the introduction of new industries. Upon receipt of this report an interdepartmental committee was appointed in Washington which studied the plan and made important modifications.[39] The Puerto Rico Reconstruction Administration, organized in 1935 to carry out this program, was allotted $42 million by the Works Progress Administration, over one-half of which was allocated to the rehabilitation of agricultural areas.[40]

In spite of these well conceived and strongly supported measures for improving the island's economic status, the political elements became increasingly critical of the United States. Whereas until 1932 Puerto Rican parties favored statehood or independence by normal political action,[41] at that time the Nationalist Party was organized by a Harvard trained lawyer, Pedro Albizu Campos, advocating the immediate constitution of the island as a republic and resistance to the authority of the United States by violent means. Numerous clashes with the police occurred, one at the University on October 24, 1935, resulting in the deaths of several Nationalists. By way of retaliation, on February 23, 1936, two young Nationalists, inspired by the exhortations of Campos, shot down in cold blood Colonel Francis F. Riggs, Chief of Police. This outrage was followed by several other attacks upon the police, and the culmination came on March 21, 1937, at Ponce, where 19 people were killed and about 100 wounded when the police tried to prevent a parade by the Nationalists.[42]

The government of the United States had not been unmindful of the growing political crisis in the island and as a preliminary step to a more

[38] Report of the Puerto Rico Policy Commission, June 14, 1934.

[39] See Conclusions of the Committee, Cong. Rec., Vol. 79 (June 28, 1935), p. 10349.

[40] See the excellent survey by Earle K. James, "Puerto Rico at the Crossroads," Foreign Policy Reports, Vol. XIII, No. 15 (Oct. 15, 1937), pp. 186-188.

[41] The Coalitionists (Union Republican and Socialist Parties) favored statehood, the Liberals split over statehood and independence.

[42] For a detailed account see the statement of Governor Winship in the Cong. Rec., Vol. 81 (June 3, 1937), pp. 5275-5280; see also the very critical "Report of the Commission of Inquiry on Civil Rights in Puerto Rico," by the New York American Civil Liberties Union (May 22, 1937).

satisfactory policy the jurisdiction of the island was transferred from the War Department to the newly established Division of Territorial and Insular Possessions in the Department of Interior.[43] A well-known liberal with considerable experience in Latin-American affairs, Dr. Ernest H. Gruening, was named as its head. Unfortunately, whether through lack of experience in colonial administration or through an alleged tendency to engage in local politics in the island, the change in administration did not prove to be as beneficial to Puerto Rico as was hoped.

When Secretary of Interior Ickes was asked to state his attitude towards the bill regularly introduced into Congress by Resident Commissioner Iglesias granting full statehood to the island, he replied that he would not put any obstacle in the way of a vote. He thought, however, that various points should be considered before such a step should be taken: it would establish a precedent by including noncontiguous territory and also by including a population of wholly different cultures, tradition, and language; there was some opposition to statehood in Puerto Rico and the rights of the people in the Union were involved; finally, statehood once gained would be permanent.[44]

The murder of Colonel Riggs brought matters to a head in the United States as to establishing the future status of Puerto Rico. Without previous warning, on April 23, 1936, Senator Tydings, Chairman of the Senate Committee on Territories and Insular Affairs, introduced, with the support of the administration, a bill giving the Puerto Ricans the option of becoming independent or remaining under the American flag, the decision to be based upon a national referendum on the island.[45] If independence were preferred, the island would retain a commonwealth status for four years and then be given complete independence. Such a bill was a bombshell in the islands where it was well known that independence meant economic ruin. Nor was the fact overlooked that for over two years the United States had been spending about one million dollars a month of its own relief funds in Puerto Rico. The reaction in the island was noticeably hostile to the bill and the Liberal party which favored independence suffered a substantial defeat in the fall elections of 1936. The bill itself was not even discussed in committee and the political future of the island remained a question mark.

A political event with great economic potentialities occurred in the autumn of 1940 with the success of the new *Partido Popular Demo-*

[43] Set up by Executive Order of May 29, 1934.

[44] *New York Times*, Apr. 17, June 2, 1935; *Cong. Rec.*, Vol. 79 (June 5, 1935), p. 8713.

[45] *Cong. Rec.*, Vol. 80 (Apr. 23, 1936), p. 5925.

crático under the dynamic leadership of Luis Muñoz Marín. This party had an elaborate program of social and economic reform which it was determined to translate into legislative enactment. Its first noteworthy achievement was the passage of the Land Authority Act in April, 1941, which set up a Land Authority—*Autoridad de Tierras de Puerto Rico*—which was empowered to acquire and distribute among the small agriculturists lands in excess of 500 acres held by corporations. Its first large purchase was 10,000 acres from a sugar concern which it allocated to small farmers. Coupled with the fact that the benefits of the Bankhead-Jones Farm Tenant Act were made available to Puerto Rico, it was made possible for farm tenants, laborers, and share croppers to obtain loans to acquire family-sized farms.

Although sugar is Puerto Rico's greatest asset at the present time, and some method of coöperation between the great sugar controls and the small farmer may be worked out, a one-crop economy is always vulnerable. For this reason serious attention is being given to restoring the island's former position as a producing area of high-grade coffee. The hurricanes of 1928 and 1932, followed by the second World War, have had disastrous results; nevertheless when the European market is again available there should be a substantial outlet for the aromatic Puerto Rican coffee which is much preferred in Europe to the coarser Brazilian bean. The taste for Café Rico is also being stimulated in the United States by an advertising campaign. Since the repeal of prohibition the production of rum in Puerto Rico has been the fastest growing industry. Ronrico and Carioca are now almost as popular as Bacardi in the United States and exports which were only valued at $40,000 in 1935 amounted to over $5 million in 1940. If Puerto Rico is successful in building up the tourist trade which the island's location, climate, and beauty easily warrant, some of these local industries will be stimulated both at home and abroad.

In his message to the second session of the fifteenth legislature Governor Tugwell, after conceding that the condition of the people reflected years of injustice and neglect, stressed the need to "set going movements which in time will lift people out of slums and will exorcise hunger.... Specifically, we must perfect and enlarge the program of land reform; give workers greater protection; constantly strive to raise the levels of nutrition; make life and living more secure; perfect the devices of government for recruiting and disciplining the public service; plan and execute public work with greater efficiency...." [46]

[46] *Message of R. G. Tugwell to the Fifteenth Legislature* (San Juan, P. R., 1942), pp. 3, 12.

The outbreak of war and the decision to make Puerto Rico the key to the defense system of the Caribbean had a quick and stimulating repercussion upon the economic conditions of the island. The program included two airplane bases for the army at Punta Boriquen and Ponce, an air base and a submarine base for the navy at Isla Grande, numerous auxiliary air fields, and a huge expansion of existing army posts. It was estimated that the United States would spend over fifty million dollars on this construction. The army's first new military department in forty years, the Military Department of Puerto Rico, was instituted July 1, 1939, in San Juan. Puerto Rico and the Virgin Islands were constituted as the tenth naval district on January 1, 1940. Since Puerto Rico is the only island base in the Caribbean which is under the sovereignty of the United States it may well become the "Gibraltar of the Western Hemisphere."

In spite of temporary improvement in the economic situation of the Island as a result of the war, the Puerto Ricans were dissatisfied with their political status, and President Truman recommended in October, 1945, that the Congress enact legislation authorizing a plebiscite in Puerto Rico whereby the inhabitants might indicate whether they wished (1) an elective governor with a wider measure of self-government; (2) statehood; (3) complete independence; or (4) a dominion form of government. When this bill was not reported out of committee, President Truman on July 25, 1946, named Resident Commissioner Jésus T. Pinero as Governor of the Island—the first native-born governor ever to be appointed. In 1947 the Organic Act was amended to permit the Puerto Ricans to elect their own governor in the 1948 elections.

In the elections held November 2, 1948, Luiz Muñoz Marín, as was expected, was elected by an overwhelming majority and was inaugurated January 2, 1949. This proved to be only the first step towards greater autonomy for the Island. In 1950 Public Law 600 was passed by the Congress authorizing the people of Puerto Rico to organize a constitutional government. The constitution when drafted would be submitted to the Congress for its approval. The new Organic Act was to be known as the "Puerto Rican Federal Relations Act." A referendum held June 4, 1951, by the people of Puerto Rico overwhelmingly approved Public Law 600. On August 27, 1951, delegates to a constitutional convention were selected which after four and one-half months' work adopted a constitution which was submitted to the people. A referendum held March 3, 1952, approved the Constitution by a vote of 373,594 to 82,877.

The new Puerto Rican Constitution was transmitted to President Truman who immediately recommended its approval by the Congress.

Congress passed a joint resolution ratifying the Constitution with three minor changes and the President signed the resolution on July 3, 1952. The Convention of Puerto Rico accepted the changes and the Commonwealth of Puerto Rico was officially proclaimed on July 25, 1952.

The new Constitution follows the model of the United States Constitution in accepting the presidential type with its tripartite check and balance system instead of the parliamentary system of Great Britain and the Continent. Its Bill of Rights is more elaborate, as for example, providing for the complete separation of Church and State and prohibiting "wiretapping." One interesting variation is a provision that if the governorship become vacant before the expiration of the four-year term the new governor shall be the Secretary of State who shall be appointed by the governor with the advice and consent of both houses. The right to amend the Constitution is vested exclusively in the people of Puerto Rico and their representatives. Although the Resident Commissioner is still without a vote in the House of Representatives, there is no taxation without representation because Puerto Ricans pay no federal taxes. The new status, perhaps unique in governmental systems, makes the Commonwealth of Puerto Rico a "free associated state" in a sort of voluntary federated association with the United States.

On January 2, 1953, Luis Muñoz Marín was inaugurated Governor of Puerto Rico for the second time but as the first governor under the new Constitution. President Eisenhower sent Governor John Davis Dodge of Connecticut to act as his personal representative during the ceremony.

Until Puerto Rico became an Associated Free State in 1952 the United States made an annual report on its status and development as a non self-governing colony to the United Nations. When in September, 1953, the United States indicated that no further reports would be made since Puerto Rico had achieved a "commonwealth status," the representative from India questioned its autonomous character. The Trusteeship Committee of the United Nations, however, approved the new status as one of a self-governing character and their decision was sustained by the General Assembly by a vote of 26 to 16 with 18 abstentions.[47] It might be noted that Mexico and Guatemala joined with the Soviet bloc in opposing the position taken by the United States. As proof of the intention of the United States to comply with the wishes of the people of Puerto Rico, Henry Cabot Lodge, the United States Delegate, declared that President Eisenhower authorized him to state that if Puerto Rico should

[47] For text of the resolution of approval see *General Assembly Official Records,* 8th Sess., Supp. No. 15, Part I, Sect. 7.

adopt a resolution favoring more complete or even absolute independence the President would immediately recommend to the Congress that such independence be granted. Under these circumstances the murderous attack from the visitors' gallery upon members of the United States House of Representatives on March 1, 1954, by four Puerto Rican Nationalists is the more difficult to understand.

As evidence of its continuing interest in the Island's social conditions, the Agricultural Housing Commission announced in February, 1953, that loans amounting to $1¾ million would be granted to Puerto Rican farmers during the following three months. The Department of Labor assisted in the unemployment situation by arranging for 11,000 Puerto Rican workers to be brought to the eastern part of the United States to help with the tobacco and vegetable crops. The migration of Puerto Ricans to the United States in recent years has been so great that it is estimated that almost half a million have settled in eastern United States.

Much has been made of the physical and economic progress of the island in the past fifty years, and these phases cannot be overlooked in attempting to evaluate the success of American rule in Puerto Rico. When the United States took over the island in 1899 there were but 267 kilometers of completed roads; in 1949 there were 3437 kilometers. In 1899 there were practically no public school buildings worthy of the name; in 1949 there were over 3000; the number of students has increased from about 45,000 to over 445,000. The University of Puerto Rico has over 11,000 students enrolled and the School of Tropical Medicine is one of the outstanding institutions of its kind in the world. Agencies for guarding public health have been introduced, such as quarantine, hospitals, and sanitary systems; some diseases, such as yellow fever and smallpox have been almost completely eliminated, while others have been brought under control. A more modern and just taxation system has been put into operation and a strict auditing system has been provided. It should also be noted that all the customs duties and internal revenue taxes collected in the island go to Puerto Rico, and these have already amounted to over $70 million. The island is exempt from federal income tax and inheritance tax, and has free trade with the United States.

It is in the volume of foreign commerce, however, that Puerto Rico has made the most phenomenal progress, having risen from $17,502,103 in 1901 to $554,469,000 in 1949. The share of the United States in this trade has increased from about 70 per cent to over 95 per cent in this period. At the present time Puerto Rico ranks fourth among the Latin-American countries as a market for United States goods.

This table, prepared from statistics found in the Annual Report of the Governor for 1948-1949 shows graphically the commercial progress of the island:

	1901	1949
Merchandise from Puerto Rico to the United States	$ 5,581,288	$195,844,000
Merchandise from Puerto Rico to foreign countries	3,002,679	8,281,000
Total trade with the United States	12,546,696	521,979,000
Total trade with foreign countries	4,955,407	32,490,000

But in spite of this imposing façade of statistics the condition of the people of the island today is not a happy one. And, paradoxically, the very improvements instituted by the United States have been one of the fundamental causes of the present tragic situation. As a result of improved sanitary and health measures, the population is greater than the island can support. It has more than doubled under American rule and in 1952 was estimated at 2,285,000, a density of over 650 to the square mile. The United States, an industrial nation, has a density of 41. It has been declared by investigators that the Puerto Rican peon "lives literally in a state of chronic starvation, crowding his filthy scarecrow body into a hut where his female counterpart and their numberless wretched children almost always share at least one of his diseases." [48] Under these circumstances, the crying need for a prompt, all-embracing program of birth control would seem to be the most fundamental requirement of the island. So long as unlimited breeding of undernourished peons continues, economic rehabilitation is impossible. Unemployment, low standards of living, social and physical degeneration are the direct results.[49]

As former Governor Theodore Roosevelt once observed, "Puerto Rico is not and almost certainly never will be an economic asset to the United States." Nevertheless, if the population pressure could be checked, and if there could be a careful redistribution of land, followed by a rigid enforcement of the "five hundred acre law," the economic rehabilitation of Puerto Rico would not be an impossible task. Certainly the vigorous efforts of Governor Muñoz Marín to encourage industries to come to Puerto Rico—"Operation Bootstrap"—which have raised the national income from $228 million in 1940 to $970 millions in 1953 give hopes for the future.

[48] E. M. Matsner and William Laidlaw, "Puerto Rico: Old Woman in a Shoe," *North American Review*, Vol. 242 (Winter, 1936), p. 277.
[49] The dissemination of birth control information has been legalized by the government but the ignorance and poverty of the *jibaro*, the influence of the Catholic Church, and the cost of contraceptives have militated against any noticeable reduction in the birthrate.

SUPPLEMENTARY READINGS

WILFRID H. CALCOTT, *The Caribbean Policy of the United States 1890-1920* (Baltimore, 1942).

VICTOR S. CLARK and Associates, *Porto Rico and Its Problems* (Washington, D. C., 1930).

B. W. and J. W. DIFFIE, *Porto Rico, A Broken Pledge* (New York, 1931).

J. E. ENAMORADO-CUESTA, *Porto Rico, Past and Present* (New York, 1929).

E. S. GARVER and E. B. FINCHER, *Puerto Rico, Unsolved Problem* (Elgin, Ill., 1945).

JOHN GUNTHER, *Inside Latin America* (New York, 1941), Chap. XXVIII.

R. T. HILL, *Cuba and Porto Rico* (New York, 1899).

PRESTON E. JAMES, *Latin America* (New York, 1942), pp. 776-788.

C. LLOYD JONES, *Caribbean Interests of the United States* (New York, 1916), Chap. VII.

———, *The Caribbean Since 1900* (New York, 1936), Chap. VIII.

LUIS MUÑOZ MARÍN, "Puerto Rico and the United States," *Foreign Affairs* (July, 1954).

KNOWLTON MIXER, *Porto Rico* (New York, 1926).

H. S. PERLOFF, *Puerto Rico's Economic Future* (Chicago, 1950).

VINCENZO PETRULLO, *Puerto Rican Paradox* (Philadelphia, 1947).

"Puerto Rico—A Study in Democratic Development," *Annals of the Amer. Acad. of Polit. and Social Sci.* (Jan., 1953).

L. S. ROWE, *The United States and Porto Rico* (London, 1904).

REXFORD TUGWELL, *The Stricken Land* (New York, 1947).

R. S. and E. K. VAN DEUSEN, *Porto Rico, A Caribbean Isle* (New York, 1931).

A. H. VERRILL, *Porto Rico, Past and Present* (New York, 1926).

W. F. WILLOUGHBY, *Territories and Dependencies of the United States* (New York, 1905), Chap. V.

❧ 12 ❧

American Interests in Haiti and the Dominican Republic

THE influence of geography upon history can hardly be over-estimated. In ancient times, when nature's highways, the seas and great navigable rivers, furnished the principal arteries of communication, this influence was unquestionably more important than today, when man's ingenuity and effort have so largely overcome the obstructive barriers of nature. But even now, although the effects of physical factors are less evident, they play an important rôle in national and international policies. No nation can ignore the consideration of geography in evaluating the bases of its historical development.

A mere glance at a map of the Caribbean Sea gives the key to the history of the island of Santo Domingo. Lying almost directly between Cuba and Puerto Rico, it would undoubtedly be discovered by Spain; like Cuba, it would probably be the sport of English and French buccaneers during the seventeenth century; and at the present time, commanding as it does both of the important routes between northern Europe and the Panama Canal, i.e., the Windward passage and the Mona passage, it would necessarily be affected in some way by the influence of the United States. This is the general setting of its history, no less than that of its neighbors. But, although the historic background of the Caribbean islands is similar, each island has had a decidedly individual foreground; and in the case of Santo Domingo it must be sketched in rather somber colors.

Santo Domingo was discovered by Columbus on his first voyage, shortly after he had discovered Cuba. The natives called the island Haiti, but Columbus named it la Española, or, as it is now generally written, Hispaniola. A small colony of Spaniards was left by the discoverer at Cape

Haitien, on the northwest coast of the island. But on his return, in 1493, he found that all had been massacred by the natives. The Spaniards exacted bloody vengeance later, and it was estimated that within twenty years of the discovery of the island the population was reduced from 1,000,000 to about 14,000.[1] To repopulate the island the slave trade was resorted to; and ultimately the blacks became the preponderant population.

The island remained under the unchallenged domination of the Spaniards until the middle of the seventeenth century, when the French established settlements in the western extremity. The Spaniards made various efforts to oust their unwelcome neighbors, but to no avail, and the treaty of Ryswick in 1697 definitely ceded the western section of the island to France. The French colonists soon made Saint-Domingue one of the most prosperous islands of the West Indies, although their great sugar, coffee, and tobacco plantations were worked entirely with slave labor. When the French Revolution broke out, in 1789, it was estimated that the population of Saint-Domingue consisted of about 40,000 whites, 28,000 affranchis, or freedmen, and about 452,000 slaves.[2]

The principles of the Revolution quickly became known in Santo Domingo, and at the earnest solicitation of the affranchis, the National Assembly, in 1791, granted full civil and political rights to free-born colored men in French possessions. This decree was resisted vigorously by the whites in Haiti, and the result was one of the most horrible servile wars in the world's history. The blacks, whose treatment at the hands of the whites had been barbarous in the extreme,[3] massacred the whites in veritable orgies of slaughter. In the wars that followed, the one bright spot was the brilliant achievements of the black leader, Toussaint l'Ouverture. Fighting, in turn, with the Spanish against the French, then with the English and Spanish, sometimes with the mulattoes, sometimes against them, but always sturdily defending the interests of his black comrades, by 1799 Toussaint l'Ouverture had gained control of virtually the entire island.[4]

It was at this period that the island came within the diplomatic horizon of the United States. In December, 1798, Rufus King, the American minister to Great Britain, heard rumors that a commercial agreement had

---

[1] Justin Placide, *Histoire politique et statistique d'Hayti, Saint-Domingue* (Paris, 1826), p. 40.
[2] J. N. Léger, *Haiti: Her History and Her Detractors* (New York, 1907), p. 41.
[3] *Ibid.*, p. 50 (note).
[4] For detailed accounts of this period see T. G. Stewart, *The Haitian Revolution, 1791-1804* (New York, 1914), and T. Lothrop Stoddard, *The French Revolution in San Domingo* (Boston, 1914).

been signed by a British officer and Toussaint.[5] King immediately approached Grenville, the British Foreign Minister, who admitted that the report was true and explained that, although General Maitland had signed the agreement wholly without authority, his government felt that in order to protect Jamaica it was wise to ratify the convention.[6] Owing to the fact that French sovereignty was still recognized in the island, and that the United States had prohibited all trade with French territories, such an agreement would be inimical to American trade interests. Therefore, early in January, 1799, King again approached Grenville, this time suggesting that if the island should become independent, concerted action between the two powers would be the most advantageous line of action. Grenville agreed, and proposed the formation of an exclusive company, composed jointly of British and American nationals, to trade with Santo Domingo. King was dubious about the power of Congress to create such a company, and he suggested as a more feasible scheme that each nation make treaties with Toussaint, confining trade to the citizens of the two countries.[7] Grenville, however, seemed to prefer the plan of a joint company, and in a communication to King he outlined a definite proposal in which all trade should be confined to Port au Prince.[8]

These proposals were laid before President Adams, who, however, feared that the independence of Santo Domingo would not be an unmixed blessing for the United States, and also objected to the idea of a joint company. He accordingly declared it to be the policy of the United States not to meddle.[9] Hamilton was more outspoken in his advice. In a letter to Pickering, the Secretary of State, dated February 9, 1799, he proposed that there be no committal regarding the independence of Santo Domingo, that there be no guaranty, no formal treaty, merely a verbal assurance to Toussaint that upon a declaration of independence commercial intercourse would be opened.[10] The whole American position was well summed up in a confidential note from Pickering to King, dated March 12, 1799, in which the Secretary of State declared: "We shall never receive from the French Republic indemnification for the injuries she has done us. The commerce of Santo Domingo presents the only means of compensation, and this I have no doubt we shall obtain. Tous-

---

[5] For a full account of this agreement see Thos. Southey, *Chronological History of the West Indies* (London, 1827), Vol. III, pp. 155-159.
[6] *Life and Correspondence of Rufus King* (New York, 1895), Vol. II, p. 476.
[7] *Ibid.*, Vol. II, p. 499.
[8] *Ibid.*, p. 504.
[9] *Works of John Adams* (Boston, 1853), Vol. VIII, p. 635.
[10] *Works of Alexander Hamilton* (New York, 1850), Vol. VI, p. 395.

saint respects the British, he is attached to us; he knows our position, but a few days' sail from Santo Domingo, and the promptitude with which we can supply his wants.... Nothing is more clear than, if left to themselves, the blacks of Santo Domingo will be less dangerous than if they remain the subjects of France.... We therefore reckon confidently upon the independence of Santo Domingo." [11]

Joint action with Great Britain seemed essential, and in April an agreement was signed, based upon the common interest of the two countries, to prevent dissemination of dangerous principles among slaves held in territories belonging to the respective countries, and to open up intercourse with the islands. [12] The result was the appointment of Mr. Edward Stevens as consul to Santo Domingo, and a proclamation by the President, dated June 26, 1799, opening up Santo Domingo to American trade, though only through the two ports of Cape François and Port au Prince. [13] By this decree Toussaint's position was both recognized and strengthened, inasmuch as Rigaud, his principal rival, had to depend upon the southern ports for his provisions and war material. As shown by his letter of August 14, 1799, to President Adams, [14] Toussaint was not entirely satisfied. But in the following year the United States gave him further support by sending war-ships to blockade the southern ports. [15]

By the opening of 1801 Toussaint was in complete control of the island, including the Spanish part; and a constitution adopted May 9, 1801, made him governor-general for life. His success was to be transient. Napoleon, who now had a breathing-spell in Europe, organized an expedition under his brother-in-law, General Le Clerc, to recover Santo Domingo. For a time Toussaint resisted, but finally, realizing the futility of continuing the struggle against overwhelming odds, he surrendered and withdrew to one of his plantations. The French, however, feared his influence, and by an act of base treachery they seized him and sent him to France. Broken in health but not in spirit, he died, less than a year afterwards, in the prison at de Joux. The French paid dearly for their action. Finding a new leader in Dessalines, the blacks renewed the struggle for independence with astonishing vigor. The death of Le Clerc aided their cause, as did also the ravages of yellow fever. When the peace of Amiens was broken, Napoleon could no longer afford to dissipate his energy in the New World to such little advantage. Santo Domingo be-

[11] *Life and Correspondence of Rufus King*, Vol. II, p. 557.
[12] For text see *Works of John Adams*, Vol. VIII, p. 639.
[13] *Amer. State Papers, For. Rel.*, Vol. II, p. 240.
[14] Léger, *op. cit.*, p. 99 (note).
[15] *Ibid.*, p. 100.

came merely a stepping-stone to a great French empire west of the Mississippi. Yet it was also the cornerstone, without whose possession the structure would be exceedingly insecure. Jefferson had already intimated that the United States would not look with pleasure upon French ownership of Louisiana, and Monroe had already been sent to negotiate for New Orleans and the Floridas. America's star was in the ascendant; and Napoleon, who did not do things by halves, suddenly ordered Marbois to sell the whole of the Louisiana territory to the United States, and at the same time instructed Rochambeau, who now commanded in place of Le Clerc, to withdraw from Santo Domingo. On December 20, 1803, the United States took formal possession of New Orleans, and on January 1, 1804, Saint-Domingue was declared forever independent of French domination. Even the French name was discarded—the island resuming its original name of Haiti.[16] The United States will always be grateful to Jefferson for his vision, and to his representative Livingston for his prompt action. But it must be conceded that no small share in the happy result was contributed by the fight for the independence of Santo Domingo so indefatigably carried on by Toussaint l'Ouverture.

It does not come within our province to consider the internal history of the island during the next few decades, except as it concerns the United States. The island's independence was not recognized by the United States when recognition was accorded to the rest of Latin America, although Great Britain officially gave recognition in 1826, and even France followed suit in 1838. The unstable character of the government was hardly a reason for our inaction, considering that one president, Jean Boyer, remained in office from 1818 to 1843. The real reason was rather the dangerous slavery question; for undoubtedly the abolition of slavery in the island was viewed by an important element in the United States as a most undesirable precedent. Even Bolívar, who had been received most cordially by the Haitians during his struggle for the independence of South America, and had been given generous supplies of ammunition and provisions, did not dare include Haiti in his invitation to the Congress of Panama.

The first official diplomatic relations that the United States had with the island were established in 1844. After the resignation of Boyer in 1843, the Spanish part of the island revolted and set up a separate government under the name of the Dominican Republic. Desirous of strengthening itself against the blacks, this republic immediately despatched an envoy to the United States to obtain recognition and, if possible, to sign a treaty

16 *Ibid.*, p. 153.

of friendship and commerce. In order to obtain unbiased information concerning resources and conditions in the island, President Polk despatched a special agent, John Hogan, on February 22, 1845, to investigate and make a report. Mr. Hogan spent about five months in the island, and ran up a heavy expense account which the government later refused to pay. But his report remained buried until 1871, when the House asked for the information.[17]

In the meantime the Dominicans, not obtaining satisfaction from the United States, and constantly harassed by the guerrilla warfare on the Haitian border, approached both France and Spain. President Souloque, of Haiti, prepared a large expedition with the purpose of forcing the Dominicans back under the control of Haiti; whereupon the threatened republic, in a circular note dated February 22, 1850, and addressed to the consuls of the United States, France, and Great Britain, urgently solicited the mediation of the governments of those countries.[18] Through the British minister at Washington, France and Great Britain proposed that the United States coöperate with them in a joint plan of action. Mr. Webster, who had succeeded Mr. Clayton as Secretary of State, nominated Mr. Robert M. Walsh as special agent to Haiti, with a view to obtaining fuller information before announcing his policy.

Mr. Walsh sailed for Haiti, January 25, 1851, and upon arriving at Port au Prince immediately got in touch with the British and French consuls. He then informed the Haitian Minister for Foreign Affairs that the government of the United States had determined to coöperate with the governments of England and France to secure the pacification of the island, and that the most feasible way to accomplish this was for the government of Haiti to acknowledge the independence of the Republic of Santo Domingo.[19] At the same time, a joint note, signed by the representatives of the three powers, demanded a definite treaty of peace, or, in lieu of that, a truce of ten years between the Empire of Haiti and the Dominican Republic. After a series of interviews and *pourparlers,* the Haitian government refused to subscribe to either proposition, but promised to continue the truce that then existed. Unable to obtain anything better, Mr. Walsh left, and in summing up his report he declared that the only way to obtain the recognition of the Dominican Republic by Haiti was by the use of force. The United States government, however, might well be content with the result achieved; for this statement not

[17] Report published in *House Ex. Doc. No. 42,* 41st Cong., 3rd Sess.

[18] *Sen. Ex. Doc. No. 12,* p. 19, 33rd Cong., 1st Sess.

[19] The complete correspondence of the Walsh Mission is found in *Sen. Ex. Doc. No. 113,* 32nd Cong., 1st Sess.

only allowed it to escape from an entangling alliance of dubious value, but was in direct accord with the American policy of looking with disfavor upon European intervention in the Western Hemisphere.

During the next decade America's relations with the island were based chiefly upon the Dominican Republic's need of protection against Haiti, and upon the means that she employed to obtain it. A protectorate under a strong power seemed the safest plan, and from 1843 onwards the Dominicans had made a series of proposals to both France and Spain suggesting such a measure; but, as one authority puts it, "neither France nor Spain was anxious to annex a hornets' nest." [20] In 1855 a proposal was made to General William L. Cazneau, the United States commissioner to the Dominican Republic, that Samana Bay be leased to the United States at a nominal rent for a naval base; but when the negotiations leaked out, France and Great Britain protested, and nothing further was done.[21]

In 1861 President Santana was successful in his efforts to obtain a Spanish protectorate; and in a fervid letter to the Queen of Spain he assured her that "The Dominican people, giving a free course to those sentiments of affection and loyalty which have been so long repressed, have unanimously and spontaneously proclaimed you as their Queen and Sovereign, and I, who have now the exalted and undeserved honor of being the organ of those sincere sentiments, lay at your Majesty's feet the keys of this lovely island." [22] By a royal decree dated May 19, 1861, the Queen accepted the offer, and Santana was made governor-general of the colony. If the Monroe Doctrine covered voluntary transfer of sovereignty, here was a clear-cut violation. But, as in the contemporary French intervention in Mexico, Seward's hands were tied by the Civil War, and he could only protest in very general terms. Although on April 2, 1861, he wrote the Spanish minister at Washington that Spanish interference in the Dominican Republic would be regarded as manifesting an unfriendly spirit toward the United States and would be met with a prompt resistance, when the news of annexation was received, and Carl Schurz, our minister to Spain, asked him for an explicit statement of policy, Seward replied that too many other subjects were occupying his attention to permit him to give full consideration to this one.[23] The Dominicans,

[20] Otto Schoenrich, *Santo Domingo* (New York, 1918), p. 55.

[21] See Moore, *Digest of Int. Law,* Vol. I, p. 598; treaty also mentioned by Hamilton Fish, *Sen. Ex. Doc. No. 17,* 41st Cong., 3rd Sess. Mrs. W. L. Cazneau gives an interesting side-light on these negotiations in an appendix entitled "The Seward Samana Mystery" in her book, *Our Winter Eden* (New York, 1878).

[22] *British Parliamentary Papers, 1861,* Vol. LXV. Papers rel. to Annex. of St. Domingo, p. 28.

[23] Frederic Bancroft, *The Life of Wm. H. Seward* (New York, 1900), Vol. II, p. 157.

however, were not long content with the Spanish rule. In 1863 a revolution, known as the War of the Restoration, broke out, and two years later, coincident with the termination of the Civil War in the United States, the Spanish Cortes passed a law relinquishing the colony.[24]

An excellent opportunity was given to Seward to indicate the post-bellum attitude of the United States toward the island when the British minister proposed, on July 25, 1865, that the United States concur with Great Britain in guaranteeing the neutrality of the peninsula of Samana.[25] Replying on August 15, the secretary declared that the United States was "sincerely desirous that the entire island of Haiti may now and henceforth remain subject exclusively to the government and jurisdiction of the people who are the dwellers and occupants thereof, and that they may never be dispossessed or disturbed by any foreign state or nation whatever." [26] He further pointed out that, while the United States was gratified at the proposal, its policy regarding political alliances with foreign states prevented its participation.

After the emancipation of slaves in the United States there was no further reason to refuse to recognize Haiti. In fact, ever since 1838 Congress had been bombarded with petitions and memorials from citizens and organizations of different states asking for such recognition. In his message of December 3, 1861, President Lincoln expressed the opinion that the independence of Haiti should be recognized; and by the act of June 5, 1862, the President was authorized to appoint a diplomatic representative. On July 12, 1862, Mr. Benjamin F. Whidden was empowered to act as a commissioner and consul-general to Haiti.[27] Two years later a treaty of amity and commerce was concluded between the two countries, and its proclamation followed on July 6, 1865.[28] Owing to the Spanish protectorate and the resulting disorder, the Dominican Republic was not recognized by us until September 17, 1866. A treaty similar to that made with Haiti was signed in the following year.[29]

In 1866 the question of Samana once more came up, and this time the Dominican Foreign Secretary proposed to lease certain keys and coal mines in Samana Bay, provided the United States would advance the republic $1,000,000 in the form of a loan. Secretary Seward thereupon

[24] A full account of this period from the Spanish standpoint is given by General Gandara y Navarro, *Anexion y Guerra de Santo Domingo* (Madrid, 1884).

[25] *For. Rel. of the U. S.*, 1865, Part II, p. 184; see also Seward's notes to Perry, pp. 522-534.

[26] *Ibid.*, p. 191; see also J. N. Léger, *La Politique Extérieure d'Haiti*, pp. 145-157.

[27] J. B. Moore, *Digest of Int. Law*, Vol. I, p. 107.

[28] W. M. Malloy, *Treaties, Conventions, etc., of the U. S.*, Vol. I, p. 921.

[29] *Ibid.*, p. 403.

sent the Assistant Secretary of State and Rear-Admiral Porter, with power to conclude a convention for the lease or cession of the peninsula and bay of Samana for the sum of $2 million, one half in cash and the other half payable in munitions of war. The Dominican government was willing to give certain concessions, but declared that the national constitution prevented absolute sale of territory. By the end of 1867, however, conditions were such that the island government decided to accede to the terms of the United States, and the negotiations were rapidly progressing when a revolution brought the downfall of the ruling authorities.[30]

The new government, under General Baez, was even more friendly to the United States; it proposed, indeed, to Mr. Smith, the commercial agent at Santo Domingo City, that the United States assume a protectorate over the republic and take possession of Samana Bay as a first step toward annexation.[31] This went beyond the ideas of even Seward; although he was soon won over to the proposal, subject to the favorable outcome of a popular referendum in the insular state. President Johnson's ill-considered message of December 9, 1868, indicated the direction of the wind.[32] In a letter to General Banks on January 29, 1869, Seward suggested that the stage was all set for annexation, and a joint resolution was introduced by Mr. Orth, of Indiana, providing for the admission of Santo Domingo, on the application of the people and government of that republic, into the Union as a territory of the United States, with a view to the ultimate establishment of a state government.[33] Congress, possessing neither the information nor the imagination of Seward, promptly laid the resolution on the table.

The Grant administration next took over the problem, and Hamilton Fish, the new Secretary of State, despatched General Babcock as a special agent to obtain full information regarding the island, particularly in regard to the disposition of the government and people towards the United States.[34] Incidentally, the new agent signed a protocol with the Dominican government in which Seward's proposal was virtually repeated, but which also provided that President Grant should use his utmost influence to make the idea of annexation more popular wtih members of Congress.[35] With this as a basis, General Babcock and Mr. R. H. Perry were authorized to sign a treaty of annexation incorporating the republic as a terri-

---

[30] See Seward's account in *Sen. Ex. Doc. No. 17*, 41st Cong., 3rd Sess., p. 5.
[31] Moore, *op. cit.*, Vol. I, p. 590.
[32] See pp. 60-61.
[33] Bancroft, *op. cit.*, Vol. II, p. 488.
[34] For instructions see *Sen. Ex. Doc. No. 17*, 41st Cong., 3rd Sess. p. 79.
[35] For text of protocol see *Sen. Report No. 234*, 41st Cong., 2nd Sess., p. 188.

tory of the United States, and also a convention giving the United States immediate possession of the Samana peninsula and bay. The cash payment to be made by the United States was $1½ million. The treaty further provided that in case of its rejection the United States should still have the right to acquire the peninsula and bay of Samana within fifty years upon the payment of $2 million.[36] The treaties were signed November 29, 1869, and communicated to the Senate in the following January.

The debate that followed brought about a serious controversy between President Grant and Charles Sumner, who was at that time chairman of the Senate Committee on Foreign Relations. The report of the committee was adverse to the treaties, and Sumner led the opposition. A vote was taken on June 30, 1870, resulting in a tie (28-28); and as a two-thirds vote was required for ratification, the opponents had won. In his second annual message, December 5, 1870, President Grant again brought up the question and strongly urged that Congress reconsider the matter on the ground that possession of the territory would be of incalculable advantage to the United States strategically, economically, and commercially, and would be "a rapid stride towards that greatness which the intelligence, industry, and enterprise of the citizens of the United States entitle this country to assume among nations." [37] Although the opposition to annexation remained as strong as ever, out of deference to the President's views it was proposed that three commissioners be appointed to inquire once more into the political and economic condition of the island. In a powerful speech, teeming with invective and heated charges, Sumner resisted this proposal.[38] The resolution passed; and the result was that Fish joined Grant in open opposition to Sumner, who was ultimately ousted from his committee chairmanship.[39]

In accordance with the congressional resolution, President Grant appointed a very eminent investigating commission, consisting of Benjamin F. Wade, Andrew D. White, and Samuel G. Howe. The three men visited the island and made an elaborate and painstaking report, which is even today a very valuable source of information.[40] They unanimously approved of the annexation, and President Grant once more, in a special message prefacing the report (April 5, 1871), indicated that his own

[36] Text of treaty and convention, Sen. Ex. Doc. No. 17, 41st Cong., 3rd Sess., pp. 98-102.

[37] J. D. Richardson, Messages and Papers of the Presidents, Vol. VII, pp. 90 ff.

[38] Works of Charles Sumner, Vol. XIV, 15 vols. (Boston, 1875-83), pp. 89-131.

[39] For a detailed account of this famous controversy see Ed. L. Pierce, Memoir and Letters of Charles Sumner (Boston, 1894), Vol. IV, pp. 426 ff.

[40] Sen. Ex. Doc. No. 9, 42nd Cong., 1st Sess.

opinion regarding the desirability of annexation had not changed. But the sentiment of Congress was similarly unchanged; so that, although the President, in his last annual message, recurred to the subject, it was merely to vindicate his attitude rather than to renew the proposal.

One of the chief arguments made by Sumner, Schurz, and their followers was the alleged overbearing attitude of the United States toward Haiti. It was asserted that, in order to prevent extraneous influences from interfering with the negotiations, our government had sent war-ships to the island, not only to sustain President Baez against internal difficulties, but also to intimidate Haiti. The instructions given by the Secretary of the Navy to Admiral Poor were, indeed, couched in no uncertain terms: "Proceed at once with the *Severn* and *Dictator* to Port au Prince, communicate with our consul there, and inform the present Haitian authorities that this government is determined to protect the present Dominican government with all its power. . . . If the Haitians attack the Dominicans with their ships, destroy or capture them." [41] Admiral Poor did not think it necessary to mask his orders by diplomatic formulæ, and he bluntly informed President Saget of Haiti that "any interference or attack by vessels under Haitian or any other flag upon the Dominicans during the pendency of said negotiations will be considered an act of hostility to the flag of the United States, and will provoke hostility in return." [42] Sumner offered a resolution in the Senate condemning these orders as involving an unlawful assumption by the President of the war-making power; but the proposal was laid on the table. [43] Secretary Fish also gave instructions during this period to Mr. Bassett, our minister to Haiti, warning the Haitian government against any interference with the Dominican Republic. [44]

For a period following the Grant administration the United States seemed to lose interest in further expansion in the Caribbean region. When, in 1882, President Salomon, of Haiti, offered to cede to the United States the island of La Tortue, Secretary Frelinghuysen said that "the policy of this government, as declared on many occasions in the past, has tended towards avoidance of possessions disconnected from the main continent." [45] Two years later a similar observation was called out from him by a proposal to cede the peninsula or bay of Le Môle or the island of Tortuga.

[41] *Sen. Ex. Doc. No. 34,* 41st Cong., 3rd Sess., p. 11.
[42] *Ibid.,* p. 13.
[43] See *Cong. Globe,* 42nd Cong., 1st Sess. (1871), Part I, pp. 232 *et seq.*
[44] Moore, *op. cit.,* Vol. I, p. 279.
[45] *Ibid.,* p. 432.

During this period the diplomatic relations between the United States and Haiti were exceedingly friendly, and in the case of the Pelletier and Lazare claims the United States acted in a manner above reproach. Pelletier, a naturalized American, had been seized and imprisoned while cruising off the coast of Haiti in 1861, on evidence of being a slaver. Escaping, he demanded damages from the Haitian government, and his claim was brought up on various occasions until finally, in 1884, Haiti agreed upon arbitration. Mr. William Strong, a former justice of the United States Supreme Court, was appointed sole arbiter, and he awarded Pelletier $57,250 instead of the two and one-half millions that he demanded. Haiti protested against making any payment, and when the case was brought before Mr. T. F. Bayard, Secretary of State, he declared the claim of Pelletier against Haiti on the facts exhibited "must be dropped, and dropped peremptorily and immediately, by the government of the United States, ... first because Haiti had jurisdiction to inflict on him the very punishment of which he complains, and secondly because his cause is of itself so saturated with turpitude and infamy that on it no action, judicial or diplomatic, can be based." [46]

The Lazare claim was for a breach of contract in the establishment of a national bank in Haiti. Here again the award of $117,500 rendered by Mr. Strong was set aside on the ground that new evidence showed the claim to be invalid, and that "the moment the government of the United States discovers that a claim it makes on a foreign government cannot be honorably and honestly pressed, that moment, no matter what may be the period of the procedure, that claim should be dropped." [47] In his message to Congress on May 12, 1887, President Salomon declared that such sentiments did honor to the statesmen who had so well expressed them. [48]

Friendly relations between the United States and Haiti were suddenly interrupted in 1888 by the seizure of an American steamship, the *Haitian Republic,* as she was leaving Saint Mare, on the ground that an effective blockade was being maintained. The reasons for the blockade were as follows: President Salomon's seven-year term ended in 1887. But he had been so successful that the constitution was modified and he was reëlected for another seven years. This brought about a revolution leading to his withdrawal in August, 1888, followed by a period of anarchy, in which one faction controlled the north and another the south. The *Haitian Re-*

[46] Sen. Ex. Doc. No. 64, 49th Cong., 2nd Sess., p. 20, or For. Rel. of the U. S., 1887, pp. 593 ff.
[47] Ibid., p. 33.
[48] Ibid., 1887, p. 629.

public had, it was claimed, transported various armed members of the Hyppolite, or northern, faction while touching at the ports of the north and northwest, and on this ground it was seized while in waters patrolled by the Légitime, or southern, faction. The United States protested vigorously against the seizure, saying that, since no notice of blockade had been given, the blockade was not effective; that the prize tribunal was irregularly constituted; and that the carrying of passengers who might have been armed between the vessels' ports of call did not constitute complicity in Haitian disorders. When the Haitian authorities refused to give up the ship, the United States sent two war-ships to Port au Prince; whereupon the disputed vessel was surrendered to the American commander.[49]

The Légitime faction, which had been hostile to the United States, was finally overthrown, and Hyppolite was elected president. Whether the United States had ever done more than manifest sympathy for the Hyppolite side the published records do not show. But about a year after the inauguration of President Hyppolite (January 26, 1891), Rear-Admiral Gherardi arrived at Port au Prince as special commissioner to obtain the Môle St. Nicholas as a coaling station for the United States, and used as one of his arguments the services rendered by the United States to the Hyppolite revolution.[50] Popular opinion, aroused by the sight of an American fleet in the harbor, was so strongly opposed that after several months of fruitless negotiations, in which such technicalities as the form of the commissioner's credentials played a leading part, the United States gave up the idea. Secretary Blaine then turned towards the Dominican Republic and proposed to lease Samana Bay. But at the mere disclosure of the proposal the Dominican Secretary of State, General Gonzales, was forced to seek safety in exile. This was the last attempt made by the United States to obtain a naval station in the Caribbean until the war with Spain created new conditions and raised new problems.

SUPPLEMENTARY READINGS

H. P. DAVIS, *Black Democracy* (New York, 1928).

J. G. GARCÍA, *Compendio de la Historia de Santo Domingo* (Santo Domingo, 1867).

SAMUEL HAZARD, *Santo Domingo, Past and Present* (New York, 1873).

RALPH KORNGOLD, *Citizen Toussaint* (Boston, 1944).

[49] For details see *Sen. Ex. Doc. No. 69,* 50th Cong., 2nd Sess., particularly pp. 171-176; also *For. Rel. of U. S.,* 1888, pp. 932-1006; and 1889, pp. 487-494.

[50] Fred. Douglass, "Haiti and the United States," *North Amer. Rev.,* Vol. CLIII (Sept., 1891), p. 343. See also Moore, *op. cit.,* Vol. I, p. 610.

MELVIN M. KNIGHT, *The Americans in Santo Domingo* (New York, 1928).

J. N. LÉGER, *Haiti: Her History and Her Detractors* (New York, 1907).

JAMES G. LEYBURN, *The Haitian People* (New Haven, 1941).

R. W. LOGAN, *The Diplomatic Relations of the United States with Haiti, 1776-1891* (Chapel Hill, N. C., 1941).

W. A. MACCORKLE, *The Monroe Doctrine in Its Relation to Haiti* (New York, 1915).

L. J. MARCELIN, *Haiti* (Paris, 1892).

L. L. MONTAGUE, *Haiti and the United States, 1714-1938* (Durham, N. C., 1940).

DANA G. MUNRO, *The United States and the Caribbean Area* (Boston, 1934), Chaps. III, IV.

BLAIR NILES, *Black Haiti* (New York, 1926).

HESKETH PRICHARD, *Where Black Rules White* (New York, 1900).

OTTO SCHOENRICH, *Santo Domingo* (New York, 1918).

W. B. SEABROOK, *The Magic Island* (New York, 1929).

SPENCER ST. JOHN, *Haiti* (London, 1889).

T. L. STODDARD, *The French Revolution in San Domingo* (Boston, 1914).

C. C. TANSILL, *The United States and Santo Domingo, 1798-1873* (Baltimore, 1938).

L. G. TIPPENHAUER, *Die Insel Haiti*, 2 vols. (Leipzig, 1892).

MARY TREUDLEY, *The United States and Santo Domingo, 1789-1866* (Worcester, Mass., 1916).

J. W. VANDERCOOK, *Black Majesty* (New York, 1928).

A. H. VERRILL, *Porto Rico and San Domingo* (New York, 1914).

PERCY WAXMAN, *The Black Napoleon* (New York, 1931).

SUMNER WELLES, *Naboth's Vineyard: The Dominican Republic* (New York, 1928).

FAUSTIN WIRKUS and TANEY DUDLEY, *The White King of La Gonave* (New York, 1931).

❧ 13 ❧

American Imperialism in Haiti and the Dominican Republic

BEFORE considering the next and more serious intervention of the United States in the affairs of Haiti and Santo Domingo, it is necessary to say a word regarding the internal history of the two island republics. Sir Spencer St. John, British minister to Haiti for a period of years, called its government "a despotism tempered by revolution and exile and occasionally by death." [1] Beginning with Dessalines in 1804, and surveying the political history of Haiti for a century, we find some twenty different presidents, of whom two were shot, one committed suicide, six were exiled, and several others were overthrown or forced to resign. The Dominican Republic can hardly boast of a better record than its unstable neighbor. In fact, in its checkered history of revolution and counter-revolution, in its unending procession of presidents *de jure* and *de facto*, the Spanish end of the island stands well towards the top in any list of revolution-tossed republics. From 1844 to 1904 we find more than twenty different presidents, in spite of the fact that Heureaux served as president for fourteen years and Baez held office on five different occasions.[2]

No nation can maintain its credit under such conditions, and when Carlos Morales was inaugurated president of the Dominican Republic in 1904 the government was hopelessly bankrupt. The claims against the government were estimated at anywhere from $30 million to $40 million. Inasmuch as many of the creditors were Europeans, who constantly urged their governments to intervene, the United States was compelled to keep in close touch with the situation. Furthermore, the

[1] Spencer St. John, *Haiti* (London, 1889), p. 272.
[2] See the "Chronology of Political Events in Santo Domingo," prepared by Minister T. C. Dawson, *For. Rel. of the U. S.*, 1906, pp. 572-600.

United States was virtually forced to intervene in the case of the San Domingo Improvement Company. This American corporation had taken over the holdings of a Holland corporation in 1892, and was authorized by the Dominican government to take over certain custom-houses, with the understanding that a stipulated amount should be paid to the government and the rest devoted to the payment of interest and sinking fund of the loan. In 1901 the Dominican government became dissatisfied with the arrangement and repudiated it. The company appealed to the United States, but the State Department urged a settlement by private negotiations. After much haggling, the Dominican government finally offered $4½ million for the company's interests; and the proposal was accepted.[3] Representatives of the two governments signed a protocol on January 31, 1903, providing for the settlement, and for a board of arbitrators to fix the details of payment.[4] The board fixed the interest rate at 4 per cent, designated the monthly payments, and secured them by the customs, revenues, and port dues of the ports on the northern coast. In case of failure to pay, a financial agent of the United States was authorized to take over certain custom-houses and carry out the award.[5]

The Dominican government never made any payments, and in compliance with the terms of the award an American financial agent took over the custom-house of Puerto Plata, October 21, 1904. This move aroused the foreign creditors, and in December of this year the French threatened to seize the custom-house of Santo Domingo City; the Italian interests also demanded the payment of their claims. Secretary Hay thereupon instructed the American minister to Santo Domingo, Mr. T. C. Dawson, to sound out the insular president as to whether the Dominican government would be willing to request the United States to take charge of the collection of duties, with a view to an equitable distribution of the proceeds among the claimants and the Dominican government.[6] President Morales was by no means averse to such a solution, and on February 4, 1905, a protocol was signed which provided that the United States should take over all the custom-houses, turn over to the Dominican government 45 per cent of the amount collected for its expenses, and use the other 55 per cent to liquidate the republic's foreign and domestic debt. The United States further agreed to grant the little republic any

[3] President Theodore Roosevelt in a message to the Senate Feb. 15, 1905, gives a complete summary of the financial and political difficulties of the republic, *ibid.*, 1905, p. 334; see also the more detailed report of J. B. Moore, *ibid.*, p. 344.

[4] For text of the protocol see *For. Rel. of the U. S.*, 1904, p. 270.

[5] *Ibid.*, p. 274.

[6] *Ibid.*, 1905, p. 298.

assistance deemed necessary "to restore the credit, preserve the order, increase the efficiency of the civil administration, and advance the material progress and welfare of the Dominican Republic." [7]

When the protocol came before the Senate, President Theodore Roosevelt urged that assent be given to its ratification, on the ground that "those who profit by the Monroe Doctrine must accept certain responsibilities along with the rights which it confers." [8] The Senate did not seem to appreciate these responsibilities and gave no indication of an intention to give its consent. The President thereupon sent another special message, dated March 6, appealing for immediate action. The Senate adjourned, however, without acting, and the situation in Santo Domingo became so alarming that President Roosevelt decided to carry out the arrangement as an executive agreement. Mr. J. H. Hollander was appointed as confidential agent to examine and report on the financial conditions in the republic, and the Secretary of War, Mr. Taft, was authorized to nominate the necessary officials to collect the customs. [9] Santo Domingo accepted the *modus operandi,* and in his message to Congress on December 5, 1905, the President declared that a temporary arrangement had been made which would last until the Senate should take action on the treaty. He also asserted that under the course taken "stability and order and all the benefits of peace are at last coming to Santo Domingo, danger of foreign intervention has been suspended, and there is at last a prospect that all creditors will get justice." [10] The Senate did not take very kindly to this alleged executive usurpation, and Senator Tillman violently arraigned the President for his unconstitutional abuse of authority. [11] The *modus operandi,* however, brought order out of chaos, and the Dominican government received more money from the 45 per cent turned over by the American officials than they had previously obtained when collecting 100 per cent for themselves. [12]

After a careful investigation, Professor Hollander found that the claims pending against the Dominican Republic on June 1, 1905, amounted to more than $40 million. [13] Of this amount, the government recognized

[7] *Ibid.,* p. 342.

[8] *Ibid.,* p. 334.

[9] *Ibid.,* p. 360.

[10] *Ibid.,* p. xxxvi.

[11] See speech of Jan. 17, 1906, *Cong. Rec.,* Vol. 40, Part II, pp. 1173 *ff.*

[12] Minister Dawson's memorandum of July 1, 1905, gives an excellent account of the events preceding and the results following the application of the arrangement; *For. Rel. of the U. S.,* 1905, p. 378.

[13] See Report of J. H. Hollander (Washington, D. C., 1907), or *Quar. Jour. of Economics,* Vol. XXI (July, 1907), p. 405.

about three-fourths as valid. But a plan was finally evolved for scaling down this amount to about $17 million, based upon a cash payment. The funds were to be obtained by the flotation of an issue of fifty-year 5 per cent bonds to the amount of $20 million. An American receiver of customs appointed by the President of the United States was to collect all customs duties until the bond issue should be redeemed; and the Dominican Republic was not to increase its public debt until full payment should be made. A convention to this effect was signed on February 8, 1907. This time, the Senate was willing to assent; and the convention went into effect on July 25.[14]

The Dominican officials themselves could not fail to realize the immediate benefits of American control, and in his annual report for 1906, Señor Velasquez, the Dominican Minister of Finance and Commerce, bore witness to the advantages gained: "The items of revenue during 1905 and those of 1906 speak clearly, with renewed eloquence, of figures, that for some time past we have been living in the public posts a life of order and honesty, where but a few years ago life with few exceptions within and without the national palace was one of shamelessness, dilapidation, cupidity, and permanent disgrace for the Republic, being the principal cause, if not the only one, why our weak state has felt itself more than once trembling on the brink of the abyss, and that for a long time we have found ourselves lacking in economic autonomy, overweighed by debts, unjustifiable for the greater part, suffering insults and humiliations." [15]

The convention of 1907 remained unchanged until 1924; and if the "eloquence of figures" is a fair basis of judgment, the effect of the arrangement has been all that could be desired. The table on page 271, made up from figures submitted in the annual reports of the general receiver of Dominican customs to the bureau of insular affairs in the War Department, summarizes the results.[16]

Despite the remarkable financial and commercial improvement due to American control of the customs, the internal history of the Dominican Republic failed to show much improvement. General Ramón Cáceres, who was elected president in 1908, and whose administration was eminently successful, was shot down in cold blood by a group of political enemies in November, 1911. A provisional government was immediately established, but it could scarcely maintain itself against the revolutionary

---

[14] Text in *For. Rel. of the U. S.*, 1907, p. 307.

[15] *Ibid.*, p. 357.

[16] The report for 1939, the last to be made, was submitted to the newly established Division of Territories and Island Possessions in the Department of Interior.

FOREIGN TRADE AND CUSTOMS COLLECTION OF THE
DOMINICAN REPUBLIC *

Year	Imports	Exports	Collections by General Receivers	Value of Trade with U. S.
1911	$ 6,949,662	$10,995,546	$3,433,738.92	$ 9,871,947
1916	11,664,430	21,527,873	4,035,355.43	27,574,786
1921	24,585,327	20,614,048	2,859,866.40	31,866,711
1926	23,677,533	24,895,871	4,714,405.25	20,006,604
1931	10,151,762	13,067,162	2,883,446.92	9,310,422
1936	9,926,567	15,149,908	2,878,789.07	9,366,817
1939	11,592,166	18,643,302	3,031,455.64	11,912,960 †

* The collections by the general receiver were by convention years to Aug. 1, 1914, but starting with Jan. 1, 1915, they have been by calendar years. For the 5-month period Aug. 1, 1914, to Dec. 31, 1914, receipts were $1,209,555.54. The imports and exports are by calendar years.
† Report of fiscal periods 1911, 1916, 1921, 1926, 1931, 1936, 1939, Dominican Customs Receivership.

outbreaks. In the fall of 1912 President Taft appointed two special commissioners to investigate the situation and recommend measures calculated to put an end to the difficulties. They were to make the trip on an American gunboat, accompanied by 750 marines, who were to be at hand to protect the custom-houses.[17] In accordance with the suggestions of these commissioners, the insular president resigned, and the Dominican congress elected as new president Archbishop Nouel, a man loved and respected throughout the country. He did his best to bring order to the distracted land; but his health could not stand the strain, and on March 31, 1913, after serving exactly four months, he resigned.

Another period of revolutionary activity followed, and in a note dated September 9, 1913, Secretary Bryan declared that the influence of the United States would be exerted for the support of lawful authorities and for the discouragement of any and all insurrectionary methods, and that President Wilson had no sympathy with those who sought to seize the power of government to advance their own personal interests.[18] The American minister finally prevailed upon the revolutionary forces to lay down their arms, upon the promise of a fair election in the near future. It should be noted however that Minister Sullivan's influence was considerably vitiated by his unauthorized promises to the revolutionists and his inexcusable participation in local party politics. He had deservedly lost the confidence of the State Department and was under suspicion of questionable financial practices by the Dominican government.

When the United States government appointed three commissioners to observe the elections, the Dominican government in power protested

[17] For. Rel. of the U. S., 1912, p. 366.
[18] Ibid., 1913, p. 425.

vigorously. The commissioners were properly received, but their presence did not prevent the government from arresting six leaders of the opposition on the grounds of conspiracy.[19] Except for this incident, which completely demoralized the power of the opposition, the elections were very peaceably conducted. In 1914 there was a repetition of the same conditions, and again the United States sent commissioners and the elections were held. Ex-President Jiménez was successful, and for a little more than a year he maintained the peace. In April, 1916, a new insurrection took place, and this time the United States, with the consent of the insular president, landed marines to maintain order. Shortly afterwards President Jiménez resigned and the Dominican congress elected Dr. Henríquez y Carvajal as temporary president.[20]

On the ground that the terms of the convention of 1907 had been repeatedly violated, the United States, however, refused to recognize the new president unless he would sign a new treaty, which should provide for the collection of customs under American auspices, the appointment of an American financial adviser, and the establishment of a constabulary force under American officers. President Henríquez refused to accept recognition on these terms, and the United States declined to pay over any revenue to an unrecognized government. Rear-Admiral Knapp finally broke the deadlock by issuing a proclamation, on November 29, 1916, declaring the Dominican Republic under the military administration of the United States. The proclamation recited that there was no intention to destroy Dominican sovereignty, but merely to restore and maintain order and carry out the terms of the convention of 1907.[21] To accomplish this, Rear-Admiral Knapp suspended the Dominican congress and, in the capacity of governor-general, appointed American naval officers to the various cabinet positions.

Colonel George C. Thorpe, who for almost two years acted as chief of staff of the brigade of marines in the occupation of the republic, thus summed up the mission of the military government: "(1) to promote education, primary and vocational; (2) to build roads; (3) to create an effective police force; (4) to cultivate a regard for law and order; (5) to place property rights on a firmer basis, particularly as to land titles; (6) to

---

[19] See report of the commission, *ibid.*, p. 449.

[20] A brief accurate sketch of these events is found in Judge Schoenrich's *Santo Domingo* (New York, 1918), Chap. VI; see also report of Rear-Admiral Snowden, *Conditions in Santo Domingo,* in report of Secy. of Navy, 1920, pp. 321-342.

[21] For text of the proclamation and American version of the situation leading up to it see *Hearings before a Select Committee on Haiti and Santo Domingo,* U. S. Senate, 67th Cong., 1st Sess., 1922, Part I, pp. 90-94; the Dominican version is given by President Henríquez, *ibid.*, pp. 51-60.

stabilize the finances of the country; (7) and at the same time to respect Dominican institutions and sentiments as far as might be." [22]

It would appear that the United States made a conscientious effort to carry out this program. In his report of October 23, 1920, to the Secretary of the Navy, Admiral Snowden noted some of the benefits of American rule. Where formerly it cost the internal revenue department 14 per cent to collect about $700,000 annually, it was costing but 5 per cent to collect almost $4½ million.

In four years of occupation more than 400 miles of roads were constructed, about one-fourth of them macadam. More than a score of bridges were built, and of them seven were large steel bridges and eight were concrete. New piers, a new custom-house at Santo Domingo City, new wharves, and other port improvements were built. In fact, a summary of amounts used by the department of public works from 1909 to 1916 shows an average annual expenditure of about $400,000; while the average expenditure annually from July, 1917, to June 30, 1920, was more than $1¼ million. Reforms in other directions were equally noteworthy. The railroads for the year 1916-17 hauled 27,866,635 kilos of freight, and the net earnings were $49,750.63. In the year 1919-20 50,272,506 kilos of freight were hauled, and the net earnings were $217,039.74. Before the military administration there were about 18,000 pupils in all schools; in 1920 there were more than 100,000. The reforms instituted in sanitary methods and public health conditions were of particular value to the people.[23]

Yet, in spite of the noteworthy improvements due to American rule, the Dominicans were by no means content under it, and in many respects they had serious grounds for complaint. Their civil and political liberties were completely taken away by the American military government; numerous cases of unjust imprisonment were proved against the American provost courts; the water torture and other more horrible methods were employed at times by the marines; and a strict and humiliating censorship of the press was maintained during the greater part of the American occupation.[24] When, finally, even the economical and financial program of the military administration was suspended through lack of funds, the discontent became so pronounced that during Secretary Colby's visit to South America the Wilson administration on December 23, 1920, author-

[22] G. H. Blakeslee, ed., *Mexico and the Caribbean* (New York, 1920), p. 233.

[23] *Report of the Secretary of the Navy, 1920*, pp. 321-342; see also memorandum prepared for Sen. Com. Hearings, *op. cit.*, Part I, pp. 96-104.

[24] See summary of abuses in the letter of Archbishop Nouel to Minister Russell, dated December 29, 1919. (*Nation*, July 17, 1920, gives excerpts); see also the protest of President Henríquez, *Current History*, Vol. XIV (June, 1921), p. 397.

ized Rear-Admiral Snowden to issue a proclamation announcing that "the United States believes the time has arrived when it may, with a due sense of its responsibility to the people of the Dominican Republic, inaugurate the simple processes of its rapid withdrawal from the responsibilities assumed in connection with Dominican affairs." [25] The only conditions attached were that a commission of Dominican citizens should be appointed, with an American technical adviser who should formulate certain amendments to the constitution and a general revision of the laws. The Dominicans, however, protested vigorously against these conditions, and the situation was turned over to the Harding administration virtually unchanged.

As a candidate, President Harding had promised to take action, and he did not delay. On June 14, 1921, Admiral Robison, who had been appointed military governor to succeed Admiral Snowden, issued a proclamation promising withdrawal within eight months, providing the Dominicans would coöperate with the Americans in establishing a government able to maintain independence and public order and to assure security of life and property. The principal conditions of the convention of evacuation were: (1) the acts of the military government should be ratified; (2) a new loan of $2,400,000 to complete the public works should be validated; (3) the duties of the general receiver of Dominican customs should be extended to apply to this loan, and also to the collection and disbursement of a part of the internal revenues if the customs were insufficient to meet the service of the foreign debt; and (4) an efficient *Guardia Nacional* should be organized under the direction of an American military commission.[26] Again the Dominicans protested, and certain of the objections were met by a new statement issued by Secretary Hughes on June 28. The military government thereupon promulgated an electoral law, and the elections were set for August 13. The Dominicans were not yet satisfied; and they organized a "Junta of Electoral Abstention," which prevented the elections from being held.

In the meantime the question had come before Congress, and a Senatorial investigating commission was appointed, with Senator McCormick as chairman. The commission spent about a fortnight in the island, and in a preliminary report Senator McCormick declared that inasmuch as the political leaders in the Dominican Republic had rejected the proposals for the withdrawal of the American forces, and since at the present time

[25] Text *Hearings before a Select Committee on Haiti and Santo Domingo*, Part III, p. 934.
[26] *Ibid.*, Part I, p. 102.

it was impossible to advise a substantial modification of the terms of the proclamation, the American troops should not be removed.[27]

Early in 1922, however, numerous conferences were held in Washington between Secretary Hughes and Señores Velásquez, Vásquez, Brache, and Peynado, the first three representing the different political parties in the Dominican Republic, the latter being the former Dominican minister at Washington. The following program was finally agreed upon:

(1) A Provisional Government of Dominican citizens selected by Dominicans will be installed to carry out such legislative and constitutional reforms as they may deem appropriate, and to hold general elections for the installation of a subsequent permanent government without the intervention of the authorities of the United States.

(2) Upon the inauguration of the Provisional Government, the executive departments of the Dominican Republic will be turned over to the cabinet ministers appointed by the Provisional President; the Military Government will also turn over the National Palace, and at the same time the United States military forces will be concentrated in one, two, or three places as the Military Governor may determine. From that time peace and order will be maintained by the Dominican national police under the orders of the Provisional Government.

(3) Dominican plenipotentiaries will be designated by the Provisional Government to negotiate a convention with the United States containing the following provisions: (a) Recognition by the Dominican government of all executive and department orders promulgated by the Military Government, contracts entered into in accordance with these orders, and specific recognition of the bond issues authorized in 1918 and in 1922; (b) the convention of February 8, 1907, shall remain in force so long as any bonds of the issues of 1918 and 1922 shall remain unpaid, and the duties of the general receiver shall be extended to include the collection and application of the revenues pledged for the service of these issues.

(4) Upon this convention being approved by the national congress and constitutional president duly elected, the American military forces will immediately leave the Dominican Republic.

In order that the United States might be advised without delay whether this agreement met with the approval of a majority of the Dominican people, President Harding appointed Mr. Sumner Welles of New York, a former Chief of the Division of Latin-American Affairs in the State Department, as commissioner, with the rank of envoy extraordinary and minister plenipotentiary, to represent him in the Dominican Republic, for the purpose of investigating and reporting upon conditions there, and to obtain the views of the Dominican people respecting an appropriate

[27] *New York Times,* Dec. 26, 1921.

agreement with the United States as a result of which the military forces of the United States might be withdrawn.[28]

A current and unbiased survey of the whole situation is found in the report of Dr. Carl Kelsey, of the University of Pennsylvania, who was selected by the board of directors of the American Academy of Political and Social Science to undertake a survey of the economic, social, and political conditions in Haiti and the Dominican Republic. He spent nine months in the island, and his report contains a wealth of valuable material about conditions on the island at that time. In his conclusions regarding the Dominican Republic he found that, although the Dominicans were not antagonistic to Americans, they were critical of the policy of our government. They felt that the troops were sent either under false pretenses or through error. They recognized their economic dependence upon the United States, and they would have welcomed better trade relations. But the United States had promised to withdraw under certain conditions, and the pledge had to be kept if the conditions were accepted.[29]

Secretary Hughes himself recognized the false position in which the United States found itself in the Dominican Republic, and in a speech delivered at Amherst College in June, 1924, he asserted that "no step taken by the government of the United States in Latin-America in recent years has given rise to more criticism, and in this instance just criticism, than the military occupation of the Dominican Republic by the armed forces of the United States in 1916 . . . it is the belief of many that the military occupation would have never occurred had President Wilson had the opportunity or the time in the excitement of that period, to become fully cognizant of the causes of the situation existing in the Dominican Republic. Likewise it is improbable that he was informed of many of the occurrences which took place in the Dominican Republic during the earlier years of the American occupation,—occurrences deeply to be regretted by every American citizen." [30]

However, in this same speech Secretary Hughes was able to state that the occupation had terminated and that a freely elected constitutional government was at the time in sole power. For although the marines

[28] *Ibid.*, July 12, 1922. Mr. Welles later published a complete narrative of the events of this period in his book, *Naboth's Vineyard: The Dominican Republic, 1844-1924* (New York, 1928).

[29] "The American Intervention in Haiti and the Dominican Republic," *Annals of Amer. Acad.*, Vol. C, No. 189 (Mar., 1922), pp. 109-200, found also in *Hearings before a Select Committee on Haiti and Santo Domingo*, Part 4, pp. 1279-1341; see also Dr. Kelsey's statement before the Senate Committee, *ibid.*, pp. 1238-1277.

[30] *New York Times*, June 19, 1924.

were not withdrawn until September, 1924, an election supervised by the United States officials had taken place on March 15, 1924, approving the plan of evacuation signed at Washington on June 30, 1922. Shortly afterwards, pursuant to the agreement of 1922, a convention of ratification or validation of all executive orders and resolutions promulgated by the military government was signed by the two governments. This treaty also specifically recognized the bond issues of 1918 and 1922 as irrevocable obligations of the Republic, and provided that no change should be made in customs tariff without previous agreement between the Dominican government and the United States. The convention of 1907 was to remain in force until both bond issues were paid and the general receiver of customs was to control the revenues pledged to these services.[31]

However, it had long been felt that the 1907 convention was forcing too large an amount of income to be used for the amortization of the loan at the expense of various projects of public works vital to the development of the country. Consequently on December 27, 1924, a new convention was signed revising the convention of 1907. The new agreement contemplated the floating of a loan of $25 million to refund all outstanding loans and to leave a surplus of some $10 million "to be devoted to permanent public improvements and to other projects designed to further the economic and industrial development of the country." The agreement made no change in the arrangement whereby the customs were to be administered by a general receiver appointed by the President of the United States, and it also provided that until the whole amount of the bonds should be paid the public debt should not be increased except by previous agreement with the United States.[32]

However, there arose in the island considerable opposition to the new agreement on the ground that the new loan would prolong the control of the United States for a period of time ranging from twenty-five to a hundred years. Some seventeen of the thirty members of the Chamber of Deputies signed a "pact of honor" not to approve the convention. Nevertheless, when three of the "pacta" group went over to the government, the convention was approved and ratifications were exchanged on October 24, 1925.

During the next few years both political and economic relations in the Dominican Republic were eminently satisfactory. President Vásquez, elected for a six-year term in 1924, was both able and popular and if his health had not become seriously impaired he might well have been re-

[31] *U. S. Treaty Series*, No. 729.
[32] *Ibid.*, No. 726.

elected. However, while he was undergoing treatment in the United States in the fall of 1929 serious differences arose between Vice-president Alfonseca and General Rafael Trujillo, commander-in-chief of the army. Although President Vásquez upon his return reëstablished harmony, his feeble health and advanced age manifestly impaired his efforts to secure reëlection. In February, 1930, a revolution broke out led by Estrella Ureña which was quickly successful, and to avert bloodshed President Vásquez resigned and through mediation of the American legation, Ureña became provisional president. In the elections held May 16, 1930, General Trujillo was elected President for a four-year term and Estrella Ureña was chosen Vice-president.

Before the end of his term President Vásquez had attempted to put into effect a complete reorganization of the economic and financial adminis-tration of the government. To assist him he had invited General Charles G. Dawes to organize a financial commission to recommend methods of improvement in the collection and control of both national and munic-ipal revenues. The commission after a three-weeks' study in the island prepared drafts of laws for a budget, for a general accounting, for finance, for the reorganization of the government departments and for a civil service.[33] Although the Dominican Congress enacted all of the program into law the downfall of the Vásquez administration nullified its en-forcement.

The administration of President Trujillo was handicapped from the be-ginning by the results of the terrific hurricane of September 3, 1930, which caused a considerable loss of life and enormous property damage. This, coupled with the world economic crisis, forced a revision of the debt payments under the 1924 convention to prevent complete national bank-ruptcy. An emergency law of October 23, 1931, diverted to governmental expenses $1,500,000 from customs revenues which were pledged to service on the foreign loans. The United States Department of State immediately ordered an investigation, but when the serious situation was confirmed by its representatives, it contented itself with following "with attention and care the developments in the Dominican Republic.[34]

In 1934 a new arrangement was made with the Foreign Bondholders' Protective Council, Inc., an organization sponsored by the United States government, whereby the General Receiver of Customs was given greater powers, interest payments were to be made in full, while amortization pay-ments were reduced so that maturities for the two bond issues originally

---

[33] *Report of the Dominican Economic Commission* (Chicago, 1929).
[34] U. S. Dept. of State, *Press Releases* (Nov. 14, 1931), p. 454.

set for 1932 and 1940 would be extended respectively to 1962 and 1970. This very substantial reduction in debt payments permitted the Dominican government to balance its budget annually.

Negotiations for a revision of the 1924 convention were begun in 1936, and a new treaty was signed in Washington September 24, 1940, and ratifications exchanged March 10, 1941. The new arrangement superseding the 1924 treaty abolished the General Receivership of Dominican customs and permitted the Dominican government instead of an outsider to collect the customs' revenues. These were to be deposited in a bank selected by mutual consent and placed under the obligation to service first the public debt. The Foreign Bondholders Protective Council protested the agreement, although it was given a representation in the depository bank. By an exchange of telegrams between the two governments the Ciudad Trujillo branch of the National City Bank of New York was selected as the sole depository bank. With the convention of 1940 in force the United States was at last free from all governmental checks or controls over the Dominican Republic.[35]

The political record of the Trujillo administration has not been immune to widespread criticism. It has been alleged that President Trujillo has established a dictatorship under which political opponents are kept impotent by a régime of repression and terror. Exile, disappearance, imprisonment, and assassination have been employed to wipe out all opposition.[36] By the end of 1931 the President was so completely in control of the political situation that his own Dominican party was the only political party functioning, and his reëlection in 1934 was uncontested. With Congress completely subservient to his wishes, President Trujillo proceeded to show what could be accomplished by the "Benefactor of the Nation." He rebuilt Santo Domingo City, whose name was changed to Ciudad Trujillo in his honor, he carried out a vast program of public works, he successfully encouraged agricultural production, and he revised and improved the entire public school system.[37]

In his relations with the neighboring Republic of Haiti, President Trujillo began auspiciously by endeavoring to settle the boundary question which had remained a threat to friendly relations since 1874. A treaty establishing a boundary commission had been signed January 21,

[35] For text see U. S. Treaty Series, No. 965.

[36] See Charles A. Thomson, "Dictatorship in the Dominican Republic," Foreign Policy Reports, Vol. XII, No. 3 (Apr. 15, 1936).

[37] For an eulogistic account of the achievements of President Trujillo see Laurence de Besault, President Trujillo, His Work and the Dominican Republic (Washington, D. C., 1936).

1929, but the commission had not been named. However, by personal meetings with President Vincent of Haiti held in both countries from 1933 to 1935 a settlement was finally reached and the commission was named and set to work. Friendly relations between the two countries were seriously disturbed, however, by reports published in October, 1937, that there had taken place on the border a wholesale massacre by Dominican soldiers of Haitian peasants who had crossed into Dominican territory in search of work. The Haitian government immediately asked for an investigation, punishment of the guilty, indemnification for the victims and assurances of protection in the future. When a month elapsed without a satisfactory settlement President Vincent on November 12, 1937, appealed to the Presidents of the United States, Mexico, and Cuba to use their good offices to attempt a settlement of the question. The three governments accepted the invitation and informal hearings were held in Washington. The Dominican Republic was at first inclined to insist upon a direct settlement between the two governments, but on December 18 President Trujillo accepted the invitation of the permanent commission set up under the Gondra treaty to participate with Haiti in an effort to settle by conciliation the dispute over the border killings. On December 20 President Franklin D. Roosevelt sent a telegram of gratification to President Trujillo for his acceptance of the peaceful procedure for the settlement of the dispute.

An agreement settling the controversy was signed on January 31, 1938, at Washington, D. C., by representatives of the two governments. By the terms of this agreement the Dominican Republic agreed to pay an indemnity of $750,000 to Haiti and to abide by the findings of the Dominican tribunals which were to continue the inquiry into the incidents which led to the dispute. The Dominican Republic also agreed "to fix the responsibility of those guilty of instigating the incidents and to give the results of the investigation full publicity." [38]

As an antidote to these gruesome events the Dominican representative to the Intergovernmental Committee on Refugees, convened at Evian in the summer of 1938 at the suggestion of President Roosevelt, offered in behalf of General Trujillo a large tract of land in the Dominican Republic for the settlement of a contingent of European refugees. The Committee investigated the tract offered and found that it could be reached by an improved road, that it already had almost 500 acres cleared for farming or grazing, that adequate water was available, and that more than a

[38] *New York Times,* Feb. 1, 1938.

score of houses had already been built by the former owner—the United Fruit Company.

The Dominican Republic Settlement Association was organized, and it brought over during 1939 about 500 refugees as a test example of the colonization scheme. The war prevented any further additions, and hardly enough time has elapsed to make a final decision as to the success. A survey of the project made in 1941 under the supervision of the Brookings Institution presented a somewhat pessimistic report based partly upon the health conditions of the Sosua tract and partly upon the small amount of unoccupied land available on the island.[39] Nevertheless it was felt that the generous offer of the Dominican government might stimulate other American governments to follow its example.

President Trujillo after his second term from 1934-1938 was succeeded by his henchman President Peynado. When the latter died in office in 1940, Vice-president Troncoso took over, but under the aegis of General Trujillo. The "Restorer of the Financial Independence of the Republic," as Trujillo was officially designated by the Congress in 1940, was reëlected President in May 1942 without any opposition. President Troncoso thereupon appointed the General to his cabinet and then resigned, thus permitting Trujillo to become president immediately without violating the constitution of the Republic. Dr. Troncoso was subsequently appointed Minister to the United States.

When in 1947 Trujillo had himself elected for a fourth term of five years, Dominicans who had escaped from his tyranny attempted to organize an expedition against him from Cuba. However, Trujillo learned about the plot and informed the Cuban government which arrested the leaders and seized the ships and planes which had been assembled. An attempt sponsored by a wealthy Dominican exile living in Guatemala in June, 1949, was equally abortive.

When President Trujillo's fourth term of office expired in 1952, he had his brother, General Hector Trujillo elected as President and himself named Generalissimo and Commander-in-Chief of the Armed Forces of the Republic, also Ambassador-at-Large to the United Nations. In the latter capacity at the meeting of the General Assembly in New York in February, 1953, it was declared that Ambassador Trujillo with his bodyguard outnumbering that of the Russian delegation by two to one was a greater attraction to the populace than the Soviet Foreign Minister

[39] Brookings Institution, *Refugee Settlement in the Dominican Republic* (Washington, D. C., 1942).

Vishinsky. While in the United States Generalissimo Trujillo signed a Mutual Military Assistance Pact with the United States.

Even before the outbreak of World War II in Europe General Trujillo had offered all available facilities of the Dominican Republic in defense of the United States. After the attack on Pearl Harbor the Dominican Republic declared war upon Japan, December 8, and upon Germany and Italy, December 11. The war affected the economic situation of the Dominican Republic favorably rather than adversely. In fact the Dominican Republic's prosperity has been so great, that in 1947 its foreign debt was completely liquidated and in 1953 its internal debt was paid in full. In the six-year period from 1947 to 1953, the income of the Republic had more than doubled, rising from 43 to 89 million pesos. Sugar is still the principal crop of the islands and the $200-million sugar mill at Rio Haina is said to be the world's largest. The Republic is seeking to increase the production of bananas and has set aside over a thousand acres for growing cotton. The country is self-sufficient in foods, has increased its production of coffee, and has great possibilities in further increasing its production of cacao.

Industries have tripled in number since 1936, capital and sales have increased commensurately, and one-third of the 1953 budget has been allocated for the construction of highways, hospitals, and schools. Dictator Trujillo apparently while enriching himself and his friends, has succeeded somewhat in meriting two of his various titles: Restorer of Financial Independence and Benefactor of the Fatherland.

The recent relations of the United States with Haiti have been very similar to our relations with the Dominican Republic. After a protracted series of revolutionary outbreaks, the financial situation became so bad in 1914 that Great Britain, tired of being put off, sent an ultimatum demanding payment of an indemnity of $62,000; and shortly afterwards Germany and France demanded the control of the customs.[40] The European war averted European interference for the time being. But, with a view to preventing it permanently, Mr. Bailly-Blanchard, the American

[40] For a detailed survey of the history of this period see Arthur C. Millspaugh, *Haiti Under American Control 1915-1930* (Boston, 1931); also R. L. Buell, "The American Occupation of Haiti," *Foreign Policy Association Information Service* 1929, Vol. V, Nos. 19-20; see also Mr. Lansing's letter to Secretary Hughes regarding Germany's intentions in the Caribbean, *Sen. Rep. No. 794*, 67th Cong., 2nd Sess., Appendix B. For a detailed account of the financial difficulties see Paul H. Douglas, "The American Occupation of Haiti," *Polit. Sci. Quar.*, Vol. XLII (June, 1927), pp. 229 *ff.* For a critical report of the American occupation by a group of American lawyers see *Cong. Rec.*, Vol. 62, pp. 8945 *ff.*

minister, presented to the Haitian government on December 10, 1914, a project for a convention similar to the agreement of 1907 with Santo Domingo, *i.e.*, providing for a customs receiver who should put the finances in order.[41] Fearing popular disapproval, the Haitian government refused, and the United States did not insist. In May, 1915, Mr. Paul Fuller, Jr., was sent as a special agent to Haiti with a new proposal. The United States now asked to protect Haiti against foreign attack and to aid in suppressing insurrection within, provided that Haiti would covenant that no rights or privileges concerning the occupation of Môle Saint Nicholas would be granted to any foreign government, and would agree to settle by arbitration the claims of American citizens.[42] Haiti accepted this proposal as a basis of negotiations, and early in June made a counter-proposal.

Meanwhile the internal conditions became so serious that Rear-Admiral Caperton was ordered to proceed to Cape Haitien with his cruiser. President Theodore had been killed, and President Guillaume-Sam was maintaining himself with difficulty. To secure himself, the latter had arrested a large number of influential citizens and political opponents, and when, in spite of this, an attack was made on his palace, he had them put to death. This so enraged the populace that they broke into the French legation, whither he had fled for refuge, shot him, cut his body into pieces, and dragged it about the town.[43] On the same day (July 28, 1915) Admiral Caperton landed marines at Port-au-Prince to protect the legation, and later he took over the custom-houses and other public services. In order to secure the coöperation of the Haitians, a presidential election was held on August 12 under American protection, and M. Dartiguenave was elected. Conditions continuing turbulent, on September 3, Admiral Caperton proclaimed martial law; and on September 16 a treaty was signed whereby the United States established a virtual protectorate.[44] At first there was strong opposition on the part of the Haitian government to approving the treaty. But on November 11, 1915, the insular senate agreed to it. Considering the fact that Admiral Caperton, under Secretary Daniels' instructions, announced to the insular President and his cabinet that the United States would remain in control until the treaty was rati-

[41] *Hearings before a Select Committee on Haiti and Santo Domingo*, Part I, p. 6; text, p. 33. A similar proposal had been made on July 2, 1914, to the Zamor government, but no action was taken. *For. Rel. of the U. S.*, 1914, pp. 347-350.

[42] *Ibid.*, p. 7.

[43] *Report of the Secretary of the Navy, 1915*, pp. 15-17; or the more detailed report of Brig.-Gen. George Barnett in the *Report of the Secretary of the Navy, 1920*, pp. 245 *ff.*

[44] *Hearings*, pp. 336, 344, 348.

fied, and that the funds collected at the customs would be available for the payment of salaries only after ratification, it is not surprising that the Haitian senate accepted the convention.[45]

The principal provisions of the convention were as follows: (1) the establishment of a Haitian receivership of customs under American control; (2) the appointment of an American financial adviser to assist in the settlement of the foreign debt and in other financial and commercial matters; (3) the organization of a native Haitian constabulary under the command of American officers; (4) the disarming of all revolutionary forces; and (5) a guaranty on the part of Haiti to cede no territory to any nation but the United States. The convention was to remain in force ten years, and was to be continued for another ten years if its objects should not have been satisfactorily accomplished within the briefer period.[46] In fact, on March 28, 1917, an agreement was reached to extend the treaty for an additional ten years, or to 1936, although the legality of the extension has been questioned, since it was approved by neither the Haitian Congress nor the Senate of the United States.

The convention was proclaimed on May 3, 1916, and remained in force until the treaty of 1932 became effective. The results, however, on the whole were less satisfactory than in the Dominican Republic. The list of grievances of the Haitians was a long one.[47] The United States was accused of not carrying out the terms of the convention, and of deliberately usurping the powers of civil government which the convention guaranteed to the Haitians. It was claimed that no attempt had been made to give the financial aid promised by the United States, and that up to 1920 no attempt was made to pay interest on the foreign debt; there had also been but one payment on the internal debt. The Haitians asserted that the United States had backed the unconstitutional methods of Presidents Dartiguenave and Borno, had suppressed the Haitian legislature, and had prevented the drawing up of a more liberal constitution. Finally, they accused the marines of indiscriminate killing of Haitians and of employing cruel and inhuman treatment towards the natives upon numerous occasions, particularly in the establishment of the corvée or enforced labor on the roads.

Unquestionably, every one of these accusations was justified to a considerable extent; but, on the other hand, a careful investigation into the voluminous testimony shows that the American intervention has not de-

[45] *Ibid.*, Part II, p. 394.
[46] *U. S. Stat. at Large,* Vol. XXXIX, Part II, p. 1654.
[47] See the memoir of the Union Patriotique d'Haiti, *Hearings before a Select Committee on Haiti and Santo Domingo,* Part I, pp. 5-33.

served the bitter criticism that it has sometimes received. The military forces have not always carried out the provisions of the convention as promptly as they should—Admiral Knapp, in his report, concedes this—but only because of the desire to do the job quickly and well.[48] Some of the officers abused their power,[49] and there were also unlawful executions of prisoners,[50] but the guilty officials were immediately court-martialed and removed from the service. The corvée was used for a time as an emergency measure, but was subsequently discontinued.

When evidence of abuses was brought to the attention of the United States government, every effort was made to get at the truth of the situation. In the summer of 1920 Rear-Admiral Knapp was ordered by Secretary Daniels to make a special investigation. General George Barnett, who commanded the marines from June, 1915, to June 30, 1920, was asked to make a complete report, and this was followed by another by General Lejeune, who took over the command. In addition, Secretary Daniels appointed a court of inquiry headed by Rear-Admiral Mayo, and consisting of Rear-Admiral Oliver, Major-General Neville, and Major Dyer of the Marine Corps, to inquire into the alleged indiscriminate killings of Haitians and unjustifiable acts by members of the United States naval service. Finally, there was the Senate investigation under Senator McCormick.

All of these reports show that abuses were the exception rather than the rule; and they indicate that the results of the American occupation have not been wholly bad. For instance, the customs collected for the fiscal year ending September 30, 1920, amounted to almost $6½ million, exceeding by more than $1 million the entire revenue collected in any of the five years before the intervention.[51] But the improvement in living conditions was perhaps the greatest achievement of the American intervention. The Rev. Charles Blaney Colmore, bishop of Puerto Rico and Haiti, writing in 1917, thus characterized it: "The marines have literally taught the Haitians how to live decently. Before their coming, sanitation, save in the crudest and most unsatisfactory forms, was unknown; fevers and epidemics were as plentiful as revolutions; a press gang was in vogue, and the country was the victim of continuous uprisings engineered by political scoundrels. . . . The entry of the United States marines ended this sorry story. . . . Sanitary systems had been installed, the towns had been cleaned up, former idlers and revolutionists were working happily for living

[48] Report of Admiral Knapp in *Report of the Secretary of the Navy, 1920*, p. 232.
[49] *Ibid.*, p. 227.
[50] Report of General Barnett, *ibid.*, p. 306.
[51] Report of Admiral Knapp, *ibid.*, p. 228.

wages, and a new spirit was animating the people. . . ." [52] Bishop James Craik Morris, writing in 1920, after visiting every important city on the island, declared: "The only opposition to Americans in Haiti is political opposition. In the southern part of the island, particularly on the peninsula, the American occupation is regarded as the salvation of the people. I heard this opinion frequently. I had under me twelve native clergymen, and neither from them nor from the many other natives I talked to did I hear one word of condemnation of the acts of the American Marine Corps." [53]

Bishop Morris appears to have struck at the very heart of the difficulty—the opposition was chiefly political. But could the United States afford to disregard political opposition? It would be impossible to do so and still adhere to the policy that has been so consistently maintained in our relations with weaker states. Nor did it seem feasible at the time for the United States to withdraw immediately and completely from the Republic. In the preliminary Senate report on Haiti, Senator McCormick declared that "the members of the committee are unanimous in the belief that the continual presence of the small American force in Haiti is as necessary to the peace and development of the country as are the services to the Haitian government of the American officials appointed under the treaty of 1915. There can be no abrogation of the treaty, and at this time no diminution of the small force of marines." [54]

Although the report of the Senate Committee gave full credit to the American administration for its establishment of peace and order and for the excellent results obtained through the improvement of sanitary conditions and the construction of highways, nevertheless it criticized the United States for its failure to develop a definite, constructive policy and for its failure to select men for service in Haiti who were sympathetic to the Haitians and able to maintain cordial relations with them. As a remedy for this situation the Committee recommended that a High Commissioner be sent to Haiti to act as the American diplomatic representative and at the same time exercise a direct supervision over the treaty officials. In accordance with this suggestion Brigadier General John H. Russell was appointed American High Commissioner in February, 1922, and placed under the jurisdiction of the Department of State.

[52] Cited in report of Gen. Barnett, *ibid.*, p. 275.
[53] *Report of the Secretary of the Navy, 1920,* p. 319.
[54] *New York Times,* Dec. 25, 1921. For Haitian opinion on the investigation see the address of Prof. Pierre Hudicourt in Washington, Feb. 2, 1922, *Cong. Rec.*, Vol. 42 (May 19, 1922), p. 7857. The detailed findings and recommendations are found in *Sen. Rep. No. 794,* 67th Cong., 2nd Sess.

A few months later the Haitian Council of State elected as President of the Republic Mr. Louis Borno, who immediately signified his intention of coöperating wholeheartedly with the new High Commissioner. As a result the financial situation improved, the American military courts ceased to function, the Haitian constabulary was efficiently organized, new highways were constructed, the Public Health Service built modern hospitals and held free clinics, and in 1924 a new technical service created a system of vocational and agricultural instruction.[55]

Nevertheless, the government of Haiti was under the complete domination of the American occupation; the American High Commissioner virtually controlled all political matters, while the American Financial Adviser dictated financial policies. Although a new constitution had been given to the Haitians in 1917—Franklin D. Roosevelt wrote it and confesses that it is a good one [56]—no elections had been held under it, nor had there been any session of the Haitian Congress since the American occupation had begun. The former ruling classes resented keenly the control of the public administration by representatives of a foreign power. President Borno, who had been reëlected by the Council of State in 1926, had become very unpopular among the politicians because of his cordial coöperation with the United States. Matters reached a climax towards the end of 1929 when the students at Port-au-Prince inaugurated a strike because the government had reduced the annual scholarship allotment.[57] The political parties took up the question and at Aux Cayes, a small seaport about a hundred miles from Port-au-Prince, on December 7, a mob of Haitians attacked the American marines, who repulsed them, killing six and wounding some twenty-eight more.[58]

In his annual message to Congress sent on December 3, 1929, President Hoover had already indicated his desire of sending a commission to Haiti to obtain the necessary information to formulate a more definite policy. The outbreak on December 7 caused him to send a special message to Congress the same day requesting the authority to despatch a commission immediately. Congress approved, and in February, 1930, a commission headed by W. Cameron Forbes was instructed to investigate and report when and how we could withdraw from Haiti after discharging our obligations.[59]

[55] For an account of this period see A. C. Millspaugh, *Haiti Under American Control*, Chap. IV.

[56] *New York Times*, Aug. 19, 1920.

[57] *Report of American High Commissioner, 1929*, pp. 7-9.

[58] *New York Times*, Dec. 8, 1929.

[59] *Report of the President's Commission for the Study and Review of Conditions in the Republic of Haiti* (Washington, D. C., 1930), p. 1.

The Commission found a serious state of unrest existing, due partly to the economic condition caused by the falling price of coffee, but even more to the hostility towards President Borno who, according to public opinion had permitted himself as well as the Council of State to be completely subservient to High Commissioner Russell. As an emergency measure, the Committee suggested the immediate election of Eugene Roy, a business man, as temporary President. He could thereupon call for the election of the legislature which might elect a President in accordance with the provisions of the constitution. The suggestion was adopted, M. Roy was elected President by the Council of State on April 21, 1930, and inaugurated on May 15. A new Congress was elected in October which forthwith chose as President M. Stenio Vincent, a strong opponent of the American occupation.

In the meantime the Forbes Commission had returned to Washington and had made its report. Although it gave the American administration credit for the remarkable progress made in health, sanitation, bridge and road building, it found little effort had been made to prepare the Haitians for self-government. In fact, the report stated that "the acts and attitude of the treaty officials gave your commission the impression that they had been based upon the assumption that the occupation would continue indefinitely." [60] In its recommendations, which were approved by President Hoover, the Commission advocated: (1) the rapid Haitianization of the administration services with the definite aim of having Haitians trained to take over the work in 1936; (2) the abolition of the office of High Commissioner and the appointment of a non-military minister to take over his duties as well as those of diplomatic representative; (3) the gradual withdrawal of the marines in accordance with arrangements to be made by the two governments; (4) a modification of the present treaty providing for less intervention in Haitian domestic affairs. [61]

In accordance with these suggestions General Russell submitted his resignation as American High Commissioner and Dr. Dana G. Munro was appointed as Minister to Haiti. Although the United States was eager to terminate its responsibilities in Haiti at the earliest possible date, it was not able to accept the Haitian government's proposal for the speedy termination of financial control. In other matters a solution was finally agreed upon and incorporated in the Haitianization Agreement of August 5, 1931. [62] According to its terms all Americans connected with the Public

[60] *Ibid.*, p. 8.
[61] *Ibid.*, pp. 20-21.
[62] For text see U. S. Dept. of State, *Executive Agreement Series*, No. 22.

Works Service, the Public Health Service, and the *Service Technique* were to be withdrawn by October 1 of the same year, while the Service of Payments and the auditing of expenditures were to remain under the control of the Financial Adviser.

The Haitianization of the Garde and the withdrawal of the marines required longer consideration, but agreement was finally reached on these subjects, and by the Treaty of September 3, 1932, it was provided that all American officers should be withdrawn from the Garde by December 31, 1934, and the withdrawal of the Marine Brigade was not to begin later than that date. It was also agreed that a Fiscal Representative appointed by the President of Haiti upon the nomination of the President of the United States should replace the Financial Adviser-General Receiver on December 31, 1934, and he should collect all customs duties with the assistance of an Haitian personnel.[63]

It soon became evident that the Haitian legislature was not satisfied with these terms and the ratification of the agreement was unanimously rejected. No further action was taken until the Franklin D. Roosevelt administration came into office. Norman Armour, a career diplomat, now replaced Dr. Munro, and he proceeded to negotiate a new settlement largely along the lines of the previous one, but in the form of an executive agreement, instead of a treaty. The Agreement of August 7, 1933, advanced the date of the Haitianization of the Garde and the withdrawal of the marines to October 1, 1934, and the date of the appointment of the Fiscal Representative to January 1, 1934, but the rest of the agreement was very similar to the 1932 Treaty.[64]

President Roosevelt's desire to make effective his "Good Neighbor Policy," and Secretary Hull's cordial attitude at the Montevideo Conference encouraged President Vincent to request a speedy renunciation of American financial control in Haiti; he was invited to come to Washington to confer on the situation. On April 17, 1934, a joint statement was issued by the two presidents stating that the commitments of the August 7 agreement would be carried out and in addition new and satisfactory commercial and financial agreements would be negotiated.[65] As a gesture of friendship, President Roosevelt asked and obtained from the Congress authorization to turn over to Haiti buildings and equipment used by the marines during their occupation.

[63] For text see U. S. Dept. of State, *Press Releases* (Sept. 10, 1932), p. 150; also Dana G. Munro, *The United States and the Caribbean Area* (Boston, 1934), pp. 190-193.

[64] For text see U. S. Dept. of State, *Executive Agreement Series,* No. 46.

[65] *New York Times,* Apr. 18, 1934.

In July President Roosevelt returned the visit of President Vincent and ordered the time for the withdrawal of the marines to be advanced to August 15. In fact, the 850 marines who still remained began to withdraw at the end of July and by the 15th of August the last marine had left and the Haitian flag flew over the former American barracks. To put an end to financial control it was agreed that the National City Bank of New York should sell back the National Bank of Haiti to the government of Haiti and all official American control be abolished. The sale was consummated July 9, 1935, subject to approval by the Haitian Senate. When a small group of eleven Senators opposed, President Vincent put the matter up to a national referendum which overwhelmingly approved the purchase of the bank. A reciprocity tariff agreement was also signed with Haiti the same year (March 28, 1935) whereby the United States lowered the tariff on rum, fruit, and cocoa in return for a freer admittance for our machinery, radios, and automobiles.

Contrary to the situation in the Dominican Republic, the European war had a serious effect upon the economic situation of Haiti since it closed her principal markets for coffee and cotton. The United States recognized this situation and by an executive agreement dated February 13, 1941, Haiti was permitted to postpone the payment of one-third of the interest due upon the bonds of 1922 and 1923.[66] On September 13, 1941, after numerous conferences the two governments signed a new agreement which replaced the one negotiated in 1933. The financial agreement of 1941, like the one concluded with the Dominican Republic, abolished the office of Fiscal Representative, transferring all funds to the National Bank of Haiti as sole depository for the Haitian government. The Bank's Board of Directors was reorganized making three of the six voting members United States citizens, one of whom should serve as Co-President and represent the holders of the 1922 and 1923 bonds. The new agreement became effective October 1, 1941, and will continue in force until the bonds shall be redeemed.[67]

The war shifted the Haitian market towards the United States even more than formerly and during the fiscal year 1940-1941 we took 87.92 per cent of her exports and provided 83.58 per cent of her imports.[68] Haiti declared war upon Japan the day after Pearl Harbor and on Decem-

---

[66] U. S. Dept. of State, *Executive Agreement Series,* No. 201. Due to an improvement in trade conditions during the last quarter of the year the postponed interest was repaid and the Oct., 1941 payment met in full.

[67] *Ibid., Series,* No. 220.

[68] Banque Nationale de la République d'Haiti, *Annual Report of the Fiscal Department: Oct. 1940—Sept. 1941.*

ber 12 extended her declaration to include Germany and Italy. To co-ördinate economic and defense arrangements, President Elie Lescot visited Washington in April, 1942, and following a series of meetings, an omnibus memorandum was issued covering various agreements which had been reached. These agreements *inter alia* provided that the Commodity Credit Corporation of the United States purchase all surplus cotton produced in Haiti during the war period; that the Export-Import Bank extend such credits to the National Bank of Haiti as were necessary to stabilize exchange; to aid in the common war effort that 24,000 additional acres of sisal be planted in Haiti; and that the United States should aid by material and by training the Haitian coast patrol and coast artillery. The two governments also agreed to carry out a number of health and sanitation projects in Haiti.[69]

The war by forcing a shortage of commodities and a raise in prices brought about a series of political disturbances in Haiti. In January, 1946, President Lescot was forced out and a military junta took over until a new Congress chose Dumarsais Estimé as President. He tried to improve the economic position of the people by a program of public works and construction of model villages, financing the development by means of an income tax. When in May, 1950, he proposed a change in the constitution to permit his reëlection, he too was forced out and again a military junta seized control. This time one of the members of the junta, Colonel Paul Magloire, was a candidate for President under an election procedure when for the first time the people voted directly for a president. Colonel Magloire won by a large majority and was still in office at the beginning of 1954 when Haiti celebrated its 150th anniversary of independence, next oldest to the United States in the Western Hemisphere.

Haiti's economic future is to a considerable extent dependent upon the Artibonite Valley irrigation project which when completed will, it is estimated, irrigate 80,000 acres of land which are at present unsuitable for agriculture. Haiti is receiving loans under both the United States Technical Assistance program and from the United Nations, and is the first Latin-American republic to sign an investment guaranty agreement with the Mutual Security Agency under which the United States affords insurance protection to new investments abroad against losses through confiscation or expropriation.

With the substitution of coöperative assistance for enforced control in Haiti, the United States had ended the last of her military interventions

[69] U. S. Dept. of State, *Bulletin*, Vol. VI, No. 147 (Apr. 18, 1942), p. 353.

in the Caribbean. From the standpoint of physical improvements the Republic had benefited considerably. The total public debt had been substantially reduced, while at the same time a program of public construction, sanitation, and instruction had been inaugurated. But the Haitian people resented an alien tutelage, nor were the people of the United States in favor of it. Haiti is now mistress in her own house—may she be successful in her future administration.

SUPPLEMENTARY READINGS

EMILY G. BALCH, *Occupied Haiti* (New York, 1927).

DANTÈS BELLEGARDE, *Haiti and Her Problems* (Rio Piedras, Puerto Rico, 1936).

MERCER COOK, *An Introduction to Haiti* (Washington, D. C., 1951).

JACQUES CROCKAERT, *La Mediterranée Americaine* (Paris, 1927).

H. P. DAVIS, *Black Democracy* (New York, 1928).

MAX UREÑA HENRÍQUEZ, *Los Yanquis en Santo Domingo* (Madrid, 1929).

ALBERT C. HICKS, *Blood in the Streets* (New York, 1946).

S. G. INMAN, *Through Santo Domingo and Haiti* (New York, 1919).

C. LLOYD JONES, *Caribbean Backgrounds and Prospects* (New York, 1931).

———, *Caribbean Interests of the United States* (New York, 1916), Chaps. VIII, IX.

———, *The Caribbean Since 1900* (New York, 1936), Chaps. V, VII.

RALPH KORNGOLD, *Citizen Toussaint* (Boston, 1944).

MELVIN M. KNIGHT, *The Americans in Santo Domingo* (New York, 1928).

JOHN D. KUSER, *Haiti, Its Dawn of Progress after Years in a Night of Revolution* (Boston, 1921).

J. N. LEGER, *Haiti: Her History and Her Detractors* (New York, 1907).

J. G. LEYBURN, *The Haitian People* (New Haven, 1941).

R. W. LOGAN, *The Diplomatic Relations of the United States with Haiti* (Chapel Hill, N. C., 1941).

MRS. HARRIET MARSHALL, *The Story of Haiti* (Boston, 1930).

ARTHUR C. MILLSPAUGH, *Haiti Under American Control* (Boston, 1931).

L. L. MONTAGUE, *Haiti and the United States, 1714-1938* (Durham, N. C., 1940).

DANA G. MUNRO, *The United States and the Caribbean Area* (Boston, 1934), Chaps. III, IV.

BLAIR NILES, *Black Haiti* (New York, 1926).

PERICLES FRANCO ORNES, *La Tragedia Dominicana* (Santiago de Chile, 1946).

DEXTER PERKINS, *The United States and the Caribbean* (Cambridge, 1947).

W. B. SEABROOK, *The Magic Island* (New York, 1929).

OTTO SCHOENRICH, *Santo Domingo* (New York, 1918).

STANLEY WALKER, *Journey Toward the Sunlight* (New York, 1947).

❦ 14 ❦

Interests of the United States in Central America

SOUTH of Mexico, stretching some six hundred miles in a southeasterly direction to the Isthmus of Panama, lie the five republics of Central America—Guatemala, Honduras, Salvador, Nicaragua, and Costa Rica. The combined area of these states is about 175,000 square miles, or virtually that of Illinois, Michigan, and Wisconsin. Their aggregate population is about eight and one-half millions.[1] The climate varies from that of the humid and suffocating coastal plains on the Atlantic side to that of the comparatively cool regions of the plateaus and mountain valleys, and again to that of the hot, dry, but healthful coast of the Pacific. The population is predominantly Indian, although it varies considerably in the different states. Guatemala, for example, is almost completely Indian, while in Costa Rica the white population predominates. In spite of the fact that the Central American states are for the most part possessed of extremely fertile soil, have considerable mineral resources, and, with the exception of Salvador, have outlets on both oceans, they must still be regarded as among the more backward regions of the western hemisphere. Spain's policy of selfish exploitation kept them in this condition while they were under her control; since they have achieved independence, mutual jealousies and revolutions have produced a similar result.

Before taking up the relations of the United States with Central America, it might be well to point out the more noticeable differences among these five republics.[2] Guatemala has the largest population, the greatest

[1] For population of the individual states, see *United Nations Demographic Year Book* (New York, 1952).

[2] For general description concerning these republics see the pamphlets issued by the Pan American Union under the names of the various countries. The best single book is D. G. Munro, *The Five Republics of Central America* (New York, 1918).

foreign trade, and is the most wealthy. This arises partly from its size, partly from the comparative peace that the republic has enjoyed until recently under its autocratic governments. Two of its despots, Carrera and Cabrera, succeeded in maintaining themselves in power for over twenty years, while President Ubico held office for more than a decade. On the other hand, Guatemala has virtually no middle class, and its wealth has been produced by the contract labor of the ignorant and oppressed Indians. It is asserted that the great coffee plantations could not be worked without a system of peonage; but such a confession if true bodes ill for the future progress of the country.

Costa Rica, although not half so large as Guatemala, is a close second to it in commerce and wealth, and is the first country in Central America in its trade per capita. Owing to its homogeneous white population and its isolation from its more turbulent neighbors, its history has been fairly free from revolutions and its prosperity correspondingly great. It justly claims first place among the Central American republics as the most progressive and most efficiently governed, and it is the country's boast that it has more school teachers than soldiers.

Although the smallest of the twenty-one American republics, El Salvador must in many ways be regarded as a very important member of the Central American group. Its climate and soil are excellent; its coast on the Pacific contains good harbors; its population has more Spanish blood than has that of either Nicaragua or Honduras; and, although its history has been very turbulent, the reason is to be found chiefly in the interference of other countries in its affairs. Salvador is the second country in Central America in population and third in trade, and is by far the most densely populated. In contrast with Costa Rica, its army is better organized than its schools, and has been a rather heavy drain on its finances. On the whole, it has been the least friendly towards the United States of all the Central American republics; and it was the only one that did not join in the first World War against Germany.

Nicaragua is the largest of the five states, and, owing to its canal possibilities, it has received more attention from foreign powers than any of its sister republics. Its political history—in which the United States has played a leading part—has been exceedingly turbulent. Next to Honduras, it is perhaps the most backward state in Central America; its communication facilities are wholly inadequate, and its arrangements for education are primitive in the extreme.

Honduras means "the depths," and the republic does not belie its name. Its population is, for the most part, densely ignorant; economically it is

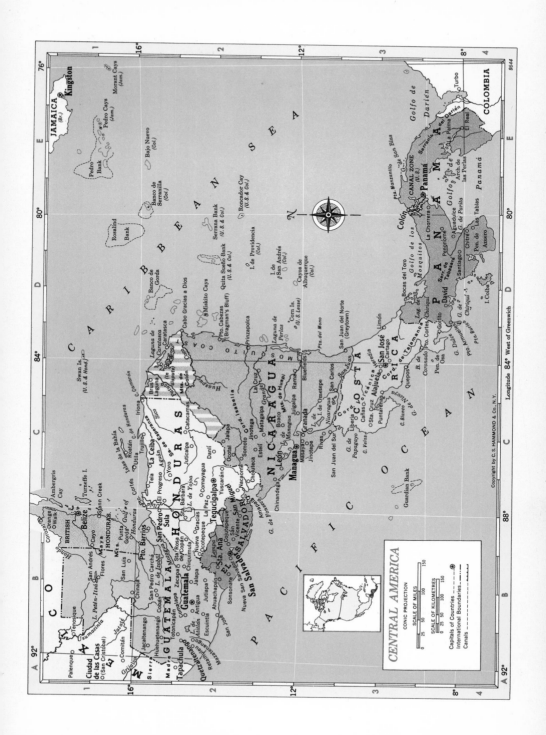

CENTRAL AMERICA

CONIC PROJECTION

SCALE OF MILES

0   25   50   100   150

SCALE OF KILOMETRES

0   25 50   100   150

⊛ Capitals of Countries

International Boundaries -----

Canals -------

Copyright by C. S. HAMMOND & Co., N.Y.

9644

the most backward; its government has generally been a military despotism; and the state has been the center of virtually every conflict in the isthmus. The result has been a tremendous foreign debt, bankruptcy, and finally American intervention.

Before its declaration of independence on September 15, 1821, the viceroyalty of Guatemala, which included the provinces of Salvador, Nicaragua, Honduras, and Costa Rica, had been the connecting link of the great Spanish Empire extending from Mexico to Patagonia. Free from the Spanish yoke, the states into which the viceroyalty disintegrated gravitated towards Mexico; and, although there was considerable opposition, particularly on the part of Costa Rica, a provisional junta decreed that the whole of Central America should be annexed to the Empire of Mexico.[3] The fall of Iturbide came before the plan could be carried into effect, and the states were once more adrift. It is interesting to note that at this time Salvador, which also opposed annexation to Mexico, passed an act annexing itself to the United States and sent two representatives to negotiate with the authorities at Washington on the subject.[4]

The idea of a federal union modeled upon that of the United States had appealed strongly from the beginning, and in 1823 a national constituent assembly was called, which declared the former viceroyalty of Guatemala free and independent and confederated into a nation under the name of *Provincias Unidas del Centro de América*. A constitution was thereupon drafted, after the American model, and ratified on September 1, 1825. Before the year was out the United States recognized the new federal state by signing, on December 5, 1825, a treaty of commerce and friendship, which was proclaimed in effect by the American Secretary of State on October 28, 1826.[5] This treaty, designated "A General Convention of Peace, Amity, Commerce, and Navigation with the Federation of the Centre of America," consisted of thirty-three articles, which granted equal privileges and rights to citizens coming from either republic into the other, and all the rights granted by one or the other to the most favored nation. It was to remain in force for twelve years. No provision was made for its continuance after that time. But it proved eminently satisfactory to both parties, and shortly before its expiration in 1838, Mr. De Witt, the *chargé d'affaires* at Guatemala, was instructed to obtain a renewal of it. A new treaty was signed on July 14, 1838.

---

[3] H. H. Bancroft, *History of Central America* (San Francisco, 1886-1887), Vol. III, p. 54.

[4] *Ibid.*, p. 64; see also *Sen. Ex. Doc. No. 75*, 31st Cong., 1st Sess., p. 94.

[5] For text see *Amer. State Papers, For. Rel.*, Vol. VI, pp. 269-276.

But, owing to a delay in the exchange of ratifications, it did not go into effect; and in the summer of 1839 Mr. J. L. Stephens was sent as special agent to bring about the exchange of ratifications.[6] In the meantime the confederation had been rapidly weakening; the last federal congress adjourned in 1838, and the last president was expelled in 1840. As a consequence, Mr. Stephens although well received was unable to accomplish the object of his mission.

Various attempts were made to reorganize the federation, but nothing permanent came of them. In 1842 Salvador, Honduras, and Nicaragua formed a confederation which lasted about two years, and again in 1849 they signed a treaty of confederation which proved equally abortive.[7] Uncertain of the situation, the United States had despatched Mr. W. S. Murphy in 1841, with instructions that if he should find any organized government of a federation of Central America, he should arrange for the ratification of the treaty of commerce. He was obliged to report that there was, at the time, no federal government in Central America entitled to the privileges, or responsible for the duties, of a sovereign power.[8] Guatemala declared herself definitely free and independent on March 21, 1847, and the United States thereupon despatched Mr. Elijah Hise to propose the adoption of the treaty of 1838 between the United States and Guatemala. He was also authorized to conclude a similar treaty with Salvador; but Secretary Buchanan did not deem it advisable to conclude treaties with either Nicaragua, Honduras, or Costa Rica until the Department secured further authentic information concerning them.[9]

Undoubtedly a more important reason for sending Mr. Hise was to obtain information about the encroachments of Great Britain upon the territories of Nicaragua, Honduras, and Costa Rica, under the guise of protecting the so-called kingdom of the Mosquito Indians. In fact, on January 1, 1849, a British man-of-war had taken forcible possession of the post of San Juan de Nicaragua; and, although the Nicaraguan troops recaptured it on January 9, the British reoccupied it three days later and maintained their hold. Inasmuch as San Juan would be the natural outlet for any isthmian canal through the state of Nicaragua, the interest of the United States was justified. Mr. Hise arrived about the first of November, and lost no time in accomplishing his mission. In a letter to the Secretary of State, dated May 25, 1849, he reported that he had already

---

6 Sen. Ex. Doc. No. 75, p. 95.

7 For full account see Bancroft, op. cit., Chap. X; also W. F. Slade, "The Federation of Central America," Journal of Race Development, Vol. VIII (July, 1917), pp. 79 ff.

8 Sen. Ex. Doc. No. 75, p. 95.

9 Ibid., p. 96.

concluded a treaty with Guatemala, and was then negotiating with the commissioners of Honduras and Nicaragua, with whom he hoped to conclude commercial reciprocity treaties; and he intimated that he also expected "to conclude a special convention with Nicaragua of vast importance to the United States and to the whole commercial world." [10] He was not disappointed, and in a despatch dated September 15, 1849, he announced that he had concluded treaties of amity and commerce with Honduras and Nicaragua, and a special convention with Nicaragua. This convention secured to the United States a perpetual right of way by land or water through Nicaragua, and the right to charter a company which should have exclusive right over the contemplated canals or roads; in return, the United States was to guarantee the sovereignty of Nicaragua over its rightful territories.[11] Although his instructions had given him no such powers—in fact, had definitely prohibited conventions with Honduras and Nicaragua—he justified his acts on the grounds that, on account of the revolutionary condition of the country, he had received no answers to his despatches. He also felt that the cession of Upper California to the United States and the subsequent discovery of gold there made this acquisition doubly valuable. Finally, he was confident of being sustained because he had received authentic information that English companies were endeavoring to procure for themselves the privileges that he had received.

Months before this, however, the new administration at Washington had recalled him, and had appointed Mr. E. G. Squier to undertake a similar mission to Nicaragua. In Squier's case, however, authority was given to conclude treaties with all five republics separately in case he should consider that there were no hopes of a new confederacy. In the case of Nicaragua, he was to obtain, if possible, for the citizens of the United States the right of free transit over any canal or railroad that might be constructed between the two oceans. But it was not deemed expedient to give as compensation any guaranty of the independence of the country through which the canal or railroad should pass.[12] The instructions of Secretary Clayton also gave a very complete résumé of the British claims to the Mosquito territory, and concluded with the opinion that they were founded upon repeated usurpations. "The United States," he declared, "would not allow the isthmian passage to be blocked by such pretensions—it desired no monopoly of the right of way for its commerce,

[10] *Ibid.*, p. 103.
[11] Text *ibid.*, p. 110; for earlier attempts to obtain a canal route across Nicaragua, see Chap. 5, above.
[12] *Sen. Ex. Doc. No. 75*, p. 120.

nor could it submit to a similar claim on the part of any other country." [13]

When Mr. Squier arrived at his post, he noticed that a very cordial relationship existed between Honduras, Salvador, and Nicaragua, and upon learning that commissioners had been appointed to arrange for a more complete and efficient union he expressed the hope that the attempt would prove successful. In a note to the Minister of Foreign Relations of the Republic of El Salvador, he declared that "it is the desire of my government that some consolidation of these states may be effected, believing, as it does, that their general interests will thus be promoted, and that they will be better enabled to resist the encroachments and thwart the designs of foreign and unfriendly powers." [14] He also noticed that the British appeared to have designs upon Tigre Island in the Gulf of Fonseca, which belonged to Honduras. Believing that its seizure by Great Britain would vitally affect the interests of the United States, he, too, exceeded his instructions, and, despatching a special courier to Honduras, he asked for a speedy treaty between the United States and Honduras which should "authorize the United States in interposing its power against the designs of the English." [15] In his despatch to Secretary Clayton he suggested that a feasible method of effecting the objects desired might be to procure the cession of the island to the United States.[16] Washington was unwilling to risk this plan; and we have shown in another chapter how the United States attempted to settle the dispute with Great Britain by the Clayton-Bulwer treaty.[17] Although Mr. Squier succeeded in obtaining a satisfactory treaty with Nicaragua, it was no more productive of results than "the most advantageous treaty that human ingenuity could devise" of his predecessor.

During the next decade Central America was a close competitor with California in furnishing an outlet for the restless energy of adventurous Americans. In fact, the two were very closely linked up, since the most practicable way to California from the eastern seaboard of the United States was by water as far as Panama, and thence, after crossing the isthmus, by way of the Pacific. We have already seen how the Panama

[13] *Ibid.*, pp. 121-128. For a more complete discussion of the British claims see *Sen. Doc. No. 27*, 32nd Cong., 2nd Sess., pp. 73-98.

[14] *Sen. Ex. Doc. No. 75*, p. 163. It is interesting to note that just three weeks earlier Señor Francisco Castellón, the Nicaraguan minister to London, had asked of Mr. Bancroft, the American minister, whether Honduras, San Salvador, and Nicaragua might be admitted into the North American Union and upon what conditions. If not, could they count upon the United States to defend the integrity of their territory? *Ibid.*, p. 302.

[15] *Ibid.*, p. 167.

[16] *Ibid.*, p. 157.

[17] See pp. 104-106, above.

Railroad Company had received a concession from Colombia in 1850, and had completed the road in 1855.[18] This company was not destined, however, to monopolize the isthmian traffic. In 1849 Colonel Vanderbilt, with several associates, obtained a concession from Nicaragua, authorizing them to construct a canal through Nicaragua, utilizing any lakes or rivers that the engineers should consider feasible in putting through the project. Having become incorporated as the "American Atlantic and Pacific Canal Company," this group proceeded actively with the plan. Soon, however, they found that it was not entirely practicable.[19] A new charter was then obtained, which gave to the Accessory Transit Company (an offshoot of the former organization) a right of way across the country and the sole privilege of steam navigation on the navigable waters of the state.[20] By 1854 a route across the country by river boats, lake steamers, and stage-coaches had been completed and was competing very actively with the Panama route.[21]

It can readily be imagined that the officials of this company would be directly interested in the maintenance of a stable government in Nicaragua strong enough to protect the transport of passengers across the country. But a stable government in Nicaragua at this time seemed quite beyond the bounds of probability. The Conservatives, with Granada as their stronghold, were in perpetual conflict with the Liberals, whose strength was centered at León. The other towns divided their allegiance between these two groups. Fifteen presidents during a period of six years makes a record for even Central American republics. In 1854 the Liberals, under Francisco Castellón, who had taken the offensive and were besieging the Legitimists in Granada, found that they were losing ground. To stem the tide, Castellón contracted with Byron Cole, an American, to bring a detachment of Americans to Nicaragua to serve in the Democratic Army.[22] Cole was a friend of William Walker, who had already attained considerable notoriety as a result of the filibustering expedition which he had led to Lower California with a view to adding it, together with Sonora, to the territories of the United States. Cole communicated the proposal to Walker, then engaged in newspaper work in California. The adventurer needed little persuasion to organize the expedition. On May 4, 1855, fifty-eight men left San Francisco for Nicaragua under his leader-

[18] See Chap. 5, above.
[19] For text of the charter see *Sen. Ex. Doc. No. 68*, 34th Cong., 1st Sess., p. 84.
[20] *Ibid.*, p. 100.
[21] L. M. Keasby, *Nicaragua Canal and the Monroe Doctrine* (New York, 1896); also E. G. Squier, *Honduras* (London, 1870), p. 241.
[22] An interesting and scholarly account of these events is given by Prof. W. O. Scroggs, *Filibusters and Financiers* (New York, 1916).

ship. In less than six months Walker had captured Granada, signed a treaty with the Legitimist leader, and had himself named commander-in-chief of the military forces of the new Rivas government. The Accessory Transit Company was not slow to appreciate the advantages of enlisting him on its side, and one of its agents offered to finance the new government and immediately made an advance of $20,000.

Walker's situation was still so critical that he could not afford to refuse such timely aid; and when the company also agreed to furnish free transportation on its steamers for recruits from New York and San Francisco, thus augmenting his forces by hundreds of valuable followers, he became hopelessly indebted to its agents. Their purpose was soon revealed. The New York and San Francisco agents, Morgan and Garrison, had determined to wrest control of the company from Vanderbilt, and Walker was to play a leading rôle in bringing about this result. Nicaragua had certain valid claims against the company, which Walker was to use as a basis for securing the revocation of the charter. He could then issue a new charter to Morgan and Garrison, who by virtue of the concession would be in a position to take over the property of the old company. Walker became a partner in the scheme, and obtained Rivas' signature to the revocation of the old charter. Morgan and Garrison received the concession. But Walker, by incurring the bitter enmity of Vanderbilt, had committed himself to a course which was to result ultimately in his undoing.

In trying to decide upon a policy regarding the filibusters, the Pierce administration found itself in a quandary. The ministers of Costa Rica, Guatemala, and El Salvador protested against the recruiting, which was going on openly, and thereupon Pierce issued a proclamation warning all American citizens against fitting out or taking part in the expeditions to Nicaragua.[23] But, in spite of the proclamation and the Attorney-General's attempts to enforce it, the recruiting went on as merrily as before. When Parker H. French arrived in Washington as the official representative of the Walker-Rivas government, Secretary Marcy refused to receive him, on the ground that those who were instrumental in overthrowing the government of Nicaragua were not citizens of the country, and that the United States would establish diplomatic relations with Nicaragua only after it appeared that the new government had the support of its citizens.[24]

Pierce was accused of catering to Great Britain by refusing to recognize the American government in Nicaragua, and there was even a chance

[23] J. D. Richardson, *Messages and Papers of the Presidents,* Vol. X, p. 388.
[24] *Sen. Ex. Doc. No. 68,* p. 57.

that it would defeat his renomination. Incensed at the treatment accorded French, Walker broke off diplomatic relations with Wheeler, the American minister at Granada.[25] A little later, realizing that French was a most unfortunate choice as minister to the United States, Walker chose Father Vijil, the curate of Granada; and when the latter presented his credentials at Washington they were accepted by President Pierce, "satisfactory evidence appearing that he represents the *de facto* government." [26]

The Costa Rican minister at Washington, Señor Molina, was particularly hostile to the Walker-Rivas government, and protested bitterly to Mr. Marcy on various occasions. In desperation, his state finally took up arms against Nicaragua, whose independence had been destroyed "by the pirates who sailed from the coasts of the United States." [27] The first engagements were decidedly favorable to the Costa Rican forces, but an epidemic of cholera so decimated the ranks that the campaign had to be abandoned. Elated by his success and by the recognition extended by the American government, Walker now proceeded to have himself elected president. The American minister, Mr. Wheeler, without awaiting instructions, proceeded to recognize the new government.[28] He was later censured for his blunder, and when the Walker government's representative reached Washington, he was not received and explanations were refused.[29]

The other republics now became alarmed at Walker's success, and, fearing for their own safety, entered into an alliance for the defense of their sovereignty and independence, recognizing the deposed Rivas as the provisional president of Nicaragua. In spite of the overwhelming superiority of the allies, Walker and his brilliant officer, General Hennington, withstood every attack, and at the end of 1856 the prospects for success were still bright. Vanderbilt now came to the aid of the allies, and, by a clever scheme ably carried out by his agents, caused the collapse of the filibuster régime. A force of Costa Ricans, aided by Spencer, a former engineer on the Transit Company's line, succeeded in surprising Walker's force guarding the steamers on the San Juan and Great Lake, thus cutting off further supplies and reinforcements. The result was now merely a question of time. Commander Davis, in charge of a United States sloop-of-war, seeing the desperate plight of the filibusters, offered his mediation, and the allied general was willing to allow them to surrender to the American commander. "Vanderbilt's man had succeeded in doing what the

[25] *Ibid.*, p. 74.
[26] *Ibid.*, p. 6.
[27] *Ibid.*, p. 131.
[28] Scroggs, *op. cit.*, p. 214.
[29] *Ibid.*, p. 215.

allied Central American states could not accomplish. It was American capitalists who set up the filibuster régime in Nicaragua, and it was an American capitalist who pulled it down." [30]

In September, 1857, the representatives of Costa Rica, Guatemala, and Salvador informed Mr. Cass that a new Walker expedition was being prepared.[31] When this was brought to the attention of Walker, he indited a letter to Secretary Cass truly remarkable in its diplomatic naïveté. He declared that this self-imposed guardianship over Nicaragua on the part of the representatives of Costa Rica and Guatemala was humiliating in the extreme, and as the rightful and lawful chief executive of Nicaragua he protested against it.[32] The United States government investigated, none the less, and finally ordered his arrest. Released on bail for hearing, he immediately set sail for Nicaragua from New Orleans, with very little interference on the part of the port authorities.[33] He landed at Punta Arenas November 24, but before he could do much mischief the U. S. frigate *Wabash,* under the command of Commodore Paulding, appeared opposite the filibusters' camp and demanded their surrender. Walker was brought back to the United States, and, although Commodore Paulding was censured for violating the sovereignty of Nicaragua, President Buchanan expressed the view in no uncertain terms that Walker's expedition was a crime, and said that such undertakings interfered at every step with the conduct of foreign affairs with Central American governments.[34]

Buchanan had already recognized Señor Yrisarri, who was serving as minister from Guatemala and Salvador, as representative from Nicaragua, and immediately signed a treaty with him providing for open transit through Nicaragua to all nations upon equal terms, and giving the United States the right to employ force, if necessary, to protect the route.[35] This treaty, however, was never signed by the Nicaraguan president, partly because of the opposition of Vanderbilt, who knew that a rival company had the concession, but principally because of the machinations of a Frenchman, M. Felix Belly, who used the fear of the filibusters as a most effective bogy to frighten the president of Costa Rica and Nicaragua. These officials went so far as to issue an elaborate manifesto against the United States, declaring that the United States openly menaced Central

[30] *Ibid.,* p. 285. For a full account of the surrender from the standpoint of the filibuster see *House Ex. Doc. No. 24,* 35th Cong., 1st Sess., p. 15.

[31] *Ibid.,* p. 4.

[32] *Ibid.,* p. 6.

[33] *Ibid.,* p. 26.

[34] Richardson, *op. cit.,* Vol. V, p. 466.

[35] Text in *Sen. Ex. Doc. No. 194,* 47th Cong., 1st Sess., p. 117.

America with annexation unless Europe should defend it; and they therefore placed their countries under the protection of England, France, and Sardinia.[36] When the United States asked whether this document was genuine, the Nicaraguan government, after considerable prodding, replied that it was signed by the President acting as a private citizen, and therefore was not an official act.[37]

Walker's third and last attempt ended the filibustering expeditions to Central America. Early in 1860 an inhabitant of one of the Bay Islands, which, by a convention signed the previous year between Great Britain and Honduras, had been put back under the sovereignty of Honduras, invited Walker to come to the islanders' aid to resist the convention's execution. Walker seized the opportunity, and was soon heading another expedition to Central America. Upon arriving, he found the British flag still flying, and after waiting several weeks he became desperate and seized the fortress of Truxillo on the mainland of Honduras. A fortnight later Commander Salmon of H.M.S. *Icarus* sent him a note declaring that the occupation was prejudicial to British interests, and that therefore he must lay down his arms and withdraw. Realizing the hopelessness of his position, Walker first attempted flight, but, being captured, surrendered to the British officer. Contrary to his promise, Salmon turned him over to the authorities of Honduras. This was equivalent to a sentence of death, and on September 12, 1860, a firing squad ended the career of the greatest of the filibusters.[38] In his annual message of December 3, 1860, President Buchanan uttered the pious opinion that "it surely ought to be the prayer of every Christian and patriot that such expeditions may never again receive countenance in our country or depart from our shores." [39]

During the next decade the relations between the United States and the Central American republics were uneventful. From the beginning of his term, Secretary Seward determined to follow a policy of friendly relations with Central America and to gain, if possible, the inhabitants' good will. In his instructions to Mr. Dickinson, the new minister to Nicaragua, dated June 5, 1861, the Secretary counseled him to assure the Republic of Nicaragua "that the President will deal with that government justly, fairly, and in the most friendly spirit; that he desires only its welfare and prosperity. . . . Let unpleasant memories of past differences be buried and let

[36] Scroggs, *op. cit.*, p. 361.

[37] *Ibid.*, p. 364.

[38] *Ibid.*, Chap. XXIII. General William Walker's account of his expeditions, *The War in Nicaragua* (Mobile and New York, 1860), is a well written, accurate, and remarkably unbiased historical narrative.

[39] Richardson, *op. cit.*, Vol. V, p. 649.

Nicaragua be encouraged to rely on the sympathy and support of the United States if she shall at any time come to need them." [40] In 1867 Nicaragua had occasion to remember Seward's promise and called upon the United States to use her good offices to obtain for Nicaragua a favorable settlement of the problems arising under her treaty of 1860 with Great Britain relative to the Mosquito territory.[41] The American minister at London, Mr. Charles Francis Adams, approached Lord Stanley on the subject, and received his assurance that the British government had no wish to embarrass Nicaragua, and had already given the Nicaraguan minister satisfactory evidence of the justice of its position.[42]

The one subject, however, upon which the United States laid greatest stress, in her diplomatic correspondence with the Central American republics during the second half of the nineteenth century, was the project of a Central American confederation. The Central American states realized very clearly the advantages of a closer union, and, after the complete dissolution of the Union in 1840 numerous efforts were made to reëstablish the Confederation. In 1842, 1849, and 1852 attempts were made by the three central states; but no permanent result came of them.[43] In 1871 President Medina, of Honduras, proposed that delegates be sent to Salvador to consider plans for a union. The presidents of Nicaragua and Guatemala seemed favorable to the idea, and it was suggested that Mr. Riotti, the American representative at León, should preside over the conference. Secretary Fish was favorably impressed wtih the idea and intimated that the project was a very desirable one in the eyes of the United States.[44] The following year a pact of union was signed in El Salvador by the representatives of Costa Rica, Honduras, Guatemala, and Salvador, "to preserve and maintain the peace between them, . . . and to guarantee the autonomies of Central America and the integrity of its territory against all aggression and pretensions of foreign powers." [45] But, within two months of the conference, war broke out between Honduras and El Salvador.

On June 24, 1874, Mr. Williamson, the American representative at Guatemala, summed up in a despatch to Secretary Fish what he considered to be the principal obstacles to a union of the Central American

[40] *Diplomatic Correspondence of the United States,* 1861, p. 419.

[41] *Ibid.,* 1867, Vol. II, pp. 690 *ff.*

[42] *Ibid.,* 1868, Vol. I, p. 151.

[43] See Munro, *op. cit.,* Chap. VIII, for a concise account of the various attempts; also P. M. Brown, "American Intervention in Central America," *Journal of Race Development,* Vol. IV, p. 409.

[44] *For. Rel. of the U. S.,* 1871, pp. 681-683.

[45] *Ibid.,* 1872, p. 520.

states: the debts incurred during the former federal union, local preju-
dices, a heterogeneous population, no identity of interest, difficulty of
intercommunication, and lack of a prominent leader to make a public
issue of the question of federation.[46] The new president of Guatemala,
J. Rufino Barrios, was destined to become such a leader. In 1876 he proposed that Guatemala annex the four other republics, but such a plan
could scarcely be expected to meet the approval of the states to be taken
in. The United States continued to manifest interest in the idea of federation, and Secretary Blaine, in a despatch to the American minister at
Guatemala City, dated May 7, 1881, declared that "there is nothing which
this government more earnestly desires than the prosperity of these states,
and our experience has taught us that nothing will so surely develop
and guarantee such prosperity as their association under one common
government. . . . You cannot impress too strongly upon the government
to which you are accredited, or upon the public men with whom you associate, the importance which the government of the United States attaches
to such a confederation of the states of Central America as will respond
to the wants and wishes of their people." [47] He repeated these sentiments
to Señor Ubico, the representative of Guatemala at Washington,[48] and to
Mr. Morgan, the American minister to Mexico.[49]

During the year 1882 President Barrios visited the United States, and
the results showed that the administration undoubtedly encouraged him
in his plans for a union. Upon his return he secured the approval of the
presidents of Salvador and Honduras, and to reconcile public opinion he
declared, in a public letter to the Liberal Party, that although he was
doing all in his power to bring about a federation of the five republics,
he had no intention of accepting the presidency.[50] Unfortunately, the
popular opposition was too great, and the scheduled convention did not
take place. Barrios now determined to resort to force. On February 28,
1885, he issued a decree declaring himself the supreme military chief
of the "Central American Union" and proclaiming the union of Central
America into one sole republic.[51] Honduras accepted immediately, but
the president of El Salvador, who had previously pledged his support,
vacillated and played for time, Nicaragua and Costa Rica rejected the
plan unconditionally, and on March 9, together with El Salvador, they

[46] *Ibid.*, 1874, p. 172.
[47] *Ibid.*, 1881, p. 102.
[48] *Ibid.*, p. 599.
[49] *Ibid.*, p. 816.
[50] *Ibid.*, 1883, p. 49.
[51] *Ibid.*, 1885, p. 75.

appealed to the United States and Mexico to intervene against the projects of Barrios.[52] Mr. Hall, the American representative at Guatemala, was authorized to use his good offices, but the day after he received the despatch news came that President Barrios had been killed in action.[53] With the death of Barrios, all further immediate efforts to form a confederation under the ægis of Guatemala were dropped. In spite of the hostilities engendered by the war, a treaty was signed on September 12, 1885, between Guatemala, Honduras, and El Salvador, providing among other things for extradition, commercial reciprocity, and a postal telegraph and monetary union; and Nicaragua and Costa Rica were invited to become parties to it.[54]

Although the invitation was not accepted, negotiations continued, and in January, 1887, the delegates of El Salvador, Honduras, Nicaragua, and Costa Rica met in Guatemala, and after a month's deliberation, on February 16, 1887, signed a treaty of peace and friendship. This document opened with the statement that it is the mutual desire of the five states to draw closer and "establish appropriate bases for the near advent of the longed-for political union of Central America." [55] The treaty was ratified by all the states except Nicaragua, who seemed to fear forcible action on the part of Guatemala and raised the issue in Washington. Secretary Bayard hastened to notify Mr. Hall, the American minister at Guatemala, that the United States strongly disapproved of a coercive union of the Central American republics, and suggested that he take an early and discreet occasion to bring these views to the attention of the government of Guatemala.[56] Guatemala denied the allegations and continued under the treaty of 1887 to work for a union. But a revolution in El Salvador in 1890 brought into power the opponents of the union, thus forcing another postponement. Selfish domestic rivalries continued to nullify all efforts toward federation.

We have already indicated the interest of Mr. Blaine in Latin-American affairs as shown by his part in the first Pan American Conference and by his efforts to further a Central American federation. Unfortunately for his popularity in Central America, he was forced to decide a number of close cases in international law against the Central American republics. Guatemala was the chief offender. In July, 1890, she had seized arms on board the Pacific Mail Steamship Company's steamer *Colima*, contrary

[52] Bancroft, *op. cit.*, Vol. III, p. 448.
[53] *For. Rel. of the U. S.*, 1885, pp. 98-99.
[54] *Ibid.*, 1887, p. 85.
[55] *Ibid.*, p. 101.
[56] *Ibid.*, 1888, Part I, p. 131.

to an agreement made with the American minister,[57] and in the following month Guatemalan officials killed General Barrundia, traveling on the same company's steamer *Acapulco*.[58] For his conduct in the second case, the American minister's acts were disavowed and he was recalled forthwith. With war ever threatening between Guatemala and El Salvador, Secretary Blaine's instructions to the new minister were most emphatic that he should make every effort to avert it. "Not only are the good offices of the United States equally ready towards averting possible causes of difference, but it is deemed the friendly duty of this government to do all that it can to prevent strife among its neighbors."[59]

In 1894 the United States had occasion to enter into negotiations with the British government in regard to the Mosquito kingdom. By the treaty of Managua, dating from 1860, Nicaragua's sovereignty over this region was recognized, but the Indians were given certain rights of self-government. In the course of time many foreigners, principally English and Americans, engaged in business enterprises in Bluefields, the capital, and the region became very prosperous. On November 2, 1893, a Nicaraguan commissioner, with a staff of officers, arrived at Bluefields and established heavy customs upon the export of bananas. When the natives protested, the Nicaraguan officials obtained reinforcements, and finally took over the whole management of the country and proclaimed martial law. On February 25, 1894, H.M.S. *Cleopatra* anchored at Bluefields, and her commander insisted that martial law be raised and the Mosquito flag again hoisted.[60] The United States was interested, and the American minister to Nicaragua was directed to visit Bluefields and make a report. He found (1) that the present provisional government imposed by the Nicaraguan authorities, coöperating with the British consul, was a bold usurpation; (2) that the Mosquito government existing before Nicaragua became an independent state was overthrown by armed violence on February 11, 1894; (3) that fully 90 per cent of all the wealth, enterprise, and commerce of the Indian reserve was American; and (4) that the extension of Spanish revolutionary rule over this reserve would inevitably extinguish the whole of this present business prosperity.[61]

Although the American minister's sympathies seemed to favor the Mosquito government, the United States from the beginning took a firm stand in behalf of full Nicaraguan sovereignty. Writing to Mr. Bayard,

[57] J. B. Moore, *Digest of Int. Law,* Vol. VII, p. 659.
[58] *Ibid.,* Vol. II, p. 871.
[59] *For Rel. of the U. S.,* 1891, p. 56.
[60] *Ibid.,* 1894, Appendix I, pp. 261-264; 276-284.
[61] *Ibid.,* p. 287.

the American minister at London, April 30, 1894, Secretary Gresham declared he was "unable to see that this joint assumption of authority by British and Nicaraguan agents was incompatible with the treaty of Managua." [62] Again on July 19 he maintained that the sovereignty of Nicaragua over the whole of the national domain was unquestionable. "No matter how conspicuous the American or other alien interests which have grown up under the fiction of Indian self-government, neither the United States nor Great Britain can fairly sanction or uphold this colorable abuse of the sovereignty of Nicaragua." [63] Further foreign intervention was eliminated by the Mosquito tribes voluntarily signing a convention, November 20, 1894, permitting the absolute incorporation of their territory into the republic of Nicaragua. [64]

The century came to an end with one more attempt on the part of the Central American states to form a federation. Nicaragua, Honduras, and El Salvador signed the treaty of Amapala, June 20, 1895, by which they were to form a single political organization for the exercise of their external sovereignty; and the agreement was ratified in September of the following year. The federal powers were to be exercised by a diet consisting of one member and one substitute elected by each congress for a term of three years. Costa Rica and Guatemala were to be invited to join. [65] President Cleveland extended recognition to this Greater Republic of Central America, discerning in the articles of association "a step towards a closer union of Central American States in the interest of their common defense and general welfare," and he welcomed it as "the precursor of other steps to be taken in the same direction, and which it is hoped may eventually result in the consolidation of all the states of Central America as one nation for all the purposes of their foreign relations and intercourse." [66]

Costa Rica and Guatemala did not join, but in 1898 the other three states adopted a permanent constitution establishing a federal republic and made plans for the election of a president. Before the successful culmination of these plans, however, a revolution in El Salvador detached this state from the group, and the other two thereupon resumed their in-

[62] *Ibid.*, p. 271.
[63] *Ibid.*, p. 311.
[64] *Ibid.*, p. 361. The relations with Great Britain were finally settled by a new treaty, signed at Managua April 19, 1905, in which Great Britain recognized the sovereignty of Nicaragua over the Mosquito Reserve. For text see *For. Rel. of the U. S.*, 1905, p. 703.
[65] For full text see *ibid.*, 1896, p. 390.
[66] *Ibid.*, p. 370.

dependence of action.[67] The close of the century found the five independent republics at peace with the world and with each other, but apparently as far as ever from the union that had so long been the goal of their endeavors.

SUPPLEMENTARY READINGS

H. H. BANCROFT, *History of Central America* (San Francisco, 1886).

FLOYD CRAMER, *Our Neighbor, Nicaragua* (New York, 1929).

SAMUEL CROWTHER, *The Romance and Rise of the American Tropics* (New York, 1929).

C. W. DOMVILLE-FIFE, *Guatemala and the States of Central America* (New York, 1913).

C. R. ENOCK, *Republics of Central and South America* (New York, 1913).

RICARDO FERNANDEZ-GUARDIA (H. W. Van Dyke, trans.), *History of the Discovery and Conquest of Costa Rica* (New York, 1913).

CHESTER LLOYD JONES, *Costa Rica and Civilization in the Caribbean* (Madison, Wis., 1935).

————, *Guatemala, Past and Present* (Minneapolis, 1940).

L. M. KEASBY, *The Nicaragua Canal and the Monroe Doctrine* (New York, 1896).

W. H. KOEBEL, *Central America* (London, 1917).

P. F. MARTIN, *Salvador of the Twentieth Century* (London, 1911).

L. A. MORENO, *Historia de las Relaciones Interstatuales de Centro America* (Madrid, 1928).

D. G. MUNRO, *The Five Republics of Central America* (New York, 1918).

FREDERIC PALMER, *Central America and Its Problems* (New York, 1910).

MAURICE DE PÉRIGNY, *Les Cinq Republiques de L'Amérique Centrale* (Paris, c. 1910).

G. P. PUTNAM, *The Southland of North America* (New York, 1913).

A. B. RUHL, *The Central Americans* (New York, 1928).

W. O. SCROGGS, *Filibusters and Financiers* (New York, 1916).

E. G. SQUIER, *Honduras* (London, 1870).

WALLACE THOMPSON, *Rainbow Countries of Central America* (New York, 1926).

WILLIAM WALKER, *The War in Nicaragua* (New York, 1860).

[67] *Ibid.*, 1898, pp. 173-178; also Richardson, *op. cit.*, Vol. X, p. 178, and W. F. Slade, "Federation of Central America," *Journal of Race Development,* Vol. VIII (Oct., 1917), pp. 210-218.

❦ 15 ❦

Recent Relations with Central America

THE events outlined in the preceding chapter indicate a fairly consistent policy of friendly coöperation on the part of the United States with the Central American republics, particularly in their efforts to obtain a successful federal system of government. American citizens had been guilty of various audacious attempts to obtain special privileges and autocratic powers in these republics, but the American government never failed to frown upon them, even when a different policy might have redounded to the country's advantage. The war with Spain, however, was destined to place the United States in a new position with regard to the Caribbean region, and a greater interest in Central America and its problems was to be expected.

The first intervention of the United States in the affairs of the Central American republics, except in the collection of a few private claims, occurred in 1906. In July of that year a war broke out between Guatemala and El Salvador, and Honduras, as usual, was drawn in, this time on the side of El Salvador. The American minister used every effort to avert it; when he failed, President Theodore Roosevelt, after securing the coöperation of President Diaz of Mexico, stepped in. He sent identical notes to President Escalon of Salvador and Cabrera of Guatemala urging the immediate cessation of hostilities, and offering the deck of the American warship *Marblehead* as a neutral place where terms of an agreement might be drawn up.[1] Both sides accepted, and on board the *Marblehead*, on July 20, 1906, a convention of peace was signed which provided that within two months a general treaty of peace, amity, and navigation

[1] *For. Rel. of the U. S.*, 1906, Part I, p. 837.

should be arranged for by a meeting, in Costa Rica, of the representatives of the three republics. The convention also provided that new differences should be submitted to arbitration, with the presidents of the United States and Mexico serving as arbitrators.[2] In appreciation of this just and peaceful settlement of the controversy, the Third Pan American Conference, which was then in session at Rio de Janeiro, passed a resolution of gratification over the successful mediation by the two presidents.[3]

The meeting in Costa Rica was participated in by representatives of all the Central American republics except Nicaragua. The results were a general treaty of peace and amity, arbitration, extradition, commerce, etc., between the four republics; also two conventions, the first establishing an International Central American Bureau in the city of Guatemala, and the second establishing a Central American Pedagogical Institute in San José, Costa Rica. Copies of these were sent to the United States by Costa Rica "as an act of courtesy to the government of the United States for an equal interest in the welfare of the Central American states."[4] Although Nicaragua had not sent representatives to the conference, copies of the treaty and conventions were sent to her, inviting her adherence. Nicaragua replied that she did not care to adhere, inasmuch as the treaty seemed to ratify the treaty of *Marblehead*, whose terms she was not willing to accept. The inference was that President Zelaya of Nicaragua, known to be hostile to the United States, was unwilling to accept the President of the United States as an arbitrator in case a dispute should arise to which Nicaragua was a party.

Hardly had Nicaragua thus announced her attitude before a situation arose which demanded arbitration. Honduras claimed that certain revolutionists and disturbers of the peace had fled across the border into Nicaragua, and that in order to suppress them its troops had been forced to cross the line. Nicaragua immediately got its forces in readiness and demanded indemnity for the infringement of its territorial rights. An attempt to settle this dispute by arbitration having failed, President Roosevelt wrote, on February 11, 1907, to the presidents of both states, expressing the strong hope that some means might be found to settle the dispute without resorting to war.[5] Receiving favorable responses from both, President Roosevelt thereupon offered his assistance. President Diaz acted in a similar fashion, but Nicaragua insisted upon reparations as a basis of arbitration, and, when Honduras refused, began operations. Hostilities

[2] *Ibid.*, Part I, p. 851.
[3] *Ibid.*, p. 852.
[4] *Ibid.*, p. 856.
[5] *Ibid.*, 1907, Part II, p. 616.

did not last long, but El Salvador was drawn in against Nicaragua, and to avoid complications the United States once more offered its good offices. With the United States minister present during discussions, a treaty of peace was signed at Amapala, April 23, 1907, between Nicaragua and El Salvador. The third article of this treaty provided that "any difference that may arise in the future between El Salvador and Nicaragua that might alter their good relations shall be adjusted by means of the obligatory arbitration of the presidents of the United States and of Mexico, conjointly." [6]

When trouble again threatened, in August of the same year, President Roosevelt, coöperating with President Diaz of Mexico, sent identic notes to each of the five Central American republics—tendering the good offices of the United States to bring about a peace conference of the representatives of the several states.[7] This overture received a very favorable response, and on September 17, 1907, the representatives of the five Central American republics at Washington signed a protocol agreeing to a joint conference at Washington, to meet November 1; in the meantime, they agreed to maintain peace and good relations among one another, and not to commit, or allow to be committed, any act that might disturb their mutual tranquillity.[8] In accordance with this protocol, President Roosevelt invited the executives of the five republics to name commissioners, to meet in Washington to discuss measures to be adopted to adjust any existing differences, and to conclude a treaty determining the general relations of their countries.[9]

The invitations were accepted by all of the republics, and they proposed that both the United States and Mexico should be represented. The conference, which met in Washington November 14, in the Bureau of American Republics began very auspiciously. In his opening address, Secretary Root made a strong plea to the delegates to banish fraternal strife from their land, and to find specific and practical measures whereby they might keep and enforce the agreements entered into.[10] The delegates showed their spirit of coöperation and friendly feeling by unanimous declarations at the first regular session that each of their countries had no claims against any of the others. But when, at the second session, Honduras proposed a scheme for the union of the five republics, a difference of opinion was quickly noticeable. Nicaragua was favorable to the

[6] *Ibid.,* p. 633.
[7] *Ibid.,* p. 638.
[8] *Ibid.,* p. 644.
[9] *Ibid.,* p. 648.
[10] Report of W. I. Buchanan, *ibid.,* p. 687.

proposal, but Guatemala opposed it, and Costa Rica objected to the consideration of the subject. The matter was finally referred to a committee of five, including one representative from each state.

The reports of this committee, which were read at the next session, showed strong divergence of views. The majority report, signed by representatives of Guatemala, El Salvador, and Costa Rica, conceded that the political union of Central America was the "greatest and noblest aspiration of patriotism," yet gave it as their opinion that conditions were not suitable for attempting it at this time. They said that it was more opportune in the present conference to consider measures tending towards preparing in a stable manner for this union, such as better means of communication, a coasting ship commerce, a unification of customs and tax laws, and the encouragement of further Central American conferences. As definite steps, they supported the idea of a Central American bureau, the Pedagogical Institute, and the creation of a permanent Central American court of international justice. The minority report, signed by Honduras and Nicaragua, declared that union alone would insure stable and efficient peace and order in Central America, and insisted that this was the time to establish it.[11]

Fearing lest this question might interfere with the constructive work of the conference, Mr. Buchanan, the American representative, supported by the Mexican representative, proposed that the consideration of both reports be postponed, and that the conference proceed to prepare projects for the several proposed conventions. This course was adopted, and the conference proceeded to frame and adopt a number of important conventions regarding peace and friendship, the establishment of a Central American Court of Justice and a Central American bureau, extradition, railway communications, and a convention concerning future Central American conferences.[12]

Undoubtedly the two most important achievements were the general treaty of peace and amity, which was to remain in force ten years, and the convention establishing the Central American Court of Justice. Among other things, the treaty provided that any disposition or measure tending to alter the constitutional organization of any of the republics should be deemed a menace to the peace of all; the territory of Honduras was made neutral in conflicts arising between the other four republics, as long as she remained neutral; political refugees and disturbers were not allowed to reside near the frontiers of any of the five republics;

[11] For text see *ibid.*, pp. 671-673.
[12] *Ibid.*, p. 673.

and all future disputes were to be decided by the Central American Court of Justice. This tribunal was to consist of five judges, one from each state, appointed for five-year terms. It was given obligatory jurisdiction over all cases arising between two or more of the states, and its decision, given in writing by a majority opinion, was to be final. The court could fix the *status quo* pending the decisions in a case, and the signatory republics bound themselves to carry out faithfully the court's orders.[13]

On the whole, the representatives had no reason to feel ashamed of the results of their labors. Although the results were only on paper, and all looked towards the future, the ideas adopted were specific and practical, and they were grounded upon a solid basis of coöperation which alone was bound to be beneficial to all. The Court of Justice naturally received the most attention. One eminent American publicist aptly remarked: "To the powers of Europe, to the great powers of the world who struggled with partial success, for four months at The Hague, to establish a court of arbitral justice, the young republics of Central America may recall the scriptural phrase, 'A little child shall lead them.'" [14]

Unfortunately for the future peace of Central America, the court was not to have the success that its advocates had hoped, and the United States, as will be seen later, bulks large in the ultimate cause of its failure. The court was installed with much acclaim in Cartago, Costa Rica, May 25, 1908, representatives from the United States and Mexico participating in the inauguration ceremonies. In his address, Mr. Buchanan, the American representative, while taking a tone of optimism, very clearly pointed out that if success were to crown the effort there must be behind this court and its decisions an elevated patriotic public conscience in each of the republics that would lift and maintain the court in every way above the plane of political purposes or necessities. In conclusion, he read a telegram from Secretary Root saying that he had been authorized by Mr. Andrew Carnegie to offer, as a mark of his good wishes for the peace and progress of Central America, the sum of $100,000 for the construction in the city of Cartago of a temple of peace for the exclusive use of the court.[15]

Another result of the Washington conference was the establishment at Guatemala City, in the following year, of the Central American Inter-

[13] For text of the general treaty and the convention see *ibid.*, pp. 692-711.
[14] J. B. Scott, *Amer. Jour. of Int. Law*, Vol. II (Jan., 1908), p. 143.
[15] *For. Rel. of the U. S.*, 1908; report of W. I. Buchanan, pp. 217-247.

national Bureau. The principal objects of this bureau were: (1) the reorganization of the Central American Union; (2) the introduction of an up-to-date educational system; (3) the development and extension of domestic and foreign trade; (4) the increase and development of agriculture and industries; (5) the reform of legal institutions; and (6) reforms in customs, the monetary system, credit, weights and measures, and sanitation. This bureau was to consist of one delegate from each republic, who should reside in Guatemala. All future Central American conferences were to be held under its auspices, and it was to publish a bulletin, *Centro América*, as a means of keeping the republics in touch with one another's progress.[16] The bureau was in many respects modeled upon the Pan American Union, and, considering its limited resources and facilities, it has been eminently successful. Mr. Dana G. Munro goes so far as to assert that of the institutions provided by the Washington conference this is the only one that had thus far fully justified its creation.[17]

While these various means were being provided to strengthen friendly relations between the Central American republics, President Zelaya of Nicaragua continued to show his unwillingness to maintain friendly relations with either his neighbors or the United States. President Davila of Honduras was under his thumb; El Salvador was constantly threatened by his machinations. A British traveler who had spent much time in Central America declared that "all travelers, foreigners, and natives alike, who happened to be in Central America at this time, were well aware of the provocative part which President Santos Zelaya was playing; for many years he had been acting as the evil genius of this republic, and his misgovernment and brutalities to his own people met with general condemnation."[18] The ultimate result was a revolution, which started at Bluefields in October, 1909. At first the United States remained neutral, but when, in November, Zelaya ordered two Americans to be shot because they were serving as officers in the revolutionary army, the United States broke off diplomatic relations with his government. In his note to the Nicaraguan *chargé* Secretary Knox strongly denounced the Zelayan régime, declaring that it had almost continually kept Central America in tension or turmoil, that it had repeatedly and flagrantly violated the

---

[16] For an account of the bureau's activities see W. F. Slade, "Federation of Central America," *Jour. of Race Development*, Vol. VIII (Oct., 1917), pp. 234-241.

[17] D. G. Munro, *The Five Republics of Central America* (New York, 1918), p. 225.

[18] P. F. Martin, *Salvador of the Twentieth Century* (London, 1911), p. 67.

Washington conventions, and that it was a blot on the history of the country.[19]

Partly as a result of the American attitude, Zelaya was unable to put down the revolution, and he finally resigned, left the country, and took refuge on a Mexican gunboat. The United States maintained an ostensible neutrality between President Madriz, who received the backing of the Zelaya faction, and Estrada, who headed the revolutionists; but when the Madriz forces wanted to bombard Bluefields, which they declared to be the vital base of the Conservatives, United States cruisers refused to permit it. The reason given was that foreigners would be the chief sufferers. But the result was a decided strengthening of Estrada's position. President Madriz protested both to President Taft and to President Diaz of Mexico; but Secretary Knox replied that the United States had taken only the customary step of prohibiting bombardment or fighting by either faction within the unfortified and ungarrisoned city of Bluefields, thus protecting the preponderant American and other foreign interests.[20] In August, 1910, Madriz gave up the struggle, and by the middle of the following month Señor Don Juan J. Estrada claimed to be in peaceful and unrestricted possession of the entire republic.

In its first note to the United States the new government promised that a general election would be held within a year and that the national finances would be rehabilitated, and to this end the Department of State at Washington was asked to obtain a loan secured by a percentage of the customs revenues, and to send a commission to Nicaragua to arrange the necessary formalities.[21] The United States thereupon appointed Mr. T. C. Dawson as special agent to Nicaragua to deal with the provisional government on these lines. The negotiations were successful, and a number of agreements were entered into which provided that Estrada should remain at the head of the government for two years, after which a free election should be held; that a claims commission, consisting of one Nicaraguan and one American and an umpire named by the American State Department, should be appointed to consider all unliquidated claims against the government; and that a loan secured by the customs receipts be raised in the United States.[22]

A special loan convention embodied the latter proposal, and President Taft urgently recommended it as contributing to the peace of Central

[19] *For. Rel. of the U. S.*, 1909, p. 455; see also President Taft's Message of December 7, 1909, *ibid.*, p. xvii.
[20] *For. Rel. of the U. S.*, 1910, pp. 751-753.
[21] *Ibid.*, p. 762.
[22] *Ibid.*, 1911, pp. 625 ff.

America; but it failed to receive the assent of the United States Senate.[23]
A loan was none the less negotiated with American bankers, and an
American, Mr. Clifford D. Ham, was put in charge of the collection of the
customs to guarantee its repayment.[24] The claims commission was also
appointed, and it began to work on May 1, 1911. The commission worked
steadily for more than three years and passed upon almost 8000 claims,
scaling them down from a total of $13,750,000 to about $1,750,000.[25] The
political part of the program, however, was a complete failure, and in
less than six months President Estrada had resigned in favor of Vice-
president Diaz. The latter soon found out that a reform program in
Nicaragua could not be put through unless the president received outside
support, and in a confidential letter to the American *chargé d'affaires*, written December 21, 1911, he confessed the need of more direct and efficient
assistance from the United States. He proposed that the Nicaraguan constitution be so amended as to permit the United States to intervene in
Nicaraguan internal affairs in order to maintain peace and the existence
of a lawful government.[26]

Practical evidences of this need were soon given. On July 29, 1912,
General Luis Mena, the Minister of War, engineered a *coup d'état* against
the Diaz government with a view to seizing the executive power. Failing
in his original attempt, he left the capital and organized an open rebellion
against the government. Fearing that he would be unable to protect the
property and lives of American citizens, President Diaz asked that "the
United States guarantee with its forces security for the property of American citizens in Nicaragua and that it extend its protection to all the
inhabitants of the republic." [27] President Taft thereupon ordered a small
detachment of marines to be landed at Managua.

When the president of El Salvador expressed the fear of serious complications if American troops should enter Nicaraguan territory, the State
Department, in a note to the American minister at Managua, dated September 4, 1912, laid down the American policy in no uncertain language.
"The policy of the government of the United States in the present Nicaraguan disturbances is to take the necessary measures for an adequate
legation guard at Managua, to keep open communications, and to protect
American life and property. In discountenancing Zelaya, whose régime

[23] *Ibid.*, 1912, pp. 1071-1078.
[24] For an excellent summary of the events of this period, embracing particularly
the financial arrangements, see Munro, *op. cit.*, Chap. XI.
[25] Otto Schoenrich, *Amer. Jour. of Int. Law*, Vol. IX (Oct., 1915), p. 958.
[26] *For. Rel. of the U. S.*, 1911, p. 670.
[27] *Ibid.*, 1912, p. 1032.

of barbarity and corruption was ended by the Nicaraguan nation after a bloody war, the government of the United States opposed not only the individual but the system, and this government could not countenance any movement to restore the same destructive régime. The government of the United States will, therefore, discountenance any revival of Zelaya-ism, and will lend its strong moral support to the cause of legally con-stituted good government for the benefit of the people of Nicaragua, whom it has long sought to aid in their just aspiration towards peace and prosperity under constitutional and orderly government." [28]

The revolution that followed proved more serious than was at first expected, owing to the uprising of the Liberals of León, who threw in their fortunes with General Mena. The United States, however, could not afford to allow the Zelaya faction to triumph, and American marines were landed at Corinto, Granada, and León; they even went so far as to storm the position overlooking Masaya. The revolutionists could hardly hope to hold out against the government thus aided by the United States, and with the seizure of General Mena, and his internment in Panama, the upris-ing collapsed. President Diaz was reëlected for a four-year term to begin January 1, 1913. Although order had been completely restored and the Diaz government was in full control, a detachment of one hundred Amer-ican marines was left in Managua, at the urgent request of the American minister, to act as a stabilizing influence.

On account of the U. S. Senate's failure to approve the loan convention, the financial situation was in even worse shape than before. American bankers had made a loan of $1,500,000 for the establishment of the Na-tional Bank of Nicaragua, the reform of the currency, and the establish-ment of the claims commission; but the hoped-for loan of $15,000,000 was dependent upon the ratification of the convention.[29] As a solution of the difficulty, Nicaragua proposed, in December, 1912, to sell to the United States, for the sum of $3,000,000, the sole right to construct a canal through her territory. As an additional inducement to the United States, the right was given to construct a naval base in the Gulf of Fonseca and one on Corn Island.[30] When the Wilson administration came in, this treaty was modified so as to prevent Nicaragua from declaring war, from making treaties with foreign governments affecting her independence or territorial

[28] *Ibid.*, p. 1043.
[29] See the memorandum on Nicaraguan finances prepared for the Secretary of State, *ibid.*, 1913, p. 1040.
[30] *Ibid.*, p. 1021. Mr. Weitsel, the American minister to Nicaragua, 1912-1913, and one of the signatories of this agreement, in a memorandum on the convention gives an excellent résumé of American relations with Nicaragua; see *Sen. Doc. No. 334*, 64th Cong., 1st Sess.

integrity, and from contracting public debts beyond her ability to pay; and it was also changed so as to grant the United States the right to intervene in her affairs, with a view to maintaining her independence and protecting life and property in her domain. The Senate refused to accept this full protectorate, and a new treaty without these provisions was signed on August 5, 1914. Again the Senate raised objections; but these were met, and the treaty was ratified on February 18, 1916, and proclaimed on June 24, following.

The Bryan-Chamorro treaty as finally approved makes the following provisions:

(1) the government of Nicaragua grants in perpetuity to the government of the United States, free from taxation, the exclusive rights necessary for the construction and operation of a canal by way of the San Juan River and the Great Lake or by any other route; (2) to protect American interests, Nicaragua leases to the United States for ninety-nine years the Great Corn and Little Corn Islands, and also grants the right to establish a naval base on such Nicaraguan territory bordering upon the Gulf of Fonseca as the United States shall select, with a right to obtain renewal of the grants for a similar period; (3) in consideration of these stipulations the United States agrees to pay the sum of $3,000,000 in gold; and (4) the following proviso is inserted: "Whereas Costa Rica, Salvador, and Honduras have protested against the ratification of the said convention, in the fear or belief that said convention might in some respect impair existing rights of said States; therefore it is declared by the Senate that in advising and consenting to the ratification of the said convention as amended, such advice and consent are given with the understanding, to be expressed as a part of the instrument of ratification, that nothing in said convention is intended to affect any existing right of any of the said named States." [31]

Despite this proviso, Costa Rica and Salvador continued to protest, and finally they attempted through the Central American Court of Justice to enjoin Nicaragua from carrying out the provisions of the treaty. Costa Rica based her case upon a treaty of limits between herself and Nicaragua, signed April 15, 1858, giving Costa Rica rights in the San Juan River and agreeing that she should be consulted before any contract should be entered into for the construction of a canal. This treaty had been held valid by President Cleveland in 1888. Costa Rica therefore argued that the present treaty would infringe her rights under the treaty of 1858. [32] El Salvador claimed an equal right with Honduras and Nicaragua in the Bay of Fonseca, and therefore asserted that Nicaragua had

[31] U. S. Stat. at Large, Vol. XXXIX, Part II, p. 1661.
[32] Complaint of the Republic of Costa Rica before the Central American Court of Justice (Washington, D. C., 1916), Appendices G and N.

no right to alienate territory clearly jeopardizing and menacing her interests without her consent. Furthermore, the Washington conference of 1907 had proclaimed the neutrality of Honduras, including its rights in the Gulf of Fonseca; therefore, it was urged, this projected agreement for the establishment of a naval base there "is an attempt to violate, in a manner both flagrant and evident, the principle of the neutrality of Honduras, and to throw overboard the legal system instituted by the conference of Washington." [33]

Nicaragua denied the court's jurisdiction in the cases of both Costa Rica and El Salvador, but the court declared itself competent to take cognizance of them. The decision in the case of Costa Rica was handed down on September 30, 1916; that in the case of El Salvador on March 2, 1917. In both cases the court held that Nicaragua, by signing the Bryan-Chamorro treaty of August 5, 1914, had violated the rights of Costa Rica and El Salvador, that she had also violated the treaty of peace and amity signed at Washington in 1907, and that she was under obligation to re-establish and maintain the legal status existing prior to the Bryan-Chamorro treaty. In both cases, however, the court admitted that it was without competence to declare the Bryan-Chamorro treaty null and void, since its jurisdictional power extended only to establishing the legal relations among the "high parties litigant." [34]

The refusal of the United States, as well as of Nicaragua, to accept the decision of the court had a very bad effect on the standing of the United States with the other Central American countries. Since the United States refused to back the very agency for settling disputes to whose establishment it had given such hearty encouragement, simply because the decision interfered with her own selfish interests, how could the Latin-American republics feel much confidence in American expressions of friendly coöperation? When the question of renewing the convention to continue the court's existence came up, nothing could be done, owing to Nicaragua's withdrawal; and on March 17, 1918, the court was formally dissolved. [35] The Bryan-Chamorro treaty thus indirectly caused the downfall of the Central American court, thereby weakening the trend towards a closer relationship among these states which it has been the avowed

[33] *Complaint of the Republic of El Salvador before the Central American Court of Justice* (Washington, D. C., 1917), Appendices A and I.

[34] *Opinion and Decision of the Court—the Republic of El Salvador Against the Republic of Nicaragua* (Washington, D. C., 1917).

[35] For a detailed account of the Court's history see the scholarly article by Manley O. Hudson, "The Central American Court of Justice," *Amer. Jour. of Int. Law*, Vol. XXVI, No. 4 (Oct., 1932).

policy of the United States to foster. In fact, when another attempt at federation was made in 1920, and a "treaty of union" was signed January 19, 1921, by representatives of Guatemala, Honduras, El Salvador, and Costa Rica, Nicaragua refused to enter because of her fears lest her rights under the Bryan-Chamorro treaty should be in some way jeopardized.[36]

It will be remembered that one of the principal results of the conference of Washington in 1907 was to establish the perpetual neutrality of Honduras. But Honduras needed a strong government to maintain its neutrality, and before this could even be hoped for, its disorganized financial condition had to be remedied. By reason of a series of loans negotiated in Europe between 1867 and 1870, to the amount of about $27 million, upon which virtually no interest had been paid, the state found itself indebted to the stupendous sum of $125 million. In 1908 the Council of Foreign Bondholders proposed a refunding scheme whose terms Honduras considered too onerous; accordingly, she turned towards the United States. Secretary Knox immediately sought to interest American bankers in a project for refunding the debt, and J. P. Morgan and Co. agreed to attempt it. They found that the debt could be adjusted for about 15 per cent of its face value without interest; therefore by the issuance of $10 million in 5 per cent bonds Honduras could wipe out both her external and internal debt, pay all claims, acquire and extend the interoceanic railway, and still have a balance of $2½ million for future internal development. Before making such a loan, however, the bankers demanded that the United States sign a loan convention with Honduras affording the necessary security to the bondholders.

Such a convention was signed January 10, 1911, by Secretary Knox for the United States and Señor Juan Paredes for Honduras. The two governments promised to consult in case of any difficulties, with a view to the faithful execution of the provisions of the contract. The loan was to be secured upon the Honduran customs, which were not to be changed during the existence of the contract without consent of the United States. The government of Honduras further agreed to appoint a collector of customs, who should be approved by the President of the United States, from a list of names submitted by the fiscal agent of the loan.[37] President Taft earnestly urged the Senate to assent to the convention, and Secretary Knox, in a statement before the foreign relations committee, May 24,

[36] See the article by Dr. Ruben Rivera on the Central American Union in the *New York Times*, Apr. 24, 1921.

[37] Text in *For. Rel. of the U. S.*, 1912, p. 560.

1911, laid down the basis of his policy as follows: "Shall the government of the United States make American capital an instrumentality to secure financial stability, and hence prosperity and peace, to the more backward republics in the neighborhood of the Panama Canal? And in order to give that measure of security which alone would induce capital to be such an instrumentality without imposing too great a burden upon the countries concerned, shall this government assume towards the customs collections a relationship only great enough for this purpose—a relationship, however, the moral effect and potentialities of which result in preventing the customs revenues of such republic from being seized as the means of carrying on devastating and unprincipled revolutions?" [38]

Despite this persuasive presentation of the advantages of dollar diplomacy, the Senate failed to agree to the convention; and the bankers refused to proceed farther. The Honduran congress also refused to ratify the convention, principally upon constitutional grounds. Although the original loan was unquestionably tainted with fraud, the lien existed, and Honduras could not establish herself upon a sound financial basis until some readjustment was made. The Morgan proposal, which was approved by a neutral expert whose services were sought by the State Department, seemed to offer an excellent opportunity for Honduras to make a new start. Yet the United States showed wisdom in refusing to urge the convention when the Honduran congress evidenced its overwhelming opposition. [39]

In its other diplomatic relations with Honduras during the year 1911 the United States was more successful. In January of that year General Manuel Bonilla staged a revolution against President Davila, and the latter, no longer having the assistance of Zelaya, asked the United States to intervene as arbitrator, and promised to deliver the presidency to any third party named or approved by the United States. [40] President Taft accepted the proposal and named Mr. T. C. Dawson as the special commissioner of the United States. A peace conference was held in February at Puerto Cortes on board the U. S. S. *Tacoma*, with Mr. Dawson presiding. A provisional government was organized, and Dr. Francisco Bertrand was named as provisional president. Peace was restored, and President Taft received a vote of thanks "for his friendly mediation

[38] *Ibid.*, p. 589.

[39] An agreement with the British bondholders was approved by the Congress of Honduras in 1926 and regular service on the debt has been maintained since January, 1927.

[40] *For. Rel. of the U. S.*, 1911, p. 297.

towards the reëstablishment of peace in the Republic of Honduras." [41]

The entrance of the United States into the European war stirred the Central American republics to enthusiastic manifestations of coöperation. All of these states, including Panama declared war on Germany except El Salvador; and she went so far as to declare a benevolent neutrality which permitted the use of her territorial ports and waters by the warships of the United States and the Allies. In the declarations of war the United States was usually expressly mentioned: "Guatemala assumes the same belligerent attitude as the United States"; "Nicaragua makes common cause with the United States"; even El Salvador, in announcing its attitude, declared that "El Salvador as an American nation could not fail to recognize, in the conflict between the United States and Germany, the solidarity which binds it to the great Republic of the North, . . . and that its condition of neutrality could not lead it to the point of considering the United States as a belligerent subject to the ordinary rules of international law." [42] During the peace negotiations the Central American republics boldly accepted the idealistic principles of President Wilson and entered the League of Nations, fearing not at all lest they be thereby drawn into the broils of Europe.

The subsequent relations between the United States and the Central American states (with the exception of Guatemala and Nicaragua, which we shall consider later) have been comparatively uneventful. When, in 1917, Costa Rica broke her long and excellent record of domestic peace by a bloodless *coup d'état*, the United States refused to recognize the Tinoco government which engineered the movement. In spite of this attitude towards President Tinoco, the United States upon several occasions protested vigorously against the raising of armed forces in Nicaragua and Honduras against this *de facto* government of Costa Rica.[43] Tinoco fell from power in 1919, and the succeeding Acosta government, being legally organized, was duly recognized by the United States on August 2, 1920.

In 1920 the Cabrera régime in Guatemala, which had originally been put in power in 1898, was overthrown. Cabrera stoutly opposed the plan of a federal union which had once again become popular, and arrested many of its chief Guatemalan adherents. The Unionists seized Guatemala

[41] *Ibid.*, p. 304.

[42] John Barrett, *Latin America and the War* (Washington, D. C., 1919), p. 28; see also P. A. Martin, *Latin America and the War*, League of Nations, Vol. II, No. 4, and P. A. Martin, *Latin America and the War* (Baltimore, 1925).

[43] *Sen. Doc. No. 77*, 66th Cong., 1st Sess.

City, and, in spite of a serious bombardment by government forces in which hundreds were killed, they held out and finally deposed Cabrera. The United States asked that the deposed president's life be spared, and upon receiving satisfactory assurances recognized the new Herrera government. This administration worked strenuously in behalf of the new federation, and on September 15, 1921, the constitution of the Federation of Central America was signed by representatives of Guatemala, Honduras, and El Salvador. On October 10, the separate governments ceased to function and the Provisional Federal Council of the new state took over the executive powers. The dream of a century seemed at last to be fulfilled. Once more, however, hope was doomed to disappointment. The Herrera government was overthrown in December, 1921, and it dragged down with it the new federation before it had been given an opportunity to prove its value.

Nevertheless, hope was only deferred, and the following year brought about a new attempt at coöperation which was to have important results. In view of the differences of opinion arising regarding the status of the treaty of peace and amity of 1907, the presidents of the three republics, Honduras, El Salvador, and Nicaragua, were invited to meet with the diplomatic representatives of the United States to these republics on the U. S. warship *Tacoma* in the Gulf of Fonseca. The result of the meeting was incorporated in the so-called Tacoma Agreement under date of August 20, 1922. The substance of this agreement might be summarized as follows: (1) the three participating states regarded the treaty of 1907 as still in force; (2) the clauses prohibiting political refugees from utilizing a neighbor's territory for preparing expeditions were to be rigorously applied; (3) the three presidents agreed to summon a new conference of the five Central American states to bring about closer coöperation "which would tend to make really practicable the political unification of Central America"; and (4) in order to make effective their purpose of maintaining peace in Central America the signatory presidents agreed to submit to arbitration all present and future disputes. The presidents of the republics of Guatemala and Costa Rica were to be invited to adhere to this convention.[44]

The United States was interested in the proposal for a new conference and issued an invitation to the five republics to convene in Washington on December 4, 1922, to negotiate treaties to make effective the provisions of the 1907 treaties which experience had shown to be most useful, and also to adopt measures for the limitation of armaments in Central

[44] *Conference on Central American Affairs* (Washington, D. C., 1923), pp. 6-10.

America, and to work out a plan for setting up tribunals of inquiry for the consideration of disputes which diplomacy had failed to settle.

Under the chairmanship of Secretary of State Hughes, the delegates of the five republics worked from December 4, 1922, until February 7, 1923, upon these proposals, and the results were incorporated in some fifteen agreements which comprised a general treaty of peace and amity, eleven conventions, two protocols, and a declaration.[45]

The general treaty of peace and amity which abrogated all previous agreements formulated by Central American conferences was largely concerned with eliminating the causes of friction between and revolution within the signatory states. Constitutional changes in one were deemed to be of interest to all, consequently not only were *coups d'état* and revolutionary activities frowned upon, but strict injunction was laid upon all against recognition of unconstitutionally chosen governments. Intervention in civil wars, or in the internal political affairs of any other Central American Republic, was strictly prohibited, and each government agreed to adopt effective measures to prevent the fomenting or organizing of political activities within its territory against a neighboring government. The principle of non-reëlection of presidents and vice-presidents was accepted, and all agreements and treaties were to be published. The treaty was to remain in force until 1934 and then continue indefinitely until denounced with due advance notice. The treaty lasted until the end of 1933 when it was denounced by El Salvador and Costa Rica in order that the latter state might recognize the government of General Martinez who had been named President of El Salvador by a military junta in December, 1931. Early in the following year Guatemala, Honduras, and Nicaragua followed the lead of Costa Rica in the recognition of the Martinez régime. When the Central American republics showed their intention so unanimously to accept the *coup d'état* method of setting up governments, it was no longer the part of the United States to follow a different policy. With our recognition of the Martinez government, the General Treaty of Peace and Amity was abrogated at least as regards the policy of nonrecognition of governments established by revolution against the constitutional régime.[46]

Mention should also be made of the convention providing for the reëstablishment of an International Central American Tribunal. Instead

[45] For texts see *ibid.*, Appendix.

[46] A Treaty of Central American Fraternity was signed by the five republics at a conference in Guatemala City March 15-April 12, 1934, supplementing the 1923 treaties which outlawed war, recognized the principle of nonintervention, and upheld the ideal of a future Central American Union.

of again setting up a permanent court as established by the treaty of 1907, a panel system of judges modeled upon the Hague Court system was adopted. The powers agreed to submit all present or future controversies not settled by diplomatic means to the court, although it was provided that "controversies or questions which affect the sovereign and independent existence of any of the signatory republics cannot be the object of arbitration or complaint." When in 1928 a long standing boundary dispute between Guatemala and Honduras [47] flared up again, the State Department recommended that the question be referred for settlement to the International Central American Tribunal. Honduras refused on the ground that the panel of judges was not adequate, and the case was settled in 1933 by a special arbitral tribunal under the chairmanship of Chief Justice Hughes.[48]

Another of the conventions recast, unified, and to a considerable extent weakened the so-called Bryan Commission of Inquiry Treaties of 1913 and 1914 between the United States and the five Central American Republics.[49] In the new convention, instead of five permanent commissions of five members each, there was provided a panel or permanent list of thirty commissioners, five from each state, and a commission of inquiry was to be formed only upon request of one party directly interested in the elucidation of the facts. Such a commission of inquiry was to consist of one of the nationals of each interested country selected from the permanent list and a president chosen by them from the neutral names on the list. The machinery was undoubtedly simplified and improved, but whereas the former treaties for the advancement of peace subjected "all disputes . . . of every nature whatsoever" to a commission of inquiry, the new convention excluded questions affecting the sovereignty, independence, honor, and vital interests of the signatory states. The new convention has been in force since June 13, 1925, for Costa Rica, Guatemala, Honduras, Nicaragua, and the United States.[50] El Salvador was consistent in refusing to accept the revised convention.

Although the conference did not attempt to set up a federal system, the various conventions relative to the establishment of uniform labor laws, coöperation in agricultural stations, extradition, the exchange of students, and the establishment of free trade between Guatemala, El

---

[47] For a detailed statement see *For. Rel. of the U. S.*, 1917, pp. 760-801.

[48] *Guatemala-Honduras, Special Boundary Tribunal, Opinion and Award* (Washington, D. C., 1933).

[49] Neither Nicaragua nor El Salvador ratified the Bryan Treaties, and Honduras failed to set up the commission provided.

[50] *U. S. Treaty Series*, No. 717.

Salvador, Honduras, and Nicaragua laid a foundation for a closer union of the republics.[51]

On account of intervention of the United States in a boundary dispute between Panama and Costa Rica, the relations between the United States and Panama during 1921 became exceedingly strained. The trouble was of long standing, and the disputed area included sections on both the Pacific and Atlantic sides of the Cordillera. In 1900 the two states had submitted the dispute to President Loubet of France, who fixed a line running from Mona Point on the Atlantic to Burica Point on the Pacific, giving to Costa Rica the Coto region on the Pacific, which had been in Panama's possession for many years, and giving Panama a strip of land on the Atlantic side bordering the Sixaola River.[52] As shown by Article I of the Porras-Anderson treaty, signed through the mediation of the United States at Washington on March 17, 1910, the award on the Pacific side was accepted by both parties. But in regard to the rest there was a disagreement, and by the terms of this same treaty both parties agreed to submit the interpretation to the Chief Justice of the United States and bound themselves to abide by his decision. Article VII specifically states that "the boundary line between the two republics as finally fixed by the arbitrator shall be deemed the true line and his determination of the same shall be found conclusive and without appeal.[53]

Chief Justice White announced his award on September 12, 1914, after a commission of American engineers, chosen in accordance with the terms of the convention, had made a prolonged and careful survey. The award gave to Costa Rica a portion of the territory claimed by Panama and to Panama a portion of the territory claimed by Costa Rica.[54] Panama, however, refused to accept the award, on the ground that the Chief Justice had exceeded his jurisdiction as arbitrator. Nothing was done to carry out the award until February 21, 1921, when Costa Rica invaded and seized the Coto region given to her by the Loubet award and conceded to her by Panama in the Porras-Anderson treaty. Panama speedily recaptured the region; but Costa Rica mustered an army and threatened war. Secretary Colby immediately protested against the use of force; and on the day after he entered office, Secretary Hughes was

[51] For a detailed account of the conference see "The United States and Central American Revolutions," *Foreign Policy Association Reports*, Vol. VII, No. 10 (July 22, 1931).

[52] For a complete summary of the dispute from 1825 to 1909, including the text of the Loubet award, see *For. Rel. of the U. S.*, 1910, pp. 785-791.

[53] *Ibid.*, p. 820.

[54] For text of the award see *British and Foreign State Papers*, 1914, Part II, pp. 429-465.

compelled to give consideration to the question. In a reply to a note from Panama, dated March 4, 1921, and requesting a declaration of the manner in which the United States understood its obligation to maintain the independence of Panama in the light of the Hay-Bunau-Varilla treaty, the new Secretary of State sent identic notes to Panama and Costa Rica, calling upon both countries to suspend hostilities until the United States could consider the question and propose a peaceful solution.

Secretary Hughes studied the matter carefully, and on March 15, in a long note to the American minister in Panama, he made clear the position of the United States. After reviewing the background of the case and the successive steps towards settlement, he reported that he could find no basis for the contention that the arbitrator had exceeded his powers; the award, therefore, by the terms of the Porras-Anderson treaty, became, he declared, "a perfect and compulsory treaty between the high contracting parties." Under these circumstances, he continued, "the government of the United States feels compelled to urge upon the government of Panama, in the most friendly but most earnest manner, that it conclude without delay arrangements with the government of Costa Rica for the appointment of the Commission of Engineers provided for by the terms of Article VII of the Porras-Anderson treaty, in order that the boundary line laid down by the decision of Chief Justice White may be physically laid down in a permanent manner and in accordance with the findings of the award." [55]

President Porras refused to accept Secretary Hughes' decision and appealed directly to President Harding. When the latter sustained his Secretary of State, President Porras called a special session of congress, which backed him in defying the United States. Costa Rica, on the other hand, expressed gratitude for the prompt and efficacious mediation on the part of the United States. Early in May, Secretary Hughes despatched another note to Panama, saying that, unless she settled the boundary dispute promptly in accordance with the White-Loubet award, the United States would take necessary steps to give effect to the physical establishment of the boundary line. The United States realized that it was bound by treaty to protect the independence and territorial integrity of Panama, but could hardly guarantee the integrity of a country whose boundary shifted according to the caprice of the government.

Panama, still protesting, sent a special mission to Washington and finally proposed that the White award be submitted to the Hague Tribunal to see if it was within the terms of the arbitration. Secretary Hughes

[55] *New York Times,* Mar. 18, 1921.

refused, and on August 18, 1921, he sent a note declaring there was no reason why Costa Rica should delay in taking possession. American marines were despatched to maintain the peace, and Panama, under protest, ordered her civil authorities to leave. Chief Justice Taft appointed two engineers to work with those to be appointed by Costa Rica and Panama to delimit the boundaries; but Panama refused to name her member of the commission. On September 9 the State Department announced that Costa Rica had taken possession of the disputed region.[56]

Diplomatic relations between the two countries were not resumed until 1928, and no further action towards a mutually acceptable settlement was taken until 1938. A treaty signed at San José, Costa Rica, September 26, 1938, established a boundary line which followed the White award from the Atlantic to Cerro Pando and the Loubet award from Cerro Pando to the Pacific. This required concessions by both states and seemed a reasonable compromise. However, President Castro of Costa Rica, threatened by serious opposition, withdrew the treaty from Congressional consideration, and President Arosema of Panama quickly followed suit. A final settlement is still to be obtained.

Of all the Central American republics, Nicaragua in recent years easily takes first place as the administration's principal *trouble fête* in the conduct of American foreign relations in the Caribbean.[57] It will be remembered that after 1912 a small detachment of American marines was ordered to remain in Managua as a counter-irritant to revolutionary symptoms, particularly of the Zelaya type. President Díaz, a Conservative, continued to prove himself most friendly to American interests, but the Liberals were discontented, and in 1916, nominated Dr. Irís, a close follower and a friend of Zelaya. The Conservatives chose Emiliano Chamorro, an able man who had served in a most acceptable fashion as Nicaraguan minister at Washington. Unwilling to see any one connected with Zelaya returned to power, the United States actively supported the candidacy of General Chamorro, who was consequently elected.

It is almost an axiom of Latin-American politics that the only certain way to win an election against a candidate supported by the party in power is by a revolution, for the party which controls the election machinery *ipso facto* receives the votes. When the party in power had

[56] A detailed critical analysis is given in W. D. McCain, *The United States and the Republic of Panama* (Durham, N. C., 1937), Chaps. VI, X.

[57] For an official account see *The United States and Nicaragua—A Survey of the Relations from 1909 to 1932,* Dept. of State, Latin American Series, No. 6.

also the moral support of a hundred American marines in the capital, its chances of success became a certainty. Such a situation to a certain extent placed the United States in the position of supporting the administration in power. To avoid this accusation, the United States Department of State in 1920 suggested to President Chamorro that the election laws be revised; but with the elections at hand the suggestion was not regarded as appropriate, and once more the Conservatives put their candidate in office.

Nevertheless the United States persisted in its efforts, and in 1922 Dr. H. W. Dodds was appointed as an expert to draft a new electoral law. Such a law was drawn and adopted by the Nicaraguan Congress, and the registrations under this law for the 1924 elections were carried on with very few charges of fraud.[58] But a split now occurred among the Conservatives when General Emiliano Chamorro returned from Washington, where he had again been acting as minister, and decided to run for president against the wishes of the Conservatives in power headed by President Martínez. The latter, unable to stand for reëlection, owing to the restriction of the constitution, formed a coalition with the Liberals and supported Carlos Solorzano, a Conservative, for president, and Dr. Juan B. Sacasa, a Liberal, for vice-president. The United States was willing to supervise the election, but the administration opposed, and the coalition won by a substantial majority and in the old-style manner.

The United States had already given notice of its intention to withdraw the marines on the first of January, 1925, but at the earnest request of President Solorzano they were permitted to remain until a constabulary might be established under the supervision of Major Carter of the United States Army.

The marines were withdrawn on August 4, 1925, and in less than a month General Chamorro had begun a revolution against the government. Gaining control over the army, and seizing the forts overlooking Managua, he expelled unfriendly members of the Assembly, had himself appointed designate for the presidency, and forced the resignation of President Solorzano.[59]

Inasmuch as such a *coup d'état* was a flagrant violation of the Washington conventions of 1923, the United States not only refused to recognize the Chamorro régime but made representations through our *chargé*

---

[58] H. W. Dodds, "The United States and Nicaragua," *Annals of Amer. Acad.*, Vol. CXXXII (July, 1927), p. 137.

[59] For a succinct summary of the facts see President Coolidge's message to Congress of Jan. 10, 1927, *Cong. Rec.*, Vol. 68, Pt. 2, p. 1324.

d'affaires expressing disapproval of the Chamorro course of action. The four Central American states followed the United States in their refusal to recognize the revolutionary government. The failure to receive recognition weakened the Chamorro government, and in October, 1926, at the suggestion of Admiral Latimer, who had been sent to Bluefields with his squadron at the request of the State Department, an armistice was arranged, and a conference took place between representatives of Liberal and Conservative factions at Corinto on the U. S. S. *Denver.* Although no agreement was reached, owing to pressure put upon Sacasa by Mexico, General Chamorro realized his inability to remain in power, and named Senator Uriza, the second designate of the Congress, as his successor. When the United States refused to grant recognition to him, he summoned an extraordinary session of the Congress to select a new designate. According to Henry L. Stimson, whom President Coolidge sent as his personal representative with full powers to investigate and suggest a solution of the Nicaraguan situation, this Congress, taking into consideration that President Solorzano had resigned, and that Vice-President Sacasa was out of the country, legally selected Adolfo Días as first designate.[60] Señor Díaz was inaugurated on November 14, and the next day he appealed to the United States to aid him in the protection of the interests of American and other citizens, agreeing in advance to approve any means chosen by the State Department.[61] Two days later he was accorded recognition by the United States. The European governments followed the lead of the United States in recognizing Díaz, while Mexico, Guatemala, Costa Rica, and most of the South American states withheld recognition.

Supported by the United States, Díaz claimed that his election was legal in that the constitution of Nicaragua provides that if the vice-president is unavailable, the Congress is authorized to entrust the office to one of its members whom it shall designate. Vice-President Sacasa however declared that he was "ruthlessly pursued after the Chamorro-Díaz coup against the legitimate president, Solorzano," and obliged to leave Nicaragua; that, inasmuch as Díaz aided in the overthrow of the Solorzano-Sacasa régime, according to the Washington compacts he had no more right to the presidency than had Chamorro; that just as soon as it was possible after the resignation of President Solorzano he had returned to the country to assume the presidency, and had set up a government at Puerto Cabezas (Dec. 2), but that its operations were daily

[60] H. L. Stimson, *American Policy in Nicaragua* (New York, 1927), p. 26.
[61] Message of President Coolidge, *loc. cit.,* p. 1325.

obstructed by the American forces.[62] Incidentally, the Mexican government had recognized Sacasa as the constitutional president shortly after his inauguration by the Liberals.

The Liberals now began a bitter struggle to oust Díaz, with substantial aid of arms and ammunitions from Mexican sources.[63] The United States increased its squadron in Nicaraguan waters to fifteen war-ships and authorized the shipment of war materials to the Díaz government. Landings of marines were made and neutral zones established at various points, particularly in the region controlled by the Liberals. For a time even a radio censorship was established by Admiral Latimer.

Criticism of the intervention of the United States now became so severe, both in the press and in Congress, that the State Department was sorely pressed to find reasons satisfactory to the public for its policy. The first landing of troops was declared to be solely for the protection of American lives and property, but there was little evidence that American lives and property were in jeopardy. A few days later our canal rights under the Bryan-Chamorro treaty were cited, but the Liberals had in no way impaired them. Two weeks later it was stated that both British and Italian governments had requested American protection for their nationals. On January 10, 1927, in a message to Congress, President Coolidge gave a clear and impartial statement both of the facts and the administration's handling of the situation. In addition to the reasons already given, he cited the shipment of arms and munitions from Mexico as especially provocative, declaring that "the United States cannot fail to view with deep concern any serious threat to stability and constitutional government in Nicaragua tending toward anarchy and jeopardizing American interests, especially if such state of affairs is contributed to or brought about by outside influence or by any foreign power." [64]

The good impression made by this speech was largely nullified by the statement given to the press by Secretary of State Kellogg on January 12, 1927, following his testimony at an executive session of the Senate Committee on Foreign Relations, which was then holding hearings on the Mexican and Nicaraguan situation.[65] The specter of Russian Bolshevist activity in Latin America was conjured but the ghost refused to walk. Resolutions of the Congress of the Red International of Trade Unions and the executive committee of the Communist International against American imperialism, some of them passed several years before, had

---

[62] *New York Times,* Jan. 10, 1927.
[63] See speech of President Coolidge, *loc. cit.*
[64] *Ibid.,* p. 1324.
[65] *Ibid.,* p. 1649.

lost their potency to inspire the fears of the Mitchell Palmer period—particularly as Foreign Minister Saenz of Mexico pointed out that the Mexican Federation of Labor had protested against the alleged propaganda activities of the Soviet Minister to Mexico on the very evidence cited by Secretary Kellogg. In the language of Senator Frazier, it was a flimsy document making a fantastic charge.[66]

But something had to be done to assist Nicaragua, which was rapidly becoming completely demoralized by the revolutionary activities of the two factions. On March 31, 1927, at the suggestion of the State Department, President Coolidge appointed Mr. Henry L. Stimson, former Secretary of War, as his personal representative to go to Nicaragua and investigate the situation with a view to working out a solution of the difficulty if possible. Mr. Stimson conferred with American Minister Eberhardt, with Admiral Latimer who commanded the naval forces, and with the responsible leaders of both factions. He found both sides willing, and even desirous, of American assistance to end the deadlock.

President Díaz finally, on April 22, agreed to make peace with the Liberals on the following terms: (1) immediate general peace in time for the new crop, and delivery of arms simultaneously by both parties to American custody; (2) general amnesty and return of exiles and return of confiscated property; (3) participation in the Díaz cabinet by representative Liberals; (4) organization of a Nicaraguan constabulary on a nonpartisan basis commanded by American officers; (5) supervision of elections in 1928 and succeeding years by Americans, who will have ample police power to make such supervision effective; (6) continuance temporarily of a sufficient force of marines to make the foregoing effective.[67]

Mr. Stimson thereupon arranged a conference with representatives of Dr. Sacasa, who agreed to the arrangement, provided it was acceptable to General Moncada, the Liberal general in the field. A conference in Tipitapa between Mr. Stimson and General Moncada took place on May 4, and the result was an acceptance on the part of the Liberal general, provided the United States would declare in a written statement that the retention of General Díaz and a general disarmament were regarded as essential conditions of the plan. This would make it easier for him to persuade his troops that they could not hope to overthrow Díaz. Mr. Stimson immediately gave such a written assurance. Finally, in a more detailed statement dated May 11, Mr. Stimson promised a free, fair, and impartial election under American auspices in 1928, and pointed out that

[66] *Ibid.*, p. 5523.
[67] Stimson, *op. cit.*, pp. 63-64.

he had recommended changes in the Supreme Court and the Congress to the advantage of the Liberals, and the appointment of Liberal *jefes politicos* in the six Liberal districts. He had already received assurance that these reforms would be carried out.[68]

General Moncada accepted the arrangement in a formal statement, and within a week Liberals and Conservatives had turned over some 9000 rifles, 300 machine guns, and 6,000,000 rounds of ammunition. The one source of trouble was a General Sandino, who, retreating to the north with his force, on July 16 attacked a detachment of marines and constabulary at Ocotal near the Honduran frontier. His repulse with heavy losses aroused a considerable stir in the United States, but General Moncada in a public statement disavowed Sandino as a renegade Liberal at the head of outlaw mercenaries.

As a proof of the fairness of the elections held November 4, 1928, under the general supervision of General Frank R. McCoy,[69] General Moncada, regarded as hostile to the United States, was elected president by a majority of almost 20,000.[70] He was inaugurated on January 1, 1929, and one of his first official acts was to appoint Dr. Sacasa as Minister of Nicaragua in the United States. President Moncada also approved the agreement signed December 22, 1927, creating a Guardia Nacional in place of a national army, with the understanding that it was to be trained and under the command of an American officer subject to the sole direction of the President of Nicaragua.[71] It was also understood that all American marines should be withdrawn just as soon as the Guardia should be able to police and protect the state effectively. In fact, the Department of State announced February 13, 1931, that it was hoped that all the marines except officers instructing the Guardia would be withdrawn by June of that year and the officers would leave after the 1932 elections. In fact, by April 1, 1932, the marine force had been reduced from its maximum of 5,673 to 753 marine and naval personnel, exclusive of the 205 officers in the Guardia Nacional.[72]

Unfortunately for the peaceful development of Nicaragua, General Sandino continued his policy of raiding and pillaging towns and villages in the mountainous interior. Taking advantage of the fact that the earthquake on March 31, 1931, had engaged all available Guardia and marines

[68] *Ibid.*, pp. 81-83.
[69] General McCoy was nominated by President Coolidge at the request of President Díaz.
[70] Dodds, *op. cit.*, p. 91.
[71] *Ibid.*, p. 100.
[72] *Ibid.*, pp. 107-108.

in relief work in Managua, he struck on the east coast and sacked the town of Cabo Gracias. During this raid, many civilians were murdered, including nine Americans. Disturbed by this situation, on April 17 Secretary Stimson informed American citizens that their government could no longer protect them in the interior of Nicaragua with American forces; therefore it urged them, if they felt themselves endangered, either to withdraw from the country or at least to the coast towns.[73] This new policy, so different from that expressed by President Coolidge in 1927, was heartily commended by Senators Borah, Capper, La Follette and Norris, but bitterly denounced by Senator Johnson. Shortly afterwards Secretary Stimson explained that his new policy was primarily due to the fact that the marines were unable to penetrate the trackless jungles where the Sandinistas operated, whereas the expanded Nicaraguan gendarmerie were being trained and equipped to stamp out this banditry in the early future. In the meantime naval vessels would stand by at all threatened ports and we would "continue to be zealous in our concern for the lives of our nationals wherever they may be found." [74]

When in April, 1932, in a raid near Ocatal four American marines and an officer were killed, Senator Lewis of Illinois introduced a resolution demanding the withdrawal of all American troops from Nicaragua. However, as the American government was already pledged to supervise the 1932 elections, such a procedure was not regarded as feasible. The elections were held November 6, 1932, with the assistance of about 400 American marines under the supervision of Rear Admiral Clark H. Woodward, who served as chairman of the board of elections. The elections provoked practically no disorders and Dr. Sacasa was elected by a majority of about 23,000 over his opponent Díaz, who was considered the "Americanista" candidate. Almost immediately after the elections the United States commenced to withdraw the marines and on January 2, 1933, the day after President Sacasa's inauguration, the last contingent of officers and men embarked at Corinto.

President Sacasa immediately began negotiations with General Sandino, who had carried on his guerrilla warfare until the marines had left. On February 2, 1933, an agreement was signed whereby the Government granted General Sandino and his followers amnesty and compensation in return for which he undertook to disarm all of his forces except one hundred men who were to be incorporated into the Guardia. He declared that he had never been animated by a spirit of ill will towards the United

[73] U. S. Dept. of State, *Press Releases,* Apr. 17, 1931.
[74] *Ibid.,* Apr. 18, 1931.

States, but had fought patriotically to end foreign intervention. Following clashes between his followers and the National Guard in the fall of 1933, it was demanded in January, 1934, that General Sandino surrender all his arms. Invited to discuss the matter with President Sacasa at the presidential palace February 21, 1934, General Sandino and his brother and his two aides were seized by guardsmen as they left the palace grounds and murdered in cold blood. No serious effort was made to discover or punish those responsible for the killing. In fact, General Somoza, Commander of the Guardia Nacional, who was accused by followers of Sandino as being responsible, was able by threats and coercion, despite his constitutional disability as head of the Guard, and as being related to President Sacasa, to have himself elected to the presidency in 1936.

Subsequent relations with Nicaragua have been concerned with renewed trouble between Nicaragua and Honduras over their boundary line. By a convention between Nicaragua and Honduras signed October 7, 1894, a joint commission was named to demarcate the boundary. When a dispute arose over the marking, the King of Spain was chosen to arbitrate and his award was made December 3, 1906. This settlement was accepted by Honduras but not by Nicaragua. The United States urged a settlement in 1914, and again in 1918 it offered to mediate, but it was only able to obtain a temporary acquiescence of the *status quo*. Finally, in 1931, a new boundary protocol was signed accepting the award of the King of Spain and appointing a commission composed of three engineers—one named by each government—and the chairman by the United States. Honduras ratified this protocol, Nicaragua did not.[75] The dispute was kindled again in September, 1937, when the Nicaraguan government issued a series of air-mail stamps picturing a map upon which the area in controversy was shown as Nicaraguan. When Honduras protested vigorously the United States on October 20, following the procedure outlined at the Buenos Aires Conference, tendered its good offices in association with the governments of Costa Rica and Venezuela. The offer was accepted and on December 10, 1937, a pact of reciprocal agreement was signed in San José, Costa Rica, whereby Nicaragua and Honduras agreed to withdraw their troops from the frontier, to refrain from further military preparations or purchase of arms, and to settle their differences by peaceful means in accordance with the Convention of 1929. Dr. Frank P. Corrigan, United States Minister to Panama, who served as chairman of the conciliation commission, made a valiant but

[75] Dodds, *op. cit.*, pp. 109-111.

vain effort to effect a settlement before the agreement expired on December 10, 1939. The question still awaits a permanent solution.

The critical situation of Europe in 1939 brought about an even closer relationship between the United States and the Central American Republics. Shortly after his inauguration as president in 1939, President Somoza of Nicaragua made a visit to the United States where he was cordially received by President Roosevelt and invited to address both houses of the Congress. As a result of his visit an elaborate program of coöperation for the development of Nicaragua with the assistance of the United States was worked out. In return for Nicaragua's promise to encourage the investment of American capital, to utilize American technical advisors, and to provide dollar exchange for its customs bonds of 1918, the United States agreed to send to Nicaragua army engineers to study the feasibility of a trans-Nicaraguan waterway to link the east coast with the populous interior of the Pacific. The Export-Import Bank agreed to set up credits of $2 million to purchase machinery and supplies for the construction of highways and other production projects and also to make available a revolving fund to $500,000 for emergency needs.[76]

A very vital feature of Caribbean defense was the section of the Inter-American Highway linking the United States with the Panama Canal. This roadway from Laredo, Texas, to Panama was 3252 miles long and by the end of 1941 substantial progress had been made towards its construction.[77] On December 26, 1941, the Congress of the United States passed an act authorizing the appropriation of a sum not to exceed $20 million to enable the United States to coöperate with the Central American Republics in the completion of the Inter-American Highway within their borders. Under the grant the United States was prepared to assume two-thirds of the total expenses incurred in each country for the survey and construction of the highway.[78] In order to speed up construction an arrangement with the five Central American states and Panama was announced on July 28, 1942, providing for the immediate linking by a pioneer road of the already completed segments between the Mexican-Guatemalan border and Panama City. This meant the im-

[76] U. S. Dept. of State, *Press Releases*, Vol. XX (May 27, 1939), p. 439. Further supplemental arrangements were agreed upon Apr. 8, 1942—*Dept. of State Bull.*, Vol. VI (Apr. 25, 1942), p. 368.

[77] The road was completed from Laredo to beyond Mexico City, and Mexico was building to the Guatemalan border. The Guatemalan section was passable; the Salvadoran was the first Central American section finished; and Costa Rica and Nicaragua were well along in their sections.

[78] *U. S. Stat. at Large*, Vol. 55, p. 860.

mediate construction of approximately 625 miles of new all-weather pioneer road.[79] Owing to the necessities of war and the need for haste a pioneer road was constructed in a most costly and wasteful manner. Sections had to be abandoned, others rebuilt, and World War II ended with the highway still uncompleted. However work is still going on and at the end of 1953 there were only the following gaps in the Middle American Section of the highway: 21 miles in Guatemala beginning at the Mexican border, 49 miles in northern Costa Rica, 133 miles in the southern part of Costa Rica, 31 miles in Northern Panama, and 310 miles in the very difficult Darien peninsula section.

All of the Central American Republics declared war against Japan on December 8, 1941, and on Germany and Italy by December 12. At the Rio Conference they supported the United States unanimously. All were granted essential requirements under lend-lease agreements and all except Honduras requested and were granted military, naval, or air missions. Agreements for the production of rubber were signed with each one of the Central American Republics according to the terms of which the United States would purchase all rubber produced which was not required for essential domestic needs for a period of five years. Although all of these republics were dictatorships, they were strenuously opposed to the totalitarian systems abroad and were willing and eager to coöperate and even to fight to protect the American system in the Western Hemisphere.

After the end of World War II a period of political instability seemed to have settled upon the Caribbean area. Revolutionary *coups d'état* followed by dictatorships in various Central American states brought about the formation of the Caribbean Legion whose members, both patriots and adventurers, were dedicated to the restoration of democratic regimes in their countries. The Martinez dictatorship in El Salvador, the Somoza dictatorship in Nicaragua, the Carías Andino dictatorship in Honduras, and the bloody revolution of 1948 in Costa Rica in which Nicaragua and the Caribbean Legion played important roles brought matters to a head. On December 11, 1948, the Costa Rican government appealed to the newly established Council of the Organization of American States to consult regarding an armed invasion from Nicaragua.

Prompt action was taken. An investigating commission with representatives of four American states was sent to the area and it reported back to the provisional Organ of Consultation. In accordance with the committee's findings, a resolution was passed holding the Nicaraguan govern-

[79] *Dept. of State Bull.*, Vol. VII (Aug. 1, 1942), p. 661.

ment responsible for failure to take adequate measures to prevent the organization and departure of elements aiming at the overthrow of the government of Costa Rica. It was also suggested that Costa Rica was responsible for harboring armed nationals and foreigners aiming at the overthrow of the Nicaraguan and other regimes. A five-member military committee was thereupon sent to the area to obtain the disbanding of the Caribbean Legion and fulfillment of the nonintervention principle. A pact of amity was signed in Washington by representatives of the disputing governments on February 21, 1949, and with its subsequent ratification hopes for peaceful coöperation were revived.

Following the adoption of the Charter of the Organization of American States another effort was made to bring about a closer union of the five republics. In October, 1951, representatives of the five Central American States met at San Salvador and drew up a charter known as the Charter of San Salvador which was promptly ratified by the five republics and came into force December 14, 1951. The Charter does not establish a federal union but proposes to strengthen the bonds uniting the five states. The machinery consists of occasional meetings of the Presidents and conferences of Foreign Ministers every two years. The secretariat—the Central American Office—was to be permanently located at San Salvador.

It would appear, however, that Communism in Guatemala may be the weak link in the Federation chain. When it was proposed and supported by all members except Guatemala that concerted action be taken against Communist infiltration in Central American governments, Guatemala opposed the proposal and when outvoted withdrew from the Organization. The meeting scheduled to convene in Guatemala May 2, 1953, failed to take place. Although the representatives of the other four states decided at San José, Costa Rica, on April 16, that the Organization will continue to function, and held a special conference on July 10, 1953, at Managua, Nicaragua, at which Communism was unanimously condemned it is doubtful whether a Central American Organization can be very effective without the coöperation of the most populous and second largest of the Central American states.

The relations of the United States with Guatemala have been somewhat clouded by the hostile attitude of the administration of President Arbenz towards American capital invested in the Republic. Basing its action upon the Agrarian Law of June 19, 1952, the government of Guatemala in March of 1953 expropriated 234,000 acres of land owned by the *Compania Agricola de Guatemala* (United Fruit Company) on the ground that this property was not being currently cultivated. In return the Guatemalan

Government offered compensation to the amount of $600,000 in 3 per cent agrarian bonds maturing in twenty-five years.

In an *Aide-Memoire* dated August 28, 1953, the United States protested the seizure both upon the valuation and the method of payment. In evaluating the properties on the basis of their tax value there "was not the slightest resemblance to a just valuation" inasmuch as the company had put many improvements on the lands and had vainly requested a new valuation. As to method of payment, the bonds of uncertain value were not considered "either prompt or effective payment." Furthermore, the allegations that the properties were not being utilized was false since they were a necessary reserve against Panama disease and they were being utilized for lumber supplies, fruit and vegetable production, and cattle raising necessary to the requirements of the company. The action of the Guatemalan government was a flagrant violation of international law and the United States government protested it as such.[80]

Nor was this an isolated case. The Electric Company of Guatemala, termed an "American imperialist monopoly," was taken over by the government to prevent an interruption of service threatened by a strike for higher wages by the workers. Inasmuch as the daily pay of the workers averaged $4.25, making them the highest paid labor in Guatemala, it was evident that the demands were somewhat unreasonable. In similar fashion the International Railway of Central America, whose principal stockholder was United Fruit Company, when threatened by a workers' strike in October, 1953, was temporarily placed under governmental control to prevent interruption of service. President Arbenz Guzman not only rejected the United States protest, but threatened to expropriate another large tract of land owned by United Fruit.

Repercussions of this procedure had an effect even in conservative Costa Rica. Although the newly elected President, José Figueres, was more liberal than his predecessor, he immediately took a strong stand against Communism. Nevertheless he declared that "temporary" foreign investments should be withdrawn after a certain number of years. In a letter to the American Ambassador, Robert C. Hill, dated December 23, 1953, President Figueres while decrying expropriation declared that the time had come for a revision of the contract with the United Fruit Company so that ultimately the production of bananas should be in the hands of Costa Ricans while the United Fruit Company might still serve as the agency of distribution. Meanwhile he suggested that the company

[80] For text of the *Aide-Memoire*, see *Dept. of State Bull.* (Sept. 14, 1953), pp. 357-360.

pay higher taxes and forego the tariff exemptions on its equipment and stores. As Milton Eisenhower phrased it in his report to the President, the Latin-American people "are on the march."

The Communist threat in Central America was brought to a head in January, 1954, by a charge of the Guatemalan Government that Nicaragua aided by the United States and the United Fruit Company was engineering a plot to invade Guatemala. A Guatemalan exile, Colonel Carlos Castillo Armas was alleged to be one of the principal conspirators implicated. In a campaign of hate, the United States was excoriated both by the Guatemalan press at home and by Foreign Minister Toriello at the Inter-American Conference in Caracas. In April, American Ambassador Peurifoy was recalled to Washington for consultation and the United States Information Agency issued a confidential report to its posts abroad noting the alarming increase of Soviet financing of contraband arms and training units in Latin America. The report declared that about 1000 Latin Americans visited the Soviet Union and other satellite countries to attend Communist front meetings during 1953.[80a]

On April 26 the Guatemalan government issued a "flat and categorical" rejection of the $15 million claim filed by the United States on behalf of the United Fruit Company. May Day offered an opportunity for a vast Communist demonstration against "Yankee imperialism" and Labor leader Gutierrez accused the United States of trying to tie Guatemala to "the voracity of the United Fruit Company."

When late in May a Swedish freighter with a cargo of ammunition from Poland assigned to Guatemala arrived at Puerto Barrios, the United States notified the other Latin American republics and sent consignments of arms to Honduras and Nicaragua. The Guatemalan army now gave evidence of resenting the Communist pressures and when towards the end of June Colonel Castillo Armas with a contingent of armed men crossed into Guatemala from Honduras he gained strength as he proceeded. President Arbenz quickly found out that his army would no longer support him and when the rebels were able to bomb successfully the government's fortress in Guatemala City he decided to resign. A military junta under Colonel Monzon aided by Ambassador Peurifoy of the United States worked out a compromise with Colonel Castillo Armas which finally resulted in the setting up of a junta with Colonel Castillo Armas as provisional president. The United States accorded formal recognition to the new government on July 13, 1954, and on July 30, President Castillo Armas

[80a] The State Department on August 7, 1954, released a blue book entitled *Intervention of International Communism in Guatemala*, Publication 5556.

declared it to be the intention of Guatemala to reincorporate herself in the Organization of Central American States and his government accepted the anti-Communist resolution of the Caracas Conference. Colonel Castillo Armas was able to put down a counterrevolution of army officers and late in August 1954 he outlawed the Communist Party in Guatemala. The most dangerous overt Communist threat to the Western Hemisphere had been effectively warded off.

Inasmuch as the term "dollar diplomacy" seems to have originated, and to have a special significance in relation to the Caribbean region, it is worth while to look briefly into the figures showing the value of products and trade of the Central American republics. All of these states are essentially agricultural and limited in their range of products. In fact, the raising of coffee and bananas has proved to be so suited to their soil and climate that these two crops have come to be grown almost exclusively. Honduras is almost entirely sustained by the banana industry; while El Salvador is almost equally dependent upon her production of coffee. Guatemala and Costa Rica raise great quantities of each, while Nicaragua receives as much income from her export of coffee as from all her other exports combined. Considering the fact that the banana industry has been developed by the enterprise of United States citizens and has been built up and supported by their capital, and that a large amount of American capital is also invested in the Central American coffee plantations, it is evident that the American government cannot wholly ignore the investment interests of its citizens in this quarter.[81]

Immediately after and partly resulting from the first World War, the United States had become by far the greatest customer of the Central American states. In the year 1920 the United States consumed about two-thirds of all the Central American exports and furnished to these republics more than three-fourths of their imported goods.[82] In fact, the United States had increased her total trade from about $35 million in 1913 to over $120 million in 1920.[83]

Nevertheless, by its wholly unreasonable Hawley-Smoot tariff bill the United States succeeded in almost wiping out this favorable position which she had held in the Central American market. For example, El Salvador, which in 1925 did a business with the United States valued at over $11 million, in 1934 was doing just about one-half that amount.

[81] For an interesting account of the banana industry as developed by the United States Company, see F. U. Adams, *Conquest of the Tropics* (New York, 1914).

[82] *Statistical Abstract of the United States,* 1920, p. 838.

[83] *Bulletin of the Pan American Union* (Jan., 1922), pp. 48-49.

Our trade with Costa Rica in 1925 was also worth about $11½ million; in 1934 it was worth a little over 5 million. Guatemala, with whom in 1925 we carried on the greatest volume of trade—valued at over $20½ million— was only doing $8½ million business with us in 1934. Even though the depression accounted for a part of this loss, a comparison with the trade of Great Britain and Germany with Central America for the same period indicates that we lost at a considerably greater ratio than did they.

Secretary of State Hull was particularly desirous of remedying this situation in the Caribbean region. The first reciprocal trade agreement with a central American state was signed with Honduras, December 18, 1935. During the year 1936 similar agreements were signed with Nicaragua, Guatemala, and Costa Rica. El Salvador was brought into the trade agreement group on February 19, 1937. The results were soon manifest. In every country except Honduras, the 1938-1939 average total trade between the United States and these countries showed a substantial increase over the 1934-1935 level. The increase amounted to 32 per cent in the case of Nicaragua, 49 per cent for Salvador, 91 per cent for Guatemala, and 110 per cent for Costa Rica. Even Honduras by 1940-1941 had increased her trade with the United States both proportionately and in value.[84] By 1940 the entire Central American block was doing approximately two-thirds of its trading with the United States and the ratio steadily increased. The average total trade of the United States with Central America for the period 1946-1950 was $413,979,000. In 1952 it had reached a total of $501,634,000.[85]

Compared with the total commerce of the United States, these figures may seem insignificant. But it must be remembered that, with perhaps the exception of Costa Rica and El Salvador, the Central American countries are comparatively undeveloped. Gold and silver are found in all of the republics, and there are large undeveloped deposits of copper, iron, lead, and zinc in certain sections. The raising of sugar and cacao has been very successful, and there are great possibilities for both of these crops. All of the countries need better transportation facilities, and they should furnish an increasingly excellent market for agricultural machinery. By geographical location the United States is ideally placed to do business with them. By chance or predilection, the people of the United States are the greatest consumers of coffee, bananas, sugar, and cacao, the leading products of their soil. By industrial development, the United States is

[84] S. S. Jones and D. P. Myers, *Documents on American Foreign Relations* (Boston, 1940), Vol. II, p. 455.

[85] *Statistical Abstract of the United States, 1953* (Washington, D. C., 1953), p. 914.

best fitted to supply these countries with cotton goods and manufactured goods of iron and steel. Having constructed the Panama Canal, and aided materially in the construction of the Pan American Highway through this region, the United States must obviously take more than a passing interest in their economic as well as their diplomatic relations.

Central America needs and desires the financial support of the United States, but it wants no interference politically. Capital, however, cannot be obtained at fair rates without reasonable guaranties. The United States has long stood staunchly for the territorial integrity and political independence of its Latin-American neighbors, and it is to be hoped that it will always do so. But it is equally obligated to protect the rights of its nationals who have legitimately invested their capital in adjacent lands— oftentimes at the invitation of the government in power—when that government is no longer able to afford them protection. The United States, therefore, should formulate a policy for the Caribbean whereby all may know that its ultimate aim is to enable its weaker neighbors to work out their own problems in their own way. Interventions have been formally disclaimed, equality of economic opportunity offered, joint consultation provided if the situation demands. Only mutual confidence is needed for the United States to aid the republics of Central America immeasurably in their struggle towards democratic stability and economic well being.

SUPPLEMENTARY READINGS

F. U. ADAMS, *The Conquest of the Tropics* (New York, 1914).

CARLETON BEALS, *Banana Gold* (Philadelphia, 1932).

G. H. BLAKESLEE, ed., *Mexico and the Caribbean* (New York, 1920), pp. 277-300.

WILFRID H. CALLCOTT, *The Caribbean Policy of the United States, 1910-1920* (Baltimore, 1942).

RAÚL DE CÁRDENAS, *La Política de los Estados Unidos en el Continente Americano* (Habana, 1921), pp. 253-263.

FLOYD CRAMER, *Our Neighbor, Nicaragua* (New York, 1929).

W. W. CUMBERLAND, *Nicaragua, an Economic and Financial Study* (Washington, D. C., 1928).

HAROLD N. DENNY, *Dollars for Bullets, The Story of American Rule in Nicaragua* (New York, 1929).

ERNA FERGUSSON, Guatemala (New York, 1937).

JOHN GUNTHER, *Inside Latin America* (New York, 1941), Chaps. VIII, IX.

Intervention of International Communism in Guatemala, Inter-American Series 48 (Washington, D. C., 1954).

C. LLOYD JONES, *The Caribbean Since 1900* (New York, 1936).

———, *Caribbean Background and Prospects* (New York, 1931).

H. K. Norton and P. T. Moon, *The United States and the Caribbean* (Chicago, 1929).

J. M. Moncada (A. C. Gahan, trans.), *Social and Political Influence of the United States in Central America* (New York, 1911).

D. G. Munro, *The Five Republics of Central America* (New York, 1918).

——, *The United States and the Caribbean Area* (Boston, 1934).

Manuel Cordero Reyes, *Nicaragua bajo el Regimen de Somoza* (San Salvador, 1944).

J. Fred Rippy, *The Caribbean Danger Zone* (New York, 1940).

W. A. Roberts, *The Caribbean* (Indianapolis and New York, 1940).

Henry L. Stimson, *American Policy in Nicaragua* (New York, 1927).

——, *A Brief History of the Relations between the United States and Nicaragua, 1909-1928* (Washington, D. C., 1928).

William S. Stokes, *Honduras, An Area Study in Government* (Madison, 1950).

The United States and Nicaragua—A Survey of the Relations from 1909 to 1932, Latin American Series, No. 6 (Washington, D. C., 1932).

A. C. Wilgus, ed., *The Caribbean Area* (Washington, D. C., 1934).

Charles M. Wilson, *Central America, Challenge and Opportunity* (New York, 1941).

——, *Middle America* (New York, 1944).

✵ 16 ✵

Argentina—The Making
of a Nation

In the fifty-year period extending from 1775 to 1825, there occurred three of the greatest revolutions in the world's history—the American Revolution, the French Revolution, and the revolt of the Spanish-American colonies. The revolution of the thirteen North American colonies against British control brought into existence a new system of government based on principles which have now come to dominate the nations of the Western Hemisphere; the French Revolution established similar principles in the Old World, and foreshadowed the end of dynastic absolutism; the revolt of the Spanish-American colonies separated once and for all the New World from the Old, and sounded the knell of empires built upon colonial exploitation. It is difficult to say just how much effect the American and French revolutions had upon the colonies of Spanish America, but no territorial limits could contain the democratic impulse born of such travail, and Spanish America speedily gave evidence of the potential influence of the new movement.

Francísco de Miranda, of Venezuela, first felt its power, and, answering its call, served in both the American and French armies of freedom. But this service was only a prelude to his real purpose, which was nothing less than to bring about a complete separation of his own country from the control of Spain. He tried to interest various governments in his schemes, and in 1798 it seemed quite possible that the United States would join with Great Britain in an attempt to foment revolutions in the Spanish colonies in the New World. Rufus King, the American minister at London, enthusiastically supported the plan, and succeeded in obtaining the backing of Hamilton.[1] Neither the British cabinet nor Secretary

[1] C. R. King, *The Life and Correspondence of Rufus King* (New York, 1907), Vol. II, pp. 250 *ff.*

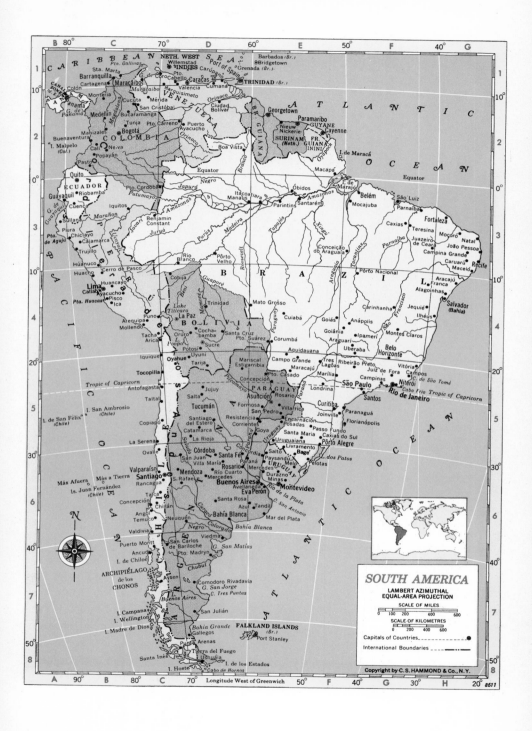

SOUTH AMERICA

LAMBERT AZIMUTHAL
EQUAL-AREA PROJECTION

SCALE OF MILES
0   100 200   400   600

SCALE OF KILOMETRES
0   200   400   600

Capitals of Countries_____●
International Boundaries_ _ _ _ _ _ _ _ _

Copyright by C.S. HAMMOND & Co., N.Y.

Pickering, however, was willing to countenance the project, and Miranda finally gave up hopes of obtaining the support of Great Britain. He thereupon visited the United States and tried to obtain help from Jefferson and Madison; but, although both personally wished him well, they were unwilling to engage the United States in an enterprise of such a nature. He was forced to content himself with organizing a small filibustering expedition in New York, without aid, but also without interference, from the United States government. This expedition, which set sail early in 1806, was a complete failure, as were Miranda's later attempts; but he deserves credit for being the first great leader in the struggle for Spanish-American independence.[2]

The real fight for independence may be said to have begun on May 25, 1810, when Buenos Aires deposed its viceroy and set up a *junta gubernativa*. Quito, in New Granada, had made a similar attempt the previous year, but this movement had been quickly suppressed. Valparaíso, Santiago, and Bogotá followed in quick succession, and on July 5, 1811, the congress of Venezuela adopted the first declaration of independence from Spain.[3] These revolutionary movements did not pass unnoticed in the United States, and in June, 1810, Joel R. Poinsett was appointed "agent for seamen and commerce" in Buenos Aires. His instructions show a keen appreciation on the part of the government of the United States of the possibilities of the situation:

As a crisis is approaching which must produce great changes in the situation of Spanish America, and may dissolve altogether its colonial relations to Europe; and as the geographical position of the United States and other obvious considerations give them an intimate interest in whatever may affect the destiny of that part of the American continent, it is our duty to turn our attention to this important subject, and to take such steps not incompatible with the neutral character and honest policy of the United States, as the occasion renders proper. . . . You will make it your object, whenever it may be proper, to diffuse the impression that the United States cherish the sincerest good will towards the people of South America as neighbors, as belonging to the same portion of the globe, and as having a mutual interest in cultivating friendly intercourse; that this disposition will exist whatever may be their internal system or European relations, with respect to which no interference of any sort is pretended; and that in the event of a political separation from the parent country and of

[2] For a complete account of Miranda's efforts see W. S. Robertson, *Rise of Spanish-American Republics* (New York, 1918), pp. 26-72; also "Francisco de Miranda and the Revolutionizing of Spanish America," by the same writer, in the *Annual Report of the American Historical Assoc., 1907*, Vol. I, pp. 189-539.

[3] For an excellent survey of the early diplomatic relations between the United States and Venezuela see W. S. Robertson, *Essays in American History* (New York, 1910), pp. 231-267.

the establishment of an independent system of national government, it will coincide with the sentiments and policy of the United States to promote the most friendly relations and the most liberal intercourse between the inhabitants of this hemisphere, as having all a common interest, and as lying under a common obligation to maintain that system of peace, justice, and good will which is the only source of happiness for nations.[4]

In the following year Poinsett was made consul-general and proceeded to Chile, a vice-consul taking over the duties at Buenos Aires and the ports on the River Plate. Similar representation was provided for at about the same time at Caracas, Venezuela. In spite of the fact that these were regularly accredited agents, there seems to have been no intention on the part of the United States to recognize the governments to which they were sent. This is not surprising when we remember that none of the revolting countries except Venezuela had declared its independence. They simply refused to recognize the Napoleonic régime in Spain. In fact, most of the colonies that had deposed their Spanish governors and had set up *juntas* claimed to be acting in the name of Ferdinand VII. Under these anomalous conditions, the question of recognition did not arise; nor did the American agents make any effort to maintain a neutral attitude. Poinsett did all in his power to aid the Chileans, giving them counsel and encouragement and supplying the names and addresses of manufacturers and merchants in the United States who would willingly furnish them with military supplies.[5] Yet, upon his return to the United States, he was congratulated by Secretary Monroe for the ability, zeal, and success with which he had conducted his delicate mission.[6]

Ferdinand was restored in 1814. Far from granting concessions to his colonies, he determined to bring them back into their former position of complete dependence. This meant a war of reconquest, and the king did not hesitate. Within a year his armies had reduced to a sullen allegiance all of the revolting colonies except Buenos Aires. It was in this state that a new and successful campaign was to originate. José de San Martín, a native of La Plata, who had served for many years in the Continental Army of Spain, had returned to give his services in the war for independence. He was given command of one of the northern Argentinian armies. Instead of using it to attack the Spaniards in Peru, he gave up the command for the governorship of the small province of Cuyo at the edge of the Andes. Here he spent two years in organizing and training

---

[4] *House Rep. No. 72*, 20th Cong., 2nd Sess.; also cited in F. L. Paxon, *The Independence of the South American Republics* (Philadelphia, 1916), p. 110.

[5] J. B. Lockey, *Pan-Americanism: Its Beginnings* (New York, 1920), p. 144.

[6] Paxson, *op. cit.*, p. 115.

a small army, with the intention of crossing the Andes and striking at the Spanish power in Chile and then marching north into Peru. It is not within our province to describe his desperate crossing of the Andes by the famous Uspallata Pass, and his victory over the Spanish army at Chacabuco, thereby opening up the road to Santiago. It is sufficient to note that he followed out his plan of freeing Chile, and when this was accomplished by the battle of Maipú, on April 5, 1818, he returned to Buenos Aires to organize a new force to carry the struggle into Peru. After two more years of preparation, he again crossed into Chile, and embarked his army upon the new Chilean fleet at Valparaíso. Aided by the brilliant strategy of Lord Cochrane, the commander of the Chilean fleet, and even more by his appeals to the Peruvians to arise and throw off the Spanish yoke, he finally, by Fabian tactics, forced the Spaniards to withdraw from Peru.[7]

While San Martín was slowly emancipating the great territories of the south and west from Spanish rule, another patriot was accomplishing the same result for the north. Simón Bolívar, a native of Venezuela, after a series of unsuccessful attempts to liberate his native state, crossed over into New Granada and defeated the Spaniards in the decisive battle of Boyacá, April 7, 1819. This province was then induced to join with Venezuela, forming the republic of Colombia. The Spaniards sought and obtained a truce during the following year; but, with the goal of complete independence clearly in view, Bolívar saw the unwisdom of parleying, and by a final blow in the summer of 1821 the north was completely freed. The Liberator now turned his attention towards the last stronghold of the Spanish forces in the highlands of what is now Ecuador, and, after a series of engagements, entered Guayaquil triumphantly on July 11, 1822. San Martín, now Protector of Peru, entered the city shortly afterwards, and the two great patriots celebrated the emancipation of South America together. Two such powerful characters, however,—one striving for a union of South America under the hegemony of Colombia, and the other insisting upon the individuality of the states,—could not agree; and, rather than force a struggle, San Martín decided to exile himself from the country he had so valiantly helped to free. To the end he remained true to his famous motto: *"Serás lo que debes ser, y si no, no serás nada* ("Be what you ought to be or else be nothing").

Although the struggle for independence did not definitely end till 1824,

[7] The standard and most exhaustive treatment of this period is Bartolomé Mitre, *Historia de San Martín y de la Emancipacion Sud Americana,* 6 vols. (Buenos Aires, 1907).

the question of recognition by foreign powers had been raised long before. Early in 1816 Buenos Aires had sent a Colonel Martin Thompson to Washington to represent its interests; but, inasmuch as no proclamation of independence had yet been issued, this envoy was not invested by his government with a public character.[8] The following year, however, the provinces of La Plata declared their independence and forthwith despatched Don Manuel H. de Aguirre "as agent of this government near that of the United States of North America";[9] and shortly afterwards Supreme Director Pueyrredón, in a letter to the President of the United States, asked that he be granted "all the protection and consideration required by his diplomatic rank and the actual state of our relations."[10] President Monroe received him confidentially, but informed him that, although he sympathized with his cause, the recognition of independence could come only after a public deliberation of Congress.[11]

In his first official note to President Monroe, dated October 29, 1817, Aguirre gave notice of the declaration of independence of the United Provinces, and in his second communication, dated December 16, he asked for recognition.[12] President Monroe had already, on April 25, 1817, written a note to Joel R. Poinsett asking him to go once more to Buenos Aires to report on the progress of the revolution; and when Poinsett declined, he had appointed a commission of three. But, as these commissioners were not ready to sail until December, the President did not feel justified in extending recognition without obtaining "in a manner more comprehensive than has heretofore been done correct information of the actual state of affairs in those colonies."[13] His attitude was shown by his message of December 2, 1817, in which, while expressing sympathy and good will for the revolutionists, he reiterated his policy of neutrality.[14]

President Monroe was undoubtedly influenced considerably by his Secretary of State, John Quincy Adams, who from the very beginning opposed recognition until independence had been clearly established.[15] But Henry Clay had already "mounted his South American great horse," and in the

[8] Amer. State Papers, For. Rel., Vol. IV, p. 174.

[9] Ibid., p. 175.

[10] Ibid., p. 176.

[11] B. Mitre, Historia de Belgrano (Buenos Aires, 1902), Vol. III, p. 98. For a full account of the Aguirre mission, see A. Palomeque, Orígines de la Diplomacia Argentina (Buenos Aires, 1905), Vol. I, pp. 39-66.

[12] Amer. State Papers, For. Rel., Vol. IV, pp. 179-180.

[13] Paxson, op. cit., p. 126.

[14] J. D. Richardson, Messages and Papers of the Presidents, Vol. II, p. 13.

[15] See note of Secretary Adams to de Aguirre (Aug. 27, 1818) in W. R. Manning, Diplomatic Correspondence of the United States Concerning the Independence of the Latin American Nations (New York, 1925), Vol. I, p. 76.

House did all in his power to force the hand of the President. On March 25, 1818, he made a brilliant speech urging recognition and the immediate appointment of a minister to Buenos Aires.[16] But apparently Congress preferred to back the President, particularly since the Florida question had already brought strained relations between the United States and Spain, and the motion was defeated by a substantial majority. Before sending his annual message of November 17, 1818, President Monroe had received the reports of his commissioners. But, inasmuch as their reports showed that the situation was still very uncertain, he declared himself satisfied with the course hitherto pursued and considered it good policy to adhere to it.[17] In his message of the following year, in spite of Adams' advice to the contrary, President Monroe gave decided encouragement to the struggling patriots. "The steadiness, consistency, and success with which they have pursued their objects, as evidenced more particularly by the undisturbed sovereignty which Buenos Aires has so long enjoyed, evidently gave them a strong claim to the favorable consideration of other nations." [18] However, in spite of the President's evident friendliness and the continued efforts of Clay, it was not until 1822 that recognition was finally accorded, and by that time the result of the contest was "manifestly settled." Incidentally the Florida treaty of 1819 had now been ratified by Spain, thereby freeing the administration of further trouble from that source.

Manuel Torres, the *chargé d'affaires* from Colombia, had the honor of being the first diplomatic agent from a Spanish-American state to be received by the United States, and he was deeply affected by it. He said that Colombia realized the importance of this recognition and that Bolívar would be extraordinarily gratified by it.[19] Mr. de Forest, the agent of Buenos Aires, laid claim to priority of recognition, but his commission was found to be inadmissible and he was required to obtain a new one. In a note to him on May 23, 1822, Secretary Adams said that in the recognition of the independence of the South American governments it was not the President's intention, by discriminating between them with regard to time, to admit any claim to prior recognition in favor of any one over the other.[20] The recognition of Buenos Aires came the following year, when Caesar Rodney, former commissioner to the South American

[16] T. H. Benton, *Abridgment of the Debates of Congress,* Vol. VI, pp. 138-145.
[17] *Amer. State Papers, For. Rel.,* Vol. IV, p. 215; for reports of the commissioners, *ibid.,* pp. 217-348.
[18] *Ibid.,* p. 628.
[19] J. Q. Adams, *Memoirs* (Philadelphia, 1874), Vol. VI, p. 23.
[20] J. B. Moore, *Digest of Int. Law,* Vol. I, p. 90, note *a.*

states, was accredited as minister to that country. As was to be expected, Spain protested vehemently against recognition, asserting that it could in no way invalidate Spain's right to her provinces or to employ any means in her power to reunite them to her dominions. In his reply Adams declared that it was the mere acknowledgment of existing facts, and that the United States expected the European countries and Spain herself soon to follow her example.[21]

Recognition did not come any too soon, inasmuch as the European powers at Verona were already planning to assist Spain to recover her colonies. Fortunately for the United States, such a plan did not fit in well with British ideas, and we have already shown how Canning approached Rush with a view to concerted action to prevent it. President Monroe's message of December 2, 1823, settled the question as far as the United States was concerned, and all South America seemed to approve of the settlement. At Buenos Aires, Las Heras, the new governor, in a message to the congress of the la Plata provinces dated December 16, 1824, declared: "We are under a large obligation towards the United States of North America. That republic, which since its formation has presided over the civilization of the New World, has solemnly recognized our independence. At the same time it has made an appeal to our national honor by supposing us capable of struggling singlehanded with the power of Spain, but it has constituted itself guardian of the field of battle in order that no foreign power may interfere to give aid to our rival." [22]

The government of Buenos Aires soon had occasion to seek a definite interpretation of the Monroe Doctrine. In 1826 the United Provinces of la Plata, with Rivadavia at their head, became involved in a war with Brazil, on account of an attempt of the Banda Oriental, now known as Uruguay, to unite itself with Buenos Aires. In this connection Rivadavia's Minister of Foreign Affairs asked the American minister, first, whether President Monroe's declaration would apply in case a European power should assist the Emperor of Brazil in his war against the United Provinces; and, second, whether "such declaration is equally applicable in a case in which the Emperor of Brazil, as King of Portugal, may attempt to draw from that kingdom . . . any kind of aid for sustaining said war." [23] After considerable delay, Secretary Clay returned his answer to these queries. Pointing out that the declaration conveyed neither pledge nor obligation, he declared that in the war between the Argentine Republic

[21] *Amer. State Papers, For. Rel.*, Vol. IV, p. 845.

[22] Quoted by W. S. Robertson, "South America and the Monroe Doctrine," *Polit. Sci. Quar.*, Vol. XXX (Mar., 1915), p. 100; *cf.* J. B. Lockey, *op. cit.*, pp. 255-260.

[23] Robertson, "South America and the Monroe Doctrine," p. 102.

and the Emperor of Brazil there was not the remotest analogy to the case that President Monroe's message deprecated. The war was strictly American in its origin and object; the European allies had taken no part; and under these conditions the policy of the United States was one of strict and impartial neutrality.[24]

In consequence of the bloody struggle between the unionists and the federalists, the next few years were very difficult for the Buenos Aires republic. By 1829 the federalist leader, Juan Manuel Rosas, was in full control of Buenos Aires and the nominal head of Argentina. He was a dominating personality, and he succeeded in remaining dictator of the province of Buenos Aires for the next twenty years.

During the early part of his régime an interesting diplomatic conflict took place between his government and the United States.[25] In 1829 the government of Buenos Aires issued a decree claiming as the successor of Spain the Malvinas, or Falkland Islands, and announcing that a governor would be appointed to reside there and regulate the seal fisheries on the coast.[26] In November, 1831, the appointee, Luis Vernet, seized certain American schooners engaged in fishing off the coasts of these islands, imprisoned their officers and crews, and sent the ships to Buenos Aires as prizes. The United States consul at Buenos Aires protested, and at the same time the U.S.S. *Lexington* proceeded to the Falkland Islands to protect American citizens engaged in the fisheries. Upon investigation, Captain Duncan of the *Lexington* found that Governor Vernet had plundered the American schooner *Harriet* of almost everything on board. Captain Duncan thereupon asked that Vernet be delivered up to the United States on charges of piracy or robbery, or that he be arrested and punished by Buenos Aires.[27] Apparently the American officer did more than protest, for on Feburary 14, 1832, the government of Buenos Aires published a proclamation stating, among other things, that "the Commander of the U.S.S. *Lexington* has invaded in a time of the most profound peace, that, our infant Colony; destroyed with rancorous fury the public property, and carried off the effects legally deposited there at the disposal of our Magistrates." [28] On the same day the government of Buenos Aires notified the American consul that, in view of his aberration of ideas and

[24] *Ibid.*, p. 103.
[25] The whole incident is well summarized from the Argentinian standpoint by Adolfo Saldías *Historia de la Confederación Argentina* (Buenos Aires, 1892), Vol. II, Chap. XIX.
[26] *British and Foreign State Papers,* Vol. XX, p. 314, note.
[27] *Ibid.*, Vol. XX, p. 319.
[28] *Ibid.*, p. 327.

irregularity of language, it had decided to suspend official intercourse with him.[29]

The situation began to be serious, and in its instructions to the new *chargé d'affaires,* Mr. Baylies, who had been hastily despatched to Buenos Aires in January, 1832, to fill the position made vacant by the death of the former American *chargé,* the United States outlined the policy that it intended to follow. The Washington government first demanded for United States citizens freedom of fishing in these regions—a right which they had held for more than fifty years at the time of Vernet's appointment. This right was now to be embodied in a treaty. With respect to the vessels seized by Vernet, their restitution was to be demanded unless they had already been recaptured. If the government disavowed his acts, the American squadron was to break up the settlement and bring him to Buenos Aires for trial.[30] Upon arriving at his post, Mr. Baylies, in a series of notes to the Argentinian Minister of Foreign Affairs, protested vigorously against the harsh and illegal treatment visited upon American whalers and sealers in this region of the Atlantic and demanded full indemnity for it. He furthermore denied the right of Buenos Aires to interfere with vessels of citizens of the United States fishing in the waters or on the shores of the Falkland Islands, Tierra del Fuego, Cape Horn, or any of the adjacent islands in the Atlantic.[31]

The Argentine government not only refused indemnity for Vernet's acts, but warmly defended him, declaring all irregularity, injustice, insult, and violence to have been the work of the American consul and Captain Duncan. It therefore demanded from the government of the United States "the most prompt and ample satisfaction for such outrages and full redress and reparation to the Argentine Republic . . . for all damages and losses in consequence of the aggressions committed by Captain Duncan." [32] Unwilling to continue a discussion in which it was evident that the Argentine government had no intention of conceding that it was in the wrong, but insisted on considering itself the injured party, the American *chargé* asked for his passports. Under the circumstances this action seemed inexcusably abrupt, and the Argentine minister protested against it and suggested arbitration by a third power.[33] Mr. Baylies, however, re-

[29] W. R. Manning, *Diplomatic Correspondence of the United States, Inter-American Affairs 1831-1860* (Washington, D. C., 1932), Vol. I, p. 72. Vernet later demanded the arrest of Consul Slocum for his statements in the official correspondence which were published by the government of Buenos Aires, *ibid.,* p. 138.

[30] Moore, *op. cit.,* Vol. I, pp. 876-883.

[31] *British and Foreign State Papers,* Vol. XX, pp. 330-355.

[32] *Ibid.,* p. 364. For Vernet's report, see *ibid.,* pp. 369-436.

[33] *Ibid.,* pp. 437-440.

mained firm, and diplomatic relations were broken off.[34] In the following year Great Britain cut the Gordian knot by sending a warship, which seized the Falkland Islands, on the ground that Spain had conceded Great Britain's right to them fifty years before Buenos Aires had achieved her independence.[35] In spite of this effective answer to Argentinian pretensions, the Argentine Republic continued to press its claim against the United States for the acts of Captain Duncan.[36] In a note dated December 4, 1841, Secretary Webster refused to consider the claim until the controversy between Great Britain and the Argentine Republic should be settled.[37] When the Argentine Republic invoked the Monroe Doctrine as against the British action, the United States refused to see its application to the case. The controversy was closed by the brusk statement of President Cleveland, in his annual message of December 8, 1885, that, "in view of the ample justification for the act of the *Lexington* and the derelict condition of the islands before and after their alleged occupation by Argentine colonists, this government considers the claim as wholly groundless." [38] Granted that the final justification of Vernet's acts depended upon his official position, nevertheless, he was exercising *de facto* sovereignty when the incident occurred. Under these circumstances the drastic action of Captain Duncan would appear to be indefensible.[39]

The historian Saldías, in his excellent work on Rosas and his times, opens his third volume with the statement that "the year 1838 began under fatal auspices for the government of Rosas." At the very time when the dictator was forced to carry on war against Bolivia in the north, and resist a new uprising of the Unitarian party at home, the French government broke off diplomatic relations and followed with a blockade of Buenos Aires and the adjoining littoral.[40] The blockade created a commercial and economic crisis which Rosas met with the greatest difficulty, but he refused to admit the French pretensions. Realizing the difficult predicament of the Argentine government, Captain Nicolson, in command of the U.S.S. *Fairfield*, offered his good offices to Governor Rosas on

[34] The United States did not accredit another diplomatic agent to Buenos Aires until ten years later (1843).

[35] Moore, *op. cit.*, Vol. I, p. 888.

[36] Manning, *op. cit.*, pp. 210-226.

[37] *Ibid.*, p. 18.

[38] Richardson, *op. cit.*, Vol. VIII, p. 324; see also note of Mr. Bayard to Mr. Quesnada, March 18, 1886, Moore, *op. cit.*, Vol. I, p. 889.

[39] According to Julius Goebel, Jr., *The Struggle for the Falkland Islands* (New Haven, Conn., 1927), President Cleveland was badly advised.

[40] Saldías, *op. cit.*, Vol. III, p. 17; see also *House Doc. No. 211*, 25th Cong., 3rd Sess., p. 33.

April 4, 1839, and outlined a basis of settlement which he thought the French would accept. Rosas received the proposal in the gracious spirit in which it was offered, but insisted upon such a radical modification that the French refused to parley further and the negotiations were broken off.[41] The United States, however, had given an indication of its amicable disposition, and the sorely pressed dictator showed his appreciation.

In the war which the Argentine republic carried on against Montevideo, the United States again had occasion to show its friendly attitude towards the government of Buenos Aires.[42] Rosas had declared a blockade of Montevideo in 1842 in order to assist General Oribe in his attempt to regain the presidency of the Eastern Republic of Uruguay, whence he had been driven by a revolution. In March, 1844, Captain Voorhees was despatched in the frigate *Congress* to Montevideo to protect the interests of the United States, but also with instructions to maintain a strict and unqualified neutrality. Instead of carrying out these instructions, the American officer, on the ground that one of General Oribe's schooners had fired upon a Montevidean fishing-boat which had sought refuge beside an American bark, declared that the act constituted piracy, in which the commander of the Argentine squadron had, by approving and adopting it, made himself an accomplice. He thereupon not only seized the offending schooner, but compelled the Argentinian squadron to surrender, and released all the Montevidean prisoners on board. He also refused to consider the port blockaded for American ships. His acts were warmly applauded by the commanding officers of the English, French, and Brazilian squadrons, but the Secretary of the Navy interpreted the law of neutrality in a different sense. Captain Voorhees was charged with disobedience on five counts, court-martialed, and sentenced to be reprimanded and suspended from the service for three years. A copy of the reprimand and sentence was communicated to the Argentine minister, with an expression of the hope that his government would see in it a satisfactory proof of the disposition of the United States to respect the rights of Buenos Aires.[43]

In the following year the United States gave another signal instance of its appreciation of the belligerent rights of weaker states. The Argentinian squadron had been maintaining a modified blockade of Montevideo

[41] *British and Foreign State Papers,* Vol. XXXI, pp. 790-801.

[42] For a critical evaluation of American methods and policy during this period see John F. Cady, *Foreign Intervention in the Rio de la Plata 1838-50* (Philadelphia, 1929), Chap. VI.

[43] Moore, *op. cit.,* Vol. I, pp. 178-182.

for over a year, but when an attempt was made to change it into a strict blockade, the French admiral refused to observe it. The American commander was thereupon forced to decide whether he would insist upon the same privileges for American shipping as the French illegally obtained, or whether he should recognize the strict blockade proclaimed and enforced by the Argentinian fleet. After carefully considering the situation, the American *chargé d'affaires,* Mr. William Brent, Jr., decided that the French admiral by his act had in reality become a belligerent, and that the United States could not put itself in the same attitude and still maintain a strictly neutral course.[44] In spite of this recommendation, Commander Pendergast decided to claim for the commerce of the United States the same immunities and advantages enjoyed by the commerce of any other country, and notified the Argentinian admiral that he would maintain this position. When the correspondence was placed before the Secretary of the Navy, he declared that Commander Pendergast was wrong, that the failure on the part of the Argentine republic to maintain her belligerent rights against the opposition of the French naval force did not justify him in refusing to conform to the strict blockade, and that the President would have been pleased if he had conformed to the advice of the United States' representative at Buenos Aires, at least until the sense of his government could be known.[45]

At the same time the French and British ministers were threatening the Argentinian government with a joint blockade by their squadrons unless it stopped trying to control Uruguay through its support of the Oribe faction. The American *chargé,* Mr. Brent, offered his good offices, but, although they were at first accepted by both parties, and preliminary bases of a compromise were laid down, the mediation fell through, owing to the exigencies of the French plenipotentiary.[46] The two powers made good their promise, and on September 18, 1845, they issued a joint declaration of blockade of the ports and coasts of Buenos Aires.[47] Mr. Brent's note to the British minister shows the American attitude: "I do not acknowledge such decision of these plenipotentiaries as having any validity whatever, as far as the United States and their citizens are concerned. . . . Nor, sir, do I acknowledge the right of the commanders of the combined squadrons of England and France to enforce any such blockade in consequence of such decision, found necessary by the English and French plenipotentiaries. . . . I therefore, sir, for the United States of

[44] *House Doc. No. 212,* 29th Cong., 1st Sess., p. 10.
[45] *Ibid.,* p. 39.
[46] Saldías, *op. cit.,* Vol. IV, p. 178.
[47] *British and Foreign State Papers,* Vol. XXXIV, p. 1266.

America, hereby protest against this so-called and misnamed blockade." [48]

The revolutions of 1848 in Europe caused both France and Great Britain to pause in their dictatorial policy towards Rosas, and by 1850 both nations had signed treaties with him. Despite his autocratic acts and often brutal methods, the United States was obliged to recognize that throughout his long tenure of power, he was a constant and powerful check upon European infringement of American sovereignty. As such, he was supported upon every occasion when the United States could consistently do so. His downfall, which came in 1851, was produced, not by the machinations of foreign powers, but by a triple alliance between his chief lieutenant, General Urquiza, governor of the rich province of Entre Rios, the Empire of Brazil, and the faction of Uruguay which had always opposed him. The historian Calderón thus summarizes the work of the great Argentinian tyrant: "His authoritative character of a Spanish patrician made him the *paterfamilias* of the Argentine democracy.... In the twenty-four years, 1829 to 1852, Rosas made federal unity a reality.... He defended the country against the territorial aggression of foreign coalitions, and his own power against conspiracy and revolts; he dominated the capital city and moderated provincialism; he painfully founded the Confederation.... His cruelty was effectual, his barbarism patriotic." [49]

With the end of the Rosas régime comes a new epoch in the history of the Argentine republic. General Urquiza, who was now in control, determined to establish a real federal republic with the least possible delay. To that end, a constitutional convention was called, which met on November 20, 1852, in Santa Fé. Every province was represented except Buenos Aires, whose attitude from the beginning was strongly antagonistic to the idea. In drawing up a constitution for a federal republic, it was but natural that the constitution of the United States should have a considerable influence, and in fact in submitting the constitution to the convention the chairman of the committee on constitutional affairs declared that "the draft of the committee has been cast in the mold of the constitution of the United States, the only model now existing for a real federation." [50] The constitution was signed May 1, 1853, and on May 25 was proclaimed the supreme law of the land.

An attempt was immediately made to obtain the acceptance of the con-

[48] *House Doc. No. 212*, p. 35.
[49] F. García Calderón, *Latin America* (New York, 1913), Chap. V.
[50] L. S. Rowe, *The Federal System of the Argentine Republic* (Washington, D. C., 1921), p. 43.

stitution by Buenos Aires, thus bringing her into the new federation; but it was not successful. The central government could not hope to become stable and strong as long as one-third of the population and one-fourth of the country's wealth remained outside, particularly since Buenos Aires controlled the sole important port of entry, the principal source of revenue. Various attempts to bring about a satisfactory arrangement were made [51]—the most important, perhaps, being the effort of Colonel Yancy, the American minister resident, in 1859. At this time Buenos Aires agreed to enter the confederation, provided that the city of Buenos Aires should not be the federal capital, and that General Urquiza should retire and occupy no public office in the new government. Colonel Yancy, representing General Urquiza, indignantly refused these conditions, and the negotiations came to an end.[52] When this last attempt failed, actual warfare broke out, resulting in a complete victory for the federal forces. Threatened by invasion and the capture of its capital, Buenos Aires became more reasonable and agreed to enter the confederation, provided that certain amendments were made to the national constitution.

A constitutional convention of the province of Buenos Aires was opened on January 5, 1860, and it proposed a number of amendments to the federal constitution. Again the influence of the constitution of the United States was apparent. The chairman of the committee on constitutional amendments said in the report submitted to the convention: "The committee has been guided in its recommendations by the provisions of a similar constitution, recognized as the most perfect, *viz.*, that of the United States. The provisions of this constitution are most readily applicable to Argentine conditions, having served as the basis for the formation of the Argentine Confederation. . . . It would therefore be both presumptuous and a proof of ignorance were we to attempt any innovations in constitutional organization, thus ignoring the lessons of experience and the manifest truths accepted by the human conscience." [53] The amendments proposed were accepted and were then laid before another national convention called for the purpose. The amendments were again ratified, September 25, 1860, thus definitely establishing the Argentine republic as a federal state with Buenos Aires included.

[51] The United States authorized its diplomatic representative, Mr. Peden, to use all his influence to bring about a reunion and as a means of pressure transferred his commission to the Argentine Confederation. When Mr. Peden continued to maintain his diplomatic connection with both governments he was severely reprimanded and sent to Panama, Manning, *op. cit.*, pp. 48-53.

[52] Mariano Pelliza, *Historia de la Organización Nacional* (Buenos Aires, 1899), p. 244.

[53] Rowe, *op. cit.*, p. 5.

Once a part of the federal republic, Buenos Aires determined to dominate it. The provincial government interpreted several clauses of the constitution differently from the national government, and when the congress put the province under martial law, war again broke out. This time General Bartolomé Mitre decisively defeated the federal forces, thereupon taking over the supreme power until the national government could be reorganized. Elections of senators and deputies took place in April, 1862, and the presidential election in October made General Mitre president for a period of six years. The new president showed himself a truly great leader. Generous and conciliatory in his methods, he succeeded in placing the federation on a basis of friendly coöperation between the national and provincial governments.

In 1865 the Argentine republic was drawn into the war against Paraguay which Brazil and Uruguay were then waging. When the question was raised regarding the good offices of the United States to settle the dispute, Seward wrote our minister to the effect that, "although we have never been eager to interfere in controversies abroad which lead to wars, or in accepting the part of mediator for the purpose of arresting hostilities, we have a natural desire, as an American power, that peace should prevail in this hemisphere. . . . If, therefore, all or either of them shall ask for our good offices, they will be bestowed with a full appreciation of the delicacy and responsibility of the trust, and with a single desire to render impartial justice and to terminate the ravages of war." [54] The differences, however, were too serious to be settled by mediation, and the war ended only with the utter destruction of Paraguay. [55]

Article V of the treaty of limits between the Argentine republic and Paraguay, signed February 3, 1876, provided that the President of the United States should be asked to arbitrate the right of sovereignty over the territory between the River Verde and the main branch of the Pilcomayo. [56] The documents were accordingly submitted to President Hayes in March, 1878. The award was rendered in November of the same year, and it stated that Paraguay was legally and justly entitled to the disputed territory. [57] Both sides thanked the President for the service which he had rendered, and as a token of recognition the Paraguayan congress voted to change the name of the principal town in the region to Villa Hayes.

With the conclusion of the Paraguayan war in 1870, the Argentine

[54] *For. Rel. of the U. S.*, 1866, Part II, p. 286.
[55] *Infra*, pp. 426-427.
[56] J. B. Moore, *History and Digest of International Arbitrations* (Washington, D. C., 1898), Vol. V, p. 4783.
[57] *Ibid.*, Vol. II, p. 1943.

republic entered upon a period of remarkable growth and commercial progress. The American *chargé* at Buenos Aires, writing February 12, 1873, notes the fact that real estate in Buenos Aires and vicinity had tripled in value within the past three years, and that there had been a tremendous increase in foreign trade. A treaty of friendship, commerce, and navigation had been signed between the United States and the Argentine Confederation in 1853; but increase of North American trade with the Argentine was hindered by the lack of direct steam communication.[58] Early in 1887 the Argentine government offered to subsidize an American line to the extent of $100,000 annually.[59] But when certain objections and delays ensued a British firm seized the opportunity and received the concession.[60]

The United States showed lack of foresight in another matter. The most important of the early exports from Argentina were hides and wool. There was no reason why the United States should not become a large customer for Argentine wool, except for a ridiculous tariff which discriminated against this wool because in its unwashed state it was heavier with grease than the Australian or New Zealand product. The discrimination was unintentional, and due to our failure to make tariff laws in accordance with the recommendations of a commission of experts rather than at the dictation of self-seeking politicians. The American minister at Buenos Aires made every effort to bring the matter to the attention of the American government, but with little apparent result. Not only was the advantage of this trade lost, but the Argentinians turned more and more to the production of cereals, thus becoming a formidable rival of the United States instead of a profitable customer. In fact, the export of wheat jumped from 109,611 kilos in 1878 to 237,865,925 kilos in 1887, while maize increased from 19,064,044 kilos to 361,456,705 during the same period.[61] While the value of trade between the United States and Argentina had increased during these same years from $5,500,000 to about $17,000,000, or about 205 per cent, Great Britain had increased hers from $15,500,000 to $51,750,000, or about 234 per cent, and Germany had increased hers from $3,000,000 to about $22,000,000, or 580 per cent.[62]

Following the excellent start made by Bartolomé Mitre, the Argentine republic was fortunate in her choice of presidents. Both Sarmiento (1868-1874) and Avellaneda (1874-1880) aided remarkably in promoting the

[58] *For. Rel. of the U. S.*, 1873, Part I, p. 35.
[59] *Ibid.*, 1887, p. 6.
[60] *Ibid.*, 1888, Part I, p. 2.
[61] *Ibid.*, p. 10.
[62] *Ibid.*, 1889, p. 4.

growth of the republic, and both were able to avoid any serious internal political troubles. The elections of 1880, however, brought on a bloody contest between Dr. Tejedor, the candidate of Buenos Aires, and General Roca, the candidate of the federal government and the provinces. The situation became so bad that Mr. Osborn, the minister of the United States, offered his good offices to prevent a further sacrifice of life and property.[63] However, the national forces soon gained control, and General Roca was duly inaugurated as president. To prevent further uprisings of a similar character, the city of Buenos Aires was detached from the province and federalized; in return for its surrender of provincial autonomy, it became the capital of the federal state.

A treaty signed between the Argentine republic and Brazil, September 7, 1889, again called in the United States to settle a boundary dispute. The territory in question was the so-called Misiones, lying between the Uruguay and Yguazu Rivers. Various unsuccessful attempts had been made to settle the question by negotiation—the last one in 1890, when there was an attempt at division. This effort having failed, the case was turned over to President Harrison in 1892, according to the terms of the treaty. Owing, however, to the delay necessary to prepare the cases, President Cleveland was called upon to make the award, which was delivered to the contending parties on February 6, 1895. The decision gave Brazil the whole territory under dispute, without assigning the reason for the judgment; but the fact that by the census of 1890 all but 30 of the 5793 inhabitants of the contested region were Brazilians (and of the 30 not one was an Argentinian) probably had something to do with the verdict. Both sides accepted the award, and the Baron de Rio Branco, head of the Brazilian special mission, declared: "I am sure that the award of the illustrious American, who, animated by an equal regard for both nations, has so carefully and conscientiously exercised his functions as arbiter, has been received with satisfaction in the Argentine republic, and that this happy and honorable event will tend, as all Brazilians desire, to tighten the bonds of friendship which unite us to our former allies of Caseros and Paraguay." [64]

A more serious dispute over boundary claims came up in 1898 between the Argentine republic and Chile. Ever since the two governments were established, the exact boundary line had been disputed; but in 1884 a protocol had established the frontier where the highest peaks of the Andes divide the watershed. The Argentinians interpreted this to mean a

[63] *Ibid.*, 1880, p. 27.
[64] Moore, *Hist. and Digest of Int. Arbitrations,* Vol. II, pp. 1969-2026.

line drawn from highest peak to highest peak, while the Chileans claimed that the highest peaks meant the highest points in the watershed. In 1895 the situation became very strained, and both sides began preparations for war. An arrangement was finally made to continue the surveys, but in 1898 a violent dispute arose regarding the northern boundary in the district known as the Puño de Atacama. Once more the situation became critical, and in August the Chilean government sent an ultimatum demanding arbitration. Fortunately for Argentina, General Roca, whose services as president in his term from 1880 to 1886, and as secretary of interior from 1890 to 1892, were so eminently valuable to his country, had just been reëlected. He accepted arbitration for not only the northern section, but also the longer and more important boundary in the south. For the Atacama region a commission of three was chosen, consisting of one Argentinian, one Chilean, and Mr. Buchanan, the American minister. Mr. Buchanan thereupon sketched the line that he considered fair according to the evidence, and divided it into sections. Possessing the deciding vote, he suggested that the commission vote on each section separately. The result was that where he favored the Argentine claims he voted with the Argentine commissioner, and where he thought Chile had the advantage, he sided with the Chilean representative. By this means the whole question was settled in three days, and, although the justice of the course was questioned, both sides accepted the award. The more difficult boundary on the south was not settled until 1902, and then only after a war scare brought both nations to the realization of the dangerous possibilities of further delays.[65]

In his message to Congress dated May 2, 1899, President Roca paid a high tribute to the efforts of the United States to bring about a peaceful solution of the boundary question. After pointing out that the delineation of the Puño de Atacama had a far greater importance than the value of the territory in dispute, since it closed the long period of uneasiness and inquietude which had been the cause of so many sacrifices on the part of Argentina and Chile, he went on to say: "The participation taken in the solution of the difficulties of which I speak by Mr. Buchanan, the American minister, has also been a motive for particular gratification. To that solution he chiefly contributed, and thus rendered both republics an eminent service. This is not the first occasion upon which it has fallen to the lot of a minister of the great confederation of the north to decisively intervene in our boundary disputes in the interest of international peace.

[65] A large bronze statue, the Christ of the Andes, was erected on the boundary line high in the Andes to celebrate the peaceful settlement.

Nor will this ever be forgotten by the two peoples whose destinies have been at stake on one or the other side of the mountain." [66]

Having finally settled its boundary disputes with Chile in 1902, the Argentine republic was able to turn its attention to the European intervention in the affairs of Venezuela. In December of that year Great Britain, Germany, and Italy established a blockade of Venezuelan ports with a view to forcing the payment of debts. The United States minister to Venezuela immediately proposed arbitration, and although the Kaiser held back, President Roosevelt was able to exert sufficient pressure to force him to terms.[67] Argentina, although not aware of the efforts of the United States at the time, came to her aid in a strong letter of protest against the European intervention. In a long letter to the State Department, Señor Luis M. Drago, Argentine Minister of Foreign Relations, thus summed up the views of his government in regard to armed intervention for the purpose of collecting the private claims of its nationals against another state: "The only principle which the Argentine republic maintains, and which it would with great satisfaction see adopted, in view of the events in Venezuela, by a nation that enjoys such great authority and prestige as the United States, is the principle already accepted, that there can be no territorial expansion in America on the part of Europe, nor any oppression of the peoples of this continent because an unfortunate financial situation may compel some one of them to postpone the fulfilment of its promises. In a word, the principle which she would like to see recognized is that the public debt cannot occasion armed intervention, nor even the actual occupation of the territory of American nations by a European power." [68] Although Secretary Hay was not willing to subscribe *in toto* to this sentiment, the American delegate to the second Hague conference introduced a somewhat similar proposal, and the result was a resolution whereby the contracting powers agreed not to have recourse to armed force to recover debts due their nationals unless the debtor nation refused arbitration, or, having accepted arbitration, failed to submit to the award.[69]

On his trip to South America in 1906 in connection with the Pan American Congress at Rio de Janeiro, Secretary Root was enthusiastically

[66] *For. Rel. of the U. S.*, 1899, p. 7.

[67] For this very interesting episode in Roosevelt's dealings with the Kaiser, see W. R. Thayer, *Life and Letters of John Hay* (Boston, 1915), Vol. II, pp. 286-288. For a contrary viewpoint *cf.* Dexter Perkins, *The Monroe Doctrine, 1867-1907* (Baltimore, 1937), p. 333.

[68] *For. Rel. of the U. S.*, 1903, p. 4.

[69] W. M. Malloy, *Treaties, Conventions, etc.* (Washington, D. C., 1910), Vol. II, p. 2254.

received at Buenos Aires, and he took advantage of the opportunity to express clearly and forcefully the United States' acceptance of the Drago doctrine. In reply to a speech in which the eminent Argentinian authority on international law declared his doctrine to be a principle of American diplomacy based upon the sentiment of common defense, just as is the traditional policy of the United States, Mr. Root answered as follows: "I am glad to be able to declare myself in hearty and unreserved sympathy with you. . . . We deem the use of force for the collection of ordinary contract debts to be an invitation to abuses in their necessary results far worse, far more baneful to humanity, than that the debts contracted by any nation should go unpaid. We consider that the use of the army and navy of a great power to compel a weaker power to answer to a contract with a private individual is both an invitation to speculation upon the necessities of weak and struggling countries and an infringement upon the sovereignty of those countries, and we are now, as we always have been, opposed to it." [70] The Monroe and Drago doctrines were seen to be in complete accord, and a better foundation for mutual understanding and appreciation between the Argentine republic and the United States was the beneficial result.

The friendly relations between the two countries were cemented the more firmly by the active participation of the United States in the Fourth Pan American Congress, held at Buenos Aires in 1910—a conference which, in the words of President Taft, had a "special meaning to the hearts of all Americans because around its date are clustered the anniversaries of the independence of so many of the American Republics." [71] Three years later, in celebration of the centenary of Argentine independence, the American citizens resident in Buenos Aires presented to the Argentine republic a fine statue of Washington. The same cordial relations continued to exist between the two countries until 1917, when the United States entered the first World War.

Until Germany declared her intention of waging unrestricted submarine warfare, the Argentine republic had no more reason for joining the Allies than did the United States. In fact, during the first three years of the war Argentina profited greatly from her neutrality through the increased value of her exports of grain and frozen meats. But when the United States refused to concede Germany's right to sink neutral vessels on the high seas and severed diplomatic relations with her, President Wilson expressed the belief that the remaining neutral states would undoubtedly

[70] *For. Rel. of the U. S.*, 1906, Part I, p. 29.
[71] *Ibid.*, 1910, p. 14.

follow our example. The Argentine republic, however, contented itself with a statement of regret that his Imperial Majesty had thought necessary to adopt such extreme measures, and by insisting that its conduct would be adjusted, as formerly, to the fundamental rules and principles of international law.[72] When, on April 6, 1917, the United States declared war upon Germany, Argentine public opinion rallied to its support, and *La Nación* published a series of articles demanding that Argentina enter the war. The government, however, determined to remain neutral, and in a note to the United States it merely recognized the justice of the causes that moved the United States to declare war.[73] In a statement published in *La Razón* on April 10, Señor Luis Drago, the former Minister of Foreign Affairs, protested against Argentina's neutral attitude, on the ground that the war between Germany and America was a struggle of democracy versus absolutism in which no American nation could remain neutral without denying its past and compromising its future.[74] But the government not only remained firm, but even passed an embargo on the export of grain, which was a decided blow to the Allies. About the middle of May the Washington government intimated that such a policy was not Pan American, and that if continued, it would force the United States to suspend all shipments of coal to Argentine ports.[75]

The United States precipitated a crisis in the relations between the Argentine republic and Germany by the publication, on September 8, 1917, of a series of despatches sent by Count von Luxburg, the German minister at Buenos Aires, to his government through the medium of the Swedish minister. These messages urged that certain small Argentine steamers either be spared or be sunk without a trace (*spurlos versenkt*). Incidentally, in one of the despatches the Argentinian Minister of Foreign Affairs was referred to as a notorious ass.[76] This brazen violation of the first principles of neutrality and hospitality provoked an immediate demand for a declaration of war against Germany. Count von Luxburg was given his passports, and both the Senate and Chamber passed resolutions authorizing the president to sever diplomatic relations with Germany. President Irigoyen, however, refused to depart from his policy of strict neutrality, declaring that Berlin's prompt disavowal of Luxburg's actions and the expression of regret accompanying it were entirely satis-

[72] John Barrett, *Latin America and the War* (Washington, D. C., 1919), p. 4.
[73] Barrett, *op. cit.*, p. 5.
[74] G. Gaillard, *Amérique Latine et Europe Occidentale* (Paris, 1918), p. 130.
[75] *Ibid.*, p. 135.
[76] For text of these messages see P. A. Martin, *Latin America and the War*, League of Nations, Vol. II, No. 4, p. 253.

factory. Various suggestions have been made to account for President Irigoyen's persistent refusal to break with Germany in the face of the almost overwhelming pressure of public opinion,[77] but in the absence of facts such speculation is futile. Whatever the cause, the president had sufficient power to maintain Argentina's neutrality to the end.

After the war Argentina was one of the fifteen Latin-American states that joined the League of Nations. At the first assembly, which met at Geneva, November 15, 1920, Señor Pueyrredón led the fight for the admission of all states to the League, including Germany. To accomplish this, it would have been necessary to amend the Covenant; so the Argentinian delegates urged the consideration of four amendments which they regarded as essential if the League was to be established upon a broad and democratic basis. These amendments included compulsory jurisdiction for the Permanent Court of International Justice, the election of members of the Council by the Assembly, and the admission of all sovereign states unless they voluntarily decided to stay outside. When the Assembly refused to consider any amendments at its first session, the Argentinian delegation refused to coöperate further and withdrew. Although regarded as a member, it was not until 1933 that the Argentine Congress gave its authorization.

Both Argentina and the United States, the former a rather uninterested member of the League of Nations and the latter wholly outside of its jurisdiction, were made active participants in the Chaco dispute between Bolivia and Paraguay partly as a failure of the League's efforts and partly as a result of their interest in maintaining peace in the Western Hemisphere. In fact, the United States has been an interested party to the Gran Chaco question ever since President Rutherford B. Hayes handed down an arbitral award in 1878 which gave Paraguay the triangular territory between the Paraguay, Pilcomayo, and Verde Rivers. However, this award merely settled the disputed boundary between Paraguay and Argentina. Their neighbor, Bolivia, had certain claims to the Chaco and immediately objected that her rights were not given proper consideration.

When defeat in the War of the Pacific shut Bolivia off from the sea, her interest in the Chaco increased, since the Pilcomayo River was the only feasible outlet to the Paraguay River and the Atlantic. Fruitless efforts were made to establish a boundary between the two states but the claimants could not reach a suitable compromise. Each could establish an excellent claim, Bolivia by title, Paraguay by possession. Treaties were

[77] As a protest the Argentinian ambassador at Washington, Señor Romolo Naon, sent in his resignation.

signed in 1879, 1887, and 1894, but none were ratified. In 1907 the two powers agreed to arbitrate the ownership of some 50,000 square miles in this area, but the President of Argentina, chosen as umpire, refused to act. A new protocol for a boundary settlement, signed in 1913, was no more successful than its predecessors. And so the negotiations continued intermittently and interminably until 1928 when diplomacy gave way to force.[78]

When the resort to arms occurred on December 8, 1928, representatives of the American nations including Bolivia and Paraguay were assembled at Washington working out treaties for arbitration and conciliation for the Western Hemisphere. The Secretary of State of the United States as chairman of the conference promptly offered the good offices of the conference. The proposal was accepted and a commission of inquiry and conciliation was appointed consisting of representatives from Colombia, Cuba, Mexico, the United States, and Uruguay and the two disputing states.

The Commission succeeded in obtaining a renewal of diplomatic relations and the reëstablishment of the *status quo* as of December 5, 1928, but failed in the fundamental task of tracing a boundary line satisfactory to both powers. The commission's recommendation that the territory of the Hayes award be regarded as Paraguayan and the port of Bahia Negra be given to Bolivia as a preliminary to arbitration was acceptable to neither power.

As a next effort the five neutrals on the commission persuaded the two states to send representatives to Washington to work out a compromise and to sign a mutual pact of nonaggression. These negotiations began November 11, 1931, and in May, 1932, the commission presented the draft of a nonaggression pact. While this draft was under consideration new clashes between troops occurred in the Chaco, each side asserting that its opponent was the aggressor.

The neighboring states became worried, particularly Argentina, whose economic interests in the area seemed jeopardized.[79] She persuaded Brazil, Chile, and Peru to offer their services to the commission of neutrals. This offer was accepted, and the immediate result was a recommendation through Mr. Francis White of the State Department, acting as chairman of the commission of neutrals, that all the American states unite in applying the so-called Hoover-Stimson doctrine of nonrecognition to the Chaco

[78] See Gordon Ireland, *Boundaries, Possessions, and Conflicts in South America* (Cambridge, Mass., 1938), pp. 66 *ff*.

[79] John C. DeWilde, "South American Conflicts, The Chaco and Leticia," *Foreign Policy Association Information Service*, Vol. IX, No. 6 (May 24, 1933), p. 60.

dispute. This suggestion was accepted, and on August 3, 1932, the countries represented in the Pan American Union, exclusive of the disputants, warned Bolivia and Paraguay that they would "not recognize any territorial arrangement of this controversy which has not been obtained by peaceful means, nor the validity of the territorial acquisitions which may be obtained through occupation or conquest of arms." [80]

While the commission of neutrals and representatives of the ABCP powers were working in Washington, hostilities increased in the Chaco, and in September the conflict had developed into sanguinary warfare. The League offered to assist, but the American powers still hoped for success. A comprehensive proposal, supported by the League and all the American states except the belligerents, was submitted on December 15, 1932, but this was refused. Independent proposals on the part of the ABCP powers were no more successful, and on May 10, 1933, Paraguay declared war on Bolivia. The League of Nations could no longer avoid responsibility, and it appointed a committee of five to visit the disputed area and work out a settlement with the two powers. [81]

The League commission, consisting of representatives from Great Britain, France, Italy, Spain, and Mexico, arrived at Montevideo on November 3, 1933, and visited Asuncion and La Paz to collect data on the controversy. Although definite figures were impossible to obtain, it was estimated that the losses were over 35,000 dead and 60,000 wounded. Bolivian troops from La Paz had to travel a thousand miles to the front, the last five hundred by truck or mule or afoot, ankle deep in dust in winter, in steaming heat in summer. Detachments had to hack their way through thickets to see the enemy. Both sides alleged cruel treatment of prisoners, and hygienic conditions were incredibly bad. [82]

The seventh Pan American Conference, which met at Montevideo from December 3 to 26, could not avoid consideration of the conflict, although the subject was not on the agenda. Secretary Hull made a special plea for peace during the conference, and an armistice was agreed upon to last from December 19 to 31. This was extended to January 6, but the League commission was unable to secure its further prolongation. At the close of the armistice Paraguay resumed the offensive and by the middle of January, 1934, had captured practically all of Bolivia's important positions and was in occupation of the entire war zone.

Determined not to permit the United States to aid the belligerents in

[80] U. S. Dept. of State, *Press Releases* (Aug. 3, 1932).
[81] *Ibid.*, June 27, 1933.
[82] *League of Nations Publication,* Official No. C. 154. M. 64. 1934. VII.

this useless slaughter, President Franklin Roosevelt succeeded in having the Congress impose an arms embargo on both Bolivia and Paraguay.[83] When Bolivia protested Secretary of State Hull declared "the government of the United States has dedicated itself to the policy of the good neighbor. It would be in the highest degree inconsistent with that policy that arms and munitions of war manufactured in the United States should continue to be sold for the purpose of assisting in the destruction of the lives of our two sister republics of Bolivia and Paraguay...."

Following up this policy of striving for peace, the Governing Board of the Pan American Union under the chairmanship of Secretary of State Hull on July 30, 1934, took the unprecedented action of adopting a resolution calling upon neutral American governments to indicate their attitude on unified action to bring the Chaco conflict to a close through arbitration.

In the meantime the League continued its efforts to bring about peace and after hearing the report of its commission and noting the refusal of both governments to accept, it decided upon more drastic measures. An extraordinary session of the Assembly on November 24, 1934, adopted a plan for settlement requiring an immediate cessation of hostilities, demobilization under the supervision of a neutral commission composed of representatives of the adjacent states, Brazil, and the United States, and the convocation of a peace conference in Buenos Aires within a month after the end of fighting.[84]

The United States agreed to coöperate with this neutral commission and also agreed to take part in the proposed peace conference at Buenos Aires. This last suggestion proved to be the germ of the ultimate settlement. When Paraguay refused the League solution it was declared to be the aggressor and the arms embargo lifted from Bolivia. Thereupon Paraguay gave notice of withdrawal from the League. However, her armies suffered from the embargo and her advance was stopped.

Seizing the opportunity afforded by the apparent stalemate in the field, Argentina and Chile on April 1, 1935, invited the coöperation of Brazil, Peru, and the United States to send representatives to Buenos Aires in a further effort to obtain peace. All accepted, and a mediation commission was set up in Buenos Aires which formulated a truce agreement. The arrangement provided for a twelve-day truce, during which a neutral military commission was to fix the positions of the armies

[83] U. S. Dept. of State, *Press Releases* (May 26, 1934). The League Assembly had already passed a resolution imposing an arms embargo on both belligerents.

[84] See Helen Paull Kirkpatrick, "The League and the Chaco Dispute," *Foreign Policy Information Service,* Vol. XII, No. 9 (July 15, 1936).

pending demobilization which must take place within ninety days. It was also agreed that each state would reduce its military effectives to 5000 men. Bolivia and Paraguay were to negotiate directly in a conference convoked in Buenos Aires by the mediators. If direct negotiations failed the whole problem was to be submitted to the World Court.

Hostilities ceased on June 14, 1935, and the truce agreement was ratified by both powers on June 21. The peace conference elected Dr. Saavedra Lamas, Foreign Minister of Argentina, president, and immediately began its sessions. At first Alexander W. Weddell, United States Ambassador to Argentina, and later Hugh Gibson, United States Ambassador to Brazil, served as the representative of the United States. When the negotiations lasted so long that they interfered seriously with the work of these men at their posts, President Franklin Roosevelt appointed Mr. Spruille Braden as ambassador-at-large and sent him as his special representative to the conference.

Although demobilization had been completed by October, 1935, nevertheless the two belligerents could not agree upon a territorial settlement. Paraguay demanded all the area in dispute and Bolivia insisted upon access to the Upper Paraguay. Paraguay refused to repatriate the thousands of Bolivian prisoners she had taken until a full settlement was reached. On two occasions early in the conference Ambassador Weddell was credited with saving the conference from a complete breakdown. Secretary Hull was so much interested in procuring a settlement that he kept in daily touch with the proceedings. Finally, on January 21, 1936, after almost seven months of delicate, nerve-wracking negotiations, the two governments were persuaded to agree upon repatriation of prisoners and the renewal of diplomatic relations.

Another seven months elapsed before repatriation was "virtually" terminated, and it was not "officially" completed until another nine months had passed. There still remained the more difficult problem of drawing up a peace treaty which should establish an acceptable boundary. The committee continued its work until a settlement was reached in spite of two revolutions in each country and through various hostile incidents— on one occasion the neutral military observers were taken into custody. A personal appeal by President Roosevelt to the presidents of Bolivia and Paraguay, and the strong support rendered to the conference by President Ortiz of Argentina were important factors in achieving a settlement.[85] The peace treaty was signed at Buenos Aires, July 21, 1938, and ratifica-

[85] See the story of the Conference by Spruille Braden in Dept. of State, *Press Releases*, Vol. XX (Jan. 7, 1939), pp. 1 ff.

tions exchanged August 29. In Bolivia ratification was approved through a constitutional convention by a vote of 102 to 9; in Paraguay a plebiscite approved 132,000 to 13,000.

The first article of the treaty definitely reëstablished peace. It provided that the dividing line in the Chaco would be determined by the presidents of the six mediatory nations acting as arbitrators on the basis of equity. Certain limitations on the fixing of the line implicitly assigned one portion of the Chaco to Bolivia and another to Paraguay—the award to be made within two months of the date of ratification. The award had to be carried out within ninety days under the supervision of the Peace Conference. The boundary award, announced on October 10, 1938, was drawn through desert and swamp, distant from Bolivian and Paraguayan posts by from 30 to 120 kilometers. As far as possible it was a natural frontier. Both states accepted the award immediately and unreservedly. One of the most serious boundary conflicts in South America was finally settled on the basis of common sense and justice through the patience and determination of the neighbors and friends of the two contestants.[86] It would take much longer to repair the human costs of the war.

The recent relations between the United States and Argentina, although officially friendly, have lacked cordiality. On his visit to South America late in 1920 Secretary Colby was received with very little popular enthusiasm in Buenos Aires. Nor did President-elect Hoover on his goodwill trip to Latin America in 1929 find the Argentinians overly eager to welcome him. The Hawley-Smoot Tariff Act of 1930 which not only penalized Argentinian imports into the United States by its high brackets, but placed unjust quarantine restrictions upon the entire Argentine livestock industry, increased the antagonism.

Argentina was quick to retaliate and in a most effective fashion. Our trade with Argentina during the years 1925-1929 averaged annually about $265 million; the average value for 1930-1934 was about $96 million, a drop of almost 65 per cent. Argentina turned towards Europe, particularly Great Britain, and by a series of bilateral agreements channeled her trade in that direction. The United States found its products discriminated against and every possible barrier raised. Nevertheless, the United States continued to buy almost 15 per cent of Argentine wool and almost 25 per cent of her linseed, hides and skins, and canned meats.

After Secretary Hull had brought the majority of Latin-American states

[86] For text of Treaty see U. S. Dept. of State, *Press Releases*, Vol. XIX (July, 1938), p. 44; for the Arbitral Award, *ibid.*, Vol. XIX (Nov., 1938), p. 263.

into his reciprocal trade agreement program, the State Department began negotiations in 1939 with Argentina. They failed, owing to the Argentine refusal to grant the United States equality of treatment with countries covered by bilateral agreements. But in 1941 when the European markets were practically unavailable, and Argentina found her elevators and store-houses overflowing with goods, she was more amenable. A reciprocal trade agreement was signed in Buenos Aires on October 14, 1941, to remain in force until November 15, 1944, and then to continue indefinitely subject to six months notice of abrogation by either party.

The most important feature of the agreement was that the United States was guaranteed equality of treatment in control regulations, import licenses, quotas, and governmental purchases or contracts. Argentina granted lowered duties or a continuation of existing duties on about 30 per cent of her imports from the United States as of 1940, whereas we granted reductions upon about 43 per cent of our imports from Argentina during the same period. The United States maintained the embargo upon chilled and frozen beef but reduced the tariff on canned meats, wool, and linseed. A new feature was the provision for joint consultation in case of any difficulty arising in operation.[87]

This trade agreement was a step in the right direction, but another cause of Argentina's attitude of unfriendliness was the quarantine re-striction against Argentine chilled and frozen beef.[88] In 1935, a Sanitary Convention, lifting the ban from areas known to be free from *aftosa* or hoof-and-mouth disease, was initialed by Secretary Hull and Ambassador Espil. President Roosevelt while in Buenos Aires in 1936 expressed a wish that the Convention might be made effective. However, up to date no action has been taken by the United States Senate to approve it, nor is there any immediate prospect of its acceptance. Nevertheless, the Sanitary Convention should have been passed not merely as a proof of the sincerity of the Good Neighbor Policy but as an indication of our willingness to base our policy upon the fundamental principles of justice and equity.

The policy of Argentina in the second World War was no more co-operative than it was in the first. During the short period when Roberto Ortiz was president, he showed himself a whole-hearted supporter of continental solidarity. In fact, when the Nazis violated the neutrality of Norway and Denmark, he authorized his Foreign Minister to approach Ambassador Armour with a proposal to change from a policy of neutrality

[87] For text of Agreement, see *Dept. of State Bull.*, Vol. V, Supp. (Oct. 18, 1941).
[88] Argentina was not even permitted to serve her chilled or frozen beef in the restaurant in the Argentine Building at the World's Fair in New York in 1939-1940.

to nonbelligerency as offering greater security to the Americas.[89] He was one of the first heads of a state to support President Roosevelt's personal appeal to Hitler and Mussolini to maintain the peace. In an interview given to the United Press, November 19, 1940, President Ortiz strongly supported a plan of coördinated action by the peoples of the Western Hemisphere against foreign perils. But with his forced retirement through ill health, Vice-president Castillo finally took over the reins of the government and followed a policy of neutrality scarcely less friendly to the Axis than to the American nations. Although on December 9, 1941, Acting President Castillo decreed that Argentina did not regard the United States as a belligerent, nevertheless Argentina took the lead at the Rio Conference in preventing the passage of a resolution looking towards an immediate and unanimous break with the Axis. Buenos Aires soon became the center of Nazi activities for all South America to such an extent that they endangered both lives and shipping in the Western Hemisphere. Even when two Argentine ships were torpedoed, the *Victoria* on April 17, 1942, and the *Rio Tercero* on June 22, the Argentine government failed to obtain the redress originally demanded. However, when in November, 1942, United States Ambassador Norman Armour delivered three confidential memoranda on Nazi activities, the Castillo government made charges of espionage against Captain Niebuhr, German naval and air attaché. When the German government refused to waive the attaché's immunity and permit his trial, the Argentine government requested his dismissal.

There were many indications that the Castillo government was not generally representative of the Argentine people. The fact that the Chamber of Deputies staunchly supported the Damonte Taborda investigation of Nazi activities and actually voted a break with the Axis is evidence of the more representative body's attitude. After Brazil's entrance into the war and Chile's break with the Axis, the position of Argentina as the only neutral in the Western Hemisphere was not an enviable one. Discontent finally resulted in a military revolt on June 4, 1943. Nevertheless, the provisional government set up gave no indication of an intention to reverse the previous policy of neutrality. General Ramírez, as acting president, agreed to control Axis communications more carefully and expressed his desire for friendly relations with the other American republics. The United States granted immediate recognition and awaited developments. They were quickly forthcoming.

[89] W. L. Langer and S. E. Gleason, *The Challenge of Isolation, 1937-40* (New York, 1952).

An exchange of letters between Argentine Foreign Minister Storni and Secretary of State Hull in August indicated the wide gap between the attitudes and policies of the two governments. The former suggested that the United States as a gesture of friendship should send airplanes and arms to Argentina. Secretary Hull, after pointing out Argentina's failure to carry out the commitments of the Rio Conference, declared that since the United States in sending arms to Latin America had been guided by considerations of hemisphere defense and Argentina had refused to coöperate, no shipments of arms under lend lease were possible. When the two notes were published in the press, Storni was forced to resign.

When Argentina severed diplomatic relations with the Axis powers January 26, 1944, the military clique forced the resignation of President Ramírez and installed Vice-president Farrell in his place. The United States decided to withhold recognition until the policy of the new government towards the Axis became evident. It was soon seen to be so pro-Axis that on July 26 the United States issued a scathing indictment declaring that the new government was giving the Axis both political and economic support. On September 7 Secretary Hull declared that Argentina was the Fascist headquarters for the Western Hemisphere and shortly afterwards all United States ships were forbidden to call at Argentine ports.

The Argentine government was sufficiently disturbed to present a formal request that a Conference of Foreign Ministers be held to consider the Argentine question. The United States countered by suggesting a conference of the states coöperating in the war effort to consider war and postwar problems. This suggestion was adopted and Argentina was not invited to the Inter-American Conference on Problems of War and Peace held in Mexico City early in 1945. The Conference, however, passed a resolution urging Argentina to change its policy and coöperate with the other American nations. Argentina finally declared war upon the Axis Powers on March 27, 1945, and her government was recognized by the United States.

Mention should be made at this point of a new inter-American policy of intervention suggested by Uruguayan Foreign Minister Alberto Rodriguez Larreta on November 22, 1945, as a result of the pro-Axis policy of Argentina. According to Larreta, nonintervention should not be a shield behind which "law may be violated, agents and forces of the Axis may be sheltered and binding obligations may be circumvented." [90] Secretary of State Byrnes, acting on the advice of Assistant Secretary of State

[90] *Dept. of State Bull.* (Nov. 25, 1945).

Spruille Braden, officially endorsed this policy on November 27, 1945.

The Argentine government, however, dominated by Vice-president Perón, continued to support the Axis and to criticize the United States. Matters came to a head in the presidential campaign of 1946 when Perón appealed to labor and to anti-American elements to support his candidacy. Ambassador of the United States Spruille Braden, who made no secret of his opposition to the Farrell-Perón government, was Perón's particular subject of attack. Unfortunately, twelve days before the election, the United States published a Blue Book of documents from the German Foreign Office proving Argentina's collaboration with Nazi Germany and noting the active role played by Perón in this policy. Perón cleverly countered by alleging that the United States was interfering in Argentina's domestic policies to defeat him—it was "the pig Braden or the patriot Perón." Perón won the election.

The United States Department of State was now in a dilemma. Numerous Senators, important military officials, representatives of business, insisted upon getting together with Perón. Other Latin-American states resented the delay in holding the next Inter-American Conference because of United States opposition to Argentina. George Messersmith, an eminent career ambassador, was sent to Argentina and instructed to patch up relations with Perón and at the same time get rid of Nazi influences if possible. He was successful in both efforts. On June 3, 1947, President Truman announced that the United States was ready to renew consultations with the other American republics, including Argentina, with reference to implementing the Act of Chapultepec. Two days later Spruille Braden resigned as Assistant Secretary of State in charge of Latin-American affairs.

The anti-Perón policy of the United States which former Secretary of State Sumner Welles called "the most sterile page in the history of American foreign policy" was completely reversed. Ambassador James Bruce, who succeeded George Messersmith, was credited by a Buenos Aires newspaper as giving the impression of representing the government of President Perón rather than that of President Truman.

However, when Argentina failed to get as much as she had hoped from purchases under the Marshall Plan and foreign exchange became scarce, a new attack was launched against Tio Sam by the Peronista press. Nevertheless, the United States was seemingly impervious to insults and when in the spring of 1950 Assistant Secretary of State Miller visited Argentina on his Latin-American tour, a loan of $125 million was granted to Argentina to repay accumulated commercial debts to American exporters. Even the subsequent suppression of the great Argentine newspaper *La Prensa* in the finest totalitarian fashion provoked only a mild expression of concern in United States governmental circles.

Perón's control of the government now seemed to be definitely established. He had engineered a revision of the constitution in 1949 permitting the immediate reëlection of the President which allowed him to succeed himself in the 1951 election. Antagonism towards Uncle Sam and stimulated fears of United States intervention were a part of his campaign strategy. Communists and Nationalists were welcomed into the Peronista fold. Subsequently President Perón helped establish a Latin American Labor Syndicate (ATLAS) with labor representatives of neighboring states which would permit "joint action against capitalist imperialism" and oppose the Regional Organization of Inter-American Workers (ORIT) which was supported by the AF of L and CIO. However, Perón's policy of achieving Argentine hegemony in South America by a series of bilateral economic agreements leading to political pacts with his neighbors was completely unsuccessful. A personal visit to Chile in February, 1953, to try to establish an indestructible political union with Argentina's most sympathetic neighbor was only productive of a limited economic accord.

The attitude of the Perón government towards the Eisenhower administration was at first noncommital. In his May Day address to the Congress President Perón denounced the American press for "spreading lies" about him and his government and temporarily suspended the publication of news from abroad which emanated from the various United States news agencies. A sudden change of attitude was evident when President Eisenhower's brother visited Buenos Aires in his fact-finding tour of Latin America; Dr. Milton Eisenhower was given a cordial reception and the controlled press joined in a paean of praise for the friendly coöperative attitude of the new Republican administration— "the new era of friendship with the United States." The United States news agencies were utilized; the *New York Times* and even *Time* magazine were permitted to be sold in Argentina. On October 17, 1953, the eighth anniversary of the Peronista movement, President Perón expressed complete friendship for the United States and declared that all former animosities had been eliminated. It should be noted, however, that Argentina still maintained her "Third Position" between capitalism and communism and the Argentine Ambassador to Moscow expressed high hopes that the recently signed Argentine Soviet Trade Agreement would bring about a substantial increase in trade between the two countries.

SUPPLEMENTARY READINGS

C. E. AKERS, *A History of South America, 1854-1904* (New York, 1912), pp. 35-129.

ROBERT J. ALEXANDER, *The Perón Era* (New York, 1951).

J. C. ASTOLFI and RAUL C. MIGONE, *Historia Argentina* (Buenos Aires, 1939).

GEORGE I. BLANKSTEN, *Perón's Argentina* (Chicago, 1953).

JAMES BRUCE, *Those Perplexing Argentines* (New York, 1953).

MIRON BURGIN, *The Economic Aspects of Argentine Confederation, 1820-1852* (Cambridge, 1946).

JOHN F. CADY, *Foreign Intervention in the Rio de la Plata, 1838-50* (Philadelphia, 1929), Chap. VI.

T. C. DAWSON, *The South American Republics* (New York, 1903), Part I, pp. 37-161.

JULIUS L. GOEBEL, *The Struggle for the Falkland Islands* (New Haven, Conn., 1927).

JOHN GUNTHER, *Inside Latin America* (New York, 1941), pp. 282-334.

CLARENCE H. HARING, *Argentina and the United States* (Boston, 1941).

HUBERT HERRING, *Good Neighbors* (New Haven, Conn., 1941), pp. 10-101.

RAY JOSEPHS, *Argentine Diary* (New York, 1944).

F. A. KIRKPATRICK, *A History of the Argentine Republic* (Cambridge, Eng., 1931).

La Política Exterior de la República Argentina (Buenos Aires, 1931).

RICARDO LEVENE (W. S. Robertson, trans.), *A History of Argentina* (Chapel Hill, N. C., 1937).

AUSTIN F. MACDONALD, *The Government of the Argentine Republic* (New York, 1942).

W. R. MANNING, *Diplomatic Correspondence of the United States, Inter-American Affairs 1831-1860* (Washington, D. C., 1932), Vol. I.

———, *Diplomatic Correspondence of the United States Concerning the Independence of the Latin American Nations* (New York, 1925), Vol. I.

GARCÍA MÉROU, *Historia de la República Argentina*, 2 vols. (Buenos Aires, 1899).

A. S. PENNINGTON, *The Argentine Republic* (New York, 1910).

VERNON L. PHELPS, *The International Economic Position of Argentina* (Philadelphia, 1938).

VIRGINIA PREWETT, *Beyond the Great Forest* (New York, 1953).

YSABEL F. RENNIE, *The Argentine Republic* (New York, 1945).

J. FRED RIPPY, PERCY A. MARTIN, and ISAAC J. COX, *Argentina, Brazil and Chile since Independence* (Washington, D. C., 1935).

L. S. ROWE, *The Federal System of the Argentine Republic* (Washington, D. C., 1921).

A. SALDÍAS, *Historia de la Confederación Argentina* (Buenos Aires, 1892).

ALEXANDER W. WEDDELL, *Introduction to Argentina* (New York, 1939).

FELIX WEIL, *The Argentine Riddle* (New York, 1944).

JOHN W. WHITE, *Argentina* (New York, 1942).

17

Chile and the United States

THE early history of Chile is a continuous record of strife and bloodshed. From the time of its discovery in the sixteenth century until the wars of independence, the Spanish conquerors of the land and their descendants were almost constantly waging offensive or defensive wars against the Araucanian Indians—the most warlike native tribes of the South American continent. Even throughout the period when the Chileans were striving valiantly to throw off the Spanish yoke their internal strife did not cease, and during the dictatorship of Carrera and his brothers, from 1811 to 1813, conspiracies and counter-revolutions followed with monotonous regularity. The factional bitterness between the Carreras and Bernardo O'Higgins, son of the old Irish captain-general and the acknowledged leader of the radical faction, became so great that the people could not unite effectively against the common foe. The result was the decisive victory of the royalist army at Rancagua, October 1, 1814, which almost annihilated the patriot hopes. Fortunately for Chile, it was shortly after this disaster that San Martín began organizing his famous army at Mendoza, and he warmly welcomed O'Higgins and the few officers who had escaped with him across the Andes.

The relations of the United States with Chile began in the troubled times of the Carreras. Joel R. Poinsett was commissioned by President Madison to visit the principal countries of South America and "to diffuse the impression that the United States cherish the sincerest good will towards the people of South America as neighbors, . . . and that in the event of a political separation from the parent country and of the establishment of an independent system of national government, it will coincide with the sentiments and policy of the United States to promote the most friendly relations and the most liberal intercourse between the inhabitants of this hemisphere." [1] Poinsett first went to Buenos Aires and then into Chile, where he arrived in December, 1811. Don José Miguel Carrera, president of the *junta gubernativa*, welcomed him enthusiastically, assuring him of the sympathy and friendship of Chile for the United States and promising close commercial relations in the future. In his reply Poinsett expressed his pleasure at being "the first to have the honorable privilege of establishing relations between the two generous nations which ought to unite as friends and natural allies." [2] Poinsett quickly became an ardent supporter of the patriot cause. The Chilean historian, Barros Arana, declares that in all of his conversations the emissary let it be known that the government and people of the United States had a keen interest in the success of the Spanish-American revolution. He also assured them that supplies and munitions could be obtained in the United States, and gave the names and addresses of various merchants and manufacturers who would be most likely to furnish them. [3] He went so far as to participate more or less directly in almost all of the public affairs of Chile, and even accompanied Carrera in his first campaigns against the Spaniards. [4] The outbreak of the War of 1812 with Great Britain, however, destroyed all immediate hope of American assistance, and early in 1914 Poinsett returned to the United States, where, in spite of his unneutral efforts in behalf of Chile, he was warmly congratulated by Secretary Monroe for the ability and success with which he had conducted his delicate mission.

The results of the Poinsett mission were seen in the attitude of more than benevolent neutrality shown by Chile towards the United States in the War of 1812. American cruisers in the southern Pacific were allowed to dispose of their prizes in Chilean ports, and the Chilean government even seriously considered purchasing some of them as a nucleus of a new navy. [5] Captain David Porter, who cruised in these waters in the U. S. frigate *Essex,* in his journal gives a picturesque account of the hospitality of the Chileans at Valparaiso. He was fêted and entertained most lavishly and given every accommodation. He confesses that it was generally believed that he had brought from the United States proposals for a friendly alliance with Chile and assurances of assistance in their

[1] F. L. Paxson, *The Independence of South American Republics* (Philadelphia, 1916), p. 111.
[2] Diego Barros Arana, *Historia jeneral de Chile* (Santiago, 1887), Vol. VIII, p. 566.
[3] *Ibid.,* p. 567.
[4] *Ibid.,* 566, note 7.
[5] *Ibid.,* Vol. IX, p. 220; also J. B. Lockey, *Pan-Americanism: Its Beginnings* (New York, 1920), p. 205.

struggle for independence; nor did it suit his purpose to disabuse the people of this idea.[6]

Poinsett's suggestion that war equipment be purchased in the United States did not fall on deaf ears. Early in 1816 Señor José Miguel Carrera landed in the United States with a view to purchasing supplies and obtaining the moral support of the United States, and he immediately looked up the two Americans whom he had formerly befriended, Poinsett and Porter. Commodore Porter, who was then living in Washington, received him cordially and introduced him to President Madison. "I was received," Carrera later wrote to his brother Luis, "as a man working for the same cause as they." Despite his friendly reception, Carrera soon perceived, however, that he could hope for no real support from the United States government. Proceeding to New York, he succeeded in interesting a number of American and French citizens in organizing an expedition; but, owing to a lack of funds and to rather uncertain security, he found great difficulty in purchasing ships and supplies. His friend Poinsett came to his aid, and he was finally able to purchase several indifferently armed ships; and, in spite of the efforts of the Spanish agents to have him arrested, he left the United States in one of his vessels, the *Clifton,* on December 3, 1816.[7]

Another attempt to obtain ships was made in the following year, when Manuel H. de Aguirre was commissioned as a private agent of Chile to obtain six war vessels in the United States, in addition to his commission as a representative of the government of Buenos Aires to obtain the recognition of the independence of the Argentine republic. After many trials he succeeded in having two sloops-of-war constructed; but before they could sail they were attached for debts at the instigation of the Spanish consul at New York. In desperation, Aguirre turned to President Monroe, asking him to purchase the vessels. Secretary Adams replied that this was impossible under the laws of the United States. He pointed out that, although Aguirre had built, equipped, and fitted for sea two vessels suitable for war purposes, yet on the ground that no proof was adduced that he had armed them he had been acquitted by the Supreme Court. "But," he concluded, "the government of the United States can no more countenance or participate in any expedient to evade the intention of the laws than it can dispense with their operation." [8] Aguirre finally settled

[6] David Porter, *Journal of a Cruise to the Pacific* (Philadelphia, 1815), Vol. I, pp. 102-112.

[7] Arana, *op. cit.,* Vol. XI, pp. 89-97.

[8] W. C. Ford, ed., *Writings of John Quincy Adams* (New York, 1913-1917), Vol. VI, p. 450.

the financial obligations and the vessels got away without further governmental interference.

During the latter part of the war of independence the relations between the United States and Chile were not so cordial as might have been expected, considering the excellent impression made by Poinsett. There were various reasons. Mr. Theodoric Bland, one of the commission of three sent by President Monroe, December 4, 1817, to investigate conditions in South America, and the only one who visited Chile, seems in some way to have become embroiled in the internal disputes between O'Higgins and the Carreras,[9] and his views, on the whole, were none too favorable to the patriots. Captain Eliphalet Smith, captain of the American brig *Macedonian,* got into difficulties upon several occasions with Lord Cochrane, the new commander of the Chilean naval forces, and the result was a series of claims filed against the Chilean government.[10] Captain Biddle, of the American sloop-of-war *Ontario,* also ran afoul Admiral Cochrane over the question of salutes. In 1819, when Lord Cochrane declared the whole coast of Peru to be in a state of formal blockade, the United States pronounced the blockade ineffective, and therefore not binding. As a consequence, a number of unfortunate disagreements arose between American merchants and ships and the blockading squadron.[11] With the final defeat of the Spaniards, this cause of friction was removed; and the independence of Chile was formally recognized by the United States on January 27, 1823, by the appointment of Mr. Heman Allen as minister plenipotentiary to Santiago.[12]

Mr. Allen did not enter upon the duties of his mission until April, 1824—the same month in which the papers of Santiago carried a report of the historic message of President Monroe. His reception was most cordial; all the highest functionaries of the state were present; and he was saluted with salvos of artillery. In reply to his speech, in which he assured the newly recognized government that no alliances or coalitions need henceforth be feared, the Chilean spokesman expressed his government's gratitude for the recognition of the independence of the new

[9] Arana, *op. cit.,* Vol. XI, p. 546 (note). In the report that Judge Bland made to the President several sentences seem to indicate that he regarded Supreme Director O'Higgins as a despot who could not hear the loud call of the people for a Congress. See *Amer. State Papers, For. Rel.,* Vol. IV, p. 309.

[10] *Infra,* pp. 384-386.

[11] Lockey, *op. cit.,* p. 210.

[12] J. B. Moore, *Digest of Int. Law,* Vol. I, p. 91. It should be noted, however, that Mr. W. G. D. Worthington had been received by the new government of Chile as Special Agent of the United States shortly after the declaration of independence February 12, 1818. Worthington was followed by John B. Prevost.

republics, and for the recent declaration of President Monroe which protected them from the proposed coalitions of the European sovereigns.[13] In spite of her appreciation of the promptness of the United States in despatching a diplomatic representative, Chile was unable, owing to internal difficulties and the emptiness of the treasury, to return the favor until 1827.[14]

Don Joaquin Campina, the first Chilean diplomatic envoy to the United States, was not entirely successful in his mission. One of the principal duties laid upon him was the negotiation of a treaty of friendship, commerce, and navigation. Another was the settlement of sundry outstanding claims. In neither of these tasks was he successful, owing to his belief that the arrangements proposed were far more favorable to the United States than to Chile. In 1830 he was transferred to Mexico. Two years later the American *chargé* at Santiago, Mr. John Hamm, succeeded in concluding a convention of peace, amity, commerce, and navigation with Chile, in which each side mutually engaged not to grant any particular favor to other nations respecting commerce and navigation which should not immediately become common to the other party. An explanatory convention was drawn up in the following year, and both treaties were ratified and proclaimed on April 29, 1834.[15] These treaties remained in force until January 20, 1850, when they were terminated on notice given by the Chilean government.

Before continuing the narrative of the relations of the United States with Chile, certain aspects of the latter's internal history must be noted. From 1823 to 1830 the country was given over to revolution and disorder. García Calderón gives a brief but vivid picture of the prevailing conditions: "The national life was chaotic—vandalism in the country, commerce paralyzed, industry at a standstill, finance in disorder, credit vanished, and politics revolutionary. . . . The political orgy continued until 1830, the Chilean people went from liberty to license, and from license to barbarism. At last the demagogy was checked by a man of superior powers, Diego Portales, founder of the Araucanian nation." [16] Portales was a man of strong mind and of practical ideas, and one who had the rare quality of being willing that others should hold the highest positions and reap

[13] Arana, *op. cit.*, Vol. XIV, p. 368. An excellent sketch of the causes and steps leading up to the enunciation of the doctrine is given by the same author, *ibid.*, pp. 469-487.

[14] *Ibid.*, Vol. XV, p. 204.

[15] *Ibid.*, Vol. XVI, pp. 173-176. For text of the conventions see *Sen. Doc. No. 47*, 48th Cong., 2nd Sess., p. 131.

[16] *Latin America: Its Rise and Progress* (New York, 1913), p. 164.

the rewards, provided that he could direct the policy of the state along the road that would lead to peace and prosperity. As minister under President Prieto, his organizing genius was given full sway—"Prieto played not illy the rôle of a Washington to Portales' Hamilton." [17] He brought about internal peace, built highways and railroads, reorganized the national finances, established schools, and, as a final legacy, gave to Chile the aristocratic constitution of 1833.[18]

This constitution, with few changes, remained the fundamental law of the country until 1925, and it made Chile the most stable of the South American republics. The half-dozen constitutions that preceded it were unsatisfactory, chiefly because of their liberality, and it was determined that there should be no criticism of this constitution because of the weakness of the government for which it provided. Although the government was vested in a president and a bicameral legislature, in actual practice it was an oligarchy, with the president wielding almost despotic powers. The presidential term was fixed at five years; but, as the constitution permitted reëlection, every president until 1871, when an amendment prohibited a second term, served for a ten-year period. During periods of domestic trouble the president was given the power to suspend the constitutional guaranties. As a result, Presidents Prieto, Bulnes, and Montt checked all uprisings with an iron hand, and were dictators in all but name. Until 1861 Chile had peace, it is true, but at the cost of almost all civil and political liberty. However, the serious uprisings during President Montt's second term showed the strength of the reaction against the despotic methods of the government. The new president, Señor José Joaquín Pérez, elected in 1861, adopted a policy that was both liberal and effective, and not once during his ten-year term did he ask for the extraordinary powers which his predecessors had found so necessary.

The diplomatic relations between the United States and Chile throughout this period were confined almost exclusively to the prosecution of claims resulting from the seizure by Admiral Cochrane of certain sums of money belonging to American citizens. The first claim was for $140,000 taken from Captain Smith of the brig *Macedonian* in 1819. This the government of Chile finally agreed to settle by the payment of $104,000 with interest.[19] The second claim was for a sum of $70,400, which was

[17] T. C. Dawson, *The South American Republics* (New York, 1904), Vol. II, p. 196.
[18] Text in amended form in W. F. Dodd, *Modern Constitutions* (Chicago, 1909), Vol. I. An exhaustive treatment of the Prieto régime (1841-51) is Raymon S. Valde's *Historia de Chile*, 4 vols. (Santiago, 1900).
[19] *Sen. Ex. Doc. No. 58*, 35th Cong., 1st Sess., p. 4. See also Barros Arana, *Un Decenio de la Historia de Chile* (Santiago, 1913), Vol. I, p. 411.

taken from Captain Smith in 1821 by a force of armed soldiers in the service of the Republic of Chile. This money was later turned over to Lord Cochrane, and distributed by him as prize-money or to discharge arrears of pay due to the officers and men in the service of Chile.[20] No claim for this sum was filed by the government of the United States against Chile until some twenty years later (May 19, 1841), when the American *chargé,* Richard Pollard, brought it to the attention of the Chilean government.[21] After another delay of two years, during which the American *chargé* at Santiago continued to press the claim, the Chilean minister for foreign affairs replied that, owing to the period of time that the interested parties had allowed to elapse, the claim was outlawed by prescription.[22] This brought a long and caustic rejoinder from J. S. Pendleton, who was now acting as American *chargé d'affaires.*[23] The interchanges finally became so heated that the Chilean minister threatened to put an end to all further correspondence. This would have been just as well, because after six months of bickering, which served only to embitter both parties, the dispute remained exactly where it started. Mr. Pendleton was finally recalled, and his successor, Mr. Crump, was instructed to press the claim, but in a courteous and respectful manner; for, as the American government conceded, the previous correspondence had been conducted "in a tone little calculated to secure an amicable adjustment of the matter in controversy." [24]

In 1846 Chile sent Señor Carvallo to Washington with a mass of documentary evidence to prove that the property siezed in the territory of the enemy was Spanish and therefore subject to capture as enemy property.[25] The documents were turned over to Mr. R. H. Gillett, solicitor of the Treasury, who, after careful consideration of the evidence given on both sides, decided that the goods belonged to American citizens. He further ruled that there had been no violation of neutrality, since the goods had been landed in an open port in Peru when that country was still under the government of Spain, and before Chile or Peru had been recognized by the United States.[26] Mr. Gillett's reply was made on May 29, 1848, and Secretary Buchanan, accepting it as conclusive, once more asked

[20] *Sen. Ex. Doc. No. 58,* p. 5.
[21] *Ibid.,* p. 30.
[22] *Ibid.,* p. 34.
[23] *Ibid.,* pp. 36-46.
[24] *Ibid.,* p. 109. For a characterization of Pendleton and his methods from the Chilean point of view see Barros Arana, *Un Decenio de la Historia de Chile,* Vol. II, p. 582, note 6.
[25] *Sen. Ex. Doc. No. 58,* pp. 126-173.
[26] *Ibid.,* pp. 173-333.

for a settlement. Señor Carvallo thereupon prepared another long answer, invoking, among other arguments, the rule of 1756 prohibiting neutrals in time of war from engaging in traffic forbidden to them in time of peace.[27] No answer was made to this until May 24, 1852, when Mr. Hunter, acting Secretary of State, stated that the United States had always denied the validity of the rule of 1756, and that, even admitting the legality of the rule, the seizure of American property by Chilean soldiers on Peruvian soil would not be justified by it.[28] Since no solution by diplomatic means seemed possible, Señor Carvallo suggested arbitration, and the King of Belgium was finally agreed upon. Even then, six years elapsed before a convention of arbitration was signed, on November 10, 1858.

Each of the contracting parties now agreed to submit to the King of Belgium the following questions: (1) Whether the claim was just in whole or part? (2) If just, what amount should be paid by Chile as indemnity for the capture? (3) Whether interest should be paid, and if so, at what rate and from what date? The question of prescription was excluded. The designated arbitrator accepted the case and handed down an award on May 15, 1863. He found the claim well founded, but that of the amount seized only three-fifths belonged to citizens of the United States. He also granted interest at 6 per cent on this sum ($42,000), but only from 1841, when the United States filed the claim, to 1848, when arbitration was agreed upon.[29] A few other claims were still pending against the Chilean government, but they were for smaller sums and all were ultimately settled by diplomatic means.[30]

The relations between the United States and Chile during the period 1835 to 1860 were not merely lacking in cordiality through the question of claims. Our various diplomatic representatives seemed unable to protect this country's interests and at the same time remain on friendly terms with the Chilean government. Richard Pollard, *chargé d'affaires* from 1835-1842, an exceedingly able diplomat, felt it necessary to stalk out in the midst of a state dinner given by the President of Chile because of a serious slight to his diplomatic standing due to his position at the table.[31] His successor, J. S. Pendleton, used such vigorous language to

---

[27] *Ibid.,* pp. 334-393.

[28] *Ibid.,* pp. 393-409.

[29] For summary of evidence and text of award see J. B. Moore, *History and Digest of International Arbitrations,* Vol. II, p. 1449.

[30] *Ibid.,* Vol. II, p. 1449, note 1.

[31] William R. Sherman, *The Diplomatic and Commercial Relations of the United States and Chile* (Boston, 1926), p. 41.

the Chilean foreign minister that the latter threatened to cease negotiations with him.[32] But the culmination of these personal unpleasant relations was reached during the mission of Seth Barton of Louisiana. He first got into a wrangle over his failure to raise the legation flag on a national holiday; shortly afterwards his horses were impounded instead of being returned when they were found as runaways; and finally he became involved in a violent dispute with the archbishop of Valparaíso who objected to his marriage with a Chilean woman of wealth and high social position, and refused to perform the ceremony. After the marriage had been performed in the legation by an American navy chaplain, the archbishop wrote urging the minister's wife to leave her husband on the ground that she was not wedded according to the Church. This communication enraged Barton and he demanded that the priest be brought to trial for insulting the wife of the American minister. When the government disclaimed authority he became so insulting that the Chilean government demanded his recall. Barton, however, left forthwith and the legation remained closed for almost a year.[33]

Other events which added fuel to the growing antagonism were Chilean sympathy with Mexico in its war with the United States; the collapse of the short agricultural boom brought about by the sale of flour to California gold-rush hordes; and the harsh treatment accorded Chileans who had been lured to California by the gold fever and had run afoul of vigilance committees. Writing in 1855, United States Minister Starkweather declared that "the United States and her citizens are the objects of constant and virulent attack and the chosen target of scurrilous abuse on the part of the press of the country ... it has even been proposed to expel them from the country and close the ports of Chile against them and their commerce." [34]

In 1865 Chile became engaged in a war with Spain in consequence of the high-handed methods of that power in dealing with Peru. Spain had seized the Chincha Islands, and Chile feared that unless the South American states stood together she would attempt to regain her authority over them. Public feeling ran high, and a riot occurred in front of the Spanish legation at Santiago. This, together with a series of other incidents which manifested an unneutral attitude on the part of Chile, brought a Spanish fleet into Valparaíso Bay, and its admiral gave the

[32] *Ibid.*, p. 45.

[33] See Henry Clay Evans, Jr., *Chile and Its Relations with the United States* (Durham, N. C., 1927), pp. 71-72; 122-126.

[34] W. R. Manning, *Diplomatic Correspondence of the United States, Inter-American Affairs, 1831-1860* (Washington, D. C., 1935), Vol. V, p. 210.

Chileans four days in which to apologize and salute the Spanish flag.[35] When this was refused, the Spanish squadron proceeded to blockade the Chilean coast. Upon several occasions the United States offered her good offices, both to Spain and to Chile, but without success. The American minister at Santiago, Mr. Thomas H. Nelson, although maintaining a correct and neutral attitude, showed clearly in his despatches that he, as well as the other members of the diplomatic corps, felt that Spain was the aggressor and that the war was both useless and unnecessary. He even went so far as to suggest to Secretary Seward that "a peaceful solution of the controversy would be much more probable if, in addition to the tender of good offices, the United States would remonstrate with Spain upon her unjust and aggressive policy toward Chile. The *moral* intervention, at least, of our government to protect the integrity of one of the American republics from unjustifiable attack on the part of a European power was never more urgently needed nor upon firmer grounds of right and justice." [36]

When, in March, 1866, news came to General Kilpatrick, who had succeeded Mr. Nelson as minister at Santiago, that the Spaniards intended to bombard Valparaíso, an unfortified town, he used every effort to prevent it. He first unofficially visited the Chilean foreign minister and tried to obtain his terms of peace, and then made a similar visit to the Spanish admiral. When this failed, he attempted to obtain the support of the British and French diplomatic representatives in asking that the United States squadron give protection to foreign property in the port and prevent the bombardment by force if necessary. As they were unwilling to interfere, the American minister did not feel justified in taking further responsibility in the matter. The bombardment took place on March 31, and the damage done to property and goods was estimated at from fifteen to twenty million dollars.[37] As a result of the failure of the United States to intervene when a squadron under Commodore Rodgers was at the very scene of action, the feeling of the Chileans towards the United States became very bitter. As General Kilpatrick phrased it: "Chile looked upon the United States as her best friend, and that friend had failed to assist her in her hour of need." [38] Secretary Seward, however, upheld the American minister's conduct and pointed out that peace was the constant interest and unwavering policy of the United States. The United

[35] For a complete account of the causes of the war from the Chilean point of view see *For. Rel. of the U. S.*, 1866, Part. 2, pp. 349-362.

[36] *Ibid.*, p. 369.

[37] *Ibid.*, p. 386.

[38] *Ibid.*, p. 408.

States would resist any effort to assail wantonly the republican principle in the Western Hemisphere, but it had no armies for aggressive warfare, nor ambition for the character of a regulator. The policy of nonintervention began with Washington and still endured.[39] In spite of this statement of policy, Seward again made a very earnest effort early in 1867 to induce both parties to arbitrate their quarrel; but Chile was still so bitter towards Spain because of the bombardment of Valparaíso that her conditions of settlement were uncompromising in the extreme. An armistice was finally arranged in 1868, which was just as good as peace, because, as the Chilean foreign minister declared, Spain could not and Chile would not resume the offensive.[40]

One important result of the war with Spain was Chile's realization of her need of a strong navy to protect her exposed sea-coast; in fact, Chile's tendency to become a militaristic nation dates from this period. Another result of the war was a temporary agreement between Chile and Bolivia in regard to the disputed boundary between the two countries in the desert of Atacama. When the two countries secured their independence from Spain, little attention was paid to this region because of its supposed worthlessness; but when, in 1841, guano was discovered, a sudden interest in the Atacama desert was manifested by both parties. In 1842 the Chilean congress passed a resolution by which all the guano in the province of Coquimbo in the littoral of Atacama, and in the adjacent islands, was thereby declared national property.[41] Hardly had the bill become law when the Bolivian representative in Chile asked that the measure, which thus extended Chile's frontiers to the prejudice of Bolivia, be revoked. Revindications continued on both sides, Bolivia insisting that her southern boundary was the twenty-seventh degree of latitude (*i.e.*, inclusive of the desert of Atacama), while Chile maintained that her territory extended north to the twenty-third degree of latitude. Inasmuch as Chile's various constitutions from 1822 to 1833 indicated Atacama as Chile's northern boundary, the Bolivian claim seemed well founded.[42] Chile, however, continued to hunt guano in the region, and in 1857 seized Mejillones and ousted the Bolivians. Bolivia protested vehemently, and when, in 1864, protests proved unavailing, she broke off diplomatic relations. Before war broke out, however, the trouble with Spain brought

[39] *Ibid.*, p. 413.

[40] *Ibid.*, p. 322.

[41] V. M. Maurtua (Pezet's trans.), *The Question of the Pacific* (Philadelphia, 1901), p. 11.

[42] *Ibid.*, p. 7. See also E. M. Borchard, *Opinion on the Question of the Pacific* (Washington, D. C., 1920), p. 6.

the two nations together in a common cause, and by a treaty signed in 1866 the boundary line was fixed at the twenty-fourth parallel. The treaty further provided that the zone lying between the twenty-third and twenty-fifth parallels should be subject to a joint jurisdiction of both governments for the exploitation of the guano and mineral deposits, and that all products of the territory between the twenty-third and the twenty-fifth and exported from Mejillones should be free of duty.[43]

Various difficulties arose under this condominium arrangement, the Chileans claiming that Bolivia failed to carry out the terms of the treaty, and the Bolivians asserting that Chile was extending its terms out of all reason. The American minister to Bolivia, writing to Secretary Fish on January 31, 1872, pointed out the increasing possibilities of trouble between the two states owing to the recently discovered silver mines in the region under joint control.[44] Bolivia, apparently fearing further Chilean encroachments, signed an alliance with Peru in 1873 under which the two parties agreed mutually to guarantee their independence and sovereignty and the integrity of their respective territories.[45] Although essentially a defensive alliance, the terms were kept secret. However, there is little doubt that Chile was fully cognizant of the treaty. In 1873 Mr. Logan, the American minister at Santiago, was asked by the Chilean foreign minister to act as arbitrator in the boundary dispute with Bolivia;[46] and when this attempt failed a direct settlement was obtained by the two powers by a new treaty signed in 1874 abrogating the treaty of 1866.

The treaty of 1874 fixed the twenty-fourth parallel as the boundary between the two republics, but provided that such guano as was left between that parallel and the twenty-third should be equally divided. The clause that brought about war between the two countries provided that for twenty-five years the export duties levied on the minerals within the zones between the twenty-third and twenty-fourth parallels should not be raised.[47]

From Melgarejo, a Bolivian dictator, a Chilean company had obtained important concessions for exploiting the nitrate in this Bolivian zone. In 1878 the Bolivian congress, with the apparent purpose of regaining

[43] Maurtua, op. cit., pp. 16-17. For a fuller discussion from the Chilean point of view see Don Gonzalo Bulnes, Chile and Peru (Santiago, 1920), pp. 8-15.

[44] For. Rel. of the U. S., 1872, p. 64. Nitrate also had been discovered in this region in 1866 by a Chilean explorer.

[45] Maurtua, op. cit., p. 28. Bulnes, op. cit., pp. 58-66. For text see The War in South America, Sen. Ex. Doc. No. 79, 47th Cong, 1st Sess., p. 85.

[46] For. Rel. of the U. S., 1874, p. 197.

[47] Maurtua, op. cit., pp. 19-21.

a small part of the wealth given away by a former executive, demanded, as a basis of renewing the contract, 10 per cent of the profits of the company—though it later changed this to read ten cents per quintal of nitrate exported. This was a clear violation of the treaty of 1874, and Chile protested and threatened to annul the former treaty. Bolivia persisted in her intentions and ordered the tax to be collected. Thereupon, on February 12, 1879, the Chilean minister demanded his passports, and two days later Chilean forces seized the disputed territory. Mr. Osborn, minister of the United States at Santiago, declared that Chile's movement was an exceedingly popular one, and that it was doubtful whether if the administration had taken any other course it could have sustained itself.[48]

Bolivia declared war on Chile on March 1, 1879, and from the beginning it was feared by Chile that Peru would take sides against her. Mr. Gibbs, the American minister at Lima, testified that public opinion in Peru was very hostile towards Chile, and the press demanded that the government declare war or resign.[49] The Peruvian government, however, seemed desirous of averting a war if possible, and sent a special mission, headed by Don José Antonio Lavalle, to propose arbitration. This mission was received with marked hostility by the Chilean populace, and when its proposals were laid before the Chilean government the latter immediately demanded an explanation of the secret alliance between Bolivia and Peru. Lavalle was unable to reply with complete frankness, and the Chileans, claiming that the mission was merely a ruse to gain time, refused to continue the negotiations unless Peru would abrogate the treaty of 1873, cease all military preparations, and promise to remain neutral. The Peruvian plenipotentiary could not accept these terms, and Chile declared war on Peru April 5, 1879.[50] Neutral opinion seems to place the burden of responsibility for the failure to find a peaceful solution upon Chile. Sir Clements Markham, the English historian, declares that Chile sought a pretext for a war against Peru to gain her nitrate wealth, and Professor E. M. Borchard, the American publicist, in a later opinion found that Peru was sincerely desirous of avoiding war.[51]

Although the United States took no official action to prevent the outbreak of the war, Mr. S. N. Pettis, the American minister to Bolivia, made

[48] *War in South America*, p. 74. For the causes of the war from the Chilean side see pp. 78-83.

[49] *Ibid.*, p. 98.

[50] For the Chilean side see Bulnes, *op. cit.*, pp. 124-160; Rafael Egana, *The Tacna and Arica Question* (Santiago, 1900), pp. 32-40; for the Peruvian side see Maurtua, *op. cit.*, pp. 43-51.

[51] C. R. Markham, *The War Between Peru and Chile* (London, 1882); Edwin M. Borchard, *op. cit.*

a special visit in August, 1879, to both Lima and Santiago in the interests of peace. This mission, undertaken without the direction or knowledge of the Washington government, was designed to acquaint each of the warring governments with the views of the other and thus to obtain a direct settlement. The United States government showed itself entirely in sympathy with his efforts by stating that, "unauthorized and even rash as Mr. Pettis' experiment might appear, the United States could not but rejoice at the result should the knowledge thus gained by the belligerents of each other's views conduce to an eventual settlement." [52] Although his mission did not succeed, Judge Pettis continued to strive for peace, and in a note to Mr. Seward, dated September 30, 1879, he urged that the United States offer to mediate, inasmuch as all the belligerents were expecting it and wondered at our delay.[53] The ministers in Bolivia and Chile were not so optimistic, and Mr. Osborn at Santiago felt that it would be most unwise for the United States to suggest mediation, since the war spirit was very strong in Chile and there seemed to be absolute confidence that Chile would conquer her enemies.[54]

Chile soon proved that she was far better prepared for war than either of her opponents, and was victorious in virtually all of the engagements on land and sea, although she was severely criticized for the cruel and harsh methods employed, for shelling unfortified towns, and for utterly disregarding the rights of noncombatants. By July, 1880, it was evident that she had won the war and that further operations would entail useless bloodshed. Therefore, on July 29, 1880, Mr. Evarts, Secretary of State at Washington, directed the American ministers in Santiago and Lima to press upon the Chilean and Peruvian governments the desire of the United States that peace be made on honorable terms.[55] Mr. Osborn thereupon offered the good offices of the United States, and Chile agreed to accept them, provided the other powers would also accept. It was finally agreed that each of the belligerents should send its representative to meet with the three American ministers accredited to the belligerent states on the U. S. S. *Lackawanna* in the Bay of Arica.

The conference convened on October 22, and Mr. Osborn, the dean of the American representatives, acted as chairman. At the first meeting Chile presented a memorandum outlining the bases upon which she would make peace. The principal provision, and the one that eliminated all

[52] J. B. Moore, *Digest of Int. Law*, Vol. VI, p. 35.
[53] *War in South America*, p. 18.
[54] *Ibid.*, p. 97.
[55] *War in South America*, p. 116.

chance of a settlement, was the demand on her part that the province of Tarapacá be ceded to her as payment for the costs of the war. As this was territory never claimed by Chile in her most extreme boundary demands, and possessed an almost boundless store of the valuable nitrates, it was not to be expected that the allies would yield it. The Bolivian delegate proposed that Chile hold the territory until a suitable indemnity had been paid, and the Peruvian delegate proposed that the United States be given full power to arbitrate the question. Bolivia heartily agreed to arbitration, but Chile declared that, while arbitration was a satisfactory method before the outbreak of war, under the changed circumstances "there was no reason whatever why she should deliver up to other hands, honorable and secure as they may be, the decision of her destinies." [56] Mr. Christiancy, the American minister to Peru, felt that the terms proposed by Chile were meant to be so extreme that the allies could not accept them; while Mr. Adams, the American minister to Bolivia, also reported that the Chilean government was not very much in earnest in its desires for peace. He declared that the main object of the Chileans was to break up the alliance between Peru and Bolivia and engage the latter republic in an alliance with themselves.[57] Both ministers thought it strange that Mr. Osborn should have let it be understood that the United States did not desire to act as arbiter on the question. Secretary Evarts was also curious on this score, and in a despatch dated December 27, 1880, he informed Osborn: "If it was your purpose to convey the impression that we would not cheerfully assume any labor and trouble incidental to arbitration in the interests of peace and in the service of justice, you have not correctly interpreted the views and ideas of this government.[58]

After the failure of the conference Chile prosecuted the war still more vigorously, and in January, 1881, she gained possession of Lima. Secretary Evarts, again desirous of putting an end to the conflict, urged the American ministers in both Lima and Santiago to use every effort in the direction of peace. Mr. Christiancy, however, informed him that the Chilean authorities in Lima declared that they would not accept the good offices of any neutral government nor those of any diplomatic official in Lima, but would treat only with the Peruvian government.[59] Owing to internal troubles in Peru, Chile refused to treat with either faction, thus remaining in control of Lima and its valuable customhouses; and Mr. Christiancy

[56] The report and protocols in full are found in *ibid.*, pp. 405-418.
[57] *Ibid.*, p. 51.
[58] *Ibid.*, p. 147.
[59] *Ibid.*, p. 448.

was of the opinion that Chile did not intend to make peace with Peru at all unless driven to do so by outside pressure.[60]

In 1881 the Garfield administration came into power, and James G. Blaine was made Secretary of State. The President immediately appointed General Kilpatrick minister to Chile and General Hurlbut to Peru. Both soon gave evidence that they were better soldiers than diplomats. The instructions to both, dated June 15, 1881, were very similar, indicating a strong opposition on the part of the United States to a transfer of territory as a basis of peace. To Mr. Kilpatrick Secretary Blaine wrote: "At the conclusion of a war avowedly not of conquest, but for the solution of differences which diplomacy had failed to settle, to make acquisition of territory a *sine quo non* of peace is calculated to cast suspicion on the professions with which war was originally declared"; and to Mr. Hurlbut: "As far as the influence of the United States will go in Chile, it will be exerted to induce the Chilean government to consent that the question of the cession of territory should be the subject of negotiation and not the condition precedent upon which alone negotiation shall commence."[61]

The two representatives interpreted their instructions in an entirely different manner. Shortly after his arrival at Lima, Mr. Hurlbut notified his colleague at Santiago that his instructions indicated that the United States wished peace, on fair and honorable terms, to be arranged as speedily as possible, but so that the integrity of Peruvian territory would be maintained. Chile, he thought, should be satisfied with a fair and reasonable indemnity for the expenses of the war.[62] To make his position clear he forwarded, on August 25, to General Lynch, commander-in-chief at Lima, a memorandum in which he thus laid down the position of the United States: "I wish to state further, that while the United States recognize all rights which the conqueror gains under the laws of civilized war, they do not approve of war for the purpose of territorial aggrandizement, nor of the violent dismemberment of a nation except as a last resort in extreme emergencies."[63] Mr. Hurlbut's statement was by no means agreeable to General Lynch, who, in a telegram to the Chilean government, asserted that the American Minister's "no annexation" declaration "complicates and endangers our occupation."[64] Thereupon the Chilean minister of foreign affairs interrogated Mr. Kilpatrick upon the forceful

[60] *Ibid.*, p. 467.
[61] *Ibid.*, pp. 157, 500.
[62] *Ibid.*, p. 513.
[63] *Ibid.*, p. 516
[64] *Ibid.*, p. 162.

declarations of his colleague in Lima. Instead of taking the matter up with Mr. Hurlbut, Mr. Kilpatrick immediately disclaimed the statements as unauthorized by the government of the United States and criticized his colleague for making them.[65] Mr. Blaine censured Mr. Kilpatrick strongly for his undiplomatic methods; nor was he entirely pleased with Mr. Hurlbut's emphatic partizanship. Inasmuch as no further friendly coöperation between the two American representatives could now be hoped for, Mr. Blaine decided to send a special envoy furnished with full powers to the three belligerent states.[66]

Mr. William H. Trescot, of South Carolina, was chosen for the task—which, indeed, had steadily become more difficult, owing to the openly manifested hostility of Chile to any interference of the United States. One evidence of this was Chile's treatment of the Calderón government in Peru. This government had been recognized by the United States in June, 1881, and in the following month the Chilean foreign minister had assured Mr. Kilpatrick that every effort would be made by Chile to strengthen it. Nevertheless, in September the Calderón government was suppressed by the Chilean authorities, and in November Señor Calderón was arrested and deported. Mr. Hurlbut interpreted this act as an attempt to continue the state of anarchy and confusion as a ground for Chilean occupation, and also as the reply of Chile to the known support of this government by the United States.[67] Mr. Blaine was inclined to accept the latter interpretation, and in his instructions to Mr. Trescot he authorized him to say to the Chilean government that if such a purpose was avowed it would be regarded by the United States as an act of such unfriendly import as to require the immediate suspension of all diplomatic intercourse.[68] His instructions further stated: "If our good offices are rejected, and this policy of the absorption of an independent state be persisted in, this government . . . will hold itself free to appeal to the other republics of this continent to join it in an effort to avert consequences which cannot be confined to Chile and Peru, but which threaten with extremest danger the political institutions, the peaceful progress, and the liberal civilization of all America." [69]

On the other hand, if Chile should receive in a friendly spirit the representations of the United States, Mr. Trescot was authorized, first, to concert such measures as would enable Peru to establish a regular govern-

[65] *Ibid.*, p. 163.
[66] *Ibid.*, p. 168.
[67] *Ibid.*, p. 561.
[68] *Ibid.*, p. 176.
[69] *Ibid.*, p. 178.

ment and initiate negotiations; second, to induce Chile to consent to such negotiations without cession of territory as a condition precedent; and, third, to impress upon Chile that she ought to allow Peru a fair opportunity to provide for a reasonable indemnity, letting it be understood that the United States would consider the imposition of an extravagant indemnity, making the cession of territory necessary, as more than was justified by the actual cost of the war, and as a solution threatening renewed difficulty between the two countries.[70] The envoy was further intrusted with the delicate task of inviting Chile to the conference of all the American republics, which Mr. Blaine was so anxious to hold in Washington.

Mr. Trescot arrived in Santiago January 7, 1882. But in the meantime President Garfield had been shot, Vice-president Arthur had been sworn in, and Mr. Frelinghuysen had succeeded Mr. Blaine as Secretary of State. Owing to the complete change in policy that followed, this change in the administration had a most unfortunate result on the mission. President Arthur decided to follow a hands-off policy in regard to the merits of the controversy, the indemnity, change of boundaries, and the personnel of the government of Peru. The clause in Mr. Trescot's instructions that contemplated the severance of diplomatic relations under certain contingencies was revoked entirely.[71] Before the revised orders were received by Mr. Trescot, he had obtained an assurance of the Chilean government that no offense was meant by the removal of Calderón, and also an acceptance of the good offices of the United States. An offer of peace was made upon the basis of the cession of Tarapacá and an indemnity of twenty million pesos payable in ten years, Arica to be occupied until payment was made.[72] However, in an interview about a week later, what was Mr. Trescot's surprise and chagrin to learn from Mr. Balmaceda, the Chilean minister of foreign affairs, that his original instructions from Mr. Blaine had been published, that new instructions had been issued, and that these were then in the hands of the Chilean government. Further parleys were, for the time at least, useless; for, as Mr. Trescot remarked, "a diplomatist of ordinary experience would conclude, when he learns that his instructions have been communicated to the government with which he is negotiating before he receives them himself, that it is time for him to be silent until he does receive them."[73] However, Mr. Trescot was

[70] Ibid., p. 178.
[71] For. Rel. of the U. S., 1882, p. 57.
[72] Ibid., p. 61.
[73] Ibid., p. 67.

finally prevailed upon to sign a protocol on February 11, 1882, in which the bases of peace were the cession of Tarapacá, an indemnity of 20 million pesos, and the retention of Tacna and Arica until payment should be made.[74]

The United States thereupon refused to be a party to peace on these terms and urged that Chile show herself more magnanimous. Mr. Trescot, however, knew that his mission had failed; for Chile would not consider any modification of her terms. Shortly afterwards he returned to Washington. From there, in a letter to Mr. Frelinghuysen dated June 5, 1882, he frankly pointed out the unfortunate consequences of the vacillating policy of the United States: "If the United States intend to intervene effectively to prevent the disintegration of Peru, the time has come when that intention should be avowed. If it does not, still more urgent is the necessity that Chile and Peru should understand exactly where the action of the United States ends. It would be entirely beyond my duty to discuss the character or the consequences of either line of conduct, but I trust that you will not deem that I am going beyond that duty in impressing upon the government that the present position of the United States is an embarrassment to all the belligerents, and that it should be terminated as promptly as possible." [75]

Mr. Frelinghuysen apparently did not realize that his ill-advised and futile efforts to obtain a peace through the moral influence of the United States were bringing his government into contempt in the eyes of all South America. Accordingly, although the United States stated in advance that under no conditions would it go beyond the tendering of its good offices, he persisted in intervening when Chile was firmly decided to make peace only upon the terms that her victory made possible. Under instructions dated June 25, 1882, Mr. Cornelius A. Logan, the new minister to Chile, was "to continue the efforts of your government to induce Chile to settle the difficulty by such moderation in her demands as you may be able to bring about, taking care to impress upon that government that any substantial concession which it may now make will be regarded as a direct and graceful recognition of the disinterested counsels of the United States." Incidentally, Mr. Frelinghuysen no longer seemed to object to the cession of Peruvian territory; for, after noting the fact that Chile was in possession of Tarapacá, Tacna, and Arica, he vouchsafed the supposition that no contingency could happen that would bring about the permanent occupation and annexation by Chile of any larger part of Peru

[74] *Ibid.*, p. 83.
[75] *Ibid.*, p. 103.

than this.[76] It is not strange that a Peruvian publicist was forced to admit that "this third attempt at mediation was still more disastrous in its results for Peru, as it was still more dishonorable for the credit and prestige of the Great Republic of the North. . . . It was no longer the glorious eagle, the emblem of the might and greatness of the United States, that came from Washington to the Pacific to compel the belligerents to lay down their arms and put an end to an iniquitous war of conquest; but the innocent and timid dove, the messenger of peace, sent by the Northern Colossus to beg the cessation of hostilities in the name of American fraternity." [77]

Mr. Logan soon showed a decided partiality for the Chilean point of view, while his colleague at Lima, Mr. J. R. Partridge, became an equally ardent supporter of the Peruvian claims. Although still a prisoner, President Calderón finally refused to negotiate further with Mr. Logan as mediator, on the ground of his over-friendliness towards Chile; and Mr. Partridge upheld him in the stand.[78] The latter even went so far as to propose common action to the representatives of Great Britain, France, and Italy; but this unauthorized proposal was immediately disavowed by Mr. Frelinghuysen, and as a result of it Mr. Partridge was recalled. Meanwhile a faction in northern Peru under the leadership of General Iglesias was corresponding directly with the Chilean government, and in return for recognition it agreed to sign a peace upon Chilean terms. Mr. Logan strongly urged that the United States recognize the government of Iglesias.[79] A protocol of peace was signed in May, 1883, and its terms were incorporated in the treaty of Ancon signed by the representatives of Chile and Peru, October 20, 1883. The third intervention of the United States had failed quite as completely as the other two in preventing the territorial dismemberment of Peru. As Mr. Alejandro Garland puts it: "This is the sad history, in as far as Peru is concerned, of the amicable intervention of the United States; . . . its unfortunate, vacillating, and contradictory policy only defeated its own ends." [80]

By the terms of the treaty of Ancon, Tarapacá was ceded in perpetuity to Chile, while the provinces of Tacna and Arica were to be held by Chile for ten years, and at the expiration of that period a plebiscite was to determine whether they should remain under Chilean sovereignty or be

[76] Ibid., 1883, p. 76.
[77] Alejandro Garland, South American Conflicts and the United States (Lima, 1900), p. xiii.
[78] Ibid., p. xv.
[79] For. Rel. of the U. S., 1883, p. 103.
[80] Garland, op. cit., p. xvi.

returned to Peru. The country then receiving the two provinces was to pay the other country $10 million.[81] This plebiscite, which should have been held on March 28, 1894, ten years after the ratification of the treaty, has never been held, and it is this question that has been called "the Alsace-Lorraine question of South America."

A well-meant attempt at settlement was President Harding's invitation of January 18, 1922, to both powers to send representatives to Washington, to thresh out the question under the auspices of the United States.[82] The invitation was accepted, and the conference was opened by Secretary Hughes, May 15, in the Hall of the Americas of the Pan-American Building. He congratulated the delegates upon the noble and conciliatory attitude animating both governments, and pointed out that this was "an auspicious time to heal old wounds and to end whatever differences may exist in Latin America," and said that there could be no more agreeable harbinger of a better day and a lasting peace upon this hemisphere than the convening of this conference of the representatives of the republics of Chile and Peru.[83] Bolivia protested vigorously at not being allowed to participate in the conference; but both Chile and Peru were unwilling to extend the scope of the conferences to include Bolivian claims. After arduous sessions for two months, a protocol was signed July 21, 1922, whereby Chile and Peru agreed to arbitration of the controversy by the President of the United States; and Secretary Hughes informed the plenipotentiaries that President Harding was ready to act as mediator.[84]

The terms of the agreement provided in substance that: (1) the arbitrator should decide whether or not in the present circumstances the plebiscite should or should not be held; (2) if held, the arbitrator should determine the conditions; (3) if not, both parties at the request of either should discuss the situation; (4) failing to agree, they would solicit the good offices of the United States.

Both sides chose their counsel, prepared their cases, and submitted them to the arbitrator on November 13, 1923. The Peruvian case was primarily an attempt to prove that, since the plebiscite to decide the ownership of the province had not been held according to the terms of the treaty, because Chile had not permitted it, and since the conditions had now changed so completely from what they were in 1894 that such

[81] For full text see British and Foreign State Papers, Vol. LXXIV, p. 349.

[82] For more extensive treatment see G. H. Stuart, "The Tacna-Arica Dispute," World Peace Foundation Pamphlets, Vol. X, No. 1 (1927), Sara Wambaugh, Plebiscites Since the World War (Washington, D. C., 1933), Vol. I, Chap. IX; W. J. Dennis, Tacna and Arica (New Haven, Conn., 1931).

[83] N. Y. Times, May 16, 1922.

[84] Ibid., July 22, 1922.

a plebiscite would be a mockery, therefore Peru should be confirmed as the undisputed owner of the territory.[85] Chile argued that since the plebiscite had not been held the arbitrator was practically limited to determine under what conditions it should be held. She then discussed these conditions with reference to the time and method of holding the plebiscite and the payment of the ten million *soles*.[86]

The award was handed down by President Coolidge on March 4, 1925, and was a lengthy document of some 17,000 words.[87] In regard to the holding of the plebiscite the arbitrator held that the provisions of Article III of the treaty of Ancon were still in effect; that the plebiscite should be held; and that the interests of both parties could be properly safeguarded by establishing suitable conditions therefor. As to the conditions of the plebiscite the arbitrator decided that all males, with the exception of military or civil employees of either country, over twenty-one years of age and able to read and write, were entitled to vote, provided that they were born in Tacna-Arica or had been living continuously in the territory for two years on July 20, 1922. A commission of three members, a Chilean, a Peruvian, and an American as presiding officer, was given complete control over the holding of the plebiscite, this commission to be appointed within three months of the date of the award and to begin work not later than six months from the date of the award. The payments to the losing state were to be made over a period of five years.

The award was received with great approval by Chile. Church bells were rung, the newspapers issued special editions, and the American ambassador, Mr. Collier, was given an ovation at every appearance in public. In Lima, however, the decision was regarded as a national calamity. A general strike began, traffic was suspended, newspapers failed to appear, and an uprising against the government was staged which was put down with the sacrifice of some forty lives. Americans were insulted and their business boycotted. Ambassador Poindexter, hitherto exceedingly popular, was given a special guard to protect the embassy from mob violence. On April 2, 1925, the Peruvian government sent an official memorial protesting against the award and requesting certain guarantees in the conduct of the plebiscite.[88] President Coolidge replied, however, that the

[85] *Arbitration Between Peru and Chile. The Case of Peru* (Washington, D. C., 1923).

[86] *Tacna Arica Arbitration. The Case of the Republic of Chile* (no place or date).

[87] *Opinion and Award of the Arbitrator. In the Matter of the Arbitration between the Republic of Chile and the Republic of Peru* (Washington, D. C., 1925).

[88] *Arbitration between Peru and Chile. The Memorial of Peru and the Ruling and Observations of the Arbitrator* (Washington, D. C., 1925).

record fully covered the question raised and that under the terms of submission they had been settled by the award "finally and without appeal." [89]

The plebiscite commission began its work on August 5, 1925, with General Pershing serving as chairman, but soon found itself unable to function effectively owing to the refusal of Chile to grant the guarantees which General Pershing felt were necessary before registration could commence. On December 9, 1925, a resolution was passed severely censuring the Chilean authorities in Tacna-Arica for not only failing to exercise their powers so as to make a fair plebiscite possible, but for using their powers unlawfully to reduce the number of Peruvian voters in the plebiscitary territory.[90] The Chilean member presented a dissenting opinion and later appealed to President Coolidge; but the latter in a decision handed down on January 15, 1926, upheld the powers of the commission.[91] On January 27, the day that the plebiscite law was approved by the commission, General Pershing returned to the United States on account of ill health, and General Lassiter took his place. He made every effort to carry out the plebiscite, but owing to the refusal of Chile to grant the guarantees approved of by General Pershing, the Peruvian members refused to participate in the registration which began on March 27.

On June 14, General Lassiter presented a report to the commission on conditions in the plebiscite area in which he declared that "suitable conditions for the plebiscite, if they have existed at any time within recent years, did not exist when the commission began its labors in August, 1925, they do not exist now and there is no prospect of their being brought into existence." [92] He then placed the blame for the situation upon the Chilean authorities, and gave specific instances of the outrages which they permitted to be perpetrated upon the Peruvians. Therefore, believing it beyond the powers of the commission to hold an "unfair and make-believe plebiscite, he recommended the termination of plebiscitary proceedings." The resolution carried.

Approximately a dozen conferences had been held in Washington for a settlement by mediation when the publication of the Lassiter report temporarily put an end to negotiations. However, in August and September it was reported that Secretary Kellogg was still conferring with the plenipotentiaries of the two powers in the hopes of settlement.

[89] *Idem.*
[90] *Amer. Jour. of Int. Law,* Vol. 20 (July, 1926), p. 607.
[91] *Ibid.,* p. 614.
[92] Full text of report in *World Peace Foundation Pamphlets,* Vol. X, No. 1, Appendix III; also in *U. S. Daily,* June 18-20, 1926. Also in Wambaugh, *op. cit.,* Vol. II, p. 468.

On November 30, Secretary Kellogg made what was reported to be the last proposal of the United States to the Chilean and Peruvian governments. In brief, it was proposed that the two powers agree to the cession "in perpetuity of all right, title, and interest" in Tacna and Arica to Bolivia upon an apportionment of equitable compensation, appropriate economic arrangements, and perpetual demilitarization of the territory. Treaties of friendship, commerce, and navigation were then to be arranged between Chile and Peru. Finally as an international memorial to the valor of Chile and Peru, a fitting monument might be erected on the Morro headland of Arica—this memorial to be internationalized.

Although this proposal was no more successful than the others—it was accepted unconditionally only by Bolivia—through the good offices of Secretary Kellogg the two states were finally persuaded to resume diplomatic relations. In October, 1928, after seventeen years of severed relations, a Chilean ambassador was received in Lima and a Peruvian in Santiago.

An era of more cordial relations had begun and the Presidents of Chile and Peru took advantage of President Hoover's good-will trip to Latin America in 1929 to bring about a settlement. At their suggestion he agreed to submit a proposal which had been carefully prepared giving Tacna to Peru and leaving Arica to Chile. The dividing line was to start at a point to be named Concordia and run parallel to the Arica-La Paz railway. Peru received an indemnity of $6,000,000 and all public works constructed in Tacna. Arica was made a free port and Peru given a wharf, customhouse and railway station there. The two governments agreed to erect a joint monument on the Morro of Arica to commemorate the settlement.[93] Ratifications of this treaty were exchanged July 28, 1929, and a month later the province of Tacna, after fifty years of Chilean control, raised the Peruvian flag, settling thereby the most thorny and long standing dispute in Latin-American diplomacy.

In addition to the protracted dispute over Tacna and Arica the United States also became seriously involved in Chilean affairs in 1891, in connection with the civil war between President Balmaceda and the Congressionalists.[94] Owing to his autocratic methods, President Balmaceda, who had been elected in 1886, was in constant conflict with Congress during his five-year term. His declared intention to dictate the

[93] For text of treaty and maps of boundary settlement, see Enrique Brieba, *Limites entre Chile y Peru,* 3 vols (Santiago de Chile, 1931).

[94] For an interesting and detailed account of this period see Sherman, *op. cit.,* C...p. VI.

choice of a successor, and an illegal decree of January 5, 1891, continuing in force the estimates of the preceding Congress, brought about an armed revolt.[95] Mr. Blaine was again Secretary of State in the Harrison administration, and Mr. Patrick Egan was the American minister to Chile. After a number of serious clashes between the two Chilean factions, Mr. Egan, together with the representatives of France and Brazil, offered their good offices, and both the government and the revolutionists accepted them. While the conferences were being held, bombs were thrown at several of the government ministers while returning from the Senate; and this so exasperated the government that negotiations were abruptly discontinued.[96] About a month later Mr. Egan again proposed mediation on the part of the United States; but, although the Balmaceda government was willing, the revolutionists refused.[97]

During the course of the revolution an incident took place that tended to arouse public opinion on the side of the revolutionists against the United States. They had despatched the *Itata* to San Diego, California, to obtain a cargo of arms and ammunition; but the Balmacedists, learning of it, warned the United States government, which immediately placed on board a United States marshal to see that its neutrality laws were respected. However, when the captain of the *Itata* learned that the cargo was ready on a schooner off San Clemente Island, he set sail without clearance, taking the United States official with him. The American agent was afterwards put ashore, but the *Itata* took on its cargo and carried it to Chile.[98] There, however, Admiral MacCann refused to allow the cargo to be landed and insisted that the boat and its cargo be returned to San Diego under a United States convoy. The Congressionalist faction conceded the justice of the act, but the rebels bitterly resented the loss of the cargo and looked upon the United States as aiding the Balmaceda government.

By the end of August the Congressionalist forces were completely victorious. Balmaceda resigned, and, fearing mob violence, sought refuge in the Argentine legation. His family and a large number of the government officials sought asylum in the American legation. The Chilean government protested against Mr. Egan's protection of the refugees, and various acts of disrespect were committed showing the hostility towards the American minister. Mr. Egan, however, refused to surrender the fugi-

[95] President Balmaceda's story of the causes is found in *For. Rel. of the U. S.,* 1891, p. 94.
[96] *Ibid.,* pp. 123-130.
[97] *Ibid.,* pp. 135, 140, 145.
[98] J. B. Scott, *Cases on International Law* (Boston, 1902), p. 732.

tives unless they be given safe conducts, and he was ultimately successful in carrying out his purpose.[99]

The constant friction between the American legation and the Chilean
authorities, the rumor which had been given wide circulation that Admiral
Brown had sent secret information to President Balmaceda regarding
the movements of the Congressionalists, the *Itata* affair, and the protection afforded by the United States representatives to the defeated faction,
all served to stir up bitter animosity towards everything Yankee. As a result, when, on October 15, 1891, Captain Schley of the U. S. S. *Baltimore*
gave shore leave to 116 petty officers and men, a concerted attack was
made upon them on the Valparaíso water-front. One petty officer was
killed, one sailor later died of his wounds, and seven or eight others
came out of the mêlée with from two to eighteen stab-wounds. Thirty-
six of the sailors were arrested, and while being taken to prison were
cruelly beaten and maltreated. An investigation made by Captain Schley
showed that the police made little effort to protect the Americans and in
some cases joined in the attack.[100] When apprised of the affair, the authorities offered no expression of regret, and a little later the Chilean
minister of foreign relations sent a most offensive note to the Chilean
minister at Washington, declaring that there was no exactness nor
sincerity in what was said at Washington.[101]

This brought matters to a head, and on January 21, 1892, after an
exhaustive investigation had been held at Mare Island directly upon the
return of the *Baltimore*,[102] Secretary Blaine notified Mr. Egan that President Harrison had come to the following conclusions. First, that the attack was upon the uniform of the United States Navy, having its origin
and motive in a feeling of hostility to this government and not in any
act of the sailors. Second, that the public authorities of Valparaíso
flagrantly failed in their duty to protect our men, and that some of the
police and of the Chilean soldiers and sailors were themselves guilty of
unprovoked assaults upon our sailors before and after arrest. Third,
that suitable apology and adequate reparation should be demanded for
the injury done to this government. Mr. Egan was further instructed
to say that the expressions imputing untruth and insincerity to the President and to the Secretary of the Navy in their official communications to
the Congress of the United States were in the highest degree offensive
to this government, and that if the offensive parts were not at once

[99] J. B. Moore, *Digest of Int. Law*, Vol. II, pp. 791-798.
[100] *Relations with Chile, House Ex. Doc. No. 91*, 52nd Cong., 1st Sess., pp. 115-118.
[101] *Ibid.*, p. 178.
[102] *Ibid.*, pp. 341-607.

withdrawn and a suitable apology offered, the President would have no other course except to terminate diplomatic relations with the government of Chile.[103] Four days later, before a reply to this note was received, President Harrison laid the whole matter before Congress in a special message.[104]

The new government that had in the meantime come into existence in Chile was more favorably disposed towards the United States, and the new minister of foreign relations returned a very courteous reply to the demands of our government. Sincere expressions of regret were offered for both the assault and the unfortunate despatch; and in regard to reparations, although the court at Valparaíso had not yet finished its investigation, Chile offered to submit to the Supreme Court at Washington the question of whether there were any grounds for reparation and in what shape it should be made.[105] This reply was entirely satisfactory to the United States, and Mr. Egan was directed to state that the President was ready to meet the friendly overtures of the Chilean government in the most generous spirit, and that, as for reparations, he had no doubt that the whole matter would soon be settled in a just and honorable fashion by diplomatic means.[106] The hope was justified; for in July of the same year Chile offered $75,000 in gold, to be distributed among the families of the sailors injured and killed in the *Baltimore* affair. The United States immediately accepted it.[107] The same year the two nations signed a claims convention whereby all other claims were to be settled by arbitration by a commission sitting at Washington.[108] The commission sat from October 9, 1893, to April 19, 1894, and awarded $240,564.35 to meet the claims of citizens of the United States.[109]

Following this period of difficulties and misunderstandings, the relations between the United States and Chile have become very friendly. During his visit to Chile in 1906 Mr. Root expressed the belief that the difficulties of the past arose primarily out of the lack of mutual acquaintance, and declared that the completion of the Panama Canal was bound to bring about more intimate relations, and that this was the time to say that these relations should be those of friendship.[110] Friendlier feelings have subsequently been shown in many ways. President Montt was

[103] *Ibid.*, p. 193.
[104] *Ibid.*, pp. iii-xiv.
[105] *For. Rel. of the U. S.*, 1891, p. 309.
[106] *Ibid.*, p. 312.
[107] *Ibid.*, 1892, p. 62.
[108] *U. S. Stat. at Large*, Vol. XXVII, p. 965.
[109] *Compilation of Treaties in Force* (Washington, D. C., 1904), p. 127.
[110] *For. Rel. of the U. S.*, 1906, Part I, p. 153.

cordially welcomed on his passage through Panama in 1910 en route to
Europe.[111] In 1911 the long-standing Alsop claim was settled by arbitration,[112] and in 1914 a treaty for the advancement of general peace was
signed, which provided that all disputes not settled by diplomatic means
should be submitted for investigation and report to an International
Commission.[113]

Chile remained neutral during World War I; and, considering the fact
that her outlook was on the Pacific, and that she was so far removed
from the seat of hostilities, her attitude was logical. Señor Beltran
Mathieu, Chilean ambassador to the United States, thus explained his
country's neutrality: "Chile was neither solicited nor compelled, because
she was not involved in the political causes of the war nor in its sphere
of action, and because no one considered that a nation so far removed
from the theater of hostilities might be useful as a military or financial
entity, while she was so as a factor of production, for which peace was
essential." [114] At the outset, however, owing to German propaganda and
German instructors in the army and the schools, there was a noticeable
friendliness towards the German cause. As the war progressed, the attitude changed, and when the United States entered the conflict, Chilean
sentiment was overwhelmingly pro-Ally. *El Mercurio* seemed to express
the common feeling: "The nations of South America, bound to the United
States by historic bonds and by the intellectual relations which are being
daily perfected, are today more than ever obliged to sustain the cause
which President Wilson defends." [115] Throughout the war the country's
vast stores of nitrate were entirely at the Allies' disposal, and the importance of this assistance cannot be overestimated. After the war Chile
joined the League of Nations, but with the express reservation that the
treaty of Ancon would not be submitted to the League.

The Alessandri government, which lasted from the president's inauguration in December, 1921, until his resignation in September, 1924, was
one of great friendliness to the United States. In fact it was in the American embassy that he sought refuge after his resignation, and the
American ambassador, Mr. Collier, accompanied him on the special train
which took him to the Argentine frontier.[116] His enforced departure was

[111] *Ibid.*, 1910, pp. 130-132.
[112] *Ibid.*, 1911, pp. 38-53.
[113] *U. S. Stat. at Large*, Vol. XXXIX, Part II, p. 1645.
[114] *Amer. Jour. of Int. Law*, Vol. XIV (Apr., 1920), p. 333.
[115] P. A. Martin, "Latin America and the War," *League of Nations* (Boston, 1919),
Vol. II, p. 257. See also C. S. Vildósola (P. H. Goldsmith, trans.), *Chile and the War*
(Washington, D. C., Carnegie Endowment for Int. Peace, 1917).
[116] Evans, Jr, *op. cit.*, p. 193.

due largely to financial difficulties caused by the reduced sales of nitrate, which cut sharply into the export tax receipts that formed a substantial part of the government's revenue. When the new government proved even less successful than the preceding, President Alessandri was invited to return.

One of his first acts was to invite a commission of financial experts headed by Professor Edwin Kemmerer of Princeton to devise measures to put Chile on a stronger financial basis. As a result of recommendations by this group, a Federal Reserve Bank was established in August, 1925, and a new banking law made effective in March, 1926. But the income from the nitrate taxes continued to diminish, and on the first of October Alessandri again resigned, owing to opposition to his policies, but not before putting into effect the more democratic constitution of 1925 which is still Chile's organic law. His successor also found himself unable to cope with the situation, and handed over the office in February, 1927, to General Carlos Ibañez, a man of strong personality whose overweening ambition and flagrant violations of the newly won constitutional guarantees brought about a *coup d'état* which sent him into exile in 1931. After another short period of revolutionary turmoil, the people welcomed back the liberal Alessandri and kept him in office from 1932 to 1938.

One of his chief accomplishments was the reorganization of the nitrate industry whose ever diminishing income was a serious blow to the nation's financial assets. This Chilean monopoly which in 1913 produced over one-half of the world's supply of nitrogen was furnishing in 1932 only about 4 per cent. In 1930 the government went into partnership with the nitrate "oficinas" and removed the export tax so as to compete with the synthetic product. When this failed to achieve the hoped-for results, Alessandri fostered a new organization to make a government monopoly of exports of nitrate and iodine under an agency known as the Chilean Nitrate and Iodine Sales Corporation. Since United States citizens had invested about $58,000,000 in the two principal nitrate companies and the United States was the principal outlet for the product, this effort to reëstablish the nitrate industry in Chile was regarded with sympathetic interest. Although the improvement was not remarkable, the average annual export since 1933 has been about 1,500,000 metric tons as against the 270,000 tons of 1932-1933.

The success of the Alessandri administration presaged the election in 1938 of the governmental candidate Don Gustavo Ross, but a *coup* in September, 1938, by Jorge Gonzalez von Marees, a Chilean impregnated with Nazi ideas, upset the political situation. The *coup* failed; von Marees and his candidate General Ibañez were thrown into prison and a considerable number of their followers shot. In the reaction which followed, the Popular Front candidate, Pedro Aguirre Cerda, was elected by a majority of a few thousand votes.

The Popular Front Government of Aguirre Cerda was a new deal for Chile with decidedly leftist tendencies. Its program included better housing for the lower classes, improved health and educational conditions, labor legislation, and additional social reforms. Its foreign policy was very friendly to the United States. Aguirre Cerda was an ardent admirer of Franklin D. Roosevelt's policies both domestic and foreign. Unfortunately Aguirre Cerda died in office late in 1941 and his successor, Juan Antonio Rios, although elected upon a platform of continental solidarity was very loath to break off relations with the Axis powers. Many reasons were offered to account for President Rios' hesitant attitude: resentment against outside pressure, Chile's 2600 miles of unprotected coastline, and the inability of the United States to assist effectively in its defense, the important Nazi element, particularly in army circles, and the unwillingness or inability of Washington to clear priority orders.

The announcement of a proposed visit of President Rios to the United States in the fall of 1942 at the invitation of President Roosevelt aroused much speculation as to an early severance of diplomatic relations with the Axis. However, when it was evident that no break would occur before President Rios began his trip, Undersecretary of State Sumner Welles declared in a public address in Boston on October 8, 1942, that certain American republics were not preventing Axis espionage which had resulted in the sinking of ships and the loss of lives in the Western Hemisphere. The Chilean government immediately entered a vigorous protest and followed by postponing the visit of President Rios. President Roosevelt voiced his regret at the postponement and expressed the hope that President Rios would come later but did not withdraw the accusation.

On October 20, 1942, the entire Chilean cabinet resigned and in the new cabinet the former Chilean ambassador to Uruguay, Joaquin Fernandez y Fernandez, took the portfolio of foreign affairs and Dr. Raul Morales Beltrami who had followed a vigorous policy as Minister of Interior in attempting to curb Axis operations was reappointed. When on November 5, the Inter-American Committee for Political Defense which was meeting in Montevideo released Ambassador Bowers' memorandum on Nazi subversive activities to the Chilean government, Dr. Morales announced that twelve Nazi suspects which the government had been investigating would be immediately expelled if found within Chilean jurisdiction. Matters now rapidly came to a head. On December 7, Minister of Interior Morales came to the United States on what was stated to be a private trip for reasons of health. Nevertheless, his conferences with President Roosevelt, Vice-president Wallace, and Undersecretary of State Welles betokened a policy of closer coöperation. Immediately upon his return he made a report to the Chilean president and cabinet, and on January 20, 1943, the Senate by a vote of thirty to ten approved the severance of diplomatic relations with the Axis powers. This action of Chile left Argentina as the only area still open to Nazi espionage and sabotage activities. As to Japan it remained to be seen whether she would carry out her threat to attack the vulnerable Chilean power stations on the long and exposed Pacific coast.

The war necessarily increased materially Chile's commercial relations with the United States. Whereas in 1939 only 31 per cent of Chilean trade was with the United States, in 1941 the figure had risen to 60 per cent. The value also increased from about $69 million to about $165 million. The United States supplies most of Chile's petroleum, iron and steel sheets, tin plate, automobiles, tires, and tubes. Chile sends by far the largest share of its principal minerals, copper and nitrates, to the United States. During the first six months of 1942 Chile's agricultural exports to the United States amounted to over $6 million, approximately 65 per cent of the total value of her exported agricultural products.

Chile's principal contribution to the war was her increased production of vital strategic materials. Not only is Chile the world's greatest storehouse of nitrates, but she holds first place in Latin America in the production of copper—her 1941 production amounted to 465,000 tons, and a rise to over 500,000 was achieved in 1942. The United States through Metals Reserve Co. contracted for a period of three years for practically all Chilean copper not sold to other American countries. Preclusive purchasing agreements were signed to cover all other strategic materials available such as manganese, lead, zinc, antimony, wolframite, molybdenum, cobalt ores, and refined mercury.

On the other hand the Export Import Bank of the United States made substantial loans to Chile for railway equipment and the purchase of industrial and agricultural products and machinery. Over $25 million was authorized and almost $10 million disbursed. The claim was made in the Chilean Chamber of Deputies during a debate in October, 1941, that the United States through lend-lease arrangements had offered Chile $50 million of which Chile only need repay $15 million. Whether true or not such a loan was contingent upon Chile's break with the Axis powers and when that failed to materialize the value of war equipment sent was limited to the amount already under contract. But when a break with the Axis finally occurred, negotiations were quickly resumed and announcement was made early in March, 1943, that a new lend-lease arrangement had been signed.

This was followed by a contract whereby the United States agreed to purchase Chilean copper at a higher price, also gold and manganese, both of which were in plentiful supply, in order to help the Chilean economy. Chile responded by coöperating effectively in checking all further subversive activities during the period of the war.

The economic situation of Chile was weakened by labor difficulties, strikes, and a drastic rise in the cost of living. When President Rios died in 1946 before his term had expired, a bitter campaign gave no candidate a majority and the Congress chose the radical Gonzales Videla who had the support of the Communist Party. The United States was much disturbed when the President gave three seats in his cabinet to the Communists. However, when the Communists began to abuse their powers and brought about a strike in the copper mines, President Gonzales Videla forced the resignation of the Communist ministers and broke off diplomatic relations with the U.S.S.R., Jugoslavia, and Czechoslovakia.

A slight flurry in the diplomatic relations between the United States and Chile occurred in 1951, when President Truman on March 26 proposed a slight revision of the Tacna-Arica settlement. Speaking, off the cuff, since the suggestion does not appear in the text of his prepared address as given to the press, President Truman declared that while talking with the President of Chile he had suggested a diversion of the waters from the high mountain lakes between Bolivia and Peru for making a garden on the West Coast of South America in return for which Chile and Peru would give Bolivia a seaport on the Pacific. The idea was not received with pleasure by the nationalists of either country and the matter was quickly dropped.[117]

During the campaign for the presidency in the spring of 1952, General Carlos Ibáñez del Campo was alleged to be opposed to the bilateral military agreement signed between Chile and the United States on April 9. However, after his election in September he declared that he wished to maintain good relations with the United States and denied any immediate intention of abrogating the United States-Chilean Pact.[118]

A serious economic situation was brought about towards the end of

[117] *Bull. of the Dept. of State* (Apr. 9, 1951), p. 568.
[118] *Ibid.* (Apr. 21, 1952), p. 630.

1953 by the fall in the price of copper and the large surplus remaining in Chilean hands. The United States made several proposals to take part of the surplus but the conditions imposed were not satisfactory to the Chilean government. Meanwhile the American copper companies (Anaconda and Kennecott) continued to seek more favorable exchange arrangements. An agreement was reached in January, 1954, whereby the price of copper was henceforth to be determined by the world market price and the United States agreed in March, 1954, to buy 100,000 tons of copper at the market price of 30¢ per pound to reduce the huge surplus on hand in Chile.

Chile and the United States have every reason to be the best of friends. Chile's oil resources have not been developed and she is utilizing all available coal, yet she must industrialize to live. The United States can furnish the hydroelectric machinery and other essential equipment required and can take a substantial amount of Chile's wealth of minerals. Chile needs rolling stock badly which the United States except in times of war can readily supply. The United States lacking Japanese labor should be able to take a considerable quantity of Chilean vegetables, fruits, and wine. Announcement was made in October, 1939, that a reciprocal trade agreement was to be negotiated with Chile. Unfortunately the opposition of United States labor and industry to concession on Chilean copper and copper products prevented its conclusion.

The Chileans have been well named the Yanquis of South America. They are a very friendly people and quite sympathetic to their cousins of the north. The North American traveler always finds the atmosphere of Chile most pleasing and congenial. With the completion of the Pan American Highway and with cheaper air and water transportation, the beauties of Chile's lakes and mountains should bring thousands of North Americans to visit the Switzerland of South America.

SUPPLEMENTARY READINGS

C. E. AKERS, A History of South America, 1854-1904 (New York, 1912), pp. 321-504.

DIEGO BARROS ARANA, Un Decenio de la Historia de Chile, 2 vols. (Santiago), 1913).

———, Histoire de la guerre du Pacifique, 2 vols. (Paris, 1881).

———, Historia jeneral de Chile, 16 Vols. (Santiago, 1887).

ENRIQUE BRIEBA, Limites entre Chile y Peru, 3 vols. (Santiago de Chile, 1931).

GONZALO BULNES, La Guerra del Pacifico, 3 vols. (Valparaiso, 1912-1919).

GILBERT J. BUTLAND, Chile (London, 1951).

F. GARCÍA CALDERÓN, Latin America: Its Rise and Progress (London, 1913), pp. 154-179.

STEPHEN CLISSOLD, *Chilean Scrapbook* (New York, 1952).

T. C. DAWSON, *South American Republics* (New York, 1904), Vol. II, pp. 135-231.

W. J. DENNIS, *Tacna and Arica; an Account of the Chile-Peru Boundary Dispute and of the Arbitrations by the United States* (New Haven, Conn., 1931).

G. F. S. ELLIOT, *Chile; Its History and Development* (New York, 1909).

PAUL T. ELLSWORTH, *Chile: An Economy in Transition* (New York, 1945).

H. C. EVANS, JR., *Chile and the United States* (Durham, N. C., 1927).

ERNA FERGUSON, *Chile* (New York, 1943).

LUIS GALDAMES, (I. J. Fox, trans.), *A History of Chile* (Chapel Hill, N. C., 1941).

JOHN GUNTHER, *Inside Latin America* (New York, 1941), pp. 234-270.

E. P. HANSON, *Chile, Land of Progress* (New York, 1941).

HUBERT HERRING, *Good Neighbors* (New Haven, Conn., 1941), pp. 167-244.

L. E. JOYCE, *Chile Today and Tomorrow* (New York, 1922).

C. A. LOGAN and F. G. CALDERÓN, *Mediación de los Estados Unidos de Norte Americana en la Guerra del Pacífico* (Buenos Aires, 1884).

GEORGE M. McBRIDE, *Chile, Land and Society* (New York, 1936).

F. J. MAITLAND, *Chile, Its Land and People* (London, 1914).

R. E. MANSFIELD, *Progressive Chile* (New York, 1913).

C. R. MARKHAM, *The War between Peru and Chile, 1879-82* (London, 1883).

V. M. MAURTUA (Pezet's trans.), *The Question of the Pacific* (Philadelphia, 1901).

HERBERT MILLINGTON, *American Diplomacy and the War of the Pacific* (New York, 1948).

G. J. MILLS, *Chile* (New York, 1914).

J. FRED RIPPY, P. A. MARTIN, I. J. COX, *Argentina, Brazil and Chile since Independence* (Washington, D. C., 1935).

W. R. SHERMAN, *The Diplomatic and Commercial Relations of the United States and Chile* (Boston, 1926).

JOHN R. STEVENSON, *The Chilean Popular Front* (Philadelphia, 1942).

G. H. STUART, "The Tacna-Arica Dispute," *World Peace Foundation Pamphlets*, Vol. X, No. 1 (Boston, 1927).

BENJAMIN SUBERCASEAUX (Angel Flores, trans.), *Chile, A Geographic Extravaganza* (New York, 1943).

RAMON S. VALDE, *Historia de Chile*, 4 vols. (Santiago, 1900).

ARTHUR P. WHITAKER, *The United States and South America* (Cambridge, 1948).

❧ 18 ❧

The United States
and Brazil

THE United States of Brazil is the giant of Latin-American countries. In fact, it is about a quarter of a million square miles larger than the United States, exclusive of Alaska, Hawaii, and Puerto Rico. It is also a very sparsely settled country, averaging only about nine persons to the square mile, as compared with forty-one to the square mile in the United States. Nevertheless, because of its size it contains as many people within its borders as all the rest of South America combined. As one writer has put it, if Brazil were as densely populated as Belgium at the outbreak of the first World War, its territory would hold more human beings than exist at present on the entire face of the earth.[1] When speaking of Brazil one is almost compelled to use superlatives. It has the greatest river system in the world; it has the longest unbroken coast-line of any country in the world; its vast tropical forests and jungles have never yet been completely explored; its mineral wealth is as yet untapped; its agricultural possibilities are boundless.

In considering the Latin-American republics, Brazil must be placed in a class by itself for other reasons than its size. Its population is primarily of Portuguese stock, whereas all the rest of Latin America is largely Spanish. Its history, too, has been cast in an entirely different mold from that of its neighbors. Discovered by a Portuguese navigator in 1500, its early settlements were made by noble adventurers who were given vast tracts of land, or captaincies, where their powers were practically supreme. Later on it was unified into a single viceroyalty. But the strong, sturdy characteristics of these feudal lords and their followers have left a lasting imprint upon the country's history.

[1] C. S. Cooper, *The Brazilians and Their Country* (New York, 1917), p. 97.

413

Napoleon Bonaparte, whose influence on the New World, although indirect, has had momentous consequences, might almost be called the founder of modern Brazil. For it was his treacherous invasion of Portugal in 1807 that caused the royal Braganza family to flee to Brazil, transferring with it to Rio the seat of its government. Thus, at a period when all the rest of South America was straining at the bonds of royal sovereignty, Brazil was binding herself even more closely with imperial trappings. The immediate result, however, of Dom John's rule was to open Brazilian ports to the commerce of the world, to introduce the latest inventions of European genius, to repeal laws impeding progress and advancement, and to give the western kingdom the advantage of a government under the direction of a cultivated and enlightened, though rather weak-minded, ruler.[2]

In the meantime a regency was governing in Lisbon. But in 1820 a revolution took place in Portugal, and the result was the formation of a *junta* which was resolved upon a constitutional government, retaining the Braganza dynasty. The revolution spread to Brazil, and Dom John wisely decided to accept the proposed constitution. Shortly afterwards he sailed for Portugal, leaving his son Dom Pedro as regent of Brazil. In parting he foretold the separation of Brazil from the mother country and urged his son to seize the crown rather than allow it to pass to some adventurer.[3] His prediction was speedily verified. In the same year the Cortes at Lisbon passed decrees recalling Prince Pedro and reducing Brazil to a provincial status. The protest from Brazil was quick and decisive. Provisional *juntas* urged Pedro to remain, and he agreed to do so. When the Cortes threatened violence he called a constituent assembly, assumed the title of "Perpetual Defender and Protector of Brazil," and on October 12, 1822, was crowned "Constitutional Emperor of Brazil." The revolution was almost bloodless, and in less than a year after the declaration of independence every Portuguese garrison was driven from Brazilian soil.

The early relations of the United States with Brazil were not so friendly as they have become today. The first American minister to the Portuguese court at Rio de Janiero was Thomas Sumpter, Jr., whose duty it was to smooth the way for a permanent and cordial relationship, both political and commercial, with whatever form of government might be established. He presented his credentials in 1810 and immediately endeavored to obtain most favored nation treatment for American goods. He was not

[2] The standard history of this period is M. de Oliveira Lima, *Don João VI do Brazil*, 2 vols. (Rio de Janeiro, 1911).

[3] F. G. Calderón, *Latin America: Its Rise and Progress* (New York, 1913), p. 182.

successful, however, and his position at the Court was not improved by his refusal to accept the very undemocratic court etiquette. When on one occasion the royal guards attempted to make him dismount at the passage of the royal family, he drew his pistols and threatened to shoot. Although Mr. Sumpter and his family became very unpopular in Rio for a period, the ultimate result was the annulment of this regulation for foreign diplomats.[4]

Another little incident occurred in 1818 to embarrass Mr. Sumpter's position. The U. S. frigate *Congress* had brought dispatches to Sumpter and during the visit one of the seamen, of Portuguese nationality, got into trouble on shore and resisted the efforts of the ship's officers to place him on board. He was later taken from the local jail by force by an American contingent. The Brazilian foreign minister objected to this action and demanded his return and an apology. The American commander apologized for the acts of his officers, but sailed away with his crew intact in spite of threats to detain him.[5]

At the beginning of the nineteenth century privateering was unquestionably a profitable source of income to many American ship-owners. Baltimore's reputation as a rendezvous of privateers became so notorious that at the conference of Aix-la-Chapelle in 1818 the Portuguese government submitted a memorial on the subject, and the powers agreed to take up the question in a friendly fashion with the United States.[6] Undoubtedly Brazil was back of the Portuguese protest, because it was Brazil that had suffered particularly through this practice. The Banda Oriental, now the Republic of Uruguay, had been seized by the Portuguese in 1816 from Artigas and his Argentinian forces. Artigas, however, could not afford to lose Montevideo; hence he engaged a number of privateers to prey upon Portuguese commerce. The Abbé Correa, the Portuguese minister to the United States, asserted that the greater part of these privateers were fitted out and manned in the ports of the United States. Adams conceded not only that this abomination had spread over a large portion of the merchants and population of Baltimore, but that it had infected almost every officer of the United States in the place.[7] He also realized that Brazil had very good cause for complaint; in fact, the

[4] Lawrence F. Hill, *Diplomatic Relations Between the United States and Brazil* (Durham, N. C., 1932), p. 7.

[5] A. M. Breckenridge, *A Voyage to South America performed by the Order of the American Government in the years 1817 and 1818 in the Frigate Congress* (Baltimore, 1819), Vol. I, pp. 92 *ff.*

[6] J. Q. Adams, *Memoirs* (Philadelphia, 1874-1877), Vol. IV, p. 317.

[7] *Ibid.*, p. 318.

situation was so serious that if the positions were reversed the United States would have considered the injuries sufficient for a declaration of war.[8] The Abbé Correa was exceedingly pessimistic over the outlook and declared that "these things had produced such a temper both in Portugal and Brazil against the people and government of the United States that . . . they were now those whom they most hated, and if the government [of Portugal] had considered the peace as at an end, they would have been supported in the declaration by the hearty concurrence of the people." [9]

Fortunately, by 1820 the power of Artigas was completely broken. In 1821 the Banda Oriental was incorporated into the Portuguese dominions of Brazil, and when the independence of the Brazilian Empire was proclaimed in 1822 this Cis-Platine province was regarded as a part of it. A more friendly relationship between the United States and Brazil now ensued, and it was confirmed in 1824, when President Monroe became the first to recognize the independence of the new empire. At the cabinet meeting where the question was brought up Mr. Wirt opposed recognition on the ground that the government was monarchical and not republican; but both Calhoun and Adams favored recognition on the basis of independence alone, leaving aside all consideration of internal government.[10]

When the Brazilian *chargé* José Rebello, was received by President Monroe, May 26, 1824, he suggested a concert of American powers to sustain the general system of American independence, and in the following year he proposed a definite offensive and defensive alliance between the United States and Brazil against European intervention.[11] Monroe declined the proposal in private to Adams; but no official reply was made until Adams became President, when Clay declared that the prospect of a speedy peace between Portugal and Brazil seemed to make such an alliance unnecessary.[12]

At the close of 1825 a war broke out between Brazil and Buenos Aires over the possession of the Banda Oriental, which once more brought about strained relations between Brazil and the United States. Brazil had declared a blockade on all Argentine ports, and the American *chargé*,

[8] *Ibid.*, Vol. V., p. 177.

[9] W. C. Ford, ed., *Writings of John Quincy Adams* (New York, 1913-1917), Vol. VII, p. 70.

[10] Adams, *op. cit.*, Vol. VI, p. 281.

[11] *Ibid.*, pp. 358, 475, 484; also J. B. Moore, *Digest of Int. Law*, Vol. VI, p. 437.

[12] See W. S. Robertson, "South America and the Monroe Doctrine," *Polit. Sci. Quar.*, Vol. XXX (Mar., 1915), pp. 82-105; also *For. Rel. of the U. S.*, 1906, Part I, pp. 116-121.

Mr. Condy Raguet, had protested on the ground that Brazil would not be able to make such a blockade effective. In the second place, he warned Brazil that the United States "have always denied the doctrine of general and diplomatic notifications of blockades as binding upon their citizens," and therefore no vessel could be seized as a prize for running the blockade unless it had been specifically warned.[13] Brazil, however, paid little attention to Mr. Raguet's protests, and even gave him further grounds for recriminations by impressing American seamen into the Brazilian navy. The constant infringement of American rights infuriated Raguet to such a point that his notes to the Brazilian government were not always couched in the most diplomatic language. A crisis was reached on March 4, 1827, when an American vessel, the *Spark*, which had cleared regularly from Rio for Montevideo, was seized just outside of the harbor by a Brazilian warship and brought back as a prize, and its crew treated almost as pirates.[14] Mr. Raguet despatched a brief note to the Brazilian minister of foreign affairs asking for an explanation. The latter replied that the brig had increased her crew in Rio, that it had a warlike equipment with no license for it, and that therefore it was seized on the suspicion of being a privateer. The American *chargé* answered that if the government had thought proper to communicate its suspicions to him before the *Spark* had cleared, he would have cheerfully lent his aid in causing the suspicions to be removed. As it was, he declined to give any explanations. The next day he asked for his passports, and the Emperor, although "surprised at this precipitate request, couched in abrupt and vague language," ordered them to be delivered, but with the notice that the American representative would be answerable to his government for the consequences which might result.[15]

Before the break in diplomatic relations came, both Clay and Adams became convinced that Mr. Raguet's language and conduct were not so reserved as they should have been, and in a note dated January 20, 1827, Clay wrote Raguet that the President would have been better satisfied if he had abstained from some of the language employed.[16] When news of the rupture reached Washington, Adams wrote in his diary: "He appears to have been too hasty in his proceedings and has made us much trouble, from which we can derive neither credit nor profit"; and later, after conferring with Clay, it was decided not to sustain him.[17] On May

[13] *House Ex. Doc. No. 281*, 20th Cong., 1st Sess., p. 9.
[14] *Ibid.*, p. 96.
[15] *Ibid.*, pp. 104-108.
[16] *Ibid.*, p. 108.
[17] Adams, *op. cit.*, Vol. VII, pp. 270, 272.

31, in a note to Mr. Rebello, the Brazilian *chargé*, Clay, although sustaining Mr. Raguet's protests, informed him that the latter's demand for his passports was without orders, and that, although there was an interruption of diplomatic relations at Rio de Janeiro, none existed at Washington. The secretary also promised to procure the appointment of a successor immediately, provided assurances were given that satisfaction would be rendered for the injuries inflicted upon American persons and property.[18] Mr. Rebello promptly accepted the conditions, and Mr. William Tudor, a merchant at Lima, was named as *chargé* at Rio.[19]

This appointment proved excellent in every way. By his tact, good judgment, and diplomatic handling of the many serious cases that came up, Mr. Tudor placed the relations between the two nations upon a firm basis of friendly understanding. This was doubly fortunate because throughout the period of the war the actions of the Brazilian naval officials were constantly provoking fresh complaints, and some of these, as in the case of the schooner *Hero*, were so harsh and uncalled for that Secretary Clay characterized the circumstances of the outrage as almost incredible.[20] Yet at the same time the commerce of the United States with Brazil was increasing at such a rate that Clay was very desirous of concluding a treaty of commerce and amity with her on terms favorable to the United States. Mr. Tudor was successful both in settling the claims and in negotiating the treaty. Virtually all of the claims were settled on the terms of the claimants and by diplomatic action alone; while the French, who sent a squadron of eleven ships, obtained only a third as much, and the British, who threatened direct reprisals, made no progress at all.[21] The treaty of commerce and navigation that Mr. Tudor concluded on December 12, 1828, was modeled upon the treaty concluded between the United States and Central America in 1825. The most-favored-nation clause was included, except for the relations between Brazil and Portugal, and the question of blockade was settled by declaring that only an effective blockade should be recognized. The treaty was to be in force for twelve years, and afterwards until notice of abrogation should be given by either party. The clauses regarding commerce and

[18] *Amer. State Papers, For. Rel.*, Vol. VI, p. 824. The whole incident is exhaustively treated in Hill, *op. cit.*, pp. 49-56.

[19] For a full and well documented account of these events see W. R. Manning, "An Early Diplomatic Controversy between the United States and Brazil," *Amer. Jour. of Int. Law*, Vol. XII (Apr., 1918), pp. 291-311.

[20] *House Ex. Doc. No. 32*, 25th Cong., 1st Sess., pp. 13, 66.

[21] *Ibid.*, pp. 152-221, 250.

navigation were terminated in 1841, but those providing for peace and friendship still hold.[22]

Some impression of the satisfactory services of Mr. Tudor in increasing the friendly attitude of the Brazilian government towards the United States may be obtained from the Emperor's appreciation of them. In a special audience with Mr. Tudor, which Pedro I himself suggested, the Emperor declared that he had high respect for the United States, and the most sincere desire to cultivate and forever maintain the most friendly relations with them, and that the United States might be assured that such were his real feelings and such would be his conduct.[23]

Emperor Pedro's assurances were never put to the test. His popularity was already on the wane, and early in 1831 he was virtually forced to abdicate in favor of his infant son. Various causes contributed—the expensive and unsuccessful war with Buenos Aires, which resulted in the loss of the Banda Oriental; Pedro's constant efforts to support his daughter's claims to the throne of Portugal against his brother Miguel; his harsh and unfair treatment of his wife; his struggles against constitutional government and continuous opposition to the Chamber; and, finally, the fact that at heart he was Portuguese rather than Brazilian. The period that followed was the stormiest in Brazilian history. The government under the regency was in continual conflict with the provinces. Finally, factions striving for control at Rio agreed to declare the young Pedro of age in spite of his fifteen and a half years. Accordingly, on July 23, 1840, Congress unanimously declared that the young Emperor had reached his majority, and Dom Pedro II entered upon his imperial functions.

During this period the relations of the United States with Brazil continued to be most friendly. In their annual messages, both Van Buren and Tyler gave evidence of the fact, and in 1844 President Tyler noted that "the commercial intercourse between that growing Empire and the United States is becoming daily of greater importance to both, and it is to the interest of both that the firmest relations of amity and good will should continue to be cultivated between them." [24] But in 1846 an incident occurred which, although trivial in itself, developed into a complete breach of friendly relations between the two countries for a short period.

[22] For text see Malloy, *Treaties, Conventions,* etc., Vol. I, p. 133; for termination, Moore, *op. cit.,* Vol. V, p. 403.

[23] *House Ex. Doc. No. 32,* p. 222. For President Adams' appreciation see Adams, *op. cit.,* Vol. VIII, p. 224.

[24] J. D. Richardson, *Messages and Papers of the Presidents,* Vol. IV, p. 340.

On October 31, 1846, Lieutenant Alonzo B. Davis of the U. S. frigate *Saratoga*, while on shore at Rio in pursuit of two deserters, found a sailor attached to his boat in a drunken brawl with two other American sailors. Davis interfered, disarmed the man, and was taking him back to the boat when a Brazilian guard came up, seized the three American sailors, and, after beating them severely, marched them off. Lieutenant Davis, having protested in vain, followed the patrol to the palace with a view of securing the sailors' release. However, upon entering the palace he also was seized and disarmed, and was kept in prison for two days. As soon as the American minister, Mr. Wise, learned of the occurrence, he protested vigorously to the Brazilian government, demanding the release of the imprisoned Americans, the disavowal of the outrage, and the punishment of the officers and soldiers of the Brazilian guard.[25] The Brazilian government freed Lieutenant Davis, but held the three seamen for further investigation, at the same time justifying both the conduct of the patrol and the arrest of Lieutenant Davis.

A long and acrimonious exchange of notes followed between Mr. Wise and the Brazilian foreign minister. The American minister insisted that inasmuch as Lieutenant Davis was in command of the sailor and was taking him back to the boat, and since no Brazilians were involved, the interference of the Brazilian patrol, its cruel treatment of the American seamen, and its subsequent arrest of the American officer were a direct insult to the American flag. The Brazilian government claimed that Lieutenant Davis had endeavored to interfere with the guard in its duty of preserving the peace within the sovereign jurisdiction of Brazil, and that therefore the Brazilian government was not only justified in its action, but had only surrendered the American officer as a proof of distinguished consideration for the United States.[26] The estrangement was increased by the action of Commodore Rousseau, commanding the U. S. squadron at Rio, who, indignant at the Brazilian stand, refused to salute on either the occasion of the baptism of the imperial princess or the celebration of his Majesty's birthday. All intercourse between the American minister and the Brazilian government thereupon ceased, Mr. Wise awaiting "calmly the first favorable and tangible occasion to come to explanations with them without danger of causing a more violent or open rupture, and not resenting their abuse in the newspapers, or their petty slights of not inviting me to a court, where the only reward for going and waiting for hours on a hot day in a hot uniform, is to make three bows forwards

[25] *Sen. Ex. Doc. No. 29*, 30th Cong., 1st Sess., pp. 5-16.
[26] *Ibid.*, pp. 20-42.

and three bows backwards, and then bob out of the imperial presence." [27]

An opportunity to resume friendly relations seemed to present itself in February of the following year, when Mr. Wise received despatches from Washington instructing him to request an audience from the Emperor to deliver in person the original of the answer of the President to a letter from him announcing the birth of a princess. Mr. Wise requested the audience, but was informed that, inasmuch as his acts were offensive in the respect due both to the Emperor and to the dignity of the nation, he could not be received till the Davis affair was settled. As a concession, however, the minister of foreign affairs offered to receive the President's letter and see that it reached "its high destination." [28]

In a reply couched in terms hardly conducive to more friendly relations, Mr. Wise informed the Brazilian minister that he was accredited minister to his Majesty the Emperor himself, and not as *chargé* to a minister of foreign affairs, and either he would present the President's note in person or it would never reach "its high destination."

In the meantime Mr. Lisboa, the Brazilian minister at Washington, had taken the matter up with Secretary Buchanan, but in a much more amicable fashion. He assured Mr. Buchanan that "the Brazilian government, animated always with feelings of good understanding and perfect friendship towards the United States of America, has regretted extremely this disagreeable occurrence and will adopt the means proper to prevent similar occurrences hereafter." [29] In his reply Mr. Buchanan declared that the President was entirely satisfied with this frank and honorable explanation and that the whole occurrence, as far as the United States was concerned, would henceforth be buried in oblivion. [30] The Brazilian government, however, now insisted upon the recall of Mr. Wise, which it had suggested before, but which the United States had refused to consider. It was convinced that friendship and harmony were always in danger while so excitable a gentleman as Mr. Wise continued to be minister. Furthermore, the Emperor had determined that this particular gentleman should never again be invited to court. As a matter of fact, Mr. Wise himself had already realized the futility of remaining at Rio and had already asked to be recalled, but in such a way that his acts would appear to be approved in the fullest degree by the United States. Mr. Buchanan had agreed to this, and he informed Mr. Lisboa that Mr.

[27] *Ibid.*, p. 45.
[28] *Ibid.*, p. 52.
[29] *Ibid.*, p. 134.
[30] *Ibid.*, pp. 135, 136. See also J. B. Moore, ed., *The Works of James Buchanan* (Philadelphia, 1909), Vol. VII, p. 209.

Wise would soon return, but at his own request and not because the United States did not approve of his conduct.[31] As a result, the Brazilian government opened the case by disapproving the *amende honorable* of Mr. Lisboa and recalling him.[32]

The authorities at Washington received unofficial advice of this action before Mr. Tod, the newly appointed minister to Brazil, left the United States; and in his instructions Mr. Tod was advised that the President would not recede from his ground, and that the recall of Mr. Lisboa would be regarded as unjust to him as well as disagreeable to the President.[33] Mr. Buchanan at the same time gave to Mr. Tod a sealed letter from the President of the United States to the Emperor of Brazil, to be delivered by Mr. Wise, and announcing the termination of his mission. Mr. Wise, however, was given the option of not asking for the audience if he was sure that it would not be granted.[34] Mr. Tod arrived at Rio August 7, 1847, and immediately got into touch with Mr. Wise. The latter, who had in the meantime made a further effort to renew negotiations and had been curtly repulsed, advised against seeking an audience, on the ground that the recall and disapproval of Mr. Lisboa and the refusal to receive Mr. Wise, who had been sustained and approved by the United States, constituted an additional insult to the American government.[35] After giving the advice due consideration, Mr. Tod felt that such action was contrary to the spirit of his instructions and decided to ask an audience of the Emperor to present his credentials. The audience was granted, and he was duly presented at court on August 28. Mr. Wise thereupon wrote a note to the Brazilian foreign minister, informing him that he had a sealed letter from the President to the Emperor, but as it had been written before the President knew of the recent insults to the American minister for acts that the President had fully approved, he felt it wholly incompatible with either the honor of his government or his own self-respect to ask an audience to present the letter; he therefore peremptorily demanded passports for himself and family.[36]

At approximately the same time that Mr. Tod arrived at Rio, despatches reached the Brazilian *chargé* at Washington, Mr. Leal, informing him that Brazil had taken serious offense at the acts committed by Lieutenant Davis, for which it required ample reparation. He was also

[31] *Sen. Ex. Doc.*, p. 139.
[32] *Ibid.*, pp. 108, 109.
[33] Moore, *The Works of James Buchanan*, Vol. VII, p. 328.
[34] *Ibid.*, p. 333.
[35] *Sen. Ex. Doc.*, pp. 114-131.
[36] *Ibid.*, p. 132.

to demand from the government of the United States a categorical decla-
ration that it had disapproved the conduct of its envoy, Mr. Henry A.
Wise, and that it ordered his recall as a mark of reparation due to Brazil.
If the government of the United States refused, but suggested arbitration,
the imperial government would agree to that expedient. Finally, if Mr.
Tod had already left the United States, Mr. Leal was to inform Mr.
Buchanan that the imperial government would not receive him in his
official character until satisfaction had been given.[37]

Mr. Buchanan's reply to these demands, dated August 30, 1847, showed
that, although the United States was anxious to do everything possible
to prevent a break between the two powers, it was determined to stand
by its former statements. After once more carefully outlining all the facts
of the Davis case, he declared that the United States would not grant
reparation to Brazil for the acts committed by Lieutenant Davis, since
reparation was clearly due from Brazil to the United States. The demand
that Wise be disapproved and recalled he considered most extraordinary,
inasmuch as the President had already publicly sustained his acts and
had already recalled him at his own request. The present attitude of the
Brazilian government following the amicable and honorable adjustment
made by their former representative, and the refusal to receive the
American minister, appeared to indicate that she intended an open
rupture. Yet, as this seemed inconceivable, the President would take
no decisive step until he learned that the government of Brazil actually
refused to receive the American minister.[38] The following day Secretary
Buchanan wrote to Mr. Tod advising him that if the Brazilian government refused to receive him without making the desired apology he was
to return to the United States.[39]

As we have already seen, the Brazilian government did not carry out
its threat to refuse an audience to the American minister. In a note to
Mr. Leal, dated November 17, Mr. Buchanan expressed his gratification
to learn that Mr. Tod had been kindly and courteously received by his
Imperial Majesty, and was also pleased to learn that a new minister from
Brazil would shortly be appointed to the United States. But in regard
to the differences between the two governments he had nothing to add
except to say that the President's views remained unchanged.[40] The same
sentiments were indicated by Secretary Buchanan in his next despatch
to Mr. Tod, with the further injunction that he should press the settle-

[37] Sen. Ex. Doc. No. 35, 30th Cong., 1st Sess., pp. 2-11.
[38] Ibid., pp. 28-41.
[39] Moore, The Works of James Buchanan, Vol. VII, p. 404.
[40] Ibid., p. 461.

ment of certain claims of American citizens which had long been outstanding against the Brazilian government.[41]

The interest of the American government now shifted from the settlement of these diplomatic difficulties to the settlement of claims, and
when Secretary Buchanan found that the Brazilian government apparently intended to allow the Davis affair to remain suspended, he urged
Mr. Tod to press more vigorously on the claims.[42] Mr. Tod followed
instructions, and on January 27, 1849, a claims convention was concluded
between the two countries, whereby the Brazilian government agreed
to place at the disposal of the United States 530,000 milreis (about
$300,000) to comprehend all the reclamations.[43] The same year Mr. Sergio
Texeira de Macedo was accredited envoy extraordinary and minister
plenipotentiary to the United States and duly accepted. The following
exchange of compliments between Mr. Clayton, the new Secretary of
State, and Mr. Buchanan throw some light on the outcome: "If I go
to the devil it will be because I am here daily engaged in covering
up and defending all your outrageous acts. . . . The Brazilian Macedo
laboured hard to revive your haughty discussion about Lieut. Davis and
the drunken seamen in Rio. I refused to revive it, assumed you were
altogether right (God assoilzie me for that) and dismissed him with
compliments." Mr. Buchanan's reply to this was that "the Brazilian quarrel, which gave fair promise at one time of producing a tempest in a
teapot, was virtually settled by your predecessor in the only effectual
manner by assuming a just and lofty attitude in support of the lamblike
Wise." [44]

The diplomatic relations between the United States and Brazil thenceforth became increasingly friendly. During the Civil War, Brazil gave
numerous examples of a friendly disposition towards the Northern government, even though it insisted upon granting to the Southern states the
status of belligerents. Upon one occasion, when the *Alabama* captured
some half-dozen American whalers in Brazilian territorial waters, and
in the meantime lay in the port of the island of Fernando de Noronha
(also under Brazilian sovereignty), Mr. Webb, the American minister,
raised a vigorous protest. The Brazilian government immediately investigated the case, and when it learned that the commanding officer of the
island had been over-friendly to the captain of the *Alabama* he was

[41] *Ibid.*, p. 462.
[42] *Ibid.*, Vol. VIII, p. 60.
[43] *House Ex. Doc. No. 19*, 31st Cong., 1st Sess., p. 1. For terms of distribution see
J. B. Moore, *Hist. and Digest of Int. Arbitrations*, Vol. V, pp. 4609-4626.
[44] Moore, *The Works of James Buchanan*, Vol. VIII, p. 359.

forthwith dismissed and proceedings begun against him. At the same time, the president of the province of Pernambuco gave the captain of the *Alabama* notice to leave the territorial waters of the empire within twenty-four hours.[45] On a later occasion information was again brought to Mr. Webb that the Confederate cruisers *Alabama, Florida,* and *Georgia* were obtaining coal and provisions in the ports of Pernambuco and Bahia in order to continue their destruction of the commerce of the United States.[46] Upon receiving Mr. Webb's protest, the Brazilian foreign minister again gave assurances that his Majesty the Emperor was firmly resolved to maintain, and cause to be respected, the neutrality of Brazil.[47]

The Confederate States, however, were not alone in violating the neutral territory of Brazil. On October 4, 1863, the *Florida* arrived at Bahia and was given forty-eight hours by the authorities to repair her boilers and obtain provisions and coal. The U. S. S. *Wachusett* happened to be in the harbor at the time, but the American consul was said to have given a pledge for the observance of neutrality by the vessel's commander. In spite of this, the *Wachusett* approached the *Florida* on the morning of October 7, and opened fire upon her. The commander of the Brazilian naval division intervened, and the firing ceased; but shortly afterwards it was seen that the *Wachusett* was towing the *Florida* out to sea. The Brazilian commander pursued but could not overtake her, and the *Florida* was brought to Hampton Roads. The Brazilian government thereupon demanded (1) a public expression on the part of the Union government that this action was regretted and condemned; (2) the immediate dismissal of the United States commander, followed by the commencement of proper process; and (3) a salute of twenty-one guns, to be given in the port of the capital of Bahia by some vessel of war of the United States, having hoisted at her masthead during the salute the Brazilian flag. In a note to the Brazilian government dated December 26, 1864, Mr. Seward replied that the President disavowed and regretted the proceedings at Bahia; that he would suspend the commander of the *Wachusett* and direct him to appear before a court martial; that the consul, who admitted having advised and incited the commander, would be dismissed; and that the flag of Brazil would receive from the United States Navy the honor customary in the intercourse of friendly maritime powers. This would be done on the ground that the capture of the *Florida* was an unauthorized, unlawful, and indefensible exercise of the naval

[45] *Diplomatic Correspondence of the United States,* 1863, Part II, pp. 1164-1169.
[46] *Ibid.,* p. 1171.
[47] *Ibid.,* p. 1177.

force of the United States within a foreign country, in defiance of its established and duly recognized government.[48] The salute was fired by Commander F. B. Blake in the harbor of Bahia on July 23, 1866, and the *Diario da Bahia* thus characterized the event: "It is thus that a great and spirited people give, in the face of the civilized world, a public and solemn proof of the sincerity of its professions of the sacred principles of justice." [49]

Just as the Civil War was coming to an end in the United States, Brazil was forced to enter a war which, although successful, imposed a heavy burden upon her people. The Paraguayan dictator, Francisco López, had been much incensed at Brazil's interference in a factional struggle in Uruguay in 1863. It was also rumored that Dom Pedro II had refused to entertain the dictator's proposals for his daughter's hand. At any rate, in the fall of 1864 López seized a Brazilian steamer on its regular trip up the Paraguayan River to Matto Grosso. He followed this up with an expedition against the southern settlements of Matto Grosso, which were wholly unable to resist his well-disciplined troops. Brazil accepted the challenge, although she was by no means equipped to combat the wonderfully trained army that López had been preparing for years. Argentina, although in sympathy with Brazil, declared her neutrality. López, however, confident of his power, deliberately invaded Argentinian territory at the Parana River in order to strike at the heart of Brazil. The result was a coalition against him on the part of Argentina, Brazil, and Uruguay, a formal alliance being signed May 1, 1865.[50]

The war lasted five years and resulted in the death of López and the almost complete extermination of the Paraguayan people. "The heroism of Paraguay overcame numbers, destiny, and death," but to no avail. Out of a million and a quarter people living in Paraguay before the war, more than a million had perished, and of the less than a quarter of a million who survived more than five-sixths were women and children. Brazil played the leading part in the war and her losses were correspondingly great. It was estimated that the war cost her more than 50,000 lives and $300 million. Considering her sacrifices, Brazil deserves all the more credit for making no effort to extend her territory at the expense of her vanquished and helpless neighbor. By a preliminary agreement of peace, signed June 20, 1870, the allies' demands were limited to the establishment of complete freedom of navigation for the warships and merchant-

[48] Moore, *Digest of Int. Law*, Vol. VII, p. 1090. See also Hill, *op. cit.*, pp. 155-158.
[49] *Diplomatic Correspondence*, 1866, Part II, p. 317.
[50] For text see *ibid.*, p. 476; for a fair summary of causes of the war see *Dip. Corr.*, 1867, Part II, pp. 248-250; the Paraguayan side is given in pp. 722-725.

vessels of the allies upon the Upper Parana and the Paraguay.[51] A definitive treaty of peace was signed between Brazil and Paraguay, January 9, 1872, whereby Brazil promised to respect perpetually Paraguay's independence, sovereignty, and integrity. The rivers Paraguay, Parana, and Uruguay were declared free to the commerce of all nations, and the boundaries between Brazil and Paraguay were to be settled by a special convention.[52]

During the progress of the Paraguayan war a number of diplomatic incidents occurred in which the United States was interested. Early in 1866 Mr. Charles A. Washburn, the minister of the United States to Paraguay, informed his government that he was being prevented by the allies from passing up the Parana River to Asunción; although it appears from his despatches that an equal source of delay was the failure of Admiral Godon, in command of the American fleet, to furnish a boat with which to run the blockade. Secretary Seward protested vigorously, both to Brazil and to Argentina; and they finally gave the necessary orders, although under protest. Even then, Mr. Washburn was delayed considerably through Admiral Godon's lack of coöperation, and it was not until a year after he had tried to return that the American minister finally arrived at his post.[53] An even more serious diplomatic controversy occurred the following year, when Rear-Admiral Davis sent the U. S. S. *Wasp* up the Parana to convey Mr. Washburn and his family back to the United States. Permission was again refused by the Marquis de Caxias, and it was only when Mr. Webb, the American minister at Rio, threatened to ask for his passports that the *Wasp* was enabled to carry out the mission.[54]

All efforts on the part of the United States to use its good offices to settle the Paraguayan struggle were refused unconditionally by Brazil. In fact, Brazil appeared less inclined than Argentina to accept mediation.[55] An attempt on the part of Mr. Washburn to secure a similar result by a personal visit to the Marquis de Caxias, the Brazilian commander-in-chief, was equally unsuccessful.[56]

[51] *British and Foreign State Papers*, Vol. LXIII, p. 322. For a survey of the operations and results of the war see C. E. Akers, *A History of South America, 1854-1904* (New York, 1904), pp. 130-188.

[52] *British and Foreign State Papers*, Vol. LXII, p. 277.

[53] *Diplomatic Correspondence*, 1866, Part II, pp. 307-326, 548-616. For an adversely critical discussion of the United States policy see Hill, *op. cit.*, pp. 187-195. The position of the United States was sound, however, according to long established precedents of international law.

[54] *Dip. Corr.*, 1868, pp. 273-299.

[55] *Ibid.*, 1867, Part II, p. 253.

[56] *Ibid.*, p. 714.

Perhaps the most satisfactory occurrence of this period to the United States was the decree of the Emperor of Brazil, dated January 22, 1866, opening up the Amazon, San Francisco, and other rivers to the merchant-ships of all nations. Ever since 1850 the United States had been sedulously striving to accomplish this result, on the ground that "this restricted policy which it is understood Brazil still persists in maintaining in regard to the navigable rivers passing through her territories is the relic of an age less enlightened than the present," and the merchant-vessels of the United States had the right to use these natural avenues of trade, not because of treaty stipulations, but because "it is a natural one—as much so as that to navigate the ocean—the common highway of nations." [57]

During the period following the war with Paraguay, Dom Pedro II was seen at his best. His upright and conservative character inspired confidence, and Brazil had little difficulty in obtaining the loans necessary to effect a financial rehabilitation. Nor did his success make him more autocratic or blind him to the need of progressive ideas. By visits to both Europe and the United States he broadened his point of view, and Brazil profited exceedingly by the statesmanlike policy of her enlightened ruler. Nevertheless, a growing sentiment in favor of republicanism was everywhere manifest. The general disposition seemed to be to allow the monarchical system to continue during the lifetime of the Emperor, but to assume that when the Princess Izabel and her unpopular consort, the Comte d'Eu, should take over the government it would be time to consider the wisdom of retaining a monarchical system in an otherwise republican continent.

The crisis came sooner than was expected. While the Emperor was traveling in Europe in 1887 for the betterment of his health, Princess Izabel, acting as regent, determined to abolish slavery. Laws had already been passed granting freedom to all children of slaves born after 1871, and to all slaves attaining the age to sixty years, but this process was considered too slow. The Princess insisted that a decree of immediate emancipation of all slaves in the empire be passed; and on May 15, 1888, the measure became law. Although there was no immediate outbreak on the part of the wealthy slave-owners and the landed aristocracy, the monarchical party, through this decree, lost its strongest prop, republican propaganda, revolutionary agitation spread rapidly, and the situation of the government became critical. Dom Pedro's return in August, 1888,

[57] Mr. Marcy to the American minister to Brazil, Aug. 8, 1853; Moore, *Digest of Int. Law*, Vol. I, pp. 640-645. For the full correspondence see W. R. Manning, *Diplomatic Correspondence of the United States—Inter-American Affairs 1831-86* (Washington, D. C., 1932), Vol. II, *passim*.

stemmed the tide temporarily, but in the following year the military element threw in its lot with the republicans and decided upon an immediate *coup d'état*. The plans were made carefully and were carried out without a hitch. Early in the morning of November 15, 1889, the imperial palace was surrounded and the Emperor and his family were arrested. A proclamation announced the deposition of the Emperor and the establishment of a republican form of government with a provisional president at the head. There was neither bloodshed nor confusion, and a few days later the Emperor and his family were sent back to Portugal.[58]

It was to be expected that the United States would look with favor upon the new convert to republican institutions, and on February 19, 1890, the Senate and House of Representatives passed a joint resolution congratulating the people of the United States of Brazil on their adoption of a republican form of government.[59] Meanwhile the American minister had been instructed to maintain diplomatic relations with the provisional government and to give it a formal and cordial recognition "so soon as a majority of the people of Brazil should have signified their assent to the establishment and maintenance of the Republic."[60]

General Deodora da Fonseca, the provisional president, summoned a national congress, which met at Rio de Janeiro on November 15, 1890, to consider a draft of a constitution submitted by the provisional government. As finally adopted on February 24, 1891, the "Law of Constitution" established a federal system of government modeled very closely upon that of the United States. A president and vice-president elected directly for a four-year term, assisted by six secretaries of state appointed by the president, constitute the executive authority. The legislature consists of a Senate of sixty-three members, three from each state and three from the federal district, elected for a nine-year term, and a Chamber of Deputies, in the proportion of not more than one for each 70,000 inhabitants, elected directly for a three-year term. The judicial power is vested in a supreme federal court of fifteen members. The states are given almost complete autonomy, except for matters that are purely national in scope. In theory Brazil now had a perfect type of representative republican government, although an arduous struggle and considerable bloodshed were required to put the theory into practice.[61]

[58] See the scholarly article by Professor P. A. Martin, "Causes of the Collapse of the Brazilian Empire," *Hispanic American Historical Review*, Vol. IV, No. 1 (Feb., 1921), pp. 1-48.

[59] *For. Ref. of the U. S.*, 1890, p. 21.

[60] Moore, *Digest of Int. Law*, Vol. I, p. 160.

[61] For text of the constitution see W. F. Dodd, *Modern Constitutions* (Chicago, 1909), Vol. I.

Before the end of 1891 President Fonseca had brought on a series of revolutionary outbreaks through his arbitrary methods, and when the navy joined in the opposition he decided "in the interests of the nation" to resign. Vice-president Peixoto, who took over the presidency, governed for a short time in accordance with constitutional prerogatives. But military training and an autocratic disposition soon overcame his newly acquired constitutional inhibitions, and he became even more despotic than his predecessor. A revolt that started in Rio Grande do Sul spread rapidly, and in the autumn Admiral de Mello and Admiral de Gama, who were in command of the naval forces and of the naval school at Rio de Janeiro, threw in their lot with the revolutionists.[62] The struggle quickly developed into a real civil war, and the question came up as to the recognition of the insurgents as belligerents.

On October 24, 1893, the American legation at Rio de Janeiro received notice from Admiral de Mello that a provisional government had been established at Desterro and requested recognition by the United States as belligerents. When the request was brought to his attention, Secretary Gresham replied that, since the insurgents had not yet established and maintained a political organization justifying recognition, such an act would be unfriendly to Brazil and a gratuitous demonstration of moral support to the rebellion. The American minister was therefore instructed to remain an indifferent spectator.[63] Commodore O. F. Stanton, in command of the United States naval forces at the South Atlantic Naval Station, happened to arrive at Rio de Janeiro in his flagship just after the revolt had occurred. On entering, he saluted the Brazilian flag with twenty-one guns, and a government fort returned the salute. Subsequently, however, he saluted Admiral Mello with thirteen guns; the salute was returned, and the next day he made an official call upon the insurgent admiral. The Brazilian government protested, and the commodore was thereupon detached from his command and ordered home. After hearing his explanation, the Navy Department decreed that he had committed "a grave error of judgment," since it was known that the United States had not recognized Admiral Mello and his forces as entitled to belligerent rights.[64]

The question of recognition of belligerency brought up a conflict between Admiral Benham, who now commanded the American squadron, and Admiral de Gama of the insurgent fleet. Inasmuch as belligerent

[62] For a short résumé of the causes see *For. Rel. of the U. S.*, 1893, pp. 68-70, or Akers, *op. cit.*, pp. 250-266.
[63] *For. Rel. of the U. S.*, 1893, p. 63.
[64] Moore, *Digest of Int. Law*, Vol. I, p. 240.

rights of the insurgents were not recognized, the naval commanders of the neutral squadrons refused to allow the insurgent forces to interfere with commercial operations except in the actual lines of fire. However, with the progress of the revolution the insurgents became inclined to interfere with neutral shipping, especially where the articles might be regarded as contraband of war. The British admiral and his European colleagues were inclined to submit to such interference. But Admiral Benham refused categorically and notified Admiral de Gama that he would use force, if necessary, to maintain American rights. An opportunity was given when several American vessels attempted to land their goods. When a shot from one of the insurgent vessels stopped the operation, the U. S. S. *Detroit* returned the fire, and the insurgents were notified that their boat would be sunk if she fired again. The threat was effectual and neutral commerce was not again interfered with. It might be noted, however, that Admiral Benham's *dictum* that the forcible seizure of contraband by the insurgents from neutrals who were engaged in supplying it to the belligerent government would be an act of piracy has hardly received the sanction of international law.[65]

With the resources of the country behind him, President Peixoto was enabled to purchase vessels in Europe and the United States, and the insurgents finally realized that further resistance was useless. Furthermore, on March 1, 1894, a civilian, Dr. Prudente de Moraes Barros, was elected president, which not only proved that President Peixoto intended to abide by the constitution but also that a more liberal régime could be expected. By summer the rebellion was completely checked, and on November 15, 1894, Dr. Moraes took over the government. The neutral attitude adopted by Admiral Benham, which had prevented a blockade of Rio de Janeiro, naturally aroused feelings of more cordial friendship towards the United States, and on the same day that the new president was inaugurated the cornerstone of a monument to the memory of President Monroe was laid in Rio.[66]

The withdrawal of President Peixoto from public life marked the end of pretorian government in Brazil. President Moraes granted full amnesty to the majority of those who participated in the revolution, and then proceeded to eliminate all military influence in the control of the government. His administration was so successful that his chosen successor, Dr. Manuel Campos Salles, another civilian, had little difficulty in securing

[65] *For. Rel. of the U. S.*, 1893, pp. 115-117; also Moore, *Digest of Int. Law*, Vol. II, pp. 1113-1120.
[66] *For. Rel. of the U. S.*, 1895, Part I, p. 48.

the election. President Salles continued the liberal and statesmanlike policies of his predecessor, governing strictly in accordance with the terms of the constitution. He was particularly successful in his financial policy, restoring Brazilian credit, which had been sorely tried by the costs of wars and uprisings and by the extravagant methods of the inexperienced republican officials. The next two presidents were also civilians, but in 1910 a soldier, Marshal Fonseca, formerly minister of war, was elected. Any doubts as to whether he would not attempt to govern after the fashion of his military predecessors were soon set at rest, and his administration was no less constitutional than those of the civilians who preceded him. However, in 1914 the country once more turned to a civilian, Dr. Braz, who had served as vice-president with President Fonseca; and the subsequent president, Dr. Epitacio da Silva Pessoa, was also drawn from civilian ranks. Republican government in accordance with constitutional limitations seemed to have been firmly established in Brazil.[67]

Since the founding of the republic, the relations between the United States and Brazil have unquestionably been more cordial than between the United States and any other South American country. President Cleveland's arbitral award in 1895 favoring the Brazilian line claim in the Misiones boundary dispute made him very popular in Brazil. The great republic maintained an attitude of friendly neutrality during the Spanish-American War.

In 1904 the Brazilian government built a beautiful palace of marble and granite for its exhibit at the St. Louis Exposition, and later it had the structure sent back to Rio de Janeiro for use as a meeting-place for international conferences and similar gatherings. It was in this building that Secretary Root made his memorable address while acting as honorary president of the Third Pan-American Conference at Rio de Janeiro, July 31, 1906; and at the close the minister for foreign affairs of Brazil, Baron do Rio Branco, announced that henceforth the palace would be known as the Monroe Palace. It is interesting to note that today this palace stands at the head of the most beautiful street in Rio de Janeiro— the Brazilians say the most beautiful street in the world—and that this street now bears the name *Avenida do Rio Branco,* in memory of Brazil's most illustrious foreign minister.

The visit of Secretary Root not only enhanced the cordial feelings of friendship that bound the two nations together, but had a very practical result in improving commercial relations. The very next month

[67] The Vargas dictatorship is discussed *infra,* pp. 438 *ff.*

a bill was introduced in the Chamber of Deputies which provided for a
20 per cent reduction of the tariff in favor of all countries importing more
than 4 million sacks of coffee annually free of duty. Inasmuch as the
United States was the only country coming within this category, the advantage was obvious.[68] This preferential tariff was renewed annually by
presidential decree until 1911, when the reduction on flour was increased
to 30 per cent. This advantage aroused the fears of the Argentine government, and the Argentine minister at Washington was instructed to
threaten an increase of its tariff on American petroleum, lumber, and other
staples if the United States attempted to secure any further concessions
from Brazil. The United States immediately denied any intention of seeking further preferential treatment and promised Argentina a notice of six
months in case unforeseen circumstances should change this situation.[69]

It was in this same year that a slight difficulty arose between the United
States and Brazil through the so-called valorization of coffee. As far back
as 1885 Brazil produced more than one-half of the world's coffee, and by
1900 it was producing more than two-thirds. In 1901 the production was
tremendously increased, particularly in the state of São Paulo, the total
crop amounting to more than 16 million sacks of 60 kilos (132 pounds).
This was more than four-fifths of the world's production and several hundred million pounds more than the world was consuming at that time.
Steps were immediately taken to prevent further planting, and, although
prices fell sharply, a fall in the Brazilian rate of exchange prevented ruin.
In 1906, however, another unprecedented crop was harvested in Brazil,
amounting to more than 20 million sacks. At that time the world's annual
consumption was estimated at about 17 million bags; there were already
on hand in the warehouses of the world about 11 million bags; and the
Caribbean region was producing almost 3 million bags annually. The
state of São Paulo faced utter financial ruin unless something radical
was done. The valorization plan was the solution. Huge loans were floated
in the United States and Europe, and São Paulo bought more than
8 million bags and stored it in various countries. A super-tax of three
francs per bag on exports enabled the state to meet the interest charges,
and diminishing crops and an increasing market in the following years
enabled the state to market its stores at a profit.[70]

In September, 1911, a report by W. T. Chantland, special assistant to
the Attorney-General, who had been detailed to investigate the valoriza-

[68] *Ibid.*, 1906, Part I, p. 135.
[69] *For. Rel. of the U. S.*, 1911, pp. 30 *ff.*
[70] For a complete account see P. Denis, *Brazil* (New York, 1911), pp. 235-266.

tion scheme in so far as it concerned the United States, stated that the plan violated Section 76 of the Wilson Act, identical with Section 6 of the Sherman Act, which gave the United States the right to seize and condemn property imported into the United States and held in restraint of trade. It was further claimed that the United States consumed 40 per cent of the entire world's output of coffee, or about 950 million pounds of coffee per year. Therefore a mere rise of six cents per pound in the cost of coffee meant $57 million a year to the people of the United States; and the valorization scheme had brought about a rise in excess of six cents.[71] The result of this report was a suit instituted by the Attorney-General in the District Court of New York against the Committee on Coffee Valorization of the State of São Paulo. The Brazilian ambassador immediately protested, and in his message to the state congress, July 14, 1912, the president of São Paulo declared that the action jeopardized in a very strange fashion the legal status of Brazilian coffee stored in New York.[72] After a series of notes the United States promised to drop the suit upon a promise of the Brazilian government that all of the stores of valorized coffee in New York would be sold in the open market before April 1, 1913.[73]

One of the results of the controversy was the temporary suspension on the part of Brazil of the preferential tariff on American goods. This entailed heavy losses for American exporters, and with the dropping of the suit the tariff concessions to the United States were revived. But, in order to cement the renewed friendly relations, the American government extended an invitation to Dr. Lauro Müller, the Brazilian minister for foreign affairs, to visit the United States to repay the visit made by Secretary Root to Brazil in 1906. Dr. Müller accepted the invitation and was enthusiastically received. He remained in the United States more than a month, visiting and traveling from New York to San Francisco. A new link of appreciation and understanding was thereby forged.

Nevertheless in a report of the United States Tariff Commission, made in 1918, the preferential treatment accorded to certain imports from the United States by the Brazilian government was deprecated as being the only arrangement then in effect which was inconsistent with the general principle of equality of treatment.[74] Inasmuch as by Brazilian law preferences in tariff rates had to be granted annually, it was customary for the American ambassador to Brazil to make each year a formal request for

[71] *For. Rel. of the U. S.*, 1913, pp. 39-52.
[72] *Ibid.*, p. 55.
[73] *Ibid.*, pp. 59-67.
[74] U. S. Tariff Commission, *Reciprocity and Commercial Treaties, 1918*, p. 285.

the preferential treatment. However no request was made by the United States for the year 1923, and by an exchange of identic notes between Secretary Hughes and the Brazilian ambassador at Washington dated October 18, 1923, each country agreed henceforth to accord the other unconditional most-favored-nation treatment.[75] As a matter of fact the result was by no means as adverse as was expected and even wheat flour, which enjoyed the largest reduction (30 per cent), practically held its own.

At the beginning of the first World War it was rather difficult to envisage what might be the attitude of Brazil. The large number of German colonists in southern Brazil, estimated at anywhere from 350,000 to 500,000, might have been expected to exert considerable influence towards a pro-German policy. The Brazilian government and the Brazilian people, however, soon gave clear indications that their sympathies were overwhelmingly on the side of the Allies. Within a week after the outbreak of the war the Brazilian Chamber of Deputies passed a motion recording its opposition to the violation of treaties and to acts violating the established principles of international law.[76] Less than a year later (in March, 1915), an organization was founded under the presidency of the eminent Brazilian statesman, Ruy Barbosa, known as the Brazilian League for the Allies. Its program included educational conferences, petitions of protest against Germany's war methods, and the raising of funds for the Brazilian Red Cross. It was at one of the meetings held by this organization, to raise funds for the establishment of a Brazilian hospital in Paris for the French wounded, that President Barbosa expressed regret that the United States had not seized the opportunity to assure itself first place among the nations by grouping about itself all the peoples of the American continent in protest against the invasion of Belgium and entering into the struggle to protect the validity of international engagements.[77]

Germany's unrestricted submarine warfare, which soon became a deadly menace to Brazil's extensive merchant marine, and the entrance of the United States into the World War, both tended to bring Brazil into the war on the side of the Allies. On April 11, 1917, immediately following the sinking of the Brazilian steamer *Parana* off the coast of France, diplomatic relations with Germany were severed. On May 22 President Braz urged Congress to revoke Brazil's neutrality in favor of the United States. In his speech he pointed out that "the Brazilian nation,

[75] U. S. Treaty Series, No. 672.

[76] P. A. Martin, *Latin America and the War*, League of Nations, Vol. II, No. 4, p. 233.

[77] Gaston Gaillard, *Amérique Latine et Europe Occidentale* (Paris, 1918), p. 44.

through its legislative organ, can without warlike intentions, but with determination, adopt the attitude that one of the belligerents forms an integral part of the American continent, and that to this belligerent we are bound by a traditional friendship and by a similarity of political opinion in the defense of the vital interests of America and the principles accepted by international law." [78]

The decree of neutrality was annulled on June 1, and in the circular note to foreign governments announcing the fact, the Brazilian government thus indicated its union of interests with the United States: "Brazil could not remain indifferent to it when the United States were drawn into the struggle without any interest therein but in the name alone of respect for international law, and when Germany extended indiscriminately to ourselves and other neutrals the most violent acts of war. If hitherto the relative lack of reciprocity on the part of the American Republics has withdrawn from the Monroe Doctrine its true character, permitting a scarcely well founded interpretation of the prerogatives of their sovereignty, the present events, by placing Brazil, even now, at the side of the United States, in the critical moment of the world's history, continue to give our foreign policy a practical form of continental solidarity—a policy indeed which was that of the old régime on every occasion on which any of the other friendly sister nations of the American continent were in jeopardy." [79]

The final break came on October 26, 1917, when a resolution recognizing a state of war was passed unanimously by the Senate and with only one vote against it in the lower house. Compulsory military service was reinstated, a mission was sent to the United States to purchase equipment and to arrange for military coöperation, a fleet of light cruisers was sent to coöperate with the British, aviators and physicians were sent to the western front, and every effort was made to increase the exportation of foodstuffs to the Allies.[80] From the point of view of the United States, the entrance of Brazil into the war was particularly important, even on purely moral grounds. The conclusion that the war was essentially just and necessary was enormously strengthened when the two greatest states of the western hemisphere, putting aside all feelings of rivalry and petty jealousy, decided to stand shoulder to shoulder in a struggle for that democracy which has ever been the ideal of the two Americas.

[78] *Brazilian Green Book*, authorized English version (London, 1918), p. 40. For expression of opinion in Brazil see Gaillard, *op. cit.*, pp. 70-90.
[79] *Brazilian Green Book*, p. 49.
[80] Martin, *op. cit.*, p. 243.

In the settlement following the war it must be conceded that Brazil was more steadfast in supporting the ideals for which she fought than was the United States. Brazil accepted the noble purposes of the League of Nations as worthy of at least a fair trial, and was deservedly honored by being elected to membership in the League Council. In his address to Secretary Colby on the occasion of the letter's visit to Rio de Janeiro in December, 1920, President Pessoa expressed regret that the United States had failed to ratify the treaty of Versailles. "Brazil," he declared, "is naturally very much interested in the beneficial purpose of the League of Nations. Therefore it is a matter of regret that the United States, which took the lead in that great project, has not retained it." [81] When the votes were cast for the judges of the Permanent Court of International Justice, Brazil showed her continued confidence in the United States by choosing as one of her candidates the American statesman whose Pan-American policy received the hearty support of all Latin America, Mr. Elihu Root. When the court was finally constituted, Brazil found herself again honored by the election to this body of her eminent statesman and publicist, Ruy Barbosa.

As further evidence of Brazil's friendliness toward the United States an arrangement was concluded between the two countries on November 6, 1922, for the sending of a commission of sixteen naval officers and nineteen noncommissioned officers for a period of four years to reorganize the Brazilian navy. Commander (later Admiral) Vogelgesang of the Brooklyn Navy Yard headed the commission. Dr. Zeballos, former Secretary of Foreign Relations of Argentina, gave voice to the resentment caused in his country by this act and claimed that it interfered with any program for the limitation of armament between A B C powers. However, according to A. T. Beauregard, a member of the mission who returned with Admiral Vogelgesang in February, 1925, the mission's purpose was not to persuade Brazil to enlarge her navy but merely to bring it up to the highest standard of efficiency.[82] In July, 1926, the State Department announced that the contract had been renewed for another period of four years as from November 6, 1926.[83]

In 1930 as a measure of economy the mission was permitted to return home, but in 1932 a new contract was signed for a smaller mission and this arrangement was renewed May 27, 1936, for another four years. As then organized the mission consisted of eight officers and five chief petty

[81] The *Independent*, Vol. CV (Jan. 8, 1921), p. 49.
[82] *Current History*, Vol. 22 (Aug., 1925), p. 815.
[83] *United States Daily*, July 16, 1926.

officers whose duties were to coöperate with the Minister of Marine and officers of the Brazilian Navy in an advisory capacity.[84] A similar agreement was signed November 13, 1936, between the two governments for a small military mission to coöperate with the general staff and assist in courses given at coast artillery instruction centers.[85]

As a result of this coöperation it was only natural that when Brazil wished to secure temporarily several United States destroyers already out of commission, for training purposes, the United States was glad to oblige. But although Brazil's neighbors did not object to the borrowing of United States naval officers for instruction purposes, they opposed very vehemently the borrowing of naval vessels. So vocal were the protests that on August 20, 1937, the United States and Brazil issued a joint statement declaring that the proposed plan was in entire harmony with the policy welcomed in many previous instances by the governments of other American republics of lending officers to them for instruction purposes or of receiving their officers for training in the naval vessels of the United States in American waters. They regretted "that a question of such limited importance should even for a few days be allowed to divert attention from the high ideals and . . . program which the 'good neighbor' policy comprises."[86]

The subsequent political situation in Brazil held a certain degree of uncertainty as to possibilities of a dictatorship after the Italian model. When Dr. Getulio Vargas took over the government of Brazil as dictator in 1930 it was regarded as merely a revolutionary *coup* to prevent São Paulo from monopolizing the presidency. The United States, insufficiently informed as to political developments, at the urgent solicitation of the Brazilian ambassador in Washington allowed itself to be persuaded to place an embargo upon shipments of arms to the revolutionists while still permitting the sale of war supplies to the federal government. When, two days later, the revolution was successful, the Department of State realized that it had made a serious diplomatic *faux pas* and tried to remedy the blunder by a prompt recognition of the new government. The bloody revolution of 1932 and the huge casualty list in its suppression indicated serious internal trouble in the federal republic. Undoubtedly the drop in the price of coffee from 24.8 cents a pound in March, 1929, to 7.6 in October, 1931, had something to do with the domestic

[84] For terms of a new agreement signed May 7, 1942, see Executive Agreement Series, 247.

[85] In 1941 a new four-year agreement covering a military and military aviation mission replaced the previous military agreement, Executive Agreement Series, 202.

[86] U. S. Dept. of State, *Press Releases* (Aug. 21, 1937), p. 162.

situation.[87] Even the new liberal constitution of 1934 could not solve the problem of the economic losses brought about by the low selling price of coffee. Nor did the destruction of some 26 million bags of coffee from January, 1931, to January, 1934, remedy the situation. Another revolution broke out in 1935 and it was again crushed by the government.

Inasmuch as the constitution of 1934 forbade the immediate reelection of the President, it was evident that a new constitution was required to permit Vargas to continue to head the government. On November 10, 1937, he assumed dictatorial powers and promulgated a new constitution establishing a centralized corporative state which dissolved all existing legislative bodies, federal and state. The new constitution increased the term to six years and declared the President to be the supreme authority of the state. Although this new government seemed to threaten a fascist form of government in the Western Hemisphere, Sumner Welles, United States Under Secretary of State, in an address made December 6 declared that the traditional friendship between the people of Brazil and the United States was not impaired by misinterpretations placed upon the Vargas *coup d'état*. He recalled that it had been unanimously agreed at the Buenos Aires Conference that no state should interfere with the internal affairs of another state.

Vargas henceforth ruled as dictator with opposition thoroughly stifled. An attempted palace revolution by the Fascist Integralistas on May 11, 1938, failed although Vargas for hours was aided only by his personal servants and a few guardsmen. The European war which finally spread to the Western Hemisphere afforded a good excuse for a government by presidential decree, and Vargas seized the opportunity and did an excellent job at that kind of administration. His government, the *Estado Nuevo* was claimed to be an "authoritative democracy," but the emphasis was clearly upon the first part of the phrase.

In the spring of 1939 Foreign Minister Aranha came to Washington and worked out an elaborate program for closer economic collaboration with the United States. Commercial transactions were facilitated by a $19,200,000 credit extended by the Export-Import Bank to the Bank of Brazil. The program also contemplated a survey of tropical agricultural possibilities by American experts, the development of certain basic industries, and the improvement of transportation facilities.[88] The following year Warren Lee Pierson, President of the Export Import Bank, after a

[87] Horace B. Davis, "Brazil's Political and Economic Problems," *Foreign Policy Reports*, Vol. XI, No. 1 (Mar. 13, 1935).

[88] S. S. Jones and D. P. Myers, *Documents on American Foreign Relations* (Boston, 1939), pp. 128-142.

survey of conditions in Brazil recommended the construction of a modern steel-producing plant in Brazil, the machinery for which could be supplied by the United States. This steel plant, to be located 90 miles south of Rio de Janeiro, was expected to produce more than half of Brazil's existing requirements for steel within two years. A loan of $20 million was made for this purpose, Brazil to supply another $25 million.

An even more elaborate economic arrangement was made with Brazil on March 3, 1942. It consisted of a series of agreements providing for a complete mobilization of the productive resources of Brazil with credits to the amount of $100 million to be made available by the Export Import Bank. Through agreements signed with the Brazilian Finance Minister and the British Ambassador, the Export Import Bank and Metal Reserve Company would finance the development of the Itabira iron mines and the Victoria Minas Railroad in order to obtain high grade ores for the United States and Great Britain. Other agreements provided for the transfer of military material under lend-lease arrangements, the development of the production of raw rubber and its purchase, and for the purchase of such commodities as barbassu and castor oil, cocoa, coffee, and Brazil nuts.[89] In the fall of 1942, a technical commission headed by an American industrial engineer, Morris Llewellyn Cook was sent to Brazil to work out the specific details of the program.

A more general economic arrangement looking towards continental solidarity but of particular interest to Brazil was the Coffee Marketing Agreement signed November 28, 1940, and ratified February 12, 1941. By the terms of this agreement fourteen American republics allocated equitably the market of the United States and that of the rest of the world among the various coffee-producing countries through the adoption of basic annual quotas for each country. According to the quotas established, the United States would take 9,300,000 bags of coffee from Brazil, 3,150,000 from Colombia, and 1,550,000 bags from the Central American republics.[90]

After the United States entered the war, Brazil gave the most wholehearted support to the cause of the United Nations. Arrangements had already been made with the United States by the agreement signed October 1, 1941, to improve Brazilian defenses through lend-lease shipments of planes, tanks, and trucks with additional funds to improve her air and naval bases. Inasmuch as the third meeting of American Foreign ministers to formulate plans for continental defense was held at Rio de Janeiro,

[89] *Dept. of State Bull.*, Vol. VI (Mar. 7, 1942), pp. 205-208.
[90] *Ibid.*, Vol. III (Nov. 30, 1940), pp. 483-488.

Foreign Minister Aranha was in a strategic position to support the United States in its desire for an all-American severance of diplomatic relations with the Axis powers. The Brazilian Foreign Minister measured up to expectations and not only supported the break enthusiastically, but when Argentina and Chile hedged upon immediate action, Brazil alone of the ABC powers took the step before the Conference adjourned.

Axis firms and individuals were placed under official surveillance and control, pro-Axis news agencies and newspapers were suppressed, and Axis financial transactions were restricted to the minimum. Following the sinking of Brazilian ships by submarines, the Brazilian government seized up to 30 per cent of the assets of Axis enterprises to guarantee compensation. Nowhere in South America did the Fifth Column receive more ruthless treatment than at the hands of Getulio Vargas. When news was received August 18, 1942, that five more Brazilian ships had been sunk within three days—one a troop transport—Brazil temporized no longer and declared war the same day. Brazil's vast stores of strategic materials, her rapidly expanding air force, and the joint defense of the strategic bulge at Natal were invaluable assets in the defense of the Americas. Upon his return from Africa in January, 1943, President Roosevelt stopped off in Brazil to see President Vargas, and both agreed that never again should the coasts of Dakar and West Africa become an invasion threat to the Americas. Brazil promised to aid in the war against the undersea menace, and it was later reported that at least ten Axis submarines had been sunk by the joint action of the air and sea forces of Brazil and the United States.

The huge airplane base constructed by the United States at Natal, which during the war was said to be the largest freight air junction in the world, was a most valuable asset in the transportation of both troops and supplies to the various fronts in Europe and Africa. In fact, when Germany surrendered in 1945, the United States War Production Board declared that "without Brazil's production of strategic materials and bridge of planes the United States could not have met its schedules."

It was generally thought in the United States that Brazil's great friendliness to the United States was due more to Foreign Minister Aranha than to President Vargas. Nevertheless, when Aranha resigned in August, 1944, through indirect pressure on the part of the President, the Brazilian government continued its coöperation with the United States, and on June 6, 1945, declared war upon Japan.

President Vargas promised free elections in 1945 but, lest he might not be able to resist the pressure of his constituents that he seize the power unconstitutionally, a bloodless revolution occurred October 30, 1945 and President Vargas was removed from his position. The elections on December 2, 1945, held under army control were fairly conducted and contrary to the belief of most of the foreign correspondents, General Enrico Dutra, the reactionary candidate favored by Vargas, won over the more liberal Brigadier Eduardo Gomes. One of the disturbing features of the election results was the fact that the Communists polled over a half million votes, winning fourteen seats in the Chamber of Deputies and electing their leader, Luis Prestes, to the Senate. Another interesting result was the return of Getulio Vargas as Senator representing his native state, Rio Grande do Sul.

As might have been expected, one of the first tasks of the new government was to provide a new constitution in place of the organic act devised by Vargas in 1937. Congress itself acted as a constitutional convention and the constitution of 1946 placed more power in the hands of the Congress as compared with the executive and returned more powers to the states in relation to the federal government.

The new administration was worried by the increase in the Communist vote in the 1947 elections. Their leader, Senator Prestes, had declared publicly that in the case of war between the Soviet Union and the United States the Communists would fight on the side of the Soviet Union. Shortly after the elections of January, 1947, the government requested the suppression of the Communist Party and in May the Supreme Electoral Tribunal declared the Communist Party to be illegal and ordered it dissolved. With the expulsion of Communist Congressmen in January, 1948, the Communists in Brazil were driven underground. The Brazilian Government had already broken diplomatic relations with the U.S.S.R. on October 20, 1947.

The Communists had attempted to provoke anti-American feeling in Brazil and the acute dollar shortage after the war played into their hands. The fact that of the total lend-lease funds advanced to Latin America, amounting to about $460,000,000 from 1941 to 1947, Brazil received more than three-fourths seemed to have been forgotten. To improve the situation a United States Brazilian Technical Commission was established in 1948 known as the Abbink Mission from the name of its chairman. This Mission after a careful investigation reported in February, 1949, recommending an elaborate program of agricultural, industrial, mineral, and power development, increased immigration, improved transportation, and a guarantee of fair treatment for United States investors in Brazil.

In October, 1950, Brazil and the United States signed the first cultural agreement of its kind, encouraging the exchange of students and professors.

In the presidential elections held in 1950 Eduardo Gomez ran for reëlection and he was opposed by Getulio Vargas. In a very peaceful campaign Vargas proved his popularity by winning with a substantial majority and was inaugurated President January 31, 1951. However by the spring of 1954 it was evident that the country was weary of the Vargas régime—his name was often hissed at public meetings and in June an attempt was made to impeach him for mishandling public funds. Toward the end of August a group of army officers forced his resignation and that same night Vargas committed suicide, leaving a note bitterly denouncing his enemies. A Communist attempt to blame the United States backfired and the new government showed itself even more friendly than the preceding one.

In the effort to disabuse the South American republics of the idea that they were orphans under the Marshall Plan to rehabilitate Europe, Secretary of State Acheson visited Brazil in the summer of 1952. In Rio de Janeiro he reminded the Latin-American republics that Soviet Communism was the common enemy and that the United States was spearheading the defense of the Hemisphere. He pointed out that bilateral military assistance agreements were being concluded with Latin-American states in accordance with which the United States would grant substantial military aid for mutual defense. Brazil had been the first state to sign such an agreement and already five others had entered into force with Latin-American governments—Ecuador, Peru, Cuba, Chile, and Colombia. Combining appropriations for the years 1951 and 1952, the United States had earmarked almost $90 million for military assistance to the Latin-American area.[91]

Although Brazil delayed in her ratification of the military assistance agreement until May, 1953, she took advantage of all other financial offers. By November, 1952, the Export Import Bank had granted loans to Brazil totaling $119 million for power and railroad development, highways, and agriculture, which was matched by an equivalent or greater amount in escudos. Early in 1953 the Bank extended to Brazil a $300 million credit to help cancel dollar debts to the United States, the largest loan ever made by the Export Import Bank to a foreign government. By the end of 1952 technical assistance loans to Brazil had amounted to

[91] *Military Assistance to Latin America,* Dept. of State Pub. 4917, Inter-Americas Series 44 (Jan., 1953).

$295 million, and at the close of 1953 a joint Brazilian-United States Commission had worked out a Point Four program covering railroad, electric power, port, merchant marine and agricultural rehabilitation and development—the largest ever attempted by the United States.

In sketching the relations between the United States and Brazil, perhaps even more than in the case of either Argentina or Chile, stress should be laid on the commercial side. Long before the establishment of the republic Brazil's trade with the United States surpassed that of all the Spanish South American republics combined. For example, in 1870 Brazil's trade with the United States was valued at approximately $31 million, while that of the Spanish South American countries amounted to about $29 million.[92] However, it must be noted that the United States imported from Brazil about four times as much as she sent in return. And this situation was due principally to the fondness of the people of the United States for Brazilian coffee. The first boat that inaugurated regular monthly steamship transport between the United States and Brazil arrived at Rio on June 7, 1878, and took back a cargo of 37,000 sacks of coffee, the largest and most valuable single cargo that had ever been shipped from the country.[93] In 1890 the total trade between the United States and Argentina was valued at approximately $14,200,000, the trade with Chile at $6,400,000, while that with Brazil amounted to more than $71,000,000.[94] At the outbreak of the first World War Brazil still held first place in United States' trade with South America, with a total value of about $154,000,000, although Argentina, with a total value of about $72,000,000, had gained more proportionately.[95]

The depression that followed the first World War, and the subsequent noxious high tariff policy culminating in the Hawley-Smoot Bill of 1930 made a drastic cut in the trade of the United States with Brazil. It was to be expected therefore that with the passage of the trade agreement act of 1934, the United States would endeavor to improve its trade relations with its best South American customer. In fact, the trade agreement between the United States and Brazil which became effective January 1, 1936, was the first signed with a South American state. According to its terms the United States agreed to cut tariff duties on such Brazilian products as manganese, Brazil nuts, and castor beans, as well as keep on the free list coffee and cocoa which were Brazil's principal exports to the

[92] For. Rel. of the U. S., 1870, pp. 283-287.
[93] Ibid., 1878, p. 67.
[94] Statistical Abstract of the U. S., 1890, p. 75.
[95] Ibid., 1914, p. 688.

United States. In return Brazil reduced her tariff on American automobiles, radios, electric batteries, cement, paints, fruits, fish, and numerous other articles. The agreement provided for most favored nation treatment and prohibited all import quotas or licenses except for sanitary purposes.

Although the results were not remarkable the figures show a substantial improvement both in imports and exports. Taking the 1934-1935 average, that is the two years preceding the agreement, and contrasting it with the 1938-1939 average, that is two years after the agreement, we find that United States exports to Brazil increased 69.5 per cent and our imports 7.3 per cent. The total trade increased in the same period from $138 million to $174 million.[96] The second World War increased both the percentage and the amount of Brazil's trade with the United States very materially. In 1940, Brazil did almost 50 per cent of her total trade with the United States, and it was valued at $273,472,000.

By 1948, Brazil's trade with the United States had passed the billion dollar mark with imports exceeding exports by some $80 million.[97] The unfavorable balance of trade kept mounting and when in the first six months of 1952 Brazil's imports from the United States were valued at over $500,000,000 whereas her exports to the United States were under $400 million the government decided to impose heavy restrictions upon imports.

The measures were so effective that in the second half of 1952 Brazil's exports to the United States were valued at about $443 million, where as imports from the United States dropped to about $243 million. The net result was a balance of over $50 million in Brazil's favor in the total trade with the United States for 1952 valued at over $1,600,000,000. Carrying this belt-tightening into the first six months of 1953, the favorable trade balance reached $330,000,000, while still maintaining a total two-way trade for the fiscal year 1952-1953 of almost $1,200,000,000.[98]

When early in 1954 the retail price of coffee in the United States passed $1.00 a pound consumers were aroused and numerous allegations were made that the high cost was due to Brazilian speculators. When the United States government appointed two committees to investigate, the Brazilian government became alarmed and invited a group of American representatives of both Congress and the public to visit Brazil and investigate the situation. Their report indicated that a heavy frost had cut

[96] *Commerce Reports,* Feb. 17, 1940, p. 169.
[97] *The Foreign Trade of Latin America Since 1913* (Washington, D. C., Pan American Union, 1952).
[98] *Brazilian Bulletin* (Oct. 1, 1953), pp. 1-2.

the coffee crop considerably but also that increased consumption in the United States and Europe had used up coffee surpluses, thereby outstripping production. By July, 1954, coffee prices had commenced to fall as a result of reduced consumption.

The United States is a natural customer of Brazil not only for her coffee and cacao but for her precious stones, manganese, woods, nuts, and rubber. Brazil needs capital, and the United States can supply it. Transportation by land, water, and air must be developed, and the United States can aid both technically and financially in its expansion. In the words of a former Brazilian commercial agent to the United States, Brazil "looks to the United States for men and money, and we stand ready to give value for value received." The United States should not find it difficult to meet these requirements.

SUPPLEMENTARY READINGS

JOSEPH AGAN, *The Diplomatic Relations of the United States and Brazil* (Paris, 1926).

G. J. BRUCE, *Brazil and the Brazilians* (New York, 1914).

E. C. BULEY, *North Brazil* (New York, 1914).

——, *South Brazil* (New York, 1914).

PEDRO CALMON, *Historia do Brasil,* 3 vols. (São Paulo, 1939-1940).

C. S. COOPER, *The Brazilians and Their Country* (New York, 1917).

T. C. DAWSON, *South American Republics* (New York, 1903), Vol. I, pp. 287-512.

PIERRE DENIS, *Brazil,* 5th ed. (London, 1926).

C. W. DOMVILLE-FIFE, *The United States of Brazil* (New York, 1911).

L. E. ELLIOTT, *Brazil To-day and To-morrow* (New York, 1917).

F. FREIRE, *Historia Constitucional da Republica dos Estados Unidos de Brazil,* 3 vols. (Rio de Janeiro, 1894-1895).

GILBERTO FREYRE, *Brazil: An Iterpretation* (New York, 1945).

L. F. HILL, *Diplomatic Relations between the United States and Brazil* (Durham, N. C., 1932).

H. G. JAMES, *Brazil After a Century of Independence* (New York, 1925).

PRESTON E. JAMES, *Brazil* (New York), 1946).

M. DE OLIVEIRA LIMA, *Dom João VI do Brazil,* 2 vols. (Rio de Janeiro, 1911).

——, *Historia diplomática do Brazil; e reconhecimiento do Imperio* (Rio de Janeiro, 1902).

KARL LOEWENSTEIN, *Brazil Under Vargas* (New York, 1942).

ROY NASH, *The Conquest of Brazil* (New York, 1926).

J. F. NORMANO, *Brazil, A Study of Economic Types* (Chapel Hill, N. C., 1935).

JOAO PANDIA CALOGERAS (P. A. Martin, trans.), *A History of Brazil* (Chapel Hill, N. C., 1939).

HENRY A. PHILLIPS, *Brazil, Bulwark of International Relations* (New York, 1945).

J. R. RIPPY, P. A. MARTIN, I. J. COX, *Argentina, Brazil and Chile since Independence* (Washington, D. C., 1935).

MARCHANT A. SMITH, *Brazil, Portrait of Half a Continent* (New York, 1951).

T. LYNN SMITH, *Brazil, People and Institutions* (Baton Rouge, 1946).

HERNANE TAVARES DE SA, *The Brazilians, People of Tomorrow* (New York, 1947).

STEFAN ZWEIG, *Brazil* (New York, 1941).

❧ 19 ❧

The Good Neighbor Policy
and After

THE typical Yankee of North America is partial to slogans. He likes to tie up his country's policies in bundles and label them. Freedom of the Seas, the Open Door, the Monroe Doctrine, and the Good Neighbor Policy are pertinent examples. Unfortunately, once formulated and labeled, the policy is accepted as a vital element in the structure of the state, but no attention is paid to its growth and development. As a result, when such a policy is challenged, no one is more surprised than complacent Mr. John Citizen. This has been particularly true with reference to our relations with the Latin-American republics to the south. We have always wanted to be "buenos vecinos" and we have found it difficult to understand how any one could possibly believe otherwise. Nevertheless, the facts of the situation have been such that hardly more than two decades ago, an objective observer would have declared that the United States, by and large, was suspected, disliked, and feared from the Rio Grande to the Straits of Magellan.

A bird's-eye view over the Latin-American attitude, as it existed at the advent of the Roosevelt administration, is very illuminating. Mexico resented the exploitation of her oil wells and mineral resources by foreign corporations which sent most of the profits out of the country. Cuba was becoming more and more restive under the Platt Amendment, which permitted legalized intervention, a flagrant infringement of her status as a sovereign state. Nicaragua, Haiti, and the Dominican Republic were either occupied by the marines or had just seen them withdrawn, with always a possibility of their return. Panama fretted under the Canal Treaty which gave the United States absolute control of the Canal Zone and an overprivileged position outside. Venezuela's oil, Peru's vanadium

448

and copper, Chile's nitrate and iron, Uruguay's meat industries, Brazil's coffee were all controlled by or dependent upon United States markets. The Colossus of the North was a tangible and threatening menace to our neighbors to the south in spite of our much vaunted anti-imperialistic intentions.

Unfortunately, the citizen of the United States had not the slightest conception of this unfriendly attitude. Had not the century-old Monroe Doctrine raised a bulwark of protection against European threats of encroachment? Had not our great Secretaries of State from Henry Clay to Cordell Hull preached the doctrine of inter-American coöperation? Had not Woodrow Wilson even tried to extend the Monroe Doctrine to the entire world? Undoubtedly in theory the United States has always believed in the good neighbor policy and on the whole has tried to follow it. But in practice the exceptions have been many and the results very profitable to Uncle Sam.

Let us draw up a bill of particulars from the Latin-American point of view. Mexico received very little protection from the Monroe Doctrine when Maximilian established a monarchy right on our border. Argentina would still possess the Falkland Islands if Uncle Sam had interpreted the doctrine to safeguard all of South America. The Mexican War had more than a tinge of imperialism south of the Rio Grande. Teddy Roosevelt and his Big Stick were not appreciated in the Caribbean and were keenly resented in Colombia. The Platt Amendment did not make for a *Cuba Libre* in the eyes of the Cuban patriots. Secretary Hughes' substitution of the euphemistic term "interposition" for "intervention" was not a satisfactory solution for the sending of the marines. In fact, to the realistic Latin American his Yankee big brother was more threatening than the European cousin because he was both bigger and closer at hand.

Added to these proofs of our aggressive tendencies, another obstacle to better understanding has been the limitless ignorance of the North American in regard to the twenty different republics to the south. To the Yankee, Latin America meant the vast continent of South America with a Central American attachment spanned by the Panama Canal and a fringe of interesting but inconsequential islands in the Caribbean. Mexico, like Canada, was so completely in our orbit that the frontier was regarded as more of a nuisance than a national boundary. Mr. John Citizen would have been much surprised to learn that these twenty republics are independent, nationalistic units, often very antagonistic to each other. It would have even startled him if he had been told that the Hondurans think of the Nicaraguans as city slickers, the Ecuadoreans regard the Peruvians as frontier highwaymen, that the Argentinians call the Brazilians monkeys because they chatter so much, and the Brazilians' retort discourteous is "wooden heads" and the wood suggested is quebracho, so tough that it resists even a machete.

Numerous incidents are related indicating our abysmal ignorance of the size, character, and even language of Brazil. Stefan Zweig in his recent fascinating book on Brazil tells of the Boston business man who wouldn't believe that Brazil was larger than the United States until shown a map, and of the English author who sent his hero to Rio to learn Spanish. Even our scholars are often surprised to learn that three countries in Latin America—Peru, Mexico, and the Dominican Republic—have universities which were established before any such institutions in North America.

The geographical factor is another obstacle which is often overlooked. Europe is closer to the United States than South America, and has always had better and cheaper means of communication. No steamship line has yet established the cabin class type of boat which has always been popular on the European runs. Although airplane service now completely spans the Latin-American area, it is very expensive and far less suitable for vacation travel.

Our salesmen rarely spoke the language of the countries to the south, firms hesitated to give long terms of credit, goods were packed improperly, and little effort was made to produce articles specifically for the Latin-American trade.

The vast and excellent literature of our neighbors to the south was unknown either in the original or in translations. Out of twenty-seven outstanding Latin-American literary works translated in the past few years almost all have been commercial losses. Latin America was a veritable *terra incognita* in the curricula of our institutions of higher learning.

Finally, as a dangerous threat to the sympathetic understanding between the United States and Latin America there was the sinister propaganda of the Nazi organization in South America. The German embassies and legations, with numerous press and so-called cultural attachés, were abusing shamefully their diplomatic privileges in order to serve as agents for Dr. Goebbel's Ministry for Propaganda and for Herr Himmler's even more dangerous Gestapo. Every instrumentality, radio programs, schools, social clubs, and relief organizations were being effectively employed to draw the Latin-American nations into the orbit of the Swastika and to undermine and sabotage the friendly approaches of the United States.

Hitler had even declared his intention of making a "great German dominion of that continent of half breeds." What better way to begin than by kindling the latent fear and jealousy of the United States in Latin-American hearts?

Fortunately for the security of the Western Hemisphere the dawn of a new era had arisen. President Roosevelt proclaimed the policy of the Good Neighbor. Determined henceforth to reconcile promises with deeds, the United States in typically Yankee fashion attacked the problem on all fronts—political, economic, and cultural.

Marines were withdrawn from every Caribbean outpost and future intervention was outlawed by specific conventions signed and ratified by the United States. Unsatisfactory agreements such as the Platt Amendment with Cuba and the Canal Treaty with Panama were revised in accordance with the wishes of these neighboring republics. No longer would we possess the legal right to intervene in Cuba in derogation of her sovereignty. In case of aggression endangering the Canal the United States and Panama would consult for mutual defense instead of Uncle Sam dictating the policy. Even the Monroe Doctrine, the Sacred Cow of American diplomacy, was overhauled and reinterpreted to the benefit of both the Americas. Instead of the United States alone determining when and if the principles of the doctrine are violated, the twenty-one American republics now consult together when any threat to this hemisphere arises. Even tariff barriers had to give way before the pressure of good will, and Secretary Hull signed sixteen reciprocal trade agreements with our Latin-American neighbors. One result has been to bring about a phenomenal increase of trade between Latin America and the United States, amounting to over $5½ billion in the fiscal year of 1948.

But the greatest accomplishment in the political field was the utilization of the Pan American Conferences to serve as effective agencies for coöperation among the twenty-one republics. At the Conference held in Lima in December, 1938, the representatives unanimously approved a declaration of principles of the solidarity of America, agreed upon joint defense against foreign intervention, and established automatic machinery to make it effective. The simple device agreed upon was to authorize the Foreign Minister of any American republic to call a meeting of all the foreign ministers when any threat arose.

Hardly was the ink dry upon this document before the Nazi war machine rolled over Poland. A conference was immediately called in Panama and a three-hundred-mile safety zone was established around the American republics and the belligerents were asked to do their fighting outside. Violations were to be followed by withdrawal of the privilege of fueling and making needed repairs.

A still greater menace arose with the subjugation of France and Holland. Both of these nations had important colonial possessions in the Western Hemisphere. Another meeting of the foreign ministers, this time in Habana, agreed that any move on the part of the Axis to take over these possessions would be prevented by joint action. If the threat was imminent any one power might act to forstall it. That is, all Latin America now trusted us sufficiently to permit the United States to enforce the Monroe Doctrine by itself if the emergency warranted. The Americas had at last recognized the famous doctrine of Monroe to mean all for one and one for all.

The devastatingly successful attack by the Japanese upon Pearl Harbor brought the war into the Western Hemisphere. Would the two Americas meet the test and carry out their promised coöperation for hemispheric defense? Would Latin America prove that the Good Neighbor Policy was a policy of reciprocity? The answer came quickly. The day after the attack, Mexico and Colombia broke off diplomatic relations and within four days the nine Central American and Caribbean republics had declared war upon the Axis powers. A meeting of foreign ministers was summoned at Rio to formulate a policy of defense of the Americas.

Since it was now evident that Axis propaganda and subversive activities were rampant throughout the Western Hemisphere and that the German embassies were the source of this pollution, the United States felt that the minimum requirement for self-protection was the severance of diplomatic relations to stamp out the evil at its very roots. A resolution recommending such a break was unanimously accepted and before the Conference ended every nation except Argentina and Chile had dismissed the Axis diplomats. Another resolution looked towards a complete economic and financial boycott of the Axis partners. Agreements were entered into for the production and exchange of strategic materials essential to hemispheric defense and envisaged the formulation of a complete and coördinated general plan for economic mobilization. To coördinate effectively the necessary measures of hemispheric defense, an Inter-American Defense Board composed of military and naval officers of the twenty-one republics was established at Washington.

As a result of the discussions with the military and naval authorities of the several Latin-American countries it seemed desirable, as far as possible, to replace foreign matériel by military or naval equipment from the United States. Since financial conditions made it impossible for the American republics to pay the entire cost, arrangements were made to supply them under the lend-lease act. A preliminary sum of $400,000,000 was allocated for these supplies, and lend-lease agreements were signed by the end of 1942 with all of the republics except Argentina and Panama.

Military, naval, and aviation missions from the United States were made available to every Latin-American republic which desired them. By June 30, 1942, some form of military, naval, or air mission was to be found in thirteen of the twenty Latin-American republics, leaving out of consideration the huge forces at Panama and the naval base in Cuba. A plan for the effective use of foreign ships in American ports was worked out so that more than a hundred of these vessels were transferred to active service in inter-American trade.

A Conference on Systems of Economic and Financial Control met in Washington in July, 1942, to supervise all commercial and financial intercourse between the Western Hemisphere and the aggressor states or the territories dominated by them for the duration of the war. Any transaction that might prove inimical to the security of the Western Hemisphere, whether international or among the American republics, was within its jurisdiction. The United States had already promulgated a black list of firms and individuals suspected of doing business with the Axis powers. A report made in 1941 by the office of the Coördinator of Inter-American Affairs indicated that of some 5000 firms in Latin America over 1000 were definitely known to be identified with anti-American activities.

The better to maintain the economic stability of the other American republics, the United States through the Board of Economic Warfare, in coöperation with the Department of State and the War Production Board, made every effort to facilitate the exchange of commodities. A quarterly allotment was made to the various Latin-American republics of specific quantities of iron and steel, chemicals, farm equipment, and other products vital to their national economics.

Preclusive purchasing agreements of strategic materials were made with various Latin-American states both to keep their supplies from the Axis powers and to keep an abundant supply available to the United Nations. For example, Metals Reserve Company made over-all agreements with Brazil for bauxite, chromite, manganese, and other minerals, with Bolivia for tungsten and tin, with Mexico for practically all of its exportable surplus of minerals, with Peru for antimony, copper, and vanadium, and with Chile for copper, manganese, lead, and zinc. Rubber Reserve

Company made similar arrangements for rubber with Brazil, Peru, Bolivia, Colombia, Ecuador, and several Central American states. Defense Supplies Corporation bought up surpluses wherever it seemed necessary, such as the reserve stock of Chilean nitrates and surpluses of Peruvian cotton.

The maintenance of health in the Western Hemisphere was also a vital feature of the coöperative war effort. An excellent illustration is afforded by the sanitation agreement with Bolivia signed July 15, 1942, whereby the government of the United States through the agency of the Coördinator of Inter-American Affairs agreed to provide up to $1 million for the coöperative development of a health and sanitation program including general disease control by clinics and public education, malaria control, yellow fever control, cure of lepers, and environmental sanitation. A group of medical and sanitation experts from the United States worked in close coöperation with corresponding officials of the Bolivian government.

The Basic Economy Department of the Coördinator's office, an agency concerned primarily with the health and nutrition of the people of the Americas, under the compulsion of war-time necessity, sponsored more than 500 projects and activities. They ranged from the establishment of health stations in the Amazon rubber country to an extensive rehabilitation program in Ecuador. A series of comprehensive health and sanitation agreements and food-producing agreements made it possible for the two Americas to coöperate effectively to strengthen the human resources of the hemisphere.

One of the most potent agencies for the coördinated economic development of the Americas was established on June 3, 1940 under the general direction of the Inter-American Financial and Advisory Committee. This agency known as the Inter-American Development Commission established national commissions in every American republic whose primary functions were to supply information on the possibilities of developing production and trade. This organization proposed not only to establish new industries, but to try and reëstablish the production of commodities such as cocoa, coconuts, copra, quinine, and rubber which were once supreme in Latin America, but which were subsequently lost to Malaya. It established a market for Brazilian tapioca in the United States and sponsored a sales campaign to stimulate the purchase in the United States of the beautiful handicraft work of the Latins.

As proof of the intention of the United States to take care that the Latin-American countries were not discriminated against during the war, an agency of the Board of Economic Operations known as the American

Hemisphere Exports Office was created to see to it that the Latin-American countries were supplied with essential commodities on a parity with civilians in the United States. By the fall of 1942 the employees of this one office numbered more than eighty.

One of the agencies under the jurisdiction of the Coördinator of Inter-American Affairs, the Institute of Inter-American Affairs, proved so useful during the war that Congress by a law of August 5, 1947, authorized its continuance for a period of three years. Its functions were to bring about a collaboration between the governmental agencies of the United States and those of the other American republics in initiating, financing, and executing technical programs and projects in the fields of public health, sanitation, agriculture, and education. Such coöperation was based upon bilateral agreements known as basic country agreements, usually continuing for a period of from three to five years. An interesting feature of the procedure was that usually the chief of the field party sent to the country coöperating was made director of the *Servicio Coöperativo* in that country, and he reported directly to the Minister in charge of the field of operations. By 1949 the technicians and field staff of the Institute of Inter-American Affairs numbered some 325 and they were providing technical and administrative supervision to approximately 9500 nationals of sixteen other republics who were carrying on the operations. In the field of health and sanitation the Institute had completed more than 1300 projects benefitting over 23 million people, or one out of every six Latin Americans. Some 107 health centers had been put into operation which were utilized by over 2,000,000. The incidence of malaria in Breves on the Amazon River in Brazil was reduced in two years from 43 per cent to .3 per cent, while in Leogani, Haiti, it was reduced from 71 per cent to practically zero.[1]

When in his message to the Congress in January, 1949, President Truman enunciated his famous "Point 4" program of technical assistance and guaranteed private investments in undeveloped areas, the Institute whose Latin-American program, according to Secretary of State Acheson, had been "the inspiration and proving ground" of the idea, was the logical organization to carry out the program in the republics to the south. Consequently, the Congress extended both the life and the scope of activities of the Institute of Inter-American Affairs. When the Technical Coöperation Administration was set up in the Department of State in October, 1950, it was decided, after careful consideration, that the Institute should

[1] For a detailed account see *The Program of the Institute of Inter-American Affairs* (Washington, D. C., Institute of Inter-American Affairs, 1949).

serve as the regional office of TCA for the other American republics, beginning November 6, 1951. The Eisenhower administration transferred TCA to the newly created Foreign Operations Administration.

The results of the program might justly be termed spectacular. In a statement made by Dr. Wilton L. Halverson, who headed a health survey team for the Institute to make a report of the health work carried on jointly by the United States and her neighbor nations south of the border in the ten years 1942-1952, he gave some very interesting figures. He found in the seventeen Latin-American states where a program was being carried out, some 150 hospitals and health centers, 12 schools of nursing, and 3 graduate schools of public health had been established. More than 1300 men and women from Latin America had been brought to the United States for postgraduate training in medicine and public health specialties. The *Servicios* have made great progress in controlling malaria, hookworms, yellow fever, typhus fever, and yaws. To eliminate intestinal infections—a Latin-American expert declared that one-half of the food consumed by the people went to feed the worms in intestinal tracts— more than 38,000 outdoor toilets had been constructed in rural areas. In many places where the water supply was limited or so foul as to make it hazardous for bathing or laundering, public bathhouses and public laundries had been built. Whereas in the beginning the United States bore most of the cost, in 1951 the Latin-American republics more than quadrupled the $3 million supplied by the United States.[2]

Next to the improvement of sanitation and health, the Institute has coöperated most effectively in aiding the producing of food. A few examples will illustrate its success. In 1952 the *Servicio Coöperativo Inter-Americano de Produccion de Alimentos,* SCIPA, in Peru had thirty-four branch offices reaching 1,000,000 families, and more than 40,000 persons consulted these offices on farm problems every year. In the Sierra the Indians are being taught to raise wheat which when the project is completed will make Peru self-supporting, as against $40 million spent for imports of wheat in 1951. Potatoes are also raised in the Sierra of Peru— some 800,000 tons annually. When an insect pest cut down the yield in an alarming fashion SCIPA specialists stepped in and not only checked the infection but increased the yield fourfold. In fact, on one demonstration farm the yield was 900 per cent higher than the previous years' bug-infested crop. Sheep and beef cattle are now being raised in the high-

[2] Wilton L. Halverson, "Health South of the Border," *Life and Health Magazine* (Jan., 1953). See also "Coöperative Health Programs of the U. S. A. and Latin America," *The Institute of Inter-American Affairs* (Washington, D. C.).

lands, dairy cows and chickens imported for productive purposes, and some $2½ million has been spent in the United States for farm machinery. The so-called boom town, Tingo Maria, near the headwaters of the Amazon in the Andes, which had a few dozen families living in poverty ten years ago, now has a well-to-do population of over 20,000 as a result of a good road and a coöperative agricultural station established through technical aid from the United States Department of Agriculture working with the Peruvian government.[3]

The agricultural program in Costa Rica which began in 1948 with a small nucleus of Institute technicians and a few Costa Ricans, by 1952 had grown to twenty-nine field offices covering all seven provinces, staffed and directed by Costa Ricans. Cotton was being grown for the first time and very profitably, abandoned slopes were being reclaimed by terracing and contour farming, rice was being farmed with modern tractors, and experiments in rubber production were being carried on. A project in raising tomatoes by the boys and girls in 4-S Clubs in one community during three months of 1951 yielded a net profit of almost $28,000. Costa Rica had contributed over a million dollars as compared with less than three quarters of a million by the United States.

In Paraguay, traditionally the country of the poor farmer, a project was begun in 1946 when some thirty-five families were each assigned fifty-seven acres in a pilot colony near Asuncion. They were given good seed and adequate instruction as to agricultural methods. The success was so great that in 1948 the Paraguayan government colonized under the guidance of the Institute some 78,000 acres near the southern border. Full payment is to be made within ten years and bank collections have already reached 90 per cent. Paraguay is now establishing two more colonies large enough to settle 100,000 Paraguayans. The President of Paraguay is said to have declared that the Institute's help in the fields of health, food production, and education were more important to the welfare of the country than all the money the United States has loaned to the southern republics.

The Eisenhower administration has already shown its sympathetic attitude towards this policy of coöperation with the Latin-American republics. Early in April, 1953, the President appointed his brother, Dr. Milton Eisenhower, to head a mission consisting of representatives of the State Department and of the Departments of Treasury and Commerce to visit the ten republics of South America to express to their

[3] See the article by George A. Wooley, "Boomtown, South America," in the Apr., 1952, issue of *Foreign Agricultural Magazine*.

governments the intention of continuing a policy of economic, cultural, political, and military coöperation. The Commission was further instructed to consider conditions affecting mutual relations and to suggest any changes which might improve them. In the report published November 18, 1953, the Commission recommended among other things that the technical coöperation program in Latin America be expanded continuing the *servicio* type of administration and that the various technical agencies operating as a part of our activities in the Organization of American States be vigorously supported. The Commission also recommended that the United States minimize tariffs and quotas and encourage greater private investment abroad with the definite understanding that economic coöperation which would raise the well-being of the people of Latin America will redound to the benefit of all.

A fundamental requirement for better understanding is an effective solidarity of mind and spirit as well as material interests. For lack of a better term this has been called cultural relations. In reality it includes every medium of communication and every facility for closer acquaintanceship. The most encouraging progress has been made in this direction.

First to encourage and make possible greater travel in both directions North and South American steamship lines with the finest accommodations link up the United States with the east and west coasts of South America. The Pan American Airways reaches every Latin-American republic, and its Flying Clipper Cruises touch not only the great seaport cities but out-of-the-way places like Quito, the ancient seat of the Incas, Cuzco, the gateway to the marvels of Machu Pichu, or La Paz, highest capital in the world. Rapid progress is being made on the great Pan American highway which within the next few years will reach from Alaska's snowy forests to the dazzling Chilean lakes.

The radio and cinema are being more effectively utilized. The Pan American Union broadcasts regularly music representative of the two Americas and the American School of the Air has been extended to the other American republics. Every American embassy and legation now possesses moving picture projectors, and films depicting our national parks, our army and navy, our agricultural development are already available. Hollywood is now producing historical films such as Júarez and Bolívar, and the Walt Disney classics such as *Saludos Amigos,* and has eliminated the sensational, highly colored Mexican bandit and Argentinian gigolo type.

Travel grants to bring outstanding Latin-American scholars, publicists, artists, and scientists are available and hundreds are being granted annually. Exchanges of students and professors are being rapidly expanded and Latin-American students enrolled in our universities have increased steadily. Books are invaluable instruments of better international understanding, and Archibald McLeish, former Librarian of Congress, has compiled a list of good books reflecting life and thought in the United States for distribution in collections to representative libraries in the Latin-American republics. *The United States Quarterly Book List,* a highly selective list of currently published books annotated by experts under the direction of the Library of Congress, is sent to libraries and cultural institutions throughout Latin America.

The United States has established some thirty major cultural centers and forty branch centers in the Latin-American republics in which instruction in English to the nationals of the state, and instruction in the national language to American residents is offered. Large centers give special courses in American history, government, and literature and are equipped with excellent libraries. American librarians are sent to these centers to catalogue the collections, establish circulation and reference services, and to train local librarians. These libraries are focal points for information on the United States and provide a natural setting for lectures by American professors, and exhibits showing the development of American art and science.

American-directed private schools are found in practically every Latin-American country. It is estimated that some 70,000 students are enrolled in them. The United States government aids them to the extent of about $125,000 annually. The Eisenhower Mission considered the support of American schools of such importance that it recommended the amount contributed should be increased to $150,000 or $175,000 a year. All of these avenues of approach are working towards the same result—better understanding and mutual appreciation.

The threat of the aggressive Communism of Soviet Russia since World War II has produced another type of coöperation in the Americas—coöperation for security. The foreign ministers of the American republics meeting in Washington in 1951 directed the Inter-American Defense Board upon which all were represented to plan for the defense of the hemisphere. In its Mutual Security Act of 1951 the United States authorized the sum of $38,150,000 for direct military assistance to Latin America, and in 1952 added an additional $51,685,750. This money was to be used to furnish military assistance to those Latin-American republics who were willing to participate effectively in the defense of the Western Hemisphere. Bilateral military assistance agreements were to be signed by each country with the United States. Three types of military assistance were available: (1) direct grants of equipment to prepare for hemisphere defense; (2) opportunities for purchasing United States weapons and equipment for country and hemisphere defense; (3) the establishment of United States Army, Navy, and Air Force missions to help train Latin-American forces.[4]

As of June 30, 1953, military aid had been supplied to Chile, Colombia, Cuba, Ecuador, and Peru. Agreements had been signed also with Brazil, Uruguay, and the Dominican Republics, and were awaiting ratification. Of the amounts appropriated, about $80,000,000 was earmarked for procurement and delivery of material, and $1,700,000 for training expenses. In the second category—purchase of equipment for cash—Argentina, Brazil, and Chile each bought two light cruisers, Peru three and Uruguay two destroyer escorts, and Colombia a frigate from United States surplus stocks, all at very low prices. Training missions whose costs are largely borne by the receiving country are now functioning in an advisory capacity in most of the Latin-American countries.

This mutual assistance program is a two-way street which permits the republics of the Western Hemisphere to work together for their mutual defense against aggression of any sort. It is aimed to protect the free flow of civilian supplies and vital strategic materials between the American republics. It makes possible collective measures for the preservation and security of the Western World.

World civilization today faces the supreme crisis. Men of good will want peace, freedom, and an enriched life for all, but they must fight together to get it and work together afterwards to maintain it. Here in the Western Hemisphere is an ideal laboratory to make the experiment of intelligent and fair international coöperation. No long festering hostilities rankle, every important boundary dispute has been settled, no lack of *lebensraum* exists, a bountiful nature has endowed us superabundantly with all essential raw materials. The twenty-one republics have formulated and unanimously agreed upon a declaration of American principles outlawing force for the settlement of disputes and accepting the principles of international law as governing their interstate relations. Territorial aggression has been repudiated and abolished. The Western Hemisphere has set up the Golden Rule as its goal for the relations between states. Justice and fair dealing no longer end at the national frontiers. Courtesy and

---

[4] *Military Assistance to Latin America,* Dept. of State Publication 4917, Inter-Americas Series, 44 (Jan., 1953).

decent conduct beget friendliness and appreciation. The most idealistic policy of the good neighbor is the most realistic policy of enlightened selfishness. The Soviet seeks in vain a security sphere by terror and slaughter; the American republics are establishing one successfully by compromise and coöperation.

APPENDIX

Charter of the Organization
of American States[*]

IN THE NAME OF THEIR PEOPLES, THE STATES REPRESENTED AT THE NINTH
INTERNATIONAL CONFERENCE OF AMERICAN STATES,

Convinced that the historic mission of America is to offer to man a land of
liberty, and a favorable environment for the development of his personality and
the realization of his just aspirations;

Conscious that that mission has already inspired numerous agreements, whose
essential value lies in the desire of the American peoples to live together in
peace, and, through their mutual understanding and respect for the sovereignty
of each one, to provide for the betterment of all, in independence, in equality
and under law;

Confident that the true significance of American solidarity and good neighborliness can only mean the consolidation on this continent, within the framework of democratic institutions, of a system of individual liberty and social
justice based on respect for the essential rights of man;

Persuaded that their welfare and their contribution to the progress and the
civilization of the world will increasingly require intensive continental co-
operation;

Resolved to persevere in the noble undertaking that humanity has conferred
upon the United Nations, whose principles and purposes they solemnly reaffirm;

Convinced that juridical organization is a necessary condition for security and
peace founded on moral order and on justice; and

In accordance with Resolution IX of the Inter-American Conference on Problems of War and Peace, held at Mexico City,

HAVE AGREED
upon the following
CHARTER OF THE ORGANIZATION OF
AMERICAN STATES

PART ONE

CHAPTER I

NATURE AND PURPOSES

Article 1

The American States establish by this Charter the international organization
that they have developed to achieve an order of peace and justice, to promote

[*] Signed at the Ninth International Conference of American States, Bogotá, March
30–May 2, 1948. (Courtesy of the Pan American Union)

their solidarity, to strengthen their collaboration, and to defend their sovereignty, their territorial integrity and their independence. Within the United Nations, the Organization of American States is a regional agency.

Article 2

All American States that ratify the present Charter are Members of the Organization.

Article 3

Any new political entity that arises from the union of several Member States and that, as such, ratifies the present Charter, shall become a Member of the Organization. The entry of the new political entity into the Organization shall result in the loss of membership of each one of the States which constitute it.

Article 4

The Organization of American States, in order to put into practice the principles on which it is founded and to fulfill its regional obligations under the Charter of the United Nations, proclaims the following essential purposes:

a. To strengthen the peace and security of the continent;
b. To prevent possible causes of difficulties and to ensure the pacific settlement of disputes that may arise among the Member States;
c. To provide for common action on the part of those States in the event of aggression;
d. To seek the solution of political, juridical and economic problems that may arise among them; and
e. To promote, by coöperative action, their economic, social and cultural development.

CHAPTER II

PRINCIPLES

Article 5

The American States reaffirm the following principles:

a. International law is the standard of conduct of States in their reciprocal relations;
b. International order consists essentially of respect for the personality, sovereignty and independence of States, and the faithful fulfillment of obligations derived from treaties and other sources of international law;
c. Good faith shall govern the relations between States;
d. The solidarity of the American States and the high aims which are sought through it require the political organization of those States on the basis of the effective exercise of representative democracy;
e. The American States condemn war of aggression: victory does not give rights;
f. An act of aggression against one American State is an act of aggression against all the other American States;
g. Controversies of an international character arising between two or more American States shall be settled by peaceful procedures;
h. Social justice and social security are bases of lasting peace;

i. Economic coöperation is essential to the common welfare and prosperity of the peoples of the continent;

j. The American States proclaim the fundamental rights of the individual without distinction as to race, nationality, creed or sex;

k. The spiritual unity of the continent is based on respect for the cultural values of the American countries and requires their close coöperation for the high purposes of civilization;

l. The education of peoples should be directed toward justice, freedom and peace.

CHAPTER III

FUNDAMENTAL RIGHTS AND DUTIES OF STATES

Article 6

States are juridically equal, enjoy equal rights and equal capacity to exercise these rights, and have equal duties. The rights of each State depend not upon its power to ensure the exercise thereof, but upon the mere fact of its existence as a person under international law.

Article 7

Every American State has the duty to respect the rights enjoyed by every other State in accordance with international law.

Article 8

The fundamental rights of States may not be impaired in any manner whatsoever.

Article 9

The political existence of the State is independent of recognition by other States. Even before being recognized, the State has the right to defend its integrity and independence, to provide for its preservation and prosperity, and consequently to organize itself as it sees fit, to legislate concerning its interests, to administer its services, and to determine the jurisdiction and competence of its courts. The exercise of these rights is limited only by the exercise of the rights of other States in accordance with international law.

Article 10

Recognition implies that the State granting it accepts the personality of the new State, with all the rights and duties that international law prescribes for the two States.

Article 11

The right of each State to protect itself and to live its own life does not authorize it to commit unjust acts against another State.

Article 12

The jurisdiction of States within the limits of their national territory is exercised equally over all the inhabitants, whether nationals or aliens.

Article 13

Each State has the right to develop its cultural, political and economic life freely and naturally. In this free development, the State shall respect the rights of the individual and the principles of universal morality.

Article 14

Respect for and the faithful observance of treaties constitute standards for the development of peaceful relations among States. International treaties and agreements should be public.

Article 15

No State or group of States has the right to intervene, directly or indirectly, for any reason whatever, in the internal or external affairs of any other State. The foregoing principle prohibits not only armed force but also any other form of interference or attempted threat against the personality of the State or against its political, economic and cultural elements.

Article 16

No State may use or encourage the use of coercive measures of an economic or political character in order to force the sovereign will of another State and obtain from it advantages of any kind.

Article 17

The territory of a State is inviolable; it may not be the object, even temporarily, of military occupation or of other measures of force taken by another State, directly or indirectly, on any grounds whatever. No territorial acquisitions or special advantages obtained either by force or by other means of coercion shall be recognized.

Article 18

The American States bind themselves in their international relations not to have recourse to the use of force, except in the case of self-defense in accordance with existing treaties or in fulfillment thereof.

Article 19

Measures adopted for the maintenance of peace and security in accordance with existing treaties do not constitute a violation of the principles set forth in Articles 15 and 17.

Chapter IV

PACIFIC SETTLEMENT OF DISPUTES

Article 20

All international disputes that may arise between American States shall be submitted to the peaceful procedures set forth in this Charter, before being referred to the Security Council of the United Nations.

Article 21

The following are peaceful procedures: direct negotiation, good offices, mediation, investigation and conciliation, judicial settlement, arbitration, and those which the parties to the dispute may especially agree upon at any time.

Article 22

In the event that a dispute arises between two or more American States which, in the opinion of one of them, cannot be settled through the usual diplomatic channels, the Parties shall agree on some other peaceful procedure that will enable them to reach a solution.

Article 23

A special treaty will establish adequate procedures for the pacific settlement of disputes and will determine the appropriate means for their application, so that no dispute between American States shall fail of definitive settlement within a reasonable period.

CHAPTER V
COLLECTIVE SECURITY

Article 24

Every act of aggression by a State against the territorial integrity or the inviolability of the territory or against the sovereignty or political independence of an American State shall be considered an act of aggression against the other American States.

Article 25

If the inviolability or the integrity of the territory or the sovereignty or political independence of any American State should be affected by an armed attack or by an act of aggression that is not an armed attack, or by an extracontinental conflict, or by a conflict between two or more American States, or by any other fact or situation that might endanger the peace of America, the American States, in furtherance of the principles of continental solidarity or collective self-defense, shall apply the measures and procedures established in the special treaties on the subject.

CHAPTER VI
ECONOMIC STANDARDS

Article 26

The Member States agree to coöperate with one another, as far as their resources may permit and their laws may provide, in the broadest spirit of good neighborliness, in order to strengthen their economic structure, develop their agriculture and mining, promote their industry and increase their trade.

Article 27

If the economy of an American State is affected by serious conditions that cannot be satisfactorily remedied by its own unaided effort, such State may place its economic problems before the Inter-American Economic and Social Council to seek through consultation the most appropriate solution for such problems.

CHAPTER VII

SOCIAL STANDARDS

Article 28

The Member States agree to coöperate with one another to achieve just and decent living conditions for their entire populations.

Article 29

The Member States agree upon the desirability of developing their social legislation on the following bases:

a. All human beings, without distinction as to race, nationality, sex, creed or social condition, have the right to attain material well-being and spiritual growth under circumstances of liberty, dignity, equality of opportunity, and economic security;
b. Work is a right and a social duty; it shall not be considered as an article of commerce; it demands respect for freedom of association and for the dignity of the worker; and it is to be performed under conditions that ensure life, health and a decent standard of living, both during the working years and during old age, or when any circumstance deprives the individual of the possibility of working.

CHAPTER VIII

CULTURAL STANDARDS

Article 30

The Member States agree to promote, in accordance with their constitutional provisions and their material resources, the exercise of the right to education, on the following bases:

a. Elementary education shall be compulsory and, when provided by the State, shall be without cost;
b. Higher education shall be available to all, without distinction as to race, nationality, sex, language, creed or social condition.

Article 31

With due consideration for the national character of each State, the Member States undertake to facilitate free cultural interchange by every medium of expression.

PART TWO

CHAPTER IX

THE ORGANS

Article 32

The Organization of American States accomplishes its purposes by means of:

a. The Inter-American Conference;
b. The Meeting of Consultation of Ministers of Foreign Affairs;

c. The Council;
d. The Pan American Union;
e. The Specialized Conferences; and
f. The Specialized Organizations.

CHAPTER X

THE INTER-AMERICAN CONFERENCE

Article 33

The Inter-American Conference is the supreme organ of the Organization of American States. It decides the general action and policy of the Organization and determines the structure and functions of its Organs, and has the authority to consider any matter relating to friendly relations among the American States. These functions shall be carried out in accordance with the provisions of this Charter and of other inter-American treaties.

Article 34

All Member States have the right to be represented at the Inter-American Conference. Each State has the right to one vote.

Article 35

The Conference shall convene every five years at the time fixed by the Council of the Organization, after consultation with the government of the country where the Conference is to be held.

Article 36

In special circumstances and with the approval of two-thirds of the American Governments, a special Inter-American Conference may be held, or the date of the next regular Conference may be changed.

Article 37

Each Inter-American Conference shall designate the place of meeting of the next Conference. If for any unforeseen reason the Conference cannot be held at the place designated, the Council of the Organization shall designate a new place.

Article 38

The program and regulations of the Inter-American Conference shall be prepared by the Council of the Organization and submitted to the Member States for consideration.

CHAPTER XI

THE MEETING OF CONSULTATION OF
MINISTERS OF FOREIGN AFFAIRS

Article 39

The Meeting of Consultation of Ministers of Foreign Affairs shall be held in order to consider problems of an urgent nature and of common interest to the American States, and to serve as the Organ of Consultation.

Article 40

Any Member State may request that a Meeting of Consultation be called. The request shall be addressed to the Council of the Organization, which shall decide by an absolute majority whether a meeting should be held.

Article 41

The program and regulations of the Meeting of Consultation shall be prepared by the Council of the Organization and submitted to the Member States for consideration.

Article 42

If, for exceptional reasons, a Minister of Foreign Affairs is unable to attend the meeting, he shall be represented by a special delegate.

Article 43

In case of an armed attack within the territory of an American State or within the region of security delimited by treaties in force, a Meeting of Consultation shall be held without delay. Such Meeting shall be called immediately by the Chairman of the Council of the Organization, who shall at the same time call a meeting of the Council itself.

Article 44

An Advisory Defense Committee shall be established to advise the Organ of Consultation on problems of military coöperation that may arise in connection with the application of existing special treaties on collective security.

Article 45

The Advisory Defense Committee shall be composed of the highest military authorities of the American States participating in the Meeting of Consultation. Under exceptional circumstances the Governments may appoint substitutes. Each State shall be entitled to one vote.

Article 46

The Advisory Defense Committee shall be convoked under the same conditions as the Organ of Consultation, when the latter deals with matters relating to defense against aggression.

Article 47

The Committee shall also meet when the Conference or the Meeting of Consultation or the Governments, by a two-thirds majority of the Member States, assign to it technical studies or reports on specific subjects.

CHAPTER XII

THE COUNCIL

Article 48

The Council of the Organization of American States is composed of one Representative of each Member State of the Organization, especially appointed by the respective Government, with the rank of Ambassador. The appointment may be given to the diplomatic representative accredited to the Government of the country in which the Council has its seat. During the absence of the titular Representative, the Government may appoint an interim Representative.

Article 49

The Council shall elect a Chairman and a Vice Chairman, who shall serve for one year and shall not be eligible for election to either of those positions for the term immediately following.

Article 50

The Council takes cognizance, within the limits of the present Charter and of inter-American treaties and agreements, of any matter referred to it by the Inter-American Conference or the Meeting of Consultation of Ministers of Foreign Affairs.

Article 51

The Council shall be responsible for the proper discharge by the Pan American Union of the duties assigned to it.

Article 52

The Council shall serve provisionally as the Organ of Consultation when the circumstances contemplated in Article 43 of this Charter arise.

Article 53

It is also the duty of the Council:

a. To draft and submit to the Governments and to the Inter-American Conference proposals for the creation of new Specialized Organizations or for the combination, adaptation or elimination of existing ones, including matters relating to the financing and support thereof;
b. To draft recommendations to the Governments, the Inter-American Conference, the Specialized Conferences or the Specialized Organizations, for the coördination of the activities and programs of such organizations, after consultation with them;
c. To conclude agreements with the Inter-American Specialized Organizations to determine the relations that shall exist between the respective agency and the Organization;
d. To conclude agreements or special arrangements for coöperation with other American organizations of recognized international standing;
e. To promote and facilitate collaboration between the Organization of American States and the United Nations, as well as between Inter-American Specialized Organizations and similar international agencies;
f. To adopt resolutions that will enable the Secretary General to perform the duties envisaged in Article 84;
g. To perform the other duties assigned to it by the present Charter.

Article 54

The Council shall establish the bases for fixing the quota that each Government is to contribute to the maintenance of the Pan American Union, taking into account the ability to pay of the respective countries and their determination to contribute in an equitable manner. The budget, after approval by the

Council, shall be transmitted to the Governments at least six months before the first day of the fiscal year, with a statement of the annual quota of each country. Decisions on budgetary matters require the approval of two-thirds of the members of the Council.

Article 55

The Council shall formulate its own regulations.

Article 56

The Council shall function at the seat of the Pan American Union.

Article 57

The following are organs of the Council of the Organization of American States:

a. The Inter-American Economic and Social Council;
b. The Inter-American Council of Jurists; and
c. The Inter-American Cultural Council.

Article 58

The organs referred to in the preceding article shall have technical autonomy within the limits of this Charter; but their decisions shall not encroach upon the sphere of action of the Council of the Organization.

Article 59

The organs of the Council of the Organization are composed of representatives of all the Member States of the Organization.

Article 60

The organs of the Council of the Organization shall, as far as possible, render to the Governments such technical services as the latter may request; and they shall advise the Council of the Organization on matters within their jurisdiction.

Article 61

The organs of the Council of the Organization shall, in agreement with the Council, establish coöperative relations with the corresponding organs of the United Nations and with the national or international agencies that function within their respective spheres of action.

Article 62

The Council of the Organization, with the advice of the appropriate bodies and after consultation with the Governments, shall formulate the statutes of its organs in accordance with and in the execution of the provisions of this Charter. The organs shall formulate their own regulations.

A. *The Inter-American Economic and Social Council*

Article 63

The Inter-American Economic and Social Council has for its principal purpose the promotion of the economic and social welfare of the American nations through effective coöperation for the better utilization of their natural resources, the development of their agriculture and industry and the raising of the standards of living of their peoples.

Article 64

To accomplish this purpose the Council shall:

a. Propose the means by which the American nations may give each other technical assistance in making studies and formulating and executing plans to carry out the purposes referred to in Article 26 and to develop and improve their social services;
b. Act as coördinating agency for all official inter-American activities of an economic and social nature;
c. Undertake studies on its own initiative or at the request of any Member State;
d. Assemble and prepare reports on economic and social matters for the use of the Member States;
e. Suggest to the Council of the Organization the advisability of holding specialized conferences on economic and social matters;
f. Carry on such other activities as may be assigned to it by the Inter-American Conference, the Meeting of Consultation of Ministers of Foreign Affairs, or the Council of the Organization.

Article 65

The Inter-American Economic and Social Council, composed of technical delegates appointed by each Member State, shall meet on its own initiative or on that of the Council of the Organization.

Article 66

The Inter-American Economic and Social Council shall function at the seat of the Pan American Union, but it may hold meetings in any American city by a majority decision of the Member States.

B. *The Inter-American Council of Jurists*

Article 67

The purpose of the Inter-American Council of Jurists is to serve as an advisory body on juridical matters; to promote the development and codification of public and private international law; and to study the possibility of attaining uniformity in the legislation of the various American countries, insofar as it may appear desirable.

Article 68

The Inter-American Juridical Committee of Rio de Janeiro shall be the permanent committee of the Inter-American Council of Jurists.

Article 69

The Juridical Committee shall be composed of jurists of the nine countries selected by the Inter-American Conference. The selection of the jurists shall be made by the Inter-American Council of Jurists from a panel submitted by each country chosen by the Conference. The Members of the Juridical Committee represent all Member States of the Organization. The Council of the Organization is empowered to fill any vacancies that occur during the intervals between Inter-American Conferences and between meetings of the Inter-American Council of Jurists.

Article 70

The Juridical Committee shall undertake such studies and preparatory work as are assigned to it by the Inter-American Council of Jurists, the Inter-American Conference, the Meeting of Consultation of Ministers of Foreign Affairs, or the Council of the Organization. It may also undertake those studies and projects which, on its own initiative, it considers advisable.

Article 71

The Inter-American Council of Jurists and the Juridical Committee should seek the coöperation of national committees for the codification of international law, of institutes of international and comparative law, and of other specialized agencies.

Article 72

The Inter-American Council of Jurists shall meet when convened by the Council of the Organization, at the place determined by the Council of Jurists at its previous meeting.

C. The Inter-American Cultural Council

Article 73

The purpose of the Inter-American Cultural Council is to promote friendly relations and mutual understanding among the American peoples, in order to strengthen the peaceful sentiments that have characterized the evolution of America, through the promotion of educational, scientific and cultural exchange.

Article 74

To this end the principal functions of the Council shall be:

a. To sponsor inter-American cultural activities;
b. To collect and supply information on cultural activities carried on in and among the American States by private and official agencies both national and international in character;
c. To promote the adoption of basic educational programs adapted to the needs of all population groups in the American countries;
d. To promote, in addition, the adoption of special programs of training, education and culture for the indigenous groups of the American countries;
e. To coöperate in the protection, preservation and increase of the cultural heritage of the continent;
f. To promote coöperation among the American nations in the fields of education, science and culture, by means of the exchange of materials for research and study, as well as the exchange of teachers, students, specialists and, in general, such other persons and materials as are useful for the realization of these ends;

g. To encourage the education of the peoples for harmonious international relations;

h. To carry on such other activities as may be assigned to it by the Inter-American Conference, the Meeting of Consultation of Ministers of Foreign Affairs, or the Council of the Organization.

Article 75

The Inter-American Cultural Council shall determine the place of its next meeting and shall be convened by the Council of the Organization on the date chosen by the latter in agreement with the Government of the country selected as the seat of the meeting.

Article 76

There shall be a Committee for Cultural Action of which five States, chosen at each Inter-American Conference, shall be members. The individuals composing the Committee for Cultural Action shall be selected by the Inter-American Cultural Council from a panel submitted by each country chosen by the Conference, and they shall be specialists in education or cultural matters. When the Inter-American Cultural Council and the Inter-American Conference are not in session, the Council of the Organization may fill vacancies that arise and replace those countries that find it necessary to discontinue their coöperation.

Article 77

The Committee for Cultural Action shall function as the permanent committee of the Inter-American Cultural Council, for the purpose of preparing any studies that the latter may assign to it. With respect to these studies the Council shall have the final decision.

CHAPTER XIII
THE PAN AMERICAN UNION

Article 78

The Pan American Union is the central and permanent organ of the Organization of American States and the General Secretariat of the Organization. It shall perform the duties assigned to it in this Charter and such other duties as may be assigned to it in other inter-American treaties and agreements.

Article 79

There shall be a Secretary General of the Organization, who shall be elected by the Council for a ten-year term and who may not be reëlected or be succeeded by a person of the same nationality. In the event of a vacancy in the office of Secretary General, the Council shall, within the next ninety days, elect a successor to fill the office for the remainder of the term, who may be reëlected if the vacancy occurs during the second half of the term.

Article 80

The Secretary General shall direct the Pan American Union and be the legal representative thereof.

Article 81

The Secretary General shall participate with voice, but without vote, in the deliberations of the Inter-American Conference, the Meeting of Consultation of Ministers of Foreign Affairs, the Specialized Conferences, and the Council and its organs.

Article 82

The Pan American Union, through its technical and information offices, shall, under the direction of the Council, promote economic, social, juridical and cultural relations among all the Member States of the Organization.

Article 83

The Pan American Union shall also perform the following functions:

a. Transmit *ex officio* to Member States the convocation to the Inter-American Conference, the Meeting of Consultation of Ministers of Foreign Affairs, and the Specialized Conferences;
b. Advise the Council and its organs in the preparation of programs and regulations of the Inter-American Conference, the Meeting of Consultation of Ministers of Foreign Affairs, and the Specialized Conferences;
c. Place, to the extent of its ability, at the disposal of the Government of the country where a conference is to be held, the technical aid and personnel which such Government may request;
d. Serve as custodian of the documents and archives of the Inter-American Conference, of the Meeting of Consultation of Ministers of Foreign Affairs, and, insofar as possible, of the Specialized Conferences;
e. Serve as depository of the instruments of ratification of inter-American agreements;
f. Perform the functions entrusted to it by the Inter-American Conference, and the Meeting of Consultation of Ministers of Foreign Affairs;
g. Submit to the Council an annual report on the activities of the Organization;
h. Submit to the Inter-American Conference a report on the work accomplished by the Organs of the Organization since the previous Conference.

Article 84

It is the duty of the Secretary General:

a. To establish, with the approval of the Council, such technical and administrative offices of the Pan American Union as are necessary to accomplish its purposes;
b. To determine the number of department heads, officers and employees of the Pan American Union; to appoint them, regulate their powers and duties, and fix their compensation, in accordance with general standards established by the Council.

Article 85

There shall be an Assistant Secretary General, elected by the Council for a term of ten years and eligible for reëlection. In the event of a vacancy in the office of Assistant Secretary General, the Council shall, within the next ninety days, elect a successor to fill such office for the remainder of the term.

Article 86

The Assistant Secretary General shall be the Secretary of the Council. He shall perform the duties of the Secretary General during the temporary absence or disability of the latter, or during the ninety-day vacancy referred to in Article 79. He shall also serve as advisory officer to the Secretary General, with the power to act as his delegate in all matters that the Secretary General may entrust to him.

Article 87

The Council, by a two-thirds vote of its members, may remove the Secretary General or the Assistant Secretary General whenever the proper functioning of the Organization so demands.

Article 88

The heads of the respective departments of the Pan American Union, appointed by the Secretary General, shall be the Executive Secretaries of the Inter-American Economic and Social Council, the Council of Jurists and the Cultural Council.

Article 89

In the performance of their duties the personnel shall not seek or receive instructions from any government or from any other authority outside the Pan American Union. They shall refrain from any action that might reflect upon their position as international officials responsible only to the Union.

Article 90

Every Member of the Organization of American States pledges itself to respect the exclusively international character of the responsibilities of the Secretary General and the personnel, and not to seek to influence them in the discharge of their duties.

Article 91

In selecting its personnel the Pan American Union shall give first consideration to efficiency, competence and integrity; but at the same time importance shall be given to the necessity of recruiting personnel on as broad a geographical basis as possible.

Article 92

The seat of the Pan American Union is the city of Washington.

Chapter XIV

THE SPECIALIZED CONFERENCES

Article 93

The Specialized Conferences shall meet to deal with special technical matters or to develop specific aspects of inter-American coöperation, when it is so decided by the Inter-American Conference or the Meeting of Consultation of Ministers of Foreign Affairs; when inter-American agreements so provide; or when the Council of the Organization considers it necessary, either on its own initiative or at the request of one of its organs or of one of the Specialized Organizations.

Article 94

The program and regulations of the Specialized Conferences shall be prepared by the organs of the Council of the Organization or by the Specialized Organizations concerned; they shall be submitted to the Member Governments for consideration and transmitted to the Council for its information.

CHAPTER XV
THE SPECIALIZED ORGANIZATIONS

Article 95

For the purposes of the present Charter, Inter-American Specialized Organizations are the intergovernmental organizations established by multilateral agreements and having specific functions with respect to technical matters of common interest to the American states.

Article 96

The Council shall, for the purposes stated in Article 53, maintain a register of the Organizations that fulfill the conditions set forth in the foregoing Article.

Article 97

The Specialized Organizations shall enjoy the fullest technical autonomy and shall take into account the recommendations of the Council, in conformity with the provisions of the present Charter.

Article 98

The Specialized Organizations shall submit to the Council periodic reports on the progress of their work and on their annual budgets and expenses.

Article 99

Agreements between the Council and the Specialized Organizations contemplated in paragraph (c) of Article 53 may provide that such Organizations transmit their budgets to the Council for approval. Arrangements may also be made for the Pan American Union to receive the quotas of the contributing countries and distribute them in accordance with the said agreements.

Article 100

The Specialized Organizations shall establish coöperative relations with world agencies of the same character in order to coördinate their activities. In concluding agreements with international agencies of a world-wide character, the Inter-American Specialized Organizations shall preserve their identity and their status as integral parts of the Organization of American States, even when they perform regional functions of international agencies.

Article 101

In determining the geographic location of the Specialized Organizations the interests of all the American States shall be taken into account.

PART THREE

CHAPTER XVI
THE UNITED NATIONS

Article 102

None of the provisions of this Charter shall be construed as impairing the rights and obligations of the Member States under the Charter of the United Nations.

CHAPTER XVII
MISCELLANEOUS PROVISIONS

Article 103

The Organization of American States shall enjoy in the territory of each Member such legal capacity, privileges and immunities as are necessary for the exercise of its functions and the accomplishment of its purposes.

Article 104

The Representatives of the Governments on the Council of the Organization, the representatives on the organs of the Council, the personnel of their delegations, as well as the Secretary General and the Assistant Secretary General of the Organization, shall enjoy the privileges and immunities necessary for the independent performance of their duties.

Article 105

The juridical status of the Inter-American Specialized Organizations and the privileges and immunities that should be granted to them and to their personnel, as well as to the officials of the Pan American Union, shall be determined in each case through agreements between the respective organizations and the Governments concerned.

Article 106

Correspondence of the Organization of American States, including printed matter and parcels, bearing the frank thereof, shall be carried free of charge in the mails of the Member States.

Article 107

The Organization of American States does not recognize any restriction on the eligibility of men and women to participate in the activities of the various Organs and to hold positions therein.

CHAPTER XVIII
RATIFICATION AND ENTRY INTO FORCE

Article 108

The present Charter shall remain open for signature by the American States and shall be ratified in accordance with their respective constitutional procedures. The original instrument, the Spanish, English, Portuguese and French texts of which are equally authentic, shall be deposited with the Pan American Union, which shall transmit certified copies thereof to the Governments for purposes of ratification. The instruments of ratification shall be deposited with the Pan American Union, which shall notify the signatory States of such deposit.

Article 109

The present Charter shall enter into force among the ratifying States when two-thirds of the signatory States have deposited their ratifications. It shall enter into force with respect to the remaining States in the order in which they deposit their ratifications.

Article 110

The present Charter shall be registered with the Secretariat of the United Nations through the Pan American Union.

Article 111

Amendments to the present Charter may be adopted only at an Inter-American Conference convened for that purpose. Amendments shall enter into force in accordance with the terms and the procedure set forth in Article 109.

Article 112

The present Charter shall remain in force indefinitely, but may be denounced by any Member State upon written notification to the Pan American Union, which shall communicate to all the others each notice of denunciation received. After two years from the date on which the Pan American Union receives a notice of denunciation, the present Charter shall cease to be in force with respect to the denouncing State, which shall cease to belong to the Organization after it has fulfilled the obligations arising from the present Charter.

[*Signed on April 30, 1948*]

INDEX